News Clippings From Orangeville, Ferron, Castle Dale & Huntington, Utah

1879 - 1897

Some of the names include: Aiken, Allen, Allred, Allside, Anderson, Behunin, Blanchard, Bolden, Boren, Bookman, Boulder, Bradley, Brasher, Bryan, Bunnacio, Bunting, Burns, Calloway, Carrol(l), Cheshire, Childs, Christensen, Collard, Conover, Cox, Crawford, Crookston, Curtis, Donaldson, Duncan, Eddington, Eden, Edminster, Edwards, Ekins, Elder, Evans, Fall, Farrer, Fillmer, Forrester, Fox, Fredrickson, Fugate, Fullmer, Funk, Gale, Gammage, Glines, Grange, Granger, Griffith, Guymon, Hales, Halverson, Hamilton, Hansen, Hatch, Haycock, Henrie, Higgs, Hinken, Hinkings, Hitchcock, Holloway, Howard, Hunley, Hunter, Huntington, Jackson, Jeff(s), Jergensen, Jewkes, Johnson, Jones, Justensen, Killman, Killpack, King, Kirby,Kofford, Lake, Larsen, Lemon, Logan, Loveless, Luke, Makin, Manning, McDonnough, McLean, Meeks, Merriam, Miles, Miller, Moffitt, Molen, Moore, More, Nay, Nells, Nelson, Nolan, Ollifant, Olsen, Osborn, Ottison, Page, Paine, Peacock, Petersen, Peterson, Petty, Potter, Poulsen, Preston, Price, Rassmussen, Redd, Reed, Reid, Robbins, Robertson, Roper, Scoville, Seely, Shaw, Shipp, Singleton, Sitterod, Smith, Snow, Sorenson, Southworth, Stepent, Stephens, Stevens, Swanson, Swazey, Tatton, Taylor, Terrace, Thomander, Thomas, Thomson, Thornton, Todman, Tuttle, VanBuren, VanNalta, Wakefield, Ware, Watt, Webb, Whitney, Welberg, Wilberg, Wilkin, Williams, Wilson, Winters, Witmer, Woodward, Wrigley, Yoxall, Zwahlen

Some of the articles are easier to read than others, please consider that they are 100 years or more old.

Newspapers with articles include Brigham City Bugler, County Register, Davis County Clipper, Deseret News, Deseret Evening News, Deseret Weekly, Eastern Utah Telegraph, Evening Dispatch, Logan Journal, Logan Leader, Manti Messenger, Manti Sentinel, Ogden Daily Standard, Ogden Herald, Ogden Junction, Ogden Daily Standard, Ogden Standard, Provo Daily Enquirer, Provo Dispatch, Salt Lake Democrat, Salt Lake Herald, Salt Lake Times, Territorial Enquirer, Utah Enquirer, Vernal Express

ISBN-13: 978-1719536790

ISBN-10: 1719536791

Deseret News
April 16, 1879

Postal Affairs.—A post office has been established at Castle Dale, Sanpete County, with Jno. K. Reid postmaster. The post offices at Leeds, Washington County, and at Lynne, Weber County, have been discontinued. John McDonald has been appointed postmaster at Silver Springs, Salt Lake County.

Deseret News
February 25, 1880

AN ACT
CREATING EMERY COUNTY.

Be it enacted by the Governor and Legislative Assembly of the Territory of Utah: That all that portion of the Territory of Utah bounded as follows, to wit: commencing at a point where parallel 38,30 north latitude crosses Green River, thence west along the said parallel to a point six miles west of the first guide meridian east of the Salt Lake meridian, thence north along the township line between ranges five (5) and six (6) east, *to the third standard parallel south,* thence east to the first guide meridian, thence north along said first guide meridian to the township line between townships eleven (11) and twelve (12) south; thence east along the last mentioned township line to Green River, thence down the main channel of Green River to the place of beginning; is hereby made and named Emery County, with county seat at Castle Dale. Which county is hereby attached to and made part of the First Judicial District.

SEC. 2. For the purpose of organizing said county, the following officers are hereby appointed: Samuel Jewks, Probate Judge, Elias Cox, Jasper Petersen and William Taylor, Selectmen, who shall qualify by taking an oath of office, conditioned for the faithful performance of the duties thereof. They shall enter upon the duties of their respective offices on the second Monday in March, A. D., 1880, appoint a county clerk, and organize a county court, and when so organized, shall appoint all county officers necessary for the full and complete organization of said county, and the transaction of all business matters therein; who shall, before entering upon the duties of their offices, qualify as the law directs. Said court shall define the boundaries of precincts, appoint judges of election, and otherwise provide for an election to be held at the time of the general election in the year 1880; said election shall be held, conducted and returns thereof made, in accordance with the election laws of Utah. Provided that the voters at said first election need not be registered.

SEC. 8. The Probate Judge, Selectmen and all other officers appointed
under the provisions of this act,
shall hold their offices until the first
general election, and until their
successors are elected and qualified.

SEC. 4. All acts and parts of acts
in conflict herewith are hereby re-
pealed.

ORSON PRATT, SEN.,
Speaker of the House of Representatives.

LORENZO SNOW,
President of the Council.
Approved February 12, 1880.

ARTHUR L. THOMAS,
Acting Governor.

Ogden Junction
May 22, 1880

Postal Routes.

The following new postal routes
are included in the act approved by
the president on the 3d inst:

From Ferron City via Castle Dale
to Huntingdon; and thence to the
point where mail route number 38,-
161 crosses Green river.— *Tribune.*

Deseret News
September 1, 1880

CASTLEDALE,
Emery County,
August 23, 1880.

Editors Deseret News:

President E. Snow, after visiting the settlements in Sanpete, with President Taylor and company, holding quarterly conference in Mount Pleasant and meetings in Spring City, Manti, Ephraim, Moroni, Fountain Green and Fairview, was met in the latter place by Elder B. Young, who came in through Spanish Fork Canyon and Thistle Valley on the evening of Wednesday, the 18th inst. On the morning of the 19th, our party, consisting of President Snow and his son Ashby, B. Young and his son George, John Gillespie, Alonzo Knight and F. M. Lyman, who were going the whole trip, and Prest. Peterson, George Farnsworth, C. J. Larson and Orange Seely who were to accompany us to Castle Valley, with one wagon, two carriages and eight horses, started in earnest upon our tour of Southeastern Utah, Western Colorado and New Mexico and Eastern Arizona.

Traversing the mountains between Sanpete and Emery Counties, which took two days, we found the roads tolerably good for new mountain roads. The country through which we passed reminded me of scenery in New Hampshire and Vermont, the mountains covered with forests of quaking asp and firs. We encountered light falls of rain in the day and frost and heavy dews at night. Being armed and equipped as the law directs, we have two shotguns, one rifle, two revolvers, one British bulldog and one Salt Lake flipper, with ammunition for the round trip. We did not count much on our flipper till our camp was startled with the word that a ground dog was moving around within a few yards of us, challenging us to shoot him, when our George took deadly aim at him with his reliable flipper, and we registered the first game killed by any of the company.

Traveling down from the mountains, the road runs down, down, through a rough canyon known as the Seely Pass, through which it has cost many dollars and hard licks to make what is now a passable road. We were unfavorably impressed with the appearance of the country and locations along the Cottonwood, which receives the little stream from Seely's Pass, and as we moved down the widening canyon into the valley of castles, my first impressions were that the more of such land a man possessed himself of, the poorer he would be, but as we approached the Castledale part of the country, we found unfenced fields and gardens that compare favorably with those of our older settled and cultivated valleys of Sanpete, Juab, Utah and Salt Lake. We arrived here at 7.15 p. m., on Friday, 20th, tired and hungry at the close of our two days' ride over the ups and downs of a mountain road 65 miles in length, from Fairview. Some of our party say it is only 60 and others 62 miles, but any one doubting my 65 mile figure is at liberty to claim it. We have been fed and so have our teams by Brothers Heiselt, Seely and others since we have been here, and have camped by the bowery which stands upon Brother Seely's ground.

I have made diligent inquiry for two days to find the County seat of Emery County, known by the name of Castledale, and it is so scattered up and down the Cottonwood, that it is very difficult to tell which is the centre of gravitation. Every man has located upon his quarter section. It is claimed that the Post Office has been the centre of attraction. The climate of this valley is said to be very fine, and our experience will sustain that reputation. There have been but three deaths, and they were of children, since the settlement of this valley, as I am told. The soil is composed of the sand and clay washed down from the white bluffs which stand up high on the west of the valley, somewhat mildly mixed with mineral. Lucern is not easily started to grow, but there are some very good pieces of it that I have seen, and I do not doubt but it will prove a successful crop, and it will be much needed, for the grass that once was plentiful has vanished before the flocks and herds that have to be pastured in this region. Good water, good land, and fine climate are inviting the industrious husbandman to come and make desirable homes for good Latter-day Saints.

All with whom I have conversed here are satisfied, and consider their chances many times better than those found in Dixie. The streams of Ferron, Cottonwood and Huntington in this valley are considered about the size of Big Cottonwood in Salt Lake Valley, and there is plenty of good land along each creek upon which to use the water.

Timber is abundant in the mountains 20 miles away, and coal mines are fabulously rich within from 10 to 25 miles distance. There are not more than 500 souls in the county.

We found the saints in good spirits, and they came together under the Bowery where I am writing, at 10 a.m., on the 21st, when a two days' meeting commenced, and the speakers were President E. Snow, Elders B. Young, Canute Peterson, George Farnsworth, C. J. Larson, John Gillespie and F. M. Lyman. The great amount of work done by the people here in a little over two years was highly commended, but their scattered condition was deprecated and they were counseled to settle as soon as possible in a town, to build school and meeting houses, to establish schools, and to hold their meetings regularly as we are required as good Saints. President Snow spoke much upon the principle of tithing, explaining its object and use and the blessings derived from the faithful observance of that law.

In the afternoon meeting of Sunday a partial organization of a Stake of Zion was effected. Brother C. J. Larson was presented by President Snow and unanimously sustained as President of the Emery Stake of Zion, and Orange Seeley was unanimously sustained as his first counselor, and I never saw men receive a better vote, for every heart seemed to go up with the hand.

Presidents Peterson and Larson and Brothers Farnsworth and Orange Seely will visit the Saints at Ferron and Huntington and hold meetings, further organizing those Wards if necessary. At 11.15 a. m. President W. H. Dame, James Houston and Israel Butt, with one wagon, one carriage and six horses, have just joined us from the south for the round trip. They bring an addition to our force of arms of two revolvers one shot gun and a needle gun. We intend to move on to Huntington Creek this afternoon. They are hurrying me up for a start. To be continued in our next.

F. M. LYMAN.

ESTRAY NOTICE.

I HAVE IN MY POSSESSION:

One dark red COW, eight or nine years old, branded T.T on left hip, T. TIDWELL on left horn, illegible brand on right ribs, downward cut dewlap on brisket, left ear cut square off.

One light roan STEER, two years old, branded T.T on left hip, downward cut dewlap on brisket, left ear cut square off.

One red roan HEIFER, one year old, downward cut dewlap on brisket, left ear cut square off.

One light roan STEER, one year old, branded ⌐ on left hip, under half crop in left ear.

One dark red COW, seven or eight years old, branded S on left hip, 55 on left ribs, resembling a heart on left hip, vented on left thigg, _K on left thigh, ⌐ on left hip, SSS on left shoulder, 55 and blotch on left horn.

If not claimed and taken away by Monday, the 16th day of August, they will be sold at 10 o'clock a. m. at the Estray pound, Castle Dale.

JOSEPH L. BOLDEN,
District Poundkeeper.
Castle Dale, Emery Co., U. T., 1880.

ON THE WAY.

DESCRIPTION OF THE COUNTRY— SHOT BY INDIANS—INTERESTING ITEMS.

MOAB POSTOFFICE, Grand Valley,
On Grand River,
Emery Co , U. T.,
August 28, 1880.

Editor Deseret News:

After I wrote to you on the 23d inst., we made some further observations of the Castle Dale county on the Cottonwood and Presidents Snow and Young gave the preference in their judgment to the townsite located by Orange Seely and approved by President Peterson on the north side of the stream, but consented for the settlers up the creek to locate upon the Reed townsite and to build a school-house, as two will be needed on the creek. They left instructions for the brethren to sink wells in different parts of the valley as it is very difficult to keep water in the ditches through the winter on account of severe frosts, and new ditches. There is a peculiarity in the atmosphere of Castle Valley that we were not able to solve; an object one mile away appears to be three or four miles, which is not the case anywhere else this side so far as I have noticed.

Our road down Cottonwood, across Huntington and up through the broken country to a high valley is tolerably good for new and little traveled road, and across the valley to the alkali spring on the south of the road the traveling is very good, but at that point it begins to be rough, and so continues past the first and second Holes in the Rocks and on to Cottonwood springs, and seven miles below from which point fifteen miles to Green River the road is chiefly solid and down hill enough for making good time. At our dry camp 2 miles east of 2d Holes in the Rocks we had our first stampede, which was not serious enough to cause great excitement. A few of the brethren went out and the stock was pacified, and the cause of fright was no doubt the breaking of a twig under the foot of a nervous pony. We camped by a surveying party at Wilsonville, on the Cottonwood, who are going to survey the unsectionized portion of Utah Territory, east of Green River. We passed them on the 24th inst., and have not seen them since.

We reached Green River, 65 miles from Castledale on the evening of the 25th, all in good condition. We prospected the crossing, blocked up the box of our baggage wagon and raised our traps in the carriages to be safe from the tide and then waited till morning of the 26th for the venture. Green River City has a postoffice, store, ferry, and three families. There is a large tract of country on each side of the river for miles up and down, covered with cottonwood forests and good land beside to make homes and farms for one hundred men "chock full of day's works," on each side of the river. This place also boasts rich coal mines within 15 miles and good timber within 35 miles. The climate is delightful, as fine as can be found in the Territory, a medium between the climate of Salt Lake and our Dixie. Last winter, so severe throughout the Territory, there was but two months of winter on Green River, January and February. Many claims have been staked off on the river, and but little more has been done. The few who are now there have worked hard, but too few to make much of a mark in a large country.

On the 26th we crossed the river safely, the water only covering the axles. We had heavy sand for two miles out from the river and the balance of the road to Bitter Water, 15 miles, was good; from there, seven miles out, the road forks, the north branch leading up to Grand River valley and the south branch leading down to Grand valley, where we are now camped. A very great excitement was caused in our camp, a few miles before we came to the forks of the road, when we discovered, a mile or two off to the southwest, in the beautiful valley through which we were traveling, an animal running at full speed, which was first thought to be a horse, but on more careful examination it was called a buffalo, an elk, deer, or some wild animal. We called a halt, hunted up our shotguns, powder, shot and caps! Our cut wads being one size too small, turned beside the ramrod, which was a little too short, fastened in the gun, and the desperate efforts made to force fingers and thumb down the muzzle to form pincers, with which to extract the ramrod, was a painful operation, and the suspense for ten minutes was almost unbearable, and when success crowned the pincer operation, it was discovered that the game was a mustang pony. Excitement subsided and the gun was once more buckled securely to the bows of the carriage. We don't anticipate such exciting times over wild game again. The good road continued across the valley, by the Rock Wells and over a beautiful pass, and down to the Court House Rock, 35 miles from Green River.

From Court House Rock and the beautiful scenery made by red and white sandstone bluffs to the west of it, we drove over 15 miles of very deep sand and rough canyon road to Grand River, which we forded without much hesitation, and no preparation, and to our surprise the water came near swimming our small horses, and run into all our wagon boxes and over the tops of some of the boxes, and things that we did not lift up hastily were well soaked and swimming. We crossed safely and drove two miles up the valley to Brother Alfred G. Wilson's, who bid us welcome, and we camped at 2 p. m. yesterday. We feasted upon watermelons for one hour, and were filled.

At 3.30 p.m., just before our dinner was spread, I saw a young man —Joseph H. Wilson, son of our host— approaching from up the valley, who seemed, at first sight, to have blacked his face, but on near approach I concluded he must have been dragged by his foot in the stirrup, but when he got down from his horse we learned that he had been shot by Indians, 21 hours before, one shot passing through from the bottom of his foot up through the instep, another grazed the thumb on the right hand and a third ball struck him just below the temple at the left corner of the left eye, passing under the eye and came out of the centre of the nose, tearing it wide open, leaving only a little of the upper part of the nose, and not to exceed half an inch of the point. He crawled five miles while thus wounded without food or water and

Remainder blurry.

LIST OF AGENTS.

The following gentlemen are authorized to canvass for the SALT LAKE
DAILY, SEMI WEEKLY and WEEKLY
HERALD; also to receive payment and
receipt for the same:

M. Muir.....Bountiful, Woods Cross and
Centreville
H. A. Lewis...Georgetown, Bear Lake Co.
Wm. Hulme,...Bloomington, Bear Lake
W. A. Stewart,..Inverury, Sevier County
John Hortin,.....Rockport and Wanship
H. Tuft, ...Monroe, Sevier County
Thos. Wallace......Ogden and Weber Co
L. T. Shepherd,.........Bear Lake County
A. W. Babbitt...........Spring Lake and
Santaquin
O. F. Lyons,................Summit County
E. Henriod ....American Fork
A. Leslie..................... Fountain Green
N. A. Rolph..............Mount Pleasant
B. W. Driggs, Jr.............Pleasant Grove
E. E. Cowdell ....Beaver County
Wm. Monteith...................Tooele County
Coöp. Store....................Spanish Fork
W. L. Watkins,.............Brigham City
D. G. Brian,..................Piute County
Thomas Crawley,.............Juab County
J. S. Moffat ....Meadowville
Walter Walker,..............Farmington
Jos. T. Ellis..................Spring City
John Shields,.................Tooele City
S R. Jewkes,..................Castle Dale
John Batty,...................Toquerville
J. K. Clark,..................Grantsville
Wm. Mendenhall................Springville
J. E. Johnson,................Silver Reef
John Pymm,....................St. George
H. McMullin...................Heber City
R. W. Hayborne................Cedar City
J. F. Walters.................Mill Creek

S. Williams....................Ephraim
F. H. Wright,..................Coalville
H. P. Miller,.................Richfield
S. Francis ....Morgan
John Swain,....................Fayette
T. Greener,....................Kanosh
Wm. Probert, Sen..............Holden
Charles C. Shaw...............Hyrum
John S. Black.................Deseret
Wm. Probert,..................Scipio
Charles Foote,................Nephi
John W. Shepherd..............Levan
William Burbeck,..............Provo
George Scott..................Manti
John Woodhouse,...............Lehi

ESTRAY NOTICE.

I HAVE IN MY POSSESSION:

One brindle and white spotted OX, about 8 years old, branded T on left side of neck, $\frac{—}{S}$ on left shoulder, swallowfork in left ear, and rounding crop in right ear.

One brindle and white speckled OX, no brands visible, underbit and upperslope and slit in right ear.

If the above described animals are not claimed and taken away on or before Monday, Nov. 18th 1880, they will be sold at 10 a.m. at the Castle Dale estray pound.

JOS. L. BOULDEN,
District Poundkeeper.

Castle Dale, Emery Co., Nov. 8, 1880.

Narrow Escape.—A correspondent to the *Enquirer* from Castle Dale, Emery County, under date of the 18th ult., gives the following particulars of a narrow escape from death of J. K. Reed and J. D. Kilpack, while crossing the mountains between Salina and Castle Dale:

"They went out to get in some goods for Christmas. The snow fell so deep that they were compelled to leave their wagons on the way, intending to hire a wagon on the other side to come as far as possible up Salina Canyon, and then pack through the snow to their own wagons. In coming up Salina Canyon, after dark and about two miles below S. Allread's ranch, and while passing over a very narrow dugway, the nigh hind wheel slid off a rock and precipitated the wagon, men and four horses a distance of 60 feet into the Salina creek. Reid was lying face downward on the hind part of the wagon and was thrown about 40 feet down the hill to the edge of a perpendicular bank, and then into the creek. The wagon went over him without injuring him. Kilpack was driving the team, and, when the wagon started to go, he sprang from the off side of the wagon and struck on the edge of the bank below, and then fell into the creek up to his waist. He crawled on to the ice and snow just in time, for the wagon and horses fell into the exact spot he had just vacated. The parties as soon as possible went to work cutting harness and getting the horses out of their entanglement. The best horse was so badly hurt that he died before morning; the others were also badly bruised, the wagon tongue was broken in twain, and the goods were smashed, scattered and wet, making the loss, including the horse, about $300. A sack of sugar was afterwards discovered, by feeling with a stick, under the ice, after it had been all night in the water.

This accident happened on the "wheelbarrow road" in Salina canyon, that was made last summer. A man would need good nerves to drive even a wheelbarrow over some of the dugways."

Deseret News
February 23, 1881

Correspondence.

CASTLE DALE,
Emery County, Utah,
Jan. 26th, 1881.

Editor Deseret News:

A great many people throughout the country do not know that there is such a place as Castle Dale in Utah. We are situated about the centre of the largest coal fields known in America. There have been three crops raised here; the first was a very small one, enough just to show that grain would grow. But anything will grow here that will grow in almost any part of Utah. There were 500 gallons of molasses raised last season at this place, and 4,000 bushels of small grain. We have about ten thousand acres of tillable land, with an abundance of water to irrigate it. The people are scattered all over the land, most of them having city lots with 160 acres in them.

The only place that there is anything like a town started or that the people seem to want to get closer together is what is known as the Reid townsite; the people there have got a school-house up and a day school is in operation, taught by a lady from Fairview, Sanpete County, who takes a great interest in teaching the young idea how to shoot. There is also a school-house built on what is known as the old townsite. The site is there, but the town is in prospective. School is taught in it under the able supervision of Emanuel Bagley, Esq. We have two Sabbath schools in operation, with J. M. Peterson superintendent of the lower house and Andrew Andersen superintendent of the upper house, with about 40 pupils at each place. Meetings are held at both houses every other Sabbath respectively; we have also Thursday night meetings, which are very well attended considering the scattered condition of the people.

We have a grist mill and saw mill in course of construction by S. Jewker & Co. At present they are running a set of French burrs by horse power, to grind Graham and corn meal, and they do a very good business. They have set the saw mill down, intending to saw out lumber by horse power, to construct the grist mill in the spring, which will be a great blessing to the people of the valley, for the appetites of the people are so good that a man with any sized family has got to be on the the road about one-third of the time to keep the bread basket full.

We hear a great deal about railroads and coal. All that we are afraid of is, that they will flood this country with railroads till they become a drug on the market. One or two would not come amiss, so that we could get out in the winter and get our store goods in; but if they build so many, they will compel us to travel on them, and it will be bad. I understand there are two companies working in Salina Canyon already; how many more I don't know. When they get to running it will then be impossible to get through with a wagon. And all their cry is, Coal! Coal! Coal!

I must not forget to mention that we have a blacksmith shop just started at this place and a good workman in it, which is the best of it. His name is Jos. Boulden. Next in order are our ditches for carrying the water to our towns and farms. President Larsen and Seely have got some of the people star ed to dig the ditch on to the townsite, some of them intending to build there this summer. There is some talk of parties starting another ditch on the same side of the river, to cover a large tract of land to the north and northeast of the townsite; if this is done a great many new settlers can get farms. It was advised by Prest. Erastus Snow, when he and company were here last summer, that this ditch should be taken out.

We expect that large crops will be put in here this spring All we want to make this once barren desert (it is a little better now) blossom like the rose is more men of muscle and energy to utilize the land and water and *bring them under subjection.*

More anon, from

E. PLURIBUS.

P. S.—I *forgot to mention* our stores of which we have two, or at least the places where they were, but owing to so much snow being in

the mountains there is nothing in them. Can't travel except on horseback.   E. P.

FERRON CREEK,
Castle Valley, Emery Co.,
Feb. 12, 1880.

Editor Deseret News:

The health of the people in this place is good, with a very few exceptions. We are continually on the increase in numbers, as settlers keep coming in. We number now upwards of 40 families, but at present we are much in need of tradesmen, especially a blacksmith and shoemaker. And as there is still land to be had, we would like any such to come out and see our country, and don't forget to visit Ferron Creek, and I would say to any intending to come here to settle that they can procure seed grain at a reasonable price. The Saints here seem to feel well in the good cause we are engaged in, that of building up the church and kingdom of God. We have had good meetings throughout the present winter; our worthy Bishop, Wm. Taylor, Sen., seems to be alive to his duties.

We are now working a road up into our canyon, that we may get timber that we may improve and fence our farms, as well as build upon our town site. We also have a weekly mail which now runs regularly, so that we have a chance to receive the news through your weekly NEWS. J. E. KING.

More Favorable.—N. T. Guymon, writing from Huntington, Emery County, on the 6th inst., states that since his last communication, the weather has taken a change for the better in that locality. For three weeks it had been more like spring. Stock was doing first rate. Prospects were good for grass and crops, and if fine weather continued, plowing would begin in a few days. General health, good.

Correspondence.

CASTLEDALE, Emery Co.,
U. T., Feb. 7th, A. D. 1881.

Editor Deseret News:

In August, 1880, this place was visited by Apostles Erastus Snow, Brigham Young, Francis M. Lyman and their company, *en route* for Colorado and Arizona, and President Canute Petersen and other brethren from Sanpete Valley, at which time we were appointed to preside over the Emery Stake of Zion.

Our homes were then in Sanpete Valley, respectively at Spring City, and Mount Pleasant. Responding to the call, we prepared ourselves to winter with the Saints in Castle Valley. We may here state, that we were not at first so favorably inclined towards this valley, but as we became better acquainted with the facilities and resources of the valley, the more are we convinced of its adaptability for homes for Latter-day Saints. A goodly supply of water from mountain streams passes through the valley, and empty their great waste into the Colorado river. These are scarcely affected by the amount of water which has thus far been taken for irrigating purposes. Among these streams are Price River, Huntington Creek, Cottonwood Creek, Ferron Creek and the Muddy. Many years will no doubt elapse, before all the available lands on either of those creeks will be utilized. Besides these, Green River with the Gunnison Valley yet comparatively unsettled, will in the future undoubtedly yield to the faithful stroke of the sturdy husbandman, furnishing homes and sustenance for thousands of souls. Small grain does tolerably well, and harvests early. The vegetable-growing properties of the soil are good. The climate and soil seem well adapted to the growing of cane and corn. With the addition of a good flour mill, which is now being built by Bro. Samuel Jewkes & Co., and will no doubt be completed by next harvest, we will consider ourselves in pretty good circumstances and established on a good foundation. A very good quality of Graham flour and also of corn meal is now being furnished by the mill.

The site recommended by the Apostles when here, as the most suitable on which to found a city at Castledale, has been purchased, and surveyed into blocks containing four lots each, each lot being 13 rods square; with streets six rods wide, and suitable public and church grounds. The ditch intended to convey water on to the townsite has been surveyed, and is now being succesfully worked. A school-house has been built on the townsite, and in consequence of the present scattered condition of the people, another school-house has been built about one mile and a half further west. Day schools are kept in each house, with an enrollment of about 50 pupils, which, in connection with two Sunday schools in the ward, and Sunday meetings, a fair opportunity is afforded for the cultivation and development of the youthful minds.

The townsite at Huntington is one mile square, surveyed into blocks containing four lots, each lot is 16½ rods square; the street are six rods wide. Much labor has already been performed on their townsite ditch. They have a very good meeting-house, dimensions 20 x 30 feet. Bishop Cox has almost completed his dwelling house on the townsite.

A townsite has also been located and surveyed at Ferron, on which Bishop Taylor and many other are building. The town lots contain one and a half acres each. They have Sunday and day schools.

In these wards, Sabbath and ward meetings are well attended.

Our county officers appear to be actively looking after the interests of the people—districting the county into precincts and suitable road and school districts.

Present appearances indicate that in the near future a railroad will be completed into this valley.

Large bodies of timber, suitable for milling, building and fencing purposes abound in the mountains, and are reasonably easy of access. Two sawmills have been built—one on Huntington Creek, and one on the head waters of Cottonwood Creek—and another is now in course of construction. From these, we believe that a sufficient amount of lumber can be obtained for building, and other necessary purposes. Square edged lumber (and of a very good quality) is sold at the mills at $1.25 and $1.50 per hundred feet.

On the low benches is an inexhaustible supply of firewood (nut pine and cedar.) Besides which the innumerable coal veins cropping out to the observing eye of the traveler, on the right and left when passing through our canyons, promise a safeguard against a monopoly of coal trade in Emery county.

The winter has been quite open—the earth is now sufficiently free from frost to admit of plowing, and the weather is fine for outdoor work. Stock has wintered well on the range.

To those seeking homes, we extend a cordial invitation to visit this place, and if they will call upon us, we will endeavor to direct them to suitable localities.

On Wednesday the 9th we will start to visit the Saints at Grand Valley.

Your most valuable paper we receive pretty regularly, and our sincere wishes are that the editor may long live to bless its numerous readers with a continuation of good reading and wise counsels.

With much interest for the welfare of Zion, we subscribe ourselves your brethren in the gospel of peace.

CHRISTIAN G LARSEN,
ORANGE SEELY.

In Castle Dale, MARIA and DORTHEA, daughters of Maria and C. A. Frederiksen; born March 18th, 1881; died March 18, 1881.

Killed.

On the 27th of April a man named Charles Rickard was killed by another named Jacob Ivie, at Ferron, Emery County, this territory. The full particulars are not obtainable, but it appears that Ivie acted in self-defense, having struck the fatal blow with a neck-yoke. A coroner's jury investigated the matter, and the result of their deliberations is found in the above, stating that to the best knowledge of the jury, Ivie acted in self-defense.

Killed with a Neck-Yoke. — A man named Charles Rickard was killed on the 27th of last month, in Emery County, by another man named Jacob Ivie. We have received no other particulars than are contained in the following verdict, rendered at the coroner's inquest upon the body of the deceased:

Territory of Utah,)
　Ferron Precinct, }
　Emery County.)

An inquisition holden at Bishop Taylor's, in Ferron Precinct, Emery County, on the 27th of April, A. D., 1881, before the justice of the peace in Ferron Precinct, in said county, upon the body of Charles Rickard, there lying dead, by the jurors whose names are hereunto subscribed. The said jurors upon their oaths do say, that the said Charles Rickard came to his death on the 27th of April, by being struck with a neck-yoke in the hands of one Jacob Ivie; and from the evidence we have, said Ivie acted in self-defense.

In testimony whereof the said jurors have hereunto set their hands the day and year aforesaid.

J. E. KING,
WM. TAYLOR, JR.,
JOS. S. THORNTON.
　　　　　　Jurors.

Witness my hand, M. W. Molen, Justice of the Peace for Ferron Precinct, Emery Co., U. T.

From the South-west.—Brother William Howard, of Huntington, Emery County, and his brother, L. A. Howard of Cottonwood, called upon us yesterday afternoon. They are both the sons of Sister Elizabeth Howard, well known as one of the leading spirits of the Ladies Relief Society. The first mentioned gentleman arrived last Tuesday from Huntington, where he has been residing since last fall He will attend to some business here and return home next Monday. Huntington is a settlement of 60 families, all "Mormon" but one, well situated in the northern part of the county, near a stream larger than Big Cottonwood Creek, and capable of supplying plenty of good water to the settlers. The soil in the vicinity is good, and an abundance of timber for building purposes is at hand. The route of the Denver and Rio Grande Railroad runs within three miles of the town, to the eastward, and as the work of grading has commenced, plenty of labor for men and teams is thereby furnished. The town was organized last Augst and is thriving. There is room for more settlers, and they would be very welcome.

DIED

In Huntington, Emery County, April 15, 1881, of worm fever, CATHERINE MARIA, daughter of Anthony and Maria Neilsen, aged 2 years, 3 months and 1 day.

Castle Dale.—Mr. J. K. Reid, of Castle Dale, Emery County, arrived in town yesterday, and made us a brief call this morning.

The settlement is the county seat of Emery, is situated about the centre of the valley, and will be about five miles from the branch of the S. V. R. R., which is to extend from the junction at Buckhorn Flat to Salina. It was located about three years ago, and already has upwards of a hundred families. When our informant first went there there were but three families. The population is daily increasing. Most of the inhabitants are engaged in farming. A saw mill is in active operation, and buildings are going up rapidly. The settlement is presided over by Bishop Jasper Peterson, and his Counselors N. P. Miller and Emanuel Bagley. The people of the place are good, industrious folks, nearly all engaged at home. One or two are away on the railroad, but even these have their crops growing. The harvest promises well, but will not be so early as in this vicinity. A great deal of ditching had to be done last spring, so that grain could not be sowed as early as it otherwise would have been. The people take water from the Cottonwood Creek, which furnishes an abundance, of excellent quality, for domestic and irrigating purposes. Among the improvements in course of construction is a grist mill, to be run by water power, from the same stream. The general health of the settlement is excellent, the climate being full of life, favorable to development and comparatively free from disease. A great deal of annoyance is caused by defective mail carriage. When Mr. Reid left Castle Dale, it had not had a mail for three weeks. It is due every week at a little place called Wilsonville, of two or three houses, and is carried there by pony express from Salina. Castle Dale is seven miles from Wilsonville, and the residents of the former place send their own messengers after the mail. Mr. Reed is postmaster at Castle Dale, duly appointed, but no regular service has been put upon the line. Repeated petitions have been sent to Washington, but although the line was established, there is no regular service in operation. The people cannot depend either upon receiving their mail, or upon its safe transmission to other points. The subject is one which should be looked into by the postal authorities. Mr. Reid is up to Salt Lake on business, and expects to return home immediately.

Deseret News
August 3, 1881

THE REPORTED INDIAN FIGHT IN CASTLE VALLEY.

HUNTINGTON,
Emery Co., Utah,
July 22nd, 1881.

Editor Deseret News:

In dispatches contained in the the Semi-weekly NEWS of June 28th, and also in an editorial in the same paper of July 2d, it is inferred that there has been an Indian fight in Castle Valley, Utah. We as settlers in this valley feel rather bad at not hearing of this fight before it came out in the papers, but from the description given of the Indian troubles, we think it must be a fight some Colorado men had with the Indians in this county, but over 100 miles east of Castle Valley.

It is 60 miles from here to Green River, 45 miles from Green River to Moab, and 25 miles from Moab to the scene of the fight, or, in other words, the fight happened at or near the line separating Utah from Colorado.

I would not take the trouble to describe the locality of this fight so much, but I have received several letters from friends asking the full particulars, they expressing great fears at our living in Castle Valley, and fearing that at any moment they may hear of us all being killed by the Indians. I will say there has been no danger here yet, and we do not expect any.

It is true the people in this valley are in a very scattered condition, in some instances being miles apart, and I think the good Latter-day Saints would justify the Lord a little in sending an Indian scare or perhaps a reality to drive the people together, for we have been counselled time and again by the authorities placed over us to get together in towns that we might attend to our meetings and send our children to school, and if the people will not take counsel and do what they are told for their best good, they must suffer the consequences.

I will again say to our friends who live in colder valleys than this, that if they want a good climate, plenty of land and water and timber handy, come and look at this valley, and they can judge of the balance themselves. We have had no frost here since the first of May, and grain, corn, potatoes and vines look splendid. Some patches look rather sickly and poor, but that is only a proof of neglect, for the man that will put his crops in in the right time and take care of them can raise just as good average crops as are raised anywhere in Utah.

Again assuring our kind friends not to fear yet awhile for scalps,

I remain,
Your brother in the gospel,
W. H.

Deseret News
August 10, 1881

DIED

At Huntington, Emery, Utah, July 17, 1881, of puerperal fever, after an illness of six weeks, EMMA SEDENIA, wife of Joseph Ottison, and daughter of Robert Gillespie and Nancy Maria Lane. Deceased was born at Fillmore, Millard County, Utah, November 22, 1860. She leaves a husband and three children to mourn her loss.

Salt Lake Herald
August 20, 1881

CLOUD BURST

Terrible Destruction of Property in Castle Valley.

(Special Telegram.)

PROVO, Aug. 19, 6.20 p.m.

Capt. R. R. Hopkins passed through here by the noon train from Castle Valley. He reports that on Sunday last about 4 o'clock at Cottonwood Springs, on the railroad grade, Castle Valley, a cloud burst and carried away his entire mercantile stores, consisting of dry goods, flour and grain for men working on the grade. Nothing was saved but a few bars of steel. He barely escaped with his life. A cloud had burst in Soldier Canyon, the main traveled road from the north to Castle Valley, and washed out the canyon road so that it is impossible to convey supplies; and also a cloud burst near Castle Dale, the county seat of Castle Valley, and did considerable damage to the place. A number of places and culverts on the grade were washed away by rain storms in various places.

CARD OF THANKS.

BEAVER, Oct. 5, 1881.

Editor Deseret News:

Allow me through your most valuable columns to tender my most sincere thanks to all who have in any way aided me in bringing before the public facts connected with the history of the Mormon *Batallion.*

Prominently among them Presidents John Taylor and George Q Cannon; Apostles Orson Pratt, church historian, deceased, and Franklin D. Richards; Cannon and Young and C. W. Penrose, editors, DESERET NEWS; Israel Barlow, for suggesting and urging me to undertake the work which met the approval of President Taylor; Captain Nelson Higgins, Lieut. James Pace Q. M. Sergeant, Redick N. Allred, Sister Eliza R. S. Smith, for revising and composing Battalion songs; Levi W. Hancock, Elizabeth Hyde, Henry Standage, Henry W. Bigler, John G Smith, Henry G Boyle, Israel Evans, James V. Williams, President John R. Murdock, Nathaniel Jones, Sister Celia Hunt, widow of the late Captain Jefferson Hunt, Fanny Mariah Huntington, Malinda Covington relict of Milton Kelly. There are numerous others, both male and female who have furnished names and facts, all of whom will please accept my best thanks and consider themselves included the same as though they were mentioned by name. Much of the *book is now in type* and I trust will soon be before the public.

Respectfully,

DANIEL TYLER.

CASTLE DALE, Emery Co., Utah,
December 14, 1881.

Editor Deseret News:

Utah seems to be taking a move, Horace Greely said, go west young man, go west. But some great impetus seems to be sending them east. I think it must be our climate, for that we can boast of, if nothing else. We have had no snow yet in the valley, and weather is as warm as in the middle of June, with the exception of nights. Our climate cannot be beat in Utah. The farmers of this valley are getting some of their pay back for the hard times they experienced in starting their homes here, in the high prices they are getting for their products, everything is high in the shape of eatables for man or beast. The railroad is bringing its accompaniments, whisky and pistols, and a man for breakfast. At Blake City the other day they had a free fight, which ended in the killing of one man and the wounding of one or two others.

I have to chronicle a sad case that happened here a few days ago; Bro. Louis Johansen's wife died, after suffering for four days. The whole community feel to sympathise with Bro. Johansen in his great bereavement. This being the first grown person that has died in this place— and it has been settled going on four years—it has caused a gloom to spread over the community.

We see through the NEWS that Prest. Taylor and party had arrived home after their extended tour south. The Saints of Emery would not have felt bad had they had the privilege of seeing and hearing them, for we are shut out to some extent from those blessings which the people have over the mountains in the older settlements. The people in this county seem to have imbibed the spirit of gathering together in towns, more than formerly, which causes a better feeling to exist, both in word and act, amongst the people. One great drawback yet is the want of a grist mill. We have one started in this place, but the parties that started it went as far as they could, and quit for a time for want of means. Enough money has left this county this fall to have built a first-class mill; it is a blessing to the people as it is, but it would have been a greater one had they received help to complete it, as they should have had.

A word on mail matters would not be out of place. The mail run through this county three times a week, by Samuel Gibson, Esq., could not be better; when run by the former company it was called a weekly mail, it got weaker and weaker till it weakened out, and the people had no pity or sorrow to express when the poor thing died. It is now run on time and good time; we get our news three days from Salt Lake, which should satisfy the most fastidious.

A SUBSCRIBER.

Deseret News
January 18, 1882

Roughs Along the Railroad.—
To-day we met Brother William Howard, of Huntington, Emery County. In consequence of the Denver & Rio Grande R.R. passing through that part of the country, bringing the usual complement of roughs, the locality is frequently the theatre of barbarous and brutal scenes. Several whisky saloons are running, and are regulated by no legal restrictions whatever.

At Lake City lately a boisterous rowdy, named Winder, drew his revolver, pointed it at a knot of men with threats of shooting. A party standing behind him made a casual remark, when he wheeled and fired at him, inflicting a slight wound. The party aimed at whipped out a pistol and shot Winder, who died a day or two afterwards.

Horse thieves are plentiful. Not long since, Major Hurd had a couple of valuable animals stolen. Recently a couple of "cowboys" rode up to the Major's camp during his absence, flourished their guns and said they were the parties who took the horses and dared the men to "come out and take them." Major Hurd is the engineer of that part of the road.

In consequence of the troublesome conduct of the rough element, the D. & R. G. Co. purpose removing their principal camp to another locality, where they will be able to have such characters under greater control.

The people are somewhat dissatisfied because of the lack of a proper or thorough civil organization, in precincts and otherwise. The looseness existing in this regard makes it impracticable to control the rougher elements now introduced into that part of the Territory.

Up to last Thursday, when Brother Howard left, there was no snow at or near Huntington, and the weather was mild in other respects.

Excitement in Emery Co.

By D. K. Reid, of Castle Dale, Emery County, the *Deseret News* is informed of the killing, on the 21st ult., of William Nugent, known as "California Bill," by William Duffy. The tragedy occurred at Blake City. The two had quarreled during the day, Duffy getting the worse of the fight. He subsequently procured a Winchester rifle with which he shot Nugent through the body, killing him. Nugent wounded Duffy in the calf of the leg, with a pistol shot. The affair raised quite an excitement, and threats of lynching Duffy were freely indulged in.

This is the second homicide in Emery County within a very brief period, D. L. Blizzard being the previous victim.

Scalded to Death.

The *Deseret News* has learned of a lamentable incident which occurred at Ferron, Castle Valley, Emery Co., on the 8th inst. Willie, a 3-year old son of Peter Hansen, while at play accidentally fell into a boilerful of hot water, by which he was fearfully scalded. After much suffering, he died at 1 o'clock the following morning. The burial took place on the 10th. The little community exhibit deep sympathy for the parents, who are greatly distressed at the occurrence.

THE KILLING OF WILLIAM NUGENT.

HUNTINGTON, Emery County,
Utah, January 26, 1882.

Editor Deseret News:

On last Saturday, the 21st inst., the inhabitants of Blake City, in this county, had rather a lively time for a couple of hours, which resulted in the death of William Nugent. The circumstances, as near as I could learn, are about as follows:

It appears that Nugent and another man by the name of Wm. Duffee had a quarrel over a lunch they were taking, when Nugent knocked Duffee down with a large bone he had in his hand, and while Duffee was down, kicked him. Duffee then drew a knife, which Nugent took away from him, then handed it back, saying he was sorry he had struck him, and that they being old friends should not quarrel in that way. Shortly after this, Duffee started away, when Nugent said, "You are going to heel yourself, Duffee?" Duffee answered, "That's all right."

In about an hour after Duffee was seen coming down the road with a Winchester rifle on his shoulder. And Nugent, on being informed of this ran between a couple of stores and called out to Duffee, "Stop, Duffee; stop! you don't want anything from me." Duffee kept right on towards him, when Nugent drew a revolver and fired. The ball striking Duffee in the calf of the leg. Nu-

-gent again prepared to fire, at the same time Duffee leveled his rifle and the two shots were fired almost together. This time Nugent missed, but Duffee's shot struck Nugent in the right breast and passed through the body, killing him almost instantly. Duffee escaped for a little while, but was finally arrested by Jos. Farrer, and held while the citizens held a mass meeting and appointed a coroner and a coroner's jury to hold an inquest over Nugent, which they did, and the evidence they received seemed to justify them in the following verdict:

The said William Nugent, Oakland, Alameda County, California, came to his death by a gunshot wound from a rifle in the hands of Wm. Duffee, and that the said murder was not justifiable.

Signed—Lawrence Bethune, foreman, B. F. Taylor, Jos. Hyde, J. T. Farrer, W. H. Coats, J. Gammage, —Burdick, Alonzo Smith, R. Hatch, L. Moore, Thos. Farrer, Jas. —sh.

The prisoner was then brought to Huntington, it being the nearest place where there was a justice of peace, (by the way, justices are few and far between in this county) Mr. Thos. Farrer and two assistants, and turned over to the justice here, who placed him in the hands of the sheriff.

As soon as the preliminary arrangements were made for an examination, the complaint was read to the prisoner, who thereupon waived an examination, preferring

... complaint should first go before

the grand jury, he (the prisoner) claiming he did the deed in self-defense. The prisoner was again turned over to the sheriff for safe-keeping until the grand jury meets in Provo.

It appears also, from what I can learn, that Nugent and Duffee were peaceable sort of men, but the quarrel they had was the result of one of the many whiskey sprees there is at Green River. There are several saloons running there, besides others in the county, without paying any license to the county, whether they do the United States or not I do not know.

Yours very respectfully,
W. H.

Deseret News
April 5, 1882

HUNTINGTON,
Emery County, Utah,
February 25th, 1882.

Editor Deseret News:

I thought a few items from this place in regard to the progress and prosperity of the Saints here would not be amiss.

The crops last season on an average were good, each man's crop being good according to the amount of care bestowed upon it. This valley being like the rest of Utah, it takes plenty of hard work to raise a good crop of any kind, but we are blessed with a splendid climate, it being fully as good if not better than that of Salt Lake. The season clear of frost being from four to six weeks longer than in Utah or Salt Lake counties. The deepest snow we have had this winter has not been over 1½ inches deep, and that did not stay on the ground long. Most of the weather has been warm and and pleasant, with nights more or less cold, but I do not think the thermometer has been down to zero yet. We have a very good day school, taught by Bro. Elias H. Cox; also a very good Sunday School, presided over by Bro. Peter Johnson.

Our Sunday meetings are very well attended. We have had a couple of very good lectures lately, delivered by Bro. Noah Y. Guymon, on the rise and persecutions of the Church. Brother Guymon having passed through most of the persecutions and mobbings of the Saints for their religion, was able to handle the subject very intelligently and with telling effect, for no true Latter day Saint can think or hear of these things without being moved to pity

r those that had to pass through
em, for the sake of worshipping
od according to the dictates of their
wn consciences. A privilege guar-
teed them by the Constitution of
e country in which we live.
ut as Joseph Smith pro-
esied it would, the time
as come when the legislators and
lers of the nation are trampling
at sacred instrument under their
et. It would appear from present
dications that there was about to
another crusade inaugurated
ainst the Latter-day Saints, but if
e will only do right and obey the
unsel given us from the Lord
rough His servants and do our
rt, God will do His part, and make
e wrath of the wicked turn to His
aise, and if trouble has to come it
ight as well come now as any
me, because if we are not prepared
w, we will never be until some-
ing comes to make us so.
But to my subject. To-day we
ve had a very interesting meeting,
e occasion of the organization of
e Relief Society of this Ward. On
e stand were (by invitation) Pre-
dents Larsen and Seely, also Bish-
Cox and his Second Counselor
illiam Avery.

After singing and prayer Bishop
ox and President Larsen gave the
sters some very good instructions.
m. Howard was appointed secre-
ry of the meeting, after which the
llowing organization was effected.
or President Sister Tilitha Avery,
st Counselor Emma Leonard,
cond Counselor Mary E, Cox,
ecretary Anna Johnson, and Treas-
er Eliza J. Avery. The above
amed sisters were then set apart
y the proper authorities.
President Larsen and Bishop Cox
ave the sisters some good instruc-
on in regard to their duties as a
ciety and as Latter-day Saints.
hus ended an important event for
e sisters of Huntington.
I will add that we feel it a bless-
g to be numbered with the Lat-
er-day Saints, for Jesus said blessed
e they who are persecuted for my
ame's sake.
After singing the meeting was
ismissed by Elder Wellington See-
y.
Yours respectfully, W. H.

Logan Leader
April 14, 1882

List of Missionaries.

Following are the names of missionaries called at the late conference:

CASTLE GATE, EMERY CO.

Rasmus Jameson, Spring City.
Henning Olsen, "

HUNTINGTON,
Emery County, Utah,
March 27th, 1882.

Editor Deseret News:

Some time ago I sent you the particulars of a two days' meeting we had in this place, but as I have not seen any reference to it, I presume you did not get it.

On Feb. 25th, Presidents Larsen and Seely visited us, and according to previous notice, meeting convened at 2 o'clock p.m. After the usual opening exercises, President Larsen said the object of the meeting on that day was to organize a Relief Society, and gave those present, especially the sisters, some very good instruction in regard to their duties, after which the following organization was effected:

Sister Tabitha Avery, president; Sisters Emma Leonard and Mary E. Cox, her counselors; Sister Anna Johnson, secretary, and Sister Eliza J. Avery, treasurer; after which the speakers were President Larsen and Bishop Elias Cox, who thanked the sisters for their good attendance.

Sunday, 26th, at 11.30 a.m., meeting opened with singing and prayer. The speakers were Elder W. Seeley, Prest. Orange Seeley, Prest. Larsen and Bishop Cox, who all spoke with the spirit of the Lord resting upon them. At the close of the meeting the universal feeling among the people was that they had enjoyed themselves very much.

We also have a very good Sunday school, presided over by Bro. Peter Johnson, with an average attendance of over 100 pupils. We also have a good day school taught by Bro. Elias H. H. Cox.

Bro. N. T. Guymon has delivered several very interesting lectures this winter on the early rise and persecutions of the Church, having passed through the trials and mobbings of the Saints in Missouri and Illinois; he was able to handle the subject with ability. There has been considerable sickness among the children here, but as far as I can learn all are better now and we all feel very thankful that there have been no deaths among us.

The heaviest snow fall we have had here this winter, (or I might say last winter, for it is nice spring weather here now), has not been over one and a half inches deep, and otherwise the weather has been warm and pleasant.

Last Saturday, March 25, 1882, there was a county convention at Castle Dale, at which Hon. C. G. Larsen was chosen to represent Emery County in the State constitutional convention to be held in Salt Lake City April 10, 1882. Elias Cox was elected his alternate. The following preamble and resolutions was introduced in the convention by Wm. Howard, and after being slightly amended was unanimously approved by said convention:

Whereas, There are now pending in the Congress of the United States several bills, having for their object the persecution and disfranchisement of a large majority of the people of the Territory of Utah, commonly called Mormons, and some portions of said bill not only strike at the religious and political freedom of the Latter-day Saints (a right that is as dear to them as it ever has been or ever will be to any of the people of the United States) but also at the Constitution of the country in which we live, an instrument we hold to be sacred, and beyond the power of Congress to make laws in conflict with, as article 1 of the amendments to the Constitution expressly declares that Congress shall make no law respecting an establishment of religion or prohibiting the free exercise thereof, and

Whereas, Some parts of said bill are bills of attainder, depriving the people of their just *rights,* without due process or law, while article five of the amendments to the Constitution declares that no person shall be held to answer for a capital or otherwise infamous crime, unless on presentment or indictment of a grand jury * * * nor be deprived of life, liberty or property without due process of law; and article six of the amendment says, in all criminal prosecutions the accused shall enjoy the right to a speedy trial by an *impartial jury* of the state and district wherein the crime shall have been committed, which district shall have been previously ascertained by law, and be informed of the nature and cause of the accusation, be confronted with the witnesses against him, have compulsory process for obtaining witnesses in his favor, and have the assistance of counsel for his defence, and

Whereas the Edmunds bill, lately passed by Congress, deprives us of these rights inasmuch as it takes from us our liberty and property which we hold in the right to vote at any election held in the County, City or Precinct in which we live, and perhaps our lives, without due process of law, and inasmuch as we hold as dear as life the privilege to worship God according to the dictates of our own consciences and what we know to be right, and also the right to speedy trial by *impartial jury,* the right to be informed of the nature of the crime held against us, and the right to be confronted with the witnesses against us and also the right of counsel for our defence. And,

Whereas our people in other more favored parts of the Territory have availed themselves of the privilege of sending petitions to Congress protesting against the enacting of such unlawful measures, and asking Congress to send a commission of honorable men to Utah to examine into its affairs that they may be properly informed of the condition of the people of Utah, which is greatly exaggerated for the worse by a small clique of our enemies who would like to possess our property, our homes, and destroy our peace and good will towards each other and our conscience void of offence towards our God and towards all truth-loving men and women (a thing they can never do), and

Whereas, Knowing as we well do that the cause of our people is just and that proscriptive legislation, whether against the people of Utah or of any other people, is not becoming the high dignity of a free and independent Republic, now, therefore, be it

Resolved, That we do heartily concur in and sanction all petitions sent by our people for that purpose, and be it further

Resolved, that the clerk of this convention send copies of this preamble and resolutions to the DESERET EVENING NEWS and *Salt Lake Herald* for publication.

Very respectfully,
WILLIAM HOWARD,
Clerk of Convention.

Ogden Herald
May 13, 1882

THE Denver & Rio Grande railway will pass within four miles of Castle Dale which is a three-year old town of 50 families, young but thrifty. The grade of the railroad is now within 20 miles of the place. Castle Dale is surrounded by immense coal deposits. —*Deseret News.*

Deseret News
May 17, 1882

Castle Dale. — Brother Samuel Jewkes, of Castle Dale, Emery Co., was in town to-day negotiating with Z. C. M. I. and Mr. Clawson for the purchase of machinery for a new grist mill about to be established at the settlement by Jewkes & Co.

The Denver and Rio Grande Railroad will pass within four miles of Castle Dale, which is a three-year old town of 50 families, young but thrifty. The grade of the railroad is now within 20 miles of the place. Castle Dale is surrounded by immense coal deposits.

Deseret News
August 2, 1882

Appointments—Elders E. Snow and John Henry Smith, of the Apostles, expect to start on Saturday, Aug. 5th, for Castle Valley. They will hold meetings with the Saints on Price River at 4 p. m. Thursday; at Huntington at 4 p. m. on Friday, and at Castledale Saturday and Sunday, 12th and 13th.

Deseret News
September 20, 1882

DIED.

At Huntington, Emery County, Utah, September 5th, 1882, of cholera infantum, ALOAH BLANCHARD, son of Ira B. and Julia M. Whitney, aged one year and ten days.

At Huntington, Emery County, Utah, August 24th, 1882, of heart disease and dropsy, THOMAS H., son of N. T. and Louisa Guyman, aged 13 years and 10 months.

CASTLE VALLEY.

Price River, Castle Valley,
August 11, 1882.

Editor Deseret News:

So this is the much talked of Castle Valley. We came in at the southern extremity and have traveled on up to this river which is at the northern end of the valley. How the idea one forms as to the appearance of any place or thing is the opposite of the reality. I supposed the valley to be a long plain encircled by blue rolling mountains, instead of which it is a rough broken country, with many hills and precipitous tabled mountains. The south end presents much the same appearance as does our own Dixie, minus the volcanic rock. The ground looks rich however and has been a splendid range for cattle. But now from one end to the other of the valley all that is left of the grass is in the memory of the oldest inhabitant and innumerable dried up parched looking stubs. Ranchers have used up this county, in a grazing point of view, so say the settlers, thousands of stock having been kept there before it began to be settled up. Coming to the Muddy, the first settlement, verily we found a muddy stream.

Some few families have made a very good start here, and grain looks well. Twenty-five miles further on we reach Castle Dale, which is to be, I have been told, the county seat. The place is more built up than the others, but the natural facilities are no better than some other places. Still traveling north, twelve miles on, Huntington is reached. Did I say that all the settlements here are built down along the banks of the streams thus making long, narrow towns? Huntington is also a stunning little place, and here as everywhere grain looks beautiful. About twenty miles north you strike the Price River. Ten miles from the crossing is the mouth of the canyon, through which the Denver & Rio Grande R. R. is fast pushing its way eastward.

The valley around Price River is much larger; in fact there are ample facilities for a good sized settlement here. The land also looks richer, the river is larger, and there is a mountain of coal near by. In my humble opinion Price River is the place in this valley. Game abounds all through the country, but here it seems more plentiful if anything. Stories are told by such men as Rhodes and Gremes that distance the tales in novels, of hunts for grizlies, fights and narrow escapes from a hugging death. One man has been killed in this valley by a bear.

Deer and antelope are very frequently seen and killed, and of course many of the smaller kinds of game. Wood is plentiful around this place, and and a saw mill is in operation 15 miles up the canyon. I am told a town is soon to be laid out on this (Price) River. And I would cordially advise any who are in search of good comfortable farms and homes, to come here, as there is no better land in Utah, plenty of wood, a very good supply of water, many fortunes in the coal abounding here, and it is on the line of the railroad. I mentioned the poor grazing facilities, but reliable men assert that there are excellent ranges up in the mountains.

Before closing I want to speak of the warm welcome we received from a young couple living here. Do you you know what a long, lonesome, hot days' travel is in a wagon, reaching your destination after dark, strangers in a strange land?" If you do, you will know how pleasant it was to be asked by the lady of the house to come right in, and have supper. Smoking venison, light dumplings and good soup, made a feast for a king. This oddly contrasted with the over thriftiness of a good man who charged ―― thirty ――ts for a small armful of wood in a place where wood was $2.00 a cord. Blessed are the hospitable for they shall be welcomed in heaven.

HOMESPUN.

NOVEMBER ELECTION.

The Utah Commissioners Make a Number of Appointments

For Judges in the Coming November Election.

Following is a list of the appointments of judges of election for the November election for a Delegate to Congress. The Commissioners have reserved the naming of the necessary officers in the four largest and most populous counties: Salt Lake, Weber, Utah, and Sanpete, as also in Garfield and Summit, for a future day, at any rate not distant.

EMERY COUNTY.

Castle Dale—Orange Seely, John K. Reid, James H. Wilcox.

Ferron—John E. King, Hiram S. Stephens, Warren S. Peacock.

Huntington—Ira B. Whitney, M. E. Johnson, C. W. Caldwell.

Moab—William H. Alred, L. B. Bartlett, Thomas M. Pritchett.

Price—Fred E. Grames Levi Simmons, Mat. Simmons.

The judges for Schofield not yet appointed.

NOVEMBER ELECTION.

Completing the Appointments for its Conduct.

List of the Presiding Judges in the Precincts.

The following additional appointments of judges of election have been made by the Utah Commission:

EMERY COUNTY.

Castle Dale—James H. Wilcox.

Ferron—Warren S. Peacock.

Huntington—C. W. Caldwell.

Moab—L. B. Bartlett.

Price—Mat. Simmons.

Schofield—Robert McKelvy.

I also take the liberty to refer thresher men to the following reliable people who have purchased the Agitator Machines:

Messrs. Robbins & Simmons, Kaysville.

Bishop Peter Barton and others Kaysville.

Woolley, Lund & Judd, St. George.

M. Badt, Wells, Nevada.

S. A. Worthington, Grantsville.

Cummins & Matthews, Grouse Creek.

Bishop H. Jensen, Manti.

H. S. Stevens, Ferron City.

Bishop S. S. Smith, Manassa, Col.

Jas. Larson and others, Malad City

Samaria Co-op., Samaria.

And many others.

THE REGISTRATION.

The Total for the Territory, 33,266

The following completes the table of registration for the territory, the other counties having been previously published:

EMERY COUNTY.

Precinct.	Males.	Females.	Total.
Castle Dale	50	37	87
Huntingdon	34	25	59
Ferron	48	33	81
Moab	16	11	27
Price	24	15	39
Schofield	24	3	27
	196	124	320

NEWS FROM EMERY.

HUNTINGTON, Emery Co., U. T.
Dec, 28th 1882.

Editor Deseret News:

Perhaps it is not too late to tell our friends in other parts of the Territory, about how we are getting along out here, in one of the back parts of Utah I have been away from home since the 1st of Oct. or I should have informed our friends of our welfare ere this, though the NEWS, (with your permission.) Last season was very favorable for the farmers of this valley. In fact they were bles- sed so much in their crops that most of the farmers on Huntington (and I presume it is the same in other settlements, as the facilities are nearly all the same) have had to en- large their stack yards, and grain bins before they could take care of their crops. Bishop Cox, has also had to have a large tithing corrall built to pretect the tithing fodder and corn that has been paid in this fall.

We have had quite a large ad- dition built to our meeting house. (It was before the largest house in the County) of 20x26, the present size of the house is 26-26x50, in the shape of a T, we also have a very good school taught by Bro. Ira Whitney, late of Iron Co., he is assisted by his wife, as there is too many scholars for one. The Relief Society, Sun- day School, Y. M. M. L. Association and Primary are also in a flourishing condition. Christmas day was a pleasant one for the little ones. The Sunday School, under the direction of Brother Peter Johnson, occupied the forenoon in recitations, songs, etc., and a dance in the afternoon for the little ones and a dance in the evening for the big folks, and every- thing went off pleasantly, but that was not the fault of one of our friends; (he is not a resident here) who brought in a couple of barrels of what some of the boys call Christmas, but what is better known as railroad whisky. He has man- aged to sell considerable here, under the impression that the Edmunds bill protects him, claiming there is no officer here that dare handle him, perhaps he is right, as there has been no effort made to stop him from selling.

The Denver and Rio Grande Rail- way Company have done consider- able in this County the last six months; they have built about sixty miles of road from the west, and I understand are now in the eastern part of this county coming from the east, they expect to connect the road sometime in February, so that will constitute another highway from the Atlantic to the Pacific, as far west at least as Salt Lake City. This road has been a blessing to this county, as no man could say he could not find work, as there has been plenty of grading, both dirt and rock work, tie chopping and hauling, also several lumber mills kept very busy furnishing bridge timbers and other building material. I believe most of the mills have stop- ped running for the winter, except that owned by parties here, it is in Price River Canyon. They calculate to run all winter, as the mill is situ- ated east of where the heavy snow falls. There has been only about two inches of snow at the mill so far this winter, and in this valley none to speak of, not over half an inch.

Bro. H. O. Crandal, the Bishop's first Counselor, of this place, while at his mill in Price River Canyon, some time ago had his leg broken but he is getting along first rate and will soon be around all right again. Since the railroad entered the valley we are very much in need of a change in our mail facilities, as our mail coming via the D. & R. G. R. R. will come from Salt Lake to Price River the first day, to the other settlements in the valley the second day. Now the mail coming by way of Salina we do well to get it the second week, some of it takes three months to get here. The postmaster here tells me he has been trying for several weeks to have the change made, but so far there has been nothing done.

Hoping it is not too late to wish you and our friends the compliments of the season,

I remain, yours respectfully,

W. H.

Deseret News
January 31, 1883

From Emery County — This morning we were pleased to receive a call from Bishop Elias Cox, of Huntington, Emery County. He reports a general time of peace and prosperity in that and other settlements of the county, the settlers not being affected by the rough scenes occasionally enacted along the line of the railroad. The railroad only touches at one town, Price, situated in Price River Valley.

Deseret News
February 14, 1883

Burglary at Castle Dale.—During the night between the 2nd and 3rd insts., the Co-op. store at Castle Dale Emery County, was broken into by burglars, who carried off what cash they could find, about six dollars, and a quantity of tobacco. They broke a panel of the door, but failing to open it, they burst away the casing to which the lock-catch was attached, with a crow bar or other strong implement, and thus gained easy entrance. We are indebted for the information of the affair to Brother Jasper Peterson.

Deseret News
February 21, 1883

ESTRAY NOTICE.

I HAVE IN MY POSSESSION:

One red COW, about 6 years old, marked with hole in each ear and underbit in left ear, branded GII on left thigh, E on left ribs, and

DC on right shoulder.

If not claimed and taken away by Feb 17, 1883, will be sold at 10 a.m. in the district pound at Huntington.

    J. F. WAKEFIELD,
      District Poundkeeper.
Huntington, Feb. 7, 1883.

Deseret News
February 28, 1883

Huntington.—We learn from N. T. Guymon, of Huntington, Emery County, that there have been a number of very severe cases of lung and inflammatory fevers at that place of late. The weather has been fine and the people are prospering.

CASTLE VALLEY.

PARTICULARS OF A TRIP AND VISIT TO CASTLE VALLEY.

For the following we are indebted to J. F. W.:

"The journey to Castle Valley, a hitherto remote, desolate region beyond the line of frequent travel, is now made with comparative ease in one day from Salt Lake City Taking the D. & R. G. train at 7.40 a.m., by courtesy of the General Agent, Mr. Lamborn, we skirted up the valley of the Jordan, often on the river's bank, through the narrows and around the northern shore of Utah Lake to Provo, where lunch is taken, and the little train pursues its way past Springville and over a wide expanse of bench land, lying below the mountains. The Spanish Fork Canyon is entered and the road becomes quite picturesque as it passes by the rugged gorges, opening on either side. In many respects, particularly in the chimney rocks, the mountain scenery resembles that of Echo Canyon about the 'Witch's Rocks' and in the vicinity of the town of Echo.

At Clear Creek station the ascent commences to be quite difficult and continues so to the summit; from the latter point, however, the train glides over the smooth steel rails very rapidly to Pleasant Valley Junction, where we arrived at five p. m., and were hospitably entertained by Mrs. Southworth, former landlady of the Lake Point Hotel. At this station, the last opened for regular travel, we boarded a lumber car on the "construction train" and sped round the point of the mountain where Fish Creek and White River join to form Price River, Along the sinuous banks of the latter, the long train of cars, having loaded with ties, dashed by the tie company's and saw mills in the canyon at fearful speed. The road is so crooked that horseshoe curves are frequent and we found it quite interesting to keep track of the North Star, appearing first on one side of the car and then the other with such rapidity as to be bewildering to the star-gazer. The scenery in Price River Canyon is very beautiful, reaching its highest attraction at Castle Gate. The latter is the opening made by the stream through a wall of rugged rock rising on one side like a slender promontory reaching into the sky. This promontory, extends from the mountain down to the roadside where it is cleanly cut from base to summit, 500 feet above, appearing like a thin slab of red sandstone set on edge.

At Price, to be called hereafter Castle Valley Station, where we arrived at 9 o'clock p.m., we were welcomed by Bishop Frandson and Counselor E. W. McIntyre. A ward has been organized here with about 35 families, scattered along the river for several miles. They, however, have located a townsite and are now engaged taking the water out to cover it. The prospects are that quite an important town will spring up at this point, as the railway company will erect a round house and perhaps some shops; it will be the market and shipping town for Castle Valley and the broad extent of land capable of cultivation when the water is brought on to it will alone surround the town with the elements of prosperity and wealth.

In the morning we left Price for Huntington, distant twenty-seven miles. The beautiful weather, balmy, warm and spring-like made the journey very pleasant, while the wonderful, ever changing scenery was a source of constant delight. The following description of this road was written by Brother Johnson, a member of the Young Men's Association at Huntington:

'The road between Huntington and Price River, Emery County, Utah, is over rolling hills and hollows, and interspersed with deep gorges and washes that have been caused by the action of the turbulent waters that had gathered from the adjacent hillsides during thunder-showers, and rushed frantically along in their wild career to the Gulf of California, far away in the Sunny South.

On either side of the road at intervals can be seen table lands or mesas, which are composed principally of slate rock covered slightly with a light blue clay. And the scene might become monotonous but for the splendid range that stretches as far as the eye can reach in every direction, dotted here and there with herds of stock ranging from one bunch of sand or Gramma grass to another, a distance of many miles.

There is also another feature of this road worthy of note, and that is, the tendency it has to create a hope within the weary traveler as he wends his way over sand-ridge and desert plain. He can always see a gentle rise of ground just ahead, and he hopes he can obtain a good view when he gains the top, and so he can (of another hill). But when he does get sight of the river he has gained the top of just a baker's dozen of these hills and crossed as many valleys or flats, and 20 miles north and 10 east. The Twin Peaks are about half way between the two traveled streams Huntington and Price.'

At Huntington conference was held. The meetings were numerously attended by Saints from all of the settlements in Emery Stake except Moab, on Green River, 150 miles away. The new log meeting house, the best of the kind we have seen in the Territory, accommodated the people comfortably. The instructions given were eminently practical, Apostle F. M. Lyman engaging with his customary interest in the spirit and business of the conference. A High Council was chosen, many ordinances attended to and the Stake and Ward organizations so far perfected as the circumstances of the people at present require Saturday evening a conference of Y. M. M. I. A. was held.

On Sunday evening we drove to Castledale, ten miles, and held meeting, and were hospitably entertained by President C. G. Larsen and family. On Monday we continued our southern journey to Ferron, distant fifteen miles, where we met with the Saints and spent a very enjoyable day at the comfortable home of brother M. W. Molen. The next day we drove early to Orangeville, ten miles on our return and held meeting in the new school house, which was packed to its utmost capacity. After dining with Bishop Robertson we drove on with Judge Elias Cox to Huntington, where we attended the regular meeting of the Young men's Association and listened to the interesting exercises.

By our return to Price we had seen enough of the Castle Valley country to convince us of its future outcome. There is land and water enough to supply a large population, the productiveness of the soil has been tested, and was found last year to be very profitable, as high as forty bushels of wheat to the acre being raised. The towns already platted and those contemplated, start with fair prospects, and through the blessing and favor of Providence the Saints of Emery Stake, who now number nearly 1,400, have every reason to expect large additions to their numbers, and that the barren wastes of Castle Valley, which they have secured, will yet bloom and 'blossom as the rose.'"

COTTONWOOD COAL.

A DESCRIPTION OF ITS QUALITY AND THE EXTENT OF THE DEPOSIT.

A correspondent of Castle Dale, Emery County, furnishes the following:

I take the liberty of giving through the NEWS a description of the coal bed in Cottonwood Canyon, ten miles from Castle Dale. Having occasion to go up to the mine I made a thorough investigation of it. There are 16 openings altogether. The largest vein is 25 feet thick, of the finest quality of bituminous coal, which cokes without any trouble in the open fire place. This vein has two tunnels. One is in 55 feet, the other 50 feet. Both are well timbered, 7 feet high, and are

in splendid condition for working a large force of men when necessary. There are two other openings on the same vein, known as air courses, which show an excellent quality of coking coal. There is another vein about 4 feet thick, of superior coal. It is as hard as rock and does not black a person handling it as other coal does. The blacksmiths in this vicinity pronounce it the best coal they ever used without exception.

There is still another vein of shale and black jet coal together, 17 feet of shale and 3 feet of black jet, and of the very best quality. The black jet article can be ignited with a match. The parties who are opening it up have one tunnel in the shale and jet coal 30 feet, and have also sunk a shaft in the bottom of the canyon through dirt and rock a depth of 16 feet, and struck the same vein of shale and coal close to the wagon road. To give you an idea of the amount of petroleum in this coal it need only be said, you can put on a fire of either of the coals and the oil will drip out of it, showing the quality of the coal.

These beds of coal are located in plenty of timber in all directions for mining purposes. I understand the parties owning these mines are intending to ship a ton of this coal to Salt Lake in a few days for the purpose of having a test made of it. It is claimed to be the best coking coal in the United States. Capital is required to operate the discovery, but much credit is due to those who have energetically opened the beds, especially the discoverer, George Matthias Makin, an old English coal miner, who thoroughly understands his work. He has sold considerable coal to residents, and it has given entire satisfaction.

The discovery is evidently one of the most important in its line ever made in Utah.

Deseret News
March 28, 1883

NEILSEN—At Huntington, Emery County, Utah, of childbed fever, Feb. 28th, 1883, Annie Kristine Neilsen.

Also on the same day her infant son.

Sister Neilsen was born on the 17th of March, 1841, in Almin City, Vibroee County, Jylan, Denmark. She embraced the gospel on the 4th of April, 1871, and emigrated to Utah in 1873. She leaves a husband and seven children to mourn her loss. She was an active member of the Relief Society of Huntington Ward, and was always willing to do any duty required of her. Her death created quite a gloom over the people of this ward who have been bereft of a faithful friend and sister.

Scandinavian papers please copy.

Deseret News
April 4, 1883

EMERY STAKE CONFERE[NCE]

The Quarterly Conference of E[m]ery Stake was held at Huntin[gton] meeting house March 3, 1883.

There were present on the sta[nd] Apostle F. M. Lyman, Junius Wells, Assistant Sup't Y. M. M. A.; President C. G. Larson a[nd] Counselors, Bishops, President[s] Quorums, etc.

After opening exercises Presid[ent] Larson congratulated the peop[le of] Huntington on having such a c[om]modious house to hold conference [in.] Spoke at some length on the bless[ings] of God to us in this fronti[er] Stake; also gave a report [of his] travels to Moab, Grand Val[ley; said] he believed the people in the diffe[r]ent wards were united both te[m]porally and spiritually in the buil[d]ing up of Zion.

Bishop Elias Cox, of Hunting[ton] Ward, Bishop Frederick Olsen, [of] Ferron Ward, Bishop Jasper Rob[ert]son, of the Orangeville Ward, a[nd] Bishop Olsen, of Castle Dale Wa[rd,] gave reports of their respect[ive] wards.

Apostle F. M. Lyman spoke [en]couragingly to the people in re[gard] to building up new settlements. [All] his instructions were listened [to] with marked attention by [the] Saints. He announced the follow[ow]ing programme of meetings in [the] different settlements:

Castle Dale at 7 o'clock Sun[day] evening, Ferron Ward Monday 2 o'clock, Orangeville Tuesday [2] o'clock, Price Ward Wednesd[ay] 2 o'clock.

Singing and benediction.

2 p. m.

After singing and prayer Eld Jos. W. Moore spoke a few words the blessings of God to our peop and gave a favorable report of High Priests Quorum.

Elder N. T. Guyman gave a g report of the Seventies of Em Stake.

Elder Junius F. Wells was prised to see so many together the first day of conference; spok some length to the young, show the blessings in store for the fa

His remarks were listened to rapt attention.

postle F. M. Lyman spoke at e length in regard to the organ on of a High Council for Emery ke, showed what kind of men e necessary to be chosen as h Councilors. Made a few re ks on the celestial law of God also on the Word of Wisdem; wed the blessings that would ac from living up to these laws. nging and benediction.

Sunday, 10 a.m.

he house was crowded to over wing.

fter opening services the statis l report was read by J. R. Reid, ke Clerk, also the report of the day schools of Emery Stake.

postle F. M. Lyman presented general authorities of the rch and Stake, who were unani usly sustained.

rest. Larsen said there was one e that was not reported this ference, on what is known as ddy Creek, it should have been rted ih the Ferron Ward.

Elder Junius F. Wells spoke in ard to the Saints instructing ir children in the doctrines of our y religion when they are young.

postle F. M. Lyman spoke a few rds on punctuality.

Singing and prayer.

uring the recess between fore on and afternoon meeting, a esthood meeting was held, at ich time the following brethren re ordained and set apart to fill e positions named: As members the High Council of Emery ake, Charles Pulsipher, Anthon ilsen, Peter Johnson, A. J. Jew , John Donaldson, Sylvester H. x, Jos. W. Moore, Andrew C. nsen, Jasper Petersen, Geo. Fran n was ordained and set apart as shop of Price Ward, with E. W. Intire and Caleb B. Rhoades as Counselors. John F. Wakefield s set apart as First Counselor to esident Jos. W. Moore, High iest's Quorums of the Emery Stake Zion. The following brethren re called as members of the High unsel: J. H. Taylor, of Orange lle; Mads Larsen and E. Homer, Ferron.

2 p. m.

After singing and prayer the Sacrament was passed. President O. Seely and President Rasmus Justensen each said a few words of encouragement to the Saints. Prest. Larsen hoped we had learned something by coming to Conference, that we would take with us to our homes and put in practice.

Apostle F. M. Lyman spoke with energy on the following subjects: the sacrament, repentance, word of wisdom and tithing. He asked for the blessing of God to be on this land and on everything pertaining thereto, that the Saints might be blessed in all things.

President Larsen said this Conference would now be adjourned until the first Saturday and Sunday in June, to meet at Orangeville.

Apostle Lyman thanked the people for coming together, also the choir and the band for making music for us. The Huntington and Orangeville choir combined, sang: "This is my Commandment."

Benediction by Elder Junius F. Wells.

J. K. REID,
Clerk of Emery Stake.

A PERILOUS ADVENTURE.

BISHOP ROBERTSON AND TWO COM-PANIONS HAVE A NARROW ESCAPE FROM DEATH.

Our correspondent, J. K. Reid, furnishes the following, written at Orangeville, Emery County, on April 18th:

Bishop Jasper Robertson, Samuel R. Jewkes, and Ole Sitturd, all of them of this place, having been down to Conference, at Salt Lake, came back on the railroad as far as Fountain Green and started to walk on snowshoes across the mountains. They started from Mount Pleasant last Saturday morning, expecting to reach this side of the mountain the same night. It had snowed the day before and there was considerable loose snow, which made it hard traveling, and the wind blew a hurricane all day long, and it was very cold. They were 1? hours getting to the top of the mountain, and were completely exhausted. They had yet three miles to go before reaching a cabin in Joe's Valley, where they could rest.

... was then upon them, and one ... their snow shoes broken. They ... five hours getting to the saw-... cabin, and when they reached ... Bishop Robertson had both ... frozen and Samuel R. Jewkes ... one foot frozen. The other ... member of the party was all right. ... completely worn out, it was ... possible for them to go any far-... without aid. They sat up the ... of the night taking care of their ... limbs. They had all they ... do to keep warm, having to ... up everything in the cabin for ... purpose as they had no bed-... with them.

In the morning the man who was ... frozen started for help. He had ... about seven miles to travel on ... shoes and then eighteen miles ... foot before he reached here. He ... nearly blind before he got ... the snow. He arrived here ... sundown.

He raised a party of twelve men ... and get the others over the ... They started about dark with ... and medicines to help the ... suffering men. They never stop-... till daylight. They made ... sleds putting six men to pull ... and went through the snow ... deep. They were ten hours in ... snow, going and coming. When ... rescuers reached the sufferers ... found they had been keeping ... feet in the snow for a consider-... time, and were greatly rejoiced ... help so soon. The two men ... put on the sleds and taken ... the snow. They got here ... ten o'clock the same night. ... a number of the rescuers were ... blind to some extent.

Bishop Robertson's feet are very ... frozen; Brother Jewkes has ... foot in about the same condi-... but they are doing as well as ... be expected under the circum-... It is to be hoped they will ... lose their toes. It will be some ... before they can get around ... They say that if there had ... fifty yards further to go they ... have frozen to death, they ... so near gone.

Great credit is due to Ole Sitturd, ... the energy he displayed in secur-... help. He had no sleep for about ... hours, and traveled all the time, ... went back with the rescuing ... The other two would certain-... have perished had he been dis-... in any way after he left them ... help, for we had no idea that ... would try to reach home by the ... mountain back.

CASTLE VALLEY.

Coal and Other Minerals---A Good Farming Section----Bright Prospects.

CASTLE VALLEY, EMERY CO.,
May 2, 1883.

Editors Herald:

I want to give you a few items regarding Castle Valley's wealth and hidden treasures, which are now being opened and developed; also regarding the increase of population, which will in the course of time, cause Castle Valley to plossom like the rose. In the last eighteen months no less than sixty-five families have come and settled in Castle Valley, and its surroundings, all of whom have now good homes. Irrigating ditches are being opened on land which, to gaze at casually, one would look upon as of no account whatever; yet some of the farms on these same ditches, cannot be purchased for as much as $3,000. A great many more families are coming here this summer. There is ample room for them here, and there are any amount of facilities for all who may come.

We have any amount of minerals here, including gold, silver, etc., and different kinds of coal. The gold and silver is found in the northeast mountains, and croppings indicate an abundance of free milling ore. The fact of good claims abounding is testified to by old and practical miners who have prospected thereabouts, particularly in the low hills which are in close proximity to the D. & R. G. Railroad line.

The coal to be found here in unlimited abundance, is of a variety of qualities. In Huntington Canyon there are four openings on an immense vein of excellent bituminous coal; it has been stripped for some twenty-seven feet, and the whole makes a splendid showing. A good, substantial house is erected on the site, for the occupancy of the miners, and there is plenty of wood and water near the mines, which renders their working comparatively cheap and easy. In the Cottonwood Canyon coal mines a number of miners are now at work under the direction of Mr. G. M. Makin. They have made three openings, and a good house is built, near which, also, there is plenty of water and timber. The vein is four feet thick and shows some coal which is bright and clean. Mr. Makin goes up the canyon to-morrow to direct the men in their search for the main vein. Mr. Makin is of the opinion that in this canyon will be found cannel coal and shale in abundance. He has a man at work there, drifting in the cannel coal vein; while the shale drift is also being opened up, and makes a splendid showing. He has some sixteen openings in the County Canyon, where there is also caanel and shale, said to be of the same quality as that found in Cottonwood Canyon. These latter mines he has been working on for a couple of years. He is selling coal to the local trade at $3 per ton at the mine. The work now in progress must be gratifying to Mr. Makin, who has practically pioneered the way to the o.ening of Castle Valley.

We have here also a steam saw mill, with an abundance of red pine in the vicinity of such growth as to make the timber very valuable.

The coal mines are principally owned by Mr. Makin, who also possesses a fine bed of excellent fire clay, so necessary for building ovens, and fire places, etc., where intense heat is required. The vein of fire clay is twenty feet through, and is on an opened road, the one going over to Sanpete Valley.

Whoever secures possession of these coal fields will have gained the means of vast wealth. A little capital and energetic workers, and a railroad through the valley, and it will become one of the most populous and productive, as it is one of the most beautiful and rich valleys in the territory. It has been usually considered a barren locality, but a visit and inspection of the vast coal fields and other mineral resources, as well as the agricultural features, will show that there is a grand field here for capital and honest labor.

H. P. HALL.

Deseret News
May 23, 1883

Toes Amputated. — Our readers will probably remember an account given in the NEWS of Bishop Jasper Roberteon and two other brethren being caught in a terrible storm in the mountains while on their way to Orangeville, Emery County, from this city, shortly after Conference. The Bishop had his feet badly frozen. He came to town a few days ago for treatment at the Deseret hospital. To-day several of his toes were amputated at that institution, the operation being performed by Doctors Anderson and Hughes.

Salt Lake Herald
June 3, 1883

DEPUTY REGISTRARS.

Following is a list of the deputy registration officers for the registration commencing on Monday, June 4, and ending on Saturday, June 9, 1883. The list is complete as to all precincts. except those in Uintah County, for which appointments have been forwarded, and doubtless accepted by the appointees, though Secretary Thomas has not yet received official notification of the fact:

EMERY COUNTY.

S. J. Harkness, Scofield precinct.
Job. H. Whitney, Castle Dale, precinct.
John D. Kilpack, Ferron prec'nct.
John F. Wakefield, Huntington precinct.
O. H. Warner, Moab precinct.
Caleb B. Rhoads, Price precinct.

GARFIELD COUNTY.

James F. Johnson, Hillsdale precinct.
James B. Thompson, Cannonville precinct.
Wm. Alvey, Escalante precinct.
John M. Dunning, Panguitch precinct.

Correspondence.

MARSHALL PASS,
State of Colorado,
June 6th, 1883.

for Deseret News:

t an elevation of 10,857 feet,
re snow is to be found many
dred feet below us, I remember
 For the last two hours we
 been circling around the tops
 these beautiful, verdant and
 ily timbered mountains. From
 re I now sit I see a tank that
 been in view from the moving
 that has appeared to circle
 nd it, at different angles for the
 70 minutes. Passengers com-
 it is with difficulty they
 the.
 e have now left the waters that
 into the Pacific—through the
 nison, Grand and Colorado riv
 and have commenced our de-
 t leaving the head waters of the
 kansas river as they speed on
 r way to the Atlantic, through
 great Mississippi.
 he engineering skill—displayed
 ying out this road and in the

construction of these massive Loco-
motives, with eight driving wheels,
drawing immense trains of loaded
cars around curves at angles so very
acute, (as to cause an engineer, it
is said to whistle "down breaks"
on one occasion, when he became a
little confused, thinking he was
about to collide with another train—
when, lo! he had mistaken the rear
end of his own train for that of another,) over a grade of 270 feet to the
mile, is something very remarkable,
to say the least, while the thrilling
sensation experienced by the traveler as he passes through the "Castle
Gate," whose massive pillars tower
400 feet above the Pass, the Castle Valley and "Black Canyon,"
present most romantic views, with
rocky heights reaching 2,600 feet
above the rapidly flowing Gunnison.

President Woodruff is now seated near me and excitedly exclaims, "If I could spare time to follow that stream for ten miles, I could supply my family with trout for a year." It appears that he got on the train at Price, Emery County, and reports to have traveled 80 miles by wagon in the last four days over Castle Valley, mostly of clay formation, very barren, as it seldom snows in winter, and rains in summer are not to be relied upon. Five meetings were held at Orangeville, where the people of the Stake assembled in Conference, under the presidency of C. G. Larsen, also one at Castledale and one at Huntington, where a good spirit prevailed amongst the Saints, and much good instruction was imparted.

In the latter place Bishop Elias Cox resigned, and Chas. Pulsipher was ordained Bishop in his stead, and two Counselors, and two High Counselors were selected and set apart to fill vacancies. The people are busy putting in crops, making ditches, etc. The five streams on the west side of the valley are quite high, the smallest of which contains as much water as Little Cottonwood, and the largest as much as the Jordan. They are known as Price, Huntington, Cottonwood, Farren and Muddy.

The Stake is prosperous and numbers over 1,600—over one-third of whom are under eight years of age. While much of the scenery on this route is magnificent, we have seen no game, with the exception of a prairie dog or two to-day.

I am just reminded by a person sitting near me that there is other game in the country as he has heard of panthers being in the mountains, and he himself and two other persons were traveling from Heber City, Wasatch Co., through the country extending south a distance of 200 miles, where their provisions gave out, and they were without food for two or three days, but they luckily found a huge porcupine, so large and fat he says it took all three of them to get it upon their pack animal. (I presume they were not as strong as the porcupine, inasmuch as they were all grown men, and they could eat little else than the soup). Upon this they subsisted two days until they reached a settlement. He, however, says game is much more plentiful in these parts, than it was then, inasmuch as the Indians do not hunt it as much and it is eight years since he passed through such a strait.

I have just met our townsman John W. Snell, who reports that he has marketed in colorado and vicinity over 1,800 bushels of Utah potatoes, in the last 30 days.
NONNAC.

Deseret News
July 11, 1883

EMERY STAKE CONFERE...

Emery Stake Conference wa... at Orangeville, June 2d and ...

There were present on the ... of the Stake authorities, Pre... C. G. Larsen, Counselor O... Seely, Bishops of the di... Wards, Counselors, and Mem... the High Council.

After singing and p... dent Larsen said he ... of our brethren of the ... us at this Conference, ... some delay they had ... yet, but he thought they ... here through the day. ... some length and gave ... instructions to the Saints.

The Bishops of the ... Wards gave in a report ... Wards; they all seemed to ... thriving condition, and all ... to the best of their ability ... up the waste places of Zi... endeavoring to live their re... Saints of God.

Elder Robert Logan said ... the first conference he ... with in this stake. But ... he was in his 79th year, he... meet with the Saints in ... many years yet. Said he ... to wear out in the service ... and his kingdom.

Brother Matthew Cald[well]
viewed some of the trial[s of the]
Saints which he w[a]s cogn[izant]
Felt to rejoice and praise [God that]
he was living in this day s[o]
the world, when God had [set]
forth His kingdom never [to]
be thrown down.

Afternoon

After singing and pr[ayer]
Counselor J. K. Reid [re]
po[r]t of the Orangeville [ward]
reports w[e]re given of [the]
Quorum and Sunday sch[ool]

Elder Stevens, of Ferr[on]
few remarks, gave a shor[t]
[sketc]h[?] life, having been in [the]
for 52 years, said he had [known]
when he was 19 years o[ld]
this was the work of God [he]
c[o]uld bear the same te[stimony]
day. He was listened to wit[h]
interest by the Saints.

Elder N. T. Gu[y]man ga[ve]
po[r]t of the Seventies of [the]
Stake.

President O. Seely made a [few]
r[e]marks encouraging the Sai[nts]
[f]a[i]thfulness.

President Larsen endorsed [all that]
had been said so far at this [confer]
[en]ce; felt pleased to have b[rethren]
with us that lived in the days [of the]
Prophet Joseph Smith.

[Elder] S. R. Jenk[in]s gave notice
[that] there would be a conference of
[Y].M.M.I.A. of Emery Stake in
[e]vening.

[Cho]ir sang an anthem. Benedic[tion]
[b]y Elder A. Anderson.

Second day.

[Pre]sent on the stand: Apostle
[Wilfo]rd Woodruff, President A. M.
[Cann]on, of Salt Lake Stake, Elder
[Thos.] E. Taylor, of Salt Lake City,
[Presi]dent Larsen and Counselor O.
[?] Bishops of Wards and mem[bers]
[o]f High Council.

[Th]e sacrament was administered.
[Bis]hop Fransen, of Price, gave a
[report] of his ward. Bishop Cox also
[gave] a report of the Huntington

[The] general Church authorities
[were] presented and sustained, also
[Emer]y Stake authorities and all
[?] authorities and were unani[mous]
[l]y sustained.

[Pres]ident Woodruff spoke at some
[length] on the great work that we
[are] engaged in, and gave some
[ver]y instructions to the Saints,
[who] were listened to with rapt
[atten]tion.

---

2 p.m.

[The] large bowery was crowded [and]
[?] overflowing.

[Sin]ging and prayer.

[Pres]t. A. M. Cannon spoke at
length in regard to living a[s the]
[tru]e Saints of the Most High
[a]lso in regard to our being
[?] as a people and in our fami[lies]
[a]dvised the Saints to try to
[advan]ce spiritually as well as tem[porall]
y.

[Eld]er Thos. E. Taylor gave some
[i]nstructions to the young; ad[vised]
[t]hem to be temperate in all
[?], so that they may qualify
[themse]lves to fill responsible pos[itions]
[i]n the Kingdom of God; said
[the ti]me was not far distant when
[you]ng would have to put their
[shoulder] to the wheel to push on the
[w]ork.

[Presiden]t. Woodruff spoke at some
[length] on the celestial law of God;
[admon]ished the young to be virtu[ous]
[an]d live up to all the laws of
[Go]d not to follow after the fash[ion]
[of] the world, as iniquity was
[?]ng rampant, and the people
[?] windling away; spoke in re[gard]
[t]o the young qualifying them[selves]
[?] to fill responsible positions in
[Kin]gdom of God; admonished
[Sai]nts to be united as wards and
[sta]kes, and God would bless
[the]m in all things.

[Pres]t. Larsen gave out that the
[?] Society would hold a confer[ence]
[at] Castle Dale the first Friday
[Sa]turday in August.

[Conf]erence adjourned to meet at
[?] Dale Ward the first Saturday
[Su]nday in September.

[A goo]d spirit prevailed through[out]
[con]ference.

[The h]ealth of the Saints of Emery
[i]s good.

J. K. REID, Stake Clerk.

Deseret News
August 8, 1883

Stake Conferences.—Apostle F. M. Lyman and Elder John Morgan purpose attending the Conference of Emery Stake, at Huntington, on the 1st and 2d of September; on the 8th and 9th, of the San Luis Stake, at Manassa. On the 15th and 16th of the same month they will meet with the Saints at Burnham, on the San Juan River, and from there they will proceed to Bluff City and attend Conference of the San Juan Stake at that place, on September 22d and 23d. They expect to return here by the 1st of October.

Deseret News
September 5, 1883

DIED.

FREDERICKSEN.—In Castle Dale, Aug. 15, 1883, Wilhelm George Fredericksen. Born April 25, 1863, in Denmark; embraced the Gospel September 22, 1878; came to Utah in July, 1883.

Correspondence.

HUNTINGTON,
Emery County, Utah,
August 15th, 1883.

Editor Deseret News:

Our Town Ditch has at last become a reality and is conducting a nice stream of water upon our beautiful townsite (which is one mile square), thus enabling us to plant our shade and other kinds of trees, flowers, garden seeds, etc., all of which look well and show that this desert land can be made to "blossom as the rose."

We have a very quiet little town of about sixty-five families, the greater part of whom are living upon the townsite. We have no whisky shops, rowdies or loafers here to mar our peace, and the people generally are living their religion, without the use of tea, coffee, tobacco, etc. There has been a marked improvement in that respect since Brothers Lyman and Wells were here in March last. We have a Y. M. and Y. L. M. I. Association, Sunday school, Relief Society, etc., all doing well. The climate here is very salubrious, the health of the people good and the husbandman is busy gathering in his bountiful harvest.

There is a grist mill at Orangeville, ten miles distant, and several saw mills in successful operation close by, and another nearly completed in Huntington Canyon. Consequently our facilities for improving are far better than heretofore. Our little place is rapidly building up, and there is yet room for a great many more good citizens. Our worthy Bishop, Charles Pulsipher, is alive to the interest and welfare of the ward. He invites people to call and see the place.

Ever praying for the welfare of Zion, I am yours in the Gospel of peace.   M. E. J.

Deseret News
October 3, 1883

Afternoon session.
Singing and prayer.
Bishop Pulsipher gave a report of the Huntington ward, Bishop Olsen a report of the Castle Dale ward. Both these wards were in a prosperous condition the Saints were alive to their duties, and striving to build up the kingdom of God.
Counselor Caleb Rhoach of Price Ward gave a report of his ward, said they had some evils to contend against owing to being on the line of the R. R., such as whisky etc, but that the Saints were striving to overcome these things, and were doing so to a great extent.
President J. W. Moore gave a report of the High Priests Quorum.
Elder F. M. Lyman gave some general instructions to the Saints on different subjects, which were listened to with attention by the congregation. At the close of his remarks he gave out that there would be a meeting at Orangeville, on Sunday evening at 7 p m., at Huntington Monday at 2 p m. and at Price, Tuesday at 2 p.m.

Correspondence.

Editor Deseret News:

Apostle Lyman and Elder John Morgan left home on the morning of Aug. 30th to visit the Saints in Emery Stake, Utah, San Luis Stake, Col., and San Juan Stake Utah

Leaving the D &R.G. train at Castle Valley station, we were cared for by the Saints of Price River Ward, and on the following morning, in company with Brothers Rhodes and Gay, who furnished us a conveyance, we started on a forty-mile trip across the barren, verdureless hills and plateaus that lie between Green River and the mountains east of Sanpete Valley.

Very little vegetation is seen, and that little is of a stunted, dwarfed character, though the soil seems susceptible of cultivation and yields remunerative crops when properly irrigated and cared for.

The country is seamed and cut by heavy washes, leading from the table lands, along the mountains, in the direction of the San Ra ael River. These washes are deep and rugged, often filled with heavy torrents of muddy water, that impede travel and are dangerous to cross.

Twenty-five miles south of our starting point the town of Huntington is located in a fish hook like bend of Huntington Creek, the waters of which they have brought out on the town site, and quite an amount of land lying adjacent to the town.

A comfortable log meeting house has been erected, a store started, a saw *mill* in process of location, and a good crop raised, the people, under the guidance and care of Bishop Chas. Pulsipher, seem happy and contented.

After enjoying the hospitality and resting with Judge Elias Cox for two hours, we continued our journey to Castle Dale, reaching the comfortable and hospitable home of President C. G. Larsen, as the shades of night were drawing on.

The conference meetings were all well attended by the people and everything connected with the welfare of the saints, reported in a fairly prosperous condition; in addition to the conference meetings, meetings were held in Orangeville, Huntington and Price Wards.

On returning to Castle Valley station, we were joined by Pres. A. O. Smoot and together continued our journey to Denver, having also the company of six Elders en-route to the Southern States Mission, with whom we parted at Pueblo.

It is scarcely worth while to undertake a description of the marvelous feats of engineering accomplished in getting the D. & R. G. R. R. established, through these mountain fastnesses, it is simply beyond description.

The mighty gorges penetrated, the dizzy heights climbed, the roaring torrents crossed, the grand scenery, all combine to make it a heavier task than can be accomplished in one short epistle.

Denver in the bright sunlight of a cloudless morning, washed clean and refreshed by a copious shower the day previous, looked pleasant and cheering.

A visit to the Mineral Exposition, a ride through its thoroughfares, a few prominent points visited and we take the cars for Colorado Springs and Manitou, the last named point reached at 6 p.m. We drove to Rainbow Falls, Ute Pass, and drink from the soda spring.

After supper we took a moonlight drive through the Garden of the Gods, and had the principal points of interest pointed out, by an enterprising Jehu, who seemed well posted, but who threw a cloud over his veracity at the very start by informing President Smoot that Johnson's army on their way to Utah in '57 passed over that identical spot.

One happy incident of our visit to Manitou, was meeting Gen. Doniphan, whom many of the Saints will readily remember. He shows the imprint of age, being 75 years old, about six feet four tall, and a firm friend to the Latter-day Saints.

An hours' stay at Colorado Springs,

and we take the Durango Express for San Luis Valley, passing Pueblo in the night, and reaching La Veta Pass as the tall dome-like tops of the Spanish Peaks are gilded by the light of the rising sun. A white frost covers the ground at the summit, 9,337 feet above the sea level. The tenderer leaves show indication of chilly winter, and the mountain sides are varegated and beautiful in their many tinted hues.

The Grand Valley of San Luis looks pleasant and cheering, and soon we are in sight of the homes of the Saints who there reside. Prest. S. S. Smith and a few friends meet us at the railroad, and we are presently greeting friends in the thriving town of Manassa.

JOHN MORGAN.

ESTRAY NOTICE.

I HAVE IN MY POSSESSION:

One red and white 7 or 8-year-old BULL, the ends of both horns broken off, branded M S on left ribs.

If said animal is not claimed and taken away in 10 days from date will be sold October 4th 1883, at Huntington District Pound, Emery County.

J. F. WAKEFIELD,
District Poundkeeper.

Huntington, Emery County, September 24th, 1883.

Salt Lake Herald
October 6, 1883

Coal Mines.

Mr. G. M. Makin, writing us from Orangeville, Emery county, in relation to some coal fields which he is engaged in developing, says: "I can sincerely say that these mines are very valuable; I am justified in saying they are equal to any in the United States. They are situated some miles from the town of Orangeville, in Cottonwood canyon, it being the county road over to Sanpete valley, twenty-five miles from my mines. If there was a railroad over this way to Sanpete valley it would go through the largest coal deposit and of the best quality; also a fine timber country, with a good stream of water close by." The gentleman states that he will soon be in Salt Lake with samples, when a better idea of what can be produced in the way of bituminous fuel in the locality referred to can be had.

Commissions.

The following are the commissions issued by acting-Governor Thomas since the last report:

Sevier county—B. H. Greenwood, selectman; W. A. Warnock, justice, Zenos Wingate, constable, Monroe; John F. Leonard, justice, Jesse A. Billingsly, constable, Gooseberry; Thomas Bill, justice, L. Loderberg, constable, Elsinore; N. E. Lewis, constable, Salina; Edward Newby, justice, Joseph; B. Wilson, constable, Glenwood.

Emery county—Elias H. Cox, jun., surveyor; E. H. Cox, superintendent of district schools; J. W. Seely, selectman; C. G. Larson, jun., treasurer; J. D. Kilpack, assessor and collector: John K. Reid, prosecuting attorney; J. H. Whitney, clerk of court; Orange Seeley, probate judge; J. K. Reid, justice, Castle Dale; A. Tuttle, constable, Castle Dale; N. H. Stevens, justice, J. E. Johnson, constable, Huntington.

San Pete county—J. B. Christensen, justice, Ephrain.

Salt Lake county—Isaac Harrison, justice, Sandy.

Cache county — David Murray, constable, Wellsville.

Rich County—George Whittington, constable, Garden City.

San Juan county—John Cullen, jun., judge of probate, San Juan county; Henry Holbrook, justice, Montezuma.

Piute county—D. S. Gellies, sheriff, Piute county.

Summit county—J. L. Frazier, constable, Wanship.

Wasatch county — E. Richman, justice, Charleston.

DIED.

GUYMON.—At Huntington, Emery County, Utah, December 3rd, 1883, of croup, Melissa Loetta, daughter of N. T. and Louisa Guymon. She was 7 years, 6 months and 3 days old when she died. She was very anxious for her next birthday to come that she might be baptized.

JACOBSON—At Huntington, Emery County, Utah, December 4, 1883, of teething, Joseph, son of Hans and Christine Jacobson. Born May 27, 1883.

EMERY STAKE CONFER-ENCE.

The Emery Stake Quarterly Conference was held at Huntington, Dec. 1st and 2nd.

Present on the stand—President C. G. Larsen and Counselors Orange Seely and Rasmus Justensen; Patriarch Robert Logan and the Bishops of the different wards, with their Counselors, and members of the High Council.

Prayer by Elder James Woodward.

Singing.

President Larsen made a few opening remarks.

The Bishops gave reports of their wards, which were all in a flourishing condition. The Saints were striving to live their religion to the best of their ability.

Dismissed till 2 p. m.

Afternoon services.

Opening exercises.

Reports were given in from the different quorums of the Stake. They were all represented as in good condition.

Elder N. T. Guyman delivered an address on the progress of the work of God in which the Saints are engaged.

President Larsen made some remarks.

Second day services.

Opening exercises.

President O. Seely spoke in regard to the condition of the Saints of Emery Stake now and their situation a short time since, showing considerable progress. He exhorted the Saints to faithfulness.

The Clerk presented the General Authorities of the Church, also the Local Authorities of Emery Stake, which were unanimously sustained. The statistical report was also read, which showed on increase since last Conference of over 100.

Afternoon services.

Opening exercises. Sacrament was administered.

Elder Jos. Birch spoke a few words on temporal affairs.

Patriarch Robert Logan spoke in regard to us living the lives of Saints of the Most High God, so that we may gain the blessings in store for the faithful.

Elder Hyrum Strong was then ordained a High Priest and set apart as first counselor to Bishop Casper Christensen, of Muddy Ward, under the hands of President C. G. Larsen.

Elder James Woodward spoke a few words on the saving principles inculcated in our holy religion.

Elder Wm. Howard made a few remarks in regard to those secret societies that were springing up, and said that the Prophet Joseph prophesied in regard to these things in these the last days.

Elder Erastus Curtis spoke on the same subject.

Elder Matthew Caldwell spoke a few words of instruction and encouragement.

President Larsen spoke on co-operation.

Singing by both choirs, "The Spirit of God like a fire is burning," the whole congregation rising to their feet and singing.

Benediction by Bishop Jasper Robertson.

President Larsen announced that next conference will be held at Orangeville.

J. K. REID,
Clerk of Emery Stake.

Deseret News
January 23, 1884

EMERY COUNTY.

CONCERNING AFFAIRS IN THAT REGION.

Brother William Howard, of Huntington, Emery County, is in the city for a few days on business, intending to return Monday. He says that matters in general are improving and on the increase in that locality. No trouble is met in raising whatever is needed by the settlers. Things are quiet and peaceable as a rule, and but little sickness prevails.

The Prosecuting Attorney for the County has been making things lively for the liquor men along the line of the D. & R. G. Railway, and has succeeded in getting them to take out licenses, the first yet issued in the County. There is no liquor sold, that our informant knows of, away from the line of the railroad.

Huntington is about 150 miles from this city and 25 miles from Price Station on the D. and R. G., the nearest railroad point to the settlement. Considerable dissatisfaction is felt and expressed over the exhorbitant rates and overcharges made by the railway company, and efforts are being put forth towards the construction of a new wagon road through Huntington Cañon to Sanpete, for freight teams, as a means of avoiding the payment of heavy railroad rates. Several teams from Castle Valley are now in this city, loading up with freight, with the same motive in view.

An instance of what the people there regard as unfair treatment from the railway, is the fact that it compels them to buy coal in car-load lots, in-

stead of by the ton, an arrangement which is not only unsatisfactory to the rich, but oppressive to the poor, who must in many cases do without the fuel in consequence. A bill will be presented at an early day to the Legislative Assembly, asking for an appropriation to help construct the wagon road above mentioned, and to build a bridge over Price River.

Huntington has much improved during the past year. About 60 or 70 new houses have been put up, and water for the home-sites got out upon the land. Our informant, a former resident of Randolph, Rich County, has been in Emery County three years. The people there have a tri-weekly mail service, which so far has given good satisfaction. Some excitement prevails among certain classes over mining discoveries in the Cedar Mountain district.

Emery Items. — Brother Orange Seely, one of the Presidency of the Emery Stake of Zion and a resident of Castle Dale, gives us a few items in relation to matters in that locality. Castle Dale, which is the county seat, numbers about 300 souls, most of them, like the inhabitants of the other settlements, engaged in farming and stock-raising.

Persons in quest of good homes and willing to work for them will find good chances to unite with the settlers there on any of the streams. A good blacksmith would be a very desirable acquisition. Twenty-one men lately started to work on a five-mile canal from the Cottonwood stream to a large tract of land immediately north of the settlement.

Huntington is going ahead in dwellings, and will eventually be the largest settlement in the county. It has but one Ward, while Castle Dale has two, about three miles apart, the other one being called Orangeville. All kinds of seeds and supplies are to be obtained there. The weather was very fine for out-door work at last accounts.

The people of Price settlement are taking steps to incorporate an irrigation company, to take water from the Price River on to their townsite. The canal is surveyed and when finished will swallow up and render needless the numerous small ditches now in use. The general health was good and everything was quiet and peaceable.

HUNTINGTON, Emery County,
Feb. 11th, 1884.

Editor Deseret News:

The people are well satisfied with their location. This valley is proving the saying that the "desert shall blossom as the rose." Those who saw Castle Valley before it was settled and have seen it of late years, especially last year, when the crops were just getting ripe, know that if ever a valley disappointed the people for the better this has done that. There has been plenty of grain raised here to provide for the wants of the people, and some to spare. There is only one thing lacking to make everybody happy, and that is a good market for their produce.

I do not know how it is in other settlements, but I know in Huntington that, although they are not very large, the tithing bins are full to overflowing, both of grain and vegetables, and I have heard the Bishop remark that he believed that with very few exceptions the people have paid their tithing up in full. There has also been quite a reformation among the people in regard to the "Word of Wisdom." I think I am safe in saying that out of about eighty families, not over one-fifth of them use tea, coffee or tobacco

It is also the general feeling among the people to sustain with their faith and prayers, and their actions the authorities of the whole Church, especially those of this Stake, whom they are more immediately associated with.

Our Sunday and testimony meetings are very well attended, as are also the Elders' Teachers' and Deacons' meetings.

The Y.M. and Y.L.M.I. Associations are in a very flourishing condition, and are well attended. At a joint meeting held a short time ago the young people almost unanimously voted against round dancing. I must not forget the Relief Society and Primary, they also hold their meetings regularly. We have a very good day school here taught by Brother Elias H. Cox, astisted by Miss Harriet Caldwell. There are 89 scholars. The average attendance at our Sunday School is over 100 scholars.

There is some talk of building a co-op. grist mill here next summer. It is something we need here very much.

The last two weeks have been very stormy. There is about eight inches of snow on the ground, with plenty of it in the mountains. In consequence of so much snow we expect traveling to be very much impeded in the spring, owing to high water. In connection with this I will say, that if ever a people who are striving to build up a new country needed a little help, the people of Emery County do. We have sent in a petition to the Legislature asking for help to build at least one bridge, and to make a road through Huntington Cañon. If we can get help to build a bridge over Price River it will give the people hope that some day we can get our mails regularly, and that the traveling public can come and go without (as it is now during high water,) a great deal of danger both to life and property.

We also need help to build and finish a road through Huntington Cañon. This route is the most practical, short and easy grade of any leading from this county. The distance by this route to the mouth of Spanish Fork Cañon is about eighty miles, while by the other roads we already have to the same point it is about as follows: By way of Soldier Cañon (which will always be a dread to the traveler) through Emma's Park and down Spanish Fork, is about one hundred and twenty-five miles. By way of Cottonwood Cañon and Joe's Valley, over five heavy summits, which can only be crossed during a short season of the year, it is about one hundred miles. By way of Salina Cañon down the Sevier and through Sanpete Valley, to the same point is about one hundred and eighty-five miles.

Although we do not claim good travel through Huntington Cañon all the year round, it can be traveled longer than any other route, except Salina, and the difference in the distance in favor of Huntington being over 100 miles, it will pay the people of this county and the whole Territory to make an effort to get this road made. I say the people of the Territory. because good roads through our country and leading from ia will make property more valuable. Consequently the people will be called upon to pay more taxes into the treasury than they would be if they were hemmed up in the future as we have been in the past.

There is considerable fault found, and justly, I think, with the Denver & Rio Grande Railway, in regard to their doing, or not doing as they agreed. I know of instances where they have appropriated to their own use private property, such as lumber and ties, that they have refused or neglected to pay for; also stock has been killed, that influential men of their road have agreed to pay for, but this has not been done. I heard of one instance of a poor man going to Mr. Wood, when he was superintendent to ask him for pay for a horse killed by an engine, when Mr. Wood told him the people ought to be sued for letting their stock run on the track to endanger the lives of passengers. There are also instances of the people being overcharged for freight that they have had to pay without any redress being given them. One of them I will mention; last summer Bishop Charles Pulsipher had a sawmill brought from Cincinnati, Ohio. The freight agent of the D. & R. G. in Salt Lake City agreed, in writing, to deliver it at Castle Valley Station for $4.10 per 100 pounds When the mill got to Castle Valley, after being six or eight weeks on the road, he was charged $469 per 100lb. When Mr. Pulsipher complained he was told to pay the bill, and forward the receipt, and *agreement* (for $410) to Salt Lake, and they would give him a rebate. They have got his papers and he has got nothing, although it is six months since this happened. Their passenger rates from Salt Lake to Price are $8,40 while to Springville nearly half way it is only $2,55. They also discriminate heavily against Utah in favor of Colorado. Parties in Salt Lake tell me they can get lumber from Montrose, three hundred and fifty miles from Salt Lake, as cheaply as they can get it from P. V. Junction, the freight being about the same. It is also a well known fact that they discharge Utah men, and bring men from Denver to fill their places. We have also got papers to show where they charged us $62.00 for a car of freight 46 miles, while at the same time they were bringing cars of lumber from Montrose for $50.00. Is it any wonder that I as well as others advise the

people of Utah to patronize the Pioneer road as much as possible between Ogden and Springville. There is one case of my own. I sent some meat by express to Salt Lake, addressed to myself, I called for it a couple of hours after the train arrived, but they had delivered it to other parties and they did not get me back all my meat and refuse to pay for what was missing.

Yours Respectfully, W. H.

A LETTER FOR THE LEGIS-LATURE.

HUNTINGTON, Emery County,
Utah, Feb. 18th, 1884.

Editor Deseret News:

A few weeks ago the citizens of this county sent a petition to the Legislative Assembly, asking an appropriation of $2,000 to build a bridge over Price River, in this county; and also for $2,000 to help to make a road through Huntington Cañon. At the time this petition was sent some of the Denver & Rio Grande Railroad officials said we might get the money for the bridge, but we would not get help for the road. Now we see by the minutes of the House of Feb. 12th, that it has turned out just about as they predicted.

There was some talk when this petition was sent that in the event the appropriation was made and the road completed, a great many would bring their supplies through this route instead of paying the D. & R. G. the exorbitant freight rates that they are in the habit of charging on local freight. The petition for the road was for and would be the greatest benefit to the people of the *whole country*, excepting the railway people, and we would like to know some of the reasons for refusing an appropriation for the benefit of the people, and making one in the interests of a railroal corporation, of course we asked for both, and not wishing to cast any reflections on the honorable committee who had our petition, and who made the report referred to, we can only say it looks strange the prediction above referred to, should be so literally fulfilled.

In connection with this we would ask our law makers if they cannot pass a law to equalize freight rates throughout the Territory, as it seems where there is no competition, the people are taxed beyond all reason, considering the way rates are charged as soon as competition ceases. Now we hold that on the same principal a railroad company charges, more for local freight in a county where there is no competition, that the county would be justified in assessing a greater tax. But as counties cannot do that, why is it that a railroad company as soon as they leave competition, raise their rates double, treble and even four times higher than they do where that competition exists.

We are having a regular old fashioned winter, with snow about one foot deep; the indications are we will have some thawing weather soon, as it has cleared up to-day.

Yours truly,
W. H.

Deseret News
March 19, 1884

EMERY STAKE CONFERENCE.

The Emery Stake Quaterly Conference was held at Huntington, March 1st, 1884.

Present on the stand President C. G. Larsen and Counselors Orange Seely and Rasmus Justensen, members of the High Council of Emery Stake, Bishops of the different wards and counselors.

Notwithstanding the inclemency of weather, there was a good attendance from all parts of the Stake, the Orangeville and Huntington choirs dispensing sweet music for the occasion.

After singing and prayer by President Justensen, President Larsen said he was pleased to see so many assembled at the beginning of Conference; he reviewed the past to some extent, and showed how the Saints had been blessed when they lived near unto God, and how the Lord was chastising Babylon at the present time.

The Bishops gave in reports from the different Wards, which were all in a thriving condition; the Saints generally were living up to the principles of the Word of Wisdom, with a very few exceptions, no saloons being in our midst, only at Price Ward, which was on the line of the D. & R. G.

Meeting adjourned until 2 p.m.

At the afternoon services more reports were given in from the wards.

President Juntersen showed the beauty of living up to the principles of our most holy faith, spoke at some length on home manufacture, showed that it was necessary in building up a new country to be self-sustaining to a great extent, advised the Saints to unite together and make their own leather and raise sheep so that they might have wool to clothe their families with instead of importing everything and selling their grain at low figures to get these things that could be made at home.

President O. Seely said that in visiting the Saints in Emery Stake he could see a great change in the people, they were trying to live nearer unto our heavenly Father, showed that when the Saints were living their religion that those who were striving to oppress this people were powerless in their designs. While the outside world were all excitement over "Mormonism" the Saints were quietly obeying the "Mormon" creed and minding their own business.

Sunday, 10 a.m.

After singing and prayer, Bishop Fransen, of Price, having just arrived, spoke a few words.

President Larsen gave a report of the Stake. He felt that the Saints of Emery Stake were a good people, and were striving to live as near the lives of Latter-day Saints as their circumstances would permit, with the many trials the people had to undergo in opening up a new country. He advised the Saints to gather together on the townsite as fast as possible, so that they might have schools for their children, and might built up and beautify the waste places of Zion.

Prest. N. L. Guyman gave a report of the Seventies Quorums of the Stake.

J. K. Reid read the statistical report of the Stake, which showed an increase of over 100 since last Conference.

2 p.m.

After singing and prayer, the sacrament of the Lord's supper was administered.

The Presidents of the different quorums gave in reports. Also reports from the Sabbath Schools.

J. K. Reid then presented the general authorities, also the local authorities of the Stake, all of which were unanimously sustained.

Remarks were made by the following brethren: Elders J. K. Reid, Wm. Howard, Joseph Birch and Matthew Caldwell, all exhorting the Saints to faithfulness and diligence in the works of God, and in regard to the word of wisdom.

Prest. Larsen spoke a few words in relation to the organization of new wards in this Stake of Zion; exhorted the Saints to live up to the instruction received at this conference and we would be blessed. Spoke in regard to the judgments of the Lord in the earth at the present time, and invoked the blessing of God on the Saints.

Conference adjourned for three months, to be held at Orangeville.

Benediction by Brother O. Seely.

J. K. REID,
Clerk of Emery Stake.

Registration.

Commissions were forwarded on Wednesday to the following named persons, by Hon. Arthur L. Thomas, secretary of the Utah Commission, as deputy registrars. Registration to commence on the first Monday (the fifth day) of May, 1884:

BEAVER COUNTY.

John Barraclaugh, Beaver.
William Smith, Greenville.
B. A. Spier, Adamsville.
Peter Lechrie, Granpion.
Henry Bowen, Granpion.
F. W. O'Connor, Star.
Luther Carter, Minersville.

BOX ELDER COUNTY,

N. P. Anderson, Bear River.
L. Snow, Jr., Box Elder.
Thomas Yates, Calls Fort.
M. D. Ochiltree, Curlew.
John Standing, Deweyville.
M. K. Parsons, Grouse Creek.
Reese Howell, Kelton.
E. R. Chase, Malad.
M. J. Barrett, Mantua.
Wm. Godfrey, Park Valley.
M. J. Richards, Plymouth.
Wm. Anderson, Portage.
Thomas Davis, Promontory.
Wm. Taylor, Jr., Terrace.
Thomas W. Brewerton, Millard.
Thomas Rowland, Logan.
Joseph Baker, Mendon.
W. D. Goodwin, Trenton.

CACHE COUNTY.

Adam Sandburg, Richmond.
Joseph Wood, Clarkston.
Aaron De Witt, Hyde Park.
Henry Griffiths, Newton.
Edward Nelson, Benson.
James Hadfield, Smithfield.
Samuel P. Hall, Wellsville.
Joseph Jordan, Peterborough.
James E. Caine, Hyrum.
W. W. Nelson, Millard.
Hyrum De Witt, Providence.
William A. Jarkey, Paradise.
Rasmus Anderson, Lewiston.

DAVIS COUNTY.

Jno. Bowman, South Weber.
Jno. H. Meredith, Kaysville.
Robt. Simpson, South Hooper.
James T. Smith, Farmington.
Parley P. Evans, Centreville.
Stephen Hales, East Centreville
A. J. Phelps, West Centreville.
Luther Burnham, South Centreville.

EMERY COUNTY.

Job H. Whitney, Castle Lake.
J. F. Wakefield, Huntington.
J. D. Kilpack, Ferron.
O. W. Warner, Moab.
J. K. Reid, Orangeville.
Caleb Rhodes, Price.
J. S. Lewis, Muddy.
A. J. Harkness, Scofield.

Salt Lake Herald
April 29, 1884

Death of a Pioneer.

Editors Herald:

This morning one of Utah's early citizens passed away in the person of John Hancock, who breathed his last at quarter past four o'clock, after one short week of illness of pneumonia. Mr. Hancock came to the Territory while very young. He was of a retiring nature before the public, but when danger was to be encountered he never flinched, one proof of which was that on the introduction of the poney express across the country, he and Billy Fisher were the first to climb into the saddles and brave storm and savages. By special arrangement Mr. H. ran the last pony between Camp Floyd and Salt Lake, after the telegraph was completed from Salt Lake to Camp Floyd. He made the fastest time on record. Could his early history have been written it would have surpassed romance, during the early days of Montana and Idaho. For about twelve years he was employed by ex-Mayor Jennings, as mining foreman in the Park and elsewhere, but through injuries received several years ago, he fell an easy victim to pneumonia.

He was born April 19th, 1842, making him 42 years of age.

Funeral services from residence of his late father-in-law, Dimick B. Huntington, in the Sixteenth ward, north-east corner Union Square.

'48.

DEATHS.

HANCOCK—At the residence of the late D. B. Huntington, in the 16th ward of this city, at 4.15 a. m. on Monday, April 28th, of pneumonia, John Hancock, son of the late Levi Hancock.

Aunt Fanny says this is the 27th of her kindred laid away since she came here with the Battalion in 1847. Deceased leaves a wife and five children.

CONDITION IN EMERY COUNTY.

Weather, Crops, Etc.

HUNTINGTON, Emery County,
May 20th, 1884.

Editor Deseret News:

We are having splendid weather here now, with occasionally a nice rain. During April and up to the middle of May, more rain fell in Castle Valley than ever known before in the same length of time. As a consequence the range is very good for stock, and the crops that were put in early look splendid.

The mountains west of us are full of snow, and we expect very high water this season; some of it is coming now, but not what there will be in a month, as it is generally from the middle until the last of June when we have our highest water. But in case any of our brethren wish to visit us at our

COMING CONFERENCE

the first and second of June, we would like to have them do so, and they will be perfectly safe as far as high water in this valley is concerned, for I am satisfied the people at Price would take them by team about five miles below Price Station to the first railroad bridge, there a team from Huntington could meet them, and a team from Castle Dale could meet them at Huntington, where there is a good foot bridge in case the water is too high to cross with a team

The health of the people here is generally very good; there has been a little sickness, but not of a very serious nature.

All of the old land and a great deal of the new is being put

UNDER CULTIVATION

this year, the Huntington canal to take water on to the townsite, and also to water several thousand acres of land south of town is proving a success. As a consequence, the town is growing very fast. There are some very good buildings going up, and lots of good gardens and a few orchards. I have got a few peach trees that were raised here by Brother N. T. Guymon, that are out in blossom and are doing well. Quite a number of

NEW SETTLERS

came in this spring and lots more are expected. Our facilities for several hundred families are good, so far as land, climate and water is concerned, as it is all good and plenty of it. Our worst difficulty at present is in regard to roads. Most of them are not five years old, and when a man takes up a piece land that has a road running through it, he plows it up, and in some cases roads that have been used for five years are served the same way, to the great annoyance of the people that have to travel them. Of course there are a few honorable exceptions to the above, but it seems the men that have the most land are the most selfish in this matter.

OUR SABBATH MEETINGS

and day and Sunday Schools and other Ward organizations are all in splendid running order, and as a general thing the people feel well, and are trying to carry out the council and instructions we receive from our leaders.

We have no common news of the day such as

MURDERS,

drunken fights, robberies, suspended firms, etc., in this place, but all are trying to live quiet and peaceful lives. If any difficulties arise between brethren that they cannot settle themselves (such as will sometimes happen in the best of families) they are generally settled in a few minutes by a couple of the Teachers.

The NEWS is always a welcome visitor. Long may it live.

Yours respectfully,   W. H.

EMERY STAKE CONFERENCE.

The Emery Stake Conference was held at Orangeville May 31st and June 1st.

Present on the stand: Counselor O. Seely, Bishops of the different wards and Counsel, also members of the High Council of Emery Stake.

President Larsen called the meeting to order.

The choir sang.

Prayer by Bishop Joseph Robertson.

President Larsen made a few opening remarks.

The Bishops gave in reports of the different wards, which were all prospering, increasing in numbers and the people trying to live nearer unto God. Some of the wards were intending some branches of home manufacture, such as furniture, brooms, etc.

President Larsen made a few remarks on punctuality and exhorted the Saints.

Singing by the choir.

Benediction by Patriarch Robert Logan.

2 p. m.

Singing.

Prayer by Elder Wm. Avery.

Reports were made by the different quorums of the Priesthood in Emery Stake, also the Sunday schools and Y. M. M. I. Associations, by the Stake Superintendents.

President Larsen spoke at some length on the temporal affairs of the kingdom of God. Said that the Presidency of the Church were working at the present time to unite the hearts of the people, both temporally and spiritually. He gave a synopsis of some of the instructions at the last General Conference at Salt Lake City, and urged upon the Saints to purge out all iniquity from ther midst and the blessings of the Lord would rest upon them.

The Orangeville choir sang an anthem: "O, How Lovely is Zion."

Benediction by Elder J. K. Reid.

Sunday morning, June 1st.

Singing by the Orangeville and Huntsville choirs combined.

Prayer by Elder James Woodward.

The satistical report was read by J. K. Reid, Stake Clerk, which showed an increase of one hundred members since last Conference.

President Larsen made a few remarks in regard to the building up of the kingdom of God.

The general and local authorities were then presented and unanimously sustained.

Patriarch Robert Logan spoke a few words. He showed what the Saints were doing, building up the kingdom of God, and the outside world were striving to pull it down, but they never would accomplish their design.

J. K. Reid made a few remarks on adopting the mountain time as it had been recommended by the Presidency of the Church.

It was then moved by President Larsen that the Saints throughout Emery Stake adopt the mountain standard time. Unanimously sustained.

Elder O. F. Anderson spoke at some length on the benefits of Mormonism. His remarks were listened to with considerable attention and were very pointed.

Elder Wm. Howard showed the ground the Saints stood on by obeying the commands of God and also by obeying the commands of man. He was in favor of obeying God and letting the consequences follow.

Elder James Woodward was the next speaker; singing; Benediction by Elder J. W. Seely.

2 p. m.

Singing, and Prayer by J. D. Hilpack. The sacrament of the Lords supper was administered.

Bishop Pulsipher spoke on the principle of Celestial Marriage.

President O. Seely spoke a few words in regard to the early settlement of this valley.

President Larsen spoke on Order in meetings and assemblies. He also dwelt at some length on Celestial Marriage, and read the revelation on the subject, as given to the Prophet Joseph Smith. The congregation sang "We thank thee O. God for a Prophet."

Benediction by Elder N. L. Guymon, sen.

J. K. REID.
Stake Clerk.

Salt Lake Herald
July 27, 1884

ELECTION JUDGES.

Appointed by the Utah Commission.

EMERY COUNTY.

Castle Dale—George Eddington, Don C. Seely, Orange Seely.

Ferron—W. S. Peacock, Hans C. Hanson, Hyrum Stevens.

Price—Charles Batteberry, R. B. Thompson, F. E. Grames.

Huntington—H. S. Loveless, E. H. Cox, N. H. Steavens.

Schofield—Robert McKeckney, D. W. Holdaway, John Eden.

A VISIT TO EMERY STAKE.

PRICE WARD, Emery Co., Utah,
September 1, 1884.

Editor Deseret News:

President Joseph F. Smith and wife, Apostle Erastus Snow and wife and Elder Andrew Jensen left Salt Lake city Friday Aug. 29th, at 11 a.m. on the D. & R. G. train for Emery Stake. Apostle F. M. Lyman accompanied the party to Provo. After a pleasant ride of 127 miles, the latter part of which was very interesting on account of the grand and beautiful scenery in Price River cañon, the party was welcomed at Price Station by Bishop Geo. Frandsen, Brother N. T. Guymor and others. At this place about 50 families of the Saints are located along the stream for nearly 14 miles, but a town site a little east of the railway station has been selected, and a meeting house, the best and largest in the county was erected thereon last winter. Owing to a little land difficulty, now about to be adjusted, none of the settlers, however, have as yet moved on to the site, but several of them intend to do so this fall.

After taking supper with Brother Birch, who lives close to the station, the party had a 25 mile moonlight ride ovenļa broken and uneven country to Huntington, at present the largest settlement in the valley. Also here the settlers are considerably scattered, but they are moving to their pleasantly loctated townsite on the right bank of the stream (Huntington Creek) as fast as possible. The present number of families on this creek is 87, but there is, according to Bishop Pulsipher's statement, land, water and other accommodations for at least 300 families. About 75 houses have been erected on the townsite during the past year.

Saturday, the 20th, the visiting brethren and a great number of the Saints from the Huntington Ward proceeded to Castle Dale, the capital of Emery County, 10 miles to the southwest. Here the quarterly conference, under the presidency of Elder C. G. Larsen, was commenced at 10 a. m. Three meetings, including the young people's conference, were held that day in a splendid new bowery, and in the evening another meeting was held in Orangeville, three miles further up the Cottonwood Creek, on which stream the two settlements, namely Castle Dale, with 48, and Orangeville, with 55 families, are located. The following day the business of the conference was attended to and completed. Among other things a new ward was organized of a part of the Ferron Ward, with Lyman S. Beach as Bishop and H. P. Rasmussen and J. D. Killpack as Counselors. The new ward was named Molen, in honor of Brother M. W. Molen, the first settler on Ferron Creek. According to the statistical report read in the conference there are now 349 families, or 1,967 souls, belonging to the eight wards of the Church in the Emery Stake of Zion, and there is yet room for thousands of thrifty Latter-day Saints, who are invited to come and cast their lot there among a truly good and God fearing people.

President Larsen and the other leading men of the Stake are very energetic and zealous in their labors to build up the country, and with more settlers they could make more and quicker advancement. Here is, indeed, a splendid chance for many of the poor unemployed brethren in Salt Lake City and other older towns to secure unto themselves and families good homes on very easy terms. Castle Valley bids fair to become a good country in due time, the soil is becoming more productive every year, and the natural advantages are very good in many respects. The land has certainly been greatly blessed of the Lord, and the prospects for future developments are promising indeed. A good crop of small grain has been raised this year, and fruit trees are doing well. We also saw some fine specimens of grapes raised here, where the climate is considerably warmer than in Sanpete. Anything that can grow in the more central regions of Utah can also be successfully raised in Castle Valley.

President Smith and Apostle Snow were under the inspiration of the Almighty, led to give the people some very excellent and practical instructions, and everybody present seemed to enjoy the meetings very much. Returning to Huntington after the close of the conference another good meeting was held there in the evening, d an to-day (Monday) the visiting brethren, accompanied by the Presidency of the Stake and a number of others, traveled to Price where a meeting will be held this afternoon, after which Brother Smith and Snow who met their respective wives, will continue their journey to Colorado. They expect to be gone about a month and will, after visiting the Stakes in Arizona, return to Salt Lake City by way of California. In view of the hard times and the scarcity of labor this season and also in consideration of the fact, that there are too many people without homes of their own in our older towns I would earnestly recommend that such of our brethren who are not afraid to take hold with a will and labor patiently and hard for a few years to subdue a new country, should turn their attention to Castle Valley, where they will be welcomed by Saints of sterling faith and true friendship, and where they will naturally grow with the country and soon become independent in a financial point of view compared with their present circumstances.

ANDREW JENSON.

Salt Lake Herald
September 21, 1884

Edward Case, of Hamilton, Ont., defeated George Reid, of Orangeville, in a half-mile race on James track, at the former place, Sept. 1, running the distance without any great effort in 2 min. 5 sec.

EMERY STAKE CONFERENCE

The Quarterly Conference was held at Castle Dale August 30 and 31, 1884. Present on the stand, Joseph F. Smith, of the First Presidency; Elder Erastus Snow, of the Twelve Apostles; Prest. C. G. Larson and Counselors, Patriarch Robert Logan, members of the High Council and Bishops of the different Wards and their Counselors.

The Castle Dale, Huntington and Orangeville choirs discoursed music for the occasion.

After singing and prayer the Bishops gave in reports which showed an increase in good works generally throughout the Stake.

Apostle E. Snow gave good instruction. He felt pleased with the improvements that were made since his last visit, and that the Lord was with this people. He advised the Saints to build close together on the town sites, that they could have good schools.

Benediction by Patriarch R. Logan.

Afternoon services. Singing and prayer.

President Jos. W. Moore gave a report of the High Priests' Quorum.

President N. F. Guymon, sen., gave a report of the Seventies Quorum of the Stake.

President S. Jenker gave a report of the first quorum of Elders, also J. L. Brasher gave a report of the second quorum of Elders.

Supt. Peter Johnson gave a report of the Sabbath Schools. All the reports were encouraging.

President Jos. F. Smith took up the remainder of the afternoon. He exhorted the Saints to faithfulness in the work of the Lord, spoke in regard to the duties of Bishops, showed that we must live up to all the laws of God to gain the blessings promised by the obedient. His remarks were timely and pointed.

Benediction by President O. Seely.

Second day.

Singing and Prayer.

Elder Andrew Jensen of Salt Lake City, spoke a few words of instruction and encouragement

J. K. Reid read the Statistical Report of the Stake, which showed an increase in the last quarter of about 100.

Apostle E. Snow took up the balance of the forenoon in giving instructions to the Saints. He showed what we were placed on this earth for and exhorted the Saints to live near to God at all times and show Him that we are willing to sacrifice all for the Gospel's sake. He spoke at some length on the spiritual things of the Kingdom, showed that we must understand these things before we can enter into the glory in store for the faithful.

Singing. Benediction by President Rassmus Justensen.

There was a meeting of the High Council, when Molen Ward was laid off on Ferron Creek in honor of M. W. Molen, being the first settler on the creek. Lyman, S. Reach was selected as Bishop, with H. P. Rassmusen as first and J. D. Kilpack as second Counselor.

Afternoon services. Singing and prayer. The sacrament of the Lord's supper was administered.

J. K. Reid presented the general and local Authorities of the Church, which were sustained unanimously. He also read a letter to the conference from the Temple committee to the Stakes in the Manti Temple District, making a call for $385 from Emery Stake to help finish the interior of the Temple.

President Larsen made a few remarks on the same subject.

President Jos. F. Smith spoke at some length on the spiritual things of the Kingdom. He showed that we were all placed on the earth to fill a mission, and explained its nature.

Lyman S. Beach was ordained a High Priest and set apart as Bishop of Molen Ward under the hands of Apostle E. Snow, Hans P. Rassmussen was ordained a High Priest and set apart as First Counselor to Bishop Beach, under the hands of President Joseph F. Smith; J. D. Kilpack was set apart as Second Counselor to Bishop Beach.

Sister Pulsipher was set apart as Second Counselor to the President of the Relief Society of Emery Stake under the hands of President Joseph F. Smith; Sisters Olive Bulkley and Johanna Curtis were set apart as nurses for the sick.

President Snow gave some instruction to the Presiding Elders of the Stake. He advised them to do the works of righteousness so that they may be examples before the Saints.

The conference adjourned to meet at Huntington in three months.

Benediction by President C. C. Larsent.

              J. K. REID,
          Clerk of Emery Stake.

Deseret News
October 29, 1884

FACILITIES AT HUNTINGTON.

PERTINENT QUESTIONS PUT AND REPLIED TO.

HUNTINGTON, Emery Co., Utah,
        October 13th, 1884.

Editor Deseret News:

In order to avoid answering from one to half a dozen letters each mail, I deem it wisdom to answer all at once through the NEWS.

I am asked, have you any room for more Latter-day Saints at Huntington? Yes.

What are the facilities and climate?

We have about 6,000 acres of land, and water enough to irrigate it. We have an abundance of cedar and pinion pine wood near by on the foot-hills; also extensive coal beds from six to ten miles distant; and plenty of saw timber and building timber from 10 to 25 miles distant.

We now have a wagon road made about fifteen miles up Huntington Cañon, which stream affords some fish, and the road gives us access to the lumber and building timber; and we hope in the near future to have the road completed to the line between this and Sanpete counties, that we may have an outlet to Sanpete, Utah and Salt Lake Counties.

But some say you have not got a good stock country.

Well we do not claim that we have, as grass is very scarce in the valley; yet we have good summer range on the mountains west of the valley, and in some parts there is winter range for small herds of stock. But as this is a farming district with no fence law, of course it is no place for large herds of stock during the farming season. Our cow herds do very well. The cows are herded during the day and corralled at night, but those have persevered, and good lucern patches can make their cows more profitable by giving them a good feed of lucern at night and morning.

But what is your climate? and can you raise fruit?

Yes, we can raise the hardy kinds of fruit for that has already been done; and I think that grapes may be raised in abundance. The soil is of a heavy clayey nature and therefore cold and backward in the spring; but when warm weather comes on vegetation grows very fast. Generally speaking the winters are cold and dry. Deer are plentiful on the mountains and we frequently have a treat on their delicious flesh.

Is the land all taken up in that vicinity?

No, there is some more to be taken up under the direction of a committee, and we contemplate laying out a ditch that will cover three or four thousand acres of land, and we propose to locate three or four men upon a quarter section so that there will not be large quantities of unoccupied land under said canal. There are also chances to buy land, with a title to it, at from five to ten dollars per acre. Our townsite, which occupies one section of land, is laid off into blocks 33 rods square, with four lots in a block, and the streets are six rods wide except two main streets, which are eight rods wide. There being but few waste lots, there are 240 good lots in the townsite.

For fear we weary the patience of your readers, we will close by saying that the frost nipped some of our late grain and corn on the 7th and 10th of September; but we trust that sufficient has been raised to bread the settlement, including the new comers.

The health of the people is, generally speaking, good.

Yours truly,

CHAS. PULSIPHER.

Deseret News
December 17, 1884

EMERY STAKE CONFERENCE.

The Quarterly Conference of the Emery Stake of Zion was held at Huntington, November 29th and 30th, 1884.

There were present on the stand President C. G. Larsen, O. Seely, Rasmuss Justenson, members of the High Council of Emery Stake, Bishops of the different wards and Counselors, and Presidents of quorums.

Singing by the Huntington choir.

Prayer by President Justensen.

Singing.

President Larsen made a few remarks on punctuality; hoped that the Saints would observe this throughout Conference and at all times. He showed that the Saints in Emery Stake had been blessed exceedingly since our last Conference, and the Lord would still continue His blessings if we would do our part and keep His commandments. Advised the Saints to take care of their grain, for the time would come when it would be needed, and that not far hence. Exhorted the Saints to faithfulness.

Brother O. W. Warner, Counselor to Bishop Stewart, gave a report of the Moab Ward. Health prevailed in that ward, and everything was prospering, although they had some outside element to content against.

At the afternoon services the Bishops gave reports of the different Wards throughout the Stake; all were in as prosperous a condition as could be expected in a new country, and all were increasing in numbers.

Prest. Larsen spoke a few words in regard to a full organization of the different Associations throughout the State. Spoke in regard to the Bishops giving recommends to parties they were not acquainted with; also on Temple donations; said the Saints were blessed at all times when we lived up to these things; said the Lord would fight our battles if we would do His will and keep His commandments.

Prest. N. T. Guymon, Sen., gave a report of the Seventies of Emery Stake. Spoke in regard to some of the prophecies that were made by the Prophet Joseph Smith, a great many of which had come to pass; some had yet to come to pass, but were in a fair way according to the signs of the times. The time was not far distant when those who would not take up arms against their neighbors would have to flee to Zion for safety.

Prest. Jos. W. Moore reported the High Priests Quorum of Emery Stake.

Father Day said he had been in the Church a long time, and never had felt to waver his belief in this Gospel and wanted to endure to the end.

Elder William Black said we had had testimony from the aged the middle aged and the young, all testifying to this work. But this was not enough, we must continue in the good work and endure to the end to gain the reward for the faithful.

Elder Lot Rowe, of Mount Pleasant, said he always felt willing to do as the servants of God required of him.

Second Day.

The congregation was so large they could not all get in the house, this being the largest conference held in Emery Stake.

President Larsen said he could see necessity of the Saints in Emery having a Stake House to hold Conference in, and hoped that they would not feel too poor at some future time to build one.

Elder P. A. Childs reported the 1st Quorum of Elders of Emery Stake, Elder John L. Brasher, reported the 2nd Quorum of Elders, Supt. Peter Johnson reported the Sabbath Schools of Emery Stake which were all in a thriving condition.

President Larson spoke a few works on Sunday schools, showed what the Sunday School Union was doing for the cause of God.

President O. Seely spoke on the blessings we were in possession of.

President Justensen made a few remarks on the responsibility resting upon the Latter-pay Saints.

Father Stevens, of Ferron, spoke on the early rise of the Church, told how the Prophet Joseph gave him a mission a short time before his martyrdom and that was to preach the Gospel to all mankind, and said testimony was that this was the kingdom of God set up in these last days, never more to be thrown down or given to another people.

Elder Mathew Caldwell made a few remarks on the labor of the Mormon Battalion.

Afternoon Services.

The Sacrament of the Lord's Supper was administered, after which, Father Joseph Allen spoke on the early rise of the Church and the persecutions he had passed through in those days; knew this work was true and never would be thrown down.

J. K. Reid then read the statistical report of Emery Stake, also presented the General Authorities of the Church also the local authorities of the Stake, who were sustained unanimously.

Elder Erastus Curtis spoke on the early days of the Church; said in listening to the aged brethren that had spoken, it made his heart rejoice in the Gospel of Christ.

Elder Wm. Howard urged the Saints to be faithful in all things.

President Larsen exhorted the Saints to look well to ourselves in regard to our salvation, both here and hereafter, and remember our obligations to one another, asked for the blessings of God to rest upon us as a people, in the name of Christ.

Singing, and benediction by N. T. Guymon, sen.

J. K. REID, Clerk.

DEATHS.

VAN BUREN. — At Orangeville, Emery County, Utah, December 28th, 1884, of bronchitis, Verona Geneva, daughter of A. C. and Lavinia Van Buren, born October 31st, 1872.

Commissions.

Governor Murray issued commissions yesterday to the following county and precinct officers, recently appointed by the county courts to fill vacancies:

William H. Hammond, justice of the peace for Toquerville Precinct, Washington County.

O. N. Stohl, county treasurer, Box Elder County.

Walter Scott, alderman, Provo.

Thomas A. Jackson, poundkeeper, Molen Precinct, Emery County.

J. T. Farrer, justice of the peace, Blake Precinct, Emery County.

H. P. Rasmussen, justice of the peace, Molen Precinct, Emery County.

A. C. Van Buren, justice of the peace, Orangeville Precinct, Emery County.

P. C. Fjeldsted, road supervisor, Molen Precinct, Emery County.

Deseret News
January 21, 1885

HUNTINGTON, Emery County,
Utah, December 27th, 1884.

Editors Deseret News:

Thinking a few items from Huntington would not be amiss, I will say that the year 1884 has been a favorable one for this place and for the whole valley. Although the grain crop was not as good as it was in 1883, mostly on account of a great many thinking that late grain was the best, this year has proven that wheat put in during March is a safer crop than that sown in June.

A great many people have located in Huntington this year, and improvements have been made at a lively rate, so much so that a person that was here a year ago would hardly know the place now. Consequently real estate has in the past twelve months

MORE THAN DOUBLED IN VALUE.

We look for more improvements, and better ones, in houses and fencing, to be made in the coming year than ever before, as it has always been very hard to get lumber heretofore, it having to be hauled from forty to eighty miles, but there has lately been a steam saw mill put up in Huntington Cañon, that is expected to make all the lumber needed for building and fencing purposes for some time to come.

We have had and are going to have again immediately after New Year's

A VERY GOOD DAY SCHOOL,

taught by Brother Terry, who seems to be well qualified for teaching the young. Our Sunday Shhool is also in a very flourishing condition, and I may say the same of all the other organizations of the Ward, namely: Seventies, Elders, Deacons and Y. M. M. I. Association; also Relief Society, Y. L. M. I. and Primary Associations.

The Spirit of the Lord has shown itself and been with the authorities of this place, and with the Elders who have from time to time been called upon to address us in our Sabbath meetings, and I believe the people never felt better spiritually. Notwithstanding this, there has been

A GLOOM CAST OVER US

lately, caused by sickness and death.
For the past several weeks the weather
has been very changeable—cold, warm
and stormy; and as a consequence a
great many children have been very
sick, and the following deaths occurred: On the first of this month, Brother Chalk buried a little child; on the
18th, Brother Chris. Johnson buried a
child; on the 23d, Bishop Chas. Pulsipher buried two children in one coffin,
both having died the night before.
One of them died through the effects of
the epidemic that seemed to prevail
among the children, the other from the
effects of a scald it got through falling
ing into a pot of boiling water. On the
24th Brother D. Washburn buried a
child, and on the 26th Brother Clark
Brinkerhoof buried one. As a consequence our Christmas festivities were
of rather a gloomy nature. At the present writing those that are sick seem
to be improving, and it is to be hoped
that the hand of the destroyer is stayed. They were mostly young babes
that died, and the people feel to say,
especially those that have been called
upon to part with their children, "Father, thy will be done."

Wishing all Israel a merry Christmas and a happy New Year,

I remain, your respectfully,

W. H.

Deseret News
March 25, 1885

DEATHS.

SCOVILL—Of consumption and old age,
March 4, 1885, Sarah Ballow, wife of Amasa
Scovill; born July 19, 1803; baptized in Mich-
igan in 1860; came to Salt Lake City in 1862;
lived at Mt. Pleasant, Sanpete County, until
1881, when she moved to Orangeville, where
she died as she had lived, a true Latter-day
Saint.

Salt Lake Herald
April 18, 1885

THE GRAND JURY.

A Rushing Day in the Secret Chamber.

The witnesses' room of the Grand Jury was thickly populated all day yesterday, and Mr. Usher Lipman was kept busy calling, ushering in and showing out the witnesses in four or five cases which the jury were investigating simultaneously. All the available citizens and citizenesses of Brighton Ward at one time seemed jammed into the broad corridors between the marshal's and the Grand Jury room. A reporter noticed Mr. and Mrs. Robert Hazen, Sr., Mr. and Mrs. Robert Hazen, Jr., Mr. William Barrow, Mrs. Louisa Harridge, Mrs. Cooley, Mary Cooley, Melissa Huntington, Mrs. Hannah Hanson and a number of others whose names he did not know, ascending and descending the Wasatch stairs. The cases on which they were summoned are those of Nathan Hanson, Bishop of Brighton Ward, A. W. Cooley, the ex-bishop, and Jas. Harridge, all of whom reside across the river. During the day several members of Mr. Henry Dinwoodey's family were also called and examined. Geo. Partington, an old gentleman, was also seen in the throng, summoned, as he supposed, in the case of Mr. Van Natta, of the Nineteenth Ward; the case of Mr. Joseph Dean, of the same ward, was also under investigation, and his son, J. H. Dean, Bishop Watson, the Corbett family, who rent Mr. Dean's house, and some others were examined as to what they knew in the premises; a lady, alleged to be the third wife, was missing.

The Grand Jury adjourned about 4 o'clock.

Salt Lake Democrat
April 28, 1885

THE ELECTION OFFICERS.

Deputy Registrars Appointed by the Utah Commissioners This Morning.

EMERY COUNTY.

Castle Dale Precinct—J. H. Whitney.
Blake—J. T. Farrar.
Fearon—Michael Molen.
Molen—J. D. Kilpack.
Price—Caleb Rhodes.
Wellington—R. B. Thompson.
Moab—O. W. Warner.
Muddy—John S. Lewis.
Huntington—C. T. Wakefield.
Schofield—S. J. Harkness.

TOOELE COUNTY.

Mill Precinct—Wm. F. Mop.
Batesville—John Hillstead.
Lake View—James Brachet.
Tooele—Robt. Scott.
Grantsville—Thomas Williams.
Ophir—John W. Thompson.
Clover—Rich. N. Burt.
St. John—Edward J. Arthur.
Vernon—Louis Stursburg.
Deep Creek—Fred Snively.
Stockton—D. B. Stover.

WASATCH COUNTY.

Heber Precinct—Thomas Smith.
Midway Precinct—Attewall Wootton.
Charleston Precinct—Jerome W. Kinney.

Wallsburgh—Joseph Kerby.

PIUTE COUNTY.

Additional new Precincts.

Graves Valley Precinct—Edward McDougle.
Kane Precinct—Hila Burgess.
Burgess Precinct—John S. Graves.

Deseret News
May 6, 1885

Deputy Registrars. — The Utah Commission yesterday appointed the following deputy registration officers:

EMERY COUNTY.

Robt. J. Whitney, Castledale.
J. T. Farmer, Blake.
Michael Nolan, Ferron.
Caleb Rhodes, Price.
John D. Kilpack, Molen.
R. B. Thompson, Wellington.
O. W. Warner, Moab.
John S. Lewis, Muddy.
C. T. Wakefield, Huntington.
A. J. Harkness, Scofield.

EMERY COUNTY ITEMS.

Sunday School Jubilee — Trapper's Outfit Wanting a Claimant — Bountiful Crops—Good Place for New Settlers.

HUNTINGTON, EMERY Co., Utah,
July 18th, 1885.

Editor Deseret News:

I have been requested to send you a report of the Emery Stake Sunday School Jubilee, which took place yesterday, the 17th.

At half-past eight a. m., the people were called together by music by the Huntington Martial Band. After the gathering a procession of the schools was formed. There was in it over 800 children, bearing flags, mottoes, etc., and representing the following wards: Huntington, Castle Dale, Price, Wellington, Ferron and Muddy. After the procession marched around the public square the several schools took seats in places allotted them in a spacious bowery erected for that purpose.

The programme both forenoon and afternoon consisted of class exercises, speeches, songs, anthems, etc., which were very well rendered by those who took part. One dialogue, entitled "Jennie and Carrie," and which brought tears to the eyes of many who heard it, was very well given by Miss Annie Lay and Miss Dora McIntire, of Price.

In the evening there was a dance for all who wished to participate, and, taking it all through, it was a day long to be remembered.

Harvest is now upon us; grain all around the settlement is now turning yellow, and some I understand are going to commence cutting next week. Our second crop of lucern is also about ready to cut, and generally the people feel that the Lord is abundantly blessing them this season.

One year ago the 4th of last May, there was brought to Brother Orange Seeley, probate judge of this county, one new three-inch steel skein Fish wagon, one span horses and harness, a lot of beaver traps and some other camp outfit, which were supposed to belong to a trapper who had been trapping on the San Raphael in this county. The property had been sent to the judge by the Tidwells, who live on the stream mentioned out near Green River. This trapper was reported by the man who brought the things as supposed to be dead. Judge Seeley has written quite a number of letters and followed up every clue he could get to try and find an owner for the property, but as yet has failed to do so; and he would be glad if this catches the eye of anyone who could give any information or clue of or about the owner, if would communicate with him about it.

I will add that if there are any people around Salt Lake or anywhere else who are wanting homes and are able and willing to work, they may find plenty of chances out here, and they will find no more drawbacks or hardships than the people did for many years in the early settlement of Utah; in fact, not nearly so many, for flour here is only $1.75 per 100 lbs., and good flour at that, made at Seeley Brothers' mills, at Castle Dale. All other products range about the same as to price; so come on and look at the country, and if it does not suit you, you need not take it. It is a free country, you know, to do as you please, so long as you don't please to worship God according to the dictates of your own conscience.

Yours respectfully,   W. H.

SAN JUAN.

Mr. F. A. Hammond's Very Valuable Narrative.

FINE OPPORTUNITIES OFFERED.

Splendid Stock Ranges—Beautiful Climate—Locations for Pleasant Homes.

(*Concluded.*)

I never saw more rapid growth of fruit and shade trees than was shown to me here by Bro. Waven, Bishop's counselor. Little slips or twigs like pipe stems when set out five years ago now measure eight to ten inches in diameter, with a dense foliage on them. I saw in Bro. Warner's orchard and vineyard the most rapid growth of a large variety of fruit trees and grape vines that I ever knew. I calculated by what he had done that five years in that climate and soil is equal to ten years here in the north, where all nature is, as it were, locked up for about one-half of the year. Bees and poultry do well here, there are great profits obtained from the bee business, for capital invested; perhaps the largest profits of any other business in that country. The working season for the bee is much longer than it is at the north.

The bee and poultry business is equally good in all of the San Juan country, as described above. One lady told me she had made $300 from the sale of her chickens and eggs, the past year, equal to the profits of a large farm here in the north. Should there be any brethren thinking of emigrating to that country, I will state in regard to the routes, there are two, one by way of Juab Valley, Salina Canyon, Grass Valley, Rabbit Valley, Blue Valley, Graves Valley, to the Colorado River, and cross it at the old Moquise crossing; thence up and over the divide between the Colorado and San Juan rivers to the junction of the new route with the old Escalanta road; thence to Grand Gulch into Coombs Reef down to the San Juan river, eight miles below Bluff City. This route can be traveled safely during the winter.

The other route would be up Spanish Fork canyon, and down Prices Creek to Green river, or through the north end of SanPete Valley, Castle Valley, and so by the way of Hunting, and Castle Dale down on to Green River, and cross it at Blake City, can be forded this season of the year, from here 35 miles to Grand River cross it at Moab; here you can also ford in the fall, from here 165 miles to Bluff passing along by the foot of the Livi Lasell and Blue Mountains, down the Recapture to Bluff. A very fair road for a mountain country.

Take light wagons, 3½ is good for 20 to 25 hundred, four horses with such a load I consider safe, take what you would need to make a beginning in any new country, should have means enough to sustain you one year at least. The last described route cannot be traveled in the winter, should not start later than 15th of October.

The Navajo Indians are our neighbors on the south, just across the river, they are friendly, and peaceable; the Utes are on the north, they are also friendly and desire our friendship. The people in that part of Colorado are very friendly, and invite us to come and improve and settle up the country; Colorado State as our neighbors are the only ones that are not prosecuting our people, who are settleing in their midst.

I hope this may be the means of drawing the attention of those who may, for any reason desire to move south, to this vast region of country, so sparsely settled, and there make to themselves pleasant homes,

I am yours very truly,

F. A. HAMMOND.

Deseret News
September 9, 1885

ESTRAY NOTICE.

I HAVE IN MY POSSESSION:

One black horse COLT, 2 years old, branded P on left shoulder, right hind foot white.

If not taken away on or before Sept. 10, will be sold at my corral, at 10 o'clock a. m.

J. L. BOULDEN,
District Poundkeeper.

Orangeville, Emery Co., Utah.
August 28, 1885.

A NOVEL BEAR HUNT.

How Two Residents of Southern Utah Captured a Bruin.

From Mr. W. Molen, of Ferron, Emery County, we learn that while driving a band of horses in the vicinity of the high mountain, southeast of Mayfield, in Sanpete County, he and a companion were considerably surprised at seeing three bears near a clump of brush just behind them. As the bears did not seem to be ferocious or belligerently disposed, Mr. Molen and his friend resolved to try and lasso one of them. Accordingly they rode around and succeeded in frightening one of the trio so badly that it ran up a tree. This position might have rendered bruin invincible and proof against futher assaults, had it not been for another tree which stood near by and which one of the pursurers quickly mounted and by a time fling of the lasso caught bruin's neck firmly within the noose. The other end was thrown to the man on the ground who wrapped it near the base of another tree and succeeded in snubbing the bewildered animal down. The bear made quite a lively and desperate struggle to extricate himself, but the courageous lassoers were too much for him, as they very soon threw a second rope around his hind legs and stretched him out on the ground. Having become convinced that, by a dexterous use of the ropes, they could probably get their refractory charge to a neighboring sheep camp, the heroes of the chase mounted their horses, and with the bear as a central figure, proceeded in the direction of the sheep camp. On their way down the mountain, the bear's course was marked by alternate walking and dragging, but it was found that one of these drags had been too prolonged, for when the rope was slackened, bruin did not move—he had been choked to death. Thus the bloodless Nimrods were compelled to leave the lifeless body on the mountain side; but they may well regard the event as one of the most venturesome of their lives. Not having time to return to the mountain, Mr. Molen and his friend gave the body to the sheep herder who skinned it on the following day.—*Home Sentinel.*

Emery County.—We had a call yesterday from Brother O. J. Anderson, of Castle Dale, Emery County, and learned from him some particulars concerning the interesting region from which he hails.

Castle Dale is the capital of Emery County, which extends over a wide area of country and embraces eight flourishing settlements — namely, Moab, Price, Huntington, Castle Dale, Orangeville, Ferron, Molen and Muddy. It is located in what used to be known as Castle Valley, one of the most barren and forbidding regions imaginable, until the blessing of the Almighty and the magic touch of "Mormon" industry converted it into one of the most fruitful districts in the Territory. In no part of this Territory, which is noted for the wonderful material development that has taken place in it since it was inhabited by the Saints, has the transformation been more marked than in Castle Valley. When first settled, not only was the surface of the ground bare and sterile in appearance, but the wind used to blow throughout the warmer portions of the year during the daytime almost a continuous gale. During the past seven years, however, the climate has seemed to change. The force and frequency of the wind storms have gradually diminished and the rainfall increased, until now it is as mild there as here, and the formerly barren surface is covered with luxuriant grass. This is not due to irrigation, for but a very small proportion of the valley has yet been irrigated. Better facilities for irrigation are seldom to be found than that valley affords. It is traversed by five large streams—Price, Huntington, Cottonwood, Ferron and Muddy, none of which are yet fully utilized; in fact, there are facilities in that valley in the shape of land, water, etc., for the support of thousands of inhabitants more than it yet contains. All kinds of grain and fruit that flourish in the older settled valleys of the Territory do well there. Very heavy crops of grain and lucern have been harvested there this year, and already the orchards are beginning to bear. President Larsen planted out a nice orchard three years ago and he has had two crops of fruit from it.

That region is also very rich in mineral resouces. Coal especially is very abundant and of excellent quality, and in the southeastern portion of the county gold and silver deposits are found. All things considered, Emery County is a a very interesting region and a desirable place to locate.

Salt Lake Herald
October 1, 1885

CAPTURE OF A HORSETHIEF.

How Charley Johnson, of Price, Earned a Reward.

On Thursday last a man rode into the little town of Price, on the D. & R. G., and reported that on the day previous a horse had been stolen from his camp, about thirty-five miles southeast of there. The owner of the animal was one of a party who were on their way to Portland, Oregon, and seemed very anxious to recover his stolen property, so anxious indeed that he offered a reward of $150 for the capture of the thief and the horse. Our correspondent "C. H." says that at the mention of the reward, Charley Johnson, a farmer and a man of very quiet disposition, was noticed to open his eyes considerably wider than usual, and those who were best acquainted with him knew that something was about to occur. After a moment's consideration, Johnson turned to the stranger and said: "I guess I'll take your $150."

The owner intimated that he woud be only too glad to hand over gold to that amount, providing the horse and thief were brought into camp. Johnson accepted the offer, and armed with the proper authority, was soon astride his trusty nag, and in keen pursuit in the direction in which it was supposed the lover of other people's horses had gone. Contrary to the general custom of people engaged in such hazardous undertaking, Johnson "rode all unarmed and he rode all alone," and save for the smile of satisfaction which was seen to overspread his countenance, one would never have imagined that he was doing other than taking a constitutional spin. But Johnson is a man of great physical strength, and is more than a match for the average man and a club combined. The pursuer tracked his man through Huntington, Castle Dale and Ferron, and soon discovered that the party he desired to interview was but a short distance in advance. He arrived at a place called Muddy, about seventy miles from Price, at 2 o'clock in the morning, and discovered the horse in question tied to a corral fence. Taking the saddle from his own jaded animal, he laid down to rest, and in a few moments discovered a man asleep, wrapped up in some quilts

CAPTURE OF A HORSE THIEF.

PRICE, Emery Co., Utah,
Sept. 29th, 1885.

Editor Deseret News:

Our quiet little burg was last Thursday aroused from its usual peaceable situation, by a party who were travelling through the country on their way to Oregon, who came to town and reported that a horse had been stolen the day previous from their camp about thirty-five miles east from here. The owner of the horse was anxious to get his animal back, and while speaking to a crowd of people present, he offered the liberal reward of $150 for the capture of the thief and the return of the horse.

Our respected townsman and farmer, Charles Johnson, who is of a very quiet disposition, and never says a great deal, after a moment's consideration remarked, "I guess I will take your $150." He was soon authorized as "deputy constable by the proper authority," and shortly after his gigantic form was seen on a horse, slowly making his way out of town in a southerly direction, as though he was taking a ride for the benefit of his health.

It is a general custom among such officers of the law, when going after a desperado, to arm themselves to the teeth, but it was different with friend Johnson; he went on his way without any weapons of any kind, relying upon his physical strength, of which a wise providence has meted out to him an abundance. He traveled through Huntington, Castle Dale and Ferron Creek, and by inquiring found that his man was only a short distance ahead of him. He traveled along and arrived at a place called Muddy, 70 miles from here about two o'clock at night, where he happened to see by moonlight the horse in question, tied to a corral fence. Our deputy concluded to camp by the same corral, so he took the saddle off his horse and sitting coolly down called in his wandering thoughts, and reflected on past, present and future. A moment after he noticed some bedding close to the house, and supposing somebody slept there he paid some little attention to the moving of the quilts

About daybreak on Friday morning the man in the bedding had perhaps had sleep enough, and commenced moving about in the quilts uncovering his face, to see if the sky was free from clouds, but suddenly a voice from our unarmed deputy came like a rushing of many waters. Arms up, young man! And although the thief had a heavy six-shooter at his side, the command given by Mr. Johnson was promptly obeyed.

in a few moments discovered a man asleep, wrapped up in some quilts About daybreak on Friday morning, the man in quilts concluded that he had probably enough sleep, and arose and made preparations to move on. But suddenly from a short distance away came the loud command, "Arms up, young man!" and notwithstanding the fact that the thief was heavily armed, he obeyed the command so quickly as to almost astonish even Johnson himself. Johnson intimated to the thief that possibly it might be a good idea for them to return to Price, as he understood Judge McIntyre was very anxious to see him in regard to some matters that would not brook delay.

Between Muddy and Ferron Creek, the prisoner snatched from Johnson the pistol, which the latter had taken from him, and attempted to escape. The officer was too quick for his man, however, and took the weapon away from him, though not before it had been discharged, the bullet passing harmlessly through the air. "Nothing happened to mar the pleasure" of the rest of the journey, however, and the two men arrived at Price on Sunday afternoon.

On Tuesday, at 9 a.m. the prisoner, who gave the name of George Wright, was arraigned before Judge McIntyre, and pleaded guilty to the two charges preferred—grand larceny and resisting an officer. Wright was placed under $1,000 bonds to await the action of the Grand Jury of the First District at Provo. C. H.

Deseret News
October 7, 1885

The man in authority told his prisoner that he guessed they would both return to Price, as he thought they had a little urgent business to attend to in Squire McIntire's office, to which the prisoner consented, and on their return they started: but, lo and behold! on the road, between Muddy and Ferron creek, the prisoner snatched from Johnson the six-shooter, which the deputy had taken from him and was carrying himself, and attempted to escape. But the officer grappled with him, got hold of the weapon and after it had been once discharged without doing harm to either of them, and after a fall to the ground the prisoner again mounted. Very little was said, but Johnson told him kindly, if he made another attempt like that, he would get hurt. Nothing happened to mar their peace during the balance of the journey, and they arrived safe at Price yesterday (Sunday) afternoon.

This morning at nine o'clock the prisoner whose name is George Wright, was brought into the justices court, where he plead guilty to the two charges preferred against him—grand larceny, and attempt to disarm an officer and judge E. W. McIntire bound him over in the sum of $1,000 to appear before the grand jury in the First Judicial District at Provo. The bond not being furnished the deputy will tomorrow take his man to Provo.

Castle Valley.—Castle Valley is a large and rather indefinitely defined region lying east of the broad range of mountains which bounds Utah County on the east. The D. & R. G., leaving Spanish Fork, passes up Spanish Fork Cañon until the summit of that range of mountains is reached, when the descent of the eastern slope of the range, through Price Cañon, is begun. Emerging from Price Cañon the road proceeds to cross the extreme north end of Castle Valley, and a few miles east of the mouth of this cañon is Price Station, to which all freight for Castle Valley points is shipped. Extending south from Price is a tri-weekly mail route, passing through Huntington, Castle Dale, Orangeville, Ferron, Muddy and to Peacock, a distance of from 50 to 60 miles. The settlements named are all new, having been founded within the last five or six years, and are all included in what is called Castle Valley. Extending down Price Cañon and much of the distance across the valley, the railroad is paralleled with Price River, a considerable stream from which the settlers in the north end of the valley obtain water for irrigation.

The wonder is that Castle Valley was not thickly populated many years ago; but this wonder is partly explained by the statement of a non-"Mormon" stock man, made some weeks ago to our informant. He said that in the fall of 1883 he and another stock man brought into Castle Valley a large herd of cattle. It was a desert region, produced little or no vegetation save greasewood, and it appeared doubtful as to whether or not the cattle could subsist during the winter. In the latter part of August last the same stock man rode horseback over the same range on which two years previously he had feared his cattle would starve to death, and for mile after mile he found the plain covered with luxuriant grass, reaching to his stirrups as he rode. A change, marvelous and incredible, had come over the land; a glistening, alkali desert had become a meadow. The "Mormon" settlers along Price river tell the same story. They declare that three or four years ago, land which now is being cultivated and is fertile, and also the range on which their cattle feed, was so barren as to glisten in the sunshine in a manner painful to the eye of a person passing over it. During the last two years frequent and copious rains have fallen in the valley, and a wonderful change in the appearance of the landscape has taken place.

The climate of Castle Valley is mild, even, and not unlike that of Utah County. Vast quantities of coal, easy of access to sellers, have been discovered in various parts of it. The soil has a whitish appearance, but is wonderfully fertile when properly cultivated. There is plenty of land in localities where facilities for irrigation are excellent, and probably no region in Utah Territory offers stronger inducements to settlers than does Castle Valley.

DEATHS.

JOHNSON—At Huntington, Emery County, Utah, November 22, 1885, of typhoid fever, Alice Malena, wife of M. E. Johnson, and daughter of Alexander and Alice McBarney Wilkins. She was born at Provo, Utah, February 23, 1857; was the mother of six children, the youngest of whom preceded her a few days to the grave. She died as she had lived, a faithful Latter-day Saint.

Arizona papers, please copy.

Commissioned. — The Governor, yesterday, issued commissions to the following officers:

M. W. Mansfield, justice of the peace; J. B. Meeks, constable, Thurber precinct, Piute County.

Ephraim Homer justice of the peace; J. S. Stephens, constable, Ferron precinct, Emery County.

L. R. Cropper, justice of the peace; J. Dewsnip, constable, Deseret precinct, Millard County.

James W. Pearson, alderman, Third ward, Park City, Summit County.

Thomas F. Roueche, selectman, Davis County.

R. M. Bush, constable, Clover precinct, Tooele County.

W. J. Robinson, justice of the peace, Grantsville precinct, Tooele County.

Caleb Parry, constable, Marriott precinct, Weber County.

Thomas Wallace, selectman, Weber County.

Chas. W. Stayner, Commissioner to Locate University Lands, Utah Territory.

Deseret News
December 16, 1885

EXCOMMUNICATED.

At a session of the High Council of Emery Stake, convened at Castle Dale, December 5th, Noah T. Guymon, Sen., was excommunicated from the Church of Jesus Christ of Latter-day Saints for the crime of lewd and lascivious conduct and adultery.

By order of the High Council.

O. J. ANDERSON, Clerk.

Salt Lake Herald
December 17, 1885

THE *Home Sentinel* is responsible for the statement that there are over fifty cases of typhoid fever in Huntington, Emery County.

From Moab.—Brother W. A. Peirce, of Moab, Emery County, who, with two other residents of that place happened to be in the city last week on land matters, made us a brief visit and gave a few items concerning the interesting region from which he hails. Moab is an Indian name for the mosquito, but why is it applied to the pleasant little settlement in Little Grande Valley is not stated. The Indians were the sole occupants of the valley until March 1879, when a few settlers from this Territory and several ranchmen from other parts simultaneously entered it and laid claim to the tillable land, which includes some 7,000 to 8,000 acres. The anticipations which these enthusiastic settlers then indulged in as to the climate and adaptability of the soil have since been more than realized. Although the altitude is considerably greater than that of Salt Lake Valley, its climate is much milder, owing probably to its being surrounded by high, precipitous bluffs. There are but two openings to the valley, one on the northwest and the other at the southeast point. All the various products of the extreme southern part of the Territory, including sweet potatoes, peanuts, etc., there flourish, and the soil seems to be very prolific, so that a person does not require so extensive a farm there to make a living upon as in most places. There is a good chance now for persons who have means to purchase a home to make a start there, as the ranchmen of the locality who are not in sympathy with the Latter-day Saints, and who prefer to keep on the outskirts of civilization, are willing to sell out their claims, of which, however, they are not yet in possession of the Government title to, and move away.

Though this settlement is in Emery County, it is hereafter to be included in the San Juan Stake, the capital of which—Bluff City—is only 80 miles distant, while the nearest settlement in Emery County—Castle Dale—is 110 miles away. The nearest railway station is Thompson Springs, on the D. & R. G. W., 35 miles away.

Indians, both Navajoes and Utes, often pass to and fro through the valley between their respective reservations, and are always friendly and peaceable. Brother Peirce acts as interpreter for those of them who do not speak English, having learned the Ute language while a boy at Springville, and acquired some knowledge of the Navajo and Spanish while living among the Navajoes on the San Juan between 1870 and 1879.

EMERY STAKE CONFERENCE.

The Quarterly Conference of the Emery Stake of Zion convened at Castle Dale Saturday, Dec. 5, 1885.

On the stand were the Presidency of the Stake, Bishops of the various wards and other presiding and local officers representing the different associations and organizations of the Stake.

At 10 a.m. the meeting was called to order by President C. G. Larsen, who, after the usual opening exercises arose and welcomed all the people and said he was very thankful for the favorable weather and every blessing enjoyed, and not the least for the peace and liberty yet granted us to meet on such an occasion as this. Our neighboring settlement, Huntington, had been put somewhat under restrictions, on account of considerable sickness among the people there, which had been called contagious and as wisdom and caution dictated, people from that ward had been counseled to stay at home.

John K. Reid, who had acted as Stake Clerk from the organization of this Stake, was, by unanimous vote of the people, honorably released from said position at his own request, and Oluf J. Anderson was honorably released from being a member of the High Council and voted in to fill the place as Stake Clerk.

Orange Seeley, first Counselor to President Larsen, addressed the congregation, saying that from all appearances it looked like our opposers intended to compel the resentment of the Saints by heaping upon us all the wickedness and abuse possible; but, thanks be to God, our leaders are preaching and teaching to us the peaceful things of the kingdom of God, and if we are willing to do our duty, we shall be able to remain faithful through all trials that may meet us on our further journey in life.

R. Justesen, second counselor to Prest. Larsen, was the next speaker; he was exceedingly grateful for the broad plan of salvation revealed to the human family. Well might it be said that a heavy cloud was at the present hovering over this people, but when he thought of the many dark hours that this people have seen before, he was reminded that there was never a night so dark but what a day dawned after it. When the big army advanced toward Utah in 1857, the "boys" were called upon to go and stop its further advancement; but it was told them that if they would go in obedience to the call and with their hearts filled with the fear of God, no shooting or destruction of human life should be necessary, which to him seemed rather a singular if not an impossible outcome of the affair, but the victory was thus at the time given the people of God without even a gun being fired with the intent of shedding blood. He was confident that the same would be the result in the pending controversy between this people and their declared enemies if the Saints only trust in God and regard their religion.

In the afternoon the Bishops of the different wards reported the condition of the same, showing a good condition in all things pertaining to the progress and well-being of the people. Good health was enjoyed all over except in Huntington Ward.

The Primary Associations and Sabbath schools were reported as effective factors in the "nursery of Zion;" the day schools received proper attention, one or two being in operation in each of the wards except Muddy, which had not succeeded in getting an efficient teacher. Ferron Ward had erected a fine meeting house, built from brick, the roof and cornice being already on. Up to the present the house had cost about $2,800, which, for a ward of about 200 inhabitants might be pronounced extremely good, but a good deal of credit for that enterprise was due to Brother M. W. Molen, who is a resident of that place.

The clerk read a communication from the First Presidency of the Church to President C. G. Larsen, stating that if agreeable to all parties concerned, the Moab Ward would be stricken off this Stake and attached to San Juan Stake, as that ward is somewhat difficult to visit from this place on account of two troublesome rivers to cross, namely Green and Grande Rivers.

President Larsen asked the Saints to manifest their feelings on this point, and the change was unanimously approved of.

President Larsen addressed the Saints in a very forcible way upon going to law, one brother with another, saying every one who did so would be held accountable for it, and would have to make public restitution. He also recommended the enforcement of the law against thieves and other transgressors that may prey upon us or may be found in our midst.

Patriarch R. Logan, being called upon, said the old ship Zion had now for over fifty years stood the breeze and the foaming sea, and was still afloat, and would go into the harbor of safety. He encouraged to good deeds, good thought and kind talk, and concluded by invoking the blessings of the Almighty upon all the Saints.

On Sunday morning, December 6, after the usual opening ceremonies, the clerk read the statistical reports, which showed a total of 2,465 souls, divided as follows: Castle Dale 359, Orangeville 351, Ferron 239, Molen 156, Muddy 119, Huntington 803, Price 416—an increase by births of 36, and by new members received of 40. The remainder of the forenoon was occupied by giving good counsel and admonition to keep firm in the faith and observe the covenants made with God and one another, that the divine favor be enjoyed, which will prove the keenest sword and the most effectual shield in all the battles we shall have to engage in.

In the afternoon the house was filled to overflowing by eager listeners. After singing and prayer the sacrament was administered and then the general and local authorities of the Church were presented to the people and unanimously sustained. After this several speakers occupied the stand and bore a powerful testimony to the divinity of the latter-day work.

The remainder of the time was improved by Prest. Larsen, who urged upon the Latter-day Saints of this Stake to watch over their children and remember that the tendency of the age is to vice and corruption. He warned the people against living beyond their means, and charged them to be wise and prudent, pay their honest debts and not run blindfolded into new obligations before they were sure that they had bread for their families and seed grain for the coming season. He concluded with the assurance that the Lord will take care of his "own work."

O. J. ANDERSON,
Stake Clerk.

Deseret News
January 13, 1886

DEATHS.

SEELEY.—In Castle Dale, Jan. 3, 1886, of an affection of the lungs, Ethel Ingra, daughter of Hannah and Orange Seeley; born Sept. 16, 1881.

CORRESPONDENCE.

EMERY COUNTY ITEMS.

HUNTINGTON, Emery County,
Utah, February 19, 1886.

Editor Deseret News:

Spring time has come, the weather is beautiful, and seed time is upon us, for which reasons the farmers feel to rejoice, and give thanks unto God for his goodness, in overruling all things for the good of His people.

We have three very

GOOD SCHOOLS

here, taught by competent teachers. There are about 150 scholars in attendance, and quite a few children of school age who do not attend. Our Sunday school is also very well attended, and our greatest trouble is to find room for all those who come. Our Y. M. and Y. L. M. I. Associations are also in good running order and well attended, which is also the case with our Relief Society and Primary Meetings. We have also a Seventies quorum presided over by President J. P. Wimmer, an Elders' quorum, presided over by President J. L. Brasher. The brethren seem to be trying hard to prepare themselves for the great work destined to fall upon the Latter-day Saints.

If it was not for the

CRUEL CRUSADE

that is being waged against the people called "Mormons," Utah could soon be made the most beautiful spot on earth.

We understand it is necessary for the persecutions of our enemies to come upon us, else how could the Church be purified, and although it makes us feel bad, and sometimes revengeful, to see and know how our brethren and sisters are persecuted and vilified by the temporary governor, judges and marshals and others who are now placed to rule over us, and who, to the worldly eyes have all power to crush the "Mormon" people, yet we cannot but feel to rejoice because we know it is one of the signs of the near coming of our Lord and Savior, who will bring peace to earth and good will to men. In that day our beautiful governor, our moral judges, our "learned" prosecutors and our spying marshals will beg for the chance to crawl through the dust to ask a "Mormon's" forgiveness for the misery and hardship they are heaping upon them now. They would do well to read the seventh chapter of St. Matthew. Perhaps it is not too late.

Was not the hand of God made manifest on the 24th day of July, 1885, when not only Utah, but the whole of the United States placed their flags at half mast—the very thing which the "Mormons" had previously been forbidden to do, and over which a warcry had been raised and men were armed and drilled and held ready at a moment's notice to march to drench Utah in blood, if the "Mormons" dared do such a thing.

Has there not been a great deal said for years about the "Mormons"

UNITING CHURCH AND STATE?

Why is not that same howl raised against Senator Edmunds for introducing into, and by misrepresentations getting passed through the Senate a bill for that very purpose? It provides among other things that the nation's chief magistrate shall appoint fourteen trustees to co-operate with the thirteen trustees of the "Mormon" church for the manipulation of its funds. What is this but a union of church and state?

Notwithstanding all this we have in Castle Valley green grass four to five inches high; the people are preparing to put in their crops as usual; we have a gardeners' club organized, and expect our fathers at Washington to furnish us a few seeds, at least we have the assurance of some from our Hon. Delegate, John T. Caine. Colts and calves continue to come, our hens lay as usual, and last, but not least or inferior by any means, we have a host of bright and intelligent children and expect many more, as there is room here yet for several hundred additions in this line.

I almost forgot to mention that there are a few young bloods in this region—new-comers, too, at that—who are ambitious for county office, who, we understand, are going to *force* the Legislature to take part of Emery, Utah, Wasatch and Sanpete counties to make

A NEW COUNTY

of their own. There are but very few, if any, of the permanent settlers of this county who would think seriously for one moment of such a thing, and there is now a remonstrance being signed by hundreds that they do not want such a thing to happen, provided those parties who live in the northern part of Emery County, and who would like to show their ability to "run" a county, present such a measure to the Legislature.

The people of Huntington do not want it, and we have good reason to believe that the people of Price will sign a remonstrance against it. We are satisfied with our county organization as it is, and do not want it changed, the reason I mention Huntington and Price is that those two settlements are in the portion of Territory about to be asked for. Offers have been made to parties here, that if they would use their influence to get the people of Huntington to sign a petition asking for a division, they (the agitators) would use their influence to get them into office, but the bait had no attraction.

Very respectfully,   W. H.

Territorial Enquirer
April 13, 1886

Mated.

A Castle Dale (Emery Co.) correspondent writes that on the 4th inst. that Mr. Harmon W. Curtis and Miss Martha Wilson, daughter of Bishop S. Wilson, of that place, were united in the bonds of wedlock. A number of guests were present and a bountiful dinner was partaken of, after which dancing was indulged in and kept up until midnight.

The ENQUIRER joins with its correspondent in wishing the happy couple a pleasant and prosperous voyage through life.

More Officials.

The Utah Commission yesterday appointed the following registration officers:

EMERY COUNTY.

Castle Dale, John Zawhalin.
Orangeville, J. K. Reid.
Ferron, M. Molen.
Molen, J. D. Killpack.
Muddy, John L. Lewis.
Huntington, C. T. Wakefield.*
Price, Caleb Rhoads.
Wellington, R. B. Thompson.
Green River, J. T. Farrer.
Moab, C. J. Boreen.
Scofield, S. J. Harkness.
Larence, C. T. Wakefield.*
*For both precincts.

FROM SATURDAY'S DAILY, MAY 1

Fatal Accident. — Castle Dale, Emery County, was the scene of a fatal accident on the 26th ult. Mrs. Caroline Miller, wife of Richard C. Miller, had just emptied some hot water into a tub for washing and stepped outside the room for another bucketful, when her three little children came in and the youngest one, Richard by name, born September 14, 1883, fell backwards into the tub, and was scalded so badly that he died after four hours' suffering.

DEATHS

DONALDSON—In Castle Dale, Emery Co., April 25, 1886, Christina Coomb, wife of John Donaldson; born in Glasgow, Scotland, Feb. 1, 1851. She lived and died a faithful Latter day Saint, and leaves a husband and five children to mourn her death.

Deseret Evening News
May 12, 1886

ESTRAY NOTICE.

I HAVE IN MY POSSESSION.

One brown HORSE, 4 years old, star in forehead, point of right ear is off, one shoe on front foot, branded RV on left thigh.

If the above described animal is not claimed within ten days from date, it will be sold to the highest bidder in front of the Co-op Store, at Ferron, Emery County, at 10 o'clock Thursday, May 13th, 1886.

R. L. STEVENS,
Precinct Poundkeeper.

Ferron, Emery Co., May 3, 1886.

Deseret News
May 19, 1886

ESTRAY NOTICE.

I HAVE IN MY POSSESSION:

One sorrel white faced HORSE, 12 or 14 years old, branded U on left thigh, also a brand resembling an anvil slantwise and vented, on left shoulder.

If said animal is not claimed and taken away within ten days from date, it will be sold at the Huntington estray pound, May 17th, at 2 o'clock p. m.

J. F. WAKEFIELD,
Poundkeeper.

Huntington, Emery Co., Utah, May 6, 1886.

ESTRAY NOTICE.

I HAVE IN MY POSSESSION:

One grey MARE, 8 years old, shoes on front feet, branded WS on left thigh.

One sorrel mare COLT, 1 year old, white strip in face, white hind feet.

If the above described animals are not claimed within ten days from date, they will be sold to the highest bidder in front of the co-op store, Ferron, at 10 o'clock a. m., Monday, May 24th, 1886.

R. L. STEVENS,
Precinct Poundkeeper.

Ferron, Emery Co., May 13, 1886.

Deseret News
June 9, 1886

ESTRAY NOTICE.

I HAVE IN MY POSSESSION:

One bay MARE, about 8 or 9 years old, branded 8 on left thigh and ⊂ on left shoulder.

One black HORSE, 1 year old, one hind foot white; no brands visible.

If the above described animals are not claimed within ten days from date, they will be sold to the highest bidder in front of the Co-op Store, Ferron, Thursday, June 10th 1886, at nine o'clock a. m.

R. L. STEVENS,
Precinct Poundkeeper.

Ferron, Emery Co., May 30, 1886.

Emery County Crops.—W. Howard writes from Huntington:

"The crops in this place, and as near as I can learn from other settlements in the County, are nearly an average of the crops of other years—not as good as in 1885, but fully as good as formerly. There will be no grain to spare for export. The reason is there are quite a few that do not farm, and also a large number of new settlers coming into the county who use up the surplus. The health of the people generally is good. The water in the county, as usual, is very high; streams dangerous to cross. The weather for a couple of weeks has been very warm."

DEATHS.

JOHNSON—At Huntington, Emery County, Utah, May 19, 1886, Ann Eliza, daughter of Phineas H. Cook and Elizabeth Johnson born Sept. 29, 1874.

NAY—At Huntington, Emery County, Utah, of typhoid fever, Nov. 8, 1885, Ormus Franklin, son of Alonzo P. and Hannah P. Nay; born Nov. 18, 1888.

NAY—At Huntington, Emery County, Utah, May 22, 1886, John Chester, son of Alonzo P. and Hannah P. Nay; born Nov. 3, 1886.

Deseret News
June 16, 1886

ESTRAY NOTICE.

I HAVE IN MY POSSESSION.

One light bay HORSE, 7 or 8 years old, white spot in face, left hind foot white, branded JП P on left thigh, also ㅐPS on left shoulder.

If not claimed and taken away within ten days from date, it will be sold at the precinct pound, Huntington, June 19th, at two o'clock p. m.

J. F. WAKEFIELD,
Poundkeeper.

Huntington, Emery Co., Utah, June 10, 1886.

HALVORSEN'S ANTICS.

Further Particulars of the Price Kleptomaniac.

Correspondence of The Herald.

A man by the name of Christian Halvorsen, who for the last seven months has been employed by D. J. Williams & Co., of Price, was arrested last night by the sheriff of this place for appropriating goods, money and store scrip out of the company's store to his own use. A search warrant was also issued, and resulted in D. J. Williams & Co. recovering about $500 in boots, shoes, hats, caps, oils, paints, dress goods, knives and forks, glassware, spades, shovels, picks, needles, flour, jewelry, and nearly every article of merchandise to be found in a general merchandise business. Nearly half a bushel of eggs were found hidden under the floor of his workshop, neatly packed in shavings and sawdust; several fine dress patterns were recovered; also motto frames, in one of which were the familiar words, nicely worked in cardboard, "In God we trust," to which was added by one of the searchers, "And Williams I bust." Search was continued nearly all night, in the hope of finding more money, as it is firmly believed by Messrs. Williams & Co. that they have missed at various times large sums of cash, and Mr. Halvorson had informed several of his neighbors that he anticipated starting a small business of his own in opposition to Williams & Co. However, he has concluded that, since last night's clearance, his stock in trade has been materially reduced, and he will abandon the project for an indefinite period. Fully two wagon loads of goods were hauled away this morning from the house of this kleptomaniac.

He appeared this morning before E. W. McIntyre, Justice of the Peace, and plead not guilty to the charge, when he was bound over in the sum of two thousand dollars to await the action of the Grand Jury, and, as it is quite probable that he cannot secure the amount, will be taken to Castle Dale, the county seat, for safe keeping.

Messrs. David Evans and A. G. Sutherland, Jr., of Provo, being here at the time trying a cattle case, have been employed by Williams & Co. to prosecute the case.

Crops on Price look well, considerable improvements are being made and the prospects for a flourishing town seem eminent. This section of the country was visited on Sunday last by a cooler in the way of an hour's refreshing rain.

Biz.

Price, Emery County, July 14, 1886.

DEATHS.

ROPER—At Huntington, Emery County, Utah, on June 26th, 1886, after two days' illness, Charlotte Elizabeth Mellor, wife of Henry Roper.

Deceased was born January 16, 1842, at Leicester, England, was baptized in 1852 and emigrated with her parents in 1856; helped pull a handcart across the Plains in Captain Martin's company. She was an affectionate wife, a loving mother of 13 children, 12 of whom survive her, and who, with her husband and numerous relatives and friends are left to mourn her departure.—COM.

HUNTINGTON, Emery Co., Utah,
July 23rd, 1886.

Editor Deseret News:

Enclosed please find the People's Ticket for Emery County, nominated unanimously by the People's candidates at a convention held at Castle Dale, July 14, 1886. The great majority of the people think the ticket a good one. There are a few exceptions, however, like there are in all communities, who think no ticket is good without their names are on it. They find fault with some of the nominees, notably E. W. Jones, who is misrepresented by some of his pretended friends. But we think he is just about as good as the rest of us, and well worthy the position. Brother Jones is a cripple, and not able to do severe manual labor, but is otherwise well qualified. There is also a little opposition to Judge Seely, but that originates from parties that cannot injure him, as as he is greatly esteemed and respected by the people.

Following is the Emery County ticket referred to above:

Probate Judge—Orange Seeley.
Selectman—James Woodward.
County Clerk—W. W. Crawford.
County Recorder—W. W. Crawford.
County Treasurer — C. G. Larsen, Jun.
Prosecuting Attorney—John K. Reid.
County Surveyor—E. H. Cox.
Coroner—T. P. Page.
Assessor and Collector—E. W. Jones.
Sherriff—H. S. Loveless.

ONE OF THE PEOPLE.

HUNTINGTON, Emery Co.,
Utah, Aug. 4th, 1886.

Editor Deseret News.

About the first of July the Central Committee of the People's Party for Emery County apportioned the number of delegates for each precinct in the county, and set the time for a general county convention to be held on the 14th day of July. The people, previous to the last named date, held their precinct caucuses and elected delegates to the county convention.

As is usual at such meetings the people instructed their delegates who to nominate and who to vote for. The convention was held and a ticket made up. There was very little opposition, and where there was two nominations made and voted upon the party receiving the highest number of votes was immediately voted for again, and the vote was made unanimous by the delegates present. Also, after all the nominations were made, the secretary wrote out the ticket and it was again voted on and made unanimous, and every delegate went home apparently well satisfied with the ticket nominated. Tickets were ordered by several of the precincts from the local job press, at Huntington, and they were headed, as they should be, "The People's Ticket."

It was but a few days after the convention that it was rumored that the ticket was not satisfactory to the people, but when the question was asked, "Who does it not satisfy?" it was traced to some of the old officers who had not been renominated by the delegates who went to the convention instructed by the people who sent them. To make a long story short, some of the disappointed ones, notably the deputy County Clerk and Assessor and Collector (and rumor has it) assisted by certain others, got up another ticket, nominating all the old officers, sent to Provo and had tickets printed, headed "The Peoples Ticket." They circulated them freely throughout the County. When those whose duty it was to circulate, advocate and encourage the people to vote the convention ticket did all they could to suppress it, and bring it into disrepute. The probate judge sent a notice to the DESERET NEWS that he did not want the office. It is to be hoped that in case he is elected he will be consistent and decline to qualify. The assessor and collector made it his business to go to several of the precincts and electioneer for himself, and in doing so he villified and traduced the character of his opponent. Brother E. W. Jones, the nominee on the genuine People's ticket, is a man of good moral character, sound on principle and well educated, but has been unfortunate in meeting with an accident that has made him a cripple, one of his eyes has been turned and through that his looks are not all a pretty man might wish for. This has been made a subject of jest and ridicule by his opponents. There is no doubt a great many voted the bogus ticket unknowingly, thinking it was the genuine convention ticket.

It is a question yet which ticket is elected. Huntington, to its honor, did not vote one of the bogus tickets, and some of these parties have got (which they justly merit) the contempt of all honorable men and women in the county. The whole business has caused a feeling that will take some time to eradicate, and some of the parties will probably never again have the confidence of the whole people as they once had it.

Emery County can boast of something that I am safe in saying no other county in Utah has ever had, and that is three People's tickets all at one election. One of them only had one name changed for probate judge, which we consider small compared to the official fraud practiced upon us. When Judge Seeley's notice appeared in the NEWS declining the nomination of probate judge, Jasper Robertson's name was placed on the convention ticket, Judge Seeley's on the bogus ticket, and E. W. McIntyre's on the Price ticket, all for probate judge. The items in this letter can be vouched for if necessary.

Yours truly, AMATEUR.

Salt Lake Herald
August 19, 1886

For an Increase of Mail.

The residents of Price, Huntington, Castle Dale, Orangeville, Peacock, Ferron and Muddy, Emery County, on mail route No. 41,151, are signing a petition to be forwarded to the Postmaster-General asking for an increase in their mail service. They now are suffering from the inconveniences of a tri-weekly system, and ask that it be changed to daily, Sundays excepted. When first established, the present system was adequate to the needs of the residents of this thrifty part of Utah, but in the last few years the population has steadily increased until now, at least 5,000 people are supplied with their mail from this route, and there are many complaints of its being entirely inadequate to the demands. Of course, the present carriers are not to be blamed for this, and they are ready and willing to commence running daily as soon as the powers at Washington authorize them to do so. It is to be hoped that the prayers of the petitioners will be granted. A daily mail for the section mentioned has grown to be an absolute necessity.

The mail for all the points mentioned above leaves the D. & R. G. W. at Price Station, and from that point to Muddy, seventy miles distant. Passengers are also carried by the Price and Muddy stage Line.

Deseret News
August 25, 1886

DEATHS.

WILBERG.—At Castle Dale, Aug. 8, 1886, from diarrhœa, Eva, daughter of Tilda and Carl Wilberg, born July 7th, 1883.

Deseret News
September 1, 1886

Deseret News
September 1, 1886

DEATHS.

CHILDS—At Orangeville, August 17, 1886, Zina Lavenia, infant daughter of Parker A. and Josie E. Childs, of inflammation of the bowels and congestion of the brain; aged 11 years.

Deseret News
September 8, 1886

Accidental Death.—Brother J. K. Reid writes as follows from Orangeville, Emery County, August 30th:

A sad and fatal accident befell Bro. Samuel R. Jewkes, of this place, on Aug. 25th. He was running the Joe's Valley saw mill and was handspiking some logs in the mill yard when a log fell back on the handspike, knocking it out of his hand and striking him in the abdomen, doing him a fatal injury, of which he died after suffering untold pain for 51 hours. Everything was done for him that was possible under the circumstances; but all to no avail.

Brother Jewkes was a prominent man in this community. He was president of the Y. M. M. I. A. of Emery Stake, leader of the Orangeville choir, assistant superintendent of the Orangeville Sunday school, and was school trustee for this district. His death has caused a gloom to overcast our town.

Bro. Samuel R. Jewkes was born in Salt Lake City, August 22, 1853, and died Aug. 27, 1886.

Some time before the accident, Bro. Jewkes told his wife that he was going to be called on a mission in a short time, and he would have to prepare to fill the same when the call came, not knowing that he would be called in this way. He leaves a wife and six children, also an aged father and mother and several brothers and sisters, and many friends to mourn his untimely loss. He died firm in the faith of a glorious resurrection.

Deseret News
September 22, 1886

ESTRAY NOTICE.

I HAVE IN MY POSSESSION:

One iron-gray MARE, six years old, branded RS on left thigh.

One dark bay MARE, five years old, branded JR combined on left shoulder and
o—
o—
JR combined on left thigh.

If said animals are not claimed and taken away within ten days from the date hereof they will be sold to the highest cash bidder, at the Huntington precinct pound, on Friday, September 24th, 1886, at 10 o'clock a. m.

J. F. WAKEFIELD,
Precinct Poundkeeper.

Huntington, Emery Co., Sept. 11th, 1886.

Commissions Issued.

Governor West has issued commissions as follows:

L. J. Long, Surveyor, Piute county; John Morrill, County Clerk, Piute county; R. A. Allen, Probate Judge, Piute county; Mahonri W. Brown, Selectman, Washington county; Robert Brown, Justice of the Peace, Greenville precinct, Beaver county; W. W. Brandon, Constable, Mt. Pleasant precinct, Sanpete county; Christian Peterson, Constable, Riverton precinct, Salt Lake county; John H. Walker, Constable, Union precinct, Salt Lake county; Lauritz Larsen, Justice of the Peace, Mt. Pleasant precinct, Sanpete county; John W. A. Timins, Notary Public, Summit county; John H. Horning, Notary Public, Millard county; Ole N. Tuft, Constable, Lawrence precinct, Emery county; A. Tuttle, Constable, Orangeville precinct, Emery county; F. A. Mitchell, of Salt Lake City, Commissioner to Locate University Lands; E. H. Cop, Surveyor, Emery county; James Woodward, Selectman, Emery county; W. W. Crawford, Recorder and County Clerk, Emery county; Jasper Robertson, Probate Judge, Emery county; H. S. Loveless, Sheriff, Emery county; John K. Reed, Prosecuting Attorney, Emery county; E. W. Jones, Assessor and Collector, Emery county; Albert A. Day, Justice of the Peace, Lawrence precinct, Emery county; D. C. Robbins, Justice of the Peace, Huntington precinct, Emery county; Brigham Moffitt, Justice of the Peace, Orangeville precinct, Emery county; Wm. Crook, Justice of the Peace, Wanship precinct, Summit county; Samuel Knight, Justice of the Peace, Santa Clara precinct, Washington county; O. B. Anderson, Justice of the Peace, Morgan precinct, Morgan county; W. C. Burton, Justice of the Peace, Second precinct, Salt Lake county; A. J. Adamson, Justice of the Peace, Brighton precinct, Salt Lake county; George D. Pyper, Justice of the Peace, Fifth precinct, Salt Lake county; W. C. Burgon, Justice of the Peace, Union precinct, Salt Lake county; John W. Grow, Constable, Huntsville precinct, Weber county; C. A. Hickenlooper, Constable, Pleasant View precinct, Weber county; James W. Burt, constable, Fourth precinct, Salt Lake county; Andrew Smith, Jr., Constable, First precinct, Salt Lake county; Alma Hardy, Constable, West Weber precinct, Weber county; L. Haag, Constable, Farmer's precinct, Salt Lake county.

DEATHS.

FULLMER—At Orangeville, Emery County, October 1st, Ronald Duval, infant son of James S. and Eliza Jane Fullmer, aged 11 months.

NAMES

OF

PRESIDENCY AND BISHOPS

OF THE

Organized Stakes of Zion.

The * indicates the President's address.
P. E., Presiding Elder.

EMERY STAKE,

Emery County, Utah.

C. G. LARSEN, President.

Orange Seely, } Counselors.
Rasmus Justovsen, }

WARDS.	BISHOPS.
*Castle Dale	Henning Olsen.
Ferron	F. Olsen.
Huntington	C. Pulsipher.
Molen	L. S. Beach.
Muddy	C. Christensen.
Orangeville	Jasper Robertson.
Price	Geo. Frandsen.
Cleveland	J. Alger, P. E.
Larence	Calvin Moore, P. E.
Upper Price	F. Ewell, P. E.
Wellington	Jefferson Tidwell, P. E.

Horse Thief Captured.

On Saturday night, the 10th instant, a pair of horses was stolen from the stables of Mr. G. W. Jacques on White River. The theft was discovered by daylight next morning and Mr. Jacques and his sons set out in search of the thief, following on his track till Sunday when Mr. Jacques took the D. & R. G. train for Provo. He and Sheriff Turner at once set their heads to work on a scheme of operations, and by the time the train, arrived, Monday, their plans were ready for action. Officers Wilkins of Provo and Hoover of P. V. Junction took the train for Price station with instructions to go and not return till they brought the thief and horses.

They traveled day and night on the trail, and when near fifty miles from Huntington they overtook him. He was on his way to Long Valley where he intended to dispose of the horses and return for some more. He and the horses which were still in his possession were brought back to Provo; and on Friday morning he was bound over in the sum of $700 to await the action of the grand jury. The name of the thief is Amos Cox and his home is in Huntington.

Mr. Jacques was in the office this morning. He feels quite jubilant over the capture and suggests the propriety of Eastern Utah and Western Colorado organizing in committees "to decorate the cedars of Emery and other counties with the d—d thieves." He praises enthusiastically the efforts of the officers and particularly of Messrs Wilkins and Hover.

Deseret News
October 27, 1886

WRIGLEY.—At Ferron, Emery County, October 9, 1886, after an illness of two weeks, Thomas, son of Joseph and Ann Wrigley, born at American Fork, Utah, March 11, 1872.

STEVENS.— At Ferron, Emery County, October 11, 1886, of typhoid fever, Charles Franklin, son of Joseph Smith and Abigail M. Stevens, born in Mayfield, Sanpete County, June 2, 1877.

Deseret News
November 10, 1886

LEMON.—At Ferron City, Emery County, October 24th, 1886, of typhoid fever, after an illness of ten days, John Carled, son of John C. and Emma E. Lemon; born March 20, 1872, at Manti, Sanpete County.
Home Sentinel, please copy.

Deseret News
November 24, 1886

Sickness at Ferron.—There seems to be a good deal of sickness at Ferron, Emery County, judging by reports we have received from there, and the frequency with which our correspondent there sends to us death notices for publication. The disease most prevalent is a species of fever, of a very tedious and stubborn character.

HITCHCOCK.—At Ferron, Emery County, October 30th, 1886, of epilepsy with which he had been afflicted seven years, James Edward, son of John C. and Fretna Hitchcock; born October 16, 1875, at Spring City, Sanpete County.

Salt Lake Herald
November 30, 1886

CHARLES STAIN, of Manti, whose feet were badly frozen while crossing the mountains between Castle Dale and Sanpete, has been brought to the city and placed in the Deseret Hospital. He is receiving every attention that can possibly be given him, but it is feared it will be found necessary to amputate one of his feet, at least.

EMERY STAKE CONFERENCE.

The quarterly conference of the Emery Stake of Zion convened at Huntington, Nov. 6th, at 10 a. m.

Present on the stand was Prest. C. G. Larsen with his first Couselor O. Seeley, also Bishops and representatives of all the wards and other local authorities in the Stake.

President Larsen called the meeting to order and after singing on page 148, prayer was offered by Wm. Black. Singing on page 51.

President Larsen thereafter made some introductory remarks and said it had pleased the authorities of the Church to change the time for our quarterly conferences, which bring it more convenient in the summer, as hitherto our conferences in June have generally been obstructed very much by the high water. The spiritual condition of the people of Emery is good and he knew of no difficulties unless they could be easily adjusted. He felt sorry that we as a people do not have that peace and good will from the inhabitants of this great republic that we desire to have, but as the controversy arises from difference of opinions in religious matters, we can not help it. Americans surely give a great deal of credit to the "Mormon" people for the development of mineral wealth and agricultural enterprises in these western mountain regions, but instead of admiration and credit our condition to-day as a people is such, that our best men, the leaders of these peculiar people, are either exiles or prisoners; but we are in the hands of God, and we are in for peace, not for war, and there will yet be a day, when all nations shall be placed upon the balance of justice. Peace will yet find a home in this land and a righteous God will yet take the reins of government, and the healing balsam shall be poured upon every wounded heart.

The Bishops of the several Wards thereof gave reports of the condition of their people, wherefrom was learned that the inhabitants of Emery County are on the onward march, improving spiritually and temporally. A medium grain crop has been raised, and with proper care the people will have bread and seed for the season. A good amount of labor has been spent on ditches and canals, and the appearance of the several settlements are greatly improved by new houses and planting of fruit and shade trees, and we have the most sanguine expectations for fruits, as some of the trees have already yielded some excellent samples of their quality.

All organizations were in fair running order. Sabbath schools well attended, but there is a lack of teachers.

The health amongst the people is good, except at Ferran, where a bad fever has left its cruel marks in several families; eight or nine persons, mostly under 14 years of age, have died.

Conference adjourned until 2 o'clock in the afternoon.

2 p.m.—Opened with singing and prayer by Boyd P. Petersen.

Counselor O. Seeley occupied a portion of the time. He endorsed the many good and timely remarks made and counsels given, and said it is necessary for the Saints to come together in conference, that our minds may be brightened up to the full sense of our duties. We may not notice our advancement as distinctly as we desire, but, like our children, when sent to school, their advancement from one week to another can not be seen so well, but by keeping them there steadily they will attain an education; so with us, diligence and faithfulness will bring us ahead.

The remainder of the time was used by the different Presidents of Quorums bearing a good testimony to the work of God, and the marked improvement in the servants of God to learn their duties, and earnestly striving to perform them.

After singing, benediction was pronounced by Joseph Evans.

On Sunday morning at 10 a.m. the meeting was called to order by President Larsen. Singing by choir. Prayer by Wm. Howard, and after another song by the choir, a few more reports were given from Wards not given the day previous, whereafter the clerk read the statistical report, which showed the total number of souls about 2,700.

On request of President Larsen, the clerk read from the DESERET NEWS "A Plea for the Poor and Suffering," after which President Larsen occupied the time by urging upon the people the necessity of attending Fast-day meetings and sending in our offerings on that day for the poor; furthermore explained about both quality and quantity of things and our obligations to God in this matter, and remember the promises from heaven for obedience to the law of tithing.

Singing by the choir. Benediction by C. Jorgensen.

In the afternoon at 2 o'clock, after singing and prayer, the sacrament was administered, whereafter the Church and also the Stake authorities were presented and all were, by unanimous vote, sustained.

The remainder of the time was used by several brethren who all encouraged the Saints to be of good courage and remember that "still she moves," and if we think we are persecuted, it becomes the duty of a follower of Christ to bear it with patience and humility. President Larsen thereafter thanked the choir and people of Huntington for all they had done to make the Conference pleasant, and after having directed some kind admonitions to the young to shun evil in acts and language and warned the elder people from bad habits of quarrels and contentions, he announced that the Conference will be adjourned till the 12th day of February.

Choir sang, "Once more we come before our God." Benediction by Henning Olsen.

OLUF J. ANDERSON, Clerk.

Deseret News
January 12, 1887

DEATHS.

ALLEN—At Huntington, December 24th 1886, Rosy Allen, daughter of Andrew J. and Salriah E. Allen; born June 3rd, 1885.

Salt Lake Herald
January 16, 1887

DIPHTHERIA is raging with considerable violence in Emery County—seven or eight deaths have recently occurred at Ferron, and nearly twenty cases were existing a few days ago.

Deseret News
January 19, 1887

Diphtheria Epidemic.—Our correspondent at Ferron, Emery County, gives an account of the terrible ravages of diphtheria in that and the neighboring ward of Molen. The disease first appeared on December 21st, and within two weeks there were twelve deaths in the two wards numbering about 10 families. There were also 16 or 18 cases still existing last Monday, when our correspondent wrote. The following is a partial list of the deaths and such particulars of birth, age, etc., as were obtainable:

Three children of Jacob A. and Charlotte E. Phillips, of Ferron. Their names were William Benjamin, Theodore and Amasa, the eldest fifteen and the youngest nearly three years old; they were born in American Fork, Utah County.

One child of Nicholas and Ellen Larsen, of Ferron.

Two children of John C. and Theresa A. Duncan, of Ferron. One of them, Sarah Jane, was born at Cedar City, Iron County, Sept. 11, 1887; died Jan. 8, 1887. The other, Jessie Agnes, was born at Salina, Sevier County, May 13, 1879; died Jan. 8, 1887.

The names of those who died at Molen have not yet been learned. The authorities in both wards have made every effort to check the disease, and to provide proper attendance and care for the afflicted ones, and it is now hoped that there will be no new cases.

Salt Lake Herald
January 28, 1887

Manti Matters.

A number of sheep in Castle Valley are dying of starvation, being compelled to stay on poor pasturage on account of the lack of snow at their old winter ranges. They are now being removed from there.

The city fathers of Manti have notified the people of Ferron that no citizen of Ferron would be permitted to come to Manti unless he has a pass; also that there has been considerable sickness of late among the children of Manti, but nothing of a serious nature, however, and all are doing well and getting along nicely at present.—*Sentinel.*

Deseret News
February 2, 1887

CROOKSTON—At Ferron, Emery County, January 14th, 1887, of diphtheria, John Crookston, born at American Fork, Utah County, in the spring of 1871. He was the son of John and Dinah Crookston.

Also at the same place, January 15th, 1887, Emma T. Duncan, born at Ferron.

Also at the same place, January 16th, 1887, Nomsa Bolle Duncan, born at Cedar City, Iron County.

Ferron Facts.—An occasional correspondent, writing from Ferron, gives us a little information in relation to a town which through modesty or neglect has not been overly represented. He says:

"This town is located on a creek of the same name as the town, about 43 miles south of Price, and consists of 52 families. The town of Ferron possesses the best public hall in the county; it is a brick structure 32x52 feet inside measurement, with an 18-foot ceiling, and when completed inside will be a very comfortable house. In the town are several pleasant homes, in fact the town is ahead of any other in that respect. The main portion of the tillable land lies to the south and east of the town in a large field. Good wells have not yet been obtained, and, as in most places in Castle Valley, the people depend on the creek for water, and in the winter have to haul it in barrels, thus putting water at a premium and is a great inconvenience to the citizens.

The town has been visited with considerable sickness for some time past; first with typhoid fever, last September and October, and since, with the dread scourge diphtheria, which has carried off several in the town. All are convalescent at the present, but it is thought best not to raise the quarantine for a week yet, to insure safety and prevent the further spread of the malady.

But very little snow has fallen in the valley, which is very detrimental to sheep interests; and if some does not soon fall, it will result in the loss of a great many. Stock also are not doing as well as usual on account of the scarcity of snow and the presence of so many sheep, which are eating off all the grass near to water. The latter does not tend to promote the most amicable feelings between the stock and sheep men, as the former assert that the latter are continually making encroachments on them and pay no attention to priority of occupation."

CORRESPONDENCE.

HUNTINGTON, Emery County,
January 26, 1886.

Editor Deseret News:

The appearance of this county is anything but inviting, as it has a sterile, forbidding appearance; in fact, it looks as though when the floods descended that this part of the country was where they struck the earth and washed it into deep washes, leaving flat-topped hills quite picturesque in appearance, some at a distance appearing feudal castles of antiquity; much so that you expect to see the sentry pass along the battlement from tower to tower or to see coming toward you a train of armored knights with all the accoutrements of feudal warfare. One might, indeed, easily look upon one of the old castellated rocks and closing the eyes dream over and of those romances that we have read in youth and imagine that one of those scenes of fiction was before him, but awakening he finds himself in Castle Valley, Emery County, Utah, and sees around him the barren, dreary look that the country at nearer view presents. And we venture to say that no people but the "Mormons" would have thought of redeeming it and causing it to yield to the husbandman, for it was naturally so forbidding and the labor to get the water out was so great that any people less united in their efforts could never have accomplished so great a task, at so great a risk, for the land before the water is applied looks as though nothing would grow. Yet by the use of fertilizers and the irrigation of it at proper times it can be redeemed and made to produce fine crops. The corn crop is exceptionally good. Vegetables of all kinds of all kinds prosper and yield an abundance in answer to proper care. Price is the first town reached in this county and has sprung into some importance since so much freight has been shipped from that point, but our agricultural district is not yet fully developed. The ditch is lagging, but it is expected to be completed in the spring.

From Price

THE ROAD TO HUNTINGTON

runs south over a broken country. The town of Huntington lies on the south side of the creek, on a gradual sloping plane inclining to the east, and is platted in squares, the roads running north and south, and east and west. The town is one mile square and is building up quite rapidly. Water has been taken out at great expense, and they are enlarging the canals now made, and another large ditch is being taken out on the north side of the creek, that will, when completed, cover about seven thousand acres of land in the district called Cleveland, which lies about three miles northeast from Huntington.

A coal vein has been developed by D. C. Robbins about eight miles from Huntington, which yields a most excellent article of coal. The vein is about eight feet thick and has a solid rock ceiling and floor.

Two marriages took place in Huntington on Monday, the 24th. Miss Emma Jane Loveless, daughter of Sheriff Loveless, to Mr. A. D. Dennie. A feast and dance followed the ceremony, in which was manifest a great amount of enjoyment. Peace prevails, all seem to be prospering and none are in want of the necessaries of life.

L.
P.

Deseret Evening News
February 19, 1887

DEATHS.

VANBUREN.—Died at Orangeville, Feb. 16, 1887, of old age, at the residence of her son, A. C. Vanburen, Lucy Vanburen, born June 14, 1813, at Utica, New York; baptized into the Church of Jesus Christ of Latter-day Saints, November 9, 1835, by Elder George M. Hinkle. She was in the mobbings of the Saints in Nauvoo and other places in the rise of the Church. She came to the Valley in 1852.

Deseret Evening News
February 23, 1887

Daily Mail Wanted.—Complaints come from Price, Emery County, that people in that region who get their mail distributed there — especially residents of Huntington, Castledale, Orangeville and Ferron—do not receive it till four or five days old from here. The mail that leaves here on Friday gets to Price the same evening and remains till the following Tuesday, and so on; and the only way this state of things can be cured is by a daily mail. We understand the people there are getting up a petition to Postmaster General Vilas, and this is the proper thing to do.

WRIGLEY.—At Ferron City, Emery County, Utah, February 18, 1887, of diphtheria, after an illness of four days, Mary Grace Wrigley, born Oct. 3rd, 1885.

Deseret Evening News
March 2, 1887

DEATHS.

HOLLOWAY. — At Orangeville, Emery County, Utah, February 21, 1887, Anna Elizabeth Callaway, daughter of Levi H. and Anna Callaway, born on the 26th of February, 1872, at Panacea, Lincoln County, Nevada.

Salt Lake Herald
March 20, 1887

H. M. FUGATE was commissioned by the Governor yesterday, as justice of the peace for Ferron precinct, Emery County.

Deputy Registrars,

The *Utah* Commission have made the following appointments of deputy registration officers:

Emery County.—Castle Dale, J. W. Seeley; Huntington, J. T. Wakefield; Lawrence, J. T. Wakefield; Price, B. H. Young; Green River, J. T. Farrer; Moab, O. J. Boren; Orangeville, J. K. Reid; Ferron, M. Molen; Molen, J. D. Killpack; Muddy, John Lewis; Wellington, R. B. Thompson; Scofield, S. J. Harkness.

Emery County Notes.—Mr. Wm. Howard, of Huntington, Emery County, sends the following, under date of April 4th:

We have had a very dry, warm winter, which has enabled us to get our canals and ditches in running order a month earlier than usual.

The farmers have been putting in crops for the last six weeks, and if we do not have a storm soon, the grain will have to be watered up.

A year ago, Huntington spent about $1,200 in fruit trees, mostly from the Geneva Nurseries, which as a general thing, have done well. Although their trees are small, yet they have splendid roots, with plenty of small fibres, which cause the tree to grow very rapidly when set out. Some that I bought from this firm last year sent forth new limbs over three feet long last season. Mr. Geo. Ipsom of this place also bought in a large lot of fruit trees from the Woodbury nurseries, but the great trouble with them was they did not have root. As a consequence, a great many of them died. Most of us feel well to think we have got splendid orchards started.

The people of Cleveland (which is destined to be a large settlement), about six miles northeast of Huntington, are now very busy on their canal. They expect to get water out soon enough this spring to raise crops this coming summer. A great many of the share holders of the canal are Pleasant Valley coal miners, who have taken up land and made some improvements on it, in most cases enough to fill the law, but who have to go back to the mines to earn means to support themselves and families. On account of no water being within six or seven miles of their land, they can as yet do no farming.

The health of the people generally is good.

DEATHS.

NIELSEN—At Castle Dale, March 13, 1887, Niels Nielsen, of typhoid fever. He was born September 8th, 1850; he leaves a wife and seven children and many friends to mourn his loss; he was highly respected by all who knew him.

Salt Lake Herald
April 29, 1887

NOTICE.

To Whom it May Concern:

THIS IS TO CERTIFY THAT I, THE undersigned, John K. Reid, of Orangeville, Emery County, Utah, did on the 12th day of March, A.D. 1883, purchase of one George Mathias Makin, ONE-HALF TENTH INTEREST in the coal mines known as the Bituminous and Cannal Coal Mines, situated in Cottonwood and Jose Valley Canyon, Emery Cou ty, Utah, and that I have never disposed of my interest in any manner; and that I am still the owner of the said one-half tenth interest in said mines, and all parties negotiating to purchase the said mines are hereby warned against purchasing the said one-ha f teoth interest only through the lawful owner t^ereof.

Any person wishing to further investigate into this matter can do so by corresponding with the undersigned.   J. K. REID,
Orangeville, Emery County, Utah.
Dated at Orangeville, April 25, 1887.   a29

Deseret News
June 8, 1887

DEATHS.

JUSTESEN—At Castle Dale, May 23, 1887, of diphtheria, Lyman Eugene, son of Rasmus and Anena Justeson, born April 28, 1882.

ESTRAY NOTICE.

I HAVE IN MY POSSESSION:

One large grey HORSE, branded P F on left hip; no other brands visible.

If not claimed and taken away within ten days from date, will be sold at Huntington precinct pound, June 4th, 1887, at 2 o'clock p. m.   J. T. WAKEFIELD,
Poundkeeper.
Huntington, Emery Co., May 25, 1887.

Deseret News
June 15, 1887

ESTRAY NOTICE.

I HAVE IN MY POSSESSION:

One sorrel MARE, 5 or 6 years old, three white feet, strip in forehead, has a Spanish brand on left shoulder, also a brand resembling JL combined on left thigh, shod on front feet.

One roan HEIFER, 3 or 4 years old, brand resembling ꓘF combined on left hip, crop off each ear.

If the above described animals are not claimed and taken away before the 17th day of June, they will be sold to the highest cash bidder.

S. P. SNOW, Poundkeeper,
Orangeville, June 7th, 1887.

Salt Lake Herald
June 15, 1887

THE CONVENTIONS.

July Ninth and Twelfth the Dates.

PREPARING FOR THE FRAY.

Thirty Delegates in the Representative Districts and Twenty in the Council.

The adjourned meeting of the People's Central Committee took place at the City Hall yesterday at noon; there were present: John Sharp, chairman; John R. Winder, E. A. Smith, J. F. Wells, John T. Caine, A. M. Cannon, Alma Eldredge, W. N. Dusenberry, A. O. Smoot, Jr., L. W. Shurtliff, Thomas D. Dee, William H. Lee, T. F. Roueche, E. B. Wells and H. S. Gowans.

The special committee appointed on the representation of delegates and district conventions made its report, which follows below.

Saturday, July 9th, was named as the time for holding all Representative conventions.

Tuesday, July 12th, was named as the time for holding all Council conventions.

The number of delegates to the convention in each Representative district was fixed at thirty.

The number of delegates to the convention in each Council district was fixed at twenty, the delegates to the Council convention to be selected by each Representative convention sending ten.

The executive committee were authorized to change the representation of the several precincts as might be found necessary to give each precinct at least one representative in the convention. After this the committee adjourned to meet at the City Hall at 8 p.m. Thursday evening, the 16th inst.

REPRESENTATIVE CONVENTIONS, JULY 9TH.

FIRST DISTRICT.

Convention to be held in Logan City, at the County Court House. Delegates apportioned as follows:

Rich County—Garden City precinct, 1; Lake Town, 2; Meadowville, 1; Randolph, 2; Woodruff, 1.

Cache County—Logan precinct, 12; Hyde Park, 2; Smithfield, 5; Providence, 4.

SECOND DISTRICT.

Convention to be held at City Hall, Hyrum City. Delegates apportioned as follows:

Cache County—Benson precinct 1; Clarkston, 2; Hyrum, 5; Lewiston, 2; Mendon, 2; Millville, 2; Newton, 2; Paradise, 2; Peterburgh, 1; Richmond, 5; Trenton, 1; Wellsville, 5.

THIRD DISTRICT.

Convention to be held at County Court House, Brigham City. Delegates as follows:

Box Elder County—Bear River precinct, 2; Box Elder, 9; Call's Fort, 2; Curlew, 1; Deweyville, 2; Grouse Creek, 1; Kelton, 1; Malad, 1; Mantua, 2; Park Valley, 1; Plymouth, 1; Portage, 2; Promontory, 1; Willard, 3; Terrace, 1.

FOURTH DISTRICT.

Convention to be held at County Court House, Ogden City. Delegates as follows: Ogden City, 30.

FIFTH DISTRICT.

Convention to be held at County Court House, Ogden City. Delegates as follows:

Weber County—Harrisville, 3; Eden, 1; Hooper, 4; Huntsville, 4; Lynne, 2; Marriott, 1; North Ogden, 4; Plain City, 4; Riverdale, 1; Slaterville, 1; Uintah, 1; West Weber, 2; Wilson, 1; Kanesville, 1.

SIXTH DISTRICT.

Convention to be held at County Court House, Farmington, Davis County. Delegates as follows:

Morgan County—Croyden, 1; Kanyon, 2; Milton, 1; Morgan, 2; Peterson, 1.

Davis County—South Bountiful, 2; East Bountiful, 3; West Bountiful, 1; Centerville, 2; Farmington, 4; Hooper, 1; Kaysville, 5; South Weber, 1.

Summit County—Henneferville, 1.
Salt Lake County—Hunter, 1; Pleasant Green, 1; North Point, 1.

SEVENTH DISTRICT.

Convention to be held at County Court House, Coalville. Delegates as follows:
Summit County—Coalville, 9; Echo, 2; Hoytsville, 2; Park City, 5; Kimball's, 2; Rockport, 1; Upton, 1; Wanship, 3; Grass Creek, 1.
Salt Lake County—Mountain Dell, 1; Sugar House, 3.

EIGHTH DISTRICT.

Convention to be held at County Court House, Tooele City. Delegates as follows:
Tooele County—Batesville, 1; St. John, 1; Clover, 1; Deep Creek, 1; Grantsville, 7; Quincy, 1; Lakeview, 2; Mill, 1; Ophir, 1; Stockton, 1; Tooele, 7; Vernon, 2; Bingham, 1; Tintic, 3.

NINTH DISTRICT.

Convention to be held at Ninth District schoolhouse, Salt Lake City. Delegates as follows:
Salt Lake County—First precinct, 30.

TENTH DISTRICT.

Convention to be held at County Court House, Salt Lake City. Delegates as follows:
Salt Lake County—Second precinct, 30.

ELEVENTH DISTRICT.

Convention to be held at Eighteenth Ward Schoolhouse, Salt Lake City. Delegates as follows:
Salt Lake County — Third precinct, 14; Fourth, 13; Granger, 2; Brighton, 1.

TWELFTH DISTRICT.

Convention to be held at City Hall, Salt Lake City. Delegates as follows:
Salt Lake County—Fifth precinct, 30.

THIRTEENTH DISTTICT.

Convention to be held at West Jordan ward hall, Salt Lake County. Delegates apportioned as follows:
Salt Lake County—North Jordan, 3; West Jordan, 6; South Jordan, 3; Fort Herriman, 2; Riverton, 2; Bluffdale, 1; South Cottonwood, 6; Union, 3; Sandy, 4.

FOURTEENTH DISTRICT.

Convention to be held at Mill Creek ward hall. Delegates apportioned as follows:
Salt Lake County—Farmers', 2; Mill Creek, 8; East Mill Creek, 3; Big Cottonwood, 6; Butler, 2; Granite, 1; Silver, 1; Alta, 1; Draper, 6.

FIFTEENTH DISTRICT.

Convention to be held at the City Hall, Spanish Fork City, Utah County. Delegates apportioned as follows:
Utah County—Lehi, 5; Cedar Fort, 1; Alpine, 2; Fairfield, 1; Goshen, 2; Santaquin, 3; Spring Lake, 1; Payson, 7; Spanish Fork, 8.

SIXTEENTH DISTRICT.

Convention to be held at County Court House, Provo City. Delegates apportioned as follows:
Utah County—American Fork, 7; Pleasant Grove, 7; Provo Bench, 2; Provo City, 13; Lake View, 1.

SEVENTEENTH DISTRICT.

Convention to be held at the City Hall, Springville, Utah County. Delegates apportioned as follows:
Utah County—Springville, 10; Thistle, 1; P. V. Junction, 2; Benjamin, 2; Salem, 3.
Sanpete County—Winter Quarters, 1.
Emery County—Scofield, 1; Castle Dale, 1; Ferron, 2; Huntington, 2; Moab, 1; Price, 1; Orangeville, 2; Muddy, 1.

EIGHTEENTH DISTRICT.

Convention to be held at County Court House, Heber City, Wasatch County. Delegates as follows:

Uintah County—Brown's Park, 2; Ashley 4.

Wasatch County—Charleston, 2; Heber, 7; Midway, 4; Wallsburgh, 2.

Summit County—Kamas, 5; Woodland, 1; Peoa, 3.

NINETEENTH DISTRICT.

Convention to be held at County Court House, Fillmore, Millard County. Delegates as follows:

Juab County—Nephi, 8; Mona, 3; Levan, 3; Juab, 1

Millard County—Deseret, 2; Fillmore, 4; Holden, 2; Kanosh, 2; Leamington, 1; Meadow, 1; Oak Creek, 1; Scipo, 2.

TWENTIETH DISTRICT.

Convention to be held at City Hall, Mount Pleasant, Sanpete County. Delegates as follows:

Sanpete County—Thistle, 1; Fairview, 4; Mount Pleasant, 7; Spring City, 3; Moroni, 4; Fountain Green, 3; Ephraim, 8.

TWENTY-FIRST DISTRICT.

Convention to be held at County Court House, Manti, Sanpete County. Delegates as follows:

Sanpete County—Chester, 1; Wales, 1; Manti, 5; Petty, 1; Mayfield, 1; Gunnison, 3; Fayette, 1; Freedom, 1.

Sevier County—Annabella, 1; Burrville, 1; Central, 1; Elsinore, 1; Glenwood, 1; Joseph, 1; Monroe, 2; Redmond, 1; Richfield, 3; Salina, 1; Vermillion, 1; Willow Bend, 1; Gooseberry, 1.

TWENTY-SECOND DISTRICT.

Convention to be held at the County Court House, Beaver City, Beaver County. Delegates apportioned as follows:

Beaver County—Adamsville, 1; Beaver City, 12; Grampion, 1; Greenville, 2; Minersville, 4; Star, 1.

Piute County—Bullionville, 1; Circleville, 1; Fremont, 2; Marysvale, 1; Thurber, 3; Koosharem, 1; Wilmont, 1.

TWENTY-THIRD DISTRICT.

Convention to be held at the City Hall, Cedar City, Iron County. Delegates apportioned as follows:

Iron County—Cedar, 6; Kanarra, 2; Parowan, 6; Paragoonah, 2; Summit, 1.

Garfield County—Cannonville, 1; Escalante, 2; Hillsdale, 1; Coyote, 1; Panguitch, 4.

Washington County—New Harmony, 1.

San Juan County—Bluff City, 2; McElmo, 1.

TWENTY-FOURTH DISTRICT.

Convention to be held at the County Court House, St. George, Washington County. Delegates apportioned as follows:

Washington County—Duncan's Retreat, 1; Hebron, 1; Grafton, 1; Gunlock, 1; Leeds, 1; Pine Valley, 1; Price, 1; Pinto, 1; Rockville, 1; St. George, 4; Santa Clara, 1; Silver Reef, 1; Shonesburg, 1; Springdale, 1; Toquerville, 2; Virgin, 1; Washington, 2.

Kane County—Glendale, 1; Johnson, 1; Kanab, 2; Upper Kanab, 1; Orderville, 1; Mount Carmel, 1; Pahreah, 1.

COUNCIL CONVENTIONS, JULY 12TH.

First Council District, composed of First and Sixth Representative districts. Convention to be held at City Hall, Kaysville, Davis County.

Second Council District, composed of Second and Third Representative districts. Convention to be held at County Court House, Brigham City, Box Elder County.

Third Council District, composed of Fourth and Fifth Representative districts. Convention to be held at County Court House, Ogden City.

Fourth Council District, composed of Seventh and Ninth Representative districts. Convention to be held at the County Court House, Coalville, Summit County.

Fifth Council District, composed of the Tenth and Twelfth Representative districts. Convention to be held at the City Hall, Salt Lake City.

Sixth Council District, composed of the Eleventh and Fourteenth Representative districts. Convention to be held at the Eighteenth Ward schoolhouse, Salt Lake City.

Seventh Council District, composed of the Eighth and Thirteenth Representative districts. Convention to be held in the West Jordan Hall, Salt Lake County.

Eighth Council District, composed of the Fifteenth and Sixteenth Representative districts. Convention to be held at County Court House, Provo City.

Ninth Council District, composed of the Seventeenth and Eighteenth Representative districts. Convention to be held at the City Hall, Springville, Utah County.

Tenth Council District, composed of the Nineteenth and Twentieth Representative districts. Convention to be held at the County Court House, Nephi, Juab County.

Eleventh Council District, composed of the Twenty-first and Twenty-second Representative Districts. Convention to be held at the County Court House, Richfield, Sevier County.

Twelfth Council District, composed of the Twenty-third and Twenty-fourth Representative districts. Convention to be held at the City Hall, Cedar City, Iron County.

Ogden Herald
June 21, 1887

TEXT BOOK CONVENTION.

The Proceedings of Yesterday—Committees Appointed.

EDITOR HERALD:—The Text Book Convention met in the University Building, Salt Lake City, June 20th, 1887, at 10 a. m: There were present Commisioner Williams, Dr. Park and a number of superintendents.

Commissioner Williams was chosen chairman and E. H. Anderson, secretary. The chairman stated that the object of the meeting was to consider the adoption of readers and spellers. It is not yet five years since the present books were adopted, and as no change could be made until the expiration of the term except by action of a special convention, it was considered best to hold this convention to comply with the law, and to so arrange matters that hereafter all adoptions would expire at the same time.

A committee on credentials was appointed, who reported the following names as members of the Convention:

Territorial Commissioner P. L. Williams.*

President Deseret University, John R. Park.*

COUNTY SUPERINTENDENTS.

Beaver—R. Maeser,* Beaver.
Box Elder—J. D. Peters,* Brigham.
Cache—W. H. Apperley,* Logan.
Davis—H. L. Steed,* Farmington.
Emery—E. A. Cox, Castle Dale.
Garfield—J. A. Worthin, Panguitch.
Iron—W. C. Mitchell, Parowan.
Juab—F. W. Chappell,* Nephi.
Kane—H. A. Broughton, Glendale.
Millard—T. C. Callister,* Fillmore.
Morgan—C. A. Welch,* Morgan.
Piute—L. G. Long, Junction City.
Rich—Wm. Rex,* Randolph.
Salt Lake—Wm. M. Stewart,* Salt Lake.
San Juan—J. A. Lyman, Bluff City.
Sanpete—W. K. Reid,* Manti.
Sevier—Victor E. Bean,* Richfield.
Tooele—J. R. Clark, Tooele.
Uintah—J. H. Black, Ashley.
Utah—Geo. H. Brimhall,* Provo.
Wasatch—Attewall Wooten,* Midway.
Washington—J. T. Woodbury,* St. George.
Weber—Edward H. Anderson,* Ogden.

Those marked * were present.

The Freedom of the house was extended to former school officers, after which Dr. Park moved the adoption of the following resolution:

"*Resolved*, that it is the sense of this convention that there exists sufficient cause to change the present adoption of school readers and spellers for this Territory, and that the chair be authorized to appoint a committee of three members who shall select and report to this convention such other readers and spellers as they may deem best for the convention to adopt for exclusive use in this Territory for the next five years, in accordance with section 16 of the school law."

After being amended so as to make the committee five, the resolution was adopted and the special convention adjourned till Tuesday at 10 a. m.

REGULAR CONVENTION.

At 11 o'clock the regular convention was called to order and organized with the same officers as the special convention.

A committee of three was appointed by the Chair on each study, as follows: Grammar, arithmetic, geography, penmanship, drawing, physiology, history and miscellaneous books. The committees were to report to the convention the results of their investigations.

Adjourned till 2 p. m. Tuesday, June 21st, 1887.

The committees were hard at work all day long listening to the claims of of the various publishers. It is reasonably certain that the readers, grammars and probably the spellers will be changed The contest in readers lies between Bancroft's & Barnes' New National.

The convention will likely adjourn on Tuesday evening.   U

SALT LAKE CITY, June 21st, 1887.

A special telegram to the HERALD this afternoon announces that the Special Convention adopted Bancroft's readers and Harvington and Harpers spellers.

Deseret Evening News
July 13, 1887

EMERY COUNTY.

Orangeville—Joseph Granger, A. Anderson, Joseph L. Boulder.

Blake—Josephus Gammage, Thomas Farrer, N. Parker.

Price—A. J Mead, R. G. McAllister, Charles Marsh.

Molen—W. S. Peacock, Hans C. Hansen, Seth Wareham.

Wellington— Lewis Benton, Allen Grames, William Tidwell.

Huntington—James Woodman, Thos. Wakefield, George W. Johnson, Sr.

Larence—Henry Roper, P. C. Burch, A. A. Day.

Muddy — Jacob Menchy, Joseph Evans, Heber C. Petty.

Ferron—John C. Duncan, Henry Mills, H. M. Fugate.

ELECTION JUDGES.

Appointments Made by the Utah Commission.

The following appointments of election judges have been announced by the Utah Commission, the first named in each precinct being the presiding judge:

Deseret News
July 20, 1887

DEATHS.

JUSTESEN—At Castle Dale, June 1; 1887 of diphtheria, Blnnehe, daughter of Rastuus and Anena Justesen. She was born November 0, 18x5.

Salt Lake Herald
July 23, 1887

JASPER PETERSON, of Castle Dale, Emery County, a young missionary to Denmark, died in that country at the city of Odense on June 23d. The sad news was communicated to his family by N. C. Flygare.

Deseret News
July 27, 1887

ELDER JASPER PETERSON,

Of Castle Dale, Dies in Denmark,

The following correspondence appeared in the *Millennial Star* of July 4th:

COPENHAGEN, June 27, 1887.

President George Teasdale:

DEAR BROTHER—It has become my sad duty to inform you of the demise of Elder Jasper Peterson, from Castle Dale, Emery Co., Utah, one of our missionaries, who died in the City of Odense, Denmark, on the 23rd inst.

Brother Petersen arrived here on the 26th of April last, from the Southern States Mission, where he had labored about six months He was ap pointed to labor in the Odense branch of Aarhus Conference. He was very anxious to fill his mission, and went energetically to work among his relatives and friends, who received him very kindly. He began to be indisposed in the latter part of May; until then he enjoyed good health, and seemed to be very robust. He suffered from chills and fever, and acute pains in his head, but, owing to the faith exercised by himself and the brethren, he was much relieved when anointed. He had a good appetite and partook of his meals up to the time of his death.

On the 22d, he felt a pain in his side and breast, he was anointed and felt better. He retired to bed, but in the night he had another attack of the pain, making it difficult for him to draw his breath. He was administered to again and received immediate relief, so he fell asleep and did not wake again until 9 a.m. At 10 a.m. he felt hungry and ate with relish the food set before him, and remarked: "Brother Hansen, it tastes pretty good." At 11:45 a.m. he fell asleep without the slightest sign of pain, and thus he died. He was conscious to the last, and occasionally remarked that he would have to go home with the first company.

Brother Peterson was a good, faithful Latter-day Saint; he died while in the discharge of his duty as a servant of God and a minister of the Gospel of Christ.

He has been properly dressed, and will be buried on the 28th. Several of the Utah Elders will be present at his funeral. The people have been very kind to our brother; many strangers have brought wreaths of flowers to be laid on his grave.

I will write to President Larsen, of the Emery Stake, and have him break the sad intelligence to his family.

With kindest regards, I remain your brother in the Gospel,

N. C. FLYGARE.

Deseret News
August 10, 1887

THE REGISTRATION.

The Number of Voters in the Various Precincts.

Below is given the number of names on the registration lists of the several precincts in this Territory, as reported to the Utah Commission by the registration officers. It will be observed that a few precincts have not been reported. It is estimated that these will aggregate from 150 to 200, making the total registration of the Territory about 20,400.

EMERY COUNTY.				
Castle Dale,	-	-	-	37
Huntington,	-	-	-	38
Laurence,	-	-	-	25
Moab,	-	-	-	69
Price,	-	-	-	59
Blake*,	-	-	-	—
Ferron*,	-	-	-	—
Thompson's Springs*,	-	-		—
Muddy,	-	-	-	28
Orangeville,	-	-	-	44
Scofield,	-	-	-	59
Wellington*,	-	-	-	—
Molen*,	-	-	-	—
				409

Deseret News
August 31, 1887

NOTICE.

Ferron Townsite.

To all whom it may concern:

NOTICE IS HEREBY GIVEN, THAT whereas Orange Seely, as the Probate Judge of Emery County, U. T., and in accordance with the laws of the United States and of this Territory, did on the 27th day of September, A. D. 1886, duly enter at the U. S. Land office, in Salt Lake City, U. T., in trust for the several owners and occupants of the lands involved, and as a townsite, to wit: The town of "Ferron," the following described tracts of land, viz: The south east quarter (SE¼) of section nine (9), and the west half of the south west quarter (W½SW¼) of section ten (10), in township twenty (20) south, of range seven (7) east, Salt Lake meridian, United States survey for the Territory of Utah, containing 210 acres of land.

I, Jasper Robertson, the successor to said Judge, duly commissioned and qualified, do now notify all persons claiming any rights whatever in or to any lot or parcel of said land, to sign a statement in writing, describing in an accurate manner the lot or parcel of land so claimed, and deliver the same to the Clerk of the Probate Court of Emery County, U. T., within six (6) months from the 31st day of August, 1887, the same being the date of the first publication of this notice, or he forever barred the right of claiming or recovering said land in any court of law or equity.

In witness whereof, I have hereunto set my hand, at Castle Dale, Emery Co., U. T., this 20th day of August, 1887.

JASPER ROBERTSON,
w3m Probate Judge, Emery Co., U. T.

ESTRAY NOTICE.

I HAVE IN MY POSSESSION:

One bay HORSE, 4 or 5 years old, branded L 5 on left thigh, white strip in face, both hind feet white, big lump on left hind leg.

One bay yearling horse COLT, not branded, white spot in forehead, right hind foot white.

If said animals are not claimed and taken away within 10 days from date, will be sold in Huntington Precinct Pound, August 18th, 1887, at 10 o'clock a.m.

J. T. WAKEFIELD,
Poundkeeper.

Deseret News
October 12, 1887

DEATHS.

JENSEN.··At Castle Dale September 17 1887, of teething, Francis, son of John J and Sarah Jensen, aged 6 months and 3 days.

Deseret News
November 9, 1887

The New Jurors.

On Saturday afternoon another open venire for petit jurors was issued out of the Third District Court. It was returned this morning with the following names:

Con. O'Keefe,   J. J. O'Reilly,
John Shuttle,   John Creamer,
John Stillwell,   Frank Glenn,
A. Mayberry,   John Goldthwaite,
Jas. McTierney,   F. B. Howland,
E. Kahn,   Jas. Hague,
W. Almy,   W. P. McKeaver,
Dan Hutchison,   Chas. Whiting,
T. J. Ward,   Alfred Godbe,
Jos. Ferran,   G. S. Ellis.

Messrs. Glenn, Howland, Hutchison, Whitney, Godbe and Ferran were excused for various causes. The remaining fourteen took the oath and were added to the list.

Ogden Herald
December 21, 1887

Never Despair.

The Manti *Sentinel* of the 19th, says that a subscriber in Orangeville has not received, since early in last September, six copies of that paper. But the *Sentinel* urges its subscriber to not despair of ever receiving the tardy papers, as they may be somewhere on the road. Judging from the length of time that it took a letter to travel from Manti to Orangeville (two months and four days), the *Sentinel* is not inconsistent in its exhortation.

Deseret News
January 18, 1888

A BLIZZARD COMING.

The Cold Wave That Will Soon Sweep From the North.

The weather has moderated somewhat in this vicinity the last day or two, and resulted in a snowstorm at noon today. This morning Sergeant Kortz, of the Signal Service Department, being asked as to the weather outlook, replied, "There will be a snowstorm in a few hours, and then look out for another cold wave. It is coming straight this way." As will be seen by the weather bulletin in another column, this wave has already struck Montana. At Fort Custer, where the thermometer registered six degrees above zero yesterday, it was today 28 degrees below, making a drop of 34 degrees in twenty-four hours. At Helena the mercury reached 30 degrees below, this morning.

The immediate prospects in the line of cold are very discouraging, especially to stockmen, many of whom have already suffered severely, and it now looks as though the worst had not yet come. One gentleman in this city, who has 2,000 sheep on the Desert, Tooele County, was asked his latest information regarding them, and stated that it was very probable that he would lose the whole flock. Deputy Marshal Cannon, returned from Tooele last night, and says that the four days he spent in that county have been the coldest he ever experienced. At Stockton the thermometer reached 28 degrees below zero. Along the northern line of the Territory the reports thus far received are exceedingly gloomy. Cattle, horses and sheep are dying by hundreds from the intense cold and the inability to get feed on the ranges, owing to the deep snow Around Emery County and Eastern Utah the condition of things is not much better. Along the roads and in the hills there, the stock is being fairly slaughtered by the severe weather. L. B. Yerxa, agent of the Pauly Jail Building Company in this city, returned this morning from Castle Dale, whither he has been to close a contract with Emery County for a $4,000 jail On the trip made from Castle Dale to Huntington he was almost frozen to death. He and his companion were loaded with as much clothing as could be put in the sleigh, but the cold was so intense that they had serious doubts of being able to get through. At Pleasant Valley Junction it was found last night that the mercury stood at 28 degrees below.

Quite a number of Utah men have sheep in Western Wyoming. In that section there has yet been comparatively little damage, as there has been plenty of feed, though the cold is just as severe as in other parts, it being claimed that one day last week the mercury froze in the bulb. Whether the later storm will affect them seriously cannot, of course, be now determined.

Utah Enquirer
January 27, 1888

Orangeville, Emery Co.

CATTLE that came off the the mountains thin, are faring very bad, a great many having died in some places, owing to the sheep herds having eaten the mountains clean last summer, and the rain coming too late for our fall grasses to mature.

WE have more snow in this county than usual at this time of the year, which is a good thing for sheep men, as they can get their herds away from the streams for feed.

THERE has been a body of shale discovered by some of our citizens in this vicinity, which bids fair, when developed, to out-rival the Australian shale for gas-making purposes.

THERE is one thing we have the advantage of here, and that is we have plenty of coal and wood with which to keep good fires in the cold weather.

WE have heard of no great loser in sheep so far, but the range is about eaten out with transient herds of both cattle and sheep.

THE weather has been very cold here, as it has been all over the Territory: but the thermometer did not go below 22 at the worst.

So far, we are blessed above other portions of Utah.

THE health of the people is generally good.

JANUARY 24th.   J. K. R.

Utah Enquirer
February 17, 1888

Orangeville, Emery Co.

We had a case of burglary at Castle Dale on the night of February 3d. About 11 o'clock a young man named David Edmonston broke into the Co-op. store of that place. He smashed the window in, and made a hole large enough to go through. There was a dance the same evening. A young man by the name of Larsen heard the noise of the glass breaking and ran and got assistance, and caught Edmonston in the store. They made him come out of the same hole he went inat. When an examination was made it was found he had broken open the lock drawer, but found no cash; the clerk, since the burglary that was committed some time ago in the same place, has carried the cash drawer home with him. The same party was accused at the time, but for lack of evidence was acquitted. He is now in the County Jail awaiting the action of the grand jury. His bonds were put at one thousand dollars, but he could not get them.

Last night we had a rain which has taken the frost out of the ground considerable.

Snow is thawing away fast.

February 13th.   E Saw.

|ORANGEVILLE.

Letter From the Pioneer Town of Emery County.

Editor Deseret News:

Orangeville is a small town in the western part of Emery County, at the mouth of Cottonwood Cañon, near a small river. There is any quantity of land and an abundance of water, which is already on the land. The inhabitants are engaged chiefly in agriculture, and raise wheat, oats, corn, etc., but the soil and climate seem to be better adapted to raising fruit and root crops. The apple, plum, peach, pear, cherry, and grape do remarkably well, and the largest sized potatoes, tomatoes, beets, cabbages, carrots, radishes, etc., are raised with little labor.

THE CLIMATE IS MILD

and the winters are not long and cold—the present winter being the coldest known here. Stock winter out and do well. The health of the people is good so there is little need of any doctors. In the beginning of the winter the children were barking and whooping with what is known as the whooping cough, but it was not very severe and is all over with now.

The day school is in a flourishing condition. The scholars, numbering over eighty, are taking a great interest in their studies in school and considering the material they have to work with, are advancing as fast as can be expected. Therefore the teacher enjoys his labors and all visitors are exceedingly pleased to see the interest taken by the pupils.

The weather is delightful at present and by all appearances is likely to continue so for some time. This seems to suit the people for they are fond of good weather.

There is barely enough snow here to cover the ground, but the young folks have had their

HORSES AND SLEIGHS

out trying to make good use of what there is, for it is not often they have that much to run their sleighs over. In addition to the amusements of dancing and sleighriding the young are busily engaged in getting up concerts, or rather entertainments, consisting of songs, recitations, dialogues, farces, etc. One of these was given on the evenings of January 11th and 12th, which was highly commendable and well attended, and it is hoped they will continue in so doing, for we all realize that it is much better for them to be thus employed than to be idling away their time during the long winter evenings.

There are two flourishing stores here which carry a medium sized stock of general merchandise and have a ready sale for the same. There is every probability of another store starting which will very likely be a co-operative institution and will be a benefit to the people at large.

There is any amount of fuel, both of wood and coal. The wood, which can be easily obtained, is about four or five miles from town, and the coal, which is of a first-class quality and easily obtained, is distant about seven or eight miles. J. J.

DEATHS.

CRAWFORD.—At Orangeville, Emery County, Feb. 20, 1888, of whooping cough and teething, Mary Cecelia, daughter of William W. and Ellen O. Crawford, born April 5th 1887.

KING.—At Ferron City, Emery County, Utah. Feb 16, 1888, of wh oping cough, Osmond Leonel, son of John E. and Mary Jane King. Born October 27, 1887.

LARSEN.—Maria Larsen died at Castle Dale October 23rd, 1887, of typhoid fever. Deceased was born October 23ed, 1864, in Odense, Denmark; emigrated with her parents when one year and six months old; both her parents died on the plains and she was brought to Mt. Pleasant, Sanpete County, by George Farnsworth; she was reared by Hana Brown, of the same place, till she was sixteen years old, when she moved to Castle Dale, Emery County, where she was married October 4th, 1883, to Carl Emil Larsen; she has been a member of the Castle Dale choir since it was organized, and at her death she was the President of the Young Ladies' Association of the ward; she leaves a mourning husband and two children—one three years and the other five months old.

Skandinavien Stjerne, please copy.

Utah Enquirer
March 13, 1888

NOTICE TO CREDITORS

In the Probate Court of Emery County, Territory of Utah.

In the matter of the Estate of Perry Miller, Deceased.

Notice is hereby given by the undersigned Administrator of the Estate of Perry Miller, deceased, to the creditors of and all persons having claims against the said deceased, to exhibit them, with the necessary vouchers within four months after the first publication of this notice, to the said Administrator at his residence in Price, Emery County, Utah, or to J. K. Reid, County Att'y., Orangeville, Emery County, Utah.

WM. MILLER,
Administrator of the Estate of Perry Miller, deceased.

Dated, Feb. 13, 1888.

EMERY STAKE CONFERENCE.

The Emery Stake quarterly conference convened Saturday, February 18, at Huntington. Present on the stand —the Stake Presidency, Bishops or representatives of the different wards, presidents of quorums. A fair number of Saints attended, although on account of the bad roads, the turnout was not as large as it otherwise would have been.

President Larsen called the meeting to order.

The Huntington choir sang, and the opening prayer was offered by Counselor Justesen.

President Larsen occupied part of the forenoon in speaking of the blessing enjoyed by the people; treated upon general principles for the well-being of the Saints of this Stake. He counseled them to live within their means and avoid contracting debts and unnecessary obligations.

Counselors Seely and Justesen followed in bearing a faithful testimony to the great latter-day work and endorsed the wise and fatherly counsels given by President Larsen. In visiting the Saints in the different wards, they had found everything in good order.

In the afternoon Bishops Henning Olsen, of Castle Dale, Jasper Robertson, of Orangeville, L. S. Beach, of Molen, and Counselor Horsley, of Price, gave reports of their respective wards. The condition of the people was favorable.

President Larsen reported Ferran Ward.

Seymour B. Young, who has just arrived from Salt Lake City, was the next speaker. He treated upon the present condition of the Saints, politically and otherwise.

Bishop C. Pulsipher, of Huntington, and Bishop C. Christensen of Muddy, reported their wards.

In the evening a Priesthood meeting was held. The time was mainly occupied by Seymour B. Young in making a few changes in the 81st quorum of Seventies. L. P. Ovesen and Jos. E. Johnson were set apart to fill vacancies in the presidency of said quorum, and a number of young Elders were ordained Seventies and enrolled in his quorum. Elder Young gave pointed instructions on a variety of subjects.

On Sunday morning the statistical report was read. It showed an increase of 257 souls in one year.

Elder Lyman B. Young was the speaker. He made a few remarks in reference to the statistical report, especially Malen Ward, which showed an unusually large number of poor for its size. This proved that there is a kind Bishop and a lively Relief Society there, hence an attraction for the poor to stay there. He then treated at length upon the resurrection.

In the afternoon the sacrament was administered, and the general and stake authorities of the Church were presented and unanimously sustained.

Henry Herriman, one of the First Seven Presidents of Seventies, now residing in Huntington, was the first speaker. He admonished the Saints to use their time, talents and means properly and be subject to the order of the house of God.

Elder Joseph E. Johnson and W. A. Guyman, both returned missionaries from the Southern States, were called on and bore a faithful testimony.

Bishop C. Pulsipher next very briefly expressed his satisfaction with the conference, and thanked all who had participated in it and helped to make it interesting.

President Larsen occupied the remainder of the time, treating upon a variety of matters.

The choir rendered finely, "O Christian Awake." Benediction was pronounced by Elder Elias H. Cox.

O. J. ANDERSON,
Stake Clerk.

EMERY STAKE CONFERENCE.

The Emery Stake quarterly conference convened Saturday, February 18, at Huntington. Present on the stand —the Stake Presidency, Bishops or representatives of the different wards, presidents of quorums. A fair number of Saints attended, although on account of the bad roads, the turnout was not as large as it otherwise would have been.

President Larsen called the meeting to order.

The Huntington choir sang, and the opening prayer was offered by Counselor Justesen.

President Larsen occupied part of the forenoon in speaking of the blessing enjoyed by the people; treated upon general principles for the well-being of the Saints of this Stake. He counseled them to live within their means and avoid contracting debts and unnecessary obligations.

Counselors Seely and Justesen followed in bearing a faithful testimony to the great latter-day work and endorsed the wise and fatherly counsels given by President Larsen. In visiting the Saints in the different wards, they had found everything in good order.

In the afternoon Bishops Henning Olsen, of Castle Dale, Jasper Robertson, of Orangeville, L. S. Beach, of Molen, and Counselor Horsley, of Price, gave reports of their respective wards. The condition of the people was favorable.

President Larsen reported Ferran Ward.

Seymour B. Young, who has just arrived from Salt Lake City, was the next speaker. He treated upon the present condition of the Saints, politically and otherwise.

Bishop C. Pulsipher, of Huntington, and Bishop C. Christensen of Muddy, reported their wards.

In the evening a Priesthood meeting was held. The time was mainly occupied by Seymour B. Young in making a few changes in the 81st quorum of Seventies. L. P. Ovesen and Jos. E. Johnson were set apart to fill vacancies in the presidency of said quorum, and a number of young Elders were ordained Seventies and enrolled in his quorum. Elder Young gave pointed instructions on a variety of subjects.

On Sunday morning the statistical report was read. It showed an increase of 257 souls in one year.

Elder Lyman B. Young was the speaker. He made a few remarks in reference to the statistical report, especially Malen Ward, which showed an unusually large number of poor for its size. This proved that there is a kind Bishop and a lively Relief Society there, hence an attraction for the poor to stay there. He then treated at length upon the resurrection.

In the afternoon the sacrament was administered, and the general and stake authorities of the Church were presented and unanimously sustained.

Henry Herriman, one of the First

Seven Presidents of Seventies, now residing in Huntington, was the first speaker. He admonished the Saints to use their time, talents and means properly and be subject to the order of the house of God.

Elder Joseph E. Johnson and W. A. Guyman, both returned missionaries from the Southern States, were called on and bore a faithful testimony.

Bishop C. Pulsipher next very briefly expressed his satisfaction with the conference, and thanked all who had participated in it and helped to make it interesting.

President Larsen occupied the remainder of the time, treating upon a variety of matters.

The choir rendered finely, "O Christian Awake." Benediction was pronounced by Elder Elias H. Cox.

O. J. ANDERSON,
Stake Clerk.

Utah Enquirer
March 30, 1888

Huntington.

WHAT we need here is a grist mill. At present Castle valley has but two grist mills, both located on Cottonwood Creek. This would be a good investment for some of Provo's capitalists, as we have some beautiful mill sites on our creek. Come on and help to reclaim the wasteplaces and build up the country.

WE have three general mercantile stores in Huntington, the Co-op store, with Job H. Whitney as superintendent, Cox & Co., and M. E. Johnson, all men of business and full of enterprise.

OUR enterprising merchant, D. C. Robbins, has lately shipped into this place a carload of farming machinery, which makes the plowman smile when he contemplates riding on Mr. Sulky.

SEED time has arrived and the people of this locality show by example what they intend to accomplish in the shape of crops this season.

The Court news and local items in the ENQUIRER are read with interest.

SNOD.

MARCH 24, 1888.

Utah Enquirer

April 3, 1888

NOTICE TO CREDITORS.

In the Probate Court of Emery County, Territory of Utah.

In the Matter of the Estate of James Woodward, Deceased.

Notice is hereby given by the undersigned administrator of the Estate of James Woodward, deceased, to the creditors of and all persons having claims against the said deceased, to exhibit them with the necessary vouchers within four months after the first publication of this notice to the said administrators, at their residence in Huntington, Emery County, Utah.

D. C WOODWARD.

Administrator of the Estate of James Woodward, deceased.

Dated March 20, 1888.

Deseret News

April 4, 1888

Orangeville.

We condense a letter from "J. J. J." dated Orangeville, Emery County, March 27th, as follows:

Everything at present is quiet and peaceful. Spring has come and the farmers are busily engaged plowing their land and putting in their crops. There is little or no sickness. The people are and have been blessed in this particular during the past winter. The weather, though not cold, is somewhat changeable.

Our amusements consist chiefly of dances and surprise parties. One of the latter took place on the evening of the 23d inst. The choir took the pleasure of surprising Samuel Jewkes their former leader. Brother Jewkes has been an earnest worker in all his undertakings and is well respected by all who have ever made his acquaintance. He is a thorough musician and a dear lover of music, and has been the leader of the choir at Fountain Green, where he formerly resided, for a great many years; and since his removal to Orangeville, in 1880, was an able leader to the choir here, until through some misfortune his sight was lost. He has been to the hospital undergoing operations to have his sight restored and has been away for three months.

ESTRAY NOTICE.

I HAVE IN MY POSSESSION:

One black HORSE, 2 years old, one hind foot white, branded ⌣⌐ on left thigh.

One sorrel MARE and colt, blaze face, one front and both hind feet white, branded 2 on left thigh, also branded WB combined on left shoulder, about 8 or 10 years old.

One brown HORSE, 3 years old, no brands visible.

If damage and costs on said animals be not paid within ten days from date of this notice they will be sold to the highest cash bidder at my yard at 2 o'clock, on the 3d day of May, 1888.

JOHN E. KING, Poundkeeper.

Dated at Ferron Precinct, Emery County, Utah, this 22d day of April, 1888.

ESTRAY NOTICE

I HAVE IN MY POSSESSION:

One blazed faced sorrel HORSE, three white feet, 3 or 4 years old, brand resembling H on left thigh.

One sorrel HORSE, about 8 years old, with white bunch above the nose, branded ⊓ on both left thigh and left shoulder.

One sorrel HORSE, about 8 years old, white strip in forehead, brand resembling ⌒ on left thigh, also IC on left shoulder.

If damage and costs on said animals be not paid within ten days from date of this notice, they will be sold to the highest cash bidder at my yard, at 2 o'clock, on the 4th day of May, 1888.

Dated at Ferron Precinct, Emery County, Utah, this 23rd day of April, 1888.

JOHN E. KING,
Poundkeeper of said Precinct.

ESTRAY NOTICE.

I HAVE IN MY POSSESSION:

One gray HORSE, about 8 years old, branded resembling O— on left thigh, also ☐ O— J on left hip.

One yellow HORSE, about 8 or 9 years old, branded resembling F O— on left thigh, also —F O— on left thigh.

One blazed face sorrel HORSE, 6 or 7 years old, one glass eye, also one hind foot white, brand resembling ⊓— O— on left thigh.

If damages and costs on said animals be not paid within ten days from date of this notice, they will be sold to the highest cash bidder at my yard, at 2 o'clock, on the 15th day of May, 1888.

Dated at Ferron Precinct, Emery County, Utah, this 4th day of May, 1888.

JOHN E. KING,
Poundkeeper.

From Huntington.

D. C. Robbins, Esq., of Huntington, Emery County, returns this evening to his home. He has been in the city on business. He reports the people of Huntington and vicinity as being well and prosperous. They have just completed a canal fifteen miles long, to take out the waters of Huntington River on farming land at Cleveland, a small settlement near the town. The cost of the ditch was $30,000.

IN CASTLE VALLEY.

A Stranger in that District Describes the Country and People.

Editor of the ENQUIRER.]

Having occasion to make a trip through Castle valley, I thought I would make a short report for publication. On arriving at Price station, on the D. & R. G. W. Ry., we found a few people located on a dry looking bench, a few hundred yards east from the station, with but little signs of life or energy. Isaiah says: "As with the priest, so with the people," and we should judge it was the case here. However, we found Mr. L. M. Olsen, General Superintendent of Emery County Mercantile Establishment, in his usual independent and dignified mood, with a beautiful stock in his line, and preparing for additional buildings.

The establishment of Mr. S. S. Jones, is run by some boys there, who seem to be wide-awake and on the push and rustle.

We also found Mr. D. C. Robins unloading two cars of harvesting machinery. As we continued our journey southward through the county, we met him in every settlement we visited, doing a lively business and making the hearts of many rejoice in furnishing them machinery at reasonable figures. He is endeavoring to open up the resources of the county, and provide ways whereby people can obtain employment He also has large and extensive fields of valuable coal, which will be of great wealth in the near future. Mr. Robins is highly spoken of by the good thinking people of the county, as a man of sterling worth to a community.

In passing from Price, en route for Huntington, we passed to our left, what was explained as the Cleveland flat, an area of country of over thirty thousand acres of choice land, crossing the Cleveland canal, which extends over fifteen miles in length, and has cost now over thirty thousand dollars. Much credit is due the hard laborers, who have completed this great successful canal. It is on this Cleveland flat that many of the Welsh people who have been engaged in the coal mines of Pleasant valley are making homes, and a great benefit has been derived from their aid in furnishing money and supplying material, as well as doing much hard work.

On reaching Huntington we found that beautiful townsite steadily improving, denoting a marked contrast from two years ago when passing through. It is without doubt the attraction of Emery County, and everything bids fair for progress and prosperity. Its natural resources are second to none. And ere long the busy hum of manufactures of many kinds, with railroad facilities will surprise the people who are now living there. The people have secured an agent for the purpose and propose to take steps to develop the great wealth that now lies dormant in that locality.

We are surprised that energetic people who are without homes, are so backward in securing independent and wealthy homes, in so favorable a locality, and when ere long it will be impossible for ethom to get a foot of land without purchasing it at an enormous price.

Continuing to Castle Dale, the present county seat of Emery County, we found several very creditable buildings and marks of industry, but why the county seat is established there is a "stumper" to intelligence, as it is very evident it is located in the wrong place.

Castle Dale is a small place with some two hundred souls or more. It is stretched along the foot of a bench, near Cottonwood Creek, which has not the resources to boom a great town. Orangeville, a nice little hamlet with signs of life and energy, has the appearance of becoming a nice little place. From here we went to Ferron city, from the name expecting to see something for the new county. We found a very creditable meeting-house erected of brick, but not completed, also some good buildings with fair surroundings Their fields look nice. We were surprised to find such a healthy growth of trees, shrubs, and in fact everything, in what is known as "that horrible Castle Valley." We could scarcely give credit to the view before us. The only regret we have to offer is in relation to a feeling of complaint and dissatisfaction. A good pruning and transplanting by a thorough "Master of the Vineyard" would result in the growth and prosperity of the people.

P. J. B. TRAVELER.

Salt Lake Herald
June 19, 1888

JOHN A. DUNCAN, of Ferron City, has been appointed a notary public for Emery County.

Deseret News
June 20, 1888

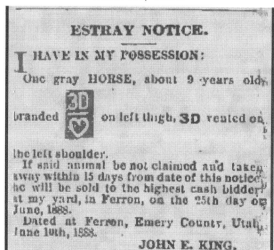

ESTRAY NOTICE.

I HAVE IN MY POSSESSION:

One gray HORSE, about 9 years old, branded 3D on left thigh, 3D vented on the left shoulder.

If said animal be not claimed and taken away within 15 days from date of this notice, he will be sold to the highest cash bidder at my yard, in Ferron, on the 25th day of June, 1888.

Dated at Ferron, Emery County, Utah, June 19th, 1888.

JOHN E. KING,
Poundkeeper.

CASTLE VALLEY.

The Home of the Prairie Dog—Immense Deposits of Coal—Improvements in a Naturally Forbidding Region — Phenomenal Increase of Bees.

HUNTINGTON, Emery County,
July 2, 1888.

Editor Deseret News:

The first account the writer ever remembers concerning Castle Valley was given by some of his comrades in an Indian expedition in 1866, who had followed a party of marauding Red Men into this region, in the hope of recovering from them some of the cattle they had stolen from Sanpete settlements, and they, like the majority of the ancient Israelites sent to spy out the promised land, did not view it with the eye of faith. They gave it a very hard character. They found it so dry and parched that scarcely any vegetation except prickly pears were to be seen, and probably not one of the whole command imagined the valley would ever be inhabited by white men. The country generally has

A MOST FORBIDDING APPEARANCE,

consisting of uneven plains, broken occasionally by deep gullies or washes furrowed out by the streams which course down from the mountains on the west or by cloud-bursts or freshets to which the region has doubtless been subjected for ages. The name of Castle Valley has been derived from the peculiar mountains which surround it, or rather hem it in on the west, and which have a castellated appearance, with their mesa tops and many colored, bare and precipitous sides as they tower up for hundreds of feet, showing the effects of the erosion which as reduced them from what they doubtless once were—an elevated level plain—to what they are today.

THE SOIL

in the valley is light colored and more or less impregnated with mineral, and the early settlers must certainly have had a good deal of faith to ever attempt to raise a crop on it. But it is a great deal better than it looks. The mineral though similar in appearance must be unlike in nature to that with which the soil in the lower portions of many other valleys throughout the Territory abounds. It does not interfere materially with the growth of crops, which when plentifully supplied with water, an element with which, fortunately, the country is bountifully provided, grow rapidly and luxuriantly though the surface of the soil may be almost white with the salts with which it is everywhere more or less impregnated. Lucern yields three good crops during the season and many other crops do as well here as in the lower valleys generally, while trees and vines grow unusually rank. The country is not, however, so well adapted for the raising of small grain as many other valleys are, although much of it is grown here.

Brother Orange Seeley, who is now one of the counselors to President C. G. Larsen of this the Emery Stake, but who was then a resident of Mount Pleasant, Sanpete, was the first to attempt a settlement of this region. He ventured into the south end of the valley with a heard of cattle in 1875 and continued to occupy it as a herd ground and experimented a little at raising a crop until 1878, when a number of others from Sanpete were called to join him in establishing settlements in the valley and contending with the numerous

PRAIRIE DOGS

inhabiting it for a subsistence. It is pretty safe to say that no people but Latter-day Saints would have been likely to succeed in the undertaking, but they have persevered in the midst of all manner of discouragements and will doubtless continue to do so until Castle Valley becomes a fruitful region and a desirable place for a home.

The first village arrived at on entering the valley by train, and the only one located on the line of railway is

PRICE.

The townsite contains, in addition to the railway station and a couple of well-patronized and thriving stores, perhaps not more than twenty-five dwellings and a saloon or two, the invariable adjunct to a railroad town, but the ward includes a great many persons living on ranches up and down Price River and about twenty families who are establishing a settlement seven miles distant, to the south-east, called Wellington. The last mentioned is likely soon to become a ward of itself and an extensive one too, as it has ample room on the broad and comparatively level plain which it occupies to spread out and plenty of water to irrigate with. Price, proper, is likely to develop hereafter faster than it has d ne, as after a long and laborious struggle the residents have at last succeeded in completing their canal and bringing water to their gardens.

Twenty-three miles south of Price, after traversing a rolling prairie which contains scarcely a green thing to break the monotony of its sterility,

HUNTINGTON,

the largest settlement of the county, is reached. The town contains perhaps 150 families, but the ward includes about fifty more, located farther down the stream eastward in what are known as the

LAWRENCE AND CLEVELAND

branches. The latter is destined to

become one of the largest wards of the Stake. It is about seven miles distant from Huntington and much of the soil it includes is as good as can be found in the valley. It has a canal fifteen miles long, just completed this year at a cost of 30,000 which is expected to irrigate 10,000 acres, but should the water prove sufficient, which is very doubtful as the whole of the stream is already utilized, at least 15,000 acres more could be cultivated and irrigated by it. Many of those who have located farms in Cleveland and helped to construct the canal are miners who are employed during a large portion of the year at Schofield. The canal at Huntington does not exceed three miles in length, and yet it cost $20,000. It passes through a tunnel 200 feet long and was was quite difficult to construct in other places owing to the unevenness of the ground.

CASTLE DALE,

the county seat, located ten miles south of Huntington, is a pleasantly situated village containing a grist mill and planing mill and some very well built residences. This settlement is well supplied with water as is also

ORANGEVILLE,

situated on the same stream, about three miles westward. The latter place is well supplied with shade trees, chiefly the native round leafed cottonwood, very similar in appearance to the Canadian poplar, and a very thrifty variety of box elder, which has a fresh looking, green bark and a differently shaped leaf to the box elder trees found in other portions of the Territory. Fruit trees and vines also appear to do well here, as indeed they do in nearly all the settlements of the valley. The writer had the pleasure of attending a Stake conference of the Y. M. M. I. A. in Orangeville and also meetings held under the auspices of the Young Men's Associations in Castle Dale and Huntington. For lack of time he was unable to visit the villages of Ferron, fifteen miles south of Castle Dale, Molen three miles east and Muddy, fifteen miles south of Ferron, but learned that those settlements were in a prosperous condition, the last mentioned being especially noted for the energy and perseverance of its inhabitants in the matter of canal making. The feats they have accomplished in that line are simply marvelous.

No country in the world is better supplied with

COAL MINES

than is Castle Valley, which, however, are as yet undeveloped. Immense veins crop out in numerous places around the mountain sides and in some instances can be traced for miles in the valley. Many veins have been consumed by fire and at least one is said to be still burning, as tradition says it has been for the last thirty years. The attention of eastern capitalists has already been attracted to the coal deposits of this region, which experts declare to be the most extensive they have ever seen, and it is not at all unlikely that the next decade will witness the construction of branch lines of railway into this valley for the development of the mine and a great influx of population. In the meantime the present inhabitants are laying the foundation for permanent prosperity by the development of the agricultural resources of the country and rendering all the more easy to extract the mineral wealth with which it abounds when the time comes to do so.

The climate of Castle Valley which is extremely dry, seems especially adopted for

THE CULTIVATION OF BEES

which seem to do better here than any other part of the Territory. Indeed, it is doubtful if any place in the world excels it in this line. Numerous cases are cited of swarms increasing three or four fold already during the present season with a prospect of their still continuing to multiply and yield honey for some months before the season is over. Thus has this region, originally so uninviting in appearance, its compensating advantages and, through the industry of its inhabitants and under the blessing of the Almighty, is it being made a pleasant abode.   G. C. L.

Emery Items.

Our correspondent at Huntington, Emery County, says:

A few days ago a 17-year-old son of Brother Harrison Herriman met with a severe accident here. He was pushing his shotgun before him through a fence, when the hammer caught, discharging the weapon. The load struck him in the palm of the left hand, making a terrible wound. He was taken to Provo to be cared for.

The streams of water here are lowering faster than they have done for years.

The crops as a general thing look well, and the health of the people is good.

The 24th at Orangeville.

Pioneer Day was celebrated here in grand style. We have never had a finer celebration since Orangeville has been settled, and everybody seemed to vie with each other to make it a complete success, which they accomplished.

There was a salute at day break by a company of musketry under Capt. Ben. F. Jewkes. At sunrise the Stars and stripes were unfurled to the breeze by Marshal of the Day James C. Woodward, while music was played by the Masquerade Band.

At 8 a. m. the people congregated at the bowery to form in procession in the following order:

1—Pioneers of 1847 with Plows, Shovels, Picks, etc.

2—String Band led by R. Johnson.

3—Mormon Battalion on foot.

4—Farmers of 1847 with Farming Implements.

5—Farmers of 1888 improved.

6—Gardeners Club, showing the cereals grown in 1888.

7—Mechanics at work doing scroll sawing and bracket work, by W. P. Stevens and S. H. Cox.

8—The Colliers of Emery County at work, by D. Griffith and R. Griffith, Welsh Colliers.

9—Blacksmiths at work, by Jos. S. Grange.

10—Twelve young men and twelve young ladies on horseback, with matched horses, and with badges representing the twenty-four counties of Utah.

11—Two wagons drawn by one span of horses, the wagons being loaded with fifty-eight of "Utah's Best Crop."

12—Masquerade Band.

The procession marched through the principal streets of the town and back to the bowery.

At 10 a. m. the people assembled at the bowery and the congregation was called to order by Marshal of the Day. Singing by the choir, appropriate to the occasion. Prayer by the chaplain, Samuel Jewkes. The choir then sang another appropriate piece.

Oration by Orator of the day, J. Robertson.

Speech by E. Curtis, in behalf of the Pioneers.

Song, the "Boys of '47," by A. G. Jewkes and chorus.

Song, "The Standard of Zion," by S. H. Cox.

Speech in behalf of the Mormon Battalion, by L. H. Callaway.

Speech by D. Wilkin, a member of the Mormon Battalion.

Music by the string band.

A recitation by Miss Alice Shipp— "The Spanish Warrior."

The choir sang the "United Band of Brethren."

Toasts and sentiments, and the chaplain dismissed the congregation to meet again at 3 p. m. for games and races.

At 3 p. m. we had foot races, horse races, climbing the greased pole, a pig race and other games, all for prizes of different kinds.

The whole concluded with dancing in the evening.

It was one of the most enjoyable times ever experienced here, and nothing to mar the enjoyment of all. J. K. REID.

ORANGEVILLE, July 25, 1888.

Deseret News
August 1, 1888

Celebration at Huntington.

"One of the Boys" writes as follows from Huntington, Emery Co., Utah, July 25th, 1888:

Editor Deseret News:

Yesterday was a gala day for Huntington. We had the best celebration of the Twenty-fourth ever held in Castle Valley. Preparations had been going on for a week previous. We had a fine bowery built, and had it well seated. It was capable of holding about fifteen hundred people, and there were plenty here to fill it. Invitations had been sent out to all the settlements to come and join us. The day was ushered in by the firing of guns and hoisting the national flag. At 8:30 the procession formed headed by the Huntington Brass Band, in the following order: Presiding authorities of wards and quorums; martial band; Mormon Battalion; Pioneers, etc.; Sunday Schools and Primaries; farmers of 1847; farmers of 1888; new machinery, wagons, etc.; carpenters and blacksmith; Brother George Johnson, Sr. with his new printing press, who printed circulars, advertisements, etc., on the march; carriages, buggies, wagons, etc.

We marched round several blocks and then to the bowery, where we went through with a programme that lasted from 10 to 12 a. m., 1:50 to 4 and 9 to 12 p. m. The programme consisted of speeches, recitations, toasts and dialogues. From 4 to 5 p. m. horse racing; 5 to 6, foot racing, in which some prizes were given. Candy was distributed to the children. A new pair of suspenders was given to Brother Wm. M. Black and a nice white silk handkerchief to Mrs. Mary J. Hill, they being the winners among

the old people. From 6 to 7 a dance
for the children was given. From 7 to
8 was choir time; 8 to 9, fireworks of
which there was a grand display, and
the first of the k___ ever given in the
county.

The bowery was well lit up with
lanterns and there was considerable
dancing on the bare ground to the satisfaction and enjoyment of all who
participated.

The committee who got up the programme were Brothers D. C. Robbins,
J. P. Wimmer, Wm. Howard and Sisters Mary Howard and Julia Wakefield. They are pleased to say that
the celebration was a grand success
and return thanks to all who took part.

Salt Lake Herald
August 14, 1888

Castle Valley Chat.

CASTLE VALLEY, August 9, 1888.

To the Editor of THE HERALD.

WE are having very pleasant weather
here the last few days and everything
seems prosperous, but the last week in
July was rather severe.

HEAVY rainstorms and frosts were
quite common, doing considerable
damage to crops, canals and roads, de-
laying travel and causing several acci-
dents, one of which I will mention. Mr.
D. C. Robbins, with two others, while
crossing Miller Creek, (a small stream
generally, but at that time quite a tor-
rent), were thrown from the buggy into
the muddy water breast deep Luckily
for them they escaped uninjured, but
the buggy was considerably broken,
one axle being twisted in two by the
strong current.

ON August 2d several places in the
valley were visited by the most des-
tructive hailstorm known for many
years. It did considerable damage to
field crops and gardens in Orangeville,
Castle Dale and Price, but missed
Huntington entirely.

THE elections passed off quietly with
no opposition to the People's ticket,
although there was considerable
scratching.

YOUR paper is appreciated by those
receiving it.

SUBSCRIBER.

A DISASTROUS STORM.

Hailstones an Inch in Diameter—All Kinds of Crops Destroyed—Bridges Carried Away and other Damage Done by Flood.

ORANGEVILLE, Emery County,
August 3, 1888.

Editor Deseret News:

We had, on the last day of July, as good a prospect for crops of all kinds as I ever saw in this section of country, but today it is quite different. On the 1st and 2nd of August the destroyer came along in the shape of hail stones. The icy chunks measured over an inch in diameter, and cut down our vegetables and vines. Everything that had a leaf on was almost denuded. Cabbage was entirely cut out by the heart; cucumber, melons, squash and all other vines were so destroyed that you could not tell where they had been. Potatoes were uncovered and lay open to sight. The lucern was left denuded of leaves. Before the storm it was ready for cutting the second time. Where there was any fruit it was literally chewed up and beaten off the trees. Even limbs and leaves were cut off the trees. I could not mention anything in the field or garden but what was completely demolished.

The streets were running a flood in every direction; our cañon road is a wreck. It will take thousands of dollars to make good bridges over washes that were good a few days ago. One cannot see a sign of where the bridges were. The timbers are all gone and the washes are cut out from ten to twenty feet wider and deeper. The labor in building up new homes has been great and they have multiplied on our hands in the last few days.

This country is liable to storms at this time of the year, but the late storms were something unprecedented in our history. The damage to crops alone cannot be estimated, but it will foot up into the thousands, and is very discouraging to poor people. Those only who have experience can sense it properly. The season for harvest is over and our yield would have been better than ever before. But our labors have almost came to naught. Even our hay that was in the stack is two-thirds spoiled. But it is said we must acknowledge the hand of God in all things and put up with our trials and losses, whatever they may be.

This morning the sun is shining as brightly as it ever did and there is not a cloud in the sky, so we can take the words of the song:

Tomorrow the sun may be shining,
Although it is cloudy today.

We look for better things in the future and thank God that we have health and are not very easily discouraged. The most of us are young and able bodied. What damage has been done in the other settlements in the county I have not learned yet. Huntington and Cleveland have been disputing over water; it is to be hoped they have got sufficient now, for this season at least, and see that it will be to their interests to divide without bringing extra cost on themselves, and keep good feelings with each other.

E. MERRY ITE.

DEATHS.

LARSEN.—At Castle Dale, August 17, 1888, Sarah Nettie, beloved wife of Joseph Larsen. She was born November 30, 1868, at Manti, Sanpete County, and leaves a husband and one child to mourn her loss. She lived and died a faithful Latter-day Saint.
Utah *Enquirer* please copy.—[COM.

Salt Lake Herald
September 7, 1888

DIED.

LARSEN.—At Castle Dale, Emery County, Sarah Annette Peacock, the beloved wife of Joseph S Larsen, and beautiful and lovely daughter of Judge George Peacock and Sarah B. Peacock.

She was born November 30th, 1868, died August 17th, 1888, after two weeks illness. She was married October 21st, 1887, by Bishop William T. Reid and went through the Manti Temple, May 30th, 1888. Her infant child died on the road from Castle Valley to Manti in its grandmother's arms. She died as she had lived, a faithful Latter-day Saint. Her latest breath was spent in exhorting her husband to be true to his covenants and to keep the faith. She leaves a mother, several brothers and sisters and a host of mourning friends.—[COM.

Utah Enquirer
September 28, 1888

LEGAL NOTICE.

In the Probate Court of Emery County, Territory of Utah.

In the matter of the Estate of James Woodward, deceased.

Notice is hereby given that Don C. Woodward, Administrator of the Estate of James Woodward, deceased, has rendered for settlement and filed in said court his final account of his administration of said Estate, together with the petition for final distribution of said estate to the legal heirs thereof; and that Saturday October 20th, A. D. 1888 at 2 o'clock p. m. of said day, at the Court Room, of said Court, at Castle Dale, Emery County, has been appointed the time and place, by said Court, for the settlement of said account and the hearing of said petition, at which time and place any person interested may appear and show cause, if any there be, why said account should not be settled and approved, and said petition be granted.

    Witness my hand and the Seal
[SEAL]   of said Court at Castle Dale, this
    1st day of Sept., A. D 1888
         W. W. CRAWFORD.
           Probate Clerk.

Ogden Standard
November 17, 1888

A PAINFUL ACCIDENT.

George Goddard, William Willis and Jas. McNiven Seriously Hurt.

The many friends of the brethren named above will regret to hear of the mishap detailed in a letter dated Nov. 14th, from our Huntington correspondent, Wm. Howard:

"Elders George Goddard and William Willis, of Salt Lake City, left there on Saturday morning, the 10th inst., to visit Emery Stake, in behalf of our Sunday schools, also to visit our quarterly conference, which convened on Sunday and Monday, the 11th and 12th, at Ferron. Arrangements had been made for these brethren to leave Price with the mail that travels through the county, but owing to the train being late they failed to reach Price in time, so had to remain there over night. Brother James McNiven, of Huntsville, was at Price, and he kindly proffered to bring the brethren over to Huntington.

"Everything went well with them on Sunday morning until nearly half way to Huntington, when they met with a serious accident. At one point on the road there is a very steep hill to go down. Just as they had started down this hill the bridles of the team broke and Brother McNiven having no control over the horses, the latter ran away, and, making a quick turn on the side of the hill, the wagon turned over, throwing the party of brethren out on a very rough place that was more or less covered with rock and boulders.

"Brother Goddard was severely bruised on the right shoulder and the left side of his head, and had one rib broken, and lay insensible for a few moments. Brother Willis was hurt very badly on his left hip and otherwise severely hurt. Brother McNiven was also badly hurt.

"After the brethren had taken care of themselves as best they could, Brother John James, of Orangeville, came along and brought them to Huntington, a distance of twelve miles. It was a very painful ride, but the brethren stood it first-rate. They were taken to Brother Elias Cox's, and have there been taken care of by many kind friends who came to see them, and who attended to them night and day. We are now glad to say that at present they are improving very fast, and expect to be able to leave for home in a few days."—Deseret News, Nov. 15.

GEORGE GODDARD and William Willes, of this city, and James McNiven, of Huntington, met with a painful accident on Sunday morning last, in Emery Country. They were on their way to Huntington by private conveyance, and in going down a steep hill the bridles of the team broke and the horses ran away, throwing all the occupants out. Mr. Goddard was badly bruised on the right shoulder and the left side of the head, in addition to a broken rib, while Messrs. Willes and McNiven were also badly bruised. At last accounts all were doing well and expected to leave for home in a few days.

VISIT TO EMERY STAKE.

Brothers Goddard and Willes Rapidly Recovering.

HUNTINGTON, Emery Co.,
Nov. 17, 1888.

Editor Deseret News:

Since the communication of your correspondent, which left here on the 14th, relative to our sad misfortune, we deem it not only a duty we owe to our many friends, but a pleasure to record the wonderful power of God, our Heavenly Father, in so rapidly restoring the shattered tabernacles of two of His fragile servants. Through the anointing of oil and the prayer of faith, we have been the recipients of God's blessings in a marvelous degree, that not only makes our own hearts rejoice, but fills our many ministering friends with astonishment and gratitude. The minor bruises and scratches have nearly all disappeared, and the more serious injuries, which caused us the most acute pain and helplessness are rapidly giving way.

One week ago this morning we left our homes and the "city we love so well," on an official visit to this Stake of Zion. We traveled on the Utah Central as far as Springville, and after partaking of the hospitality of Bishop Packard and family, were detained four hours on account of an accident on the D. & R. G. This delay made it about 10 o'clock p.m. when we arrived at Price, Emery County. We then wended our way to Elder Lars M. Olsen's house. He having gone to conference to be held at Ferron, 50 miles distant, his house was left in charge of a housekeeper, who had retired to rest.

We were soon ensconced in a warm room, and also refreshed in our inner man. After a good night's rest, and an early breakfast we looked around for a conveyance to take us to Huntington, and thence to Ferron, where the quarterly conference was held. We found two teams about to start, one owned by Brother Howard, son of William Howard of Salt Lake City, and the other by Brother McNiven. Either of them offered to take us, but one of Brother Howard's horses being sick, it was deemed wisdom to accept the kind offer of the latter, and after carefully wrapping us up in blankets and quilts, to keep us warm, we started on our journey of twenty-three miles. We shall never forget the careful and unselfish treatment we received at his hands. On reaching the verge of that steep and ever to be remembered descent, he got out of the wagon and cautiously examined the same before starting down, little dreaming what an experience awaited him that had never transpired with him before, for we had no sooner passed the brow of the hill, his horses being held with a tight grip, than one of the bits broke in the mouth of one of the horses, and the ring also on the other bit, thus loosening their head gear, and away they went, turning over the wagon and all its contents.

The result of that fearful occurrence having been stated in a previous communication, we will simply say that we feel ourselves so much improved that we anticipate with the help of the Lord a glorious time tomorrow (Sunday) in meeting with the children in their Sunday school, and also with the Saints of Huntington in their general assemblies. It is difficult for us to imagine any circumstance to arise that could draw deeper on the sympathy and the most unremitting attention and generosity of the Saints of Huntington. Long will be cherished in our memories their love and tender regard towards us.

On Thursday night our room was literally besieged with about 20 of the sweet singers of Israel, making over 30 occupants for over two hours. After their beautiful serenade, some remarks were called for, and made by one whose name is attached to this letter. It was a soul stirring time, and we are here in the midst of our friends, resting and taking care of ourselves. We are glad and thankful to the Lord that we came to Emery County, and though it is our first, we sincerely hope and believe it will not be our last visit.

We labor in the interest of the Sunday Schools of Zion; it is our meat and our drink and has been for many years, and going around from school to school, to offer a few words of encouragement to both children and teachers, and to give timely suggestions to Stake and local superintendents, and sometimes an occasional song, all backed up by the blessing of the Lord, fills our cup of rejoicing.

Should no unforeseen circumstance arise, we may possibly leave here on Monday, travel as far as Price, and on Tuesday afternoon start for home per the D. & R. G. as far as Springville, then per the Utah Central to Salt Lake City, on Wednesday.

GEORGE GODDARD,
WM. WILLES.

DESERET NEWS' AGENTS.

The following are the Authorized Agents for the DESERET NEWS in their respective towns:—

A. Allen, Rockland Creek, via American Falls, I
S. H. Higginbotham, Nacleyville, American Falls
American Fork Co-op.......American Fork
William Grant...............American Fork
H. S. Lewis.........Albion, Cassia Co., Idaho
A. Marsh. ....Alpine
J. F. Hunter. ....Alma, Weber Co., Utah
James Bowns.....................Alma
S. F. Heywood....Alpine, Apache Co., Arizona
C. C. Bartlett...............Ashley, Uintah Co
H. Van Leuven....................Aurora
Brigham City Co-op............Brigham City
W. Hulme ....Bloomington, Idaho
Bear River Co-op............Bear River City
E. Bunker, jun...........Bunkerville, Nevada
D. B. Brinton.................Brinton
T? Rogers. ....Benson
Beaver Co-op...................Beaver
C. C. Burr.....................Burrville
L. H. Redd, Jun................Bluff City
R. W. Heyborne................Cedar City
Jacob G. Bigler..Central, Graham Co., Ariz.
Jas. Kirkham..............Cedar Valley
William Hodson...............Coalville
Jasper C. Peterson.............Castle Dale
H. N. Howell............Clifton, Idaho
Co-op. Store...............Charleston
L. D. Morrill.....Circleville, Piute Co., Utah
J. A. Eldredge, Chesterfield, Bingham Co., Id
John Jardine...............Clarkston
R. R. Allred..................Chester
Joel Parrish..................Centerville
H. J. McCullough........Coyote, Garfield Co
J. C. Davey..................Deseyville
James Jenson.................Draper
Joshua Bennett................Deseret

Jas. Thomas, Eagle Rock, Bingham Co., Idaho
W. M. Parker.....Egin, Bingham Co., Idaho
D. H. Ward..........Elba, Cassia Co., Idaho
James A. Thompson.....................Eden
R. Wickle..............................Echo
James Brown............Evanston, Wyoming
S. Sorensen...........................Elsinore
R. P. Allen.........................Escalant
Ephraim Co-op.......................Ephraim
P. Rasmussen.....Ephraim, Conejos Co., Colo
Mrs. S. L. Goss ....Eureka, Juab Co
W. Taylor, jun........Ferron, Emery County
J. L. Robinson.......................Fillmore
Co-op. Store.................Franklin, Idaho
H. W. Sanderson....................Fairview
W. J. Underwood...Fairview, Oneida Co., Id
R. R. Lewellyn..............Fountain Green
H. Snyder ....Fairfield, Utah Co
John Bartholomew....................Fayette
L. H. Kennard....................Farmington
A. J. Allred.............Fremont, Piute Co
J. Stock..........................Fish Haven
Gunnison Co-op.....................Gunnison
W. Foote............................Glendale
A. Hepler...........................Glenwood
C. W. Peck....Gentile Valley, Oneida Co., Id
B. F. Cook.......................Grouse Creek
J. B. Johnson......................Goshen
T. Williams......................Grantsville
B. H. Allred.....................Garden City
H. A. Lewis.......................Georgetown
Seth Johnson.......Georgetown, Garfield Co
M. Jeffs..........................Heber City
A. Hatch & Co.....................Heber City
H. W. Manning..................Hooper City
J. G. Crane........................Herriman
Charles Pulsipher.................Huntington
James A. Daines...................Hyde Park
C. Wood...............................Holden
B. H. Tolman......................Honeyville
James Unsworth.......................Hyrum
Robert Jones.........................Hennefer

Peter Later................................Harrisville
W. D. Pace........................ ......Harmony
W. Feit................................Huntsville
T. S. Terry............................Hebron
F. M. Christensen............ .....Inverury
Hy. Seeley............................Indianola
G. A. Murdock......................Joseph City
John Morrill..........................Junction
Joseph Warr...... ....Kamas
Kanab Co-op..........................Kanab
Willard Bishop..... ....Kaysville
A. B. Griffin.............. ....Kanarra
A. C. Nelsen..........................Koosharem
A. Nadauld............................Kanosh
S. J. Allen............................Lewiston
William Yates........................Lehi
George Morrison......................Leamington
Joseph Irwin..........................Laketown
C. B. Robbins........................Logan
J. W. Shepherd......................Levan
B. Y. McMullen......................Leeds
Barton & Co..........................Layton
S. C. Berthelsen....................Lajara, Col
J. T. Lazenby............Lou, Piute Co
R. F. Jard.......Louisville, Bingham Co., I
T. E. Jones..., Lehi, Maricopa Co., Arizona
Co-op. Store............Lake Shore, Utah Co
John King............................Millville
A. N. Rosenbaum......................Mink Creek
Ed. Burgoyne................Montpelier, Idaho
F. E. Jones................Malad, Idaho
D. Van Wagenen......................Midway
N. R. Peterson......................Manti
Mendon Co-op...... ....Mendon
J. H. Stott............................Moroni
Lauritz Larson ....Mount Pleasant
W. H. Stott...... ....Meadow
M. Christensen............Manassa, Colorado
John Williams........................Mayfield
Casper Christiansen....Muddy, Emery County
W. A. Pierce............Moab, Emery County
W. N. Stevens...Menan, Bingham Co., Idaho
S. Simonsen..........................Monroe

William Wood, sen....................Minersville
W. J. Jolly........ ....Mt Carmel
P C. Jensen..........................Mantua
J. S. Fones..........................Mona
R. Fry................................Morgan City
John Morgan........Mill Creek, S. L. County
J. H. Barker..........................Newton
John Neff................Neff's, Salt Lake Co
L. A. Bailey..........................Nephi
J. W. Rex............................North Ogden
C. A. North..........North, S. L. County
Lorenzo Brown, Nutrioso, Apache Co., Arizona
Jos. A. Lyman........................Oak Creek
Thomas Chamberlein..................Orderville
C. Crowshaw..................Oxford, Idaho
Joseph Hall..........................Ogden
J. K. Reid............................Orangeville
P. M. Larsen............Oneida City, Idaho
Oakley Co-op..................Ockley, Idaho
H. M. Taylor....Olio, Rio Arriba Co., N. M
J. W. Crosby.. Overton, Lincoln Co., Nevada
A. M. Findlay........................Panacca, Nevada
J. W. Crosby..........................Panguitch
H. Florence..........................Porterville
W. H. Branch.......Price, Emery Co., Utah
J. H. Nuttall....Pima, Graham Co., Arizona
Paris Co-op,..........................Paris, Idaho
J. F. Maddison......................Providence
Gladys Coombs........................Payson
J. W. Bean............................Provo
Parowan Co-op........................Parowan
David Edwards........................Paragoonah
C. E. L. Jackson......................Park Valley
Pleasant Grove Co-op........Pleasant Grove
James H. Hess.......Plymouth, Box Elder Co
O. D. Gibbs............................Paradise
William Geddes......................Plain City
W. C. Parkinson............Preston, Idaho
J. H. Harrison......................Pinto
J. A. Marchant......................Peoa
N. W. Anderson......................Peterson
R. B. Gardner........................Pine Valley
G. M. Pace..........................Park City

Geo. A. Cordon...................Rigby, Idaho
James Woolf........Riverdale, Oneida Co., Id
R. G. Jolley............Ranch P. O., Kane Co
H. P. Miller.......................Richfield
T. Gibbons.....................Rockport
M. W. Merrill, Jr.......................Richmond
R. M. Kinnon.......................Randolph
C. N. Smith.......................Rockville
W. Paul..................Rexburg, Idaho
John Johnson.......................Redmond
J. L. Peacock.......................Stirling
Lars Mortensen...Sanford, Conejos Co., Colo
William Bramall.......................Springville
Spanish Fork Co-op...........Spanish Fork
G. H. Crosby, Springerville, Apache Co., Ariz
Smithfield Co-op.......................Smithfield
Wm. McFadyen.......................Salina
L. Suhrke...............Soda Springs, Idaho
John Holt.......................South Jordan
Co-op. Store.......................Scipio
Wm. M. Allred ....St. Charles Idaho
F. R. Snow.......................St. George
J. Evans.......................Samaria, Idaho
Rush Valley Co-op.........St. John's, Utah
J. McRae...St. Davids, Cochise Co., Arizona
A. Engberg.......................Salem
Santaquin Co-op.......................Santaquin
T. J. Parmley...........Scofield, Emery Co
J. N. Smith.......................Snowflake, Arizona
A. Goodliffe.......................Snowville
George Marriott.......................Sandy
Annie M. Dalley.......................Summit
John McLaws...............St. Joseph, Arizona
Joseph Crosby...............St. Johns, Arizona
R. Blain.......................Spring City
T. Gottfredson.......................Sigurd
Jesse M. Baker...............Teton, Idaho
James Lewis...............Taylor, Arizona
F. W. Young.......................Teasdale
E. W. Wade.......Tyner P. O., Box Elder Co
G. W. Stringham.......................Thurber
J. Percival Ltt.......................Thatcher
Tooele Co-op.......................Tooele

J. B. Jardine......Trenton, Cache Co., Utah
John Batty.......................Toquerville
Charles Denney.......................Union
A. J. Workman.......................Virgin City
J. C. Sharp.......................Vernon
J. D. Gibbs.......................West Portage
W. Crook.......................Wanship
Wellsville Co-op.......................Wellsville
H. Goff.......................West Jordan
W. E. Nuttall.......................Wallsburg
J. F. Moon......Woodland, Summit Co., Utah
G. M. Crawford.......................Washington
T. W. Brewerton.......................Willard
A. E. Eastman......Woodruff, Rich Co. Utah
J. E. Rees.......................White
J. H. Clark.......................Weston, Idaho
J. C. Owen....Woodruff, Apache Co., Arizona
Geo. Passey.......................Eenos Arizona

EMERY STAKE.

General Condition.—Items of Conference News.

HUNTINGTON, Emery Co.,
Utah, Nov. 24. 1888.

Editor Deseret News:

The people of Emery County in general, and Huntington in particular, so far as my knowledge goes, have been greatly blessed the past season in their labors. Crops have been very good; there has been enough grain raised to supply the wants of the people until next harvest, provided they do not let some contractor buy it up and ship it out of the country, which has been the case several times in the past.

The once dried up and barren benches along the streams of this valley have greatly changed in the last few years. Where you would once find a patch of prickly pears and once in a while a sickly looking bunch of salt weed, you will now find young orchards, nice gardens, lucern patches and fields of grain. Instead of paying eight to ten dollars for a load of dry wheat straw, which I had to pay eight years ago when I first came here, you can get all the good lucerne hay you want for that price. By the looks of the nice haystacks you can see at nearly every house as you pass through the settlements, one would think this a splendid hay country; and I think it is as good a lucern hay country as there is in Utah. I do not know how it is in other settlements, but I know the tithing yard in Huntington had to be enlarged to hold the hay donated by the people of this place.

We were very glad to hear of the safe return home of Brothers Goddard and Willes, who had such a sad experience in their late visit to us; and we feel very thankful for their good, kind counsel and the advice they gave before leaving us. The result is there are masons and laborers going to work at a foundation, teams hauling rock and sand, others teams and men getting ready to go to the cañons for lumber and shingles, and we expect, if the present good intentions do not change, to have a nice large hall built, where the people can meet to worship God or otherwise enjoy themselves.

It is well known, by a few at least, outside of our county, and I guess by nearly all in it, that there has not been the best of feeling among some of the brethren here for the last few years. But about six weeks ago a couple of peacemakers from Salt Lake City came down here and held several meetings with us. Where we needed reproof we got it; where we needed fatherly advice and good council, we got them; where those who took a prominent part, either in permitting wrong or showing it up, had faults, they were shown to them; and while the brethren were here several acknowledged their faults and made them right, and the result is, so far as I am concerned, and I think I speak the feelings of a large majority, there is a better feeling existing in Emery Stake now than there has been for a long time; and I hope it will continue to be so. This feeling was very prominently shown at our late quarterly conference, for there was not one contrary vote to any Stake or Ward officer.

At the request of Brother O. J. Anderson, the Stake clerk, who was with us at conference, but who is now on a visit to the "pen", I will send you a few items of conference news.

The quarterly conference convened at Ferron at the appointed time. There was present of the Stake presidency, C. G. Larson and Orange Seeley, and the Bishop of every ward in the Stake, most of the High Council, and other leading men of the county. The reports of the Bishops were very favorable, showing in most instances an increase of faith and good works among the people; and also showing that our different quorums and Sunday schools were in good running order.

On Sunday evening there was a general Priesthood meeting, at which some very good counsel and instruction were given.

On Monday morning at 8 o'clock there was a meeting of the High Council to transact some business for the Stake, Brother Justison, President Larsen's second counselor, was with us on Monday, and owing to his business interests being in other places, which called him away most of his time he felt that he could not do justice to the office he held. He therefore offered his resignation, and it was accepted, and he was honorably released.

There was quite a number of speakers during conference, and all seemed to be imbued with a good spirit, as the counsel and instructions given were all of the best kind. President Larson spoke several times during conference and the council. The instruction and advice he gave were very good and appreciated by all who heard him. Take it all through, I think it was as good a conference as was ever held in Emery Stake.

Yours very respectfully,

W. H.

Salt Lake Herald
December 22, 1888

A. TUTTLE was commissioned yesterday a constable of Orangeville.

Utah Enquirer
March 12, 1889

TO BUILD TO EMERY CO.

The Utah Central to Run a Branch Line From Juab.

It is stated on good authority, that some very important business is to be transacted at the stockholders' meeting of the Utah Central Railroad Company to be held Saturday week. Besides the amending of the articles of association to permit of the company extending its southern terminus to the western line of the Territory of Utah, with a view to building a line to the coast, steps will be taken to construct a branch line from Juab to some point in Emery County, presumably either Huntington or Castle Dale. The company intends doing some extensive building, and we can hardly see where they could do it to better advantage than in this latter connection.

Another item of business to be done at this meeting will be that of changing the name of the company to some term that will convey more forcibly its extensive operations. Besides this the capital stock will be increased, and the directory enlarged.

SUICIDE AT PRICE.

Mat. Simmons Shoots Himself.

HE IS FOUND GULTY OF STEALING. CATTLE,

And, Failing to Secure Bondsmen, Takes His Life.

The news has reached us of the suicide of Mat Simmons, at Price, Wednesday morning. It seems that Simmons had stolen a steer, killed it, sold part of the meat, and eat the balance in his family. Then he took the hide, and after cutting out the brands, sold it to Orange Seely, at Castle Dale, Emery county. Seely inspected the hide, and finding the brands gone, became suspicious; but he paid Simmons his price, and said nothing. After Simmons had gone, Seely referred the matter to Mr. Ballenger, the prosecuting attorney of Emery county, who identified the hide as that belonging to an animal of his. A warrant for the arrest of Simmons followed, and he was arrested. On Tuesday Simmons had an examination at Price, found guilty, and bound over to await the action of the grand jury on a charge of grand larceny. He started out to secure bondsmen, but was unsuccessful. He was then taken to a log house, near the depot, for imprisonment. When the attention of the sheriff was turned from

him, he put two holes through his breast, just above the heart. He lived but fifteen minutes. An inquest was held in the afternoon, and a verdict in accordance with these facts was rendered. Simmons leaves a wife and six children.

Since the above was in type, "Emery," writing from Price, on Wednesday, sends us a more detailed account of the circumstances leading to the unhappy affair. He says:

A short time ago Matthew Simmons, of this place, went to the Seely grist mill, at Castle Dale, to procure some flour. He made payment for the same with two hides, a steer hide and a calf hide. They were frozen badly and crumpled up. Mr. Seely, at the time of purchase, felt impressed that there was "a screw lose," and he spread open slightly the frozen hide, and discovered a large hole in one side. He thereupon soaked it and stretched it out. Upon close examination he detected a brand on the hide which he knew belonged to A. Ballenger, our county prosecuting attorney. The hide was thereupon sent by stage to Price. This lead to the arrest of Simmons, and an examination, at which sufficient evidence was adduced to bind him over to await the action of the grand jury. Sheriff Loveless was very lenient with Simmons all through the affair. On Tuesday Simmons, as he thought, had secured bondsmen, and so reported to Sheriff Loveless, upon which he was permitted to go home and stay with his family. The result was, however, that the bonds had been signed on conditions, those conditions being that Simmons' relatives should secure the requisite bondsmen, which they declined to do.

The sheriff on learning these facts proceeded to Simmons' farm four miles down Price river, from Price station. When he got there he found that Simmons had started up. He then returned and soon overtook Simmons, who appeared to be in good spirits. On arriving at Price station, Simmons enquired of Mr. Davidson, why he refused to go on his bonds. Mr. Davidson replied, "When your friends go back on you, you cannot expect strangers to go your bonds." Simmons thereupon said that he would go and see Messrs. Mulholland & Conway, and asked the sheriff to permit him to go up to Mr. Noyses, where Mr. Conway, was at work. The sheriff granted permission, on starting out, Simmons met Mulholland, and asked him to go his bonds. Mulholland kindly declined, Simmons then made excuse to see Mr. Conway. When near Noyses' house, he tied his horse, and entered the front door. There was a gun standing in the corner of the house and with this instrument he fired two shots into his left breast, death resulting soon afterwards. An inquest was held before E. W. McIntire, J. P., the following being the verdict:

TERRITORY OF UTAH, }
  COUNTY OF EMERY, } ss.
    PRECINCT OF PRICE. }

    An inquest held at Price, in Price Precinct, County of Emery and Territory of Utah, on the 13th day of March, A. D., 1889, before E. W. McIntire, Justice of the Peace of said Precinct, upon the body of Mathew Simmons, there lying dead, by the jurors whose names are hereunto subscribed. The said jurors upon their oath do say that he came to his death by two (2) gun-shot wounds in the left breast; administered by a gun in his own hands.

    In testimony whereof the said jurors have hereunto set their hands the day and year aforesaid.

C. H. VALENTINE,
FRED. E. GRAMES.
H. S. LOVELESS.

    Subscribed and sworn to before me this 13th day of March, A. D, 1889.

E. W. McINTIRE.

Justice of the Peace.

    It is earnestly believed that had those who should have been interested in Mr. Simmons' interest, shown a willingness to secure his bonds, this sad affair would have been avoided. Mr. Simmons was 38 years old, and was a large, well-made, powerful man. He leaves a wife and five children. The sympathy of the community is with the bereaved family.

SHERIFF H. S. LOVELESS and Oliver Hansen came in from Huntington, Emery county, yesterday, bringing with them an unfortunate man who has recently gone insane. His name is S. W. Makleprang, and he lost his reason about two weeks ago. No particular reason can be assigned for his unfortunate condition, other than the fact that his mind is given to deep study on religious subjects. Mr. Mackleprang is a large, powerfully built man. It is a pitiful sight to behold him now—a mental wreck. Nine years ago he was similarly effected for about four months, but his condition then was not as bad as now. Sheriff Loveless says he is a good citizen, an honest and industaious man. He leaves at home a wife and ten children in indigent circumstances, which makes the case more pathetic. The asylum board of examination met yesterday afternoon and committed him to the asylum.—*Provo American.*

Salt Lake Herald
April 10, 1889

THAT DRAWING.

An Ogden Man Draws Prize Number One.

THE MUSCATINE LOT GOES NORTH.

The 1,250 Prizes are Distributed With Accuracy and Despatch—List of the Most Valuable.

At 12 o'clock noon yesterday, the hour set for the long advertised distribution of prizes to subscribers of the SEMI-WEEKLY HERALD, the Salt Lake theatre was thrown open and fully four hundred persons assembled to witness the *modus operandi* of the distribution and to satisfy themselves on the burning question as to whether or not their names were among the lucky numbers. The great bulk of the subscribers were not present, being content to wait for the announcement in the HERALD, and satisfied from the manner in which the previous drawing had been conducted that everything would be fair and equitable.

Promptly on the stroke of 12, R. W. Sloan, business manager of THE HERALD, called the assemblage to order, and announced that the drawing would be placed in the hands of the subscribers themselves; that clerks from THE HERALD counting rooms were on hand with the books, stubs, and duplicate numbers, and that the company were ready to satisfy the subscribers that every receipt had its proper duplicate number in the pile of checks which lay on the table, and that none but numbers which had been issued were included in the dupli-cates. He suggested that a committee of five be appointed to make an investigation of the books, checks and stubs. A motion to this effect was immediately made and carried, and the following nominations were made from various parts of the house and unanimously sustained:

Bishop Joseph Kimball, Meadowville.
Judge J. Z. Stewart, Logan.
E. H. Pierce, Brigham city.
Jedediah Earl, Honeyville.
George E. Blair, Salt Lake.

The committee then retired with the books to the green room of the theatre, and during their absence Mr. Sloan announced that the number of SEMI-WEEKLY subscribers who had availed themselves of the premium offers, was 2,729, which made a trifle less than one prize to every two sub-scriders; a number of questions were asked from the audience, to all of which Mr. Sloan made answer, explaining fully the methods proposed to be employed, but first submitting all suggestions for the approval of the assemblage.

After being out fifteen minutes the committee returned and reported that they had examined the books, and were satisfied that everything was "straight and regular," and that every number issued had its duplicate in the pile of checks. Their report was approved on motion, and the 2,729 checks were emptied into a glass wheel which stood on a table in the centre of the stage. Miss Tessie Clawson was then selected from the audience to draw the first 100 numbers from the wheel, after which a second young lady, Miss Jacobs, was selected, in order that the drawing might be expedited.

The first number was drawn from the wheel at 12:30 exactly; the 1,250th at 3:30 exactly, 545 numbers being drawn in the last hour. There was the most wrapt attention to the close, and on every hand it was conceded that everything had been conducted in a speedy, fair and business like manner.

The names of the parties drawing the first sixty-nine prizes (ending the $3.50 valuations), are given below. The full list of the 1,250 fortunate ones will appear in the DAILY this week, and complete in Saturday's SEMI. Parties having drawn prizes are requested to send for them at once. All prizes forwarded by THE HERALD go at owner's risk and expense.

No. 902—W. W. Tracy, Ogden, one city lot, Muscatine subdivision; $300.

No. 2786—Dilbert Allred, Lehi, one thoroughbred Holstein bull, sire Jacob Witts Bardolph; dam, Suade; $200.

No. 2887—John W. Jones, Schofield, one Kimball organ; $110.

No. 967—Mrs. A. Hoagland, city, one thoroughbred Jersey heifer, from Hon. F. Armstrong's herd; $100.

No. 403—John Andrews, Richmond, one plan for country home and surroundings, by R. Kletting, architect; $100.

No. 1521—Ole K. Olsen, Ephraim, one acre in Rollin P. Saxe & Co.'s Prospect Park Subdivision of Ogden; $80.

No. 1291—L. Bean, Richfield, one Walter A. Wood Mower; $75.

No. 2425—T. R. Bess, North, one Gay Cart; $55.

No. 1935—J. Barlow, Bountiful, one Jay-Eye-See Sulky Plow; $55.

No. 2469—Rufus Patrick, Tooele, one Imperial Sulky Plow; $55.

No. 1183—F. Merrill, Logan, one lot Fruit, Shade and Flowering Trees; $50.

No. 554—William P. Guerney, Lehi, one Sewing Machine; $40.

No. 393—S. M. Pack, Kamas, one Sewing Machine; $40.

No. 1151—E. Stephenson, North, one Sewing Machine; $40.

No. 2853—John Duncan, Centerville, one Sewing Machine; $40.

No. 2848—George Miller, Union, one Sewing Machine; $40.

No. 450—Charles Abbott, Nephi, one Bedroom Set; $40.

No. 2520—P. Knudsen, Brigham, one fine New York Professional Guitar; $35.

No. 1883—B. A. Hendricks, Lewiston, one double bedroom lounge; $32.

No. 2376—A. Tuttle, jr., Orangeville, one lot ornamental trees; $30.

No. 1274—W. S. Reed, jr., Ogden, one set (8 vols.) Chambers' encyclopedia; $30.

No. 1231—A. Woolf, Hyde Park, one Oliver chilled walking plow, hand painted; $25.

No. 551—Milo Brown, Coalville, one baby carriage; $25.

No. 2705—Lars Hansen, Oasis, 100 pounds Alaroma coffee; $25.

No. 2325—Richard Hunter, Schofield, one suit home made clothes; $25.

No. 2723—Mrs. L. Frieze, city, one Franklin faultless heating stove; $22.

No. 2406—Thomas Garn, Coalville, one fine steel engraving, framed; subject, "Consolation;" $20.

No. 806—William Wood, Minersville, one fine steel engraving framed—subject, "The Mother's Joy;" $20.

No. 2115—James Howells, Tooele, one fine steel engraving framed—subject, "Foxes Playing;" $20.

No. 1240—C. E. Smith, Payson, one fine steel engraving framed—subject, "The Holiday;" $20.

No. 2262—Theodore Rogers, Deseret, one lot ornamental trees; $20.

No. 1866—Samuel Young, Brigham, one fine saratoga trunk; $20.

No. 610—William Barton, Kaysville, one show case; $20.

No. 2558—Jens Madsen, Honeyville, three volumes Popular Science Monthly (18 numbers) bound; $15.

No. 2403—B. Simmons, Spanish Fork, one pair hunting boots; $15.

No. 853—Fred Arbon, Grantsville, one lot of ornamental trees; $15.

No. 781—William Osborn, Spring City— 500 pounds Peerless flour; $15.

No. 2810—Miss A. Ballantyne, Ogden, one box groceries; $10.

No. 1957—John E. Barker, Kaysville, one lot ornamental trees; $10.

No. 2770—J. H. Whitlock, Mayfield, two volumes of Popular Science Monthly (12 numbers) bound; $10.

No. 1513—D. W. Sorenson, Ephraim, two volumes Popular Science Monthly (12 numbers) bound; $10.

No. 499—P. J. Stewart, Benjamin, two volumes Popular Science Monthly (12 numbers) bound; $10.

No. 2013—A. Pierce, Springville, two volumes Popular Science Monthly (12 numbers) bound; $10.

No. 1354—W. Sorensen, Park city, one year's subscription to the SALT LAKE DAILY HERALD; $10,

No. 2580—L. N. Boothe, Honeyville, one year's subscription to the SALT LAKE DAILY HERALD; $10.

No. 414—Joseph Richardson, Smithfield, one year's subscription to SALT LAKE DAILY HERALD; $10.

No. 2318—Mrs. A. Morgan, Schofield, three volumes supplement Popular Science Monthly (fifteen numbers) bound; $9.

No. 1815—Thomas Bridge, Tyner, one pair calfskin boots; $9.

No. 2441—W. F. Moss, Lake Point, one copy Bradbury's Encyclopedia of Practical Information; $8.

No. 125—F. Walters, Tooele, one upholstered chair; $7.50.

No. 2055—Annie Ennis, Draper, one full dress pattern, henrietta cloth; $7.50.

No. 1614—Sol Hale, Jr., Lago, one set (five volumes) Macaulay's History of England; $7.50.

No. 654—Rufus Garner, Uintah, one set (five volumes) Macaulay's History of England; $7.50.

No. 2853—Joseph S. Douglas, Payson, one set (five volumes) Macaulay's History of England; $7.50.

No. 11—P. A. Droubay, Tooele, one set (five volumes) Macaulay's History of England; $7.50.

No. 557—D Cook, Layton, one set (five volumes) Macaulay's History of England; $7.50.

No. 2673—John H. Dixon, Payson, one set (five volumes) Macaulay's History of England; $7.50.

No. 42—T. Passey, Montpelier, one set (five volumes) Macaulay's History of England; $7.50.

No. 1001—Charles A. Cox, Manti, one set (five volumes) Macaulay's History of England; $7.50.

No. 354—John Corbridge, Franklin, one set (five volumes) Macaulay's History of England; $7.50.

No. 2626—C. W. J. Hecker, Pleasant Grove, one set (five volumes) Macaulay's History of England; $7.50.

No. 896—John L. Wilson, Ogden, one set glassware, eight pieces; $6.

No. 1385—Mrs. E. P. Snider, Park city, one volume "Life of Joseph Smith," bound in morocco and gilt, by George Q. Cannon; $6.

No. 503—Jos. Y. Boise, Oxford, one volumn "Life of Joseph Smith," bound in leather; $5.

No. 754—O. D. Merrill, Richmond, one copy "The World's Great Nations"; $5.

No. 87—Chas. Windley, St. Charles, one volume "Tullidge's History of Salt Lake city"; $5.

No. 1396—Tork E. Torkenson, city, one barrel Excelsior flour; $5.

No. 501—B. A. Rund, Lago, Gentile valley, one volume "Life of Joseph Smith" by George Q. Cannon, bound in cloth; $3.50.

No. 1786—R. Porter, city, one volume "Life of Joseph Smith," by George Q. Cannon, bound in cloth; $3.50.

Salt Lake Herald
April 20, 1889

THE UTAH COMMISSION.

The Complete list of Deputy Registrars Appointed Yesterday.

The following deputy registrars were appointed by the Utah commission yesterday:

BOX ELDER COUNTY.

Precinct.	Name.
Bear River	George Horse
Calls Fort	Thomas W. Wheatly, Jr
Curlew	M. D. Ocheltree
Deweyville	John Germer
Grouse Creek	Naham Eager
Kelton	George T. Rogers
Malad	E. Ryan
Portage	John Kelly
Promontory	Thomas G. Brown
Park Valley	Jonathan Campbell
Plymouth	Jedediah Earl
Terrace	Frank Sickles
Willard	Oliver H. Dudley

SAN JUAN COUNTY.

Precinct.	Name.
Bluff	Peter Allen
Buena	Hans Walker
Mt. Elmo	Joseph Dougherty
Montecillo	W. E. Hyde

EMERY COUNTY.

Precinct.	Name.
Castle Dale	Carl Wilberg
Blake	J. F. Farrer
Malen	J. S. Killpach
Ferron	J. W. Williams
Muddy	John T. Lewis
Orangeville	J. K. Reed
Price	A. Ballinger
Wellington	R. B. Thompson
Huntington	J. T. Wakefield
Larence	Elias Thomas
Scofield	S. J. Harkness

SUMMIT COUNTY.

Precinct.	Name.
Coalville	Wm. H. Smith, Sr.
Echo	Edward C. Morse
Grass Creek	Thomas Thomas
Hennefer	Geo. Roberts
Hoytsville	Geo. Daniels
Kamas	Erasmus Sorensen
Park City	Jos. M. Cohen
Parley's Park	Gideon Snyder
Peoa	Wm. H. Stevens
Rockport	Wm. Reynolds
Upton	Wm. H. Smith, Jr
Wanship	Geo. W. Moore
Woodland	Joseph J. Jenkins

UTAH COUNTY.

Precinct.	Name.
Alpine	Geo. Y. Meyers
American Fork	James Chipman, Jr
Benjamin	Joshua Hone
Cedar Fork	John M. Farlan
Fairfield	Wm. Thomas
Goshen	Geo. White
Lehi	Robert Gilchrist
Lake View	Geo. Smoot
Lake Shore	H. S. Brooks
Pleasant Grove	John Richins
Provo Bench	D. C. Daniels
Provo	R. A. Hills
Springville	D. C. Huntington
Spanish Fork	John S. Thomas
Salem	W. H. Taylor
Santaquin	Alex. Evans
Spring Lake	W. W. Barnett
Thistle	Geo. A. Hicks
P. V. Junction	J. W. Coburn
Payson	W. H. Fairbank

ESTRAY NOTICE.

I have in my possession the following described animals impounded as estrays. or for trespass :

One brown horse, 2 or 3 years old, star in forehead, both hind feet white, branded S2 on left thigh.

One light bay mare colt, 2 years old, star in forehead, left hind and left front foot white, no brands visible.

If damages and costs on said animals be not paid within 15 days from date of this notice, they will be sold to the highest cash bidder at my yard in Ferron City a: 1 o'clock p m., on the 11th day of May, 1889.

Dated at Ferron Precinct, Emery County, Territory of Utah, this 26th day of April, 1889.

J. E. KING.

Poundkeeper of said Precinct.

STATEMENT

Of the Receipts and Expenditures of Emery County for the Seven Months Ending December 31st, 1888.

RECEIPTS.

From Taxes as per Duplicate Assessment Roll, Sept., 1888.		$5,422.39
Less remitted taxes $	24.75	
" on tree culture	28.92	
" Amount due from the Collector........	3,572.64	$3,626.31
Total Amount Received from Taxes of 1888.............		$1,796.08
From Taxes of 1887........		121.08
" Licenses.............		1,070.50
" Fines...............		189.25
Total Receipts.......		$3,176.91
Balance on hand in Treasury May 31, 1888............		1,026.73
Total		$4,203.64

EXPENDITURES.

For roads and bridges	$	686.12
"	Books, Stationery and Printing, etc	270.92
"	Light and Fuel	20.00
"	Improvement of Court-house and lot	15.00
"	Special Collection of Licenses and Fines	45.00
"	County Jail and Sur-roundings	814.91
"	Bounty on Wild Animals	49.00
"	Abstracting to County Recorder	50.00
"	Committee work on Gov-ernment Bill	25.50
"	Bee Inspector	5.00
"	Quarantining contagious diseases	30.00
"	Insane and Poor	90.98
"	Criminal Cost	339.03
"	Plows and Plow and Scraper Extras	53.70
"	Road Supervisors	207.75
"	Board of Examiners of School Teachers	30.00
"	Probate Judge	90.00
"	County Clerk	450.00
"	County Attorney	212.80
"	County Sheriff	142.60
"	Surveyor	45.00
"	Coroner	16.25
Ex-Collector of Taxes		16.60
"	Selectmen	225.20
"	Supt. Dist. Schools	170.00
	Total Expenditures	4,101.36

Less County Warrants is-sued during fiscal year and in circulation at date.		103.25
	Total	3,998.13
Amount on hand in Treas-ury December 31, 1888.		205,51
	Total	4,203.64

LIVE STOCK FUND.

Amount on hand in Treas-ury January 1, 1888.	2.10
Received from sale of estrays	28.15
Total	30.25

LIABILITIES.

To Notes outstanding	1,737.76

The foregoing report is respectfully submitted.

[SEAL]   W. W. CRAWFORD,
Clerk of Emery County.

CASTLE DALE, January 1, 1889.

Audited and found correct March 14, 1889.

JASPER ROBERTSON,
Probate Judge.

W. W. MOLEN,
J. T. BALLANTYNE,
Selectmen.

TERRITORY OF UTAH, }
County of Emery. } ss.

I, W. W. Craw-ford, of the County Court of Emery County, hereby certify that the fore-going is a full, true and correct copy

of the financial report of the County
Clerk of Emery County, in the Territory of Utah, for the seven months
ending December 31, 1888, as audited
and approved by the County Court of
said county, and of their certificate of
auditation thereon endorsed.

Witness my hand and the seal
of the County Court of said
[SEAL.] county, at my office, in Castle
Dale, Utah, this 27th day of
March A. D. 2889.

W. W. CRAWFORD,
Clerk.

Utah Enquirer
June 21, 1889

THE PEOPLE'S PARTY.

Advice From the Territorial Central Committee.

WHEN AND WHERE THE CONVENTIONS ARE TO BE HELD.

Arrangements for Primaries—Active
Work Recommended.

HEADQUARTERS PEOPLE'S TERRITORIAL
CENTRAL COMMITTEE,
SALT LAKE CITY, UTAH, June 15, 1889.

It having been represented to the
People's territorial central committee
that several of the council district
conventions held in July, 1887, failed to
provide for the calling of future representative conventions, to avoid any
lapse or misunderstanding, council and
representative district conventions of
the People's Party of Utah are hereby
called to convene at the times and
places hereinafter named, for the purpose of placing in nomination candidates
for members of the council and house of
representatives: of the twenty-ninth
session of the legislative assembly, to
be voted for at the general election,
on the first Monday in August, 1889.

The representative district conventions will be composed of thirty delegates, selected from the several precincts of the district, according to the apportionment hereinafter named, and will meet at the place indicated on Saturday, July 6, 1889, at 12 m. In addition to nominating a candidate to represent a district in the house of representatives, each convention will elect ten delegates to represent the district in the convention of the council district to which it is attached.

The council district conventions will be composed of twenty delegates to be selected by the representative district conventions, one-half from each district, and will meet at the places hereinafter mentioned on Wednesday, July 10, 1889, at 12 m. and nominate candidates to represent their several districts in the council of the Legislative assembly.

Primaries for the selection of delegates to several representatives district conventions will be held in each precinct of the territory at the usual place of holding elections therein on Monday, July 1, at 8 p.m.

County conventions for placing in nomination candidates for county offices to be filled at the ensuing election will be held at such time and place as the county central committee may appoint.

Representative conventions July 6, 1889.

Place of meeting and appointment.

FIRST DISTRICT.

Convention to be held in Logan city at the county court house, delegates as follows:

Rich county—Garden city precinct 1, Lake Town 2, Meadowville 1, Randolph 2, Woodruff 1,

Cache county—Logan 12, Hyde Park 2, Smithfield 5, Providence 4.

SECOND DISTRICT.

Convention to be held at city hall, Hyrum city. Delegates as follows:

Cache county—Benson precinct 1, Clarkston 2, Hyrum 5, Lewiston 2, Mendon 2, Millville 2, Newton 1, Paradise 2, Peterboro 1, Richmond 5, Trenton 1, Wellsville 5, Coveville 1.

THIRD DISTRICT.

Convention to be held at county court house, Brigham City. Delegates as follows:

Box Elder county—Bear River precinct 2, Box Elder 9, Calls Fort 2, Curlew 1, Deweyville 2, Grouse Creek 1, Kelton 1, Malad 1, Mantua 2, Park Valley 1, Plymouth 1, Portage 2, Promontory 1, Willard 3, Terrace 1.

FOURTH DISTRICT.

Convention to be held at county court house Ogden city. Delegates as follows:

Ogden city, 30.

FIFTH DISTRICT.

Convention to be held at east school house, Harrisville, Weber county. Delegates as follows:

Weber county—Harrisville 3, Eden 2, Hooper 4, Lynne 1, Marriatt 1, North Ogden 4, Plain City 4, Riverdale 1, Slaterville 1, Uintah 1, West Weber 2, Wilson 1, Kanesville 1.

SIXTH DISTRICT.

Convention to be held at county court house, Farmington, Davis county. Delegates as follows:

Morgan County—Croyden 1, Kanyon 2, Milton 1, Morgan 2, Peterson 1.

Davis County—South Bountiful 2, East Bountiful 3, Centerville 2, Farmington 3, West Bountiful 1, Hooper 1, Kaysville 4, South Weber 1, Syracuse 1, Layton 1,

Summit County—Henneferville 1.

Salt Lake County—Hunter 1, Pleasant Green 1, North Point 1.

SEVENTH DISTRICT.

Convention to be held at county court house, Coalville. Delegates as follows:

Summit County—Coalville 8, Echo 2, Hoytsville 3, Park City 3, Parley's Park 2, Rockport 1, Upton 1, Wanship 3, Grass Creek 1, Kimballs 2.

Salt Lake County—Mountain Dell 1, Sugar House 3.

EIGHTH DISTRICT.

Convention to be held at county court house, Tooele County. Delegates as follows:

Tooele County—Batesville 1, St. Johns 1, Clover 1, Deep Creek 1, Grantsville 7, Quincy 1, Lakeview 2, Mill 1, Ophir 1, Stockton 1, Tooele 7, Vernon 2,

Salt Lake County—Bingham 1.

Juab County—Tintic 3.

NINTH DISTRICT.

Convention to be held at Ninth District school house, Salt Lake city. Delegates as follows:

Salt Lake County—First precinct, 30.

TENTH DISTRICT.

Convention to be held at county court house, Salt Lake city. Delegates as follows:

Salt Lake County—Second precinct, 3.

ELEVENTH DISTRICT.

Convention to be held at Seventeenth District school house, Salt Lake city. Delegates as follows:

Salt Lake County—Third precinct, 14; Fourth, 13; Granger, 2; Brighton, 1.

TWELFTH DISTRICT.

Convention to be held at city hall, Salt Lake city. Delegates as follows:

Salt Lake County—Fifth precinct, 30.

THIRTEENTH DISTRICT.

Convention to be held at West Jordan, Wall hall. Delegates as follows:

Salt Lake County—North Jordan, 3; West Jordan, 6; South Jordon, 3; Fort Herriman, 2; Riverton, 2; Bluff Dale, 1; South Cottonwood, 6; Union, 3; Sandy, 4;

FOURTEENTH DISTRICT.

Convention to be held at Mill Creek ward hall. Delegates as follows:

Salt Lake County—Farmers' 2, Mill Creek 8; East Mill Creek 3; Big Cottonwood 6; Butler 2, Granite 1, Alta 1, Draper 6.

FIFTEENTH DISTRICT.

Convention to be held at the city hall, Spanish Fork city, Utah county. Delegates as follows:

Utah County—Lehi 2, Cedar Fort 1, Alpine 2, Fairfield 1, Goshen 2, Santaquin 3. Spring Lake 1, Payson 7, Spanish Fork 8.

SIXTEENTH DISTRICT.

Convention to be held at county court house, Provo city. Delegates as follows:

Utah County—American Fork 7, Pleasant Grove 7, Provo bench 2, Provo city 13, Lake View 1.

SEVENTEENTH DISTRICT.

Convention to be held at the city hall, Springville, Utah county. Delegates as follows:

Utah county—Springville 10. Thistle 1. P. V. Junction 2, Benjamin 2, Salem 3.

Sanpete county—Winter Quarters. 1.

Emery county—Scofield 1, Castle Dale 1, Ferron 2, Huntington 2, Moab 1, Price 1, Orangeville 2, Muddy 1.

EIGHTEENTH DISTRICT.

Convention to be held at county courthouse, Heber city, Wasatch county. Delegates as follows:

Uintah county—Brown's Park 2, Ashley 6.

Wasatch county—Charleston 2, Heber 6, Midway 3, Wallsburgh 2.

Summit county—Kamas 5, Woodland 1, Peoa 3.

NINETEENTH DISTRICT.

Convention to be held at county court house, Fillmore, Millard county. Delegates as follows:

Juab county—Nephi 8, Mona 3, Juab 1.

Millard County—Deseret 2, Fillmore 4, Holden 2, Kanosh 2, Leamington 1, Meadow 1, Oak Creek 1. Scipio 2.

TWENTIETH DISTRICT.

Convention to be held at city hall, Mount Pleasant, Sanpete county. Delegates as follows:

Sanpete county—Thistle 1, Fairview 4, Mount Pleasant 7, Spring City, 3, Moroni 4, Fountain Green 3, Ephraim 8.

TWENTY-FIRST DISTRICT.

Convention to be held at county court house, Manti, Sanpete county. Delegates as follows.

Sanpete county—Chester, 2, Wales 1, Manti 5, Petty 1, Mayfield 1, Gunnison 5, Fayette, 1, Freedom 1.

Sevier county—Annabella, 1; Burrville, 1, Central 1, Elsinore 1, Glenwood 1, Joseph 1, Monroe 2, Redmond 1, Richfield 3, Salina 1, Vermillion 1, Willow Bend 1. Gooseberry 1.

TWENTY-SECOND DISTRICT.

Convention to be held at the county courthouse, Beaver city, Beaver county. Delegates as follows:

Beaver county—Adamsville, 1; Beaver city, 12; Grampion, 1; Greenville, 2; Minersville, 4; Star, 1.

Piute county—Bullionville, 1; Circleville, 1; Fremont, 2; Marysvale, 1; Thurber, 3; Koosharem, 1; Wilmot 1.

TWENTY-THIRD DISTRICT.

Convention to be held at the city hall, Cedar city, Iron county. Delegates as follows:

Iron county—Cedar 6, Kanarra 2, Parowan 6, Paragoonah 2, Summit 1.

Garfield county—Cannonville 1, Escalante 2, Hillsdale 1, Coyotte 1, Panguitch 4.

Washington county—New Harmony 1.

San Juan county—Bluff city 2, McElmo 1.

TWENTY-FOURTH DISTRICT.

Convention to be held at the county courthouse, St. George, Washington county. Delegates as follows:

Washington county—Duncan's Retreat 1, Hebron 1, Grafton 1, Gunlock 1, Leeds 1, Pine Valley 1, Price 1, Pinto 1, Rockville 1, St. George 4, Silver Reef 1, Shonesburg 1, Springdale 1, Tokerville 2, Virgin 1, Washington 2.

Kane county—Glendale 1, Johnson 1, Kanab 2, Upper Kanab 1, Orderville 1, Mount Carmel 1, Pahreah 1.

COUNCIL CONVENTIONS.

Council conventions, July 10, 1889. Districts and places of meeting:

First council district, composed of First and Sixth representative districts. Convention to be held at city hall, Kaysville, Davis county.

Second council district, composed of Second and Third representative districts. Convention to be held in Wellsville city hall, Wellsville, Cache county.

Third council district, composed of Fourth and Fifth representative districts. Convention to be held at county courthouse, Ogden city.

Fourth council district, composed of Seventh and Ninth representative districts. Convention to be held at Ninth district schoolhouse, Salt Lake city.

Fifth council district, composed of the Tenth and Twelfth representative districts. Convention to be held at the city hall, Salt Lake city.

Sixth council district, composed of the Eleventh and Fourteenth representative districts. Convention to be held at the Seventeenth ward schoolhouse, Salt Lake city.

Seventh council district, composed of the Eighth and Thirteenth representative districts. Convention to be held in the county courthouse, Tooele city, Tooele county.

Eight council district, composed of the Fifteenth and Sixteenth representative districts. Convention to be held at county courthouse, Provo city.

Ninth council district, composed of the Seventeenth and Eighteenth representative districts. Convention to be held at the city hall, Springville, Utah county.

Tenth council district, composed of the Nineteenth and Twentieth representative districts. Convention to be held at the county courthouse, Nephi, Juab county.

Eleventh council district, composed of the Twenty-first and Twenty-second representative districts. Convention to be held at the county courthouse, Richfield, Sevier county.

Twelfth council district, composed of the Twenty-third and Twenty-fourth representative districts. Convention to be held at the city hall, Cedar city, Iron county.

The county and precinct committees are respectfully requested to take the initiative in making arrangements for holding of the primaries in the several precincts, and all members of the People's Party are urged to attend these meetings, that a full attendance may be secured and representative men placed in nomination, through whose efforts the rights and liberties of the whole people of the territory may be preserved.

By order of the People's territorial central committee.

JOHN R. WINDER, Chairman.
ELIAS A. SMITH, Secretary.

Utah Enquirer
July 26, 1889

SAD FATALITY.

A Resident of Emery County Meets His Death in a Saw Mill.

A fatal accident happened to a resident of Orangeville, Emery County, at Jose Valley shingle mill on the 18th inst. While William P. Stepent was feeding a lathe saw that he had just set in motion, the lathe gauge moved up to the saw, throwing the board being sawed on the top of the saw, sending the board back with fearful velocity, striking Mr. Stepent between the thumb and fore-finger of the right hand, tearing the flesh away. The board then struck him in the abdomen. He was then carried into a house close by and examined. Two small marks was all that could be found where the board struck. A doctor was immediately sent for from Mount Pleasant. All was done for him that could be done, but he succumbed to the hand of death after suffering intense pain for sixty-eight hours. The doctor stated that the blow caused paralysis of the bowels. The body was taken to his home and was buried there on Monday. He was 32 years of age, and leaves a wife and three small children to mourn his loss. He was a very enterprising man, and was well respected in the community. His demise brings forcibly to our remembrance, says our correspondent, the death of our late townsman, Samuel R. Jewker, who was struck with a hand-spike in the same part of the body, almost in the same spot, in Jose Valley, three years ago the 27th of August, and died after fifty-one hours suffering. The coincidene is strange.

CURRENT EVENTS.

Edmunds Law Prosecutions.

Deputy Whetstone arrested Mr. Tittensen, of Coveville, on the charge of unlawful cohabitation, on August 8th.

Appointment.

To the Presidents and Members of the General Seventies Quorums, throughout all the Stakes of Zion:

Brother John M. Whitaker has been appointed Secretary and Treasurer *pro tem* for the Seventies, to act for us in the place of Brother Robert Campbell, during his illness. All communications from the quorums should be addressed to John M. Whitaker, 47 s. First West Street, Salt Lake City, Utah.

By order of the First Seven Presidents of Seventies.

JACOB GATES, Presiding.

Emery County Election.

The returns from the following precincts in this county are:

	Hatch (People.)	Robbins ("Liberal.")
Huntington.	61	19
Orangeville.	16	27
Ferron.	38	2
Molen.	19	1
Lawrence	17	1
Cleveland	12	1
Price.	31	9
Scofield.	63	18
Castle Dale.	35	
Total.	292	78

There are a few more small precincts that will increase the People's majority.   W. H.

HUNTINGTON, Emery County, Utah, August 7th, 1889.

CANVASSING THE RETURNS.

The Total Vote Cast in Utah County Totals Up to 2,516

The Territorial Board of Canvassers, who commenced their operations in Salt Lake City on Monday morning, have made great headway in their work, and by the close of the third day of their labors had canvassed the returns of twenty-two counties. We give herewith the returns of those counties of particular interest to our subscribers:

EMERY COUNTY.

Blake	20
Castle Dale	11
Cleveland	21
Ferron	30
Huntington	18
Larence	3
Moab	9
Molen	18
Muddy	25
Orangeville	43
Price	44
Scofield	60
Wellington	10
	312

UNITED STATES ATTORNEY VARIAN has filed a protest against the petition praying for the pardon of David Edmonstor, who wos sentenced to a term in the penitentiary for attempting to take money from the till of the co-op. store at Castle Dale.

A RESIDENT of Emery county was yesterday giving on an account of the exploits of Apostle JOHN HENRY SMITH, on the Sabbath preceding election, to defeat DON ROBBINS. He preached in the morning at Castle Dale, in the afternoon at Orangeville, and then, riding thirty miles to Price, whooped up the brethren there until 11 p. m. The burden of his sermons was a dissertation on a TRIBUNE editorial. Now, if it is wicked for a lay member to buy and read THE TRIBUNE, how much more wicked is it for an Apostle to call the people's attention to what THE TRIBUNE says? And if the Apostle keeps reading THE TRIBUNE, what assurance have the people that the Apostle is not on the road to apostacy? What assurance has the Apostle himself that, if he keeps up that reading, he will not be converted? We warn him that he is treading on dangerous ground.

Salt Lake Herald
September 1, 1889

IN CASTLE VALLEY.

Its Wondrous Wealth of Black Diamonds.

THE TOWNS AND SETTLEMENTS.

The Beautiful Park—The Vari-Colored Cliffs and Weird, Fantastic Shapes—Crops Are Looking Well.

ON THE ROAD, Aug. 27, 1889.—[Correspondence of THE HERALD.]—We went up the Salina cañon and found more natural crooks to the mile than ever occurred to us in the same distance. The engineer who made the road was on the narrow track, and the road was just wide enough, if you are very careful in driving, to always afford a clear and distinct view of the bottom of the cliff or dugway which you may be driving along. You cross the creek about twenty times, and when there are bridges you wish they were better or none, and when you are across you begin to dread the return trip. An old resident of Castle valley assures us that he always fastened his wagon cover down while in the cañon so his wife could not see out, consequently she was not alarmed at the close shaves he made of going into the creek. About fifteen miles up the cañon it widens into

A BEAUTIFUL PARK

and must be a lovely place to spend the summer. The road is graded most of the way for a railroad, the Denver & Rio Grande having spent something like five hundred thousand dollars, so our informant said, making this so far useless grade. It extends to Green River. After what seems and intolerable climb, you reach the summit and descend a broad cañon to Red creek. A short distance below is Ivy creek, both rather small. There are a few scrubby pines to the right and considerable scrub cedar, with a few small knotty, scrubby cottonwoods. As you go down farther a board is set up with the legend "No Thoroughfare" on it. We did not want to go that road. One road was all we cared for, and if that was a fair sample of the rest we had no use for it. One guide informed us there was a ranch somewhere there of mammoth proportions: we simply took his work for it. But if the interior is like that bordering the road we would hate to have a jack rabbit of ours lost on it for it would starve to death sure.

THE FIRST VIEW OF CASTLE VALLEY

is not calculated to inspire any great amount of enthusiasm. It is so vast, so sterile and desolate-looking that the ordinary mind cannot grasp it all at once, but, like watering clay land, have to just let it soak in. There is some vegetation in places—what the settlers call salt grass. I thought it a species of salt pigweed, common on badlands or alkali flats. The ox-eyed daisy was there; also an occasional tuft of sage brush. There is also the stinkweed, or spider grass, common in Salt Lake valley, from two to four feet high. It grows about four to six inches in Castle valley. There were a few other weeds and a little grass occasionally, the latter a species of sword grass, as tough when green as buckskin. What it would be when dry is hard to say.

The first sign of civilization you came to is on a creek called Quichumpau, whose waters taste just like its name sounds. Here some enterprising persons had put in some lucern. It was trying to live, at least a part of it. Here we saw the first evidence of

THE SUPERABUNDANCE OF COAL

in the valley, as nearly every hill had more or less of it in plain sight. We had already seen from ten to twenty veins of coal in Salina cañon from an inch thick to about four feet, but did not expect to see it in the valley. The next place on the road is the new town called the Muddy. The situation is fine, being on a gentle slope with good looking soil. They have only got the water out recently. Water here is the enchanter's wand or the philosopher's stone that transmutes all it touches into gold. And this place, now a desert, will be a garden in a year or two. Two miles from the little town we came to the Muddy creek, about the size of Little Cottonwood. Farms and houses seemed to be scattered promiscously up and down the creek. Twelve miles from here is Ferron creek and town. At Ferron there are a number of good houses, fine pastures on the creek and crops looking well, particularly lucern, which seems to thrive better here, as the soil is very deep, but has a tendency to wash, so much so that the water should be watched constantly. It is the same nearly all over the valley.

Molen is a small settlement on Ferron creek, about three miles east of Ferron. Here the public generally live on their farms. There is no town. The land seems to be heavier—more like that of Sanpete than other places I have seen in this valley. Twelve miles north from Ferron is Cottonwood, a stream apparently half as big as the Provo river. Orangeville and Castle Dale are situated on this stream. Both are

THRIFTY LOOKING PLACES.

I asked a farmer what his average crop was last season. He said, wheat, corn and oats inclusive, thirty bushels to the acre, while I was told by a resident of Molen that he raised 150 bushels of potatoes on a quarter of an acre of land. There is a considerable amount of fruit trees, some bearing. Peaches, grapes, tomatoes, melons, squash, etc., do extremely well here. There is a thirty foot vein of excellent coal seven miles west of Orangeville. They have made a small hole in it to get what they can use themselves.

Ten or twelve miles north of Cottonwood is Huntington town and creek, the latter about a third larger than Big Cottonwood. The town has an extremely new look about it although it is the largest one in Castle Valley. It is situated on a gentle slope and covers considerable ground. There are several stores. The lack of foliage detracts from its looks at present. I shall not attempt to describe the lofty pillars and fantastic shapes into which hills have been carved by wind and storm. The clifts on the west look as if they were hand painted with different colors. The Huntington

cañon has some as artistically carved columns as were ever made by man. The road through the cañon and over the mountain is a shade better than the Salina road, but you have to cross the creek about twenty times and each crossing seems a little worse than the last. Near the summit are several fine coal mines, four or five saw mills, etc.   N. G.

Salt Lake Herald
November 19, 1889

COMMISSIONS as follows were yesterday issued to precinct officers elected at the August election: Cyrus W. Robbins, constable of Snowville precinct, Box Elder county; John C. Duncan, justice of the peace of Ferron precinct, Emery county; John T. Sullivan, constable of Tintic, Juab county; Charles F. Stillman, constable of East Mill Creek, Salt Lake county.

Salt Lake Herald
November 28, 1889

Mr. Arthur Henrie has returned to Manti. It is his intention to be engaged teaching school this winter at Ferron, Emery county.

Deseret Weekly
November 30, 1889

Stake convened at Ferron on Sunday and Monday, November 10th and 11th. Two meetings were held each day and the Social Hall was filled on each occasion. The time was mainly occupied by Apostle F. M. Lyman, whose excellent counsel was greatly appreciated by all present. The remainder of the meeting was occupied by the Stake Presidency, and Bishops from the different wards presenting their reports. From these it was learned that the people of Emery, considering everything, are doing well. F. M. Rynalds of Castle Dale was sustained to fill a vacancy in the High Counsel. William Taylor, Sen., of Ferron, was set apart as President over the High Priests of Emery Stake, with John Fwahlan and Niels P. Miller as his counselors John F. Wakefield of Huntington was sustained as Assistant Superintendent of Sabbath Schools in the Stake, and John Heber Stowell as Bishop of Glenn Spring Ward, which formerly belonged to Price.

O. J. ANDERSEN,
Stake Clerk.

EMERY.
The Quarterly Conference of this

Ogden Standard
November 30, 1889

FERRON, Utah,)
Nov 15th, 1889)
Ed'tor *Tribune* —On
the 30th day of Octo-
ber, 1889, John C.
Hitchcock and Ed-
ward Huntsman left
Ferron, Emery coun-
ty, Utah, to go to Salt
Lake City, Utah, for
the purpose of regis-
tering to be able to
vote at the election in
February (so I am
told). * * * I un-
derstand that the
bishops are sending
men from all the
towns for the same
purpose, *how true the
statement is I cannot
say*
H. W Curtis,
(Liberal).
—*S L Tribune*

Salt Lake Herald
February 4, 1890

FOR ALL IT IS WORTH.

The Racket Being Worked by our Worthy Registrars.

THE NAMES ACTED ON MONDAY.

The Greater Portion of the Challenges are Denied—Some Taken Under Advisement
—Others Sustained.

The registration courts were in full blast again yesterday. It seems that the Liberals have taken a flock shot in these challenges, as a majority of them were overruled. In many cases persons were summoned to appear to answer the charge of not being bona fide residents of Salt Lake city who have resided here all the way from twenty to forty years, as was shown by the evidence.

BEFORE WINTERS.

This gentleman held court in the morning and disposed of numerous cases. At the close of the examination he was heard to say the challenges in the following cases have been withdrawn: Heber M. Wells, Alfelas Young, Joseph Openshaw and Sidney Clawson. His docket was then folded like the Arab's tent, and presently he vanished.

BEFORE MORRIS.

Thomas Loyd—Came here from Draper in November. My cousin got a job for me. Never calculate to go back there to live. This is my home. Taken under advisement.

David Smellie—Challenge denied.

Andrew A. Johnson—I moved here from Santaquin April last. Have been working for the street car company. Have no other home than this city. Under advisement.

Thomas Cunnington—Have lived here since the 13th of November. Came from American Fork to work. Have a house and lot in American Fork. No one is living in it now. Taken under advisement.

August Lindholme—Have lived here three years. Denied.

Peter Lindholme—Denied.

James White—Taken under advisement.

Edward Snelgrove—Was married to my first wife in 1843, married another some years later but she died in 1881. Have lived with but one since 1881. Taken under advisement.

A. G. Livingston—Denied.

John August Johnson—Have lived here three months, came from Gunnison May 29, 1889. My wife came up here and locked the house. I am a carpenter. Intend to make this my permanent home. Passed for the present.

Elias M. Jones—Not present.

J. S. Curtis—Not present.

Edward H. Pattengales—Came here two or three months ago from Willard. This is now my only home. Under advisement.

Hamilton G. Park—My home has been on the same spot for over twenty years. Was married nearly fifty ago to my wife "and she still lives, bless her dear, good soul." Was sealed to some one else for my father. Never was married to anyone but my wife. Challenge denied.

L. Christensen - Have lived here since November 13 Came here from Sanpete. I am single. Am working for the city. I can make better wages here and intend to stay. Taken under advisement.

Guy C. Wilson—Not present.

John Judd—Not present.

Samuel Baxter—Have lived here constantly for nineteen years. Challenge denied.

James E. Howell—Have lived in the city nine months. Came from Bluff Dale. My wife came with me. I am working on the Utah Central railway. No property anywhere. I lived five years in the city previous to going to Bluff Dale. This is my home. Challenge denied.

Joseph S. Barlow — Mr. Ferguson answered for Mr. Barlow, and submited to the striking off of the name saying Mr. Barlow had changed his residence.

R. D. Roberts—Have lived here three months. Came here from Castle Dale, I am a carpenter. I don't make my permanent home anywhere. Just now this is my home. Taken under advisement.

G. Darton—Not present.

James F. Fritz. Not present.

Henry P. Burns—Have lived constantly where I now reside for four years. I am building a home at Hunter's and have squatted on some land there. Am working for the city. I make my home here but keep my family there. Have lived in the city sixteen years. Have a contest in the court now over the land. Under advisement.

Edwin Hanson—Came here from Morgan county three months ago. Am a shoemaker at Z. C. M. I. factory. I came here for my health. Have the rheumatism. I intend to make this my home. Taken under advisement.

BEFORE M'CALLUM.

The following cases were all overruled: Anthony W. Nelsen, W. C. McDonald, John A. Neilsen, J. J. Sorensen, Nels E. Christensen, Alex Olesen, Nils Christensen, Willard Rees, John U. Sandburgh, W. F. F. Neilsen, John Sidoway, Gordon Lindsay, Emile H. Lund, And. Swensen, John Rees, Peter Neilsen, Hon Sorensen, William Sidoway, Joseph Swaner, Joseph Thorup, Joseph Childs, Peter Cunningham, John L. Crane, W. J. Peirson, James E. Paul, T. Cowan, C. H. Wilkinson, W. Fereman, Mr. Goodmansee, William White, George Paremore, Ed. L. Millard, Robert W. Jones, Carl A. Hadmund, John Hingley, H. C. Lett, Nicola Gulbransen, John Hankinson, Robert Sidoway, Julius Halverson, Henry C. Hicks, David Bollick, Arthur Fargergreen, Robert T. Morris, Henry Pugh.

The following made default: G. J. Lund, Henry Taylor, Francis Brown, James Curry; and the following were taken under advisement: Daniel Corbitt, William H. Nisenger, Peter Frost, Randolph Blather, Daniel Duncan, Alma Huish, James C. Jensen, George A. Lea, Asa Coates.

Utah Enquirer
February 18, 1890

THE COURT CALENDER.

Important Cases Set For Next Term.

WHAT LAWYERS HAVE CASES.

The Appeals — Cohabitation Cases — Criminals Who Will be Tried — A Long List.

Herbert W. Shaw vs. A. D. Ferron; Henry Adams; demurrer to complaint; Hoge & Burmester.

WORK DONE THURSDAY

Half of the Legislative Session now Passed.

THE FISH AND GAME PASSES.

Claims of Public Officers—A Bill Regulating the Territorial Library—Other Busines.

In Thursday's session of the Legislature the following business was transacted·

THE COUNCIL.

Mr. Richards, of the committee on judiciary, reported on C. F. 25, authorizing the estates of decedents and minors to be mortgaged or leased in certain cases, recommending that the bill pass. Report adopted and bill filed for second reading.

The committee on printing reported that the proper amendments to C. F. 16 had been printed.

The committee on enrollment reported that C. F. 5, to enable persons to become a body corporate to loan money to its members only, had been properly enrolled and sent to the Governor for his approval.

Mr. Richards introduced by request C. F. 30, a bill providing for cesspools, registration of competent plumbers and the establishment of a system of inspection of cesspools, etc. Referred to the committee on municipal corporations and towns.

C. F. 25, providing for estates of minors or decedents to be mortgaged, was taken up, and after amendments, passed its second reading.

C. F. 33, referring to regulations of the Territorial library, was taken up on its third reading and after amendments, further consideration was postponed until to-day.

A House communication announced that that body had refused to concur in Council amendments to H. F. 10, the stock bill, and asked that a conference committee be appointed. Councilors Seegmiller and Bryan were appointed from the Council.

Adjourned.

THE HOUSE.

Mr. Wood presented a communication from residents of Sanpete county, requesting favorable action on the petition of W. G. Sharp and others, asking that Winter Quarters precinct be attached to Emery county.

A similar communication also came from Orange Seeley and others of Castle Dale.

Mr. Creer, from the committee on claims, reported favorably on the claim of the *Deseret News* company, for blanks and rebinding records injured in the fire at Beaver.

Mr. Allen made a verbal minority report protesting against the payment of $143.77 of the bill, which was for blanks to be used in the office of the clerk of the First district. He thought that, the clerk being dead, some one must lose that money. but the *News* was just as well able to bear the loss as was the Territory. It was probably hard upon the *News*, but that was no reason why the Territory should pay it to him.

Mr. Creer thought under the circumstances the claim could be allowed. The records in the court house at Beaver were burned and the clerk who had ordered these blanks had committee suicided. The *News* had acted in good faith in printing the blanks, and there was no recourse save upon the estate of the deceased clerk.

Mr. Thurman wanted the bill referred to the committee, with instruction to get a detailed statement from the *News* company, giving just what amount of the blanks was for civil and what was for criminal business.

Mr. Howells objected, but the report was recommitted.

The committee on rules, to whom had been referred the amendment to certain rules, offered by Mr. Russell, reported adversely thereon.

Mr. Russell objected to the adoption of the report. He thought it only common courtesy that each man who presented a bill should be informed why it was rejected.

Mr. Thurman thought if the real reasons for rejecting some bills were given, the fathers of the measures would probably feel more badly about it than if the facts in the case were not given.

The report of the committee was adopted.

Mr. Johnson, of the committee on live stock, reported on H. F. 10 (substitute), with Council amendements, recommending that the House do no not concur, and that a conference committee be appointed. Porter and Johnson were named.

The committee on conference on House amendments to C. F. 2, reported a disagreement and recommended that the House do not concur. Adopted.

H. F. 47, reducing the numbers of councilmen in cities of the third class from seven to five came up on second reading, was read, and on motion the rules were suspended. It was read the third time and placed upon its passage.

Mr. Creer objected to the passage of the bill. Cities of the third class ran all the way up to 5,000 inhabitants, and a city council of seven members was small enough for a city say like Provo—.

Mr. Thurman—I object to Provo being called a third-class city.

Mr. Creer—If this bill passes, a quorum to transact business would be three. A majority of these could grant franchises to street railways, electric light companies, etc.

The bill was finally rejected.

H. F. S. (substitute), the fish and game bill, was brought up on its third reading, amended slightly and passed—15, 2 nays.

A communication from a number of prominent Salt Lakers represented that they thought $500 a year, as salary for A. M. Musser, acting fish commissioner, was about the right thing. Referred to committee on fish and game.

Deseret Evening News
February 24, 1890

Emery Stake Conference.

The Quarterly Conference of Emery Stake convened at Huntington on Sunday, February 9th. On the stand were the Presidency of the Stake and representatives of the Bishopric from every ward, also from the different Quorums and organizations in the Stake. Four very spirited meetings were held during the two days, and a good portion of each meeting was profitably occupied by Prof. Karl G. Maeser, who visited us in the interest of our projected Stake Academy. He gave an eloquent address upon the object of the Saints gathering to these mountains and upon the great and important mission which parents have to perform. Having enlarged upon the subject of education, Professor Maeser said he felt very glad the time had come for this Stake to have an academy. He admonished the people to sustain it with their faith and prayers, and in return they would realize joy and satisfaction.

Reports were presented from the Presidency of the Stake and the Bishops of wards. These all showed favorably for Emery County; that the Sunday schools, day schools and all other organizations were in fair running order, that the poor were looked after, and no one was suffering. Timely advice was given to the people generally.

At a special Priesthood meeting, the question of location for the Stake Academy, was brought up, and after some explanations and advice from Brother Maeser, a vote was taken showing ten in favor of Huntington and twenty-nine in favor of Castle Dale.

Alexander Jameson, late of the B. Y. Academy was sustained as principal of the new institution.

The speakers during Conference, besides the leading authorities referred to, were Uriah Curtis and Warren Peacock, recently returned missionaries; also Alexander Jameson. L. M. Olson, Superintendent of District Schools gave some appropriate instructions.

The Woman's Suffrage Association had a well attended meeting, and the question of "emancipation" was handled, with fond hope for its speedy consummation.

All the meetings were filled to overflowing. The Huntington choir, under the leadership of Brother Fowler, deserve worthy mention. Their sweet music greatly added to the pleasure of the occasion.

O. J. ANDERSON, Stake Clerk.

Salt Lake Herald
March 1, 1890

THE following deputy registrars for Emery county were appointed by the Utah commission yesterday: Blake, J. J. Ferron; Wellington, R. B. Thompson; Price, A. Ballinger; Huntington, J. F. Wakefield; Lawrence, Elias Thomas; Castle Dale, Carl Welberg; Orangeville, J. H. Reid; Molen, J. D. Killpack; Muddy, J. J. Leevis; Scofield, S. J. Harkness; Moab, Henry Crouse; Ferrin, J. W. Williams.

Desert Weekly
March 15, 1890

The inhabitants of the eastern part of Emery County have long labored under great disadvantages on account of having to travel so far —nearly 200 miles—in order to reach the county seat, Castle Dale. It is, therefore, an act of justice to them to give them a county of their own, which the bill creating Grand County aims to do. It is true the population will be sparse, but it will increase rapidly, and there exists no sufficient objection to the creation of the new county.

Deseret Evening News
March 24, 1890

EMERY STAKE.

PRESIDENT.—C. G. Larsen, Castle Dale.

COUNSELORS.—Orange Seeley, Castle Dale; Wm. Howard, Huntington.

Emery County, Utah.

WARDS.	BISHOPS
Castle Dale	Henning Olsen
Ferron	F. Olsen
Huntington	C. Pulsipher
Molen	L. S. Beach
Emery	C. Christensen
Orangeville	Jasper Robertson
Price	Geo. Frandsen
Cleveland	Samuel N. Alger, P. E.
Lawrence	Calvin W. Moore
Spring Glen	Heber J. Stowell
Castle Gate	William Lamph, P. E.
Upper Price	F. Ewell, P. E.
Wellington	Jefferson Tidwell, P. E.
Wilsonville	Sylvester Wilson, P. E.

THE DISTRIBUTION.

J. S. Holland, of Montpelier, Gets the Piano.

W. L. EVANS, OF KAMAS, THE BAIN

The Lucky Parties Who Are Awarded the First Hundred Premiums—The Prizes Are Widely Distributed.

The third annual distribution of premiums to subscribers of the SEMI-WEEKLY HERALD, occurred at the Salt Lake theater yesterday at 11 o'clock a. m. Three thousand three hundred and fifty-six subscribers to that issue had availed themselves of the opportunity to secure numbers, but there were not more than one hundred and fifty or two hundred in attendance, which evinces something of the widespread confidence with which the distribution has come to be regarded. The estimate of the total number of receipts which would be issued had been placed at 3000 by THE HERALD canvassers, but the rush during conference had been much larger than anticipated, and the total was 3,356.

The following committee was chosen from the body of the house:

H. H. GODDARD, Ogden,
WILLIAM HARKER, Taylorsville.
W. G. FARRELL, Franklin,
JAMES HOWELL, Tooele.
JOHN KINKE, Mona.

These gentlemen at once took charge of the stubs of the 3,356 receipts which had been issued, together with all the duplicates of the numbers designed to be put in the wheel. The wheel, made of glass, was placed on the table in the centre of the stage. While the committee retired to examine the books, stubs and dupli-
cates, Prof. Daynes and one of his pupils, Miss Romney, entertained the assemblage with several four-hand selections rendered in brilliant style on the prize Fischer piano, which stood at one side of the stage and was the admired of all beholders. In about fifteen minutes the committee returned and Mr. Goddard, the chairman, stated that they had examined all the books, found that 3,356 numbers had been issued as stated and that a duplicate of every number issued was on hand ready to be put into the wheel. To the question how some receipts were numbered higher than 3,356, it was answered that 4,800 receipts had been printed, so that books could be sent to all HERALD agents, but that in many cases only parts of books had been used. All the numbers were then put into the wheel and all were well shaken up. A boy named Major was chosen to draw the numbers forth, and amid a deep silence the drawing began by the judges calling the numbers, and a clerk calling back the number of the prize to which it was entitled. When the first number (4279) came out, and it was announced that it was held by J. S. Holland, of Montpelier, Idaho, and that he would be awarded prize number one, the Fischer piano, there was a round of applause. The first 100 prizes awarded are as follows:

1—A Fischer grand upright piano, F. E. Warren Mercantile company, 10 E. Second South, Salt Lake city, value $500, No. 4279, J. S. Holland, Montpelier.

2—A thoroughbred Holstein bull, Jordan stock farm, value $200, No. 847, W. F. McLean, Castle Gate.

3—An elegantly finished Bain wagon, Co-op Wagon and Machine company, value $175, No. 118, W. L. Evans, Kamas.

4—A lot in Garden city, Senior & Rand agents, value $150, No. 986, R. Tidwell, Smithfield.

5—A yearling Holstein Jersey heifer, Jordan stock farm, value $125, No. 3739, B. Hanks, Franklin.

6—A purse of one hundred dollars gold, No. 290, Mary V. Pritchett, Fairview, Utah.

7—A lot in Lake city, value $100, Pratt Bros., No. 3119, Joseph Wilde, Coalville.

8—A Domestic sewing machine, Young Bros.' company, value $70, No. 3967, W. M. Stookey, St. John.

9—A new Piano mower, Studebaker Bros.' Manufacturing company, value $85, No. 3710, O. C. Loveland, Deweyville.

10—A purse of fifty dollars gold, No. 581, Charles Alley, Lake Town.

11—A combination fence machine, Burton, Gardner & Co., value $50, No. 4678, N. Williams, Provo.

12—A fine saddle, N. C. Christensen & Bro., value $45, No. 714, W. E. Partington, Logan.

13—A breech-loading shotgun, Browning Bros., Ogden, value $40, No. 2837, J. B. Crawford, Orangeville.

14—A Roster fanning mill, Folsom & Scofield, value $50, No. 3967, William Groves, Red Cañon.

15—A set of Collier's American Chambers' encyclopedia, Collier & Co., HERALD building, Salt Lake, value $30, No. 1,448, Thomas Eyman, Rock Springs.

16—A life-size bust photo, Morris & Co., Salt Lake, value $30, No, 1,224, H. E. Lewelyn, city.

17—A purse of $25 gold, No. 1,446, J. Peart, Farmers' ward.

18—A purse of $25 gold, No. 460, F. Robinson, Richmond.

19—A set of "V. T. R." family remedies, C. E. Johnson, value $25, No. 3,019, J. H. Cederlund, Montpelier.

20—An elegant toilet set, Johnson, Pratt & Co., value $25, No. 8, Charles Walter, Murray.

21—A selection of fruit, shade or flowering trees, Utah Nursery company, Salt Lake, value $25, No. 1,921, Paul Poulson, Ephraim.

22—A selection of fruit, shade or flowering trees, Utah Nursery company, Salt Lake, value $25, No. 1,311, S. Rust Koosharem.

23—A set of Dickens complete works, 15 volumes, ½ calf, H. Pembroke's, value $25, No. 168, J. W. Lee, Coalville.

24—A single buggy harness, W. Jenkins & Sons, Salt Lake, value $25, No. 3,283, O. Sanderson, Fairview.

25—One fine steel engraving, gilt frame, "Consolation," value $20, No. 476, Joseph Crook, Payson.

26—One steel engraving, "Mother's Joy," value $20, No. 1,099, H. H. Watson, city.

27—One steel engraving, The Holiday, value $20, No. 8272, A. Anderson, Red Canyon.

28—One steel engraving, Foxes at Play, value, $20, No. 1907 J. P. Peterson, Ephriam.

29—A Browning rifle and 100 cartridges, Browning Bros., Ogden, value $16, No. 566, J. Atwood, Kamas.

30—A set of dishes, Hoock & Clawson's, Salt Lake and Ogden, value $15, No. 3960, O. F. Maltinberg, Santaquin.

31—One heating stove, "Rival Universal," Cooper, Piper & Co., Nephi, value $15, No. 32, John Richens, Pleasant Grove.

32—An elegant banjo, value, $15, No. 1031, E. E. Shoebridge, Provo.

33—A bolt of dress flannel, Cutler Bros, Salt Lake, value $12, No. 2807, Wm. Defrieze, St. George.

34—Hanging lamp, Hoock & Clawson, Salt Lake and Ogden, value $10, No. 2578, W. K. Vanboden, Cub Hill.

35—An easy chair, P. W. Madsen, Salt Lake, value, $10, No. 4481, Emma Daily, Springville.

36—One year's subscription to the SALT LAKE HERALD, value $10, No. 3,59, Jas. Shaw, Elsinore.

37—One year's subscription to THE SALT LAKE DAILY HERALD, value $10, No. 4,100, John P. McComie, Murray.

38—One year's subscription to THE SALT LAKE DAILY HERALD, value $10, No. 1,414, C. Moslander, Wellsville.

39—One year's subscription to THE SALT LAKE DAILY HERALD, value $10, No. 4,300, O. B. Ostler, city.

40—One year's subscription to THE SALT LAKE DAILY HERALD, value $10, No. 3,655, H. M. Rawlings, sr., Cub Hill.

41—One year's subscription to THE SALT LAKE DAILY HERALD, value $10, No. 2,111, A. Challis, Franklin.

42—One year's subscription to THE SALT LAKE DAILY HERALD, value $10, No. 969, R. Miller, city.

43—One year's subscription to THE SALT LAKE DAILY HERALD, value $10, No. 39, D. Morgan, Samaria.

44—One year's subscription to THE SALT LAKE DAILY HERALD, value $10, No. 4,670, William Hudson, Provo.

45—One year's subscription to THE SALT LAKE DAILY HERALD, value $10, No. 363, W. E. Smith, Kaysville.

46—One year's subscription to THE SALT LAKE DAILY HERALD, value $10, No. 4,021, W. F. Burton, Ogden.

47—One year's subscription to THE SALT LAKE DAILY HERALD, value $10, No. 3,475, H. W. Burgess, Schofield.

48—One year's subscription to THE SALT LAKE DAILY HERALD, value $10, No. 3,838, John J. Banks, Spanish Fork.

49—One year's subscription to THE SALT LAKE DAILY HERALD, value $10, No. 3,541, George Kelly, Springville.

50—One year's subscription to THE SALT LAKE DAILY HERALD, value $10, No. 4,697, A. J. Hoover, Provo.

51—A purse of $10 in gold, No. 3638, E. Curtis, Granger.

52—A purse of $10 in gold, No. 569, James Williams, Kamas.

53—A purse of $10 in gold, No. 140, William Cottrell, Farmington.

54—A purse of $10 in gold, No. 3057, R. H. Adam, Heber.

55—A purse of $10 in gold, No. 403, George Lyon, Hyde Park.

56—A purse of $10 in gold, No. 3,401, B. W. Scott, Deseret.

57—An elegant eight-day striking alarm clock, S. P. Teasdel's, value $10, No. 1,532, J. Fosgreen, Brigham.

58—A set Handy Shakespeare, 13 volumes, Margetts Bros., value $10, No. 4,480, W. K. Johnson, Springville.

59—A pair of calf-skin sewed boots, Z. C. M. I. shoe factory, value $10, No. 4,104, Mrs. A. Smith, city.

60—A set, 8 volumes, Knight's history of England, presented as a special prize by W. H. Rowe, value $10, No 3,708, C. D. Bronson, Deweyville.

61—An enlarged photograph of Joseph Smith, the prophet, framed, value $10, No. 2,034, Joseph Tattersall, Beaver.

62—An enlarged photograph of President Brigham Young, framed, value $10, No. 1,095, George Gray, Milford.

63—One box groceries, Thomas Bros., Ogden, No. 4,370, A. Marr, Erda.

64—One full silk dress pattern, The West

Store, Provo, J. A. Harris, proprietor, value $10, No. 4,087, Joseph Perkins, Bountiful.

65—An elegant marble top centre table, Gates & Snow, Provo, value $10, No. 2,852, D. C. Sabin, jr., Salem.

66—A variety of fruit and shade trees, Pleasant Grove nursery, D. M. Smith, proprietor, value $10, No. 3,305, D. M. Griffith, Mona.

67—"Around the World with General Grant," two volumes, Felt, Olsen & Co., Provo, value $9, No. 3,506, A. Parker, Tooele.

78—A crayon portrait, enlarged from any photo, by J. B. Fairbanks, artist, Payson, value $9, No. 3,002, John Olsen, Moroni.

69—One full dress pattern, People's Emporium, Provo, S. S. Jones, proprietor, value $8, No. 1,935, C. J. Larson, Castle Dale.

70—One volume Book of Mormon, morocco, revised edition, by Orson Pratt, value $6, No. 4155, C. Workman, Asays.

71—A canary bird and cage, Hoock & Clawson, Salt Lake and Ogden, value $5, No. 347, P. Edmunds, Wales.

73—A purse of $5 gold, No. 3,880, Mrs. Fannie E. Dunn, Provo.

74—A purse of $5 gold, No. 3,745, W. R. Van Orden, Fairview.

75—A purse of $5 gold, No. 1,865, Jos. R. Reese, Oakley.

76—A purse of $5 gold, No. 240, G. R. Thackery, Croyden.

77—A purse of $5 gold, No. 3,517, J. D. Wood, Farmington.

78—A purse of $5 gold, No. 4,371, J. S. Rawlings, Taylorsville.

79—A purse of $5 gold, No. 1,029, Wm. Corkins, Payson.

80—Six months' subscription to THE SALT LAKE DAILY HERALD, value $5, No. 3,142, John Ingram, Nephi.

81—Six months' subscription to THE SALT LAKE DAILY HERALD, value $5, No 3,206, Thos. Adams, Porterville.

82—Six months' subscription to THE SALT LAKE DAILY HERALD, value $5, No. 3,157, A. Hendrickson, Levan.

83—Six months' subscription to THE SALT LAKE DAILY HERALD, value $5, No. 4,129, John Lowry, sr., Manti.

84—Six months' subscription to THE SALT LAKE DAILY HERALD, value $5, No. 1,324, John Hirshi, Inverwry.

85—One volume Life of Parley P. Pratt, Pratt Bros., value $5, No. 1,118, Chas. Barnes, jr., Lehi.

86—One volume Popular History of the Mexican People, Bancroft, value $5, No. 4,527, John Woods, American Fork.

87—One volume Every Day Life of Abraham Lincoln, value $5, No. 3,970, John Chorington, Holden.

88—20 pounds best grade of roller process flour, Excelsior mills, Provo, John W. Hoover, manager, value $5, No. 3668, M. Hall, Centreville.

89—One fine steel engraving (artist's proof, unframed) of President Brigham Young, Contributor company, value $5, No. 2019, W. Schofield, Beaver.

90—One pair of French calf shoes, A. Hedquist, Provo, value $5, 4140, A. Smith, Smithfield.

91—Five pecks of Thoburn's extra early seed potatoes, C. 12's, green grocer, Provo, value $5, No. 2536, Richard Birch, Coalville.

92—One set, six volumes, Hume's history of England, value $5, No. 1385, I. Huntsman, Glenwood.

93—One set, six volumes, Hume's history of England, value $5, No. 1008, R. Gough, Payson.

94—One set, six volumes, Hume's history of England, value $5, No. 3091, J. S. Houtz, jr., Rexburg.

95—One set, six volumes, Hume's history of England, value $5, No. 4007, R. Drake, Conant.

96—One set, six volumes, Hume's history of England, value $5, No. 1820, P. C. Anderson, Ephraim.

97—One set, six volumes, Gibbon,s Rome, value $5, No. 3159, J. Gledhill, Mona.

98—One set, six volumes, Gibbon's Rome, value $5, No. 2979, D. H. Robinson, Pleasant Grove.

99—One set, six volumes, Gibbon's Rome, value $5, No. 2401, P. F. Boyack, Spanish Fork.

100—One set, six volumes, Gibbon's Rome, value $5, No. 644, Julius Smith, Brigham.

THE REMAINING 1,400

consists of 1,400 volumes of $1 books of standard history, fiction, poetry, etc., now on exhibition at D. M. McAllister & Co.'s. The full list of persons who draw them will be published in next week's SEMI-WEEKLY.

Telegrams of congratulation were last evening sent to Mr. Holland and several others of those who drew principal prizes. Copies of to-day's daily have also been mailed to the one hundred persons whose names appear above.

The prizes are all ready for delivery and the owners are requested to call around for them as soon as practicable. The postage on books is 10 cents per volume. Parties who do not call or send for their prizes will receive an order for them by mail. Bank checks for the purses of gold will be mailed to the addresses of the parties owning them to-day. All those who drew subscriptions to the Daily HERALD are requested to forward the addresses to which they desire the papers sent. THE HERALD will see that all prizes which require boxing or wrapping are properly forwarded, but at the risk and expense of parties owning the same.

It is a matter which will be a source of satisfaction to all, whether they were among the fortunate ones or not, that the large prizes go in nearly every instance to people in the country towns whose circumstances will make them more than usually welcome.

Deseret Evening News
May 17, 1890

Notes From Emery County.

ORANGEVILLE, May 11, 1890. [Correspondence of the DESERET NEWS.]—As one enters Castle Valley from the south, low mountains, with here and there a dry barren plain, together with natural castles, many of them towering hundreds of feet high, seem to be the only objects on which to feast the mind and charm the gaze of man; still nestling behind some barrier you will emerge upon a number of beautiful valleys, where the hardy husbandman has made "the desert to blossom as the rose."

When one beholds the many changes that have taken place, he cannot but wonder at the progressiveness of man. As one proceeds on his way he views many comfortable and cheery homes. The first place that shows any signs of life is the Muddy, which is yet in its infancy; still, with some skill and energy, the people of the Muddy will prosper; but at present the place presents very little to charm the incomer. Judging from the amount of tillable land within its vicinity, there will yet many come to build them homes and reclaim the land for an inheritance.

Some ten miles to the north you enter the beautiful valley of Ferron, which is some eight miles from east to west and four from north to south, seeming to be one continuous field of lucern and farming land, all well watered, which shows that the people are industrious and persevering.

Ferron settlement is situated in the north side of the valley, on a rising bench, commanding a beautiful view of the valley. Some 70 odd families have built them comfortable homes. Many of these would do credit to some of the older districts, as they consist of new brick and frame houses of comfortable dimensions, surrounded by the beautiful and towering poplar, the balm of Gilead and other shade trees. The town is laid off in five acre blocks, with six rod streets and eleven feet sidewalks, and these are being ornamented with nature's best fruit trees in abundance. It contains a commodious two-story school-house with a bell in the tower, a pleasant social hall, and two stores doing a thriving business. The settlers being mostly young people who seem wide awake, Ferron is bound to grow, as the natural facilities are such as to invite men of means to come and settle and help develop the resources of the country.

Almost every family lives in their neat comfortable frame, adobe or brick houses of fair dimensions, with good sheds, and orchards in a thriving condition. The place supports two private and one co-op. stores, one grist mill, a nice, commodious school house fitted with modern apparatus, a large social hall with ample stage room, and home talent sufficient to amuse the people during the long winter months. The people are charitable and free, and hope some day to become independent. They extend the hand of fellowship and greeting to those who may wish to come and help beautify their situation.

This valley being the leading winter range for stock and sheep, the people find a ready local market for their produce at reasonable prices. Other settlements of the county are Castle Dale, a beautiful situation; Huntington, Price, and some minor places.

Proceeding on the way twelve miles further north, the pride of Emery — Orangeville — feasts your view, as it is situated in a most beautiful valley on the banks of Cottonwood Creek. The townsite contains some 120 acres laid off in five acre squares with broad streets, giving ample room for sidewalks, and these are lined with beautiful shade trees, giving it the appearance of a young forest viewed from the distance. It contains some of the most productive soil in Utah, and I doubt if there is a better fruit-growing district outside of the sunny south. Trees have been known to make over seven feet of wood in one season, and fruits, berries, vegetables and grasses grow in abundance.

Mr. E. H. Olliffant, formerly of Salt Lake, has started quite an extensive nursery covering a number of acres—an industry much needed in any County but much neglected in Utah. His varieties of fruit, shade, and ornamental trees are the best and choicest to be had, and he is in hopes ere long to be able to supply this as well as some of the adjacent counties with all the shrubbery they may need.

Dr. More, formerly of Mt. Pleasant, has settled in Castle Dale, having resolved to work at his profession there.

Coal is found in abundance, each settlement throughout the county owning its own coal deposit. Wood is near and lumber can be bought at a fair figure. Prosperity, peace and happiness seem predominant.

Success to Emery. May her towns grow in wealth and increase in population; may her people never witness the misery of famine or vice; but may she become prosperous and great in the valleys of Utah.

W. W. B.

NOTES FROM EMERY COUNTY.

As one enters Castle Valley from the south, low mountains with here and there a dry barren plain, together with natural castles, many of them towering hundreds of feet high, seem to be the only objects on which to feast the mind and charm the gaze of man; still nestling behind some barrier you will emerge upon a number of beautiful valleys, where the hardy husbandman has made "the desert to blossom as the rose."

When one beholds the many changes that have taken place, he cannot but wonder at the progressiveness of man. As one proceeds on his way he views many comfortable and cheery homes. The first place that shows any signs of life is the Muddy, which is yet in its infancy; still, with some skill and energy, the people of the Muddy will prosper; but at present the place presents very little to charm the incomer. Judging from the amount of tillable land within its vicinity, there will yet many come to build them homes and reclaim the land for an inheritance.

Some ten miles to the north you enter the beautiful valley of Ferron, which is some eight miles from east to west and four from north to south, seeming to be one continuous field of lucern and farming land, all well watered, which shows that the people are industrious and persevering.

Ferron settlement is situated in the north side of the valley, on a rising bench, commanding a beautiful view of the valley. Some 70 odd families have built them comfortable homes. Many of these would do credit to some of the older districts, as they consist of new brick and frame houses of comfortable dimensions, surrounded by the beautiful and towering poplar, the balm of Gilead and other shade trees. The town is laid off in five acre blocks, with six rod streets and eleven feet sidewalks, and these are being ornamented with nature's best fruit trees in abundance. It contains a commodious two-story school-house with a bell in the tower, a pleasant social hall, and two stores doing a thriving business. The settlers being mostly young people who seem wide awake, Ferron is bound to grow, as the natural facilities are such as to invite men of means to come and settle and help develop the resources of the country.

Almost every family lives in their neat comfortable frame, adobe or brick houses of fair dimensions, with good sheds, and orchards in a thriving condition. The place supports two private and one co-op. stores, one grist mill, a nice, commodious school house fitted with modern apparatus, a large social hall with ample stage room; and home talent sufficient to amuse the people during the long winter months. The people are charitable and free, and hope some day to become independent. They extend the hand of fellowship and greeting to those who may wish to come and help beautify their situation.

This valley being the leading winter range for stock and sheep, the people find a ready local market for their produce at reasonable prices. Other settlements of the county are Castle Dale, a beautiful situation; Huntington, Price, and some minor places.

Proceeding on the way twelve miles further north, the pride of Emery — Orangeville — feasts your view, as it is situated in a most beautiful valley on the banks of Cottonwood Creek. The townsite contains some 120 acres laid off in five acre squares with broad streets, giving ample room for sidewalks, and these are lined with beautiful shade trees, giving it the appearance of a young forest viewed from the distance. It contains some of the most productive soil in Utah, and I doubt if there is a better fruit growing district outside of the sunny south. Trees have been known to make over seven feet of wood in one season, and fruits, berries, vegetables and grasses grow in abundance.

Mr. E. H. Ollifant, formerly of Salt Lake, has started quite an extensive nursery covering a number of acres—an industry much needed in any county but much neglected in Utah. His varieties of fruit, shade, and ornamental trees are the best and choicest to be had, and he is in hopes ere long to be able to supply this as well as some of the adjacent counties with all the shrubbery they may need.

Dr. More, formerly of Mt. Pleasant, has settled in Castle Dale, having resolved to work at his profession there.

Coal is found in abundance, each settlement throughout the county owning its own coal deposit. Wood is near and lumber can be bought at a fair figure. Prosperity, peace and happiness seem predominant.

Success to Emery. May her towns grow in wealth and increase in population; may her people never witness the misery of famine or vice; but may she become prosperous and great in the valleys of Utah.

W. W. H.

ORANGEVILLE, May 11, 1890.

people find a ready local market for their produce at reasonable prices. Other settlements of the county are Castle Dale, a beautiful situation; Huntington, Price, and some minor places.

Proceeding on the way twelve miles further north, the pride of Emery — Orangeville — feasts your view, as it is situated in a most beautiful valley on the banks of Cottonwood Creek. The townsite contains some 120 acres laid off in five acre squares with broad streets, giving ample room for sidewalks, and these are lined with beautiful shade trees, giving it the appearance of a young forest viewed from the distance. It contains some of the most productive soil in Utah, and I doubt if there is a better fruit growing district outside of the sunny south. Trees have been known to make over seven feet of wood in one season, and fruits, berries, vegetables and grasses grow in abundance.

In Emery County.

The people who settled on the Muddy have now got the water on their townsite. No body of settlers ever struggled more heroically to overcome obstacles to settlement than those who are now located on the Muddy in the townsite called Emery, and, judging from present prospects, their efforts will be crowned with success.

The crops that have been planted promise to yield a good harvest.

W. G. Petty is now Bishop of the ward. Ferron is still growing, and a great breadth of land further south is already under cultivation. Orangeville presents the most thrifty appearance of any town in the county, owing perhaps to more extensive planting of trees, which tends to give the place a home-like look. New canals are being taken out above the town, which will bring in a great quantity of additional land, extending nearly half way to Ferron.

Castledale, though the capital of the county, will have to show more thrift and energy or be left far in the rear by some of her more energetic neighbors.

The people of Huntington are making another effort upon their meeting-house. More acreage is under cultivation here than usual, and a large quantity of lucern is being raised. Cleveland will this year raise good crops, so that the patient settlers there will soon begin to obtain results from their patience and toil. Want of water has been the drawback for years, but this season there appears to be plenty for all.

The inhabitants of Price are more hopeful, and great pains are being taken by them to cultivate their lots. The towns above mentioned are the main places in Castle Valley, and are strung out on a line north and south to the extent of about fifty-eight miles.

A sad and fatal accident happened on Thursday, a short distance above Orangeville, in the Cottonwood canyon. A. Cloward and his family, accompanied by his father, James M. Cloward, had camped on Wednesday night near the coal beds. They had an open one horse buggy and a heavy two-horse wagon. When they started from camp in the morning the single horse backed on a hill, frightening Mrs. Cloward, who was driving. The men went to her assistance and she alighted from the buggy. Young Mr. Cloward wanted to drive the horse and force him up the raise, but his father thought he could himself manage. He had not proceeded far, however, when the horse began to back on a dugway, and presently the horse, vehicle and all its occupants fell over the bank, throwing the old man out. When the son reached him he was dead, his neck having been broken by the fall.

James M. Cloward had been a resident of Moroni, Sanpete County, for about twenty years, and had been in Castledale for the last two months. He was 62 years of age. The body will be taken to Thistle on the R. G. W. Railroad, and thence to his former home in Moroni, for interment. TRAVELER.

EMERY STAKE CONFERENCE.

The quarterly conference of this Stake was held at Price, on Sunday and Monday, May 11th and 12th. On the stand were Apostle Heber J. Grant, C. G. Larsen and Orange Judd, of the Stake Presidency, representatives of the Bishopric from each ward and from the different organizations in the Stake.

After the usual opening exercises President Larsen expressed his pleasure in meeting with the Saints at Price under such favorable circumstances. In connection with his counselors he had visited the different wards of the Stake and found the people willing to serve God and respect His laws. The health of the people generally is good and the present prospect for grain and fruit promising.

Apostle Grant occupied the remainder of the forenoon. The Latter-day Saints, he said, are accomplishing the work of our Heavenly Father, although they are passing through much trial and tribulation. The prophecies of Joseph Smith are being fulfilled daily, and our present peculiar position to the American nation and the whole world today are indisputable proofs thereof. But we should bear with patience the indignities heaped upon us and learn to "suffer and be strong."

The afternoon meeting was also occupied by Apostle Grant, who read from the Doctrine and Covenants—that intelligence obtained in this world will continue in the world or life to come.

The blessings of God cannot be measured by dollars and cents. If such were the case we would find that men who acknowledge not God and regard not His divine laws are accumulating wealth by the million, while the humble, God-fearing and prayerful man is poor and sometimes destitute. The greatest riches that mortals can accumulate is knowledge of life eternal, which is the knowledge of God, and for this we as a people should strive.

On Sunday evening there was a general Priesthood meeting. The following brethren were presented: Arly Day as Counselor to Bishop Calvin W. Moore of Lawrence. Hans C. Wickman as Counselor to Bishop W. G. Petty of Emery. Albert E. McMullen as Bishop of Wellington Ward (lately organized) and Soren Frederiksen of Ferran to be ordained a High Priest, all of whom were unanimously sustained.

Monday morning conference was resumed. The statistical report was read and showed a total number as follows: Patriarch, 1; Seventies, 145; High Priests, 106; Elders, 207;

Priests, 17; Teachers, 26; Deacons, 144; members, 1340. Children under eight years, 1198. Total of souls, 3154.

The speakers in the forenoon were Orange Sealy, of the Emery Stake Presidency, and Brother Bean, of the Sevier Stake Presidency, who bore testimony to the truth of th work in which the Saints are engaged.

Bishops Frandsen, of Price, Pulsipher, of Huntington, and Olsen of Castle Dale, reported their wards in good condition. The remainder of the time was occupied by Apostle Grant.

At the afternoon meeting, the general and Stake authorities were presented and unanimously sustained. Representatives H. J. Stowell, of Spring Glenn, Calvin Moore, of Lawrence, W. G. Petty, of Emery, and A. Anderson, counselor of Orangeville, gave favorable reports of their wards.

Apostle Grant urged upon the Saints the great responsibility of teaching their children the principles of the Gospel, both by example and precept.

President Larsen offered a few closing remarks, thanked the choirs for the music and all who had aided in making the conference interesting.

Price and Spring Glenn choirs joined and rendered the anthem, "Jerusalem, my glorious home," in an excellent manner.

Benediction was pronounced by Elder O. J. Anderson and conference adjourned to be held at Castle Dale, August 10 and 11.

O. J. ANDERSON, Stake Clerk.

Ogden Standard
June 15, 1890

AN ACT

To amend section 76, s. 1, of the compiled laws of Utah of 1888, relating to the boundary of Emery county

SECTION 1. *Be it enacted by the Governor and Legislative Assembly of the Territory of Utah:* That section 76, s. 1, of the compiled laws of Utah of 1888, is hereby amended to read as follows:

Section 76, s. 1. All that portion of the Territory of Utah bounded as follows, to-w't: Commencing at a point where parallel 38 deg. 30 min. north latitude crosses Green River, thence west along said parallel to a point six (6) miles west of the first guide meridian east of the Salt Lake meridian; thence north along the township line the third standard parallel south; between range five (5) and six (6) east, to thence east three (3) miles to the section line running north through the middle of rang six (6) east; thence north along said section line to the township line between township eleven (11) and twelve (12) south; thence east along the last mentioned township line to Green River; thence down the main channel of Green River to the place of beginning, is hereby made and named Emery county, with the county seat at Castle Dale, which county is hereby attached to and made a part of the first judicial district.

SEC. 2. This act shall take effect upon its approval.

Approved March 13, 1890.

Salt Lake Herald
June 17, 1890

Decoration Day at Orangeville

It being rather cold on the first of May, the superintendency of the Sunday school put off their May day festival until Decoration day, thereby killing two birds with one stone. As early as eight o'clock in the morning many children were seen skipping along the streets, and soon sweet strains of music were floating over the beautiful burg of Orangeville, emanating from the brass band. As soon as the gong struck ten, with the band in lead the Sunday school formed into line to the number of nearly three hundred, with a company of young ladies carrying the banner, on which was inscribed, "Suffer little children to come unto me,"etc., which also represents Jesus blessing little children.

After marching through the principal streets, they then repaired to the Social hall which had been prepared for the occasion, and listened to a programme of songs, recitations, etc. Mr. Alexander Johnson, principal of Emery Stake academy, briefly reviewed some of the scenes through which our forefathers passed, and why the 30th of May was set apart for the decoration of the graves of those who had fought and died in the cause of truth and right. In the afternoon to the inspiring strains of music the children enjoyed themselves in the dance, and in the evening the young people of Orangeville and Castle Dale tripped the light fantastic untill all seemed willing to retire to their peaceful slumber. Take the day as a whole it was one of enjoyment and recreation of mind and body, and one that all seemed to enjoy—both old and young.

Prospect of a bountiful harvest is good, and you hear some of the farmers surmising, what are we going to do with our lucern. Hay cutting will commence in about two weeks and from that time until fall work will be more plentiful than men, as it seems each man has more hay than he can take care of. But they have push and muscle.

Mr. D. Wilkin has just completed his new frame house by the addition of a new veranda in front. He is the leading merchant and always keeps on hand a choice selection of the necessities, and affable clerks to wait on the buyer.

The people of Orangeville have also organized a Co-op institution, which is doing a creditable business for the time that it has been in operation and the amount of capital invested. Under proper management it will thrive and prosper. Mr. J. K. Bird keeps also on hand a good line of groceries, fancy notions, etc.

The Sunday school, under the able management of John Snow as superintendent, and U. A. Curtis and Adelbert Childs as assistants is in a prospering condition.

The Sunday meetings could be better attended, still those who meet together seem to enjoy the spirit of the gospel. The people listened to the kind and encouraging remarks of Elder C. H. Ollifant, W. W. Billings and A. Burkley. After the Sunday services were over the ladies held their meeting to discuss and sift the question of woman's rights.

The district school under the management of Mr. Billings from Manti, is in a fairly prosperous condition, having an enrollment of eighty eight pupils.

The Cottonwood from which the people receive their supply of water is booming. If some of the surplus of these parts could be transferred to the beautiful country south of Beaver to Parowan, how many sorrowful hearts could be made happy. But as it is it goes tumbling and roaring in its course to the placid bosom of the Pacific, when perhaps it is again changed by dame nature, and precipitated to mother earth to bring forth fruit meet for man.

The people own and work for home consumption, some of the grandest coal mines in the west, and they are looking forward to the day when some railroad magnate will see fit to build a road to their coal fields, and, thereby develop the resources of this valley.   W. W. B.

Orangeville, June 3, 1890.

A SENSIBLE MAN THIS.

Ferron, June 19, 1890.

Editor REGISTER;—I am pleased to notice the steps taken in the interest of our isolated county by the REGISTER for I learn that the opinion of the people at large in the neighboring counties is much worse than the county deserves.

A friend of mine from San Pete Co., visted me a few days since, and was so pleased with the country that he is preparing to settle here.

I did the same six years ago and think that there is many a young man in the older settlements that would do well to do like-wise.

H. C. Hansen.

There are twenty-three signal and observation stations in this Territory. which occasions the remark that they might be grouped into a Territorial department with the Salt Lake office at the head. In that way all the valuable data about Territorial precipitation and meteorology generally might be secured with much more facility and reliability than ever before, and a digest published monthly. The stations are Salt Lake, Ogden, Provo, Park City. Duchesne, Beaver, Nephi. Castle Dale. St. George. Mt. Carmel, Mt. Pleasant, Richfield, Moab, Taylor's Ranch, Lossee, Price. Stockton, Brigham, Deseret. Snowville, Logan, Grouse Creek, Riverview.

Notice of Homestead Final Proof.
No. 516.

Land Office at Salt Lake city, Utah. July 16th, 1890.

Notice is hereby given that the following-named settler has filed notice of his intention to make final proof in support of his claim, and that said proof will be made before the Probate Judge, or in his absence the county clerk, at castle Dale, Emery county, Utah, cn September 6th.

Also Samnel Grange, rl. k. 6276, for the S.½ S. E.¼ of Section 28, N. E.¼ N. E.¼ Section 33, N. W.¼ N. W.¼ Sec 34, Tp. 17 S. R 9 E.

He names the following witnesses to prove his continuous residence upon and cultivation of, said land, Viz:

Thomas E, Cheney, Nathan H. Stevens, William A. Guyman, and Thomas Kirby all of Huntington, U. T.

FRANK D. HOBBS
Register

Salt Lake Herald
August 16, 1890

The Busby Mining Co.

The articles of association of the Busby Mining company were filed in the county clerk's office yesterday.

The object of the company is to operate and develop mines of all kinds and characters, including coal and stone of every description, in Emery and other counties in Utah.

Salt Lake is named as the principal place of business, and the capital stock is placed at $500,000, divided into shares of the par value of $5.

The stock is held as follows:

Name.	Shares.
C. C. Raynolds	1,428 4-7
Geo. M. Makin	1,428 4-7
John Hadley	1,428 4-7
Matilda M. Busby	1,428 4-7
H. W. Hooton	1,428 4-7
H. A. Ferguson	1,428 4-7
Thos. Kane	714 2-7
W. C. Reilly	714 2-7

The consideration of said company issuing and delivering 10,000 shares of the capital stock to the incorporation is as follows: The Coal Fork Makin mine, located upon unsurveyed government lands, about eight miles from Castle Dale, Emery county, in what is commonly known as Coal Fork cañon; the Mysterious, in Straight cañon; the Liverpool Boy, in Huntington cañon.

C. C. Reynolds is president; H. A. Ferguson, vice-president; H. A. Hooton, secretary; Matilda M. Busby, treasurer.

County Register
August 21, 1890

Notice Of Pre-emption Proof.
No. 539.

Land Office at Salt Lake City, Utah. Aug. 7th, 1890.

Notice is hereby given that the following named settler has filed notice of his intention to make final proof in support of his claim, and that said proof will be made before the County Clerk, at Castle Dale, Emery county, Utah, on September 20th, 1890, viz:

Arch Kinder, D. S. 11401, for the N.½ of N. W.¼. Sec. 15. Tp 17 S, R. 8. E.

He names the following witnesses to prove his continuous residence upon and cultivation of, said land, Viz:

Leawder Lemon, Christian Ottosen, Hyrum Jones, and George E. Palmer, all of Huntington, Utah.

FRANK D. HOBBS,
Register.

County Register
September 18, 1890

EMERY CO., ITEMS.

Water-melons of the finest type are now displayed at Ferron Co-op.

Harvest is nearly over and the sound of the Thresher may be heard reverberating among the everlasting clay-banks.

Thursday evening Sept. 4th, was visited by a cold piercing wind which had the effect of injuring the more tender vegetables, corn etc.

The citizens of Ferron were somewhat excited last Saturday evening, Sept. 7th. by finding that a family of travellers had arrived in the city with the corpse of a child. Mr. Cook the head of the family, states that he and company left Gooseberry a short time ago for Ashley. The child as stated above was ill before the journey, and after travelling through heat in the day-time and cold at night died when about one half mile south of Ferron.

Mrs. Jos. Stevens, who is always ready to lend a helping hand, took the child to her home and otherwise added to the comfort of the bereaved family.

The people of Ferron contributed a casket and Sunday evening the remains were removed to the cemetery.

Deseret Evening News
November 15, 1890

Called at Castle Dale.

Brandan, now deputy marshal of Mount Pleasant, dropped into our burg very quietly yesterday. After lighting his pipe he made a raid upon President Larsen's residence and can now swear to the size and location of every room in the house. After finding he could find nothing he turned his face toward Orangeville.

BRUTUS.

CASTLE DALE, Nov. 9, 1890.

A GREAT VICTORY.

The Official Returns of the Recent Election

GIVEN IN FULL BY PRECINCTS.

A Comparison with the Vote Cast for John T. Caine and R. N. Baskin two Years Ago.

The returns of the recent election for delegate to Congress, as announced by the canvassing board, have already been published in THE HERALD. The official returns by precincts were as follows:

BEAVER COUNTY.

	Caine.	Goodwin.
Adamsville	16	5
Minersville	33	5
Greenville	25	1
Star	6	21
Grampion	10	17
Beaver	214	33
Total	304	77

BOX ELDER COUNTY.

Promontory	—	10
Deweyville	10	11
Kelton	—	—
Terrace	2	41
Willard	85	7
Plymouth	37	7
Calls Fort	51	3
Mantua	55	1
Bear River City	44	3
Malad	1	19
Grouse Creek	17	4
Curlew	10	1
Portage	43	—
Park Valley	13	3
Collinston	9	10
Snowville	—	—
Box Elder	238	13
Junction	9	6
Total	624	130

CACHE COUNTY.

Mendon	59	7
Paridise	71	7
Benson	19	4
Richmond	81	6
Clarkson	39	—
Newton	39	1
Logan	363	65
Hyde Park	53	—
Smithfield	125	9
Trenton	20	3
Wellsville	161	6
Hyrum	163	4
Providence	55	2
Peterbore	7	7
Millville	64	1
Coveville	23	—
Lewiston	76	1
Total	1,416	128

DAVIS COUNTY.

East Bountiful	118	9
West Bountiful	56	2
South Bountiful	64	4
Kaysville	123	10
Farmington	86	4
Centreville	50	4
South Weber	20	10
South Hooper	19	10
Layton	91	10
Syracuse	26	—
Steed	10	2
Total	651	75

EMERY COUNTY.

Blake	..	27
Castle Dale	40	..
Castle Gate	6	16
Cleveland	8	..
Ferron	45	5
Huntington	78	1
Larence	19	..
Muddy	39	2
Malen	26	2
Orangeville	50	3
Price	32	6
Scofield	31	25
Wellington	18	1
Total	392	86

GARFIELD COUNTY.

Cannonville	..	..
Escalante	..	..
Hillsdale	..	..
Panguitch	..	..
Total	216	24

IRON COUNTY.

Cedar City	115	2
Kanarra	26	5
Summit	10	2
Parowan	99	6
Paragoonah	35	--
Total	**285**	**15**

JUAB COUNTY.

Eureka	44	141
Juab	22	1
Levan	50	5
Mona	44	5
Mammoth	4	36
Nephi	289	33
Silver City	1	21
Total	**459**	**242**

KANE COUNTY.

Glendale	25	—
Georgetown	8	—
Johnston	—	—
Kanab	40	—
Mount Carmel	20	—
Orderville	22	—
Upper Kanab	12	—
Pahrea	—	—
Total	**127**	**—**

MILLARD COUNTY.

Deseret	68	3
Fillmore	88	10
Holden	32	6
Kanosh	58	5
Leamington	20	—
Meadow	32	1
Oak Creek	23	—
Oasis	27	—
Scipio	52	15
Total	**400**	**40**

MORGAN COUNTY.

Cañon Creek	56	—
Croyden	16	3
Milton	25	3
Morgan	94	8
Peterson	20	5
Total	**211**	**29**

SAN JUAN COUNTY.

Bluff	14	—
Benna	—	—
Monticello	11	—
Total	**25**	**—**

SEVIER COUNTY.

Anabella	21	2
Burrville	11	4
Central	23	2
Elsinor	41	2
Gooseberry	4	2
Glenwood	44	2
Joseph	51	2

PIUTE COUNTY.

Beaver Creek	8	2
Bullion	11	28
Burgess	—	—
Circleville	48	3
Deer Trail	10	4
Fremont	37	—
Graves Valley	4	1
Cainesville	11	1
Koosharem	15	6
Loa	51	1
Pleasant Creek	3	2
Thurber	28	2
Teasdale	27	—
Wilmont	3	10
Junction	24	4
Total	**270**	**65**

RICH COUNTY.

Garden City	30	1
Lake Tower	35	—
Meadowville	15	2
Randolph	45	12
Woodruff	35	10
Total	**160**	**25**

SALT LAKE COUNTY.

Salt Lake City	2264	2558
Big Cottonwood	79	4
Butler	26	18
Brighton	12	8
Bluff Dale	19	3
Bingham	16	145
Draper	104	3
East Mill Creek	35	13
Farmers	50	13
Fort Herriman	23	—
Granite	17	3
Granger	39	3
Hunter	19	7
Little Cottonwood	1	39
Mill Creek	140	27
Mountain Dale	10	3
North Point	14	—
North Jordan	55	9
Pleasant Green	35	1
Riverton	35	—
South Cottonwood	130	22
Silver	—	21
Sugar House	77	36
Sandy	89	59
South Jordan	34	3
Union	56	16
West Jordan	126	25
Total	**3515**	**3 9 3**

Monroe	74	13
Redmound	35	4
Richfield	91	21
Salina	50	29
Vermillion	27	3
Willow Bend	27	2
Total	**499**	**93**

SANPETE COUNTY.

Chester	19	1
Ephraim	201	17
Fayette	29	6
Fountain Green	79	—
Fairview	119	3
Gunison	98	23
Mayfield	36	1
Manti	181	21
Moroni	106	3
Mount Pleasant	182	75
Melbourne	19	4
Petty	21	2
Spring City	88	6
Thistle	10	2
Wales	29	5
Total	1,216	174

SUMMIT COUNTY.

Coalville	109	23
Echo	15	23
Grass Creek	3	4
Henefer	44	6
Kamas	44	7
Peoa	46	12
Hoytsville	40	4
Park City	9	895
Parley's Park	8	11
Rockport	16	2
Upton	21	5
Wanship	31	5
Woodland	22	4
Total	408	1001

TOOELE COUNTY.

Batesville	13	52
Clover	16	—
Deep Creek	—	8
Grantsville	91	2
Lake Point	21	1
Lake View	19	1
Ophir	6	27
St. Johns	24	—
Stockton	2	43
Tooele	115	19
Vernon	18	7
Total	323	103

UINTAH.

Ashley	50	6
Brown's Park	—	—
Mountain Dell	26	—
Riverdale	—	—
Vernal	88	19
Total	173	25

UTAH COUNTY.

Alpine	59	9
American Fork	212	22
Benjamin	33	14
Cedar Fort	18	2
Fairfield	8	8
Goshen	44	8
Lakeshore	47	16
Lakeview	39	2
Lehi	221	15
Payson	216	55
Pleasant Grove	176	18
Provo Bench	29	4
P. V. Junction	5	12
Provo	496	150
Spanish Fork	280	29
Santaquin	100	6
Springville	294	60
Salem	68	12
Spring Lake	8	2
Thistle	11	4
Total	2,364	457

WASATCH COUNTY.		
Charleston	58	—
Heber	169	16
Midway	93	—
Wallsburg	49	1
Total	369	17

WASHINGTON COUNTY.		
Bloomington	14	—
Duncan's Retreat	7	—
Gunlock	12	—
Grafton	15	—
Leeds	25	3
Pine Valley	35	—
Rockville	26	—
Silver Reef	1	15
St. George	153	1
Santa Clara	21	—
Shonesburg	7	—
Springdale	13	—
Toquerville	34	—
Virgin City	42	—
Washington	34	—
New Harmony	—	—
Heber	—	—
Hamilton	—	—
Pinto	—	—
Total	438	19

WEBER COUNTY.		
Eden	40	6
Hooper	71	11
Huntsville	77	14
Harrisville	65	4
Kanesville	21	3
Lynne	48	38
Marriott	31	7
North Ogden	103	8
Ogden	687	758
Pleasant View	44	2
Plain City	88	32
Riverdale	32	7
Slaterville	40	27
Uintah	25	10
Wilson	32	14
West Weber	78	2
Total	1,482	943

TOTAL NOTE.

Caine	16,353
Goodwin	6,906
Scattering	28
Total	23,287
Caine's majority over Goodwin	9,441
Over all	9,419

In 188 the vote was:

John T. Caine	10,127
Robert N. Baskin	3,484
Samuel R. Thurman	511
Total vote	14,122
Caine's majority over Baskin	6,643

Salt Lake Herald
November 26, 1890

B. W. Driggs, of this city, is authority for the statement that the Castle Valley road, projected to run from Price, Emery county, through Cleveland, Huntington, Castle Dale and Orangeville to the Pittsburg mine, a distance of fifty miles, is well under way.

IN CASTLE VALLEY.

Description of the Various Wards of the Emery Stake of Zion.

[Correspondence of the DESERET NEWS.]

For the purpose of making a tour through the Emery Stake of Zion in the interest of Church history, I left Salt Lake City on the 8th inst. and arrived at Price station (125 miles from the city) in the evening. Next morning in company with Prest. Geo. Q. Cannon and Elder John Morgan, who had arrived during the night, I continued the journey by team (Bishop Geo. Frandsen, of Price taking us in his carriage) to Orangeville, a distance of 32 miles, where we attended the Stake quarterly conference on that and the following day. After the conference Prest. Cannon and Elder Morgan returned home and I proceded to gather historical information concerning the Emery Stake of Zion. In visiting the various wards and settlements for that purpose I have held meetings with the Saints in nearly every place and have had a good time generally. Last Sunday evening I also spoke to a respectable congregation of Saints and strangers in Castle Gate, a mining town in Price Canyon, and yesterday attended a ward conference at Spring Glen, where the Stake Presidency was in attendance, and today, in connection with that Presidency and Bishops Geo. Frandsen of Price, and H. J.

Stowell of Spring Glen, I attended the ward conference at Wellington on which occasion the Bishopric of that new ward was made complete by the setting apart of Geo. W. Eldredge to act as first and Robert A. Snyder as second counselor to Bishop A. C. McMullen. In these ward conferences much good and practical instruction was given suitable for the circumstances surrounding the Saints in this new country, and the Spirit of God was poured out in a great measure upon all present causing the hearts of the Saints to rejoice exceedingly. After the afternoon meeting today Prest. C. G. Larsen and his counselors (Orange Seely and William Howard) returned to their homes in Castle Dale and Huntington, and I returned to Price, where, in the hospitable home of Bishop Geo. Frandsen, I am finishing my historical gleanings as regards the Emery Stake, preparatory to leaving for other parts of the country.

The Emery Stake of Zion embraces nearly all of Emery County, Utah, and consists of eleven organized wards, which, named in geographical order, commencing from the north, range as follows: Spring Glen, Price, Wellington, Cleveland, Huntington, Lawrence, Castle Dale, Orangeville, Ferron, Molen and Muddy. Three of these settlements are situated on Price River, three on or near Huntington Creek, two on Cottonwood Creek, two on Ferron Creek and one on Muddy Creek, all in what is generally known as Castle Valley. This valley has well defined boundaries on the west and north where lofty mountains separate it from other valleys and tracts of country, but on the

east and south it extends into an almost unexplored region so far that even the earliest settlers here are unable to define its boundaries. It is, in fact, an open country, traversed by low mountain ranges, barren hills, deep gulches and washes, etc., and in many places it is absolutely impassable for teams. Even men on horseback often encounter great difficulties in getting through, and in some instances are compelled to travel a distance of twenty-five miles or more in order to advance five miles in a straight line. But in the western part of the valley, near the eastern base of the Wasatch mountains, where all the settlements are located, there are comparatively fine tracts of country, which after being brought under cultivation, can most properly be termed an oasis in the desert. Generally speaking, Castle Valley is more suited for pastural than agricultural pursuits. Still the people have made, and are now making, farming a decided success, as in many instances the amount of grain raised per acre compares very favorably with that produced in the most fertile parts of our Territory. The culture of bees has, of late years, been proven to be a very successful industry and it is now generally acknowledged that Castle Valley produces the best honey in Utah, and perhaps the best in the United States. As an example of what can be done as regards quantity I may state that during the past summer Brother Caleb B. Rhoades of Price, produced 5,300 pounds of honey from 22 stands of bees. Noah T. Guyman of Orangeville, and John Zwahlen of Ferron, have been nearly equally successful in their bee culture the present season. The great natural wealth of Castle Valley, however, seems to be its immense coal fields. The coal is found in inexhaustable quantities in the several canyons in the mountains west. The veins, so far discovered, ranges from six to eleven feet in thickness and the coal is of the most excellent quality. But until railways shall have been built to the different places where these immense coal deposits have been discovered they are of course comparatively valueless, except for local consumption.

The Saints in Castle Valley have made great progress during the last few years, and their towns and villages begin to assume the appearance of comfort and prosperity. More settlers, however, are needed and anyone in need of a home who is not afraid to face the hardships and dangers of a new country, will be made heartily welcome by the people of this valley.

Castle Dale, pleasantly situated on the north bank of the Cottonwood Creek, 32 miles southwest of Price, the nearest railway station, is the headquarters of the Emery Stake and the county seat of Emery County. It contains the best flouring mill in the county, and the only one, except the little Pioneer mill at Orangeville on the same creek (Cottonwood). Castle Dale has 58 families belonging to the Church and a few non-members. Henning Olsen is Bishop. A new meeting house, which, when completed, will be the most commodious public building in the county, is in course of erection, and will probably be completed next spring. Two of the Stake Presidency (President C. G. Larsen and his first counselor, Orange Seeley)

his first counselor, Orange Seeley) reside in this place.

Orangeville is the other town on Cottonwood Creek. It is situated about three miles west of Castle Dale, not far from the mouth of Cottonwood Canyon, in which very extensive coal-fields have been discovered. There is considerable talk just now about constructing a railway from a point on Price River to these mines. Orangeville can boast of having produced more fruit, so far, than any other settlement in Emery County, and is also surrounded by some choice farming lands. This town has 66 families belonging to the Church, over whom Jasper Robertson presides as Bishop. He is also probate judge of the county.

Ferron, a fine little town on Ferron Creek, is reached by traveling 11½ miles in a southwesterly direction from Castle Dale. The town is situated on the north bank of the creek on a hill side sloping gently to the south. Across the creek, south of the townsite, is a compact body of good farming land. Ferron has the finest and most commodious meeting-house (known as the Social Hall) in the Emery Stake, and a number of comfortable private residences. The strength of the Saints here is 63 families, and Frederick Olsen, a man of sterling qualities, is the Bishop.

Three miles east of Ferron is Molen, an outgrowth of Ferron. It is a pleasant little neighborhood, and the townsite is situated on the north side of Ferron Creek, near where the old Gunnison trail crosses that stream. There is some of the best farming land in the county, but as the quantity is very limited as also water wherewith to irrigate it, Molen will perhaps never become a very large place. Lyman S. Beach, with H. P. Rasmussen and Hans C. Hansen, presides as Bishop over the 25 families of Saints who reside here.

After traveling 16 miles through a genuine desert country—broken and desolate—in a southwesterly direction, the townsite of Emery (formerly called Muddy) is reached. It is situated in the north end of a large valley extending toward the Fish Lake Mountains on the south. From here the lofty peaks of the Henry Mountains are also seen toward the southeast. To convey the water of Muddy Creek onto the lands where Emery is situated a long and expensive canal had to be constructed, which for a distance of 1240 feet is tunnelled through a mountain-ridge. This was done at an expence of nearly $50,000. And as the community which had to do this immense labor was poor, it has indeed been a heavy task. But it has been accomplished, and the prospects before the enterprising people of Emery are now very bright compared to what they were a few years ago. The Emery Ward numbers 46 families of Saints, and Wm. G. Petty, one of the founders of Pettyville, Sanpete County, presides here as Bishop.

Lawrence, named in honor of C. G. Larsen, President of the Emery Stake, is a village and farming district situated on Huntington Creek, eight and one-half miles northeast of Castle Dale. To it has the reputation of being the best grain producing district in the county. In 1868 13,000 bushels of small grain was raised in this little settlement, which numbers only twenty-four families. No other settlement in the Stake, even those much larger, produced an amount equal to that. Calvin W. Moore, formerly a member of the "Mormon" Battalion, is the Bishop of Lawrence Ward.

Huntington, the metropolis of Emery County, is pleasantly situated on the north bank of Huntington Creek, nine and one half miles northeast of Castle Dale, surrounded by good farming land. This growing town is the home of 133 families of Latter-day Saints, presided over by Bishop Charles Pulsipher, a son of the late President Zelah Pulsipher. Here also reside Henry Harriman, one of the first seven President, of the Seventies, now over eighty-six years of age, Geo. W. Johnson, another Church veteran, Wm. Howard, second Counselor in the Stake Presidency, and others of prominence and note. A fine meeting house is here also in course of erection, and the town is fast assuming the appearance of comfort and wealth.

Northeast of Huntington is a fine open tract of country, said to be the finest in the county, in the midst of which the settlement known as Cleveland is pleasantly situated. The recently surveyed townsite on which the people are now preparing to build, is seven miles northeast of Huntington, but as yet the settlers live in a very scattered condition on their respective quarter sections. They number thirty families of Saints and have recently been organized into a ward, with Lars P. Oveson, a man of enterprise and ability, as Bishop. To convey the water of Huntington Creek onto the farming lands of Cleveland, a canal, fifteen miles long, had to be constructed, at a cost of $35,000.

Price, on the Rio Grande Western Railway, is favorably situated on the north bank of Price River, 125 miles from Salt Lake City and twenty-two miles northeast of Huntington. The "Mormon" population of Price Ward, consisting of forty-five families, reside mostly on the townsite near the railway station, and are commencing to feel more comfortable and satisfied than formerly. It has required considerable hardship and energy to redeem this part of the county from its desert sterility, but through perseverance and patience the object has been accomplished, and Price now has the appearance of comfort and enterprise. This is the shipping point for the whole country lying southward, and also to the government post situated ninety miles to the northeast. George Frandsen, late of Mount Pleasant, Sanpete County, presides as Bishop over the Price Ward.   *

Wellington, named for Justus Wellington Seeley, Jr., one of the early settlers and leading men of Emery County, is a scattered settlement lying on both sides of Price River below Price Station. The townsite, which was partly surveyed yesterday, is on the north side of the river, about six miles southeast of Price. The people intend to build on it at once, and move together as fast as possible. Jefferson Tidwell is the pioneer settler of this part of the country, which now has thirty-three families of Saints, presided over by Bishop Albert E. McMullin. This ward is an outgrowth of the Price Ward.

Spring Glen is another outgrowth of the Price Ward. It contains all the Saints (23 families) residing in and below Price Canyon. The recently surveyed townsite is situated in a fine cove on the east side of the river, six miles northwest of Price Station, and a number of the settlers have already built on it, although the canal which is to convey the water of Price River on to the site and surrounding farming lands, is not yet completed. The cost of constructing said canal will perhaps amount to $15,000 or more, as it must be tunneled part of the way through a rocky ridge. But as this tunnel which is 340 feet long, is nearly completed, the water will perhaps be brought on to the lands for which it is intended next spring. About six miles above Spring Glen townsite is the mining town of Castle Gate, which has sprung into existence during the last two years. Here coal mining and coke burning is carried on already on a large scale, and about five hundred men are employed. The

rocks and mines belong to the
Pleasant Valley Mining Company
and is superintended by Mr. Sharp,
son of Bishop John Sharp, of Salt
Lake City. Among the men employed by the company are quite a
number of brethren who have
recently been organized into a
branch of the Church under the
Presidency of Wm. T. Lamph. as a
part of the Spring Glen Ward.
Regular meetings and Sunday
schools, which are often visited by
strangers employed at the mines,
are held every Sabbath, and everything points in the direction of a
Ward being organized here in the
near future.

ANDREW JENSON.
PRICE, Emery County, N. S.,
November 25, 1890.

Deseret Weekly
December 6, 1890

IN GRASS VALLEY.

For the purpose of making a tour
through the Emery Stake of Zion in
the interest of Church history,
I left Salt Lake City on the 8th
inst. and arrived at Price station
(125 miles from the city) in the
evening. Next morning in company with Prest. Geo. Q. Cannon
and Elder John Morgan, who had
arrived during the night, I continued the journey by team (Bishop
Geo. Fraudsen, of Price taking us
in his carriage) to Orangeville, a
distance of 32 miles, where we attended the Stake quarterly conference on that and the following day.
After the conference Prest. Cannon
and Elder Morgan returned home
and I proceeded to gather historical
information concerning the Emery
Stake of Zion. In visiting the
various wards and settlements for
that purpose I have held meetings
with the Saints in nearly every
place and have had a good time
generally. Last Sunday evening I
also spoke to a respectable congregation of Saints and strangers in
Castle Gate, a mining town in Price
Canyon, and yesterday attended
a ward conference at Spring Glen,
where the Stake Presidency was in
attendance, and today, in connection
with that Presidency and Bishops
Geo. Fraudsen of Price, and H. J.
Stowell of Spring Glen, I attended
the ward conference at Wellington,
on which occasion the Bishopric of
that new ward was made complete
by the setting apart of Geo. W.
Eldredge to act as first and Robert
A. Snyder as second counselor
to Bishop A. E. McMullen.
In these ward conferences much
good and practical instruction was
given suitable for the circumstances
surrounding the Saints in this new

country, and the Spirit of God was poured out in a great measure upon all present causing the hearts of the Saints to rejoice exceedingly. After the afternoon meeting today Prest. C. G. Larsen and his counselors (Orange Seely and William Howard) returned to their homes in Castle Dale and Huntington, and I returned to Price, where, in the hospitable home of Bishop Geo. Frandsen, I am finishing my historical gleanings as regards the Emery Stake, preparatory to leaving for other parts of the country.

The Emery Stake of Zion embraces nearly all of Emery County, Utah, and consists of eleven organized wards, which, named in geographical order, commencing from the north, range as follows: Spring Glen, Price, Wellington, Cleveland, Huntington, Lawrence, Castle Dale, Orangeville, Ferron, Molen and Mud'y. Three of these settlements are situated on Price River, three on or near Huntington Creek, two on Cottonwood Creek, two on Ferron Creek and one on Muddy Creek, all in what is generally known as Castle Valley. This valley has well defined boundaries on the west and north where lofty mountains separate it from other valleys and tracts of country, but on the east and south it extends into an almost unexplored region so far that even the earliest settlers here are unable to define its boundaries. It is, in fact, an open country, traversed by low mountain ranges, barren hills, deep gulches and washes, etc., and in many places it is absolutely impassable for teams. Even men on horseback often encounter great difficulties in getting through, and in some instances are compelled to travel a distance of twenty-five miles or more in order to advance five miles in a straight line. But in the western part of the valley, near the eastern base of the Wasatch mountains, where all the settlements are located, there are comparatively fine tracts of country, which after being brought under cultivation, can most properly be termed an oasis in the desert. Generally speaking, Castle Valley is more suited for pastural than agricultural pursuits. Still the people have made, and are now making, farming a decided success, as in many instances the amount of grain raised per acre compares very favorably with that produced in the most fertile parts of our Territory. The culture of bees has, of late years, been proven to be a very successful industry and it is now generally acknowledged that Castle Valley produces the best honey in Utah, and perhaps the best in the United States. As an example of what can be done as regards quantity I may state that during the past summer Brother Caleb B. Rhoades of Price, produced 5,300 pounds of honey from 22 stands of bees. Noah T. Guyman of Orangeville, and John Zwahlen of Ferron, have been nearly equally successful in their bee culture the present season. The great natural wealth of Castle Valley, however, seems to be its immense coal fields. The coal is found in inexhaustable quantities in the several canyons in the mountains west. The veins, so far discovered, ranges from six to eleven feet in thickness and the coal is of the most excellent quality. But until railways shall have been built to the different places where these immense coal deposits have been discovered they are of course comparatively valueless, except for local consumption.

The Saints in Castle Valley have made great progress during the last few years, and their towns and villages begin to assume the appearance of comfort and prosperity. More settlers, however, are needed and anyone in need of a home who is not afraid to face the hardships and dangers of a new country, will be made heartily welcome by the people of this valley.

Castle Dale, pleasantly situated on the north bank of the Cottonwood Creek, 32 miles southwest of Price, the nearest railway station, is the headquarters of the Emery Stake and the county seat of Emery County. It contains the best flouring mill in the county, and the only one, except the little Pioneer mill at Orangeville on the same creek (Cottonwood). Castle Dale has 58 families belonging to the Church and a few non-members. Henning Olsen is Bishop. A new meeting house, which, when completed, will be the most commodious public building in the county, is in course of erection, and will probably be completed next spring. Two of the Stake Presidency (President C. G. Larsen and his first counselor, Orange Seeley) reside in this place.

Orangeville is the other town on Cottonwood Creek. It is situated about three miles west of Castle Dale, not far from the mouth of Cottonwood Canyon, in which very extensive coal-fields have been discovered. There is considerable talk just now about constructing a railway from a point on Price River to these mines. Orangeville can boast of having produced more fruit, so far, than any other settlement in Emery County, and is also surrounded by some choice farming lands. This town has 66 families belonging to the Church, over whom Jasper Robertson presides as Bishop. He is also probate judge of the county.

Ferron, a fine little town on Ferron Creek, is reached by traveling 11½ miles in a southwesterly direction from Castle Dale. The town is situated on the north bank of the creek on a hill side sloping gently to the south. Across the creek, south of the townsite, is a compact body of good farming land. Ferron has the finest and most commodious meeting-house (known as the Social Hall) in the Emery Stake, and a number of comfortable private residences. The strength of the Saints here is 63 families, and Frederick Olsen, a man of sterling qualities, is the Bishop.

Three miles east of Ferron is Molen, an outgrowth of Ferron. It is a pleasant little neighborhood, and the townsite is situated on the north side of Ferron Creek, near where the old Gunnison trail crosses that stream. There is some of the best farming land in the county, but as the quantity is very limited as also water wherewith to irrigate it, Molen will perhaps never become a very large place. Lyman S. Beach, with H. P. Rasmussen and Hans C. Hansen as Counselors, presides as Bishop over the 26 families of Saints who reside here.

After traveling 16 miles through a genuine desert country—broken and desolate—in a southwesterly direction, the townsite of Emery (formerly called Muddy) is reached. It is situated in the north end of a large valley extending toward the Fish Lake Mountains on the south. From here the lofty peaks of the Henry Mountains are also seen toward the southeast. To convey the water of Muddy Creek onto the lands where Emery is situated a long and expensive canal had to be constructed, which for a distance of 1240 feet is tunnelled through a mountain-ridge. This was done at an expence of nearly $50,000. And as the community which had to do this immense labor was poor, it has indeed been a heavy task. But it has been accomplished, and the prospects before the enterprising people of Emery are now very bright compared to what they were a few years ago. The Emery Ward numbers 40 families of Saints, and Wm. G. Petty, one of the founders of Pettyville, Sanpete County, presides here as Bishop.

Lawrence, named in honor of C. G. Larsen, President of the Emery Stake, is a village and farming district situated on Huntington Creek, eight and one-half miles northeast of Castle Dale. It has the reputation of being the best grain producing district in the county. In 1888 13,000 bushels of small grain was raised in this little settlement, which numbers only twenty-four families. No other settlement in the Stake, even those much larger, produced an amount equal to that. Calvin W. Moore, formerly a member of the "Mormon" Battalion, is the Bishop of Lawrence Ward.

Huntington, the metropolis of Emery County, is pleasantly situated on the north bank of Huntington Creek, nine and one-half miles northeast of Castle Dale, surrounded by good farming land. This growing town is the home of 133 families of Latter-day Saints, presided over by Bishop Charles Pulsipher, a son of the late President Zerah Pulsipher. Here also reside Henry Harriman, one of the first seven Presidents of the Seventies, now over eighty-six years of age, Geo. W. Johnson, another Church veteran, Wm. Howard, second Counselor in the Stake Presidency, and others of prominence and note. A fine meeting house is here also in course of erection, and the town is fast assuming the appearance of comfort and wealth.

Northeast of Huntington is a fine open tract of country, said to be the finest in the county, in the midst of which the settlement known as Cleveland is pleasantly situated. The recently surveyed townsite on which the people are now preparing to build, is seven miles northeast of Huntington, but as yet the settlers live in a very scattered condition on their respective quarter sections. They number thirty families of Saints and have recently been organized into a ward, with Lars P. Oveson, a man of enterprise and ability, as Bishop. To convey the water of Huntington Creek onto the farming lands of Cleveland, a canal, fifteen miles long, had to be constructed, at a cost of $35,000.

Price, on the Rio Grande Western Railway, is favorably situated on the north bank of Price River, 125 miles from Salt Lake City and twenty-two miles northeast of Huntington. The "Mormon" population of Price Ward, consisting of forty-five families, reside mostly on the townsite near the railway station, and are commencing to feel more comfortable and satisfied than formerly. It has required considerable hardship and energy to redeem this part of the county from its desert sterility, but through perseverance and patience the object has been accomplished, and Price now has the appearance of comfort and enterprise. This is the shipping point for the whole country lying southward, and also to the government post situated ninety miles to the northeast. George Frandzen, late of Mount Pleasant, Sanpete County, presides as Bishop over the Price Ward.

Wellington, named for Justus Wellington Seeley, Jr., one of the early settlers and leading men of Emery County, is a scattered settlement lying on both sides of Price River below Price Station. The townsite, which was partly surveyed yesterday, is on the north side of the river, about six miles southeast of Price. The people intend to build on it at once, and move together as fast as possible. Jefferson Tidwell is the pioneer settler of this part of the country, which now has thirty-three families of Saints, presided over by Bishop Albert E. McMullin. This ward is an outgrowth of the Price Ward.

Spring Glen is another outgrowth of the Price Ward. It contains all the Saints (23 families) residing in and below Price Canyon. The recently surveyed townsite is situated in a fine cove on the east side of the river, six miles northwest of Price

Station, and a number of the settlers have already built on it, although the canal which is to convey the water of Price River on to the site and surrounding farming lands, is not yet completed. The cost of constructing said canal will perhaps amount to $15,000 or more, as it must be tunneled part of the way through a rocky ridge. But as this tunnel which is 340 feet long, is nearly completed, the water will perhaps be brought on to the lands for which it is intended next spring. About six miles above Spring Glen townsite is the mining town of Castle Gate, which has sprung into existence during the last two years. Here coal mining and coke burning is carried on already on a large scale, and about five hundred men are employed. The rocks and mines belong to the Pleasant Valley Mining Company and is superintended by Mr. Sharp, son of Bishop John Sharp, of Salt Lake City. Among the men employed by the company are quite a number of brethren who have recently been organized into a branch of the Church under the Presidency of Wm. T. Lamph, as a part of the Spring Glen Ward. Regular meetings and Sunday schools, which are often visited by strangers employed at the mines, are held every Sabbath, and everything points in the direction of a Ward being organized here in the near future.

ANDREW JENSON.

PRICE, Emery County, U. T., November 25, 1890.

WEDDING BELLS

On Wednesday, Dec 23rd, in the Manti Temple, Mr. Wm. Moffit of Orangeville, Emery Co., and Miss Luella Snow of Manti, were united in the bonds of matrimony. In the evening a reception was held at the residence of the bride's parents where nearly a hundred friends and relatives of the family were sumptuously entertained. To say that the supper was a marvel of culinary skill goes without saying, when we know it was prepared under the supervision of Mrs. Snow. Also, on New Year's Eve. at the residence of the bride's parents, Mr. Hyrum Harmon, of Holden, and Luella Tuttle. Mr. Alex Tennant, justice of the peace, preforming the ceremony. After the congratulations were over a sumptuous repast was served to nearly 100 invited guests. Singing and instrumental music consisting of selections on the organ, guitar and violin were important features in evening festives which were prolonged till a late hour or rather till an early hour next morning.

Both young ladies have been active workers in the Sunday School, and other organizations.

The young people have chosen an auspicious time for beginning life's voyage with the New Year, and they have the best wishes of their numerous friends for their success and happiness.

NOTICE FOR PUBLICATION.

No. 617.

Land Office at Salt Lake City, Utah
Oct. 1st, 1890

Notice is hereby given that the following-named settler has filed notice o his intention to make final proof in support of his claim, and that said proof will be made before the County Clerk o Emery Co., Utah, at Castle Dale, Utah on Nov. 29th, 1890, viz:

Hiram A. Southworth, D S No 10876 for the N ½ N E ¼ Sec 7, Tp 14 S, R 10 E.

He names the following witnesses to prove his continuous residence upon, and cultivation of, said land, viz:

Heber J. Stowell, Frank M. Ewell Harry Thompson, Walter Grimes, all of Spring Glen, Emery Co., Utah.

FRANK D. HOBBS, Register.
BOOTH, WILSON & WILSON, Atty's.

The communication from W. W. Crawford, of Orangevill, was received too late for publication.

DURING our short stay in Utah we have made one trip of observation through the towns of Huntington, Castle Dale and Orangeville, to the south of Price, and were surprised to find on our trip so many people, such fine land, and such valuable improvements as are to be found in the localities mentioned. The town of Huntington, we believe the largest in the county, is situated on Huntington river, and the towns of Castle Dale and Orangeville on the Cottonwood river. Surrounding each is a fine body of agricultural land, under as fine a system of irrigation as could be found in any county, and the farmer, to raise a crop, only has to use ordinary deligence in planting and cultivating, and the yield is assured. Not like portions of Kansas, Nebraska, and Colorado, where rain is a scarce article and there is no water supply with which to irrigate the too frequent result is a failure of crops and a consequent depression of business and general hard times among both farmers and business men. We also noticed that lying just to the west of each of these towns are fine veins of coal cropping out of the mountain side for miles with an average thickness of sixteen feet. This coal is of a fine quality and, we were informed, is a good coaking coal. In the gulches and on the top of the mountains can be found an abundance of timber and numerous saw mills are running in full blast, which furnishes most of the lumber consumed. This side of Huntington is the new town of Clereland which is situated in a fine valley the land of which is being converted into fine farms, which in a short time promises to be the garden spot of Utah. These lands are supplied with water from the Cleveland Irrigating ditch, the head of which takes its water supply from some place in the mountains, the d'tch being over ten miles in length and having been constructed at a cost of over $30,000. This is one of the finest irrigating ditches in the county and will furnish thousands of acres of land with water.

This item is only a casual mention of the southern portion of the county, the facts having been gathered from a one days trip, and contains no mention of Farron, Lawrence, Muddy and other points south which we have not visited, but will give space to in an early issue of the TELEGRAPH.

THE JURY LIST.

Names that have been Selected

FOR THE COMING TERM

By Deputy Clerk B. Bachman, Jr. and Judge J. D. Jones.

UNITED STATES OF AMERICA, ⎫
TERRITORY OF UTAH ⎬ s. s.
COUNTY OF UTAH. ⎭

In pursuance of Section Four (4) of an Act of Congress in relation to courts and judicial officers of the Territory of Utah, approved June 23. 1874, and title three (3) chapter one (1) of the laws of Utah; B. Bachman, Jr., deputy clerk of the District Court for the First Judicial District, of the Territory of Utah and Hon. Joseph D. Jones, probate judge of Utah county, Utah Territory, met at the office of said probate judge, at Provo city and County and Territory of Utah, on the 15th day of January, A. D. 1891, and then and there prepared a jury list from which list Grand and

Petit jurors are to be drawn to serve in the District Court for the First Judicial District of the Territory of Utah, to be held in the counties of Utah and Weber, pursuant to the provision of said act and the proclamations of his Excellency, the Governor, and until a new list shall be made as provided by said act; names composing said list being alternately selected by said clerk and said probate judge from among the male citizens of the United States who have resided in said judicial district for six months next preceding, and who can read and write the English language.

The names and places of residence of each person so selected is hereunto appended and is as follows, to-wit:—

No.	NAMES.	RESI'CE.	COUNTY.
1	J C Moses	Provo City	Utah
2	Hans Poulson	"	"
3	H C Edwards	"	"
4	Don R Coray	"	"
5	J A Pemberton	"	"
6	Ephriam Homer	"	"
7	A L Hamilton	"	"
8	Wm McKenzie	Springville	"
9	Ben R Eldridge	Provo City	"
10	Wm McBeth	Payson	"
11	Thomas Burt	Springville	"
12	Grant Simmons	Payson	"
13	Milan Packard	Springville	"
14	Crispin Taylor	Payson	"
15	W J Thomas	Spanish F'k	"
16	C C Harper	Payson	"
17	James M Boyle	"	"
18	Peter Nielson	Goshen	"
19	James M Boyle	Payson	"
20	Lewis Lewis	Alpine	"
21	G W Williams	Payson	"
22	James Chipman	American F'k	"
23	R W Bennett	Alpine	"
24	J C Jay	Ple'n't Grove	"
25	H Adamson	American F'k	"
26	C E Sterrett	Pleas't Grove	"
27	John Brown Jr	Lehi	"
28	Chas I Brown	Midway	Was'tch
29	Archie Sellers	Heber	"
30	Wm Horner	"	"

31	Wm Bridges	Schofield	Emery
32	Geo Bonner Jr	Midway	Was'tch
33	D Mcmurphy	Eureka	Juab
34	J's Mendenhall	Mona	"
35	Charles Hanks	Eureka	"
36	Ruben Thomas	"	"
37	Robert C May	"	"
38	L E Riter	Silver City	"
39	Hall F Gear	Eureka	"
40	Wm Stout	Nephi	"
41	Jno H Hornung	"	"
42	Samuel Wilkie	"	"
43	Thos A Foote	"	"
44	Gidson Wilson	"	"
45	Ole Orisen	Mt Pleasant	Sanpet'
46	Lorenzo Webb	Nepi	Juab
47	Henry Coats	Mt Pleasant	Sanpet'
48	John S Cooper	Nephi	Juab
49	Peter Almartz	Mt Pleasant	Sanpet'
50	Peter Nielsen	"	"
51	W C Stone	"	"
52	M Rasmussen	Ephriam	"
53	C A Larsen	"	"
54	Ole Nielsen	Manti	"
55	Rich' Maxfield	Spring City	"
56	Peter Domgaard	Manti	"
57	Wm Kofford	Spring City	"
58	Parley Draper	Moroni	"
59	Walter Jenkins	Milburn	"
60	Benj Conrad	Chester	"
61	Robt Bridges	Joseph City	Sevier
62	T Christensen	Gunnison	Sanpete
63	C Fairbanks	Glenwood	Sevier
64	William Wing	Fairview	Sanpete
65	Andrew Nielsen	Monroe	Sevier
66	Wm H McCarty	"	"
67	M. Keign	Vermillion	"
68	H N Fugate	Ferron	Emery
69	A Peterson	Richfield	Sevier
70	Frank Carro'l	Orangeville	Emery
71	Joseph J Jensen	Richfield	Sevier
72	Samuel P Snow	Orangeville	Emery
73	B Middlemass	Richfield	Sevier
74	John H Scott	Huntington	Emery
75	Peter Erickson	Richfield	Sevier
76	Frank P Long	Price	Emery
77	P Gallagher	Salina	Sevier
78	W A Montgomery	"	"
79	James F Barnard	"	"
80	D C Sagers	"	"
81	William Miller	"	"
82	B S Kesler	"	"
83	James George	Kanosh	Millard
84	John T Leonard	Salina	Sevier
85	W W Dame	Fillmore	Millard
86	H H Noyes	"	"
87	T Scottern	"	"
88	John Larsen	Willowbend	"
89	Ole Madsen	Scipio	"
90	P C Nielsen	"	"
91	George Porter	"	"
92	Samuel Rowley	"	"
93	John Rogers	Deseret	Milla'd
94	Wm. Memmott	Scipio	"
94	Charles Webb	Deseret	"
96	Wm Rogers	"	"
97	Wm Atchinson	Burbank	"
98	And. Bertelson Jr	Elsenore	Sevier
99	John L Gates	Salina	"
100	Neil McMillen	Plateau	"
101	W F Critchlow	Ogden	Weber
102	E S Laty	"	"
103	Chas E Lane	"	"
104	Jno Saltenburger	"	"
105	Ambres Shaw	"	"
106	Robert Robinson	"	"
107	Jno M Browning	"	"
108	Chas P Goodrich	"	"
109	Leo Harris	"	"
110	R L Armstrong	"	"
111	Geo Murphy	"	"
112	J D Gill	"	"
113	Thos Emmett	"	"
114	Chas Robinson	"	"
115	Robert Shaw	"	"
116	Jas Thompson	"	"
117	O P Herrimon	"	"
118	E R Ridgely	"	"
119	George Stetson	"	"
120	W M Anderson	"	"
121	Jas Browning	"	"
122	Philip Rank	"	"
123	Thos Ballentyne	"	"
124	Robert Ross	"	"
125	John McManis	"	"
126	William Harcombe	"	"
127	J T McIntosh	"	"
128	James Allen	"	"
129	Robert Harris	Harrisville	"
130	George H Tripp	Ogden	

131	Harvey Taylor	Harrisville	
132	G J Wright	Ogden	
133	P Wingagard	Huntsville	
134	A W Meek	Ogden	
135	Neils Knudsen	Huntsville	
136	Geo B Douglass	Ogden	
137	Lymon Skeen	Plain City	
138	E J Hulaniskin	Ogden	
139	Henry Taylor	Plain City	
140	Geo W Harris	Ogden	
141	Thomas Slater	Slaterville	
142	Wm Jenkins	Ogden	
143	John Slater	Slaterville	
144	O W Hostmark	Ogden	
145	Jos Manning	Hooperville	
146	McLaren Boyle	Ogden	
147	Thomas Ritter	Eden	
148	John Randall	North Ogden	
149	Ira Fowler	Corinne	Box Elder
150	James Walker	N Ogden	Weber
151	R Wilson Jr	Brigham	Box Elder
152	Patrick Martin	N Ogden	Weber
153	W H Booth Jr	Brigham	Box Elder
155	L Barnard	Calls F'r	Box Elder
156	E M Smout Jr	Slaterville	Weber
157	R S Barnes	B'x Eld'r	B'x Elde'
158	John Wood	Slaterville	Weber
159	A W Carr	Smithfield	Cache
160	G A Bradshaw	Slaterville	Weber
161	J B Surten	Smithfield	Cache
162	John Groger	Harrisville	Weber
163	E O Wattis	Uintah	Cache
164	Robert Fisher	Harrisville	Weber
165	Mich'el Murphy	Menden	Cache
166	Robert Davis	Plain City	Weber
167	W Y Owen	Logan City	Cache
168	James Skeen	Plain City	Weber
169	W D Goodman	Logan	Cache
170	Jas' Robinson	Plain City	Weber
171	J R Edwards	Logan	Cache
172	Wm Smith	Huntsville	Weber
173	Sam Hall Jr	Wellsville	Cache
174	John Farrell	Eden	Weber
175	J Williamson	Wellsville	Cache
176	Peter Lowe Jr	Hooper	Weber
177	Sim' Huffaker	Woodruff	Rich
178	W W Child	Hooper	Weber
179	W G Frazer	Woodruff	Rich
180	C De L'Baume	Uintah	Weber
181	D Shurtliff	Morgan	Morgan
182	Wm Bowman	Riverdale	Weber
183	W N Cleveland	Morg'n	Morgan
184	Wm Fronk	West Weber	Weber
185	P Hollingreen	Bear river	B'x Eld'
186	Wm Sowell	Wilson	Weber
187	John Johnson	Randolph	Rich
188	H D Peterson	West Weber	Weber
189	John Green	Enterprise	Morgan
190	C L Peedles	Ogden	Weber
191	John Durby	Promontory	B'x El'd
192	M Biel	Ogden	Weber
193	C H Bevans	Hyrum	Cache
194	A J Chamberlain	Ogden	Weber
195	Paul M Poulsen	Petersbrough	Cache
196	C Crabtree	Ogden	Weber
197	Jas England	Hampton Spg's	Cache
198	T M Douglass	Ogden	Weber
199	Wm Garland	Collinston	B'x Eld'
200	Geo G Griffith	Ogden	Weber

TERRITORY OF UTAH, } s. s.
COUNTY OF UTAH,

We, the undersigned, do here by certify that the foregoing and annexed list, is a true and correct list of the names prepared and selected by us, on the 15th day of January, 1891, as in the caption thereof set forth, and pursuant to the Act of Congress above mentioned, to be filled in the Office of the Clerk of the First Judicial District Court of Utah Territory, and a duplicate copy to be filled in the office of the Probate Judge of said county.

And we further certify, that the said list contains the names, to the best of our knowledge, information and belief, only of persons eligable to serve as Juror's under said Act of Congress and the laws of said Territory.

IN WITNESS WHEREOF, we have hereunto set our hands, and the Seal of said Courts, at Provo City, Utah, this 15th day of January, A. D. 1891.

[Seal]   B. BACHMON Jr.
Deputy Clerk, First District Court of
    Utah.

[Seal]   J. D. JONES,
Probate Judge, Utah County, Utah Territory.

Salt Lake Times
January 20, 1891

Paragraphs Condensed Into Briefest Possible Space for Those Who Run and Read.

It is estimated that there are over $5,000 acres of land under cultivation in Emery county.

The First ward Mormon meeting house at Ogden was burned down yesterday. Loss $11,000; insurance $5000.

The Eastern Utah Telegraph, published at Price, is a new venture in journalism that has reached us. Good luck go with it.

Martin Olsen, an aged Scandinavian, of Goshen, was brought to Provo yesterday morning to answer to the charge of unlawful cohabitation.

The mill and real estate of the North American Asphalt company at Thistle have been attached by St. V. Le Sieur, for services, aggregating over $1900

It is proposed to incorporate a company with a capital stock of $15,000 and sink prospect artesian wells at Huntington, Castle Dale, Orangeville, Ferron, Muddy and Price.

The town of Castle Gate, but little more than a year old, is a veritable little city with its electric lights, coke ovens, and the extensive coal works of the P. V. Coal company.

The Utah Valley Gazette has again changed hands. This time James H. Wallis of the Nephi Ensign takes the wheel and compress and will henceforth guide that vessel over the troubled waters of journalism.

—The County Superintendent of this county has made the following disposition of federal school funds in this county:

Wellington	$305 67
Price	722 o9
Scofield	93o 3o
Huntington	1355 58
Cleveland	3o5 67
Lawrence	323 o9
Castle Dale	877.79
Orangeville	7o8 8o
Ferron	478 11
Molen	221.5o
Emery	385.41
Green River	
Castle Gate	429.71
Total	**$6844 35**

Orangeville Items.

Fine Weather, clear cold nights.

District school closed its first term on the 2nd inst., on the 5th the second term commenced with 108 scholars enrolled A great many could not gain admittance and Tuesday morning, 13th inst, another department was opened in the Social Hall.

Total number enrolled 136, 3 teachers—W. W. Crawford, Principal.

Dr. Blanchard is doing the town in dentistry.

Health of the people, good.

Dr. E. M. Moore is always at his post.

Our three stores are doing a fairly good business.

When was America first discovered by Columbus? on what day of the month? I have three different Histories with different dates, Oct. 11, 12 and 13th. Which is right?

County Registry
January 29, 1891

Notice for Publication
NO 726

Land Office at Salt Lake City, Utah,
Nov. 28th, 1890.

Notice is hereby given that the follow-ing-named settler has filed notice of his intention to make final proof in support of his claim, and that said proof will be made before the Probate Judge or in his absence the Clerk of the County Court of Emery County, Utah, at Castle Dale Emery Co, on Jan. 23rd, 1891, viz. Andrew E. Smith, H. E. No, 6621 for the E, ½ S E ¼ Sec. 20, N W ¼ S; W, ¼ Sec 21 & N E ¼ N E ¼ Sec 29 T P 18 S, R 9 E.

He names the following witnesses to prove his continuous residence upon, and cultivation of, said land, viz.

Arthur J, Jeffs, C. P. Andersen, James H. Wilcox, of Castle Dale and, Arlington A. Day, of Lawrence, Emery Co. U. T

FRANK D. HOBBS, Register

NOTICE FOR PUBLICATION.
No. 627.

Land Office at Salt Lake City, Utah
Oct. 1st, 1890

Notice is hereby given that the fol lowing-named settler has filed notice o his intention to make final proof in sup port of his claim, and that said proo will be made before the County Clerk o Emery Co., Utah, at Castle Dale, Utah on Nov. 29th, 1890, viz:

Hiram A. Southworth, D S No 10876 for the N ½ N E ¼ Sec 7, Tp 14 S, R 10 E.

He names the following witnesses to prove his continuous residence upon, and cultivation of, said land, viz:

Heber J. Stowell, Frank M. Ewell, Harry Thompson, Walter Grimes, all of Spring Glen, Emery Co., Utah.

FRANK D. HOBBS, Register.
BOOTH, WILSON & WILSON, Atty's.

Eastern Utah Telegraph
February 5, 1891

EMERY COUNTY STAGE LINE.

Runs dailly between Price, Cleveland, Huntington, Castle Dale, Orangeville and Ferron.

Good Teams and Stages

MILES & CURTIS
Preprietors.

Notice for Publication,
No 676.

Land Office at Salt Lake, Utah, Oct., 31st, 1890

Notice is hereby given that the following named settler has filed notice of her intention to make final proof in support of her claim, and that said proof will be made before the Judge, or in his absence th County clerk of Emery county, Utah, at Castle Dale, on Dec. 18th, 1890, viz:

Christena Sorensen, H. E. 8886, for the $S\frac{1}{2}$ S. W. 1-4 and $W\frac{1}{2}$ S. E. 1-4, Sec. 35, Tp. 14, S, R, 10 E, S. L. M.

She names the following witnesses to prove her continuous residence upon, and cultivation of, said land, viz:

Geo. Eldredge, Peter T. Olson, Green W. Allred and George Downard, all of Price P. O., Emery co Utah.

FRANK D. HOBBS, Register.
Wilkes & Chadwick Attorneys for claimant.

Eastern Utah Telegraph
February 12, 1891

The County Superintendent has
made the following distributions of
the county school funds

No 1 Wellington,	$ 86 25
" 2 Price	203 75
" 3 Scofield	262 50
" 4 Huntington	382 59
" 5 Cleveland	86 25
" 6 Lawrence	9I 25
" 7 Castle Dale	191.2b
" 8 Orange.ille	200 00
" 9 Ferron	135 00
" 10 Molen	62 50
" 11 Emery	109 75
" 13 Castle Gate	121.25
	$1931.25

Districts 12 and 14 are not included.

Salt Lake Herald
February 14, 1891

IN CASTLE VALLEY.

A Rich Section of Country That Could Be Easily Improved.

For nine or ten years the central and southern portions of Castle valley have been settled and improved, and thousands of acres of land are under irrigation with each year, large additions being made to the different settlements. Immediately surrounding the town of Ferron can be seen some of the finest farms in the county—there being between 6,000 and 10,000 acres under ditch. There is plenty of water in the river to irrigate the land now under cultivation and with reservoirs constructed in the mountains for the storage of water, ten times as much land can be supplied with water in that valley. This is true of the whole of eastern Utah and if the people will only expend a little time and money in the construction of reservoirs all of the land lying in the valleys can be turned into fine productive farms. There are only about three months during the heat of summer that water is needed for irrigation and a few reservoirs constructed in the mountains at the head of the different streams flowing through eastern Utah will do a great deal toward turning the lands now lying idle into productive farms.—*Price Telegraph.*

Salt Lake Herald
February 20, 1891

The Emery County Railway.

The new railroad contemplated from Price south through Emery county would certainly be a paying investment and would make a good feeder for the R. G. W., road, which company is undoubtedly interested in its construction. Even if the R. G. W. is not building the line, the freight hauled over the new road would have to be turned over to the R. G. W. at Price for transportation and all freight shipped into the country for the southern portion of the county would be received by the new road for shipment after being hauled over the R. G. W. to Price. By the new line all of the towns south of here would be supplied with a road as it would undoubtedly run through each of them and the R.G.W. road would occupy territory, the best in Eastern Utah, that unless soon claimed by it, will be taken by some of the numerous companies that are now about to build through to Salt Lake from the east. The new line will likely go through Salina cañon joining the Manti extension of the R. G. W. road, in Sanpete county, making a complete system with an outlet east and west of the range and supplying south-eastern Utah with railroad facilities now so much needed.

Along this proposed line of road from Price to Salina cañon, for a distance of seventy-five miles there are continuous coal viens, one of the viens south of Ferron being twenty-four feet thick, all of which would be handled by the new road. In the course of a few years this entire country will be lined with coal mines and coke ovens, and a railroad into this territory cannot help but be a paying investment from the start. These mines have been laying idle in the past for the want of railroad facilities to assist in the transportation but they will soon be supplied, as several roads are looking for routes through Eastern Utah, and Castle valley will get her share.—*Price Telegraph.*

Eastern Utah Telegraph
February 26, 1891

—W. Taylor Jr, of Ferron, called at this office Tuesday and subscribed for the TELEGRAPH

BOUNDARIES OF THE HUNTINGTON MINING DISTRICT.

Commencing on the South boundary, at a point where the District line between Huntington and Castle Dale school district crosses the county road, and running on said district line east to where it intersects Huntington creek; thence, down said creek to the San Rafael river; thence, down said river to the western boundary line of the Green River Mining District; thence, North to the district line between Cleveland and Wellington school district, thence, West on said line to a point two miles east of where the county road goes on the Sage Brush Bench, thence, Northerly to the bridge across Price river, thence Westerly to a point on the west line of the Price school district three miles north of the district line between Huntington and Scofield school districts; thence, due West to the west boundary line of Emery county, thence, South on said line to the north west corner of Orangeville school district, thence, East on the north line of Orangeville district to the north east corner of said school district; thence, South to the north west corner of Castle Dale school district, thence due East to the place of begining.

Very Respectfully, Your Committee,

Elias H. Cox.
Hirom Burgess.
D. G. A. Smith

Upon motion the report was approved and a recommendation submitted for the above described boundary to be plated and with a copy of descriptions, filed in the Recorders office, carried.

The chairman announced the next business would be to hear the report of the committee on Rules and Regulations or By-Laws The following being submitted to the chairman and members of the Huntington Mining District:

UTAH COMMISSION

Met Today and Appointed These Deputy Registrars.

San Pete County—Mt. Pleasant, F. C. Jensen; Fairview, Joseph S. Wing; Milburn, George Zabriskie; Thistle, W. N. Tidwell; Spring City, Jacob Johnson; Moroni, N. L. Eliason; Fountain, James A. Holman; Wales, H. C. Lamb; Chester, E. J. Conrad; Ephraim, Peter Schwalbe; Manti, E. W. Fox; Petty, Thomas J. Patten; Gunnison, James M. Robbins, Fayette, G. M. Clark; Mayfield, Henry Jensen.

Emery County—Blake, Scott M. Miller; Wellington, H. F. Hanson; Price; A. Ballinger; Huntington, John H. Scott; Larence, Elias Thomas; Orangeville, Frank Carroll; Ferron, J. W. Williams; Molen, James H. Cook; Muddy, Rasmus Johnson; Scofield, A. H. Earle; Castle Dale, Carl Wilberg; Castle Gate, J. X. Ferguson; Cleveland, J. T. Wakefield.

DISTRICT COURT.

Swazey Cattle Stealing Case.

U. C. ARRAIGNMENTS.

William Howard and Benjamin Bennett Receive Sentence-Other Cases.

TUESDAY MORNING.

John A. Moweor withdrew his plea of not guilty and entered one of guilty to the charge of adultery.

He was also charged with unlawful cohabitation and plead not guilty.

Benjamin Bennett came up for sentence having been indicted for fornication. Mr. King vindicated his character before the Judge, who ordered him to pay a fine of $100 and costs.

William Howard plead guilty to the charge of unlawful cohabitation and was sentenced to pay a find of $100 and costs.

Martin Olsen was arranged on a charge of unlawful cohabitation. Took until 2 o'clock to plead.

Richard Jenkins came up on a charge of unlawful cohabitation. Took until 2 o'clock to enter his plea.

The case of Rod Swazey came up for trial. The indictment charges the defendant with cattle stealing committed in Emery Co. about March 1st, 1885.

A. G. Sutherland appeared for the defense and Mr. Varian for the Prosecution.

The first witness was called.

Fredrick Otterson—I live in Emery Co. Own two head of calves. The calves were born in the spring. I had lost them and not seen them for 14 days. The calves were in the field. I found them in San Rafael canyon branded with a cone and bar. There were many cattle there. Some were branded R D, and somebody claimed the calves when I got them home.

To Mr. Sutherland, defense—I learned to make the brands from seeing them on the calves. The E L is E. Larsen's brand. The brand is fresh and sores not healed up. I don't know whose brand the cone and bar is. No one claimed the calves when I got them home.

The grand jury came in and rendered a verdict in the case of E. J. Hanson for unlawful cohabitation. Sentence was set for 2 o'clock.

I went before the court at Orangeville and swore out a complaint against Rod Swazey. He said he bought the calves of Smith in Colorado. Rod Swazey said he had a bill of sale and held a paper in his hand.

Peter Otterson was called— Fredrick Otterson is my father. We did not brand our calves. We had them in the field about a mile and a half from the house. One of E. Larsen's calves was with ours. We missed the calves in the last of Oct. I went out in the field three days after and missed the calves Emile Larsen and I went to San Rafael found the calves about 14 miles from town. The calves were just branded a few days before. The brands were sore yet. The Larsen calf was branded with some brand over the E. L.

We caught the calves and tied them up until morning, had a trial a few days after. Rod Swazy said at the trial, he bought the calves of Tommy Smith—I don't remember whether he showed a bill of sale. The examination was of Sid Swazey. To Mr. Sutherland. Am 18 years old can remember back to 1885.

Father accused Sid Swazey of stealing the calves. The case was turned on to Rod Swazy. Herds of cattle were driven through that country. Know Charley Swazey. We heard that a herd of stock was driven through to San Rafael—They drive stock over the hills. I did not see the calves for about three weeks after we turned them out.

Witness to jury—Swazey did not claim the brand on the calves.

Don. C. Seeley was called. I live at Castle Dale. I sold that calf to E. Larsen's wife. I saw the calf with E. Larsen's brand on it. The brand on top of E. L. is known as Sid Swazey's brand and is called the anchor brand. The brand looked like it had been made with an iron and not with a brand. Rod Swazey said that he owed Sid a calf on a horse-trade and he branded the calf for Sid. The calves were found about ten or twelve miles from the settlement. Swazey said he got the calf from Thomas Smith, and that he could show his bill of sale.

To Mr. Sutherland.—I have lived on the head of the San Raefel for about eight years. William Howard was Sid Swazy's attorney. I dont remember whether Sid or his attorney showed the bill of sale they spoke of. I know the anchor brand to that of Sid Swazy's. Mr. Olson was called.—I helped to hunt the calves. Hunted three days. I had lost a calf too. Saw Mr. Larsen's calf before. I live about one and a half miles from Attersen's. The brands on the calves looked like they had been done with a hot iron. The brands were all fresh. I did not help take them home.

I was in court when Sid Swazey was tried. Rod Swazey said he owned a calf to Sid and branded that one for him. He said he bought the calf from Tom Smith at Wilsonville. Swazey said he had a bill of sale, I did not see it.

To Mr. Sutherland, have lived in that country since 1882. A good many stock are driven through that country. Swaezy's drove their stock down to the San Raefel every fall in about October.

James Peterson testified—I know Mr. Larsen and the calf we talk about. Saw the calf after it was branded E L. Saw the calf about three weeks after with the anchor brand over it. I was in court when Rod Swazey got up in court and said he branded the calf for Sid. He said he branded it late in the evening and could not see the brand E L. He said he bought the calf from Tom Smith at Wilsonville. Rod Swazey did not say why he carried Sid's brand around

To Mr. Sutherland—I have lived in the country since 1882. I know that Swazey's had stock there they called their own. I don't know where Sid lives most of his time. He has lived there most of the time since 1885. Rod walked out of court as any other man would. I know Mr. Hatch. The putting in of the anchor brand would make the E L blotch.

The E L was on the ribs and the anchor brand placed over it.

San Raefel is the winter range for stock. They start to drive stock about the first of October and November. Rod said he branded the calf at Charley Swazey's corral at Wilsonville.

To prosecution. Don't know whether old man Swazey leased his stock to the boys, have seen the anchor brand on several cattle.

R. H. Seeley was called. I understand that the R. D. brand was the Swazey company brand. Am a farmer and stock-raiser. My attention was called the brand on Larsen's calf, at the trial the E. L. brand was dry and the anchor brand green showing that it had been put on later. It entirely spoiled the E. S. brand. The anchor brand looked like it was made with a bar of iron to deface the E. S. brand.

To Mr. Sutherland—Have never run a brand with an iron. Can't make mine with an iron. Know that the anchor brand is Sid Swazey's. I live in Castle Dale. Don't know where Sid Swazey lives.

Recess was taken until 2 o'clock.

ᵖent for, but could not attend to tᵗ sufferer that same day, consequentˡ Mɪ Larsen had to endure the pᵃˡ through the long hours of the follᵒ ing night and until noon on the 2ᵗ before the Lr could give relief

Yesterday, March came in blustᵗ ing with heavy winds

The health of the people is gᵒ

The farmer rejoices over the pˡᵉⁿ ful snowfalls in the mountains.

We have beautiful weather snow in town, but mud plenty.

Our schools are in a prospeᵣ condition. The Academy has tʰ threu students, and the district seᵗ has sixty six which makes a totᵃˡ nint, nⁱⁿᵉ attending school present.

The Academy is not supporteᵈ it should be, the whole burden ᵣ upon Castle Dale, but we hᵃ hopes, that in the near future good people of Emery will givᵉ aid and assistance to this Insᵗᵗᵗ

A CASTLEIᵗᵉ

Castle Dale News.

Last Friday February 27, 1891 one of our worthy citizens, C. E. Larsen, of this town, had his left shoulder dislocated by a fall of a horse, which he was riding. Dr. Moore was

County Register
March 7, 1891

NOTICE FOR PUBLICATION,
No. 749.
Land Office at Salt Lake City, Utah,
Jan 29, 1891.
Notice is hereby given that the follow-
ing-named settler has filed notice of his
intention to make final proof by Com-
mutation in support of his claim, and
that said proof will be made before the
Judge or in his absence the Clerk of the
County Court of Emery County, Utah, at
Castle Dale, Utah, on the 14 of March,
1891, viz:
Josephus Gammage Homestead Entry
No 5992 for the E ½ N. W. ¼, N. W. ¼ N.
W. ¼ Sec. 16 and S. E. ¼ S. W. ¼ Sec. 9
Tp 21 S. R. 16 E.
He names the following witnesses to
prove his continuous residence upon, and
cultivation of, said land, viz:
Robert Hatrick, Harry Farrar Alfred
Farrar, J. T. Farrar all of Blake, Emery
County Utah.
FRANK D. HOBBS,
Register.
Bird & Lowe Atty's for Claimant.

Ogden Standard
March 10, 1891

B. T. Higgs, of Orangeville, Emery
county, Utah, asking prices on 600
feet of old wooden pipe, was referred
to committee on water supply.

Provo Daily Enquirer
March 10, 1891

Sheriff Fowler would not accommo-
date the fourteen "Dagos" who were
brought in from Castle Dale last night,
in the County Jail. They had to be
herded around town.

"Rise William Riley."

The following communications were handed to us yesterday. They explain themselves

Price, Utah, March 9 1891.
Hon Jasper Robertson.
Judge of Probate, Castle Dale, Utah

Sir —Referring to my communication to you, 2nd, inst, bidding $250 for jail and lot, I would respectfully ask why the same was ignored and the property sold for $202. I hope you will not think me presumptuous in inquiring if you recieved my letter making such offer?

I mailed the same under cover of Special Delivery Stamp and I am credibly informed that the mail arrived at Castle Dale (your official residence) on the above mentioned date, at 3 o'clock p m, giving the Postmaster ample time to deliver said letter.

Be pleased to inform me at what time the letter was delivered, if at all?

I presume it unnecessary for me to add that through this gross carelessness Emery County has been defrauded and I will endeavor to locate the blame where it belongs

It appears that the county has been defrauded in this matter for the purpose of benefitting a few at the chagrin of many citizens of Price.

Very Respectfully,
J. P. Keller.

Land Office at Salt Lake City, Utah, March 4, 1891.

Notice is hereby given that Hyrum S Loreless, of Huntington, Emery County, Utah, has filed notice of intention to make proof on his desert-land claim No 249, for the South-West ¼ Sec 13, Tp 17 S R 9 E, before the Probate Judge or the Clerk o Emery County Utah at Castle Dale, Emery County, Utah on Saturday the 25 day of April 1891

He names the following witnesses to prove the complete irrigation and reclamation of said land

John Z. Alger, Roman Oviatt, Albert Hanson and Andrew Johnson, all of Cleveland, Emery County, Utah

FRANK D. HOBBS, Register

19-014

Land Office at Salt Lake City, Utah, Feb, 26, 1891

Notice is hereby given that the following named settler has filed notice of his intention to make final proof in support of his claim, and that said proof will be made before the Probate Judge or, in his absence the County Clerk of Emery County Utah, at Castle Dale, Emery County Utah, on Monday, April 20, 1891, viz James H Hill, H. E No 7501 for the S ½, N. E ¼, and N ½, S. E ¼, Sec. 11, Tp 13, S. R 10 E

He names the following witnesses to prove his continuous residence upon, and cultivation of, said land, viz

Thos Zundal, George Milner, Robt. A Snyder and George Yeager, all of Emery County, Utah

FRANK D Hobbs Register

9-14

Eastern Utah Advocate
April 2, 1891

—R. G. Mc Donnough, of Castle Dale, spent the fore part of the week on our streets.

EMERY COUNTY.

A Rich but Neglected Section of the Territory.

Thousands of Acres of Coal, Asphaltum and Mineral Wax Lands—The Work Already Done.

Emery county ranks fourth in the order of the counties of Utah in increase in population during the last decade, the census showing an increase in its population of 4,210. This speaks well for Emery county and we predict more development for it during the coming two years and a greater increase in population than it had during the past ten years. The railroad building and improvements to be made during the coming summer, and the mines that will be opened up will bring a great many people into the county. There are thousands of acres of coal, asphaltum and mineral wax lands in this county which are being opened up, and a great portion of which will be developed as soon as the new road is built south from Price. Also northeast of Price, the new Denver company has commenced work in its mines and is running a large force of men and teams, filling a Denver contract of 1,500 tons with asphaltum for paving. This same company intends to open up mines on its coal land and put in one to two hundred coke ovens. At Orangeville and Huntington we understand coke ovens will be erected at the mines as soon as the road is completed, and before the end of the year we confidently expect to see at least five hundred coke ovens in full blast in the county. With the coal and asphaltum in Emery county, it can be made one of the richest counties of Utah.—*Price Telegraph.*

County Register
April 14, 1891

Judge Johnson, of San Pete county, in company with Bishop Frandsen, called at our office last Saturday. The judge accompanied Mrs. Johnson as far as Price and then returned home, Mrs. Johnson continuing her journey to Ferron, where she will visit with friends.--Price *Telegraph*.

Eastern Utah Telegraph
April 16, 1891

—Abe Hatch recieved by freight a new three-seated spring wagon which will be used on the stage route from here to Ferron. It cost $140 and is a "daisy."

Report of the Grand Jury.

The following is a copy of the report of the grand jury in the First Judicial District of Utah, for the February term, 1891:

To the Hon. Judge Blackburn.

We the grand jury in and for the First Judicial District, respectfully submit the following report for your consideration:

We have been in session 22 days, having spent 16 days in the discharge of United States business and six days in Territorial business.

We have heard 84 cases, 42 cases of which were United States cases. Of these 20 indictments were found and drawn, 19 cases ignored and three resubmitted to the next grand jury. The remaining 42 cases were Territorial cases, of which 24 indictments were found and drawn, 19 cases ignored and one resubmitted to the next grand jury.

The Territorial Insane Asylum was inspected and found to be in good condition, but somewhat crowded.

The county jail of Utah county was visited and also found in good condition. Credit is surely due the officers in charge of the above mentioned institutions for the efficient manner in which their respective institutions are managed.

The Provo City jail was visited and found to be entirely unfit for the uses to which it is put, and it is the candid opinion of the grand jury that it would be hard to conceive a place better calculated to breed disease than the Provo City jail.

It is an evident fact that the City marshal can in no way be held responsible for the condition of the place as it is now constructed, and we would hereby recommend and request that the Provo City council, out of respect for common humanity, at once take such steps as will be necessary to make said institution such a place as it should be.

The grand jury further recommend that the Provo City council enforce the ordinance in reference to the keeping clean of corrals and the burying of dead animals within the city limits.

By investigation it is found that dead animals are being left at the foot of the mountains east of Provo, in such a manner that prevailing winds carry offensive odors, to the Territorial Insane Asylum, greatly to the annoyance of the officers and inmates thereof, and we recommend that action be taken by the proper authority and the nuisance removed.

Many cases are referred to the Grand jury by Justices of the peace, that could easily be disposed of in the Justice's court and thereby avoid unnecessary expense upon the Territory where there is no cause for action.

In a case entitled the People vs Morgan Moore, et. al., eight witnesses appeared before us from Orangeville, Emery county, and upon investigation we found no possible grounds for indictment and the case was ignored. The witnesses' fees and mileage, amounted to about $150 and we would respectfully suggest that the Justices of the peace in the district investigate the details of a case more thoroughly before sending the same before the grand jury, and thereby often save unnecessary expense upon the Territory.

Inquiries have been made of the officials in the various other counties in the district, regarding county buildings etc., and they report the same in good condition.

Attest.

H. F. GEAR, Foreman of the Grand Jury.

H. C. EDWARDS, Clerk.

Frank Carroll, of Orangeville, spent some time with our merchants last week purchasing goods for the firm of Cox & Carroll.

ESTRAY NOTICE.

I have in my possession the following described animals impounded for trespass. One light red cow and calf branded thus. S-C and vented on left ribs, crop and under slope in right ear and crop in left ear.

If damage and costs on said animal be not paid within ten days from date of this notice they will be sold to the highest cash bidder at Castle Dale court house at 2 o'clock on the 14 day of May 1891

R. H. McDonough.
Poundkeeper.

Dated Castle Dale May 4 1891.

A Sad Affair.

We are informed that a sad tragedy occurred at Ferron last Friday. Willie Petty, a lad twelve years of age was herding cows near the settlement. His father had refused to allow him to take a horse fearing he might get hurt. While in the field about a mile from home one of his companions who was on horseback asked Willie to hand him a coat lying on the ground which the little fellow started to do. While reaching the coat the horse kicked him in the chest. Word was brought to the parents, and in a short time willing hands were ready to do all in their power for the sufferer. It was found impossible to take him home as the pain was more than he could stand. The little fellow bore up bravely, although his suffering must have been intense. Death relieved him in a few hours. His parents have the sympathy of the entire community in their great loss.—Sentinel.

Notice To Creditors.

Notice is hereby given by the undersigned administratrix of the estate of David Wilkin deceased, to the creditors of, and all persons having claims against the said deceased to exhibit them with the necessary vouchers within ten months after the first publication of this notice to the said administratrix at her residence in Orangeville precinct, Emory county, Utah Territory, the same being the place for the transaction of the business of said estate.

JANE WILKIN,
Administratrix of the estate of David Wilkin deceased,

Dated April 22, 1891.

—B. Bryan, the new mail contractor who succeeds L. L. Miles on the line between Price and Ferron, contemplates putting on two more teams using twelve horses on the line and changing teams at Cleveland and Castle Dale This arrangement will give each teem about eighteen miles of a drive and will be quite an advantage to the line.

—H. S. Stevens, of Ferron, is in town today and will start for the Fort in a day or two with a load of freight.

—We are having an abundance of rain this spring and the result will be fine feed during the summer for the thousands of sheep and cattle that range in Castle Valley.

The New Emery County Road.

While in Salt Lake last Friday, we called at the office of Johnson & McDowell and had a conversation with them concerning the new road from Price to southern Emery county. Mr. Johnson stated that he and Mr. B. W. Driggs were engaged in incorporating a company to build the line and were desirous of perfecting arrangements as soon as possible. During our interview a gentleman was present, who represented some eastern men and who he stated would take stock in the company if the plan of the road could be made to appear feasible to them. At our request to bring the parties to Emery county so they could look over the ground for themselves, Mr. Johnson promised to do so, and thought they would be down in a week or ten days. The road will be started from Price, instead of Dead Horse crossing, and run south as far as Orangeville and perhaps to Salina canyon. It behooves the people in Price, and all of the towns south, to wake up and do what they can to forward this enterprise. The right of way for the road and depot grounds should be donated the entire distance and everything done by the people that possibly can be done to have the road completed this summer. Mr. Johnson is spending a great deal of time and money in agitating the building of the road and deserves the thanks and unanimous support of the people of Emery county.—*Price Telegraph.*

Summons.

IN THE JUSTICES COURT OF ORANGE-
VILLE PRECINCT, TERRITORY OF UTAH
COUNTY OF EMERY.

Wm. Tatton, Plff,
      vs.   DEMAND $1.
John Doe, Deft.

To John Doe, whose name is otherwise unknown greeting.

You are hereby summoned to be
and appear before me the undersigned at my office in Orangeville precinct county of Emery Territory of
Utah on June 3, A. D 1891,
at nine o'clock a. m. to answer a
complaint filed against you in this
court by the above named plaintiff
on May 25 A. D. 1891.

Said action is brought to recover from
you the sum of 75 cts. for damage
done to the said plaintiff by the
following described animals now in
his possession. One light bay mare
about 4 years old 3 white feet branded
U⊓⊓ on left snoulder.

And you are hereby notified
that if you fail to so appear and
answer as above required the plaintiff
will take judgement against you for
the said sum of 75 cts and for costs of
keeping said animals and for costs of
suit.

To the sheriff or any constable of
said county greeting, make legal service and due return thereon.

Given under my hand this 27th day
of May A. D. 1891.

            GEORGE FOX,
            Justice of the Peace.

Our youngmen's conference which was held in Castle Dale this week, was well attended. The next confer-ence will be held at Orangeville on the last Saturday and Sunday in Oct. '91.

To Whom it May Concern.

We the undersigned residents of Orangeville Emery County Utah, owners of the Joes Valley Saw and Shingle Mills, in Emery county being desirous to cut the timber in the vicinity of the said mills to dispose of to the residents and farmers of Emery county hereby give notice to farmers and others having adverse interests who desire to have forrests preserved in the interests of the water supply for irrigation or other purposes, that they intend to make application in writing to the Secretary of the Interior for the privilege and right to cut timber for the purpose above stated in the following described locality which is unsurveyed land in Emery county Utah and bounded as follows. Commencing at the Joes Valley saw mills running north two miles thence West to the line between Emery and San Pete counties thence south two miles thence east to place of beginning

NOAH L GUYMAN, Sen
A. TUTTLE,
A C, VANBUREN,
A. SCOVILT,
THOS FULLMER

Dated Orangeville this 3rd day of June A D 1891

—President Larsen, was in Price Monday. He st.. .s that the prospects for crops were never better around Castle Dale, and fruit could not look finer.

Orangeville is anticipating quite a boom with a prospect of a railroad from Price and the erection of coke ovens in the vicinity. There is an abundance of coal in the adjacent hills, which is said to be excellent for coking purposes.

The towns of Ferron and Molen are also steadily progressing. A new canal is being made to supply the last-named town with better water for culinary purposes.

This is one of the oldest settlements in the county, and the residents have established good homes, and are blessed with fine orchards which produce an excellent quality of fruit. About three miles below is the county seat of Emery—the old town of Castle Dale.

Very little progress has been made of late years and its growth is not as observable as that of other towns in the county. A stake academy has been conducted during the past winter, in the upper rooms of a dwelling house which were not well adapted to the requirements of such a school. Brother Day, the principal, labored energetically and accomplished good results, considering the disadvantages and lack of necessary apparatus, or seating. This, however, will be remedied in the future. as orders have been placed for a full supply of of these appurtenances.

A new meeting house is being erected, and this gives the town quite an imposing appearance. The district school house is well furnished but is much too small.

GOT THEM BOTH.

Sheriff Fowler's Latest Counterfeit Exploit.

He Nabs Two Forgerers While Plying Their Work at Price Station.

One of His Birds Gets Away From Him, but He Bags It Again.

Sheriff Fowler left Provo last Friday with a man in charge, supposed to be a deserter from Fort DuChesne, as the officers of the Fort wired him to take the man to Price and they would meet him. Arriving at Price he was made aware of the fact that a forgery had been committed there that same morning.

"It appears," said Sheriff Fowler to a DISPATCH reporter, "that two men had cashed a check for $147 at the bank run by the Emery County Mercantile company, which they paid in gold. After being put in possession of the facts by the proprietors of the store and bank, I started to work on the case. Having secured a minute description, I posted the men on train No. 2, giving the conductor a complete description. as I thought the two men would be likely to board the train somewhere between there and Green River. I took the first west-bound train to look out for them on this side, and by the time I had reached Thistle I received a message from the conductor of No. 2, that two men answering the description had got on the train at Lower Crossing, with tickets for Grand Junction. I immediately wired the sheriff at that place to meet train No. 2, and get the men. I took the next train, arriving in Grand Junction on Saturday morning. I found the men there, and in searching I discovered a certificate of membership of the detective agency of E. A. Franks, Salt Lake City, with the true signature and photo of E. A. Franks. I also found three checks made out on the Utah Commercial and Savings bank, Salt Lake City, for $144 each. and made payable to J. C. Moore, of the Pinkerton Detective Agency. The check cashed at Price was also made payable to J. C. Moore, and was endorsed by one of the two men who signed himself J. C. Moore. He had a J. C. Moore detective badge pinned to his vest, which helped to convince the cashier that he was the right man. cards, etc., in the valise carried by the men, and $130 in gold. As they had paid their fares to Grand Junction this money accounted for the shortage from the amount obtained from the bank. They gave their names as Woods, and claimed to be half brothers. Their story is to the effect that they had seen J. C. Moore at Price and he had given them the checks and also the badge, telling them it might help them in cashing the checks. They had been paid $10 for cashing the check, and the alleged J. C. Moore had departed with the rest of the money.

"I brought the men back to Price on Monday morning, about 2 o'clock, and took them to the hotel and stood guard over them until morning. When morning came I washed and went down stairs and sent a boy to bring the Justice of the Peace to the hotel. While there engaged one of the prisoners came down stairs. I asked him where his partner was. He replied, 'I don't know; didn't he come down with you?' I knew he was lying, so upstairs I went, and there found my bird had flown. I secured the other one in irons and then started in pursuit of my flying hero. I found he had taken to the brush, and I followed him a considerable distance and then lost the trail. I returned and got a horse and started others on the trail by offering a reward of $50 for his capture. We kept on the trail until nearly noon, when he was discovered by two boys. He was laying under a large flat rock, where he had crawled, leaving only his head visible. Some of the men stepped forward and got hold of him. He was taken back to Price and both were examined before the Justice of the Peace and bound over, to await the action of the grand jury in the sum of $1,500 each. They were given into the hands of the sheriff of Emery county and will languish in the county jail at Castle Dale."

The two men after leaving Price must have walked at a rattling pace, as the distance from Price to Lower Crossing is forty miles, which they accomplished in a few hours.

Salt Lake Times
June 23, 1891

A child of Amasa Scoville's was drowned in the water ditch in front of its parents' home in Orangeville, Emery county, on the 10th inst.

Provo Daily Enquirer
June 24, 1891

We had a pleasant visit today from President C. S. Larsen and Bishop H. Olsen, of Castle Dale, Emery county.

Final Proofs.

No. 1012.

Land Office at Salt Lake City, Utah, June 19, 1891

Notice is hereby given that the following named settler has filed notice of his intention to make final proof in support of his claim, and that said proof will be made before the Probate Judge of Uintah County, Utah, at Ashley, on August 12, 1891, viz: DAVID AMLIN, H E, 1012, for the N ½ N W ¼ Sec. 12, S 4 5 W ¼ Sec ? Tp. 4, S R. 21 E.

He names the following witnesses to prove his continuous residence upon and cultivation of, said land, viz: Isaac Slaugh, John Slaugh, Jr., William Gillman and Thomas Robins, all of Naylor, Uintah county, Utah,

FRANK D HOBBS, Register

W. Imley, attorney for claimant.

J26-A28.

President C. G. Larsen and Bishop H. Olsen of Castle Dale, Emery county, were arraigned before Commissioner Hill of Provo on the charge of unlawful cohabitation. Each was bound over to wait the action of the grand jury in the sum of $500, and the alleged plural wives in the sum of $200 each.

Provo Dispatch
June 27, 1891

MADE HIS ESCAPE.

From the Interior of Emery County Jail.

Sheriff Fowler Will Watch at This End for the Forger.

Sheriff Fowler received a telegram yesterday afternoon from Castle Dale to the effect that one of the forgers he succeeded in capturing a few days ago had escaped. This is the same fellow that the sheriff had such a chase after at Price. Sheriff Fowler lost money in effecting his capture before, and as no inducement has been offered for his recapture, the sheriff will stay at Provo and watch for his man.

Eastern Utah Telegraph
July 3, 1891

—Miss Emily Larsen, daughter of President Larsen of Castle Dale is employed as a clerk in the Emery County Mercantile Company's store

Summons.

TERRITORY OF UTAH,
COUNTY OF EMERY } ss.

IN THE JUSTICE'S COURT, FERRON PRECINCT

William Taylor, Plaintiff,
versus
John Doe, Defendant. } Demand, $2.50

The people of the Territory of Utah send greeting to John Doe (whose name is otherwise unknown) defendant.

You are hereby summoned to appear before me, at my office in Ferron, in the County of Emery, Territory of Utah, on the 8th day of July, A D., 1891, at 10 o'clock a. m., in an action brought against you by said plaintiff, to answer the complaint of the above-named plaintiff. Said action is brought to recover from you the sum of two and a half dollars for damage done to plaintiff by the following-described animals to-wit: One black mare; star in forehead; branded Z on left thigh, three or four years old, with suckling colt.

One brown horse-colt; two years old; branded O on left side of neck; white hind feet; small white spot in forehead.

One roan horse; about eight years old, white spot in forehead, white spot on nose, white hind feet, branded V on left shoulder and thigh crop off right ear.

One bay horse; three or four years old; white strip in forehead, branded ofo on left thigh.

One sorrel horse, three or four years old, right legs white nearly to the knee and hawk joints, large white strip in face; branded T on left shoulder and thigh.

If you fail to appear and answer, the plaintiff will take judgment against you for the sum of $2.50, together with feed bill and costs of court.

To the sheriff or any constable of said county of Emery, GREETING:

Make legal service and due return hereof.

Given under my hand this 29th day of June, A D., 1891.

JOHN C DUNCAN,
Justice of the Peace, Ferron Precinct

Summons.

TERRITORY OF UTAH, }
COUNTY OF EMERY } ss.

In the Justice s Court, Castle Dale Precinct

Before R. H. McDonough, Justice of the peace.

Mrs. Emma Jeffs, Plaintiff, }
vs. } Demand,
Hans Brothersed, Defendant, } $35 & 1 100.

To Hans Brothersen, Greeting:

You are hereby summoned to be and appear before me, the undersigned, at my office in Castle Dale Precinct, in Emery County, Territory of Utah, and answer a complaint filed against you by the above named plaintiff on the 27th day of June, 1891.

Said action is brought to recover from you the sum of thirty-five, and $1 100 dollars. For goods, wares and merchandise received by you; and at your special instance and request at different times in the year 1889 and 1890.

If you fail to appear and answer, the Plaintiff will take judgment against you for the sum of thirty five and $1 100 dollars, with interest at one per cent. per month. And costs.

To the sheriff or any constable of said county, Greeting:

Make legal service and due return hereof.

Given under my hand this 27th day of June, A. D., 1891.

R H. McDONOUGH,
Justice of the Peace of said Precinct.

More Election Judges.

Orangeville—E M Moore, E W Fox, S P Snow.

No 1024

Land Office at Salt Lake City, U T., June 26, 1891

Notice is hereby given that the following named settler has filed notice of his intention to make final proof in support of his claim, and that said proof will be made before the County Clerk of Emery County, U T., at Castle Dale Emery County, U T., on Saturday August 15th, 1891, viz JOHN EDEN, H E., No 7020, for the S ½ N E quarter S. E. quarter N W quarter, N E quarter, S E. quarter Sec 11 Twp 17, S, R, 9 E.

He names the following witnesses to prove his continuous residence upon and cultivation of said land, viz

Rasmus O Rasmussen, George H Richards, Thomas Furish, all of Cleveland, Emery county, U T, Jacob B Johnson

FRANK D HOBBS

125-0a30   Register

No. 1023.

Land Office at Salt Lake City, Utah, June 26, 1891.

Notice is hereby given that the following named settler has filed notice of his intention to make final proof in support of his claim, and that said proof will be made before the County clerk of Emery county, U. T., at Castle Dale, Emery County, U T., on Saturday August 15th, 1891, v.z THOMAS FARISH, H E., No. 7488 for the N. W. quarter, Sec. 15, Twp 17 S., range 9 R.

He names the following witnesses to prove his continuous residence upon and cultivation of said land, viz:

John Eden, George H Richards, Lewis Larsen, Sr., William E. Cowley, Jr., all of Cleveland, Emery county, U. T.

FRANK D HOBBS,

125-0a30.   Register.

Eastern Utah Telegraph
August 7, 1891

—The returns from the county indicate that L M Olson is elected county superintendent and H M Fugate and L P Oveson are elected selectmen Geo W Fox, of Orange ville, is undoubtedly our future surveyor

—Notice the "ad" of the Price-Ferron stage line in this issue Bryant Bryan is the proprietor and will give you first-class accommodations The stages will soon have covers to protect passengers from rain and dust.

Eastern Utah Telegraph
August 14, 1891

—J. Stevens, of Ferron, is assisting B. Bryan in carrying the mail.

Ogden Standard
August 28, 1891

Harvesting has commenced at Orangeville, Emery county, and the crops look well, better than ever before. The fruit is also good, apples, peaches and apricots are ripe and grapes are turning.

No 1003.

Land Office at Salt Lake City, U. T., July 2, 1891

Notice is hereby given that the following named settler has filed notice of his intention to make final proof in support of his claim, and that said proof will be made before the County Clerk of Emery County, U T. at Castle Dale, Emery County, U. T., on Saturday, August 2nd, 1891, viz

JOHN L. BRASHER, H E, No. 6596, for the W. ½ S. E. quarter and N E quarter of S. E. quarter and S. E. quarter N E. quarter, Sec 14, Tp 17, S. R. 8 E.

He names the following witnesses to prove his continuous residence upon, and cultivation of, said land, viz

Wm. Howard, Samuel S. Grange, Erin A. Howard, and George A. Sherman, all of Huntington, Emery county, U. T.

FRANK D HOBBS.

(26-oa31   Register.

No. 1004

Land Office at Salt Lake City, U. T., Aug 22, 1891.

Notice is hereby given that the following named settler has filed notice of his intention to make final proof in support of his claim, and that said proof will be made before the Clerk of the County Court of Emery County, U. T., at Castle Dale, U. T., on Saturday, October 10, 1891, viz Thomas Gale, H E., No. 8405, for the N W. ¼, of N E ¼ and E. ½ N W. ¼ Sec. 7 and S. E. ¼ of S W ¼, Sec. 6, Twp. 15 S., R 11 E.

He names the following witnesses to prove his continuous residence upon and cultivation of said land, viz

Thomas Lundal, Robert A. Snyder, Edgar Thayn, William J. Tidwell, all of Wellington, Emery County, U. T.

FRANK D HOBBS,

133-oa32.   Register.

Final Proofs.

No. 1006.

United States Land Office, Salt Lake City, Utah, Aug 1, 1891

Notice is hereby given that the following-named settler has filed notice of his intention to make final proof in support of his claim, and that said proof will be made before the Clerk of the County Court, of Emery County, U T., at Castle Dale, Emery County, U T., on Saturday, September 12, 1891, viz Thomas J Kirby, H E., No. 7457, for the N E quarter N E quarter, Sec 29, W half S. W. quarter, and S. E. quarter S W quarter, Sec. 28, Tp. 17 S. R. 9 E.

He names the following witnesses to prove his continuous residence upon, and cultivation of, said land, viz

Albert Guymon, Samuel Grange, Thomas Chrosney, Thomas Wakefield, all of Huntington, Emery County, U. T.

FRANK D HOBBS, Register.

130-oa32.

Eastern Utah Telegraph
September 4, 1891

—While in Huntington last Satur
day the editor of the *Telegraph* in
company with Mr Frank Carroll of
Orangeville, took dinner with Mr
and Mrs D. C. Robbins and as we
were very hungry after a ride over
the desert enjoyed their hospitality
very much

Eastern Utah Telegraph
September 11, 1897

No 109
Land Office, Salt Lake City, Utah, July 20,
1891

Notice is hereby given that the following
named settler has filed notice of his intention
to make final proof in support of his claim
and that said proof will be made before
County Clerk of Emery County, Utah at
Castle Dale, Utah, on Sept. 11th, 1891, viz
LEVI FARRER, Declaratory Statement No.
11,148, for the S W quarter S E. quarter, Section 4, and W half N E quarter and N E,
quarter N W quarter, Section 3, Township
21 S R. 16 E., S. L. M., Utah.

He names the following witnesses to prove
his continuous residence upon and cultivation
of, said land, viz

Mathias Hartman, Herman Dahling Matt
Riley, John Mauln, all of Blake Emery
County, Utah.

t3l-oa33.   FRANK D HOBBS,
                                  Register
T C BAILY, attorney

No 1006
Land Office at Salt Lake City, U T
July 20, 1891

Notice is hereby given that the following
named settler has filed notice of his intention
to make final proof in support of his
claim and that said proof will be made before
the clerk of the County Court of Emery
County, U T, at Castle Dale, Emery County,
U T., on Saturday September 5th, 1891, viz
Lars Jensen, D S., No. 11 83", for the S half
S E quarter, Section 9, Township 12, S R
7 E.

He names the following witnesses to prove
his continuous residence upon and cultivation of, said land, viz:

Lafayett Granger, Thomas Lloyd, Anthon
Cramer and J K. Farcell, all of Scofield,
Emery County, U T

                    FRANK D HOBBS, Register

No. 1087

Land Office at Salt Lake City, Utah, August 17, 1891

Notice is hereby given that the following named settler has filed notice of his intention to make final proof in support of his claim and that said proof will be made before the Clerk of the County Court of Emery at Castle Dale, Utah, on October 3, 1891, viz. James H. Van Natta, Homestead Entry 8123, for the E½ of S E ¼, Sec 13, Tp. 13 S. R. 9 E

He names the following witnesses to prove his continuous residence upon and cultivation of said land, viz

E. D. Fullmer, H. J. Stowell, Harrison Miller, A. J. Simons, all of Price, Emery County, Utah

FRANK D. HOBBS, Register

Bird & Lowe, attorney for claimant.

No 1104

Land Office at Salt Lake City, U. T., Aug 27, 1891

Notice is hereby given that the following named settler has filed notice of his intention to make final proof in support of his claim, and that said proof will be made before the Clerk of the County of Emery County, U. T. at Castle Dale Emery County, U. T., on Saturday October 17 1891, viz

SAMUEL JACKSON, H. E. No. 8412, for the S E. quarter on Sec. 9 Twp 19 S R. 8 E

He names the following witnesses to prove his continuous residence upon and cultivation of said land viz

Andrew Rasmussen, Rhoden H. McDonough, Carl E Larsen, and Richard C Miller, all of Castle Dale, Emery County, Utah Territory

FRANK D. HOBBS, Register

134-oa39

Salt Lake Tribune
September 24, 1891

NOTES.

Deputy Marshal Bachman arrested James M. Peterson from Castle Dale, last night, for unlawful cohabitation. He also arrested the alleged plural wife, Caroline Peterson.

Eastern Utah Telegraph
October 16, 1891

—Dr. Moore of Orangeville is a new subscriber to the TELEGRAPH, and also has a card in this issue of the paper. We have heard the Dr recommended very highly as a physician.

Eastern Utah Telegraph
October 23, 1891

Summons.

TERRITORY OF UTAH, } ss.
COUNTY OF EMERY }

IN THE JUSTICE's COURT OF CAST E DALE
PRECINCT, BEFORE R. H. M LENOUGH JUS
TICE OF THE PEACE

Bort Staply, Plff.,
vs
John Doe Deft
} Demand, $2.50

To John Doe, whose name proper t not
known Greeting

You are hereby notified to appear before
me, the undersig d, at my office in Castle
Dale precinct, in Emery County, Territory of
Utah, and answer a complaint fi ed again t
you by the above named on the 21th, day of
October 1891 Said action is brought to recover from you $2.50 on the foregoing descri
bed ar mals to wit: One bay mare about 7
years old. D 3 on left shoulder _ E F on left
thigh, 1 bay mare 2 years old and 1 brown
m are, 2 years old, both branded 00 and a bar
above, on le t should'er. 1 sorrel 3 year ol
mare branded 3 circle above, on left thigh 1
gray mare 4 years old, branded, diamond with
quarter circle above on the right shoulder

If you fail to appear and answer, the Plaintiff will take judgement against you for the
sum of $2.50 two dollars and fifty cents, a d
costs. To the sheriff or ary constable of said
county, Greeting make legal service and due
return hereof Given under n y band this
11th, day of October, A. D 1891

R. H. McLENOUGH.
Justice of the Peace of said Precinct.

No 1171
Land Office, Salt Lake City, Utah, Oct, 21b,
1891.

Notice is hereby given that the following
named settler has filed notice of his intention
to make final proof in support of his claim,
and that said proof will be made before
the Clerk of the County Court of Emery County
Utah, at Castle Dale, Utah, on Saturday, Nov
28th, 1891, viz: ALEXANDER McLEAN
D E No. 11,670, for the S. 1/4 S. W. 1/4 and N. W.
1/4 S. W. 1/4 and S, W. 1/4 N. W. quarter Section
8 Tp. 13 S. R. 7 E.

He names the following witnesses to prove
his continuous residence upon, and cultivation of, said land viz Thomas Lord Lars

Land Office at Salt ake ty, Utah, October
5, 1891

Notice is hereby given that the following
named settler has filed notice of his intention
to make final proof in support of his
claim, and that said proof will be made before
the Clerk of the County Court of Emery County
Utah, at Castle Dale Emery County Utah, on
Saturday November 28, 1891 viz: JOHN
WILLIAMS, H E No. 787, for the S. W
quarter of section 15, Tp. 17 S. R. 9 E.

He names the following witnesses to prove
his continuous residence upon, and cultivation
of, said land, viz John Eden Thomas Farish,
Lewis Whinspey, Ole Johnson, all of Cleveland, Emery Co Utah

140 oa13   FRANK D HOBBS Register

Ogden Standard
October 30, 1891

Price *Telegraph:* John O. Lemon
of Ferron, will soon make proof on
his tree claim near that place. He
has one of the finest ranches in the
county and has fully complied with
the timber culture law as to planting
and cultivation of trees.

Eastern Utah Telegraph
November 6, 1891

Teachers Meeting
Program of an informal meeting of the school teacheres of Emery County, to be held at Orangeville District school house, Sunday Nov. 8th, 91, at 5 o'clock p. m.

Eastern Utah Telegraph
November 13, 1891

Report of Teachers meeting, held at Orangeville Nov. 8th 1891.

Meeting called to order at 5.15 p. m. by W. W. Crawford of Orangeville.

Murry Larsen of Ferron, was chosen praident, and F. I. Page Sec.

The following program was rendered.

Music by the Choir.

Prayer, by Arthur Dall.

Music by the Choir.

Subjects presented were.

Primary writing, W. W. Crawford.

Primary spelling, Arthur Dall.

Geography. B. F. Luke.

History, J. W. Nixon.

Grammar, A. Wall.

A plea for reading educational journals, by J. W. Nixon.

Adjourned.

The subjects presented fully and ably discussed by the teachers of Emery Co., before a good sized attentive, and appreciative audience.

We thank the Orangeville Choir for their excellent services.

Altogether, the Teachers meeting was a benefiting, and a pleasurable affair, and it is to be hoped that we may have had many more of a similar character.

The only disappointment, being the fact that Dr. Moore did not materialize to address us upon the subject of "Schoolroom Hygiene." his really was a disappointment to the audience and it is to be regretted been refused, to attend.

F. I. Page, sec.

Brigham City Bugler
November 14, 1891

THE TELEGRAPH wants a live correspondent in Castle Dale, Cleveland, Orangeville and Ferron. Who will respond?---Price Telegraph.

No 1169

Land Office at Salt Lake City, Utah, October 3, 1891

Notice is hereby given that the following named settler has filed notice of his intention to make final proof in support of his claim, and that said proof will be made before the Clerk of the County Court of Emery Couty Utah, at Castle Dale Emery County Utah, on Saturday November 28, 1891, viz: JOHN WILLIAMS, H. E No. 7573, for the S W quarter of section 15, Tp. 17 S R. 9 E.

He names the following witnesses to prove his continuous residence upon, and cultivation of, said land, viz John Eden, Thomas Parish, Lewis Whinspey, Ole Johnson, all of Cleveland, Emery Co. Utah

140 oa43   FRANK D. HOBBS, Register

No. 119

Land Office at Salt Lake City, Utah, November 7th, 1891

Notice is hereby given that the following named settler has filed notice of his intention to make final proof in support of his claim and that said proof will be made before the Clerk of the Court of Emery County U T at Castle Dale, Emery County Utah, on Dec., 26th, 1891 viz CHARLES H HALES H E 7583 for the NW quarter Sec. 4 Tp 18 S R 9 E.

He names the following witnesses to prove his continuous residence upon, and cultivation of said land viz Calvin W Moore, P C Birch Sam D Dunell, William A. Staker, all of Lawrence Utah

141-oa19   FRANK D HOBBS, register

No 1181

Land Office at Salt Lake City, U T October, 21 1891

Notice is hereby given that the following named settler has filed notice of his intention to make final proof in support of his claim and that said proof will be made before the clerk of the County Court of Emery County, U T, at Castle Dale, Emery County, U T, on Saturday, December 12th, 1891, viz: ELIAS W THOMAS, H E No. 8445 for the SW quarter SW quarter Sec, 27 and E½ SE quarter and NW quarter SE quarter Sec 31, Tp 17 S R 9 E.

He names the following witnesses to prove his continuous residence upon, and cultivation of said land viz Calvin W Moore, Samuel Dunnell, Mathew Lrens, Samuel Coombs, all of Lawrence, Emery County U T

142oa5   FRANK D HOBBS, Register

Eastern Utah Telegraph
December 18, 1891

Notice to Creditors.

Notice is hereby given by the undersigned, LOVISE PETERSEN Administratrix of the Estate of Jasper Petersen deceased, to the Creditors of and all persons having claim against the said dveeased to exh'bit them with the necessary vouchers, within four months after the first publication of this notice to the said Loviso Petersen at Castle Dale Emery County, Utah.

LOVISE PETERSEN,
Administratrix of the estate of Jasper Peter sen decrased

Dated Castle Dale November 19th 1891.

—On our trip to the South part of the County we were favorably impressed with the appearance of Orangeville. But when we stopped to think what a few subscribers we had at that place it almost made us blush, but however we added quite a number to our list.

Eastern Utah Telegraph
December 25, 1891

—Miss Hellen Fox, of Manti, who is employed as assistant of the Ferron school, attended the examination at this place last Saturday, and left on the early morning train Sunday, for her home in manti, where she will spend the holidays.

CASTLE DALE

MILLS

SEELY BROS

PROPRIETORS.

Dealers in

FLOUR AND FEED.

Castle Dale,   Utah.

INGLEWOOD.

Imported 1890, by E. Bennett & Son of Topeka Kansas.

Inglewood is a Full Blood Clydesdale Stallion, a bright Bay, four year old, sixteen and one-half hands high and weighs sixteen hundred and forty pounds

Service Fee: Inglewood will make the season of 1892 at Orange Seely's barn at Castle Dale as follows:

For season $15,00; Leap $10,00; To insure $30,00

The Clydesdale Horse Company.

Castle Dale,   Utah.

EMERY COUNTY

was created by an act of the Legislative Assembly in 1880 out of the vast territory known as Sanpete Co

Emery County as bounded by the act of 1880 contained 8,762 square miles or 5,607,680 acres The population of the new county numbered 672 souls.

The following county officials were appointed by the Gov.:

Samuel Jenkes Probate Judge, Elias Cox, Jasper Peterson and William Taylor Selectmen, who were required to enter upon the duties of their respective offices on the second Monday in March 1880 On said date they appointed a Co Clerk and organized a County Court and appointed all county officials necessary for full and complete transaction of all business matters therein. Emery County is and always has been a part of the 1st Judicial District.

The first county officials, so we are told, served two years for the county without compensation during its early existence.

The Legislature of 1890 amended the act of 1880 and the boundry of Emery County is as follows

Commencing at a point where parallel 38 deg and 30 minutes North Latitude crosses Green River, thence West along the said parallel to a point 3 miles West of the first guide meridian East of the Salt Lake Meridian, thence North along the Township line between Ranges 5 and 6 E to the 3rd Standard parallel South, thence East 3 miles, thence North to the Township line between Townships 11 and 12 South, thence East along the last mentioned Township line to Green River the place of beginning.

The officials of Sanpete Co differed with those of Emery County upon the interpretation of that part of the boundary relating to the 1st Guide Meridian East of the Salt Lake Meridian and in 1890 brought suit in the Courts to obtain that portion of Emery Co known as Pleasant valley, a region rich in coal and other valuable mineral deposits. The suit resulted in a victory for Emery Co.

The resources of Emery County are vast and va... in her boundries are fo... l, Deposits of S... Beds ... n, Quar ...rest's of Pine ...the fertility of soil

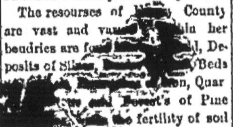

...and the irrigators
... that is required to pro-
...cest crops of cereals and
...es adapted to the latitude.
...eport of Gov Thomas show
...nery County ranks 1st in
... Lucerne, and occupies the
...o in column of production.
...e report show that the 2,277
... wheat harvested in the Co
... averaged 23 bushels per
...783 acres of oats grown in the
...averaged 43 bushel per acre,
...ood showing for corn, rye,
...nd fruit.
...tock growing business is at.
...y that ranks with the agri
...nd mineral products, and
... pays large returns on the
...invested.
Emery County has no less than
13 flourishing towns ranging in pop-

ulation from 800 to 900. Hunting
ton is the largest, and is situated in
the famous Castle valley 20 miles
south of Price. Also Cleveland
Lawrence, Castle Dale, Orangeville
and Ferron are situated in Castle
valley and all possess attractions
peculiar to themselves weich time
and space prevents our describing
Public improvements are character-
istics of the people of the towns
mentioned, and their efforts in that
direction are very commendable.

Schofield, Castle Gate and Winter
Quarters are flourishing mining towns
while Helper, and Green River
represent the Rail Road towns

There is 14 Post Offices in the Co.
and several more badly needed A-
bout 100 miles of Rail Road in operation, and as much more graded and
most ready for the rails.

Castle valley comprises the greater portion of the agriculture lands
of the County, and the products of
the valley are such as to cause the
farmers to take great pride in their
possessions.

The assessed valuation of the Co
for the year 1891 reached the snug
sum of $1,294,926,00. The County
is in a prosperous condition, low taxes with money in the Treasure. The
population of the County increased
from 4 866 in 1890 to 5 706 in 1891.
A net gain of 840 for the year.

What is said of Emery, Uintah
and Grand Counties is true of Piute,
San Juan and the balance of Eastern
Utah.

J. K. REED

of Orangeville is the Pioneer merchant of Emery County. He commenced business at Orangeville in the year 1878 with a small stock of goods. Mr Reed was the first Post Master commissioned East of the Wasatch range of mountains The people at that time were very scattering, his nearest neighbor being one mile distance and the total population of cottonwood creek numbered fifteen souls. No rail roads were then nearer than Salt Lake City and their supplies had to be hauled from that point by wagon. During the winter season when the snow was deep and roads impassable for wagons, goods were carried in on pack horses to supply the wants of the people. The early settlers of Emery County were compelled to undergo a great many hardships during the settlement of the county. Mr. Reed and a hired man were on one of their excursions during the winter of 1879—known as the hard winter—and become snow bound in the mountains and for two days and nights were without food or shelter. In Mr. Reeds language he says "We thought at times we would have to give up in despair and succumb to the inevitable." During another time when after goods in the season he and a companion were precipitated into the Salina creek with four head of horses and wagon. They fell a distance of fifty feet, killing one horse and narrowly escaping with their own lives, loosing most all of their goods.

The subject of this sketch is still at the old stand with a large and varied stock of general merchandise, and the largest stock of drugs in the county.

Mr. Reed has served three terms of two years each as County Attorney.

Petition

A petition from the people of Orangeville, relative to changing the county road so as to run through Orangeville and past Jenk's mill, signed by A. Tuttle and 78 others, was presented and on motion the same was laid over for further consideration in this session.

FINAL PROOF NOTICES.

No. 122.

Land Office at Salt Lake City, U. T
December 9, 1891

Notice is hereby given that the following named settler has filed notice of his intention to make final proof in support of his claim and that said proof will be made before the Probate Judge, Emery County, U T, at Castle Dale, Emery County, U T, on January 30th, 1892, viz: IRENA K. SOUTH WORTH, D S 11732, for E ½ NE. quarter SE. quarter, Sec 1, Twp. 14 S R 9 E. and Lot 4 and NE. quarter SW quarter, Sec. 6 Twp 14 S R 10 E.

She names the following witnesses to prove his continuous residence upon, and cultivation of said land, viz: Heber J. Stowell, Walter Grimes, Charley Grimes, James Garley all of Spring Glen, Utah

FRANK D. HOBBS,

Hobbs&. Register.

Eastern Utah Telegraph
January 8, 1892

Orangeville Items

Thinking that a few items from the thrifty little village of Orangeville would not be amiss for publication I forward the following items

The Holidays passed quietly here Dancing, Suppers and Sleighing were in vogue during the Holidays

The firm of Cox & Carroll done a rushing business during the Holidays

J K. Reid carries a good line of drugs Prescriptions carefully filled night or day on short notice,

The Orangeville Co op_____ _____ l__ of _____ _____ a and _ sells cheap general merchandise

Wm Peacock has been busy plastering for the past two months. Will can do a good job of plastering.

S. P Snow, Dr E M Moore, War ren Peacock, George Fulmer, C _ ar- Fox and H Tuttle are all _ george their new resi lences, _ living in

The eight year _ rected in '91. Oa___ _mat. Jr. old son of N. T. A comp__ was kicked by a horse a cor _ of weeks ago and received D- _ pound fracture of the skull _ Moore removed a small piece of the skull and the boy is doing well

It is very inconvenient for part of the town to have to haul water from the canal in the winter We hope provisions for a water master will be made before another winter

The Orangeville schools controlled by three teachers are doing well

Dr Moore wishes it understood that h's fees have nothing to do with the druggists fees, furthermore the doctor wishes the public to understand that persons from other settlements must make him secure for his fees before he will respond to their call,

Frank Carroll is a busy merchant.

A. Tuttle, our Constable, keeps the youth quite tame after they have imbibed a few ounces of elixir of snake juice.

Some of the boys have sworn off for a year.

Stay with it boys

The armless violinist, Owens, gave an entertainment last Saturday eve, and drew quite a crowd

Democrat.

Deseret Weekly
January 23, 1892

DEATHS.

ROBERTSON.—At Orangeville, Emery county, Utah, January 5th, 1892, of general debility, Jane, relict of Nichols Robertson, born August 7th, 1807. Deceased joined the Church with her husband at an early day in its history. She was in the persecutions and mobbings in Missouri and at the exodus of the Saints from that State. Returned to Illinois and there shared in the privations and sufferings of the Saints. She was the mother of seven sons and had the satisfaction of seeing them all emigrate to Utah in the year 1862, with the exception of one, who enlisted to defend his country in the late war and died in the service. She was a good wife, a kind mother and a true Latter-day Saint. She passed from this life at the residence of her son, Bishop Jasper Robertson, of Orangeville, at the ripe age of eighty-two years, six months.

Manti Sentinel
February 6, 1892

PRICE.

Emery Co. clipped from the Telegrap of Jan. 29

C H Taylor is figuring on a new residence.

The Licens collected for the last year amounts to over $7,000,00.

Mr D J Williams will erect a number of cottages, in Price, in the spring.

The jail cages are being put in place this week. In the future it will not be necessary to cart a prisoner across the country to Castle Dale only to be brought back in order to attend court. This will save the county some expense.

THE AMERICANIZED.

List of Those Who Have Purchased the New Encyclopedia Britannica.

Probably no book of the age that was ever offered in Salt Lake has had a more popular run than the new Americanized Encyclopedia Britannica, which is offered in the west only in connection with THE HERALD. It cost the publishers, Belford, Clark & Co., about $3,000,000 to re-edit the old work, expunge and curtail obsolete subjects and insert modern subjects —especially American themes—into the work. It is the triumph of modern literature, and everywhere it has had a tremendous sale. The very low price at which it is offered with THE HERALD is made possible by the fact a special rate has been accorded the prominent newspapers which offer the works with their issues. The *Examiner*, the Denver *Republican*, the Louisville *Courier Journal*, as well as THE HERALD are offering the new encyclopedia, which is in three styles of binding, and is sold on the installment plan with either the daily, Sunday or semiweekly edition.

Those who have obtained the Americanized Encyclopedia Britannica up to February 26, 1892, are as follows:

Arthur William Brown, Salt Lake city
George F. Felt, Salt Lake city.
Willard C. Burton, Salt Lake city.
A. A. Moulton, Salt Lake city.
James Noble, Salt Lake city.
Richard H. Cabell, Salt Lake city.
N. A. Reeves, Salt Lake city.
John Henry Hamlin, Salt Lake city.
James Gallacher, Salt Lake city.
J. H. Heron, Salt Lake city.

A. W. Stevenson, Salt Lake city.
Hiram E. Booth, Salt Lake city.
G. A. Gibbs, Salt Lake city.
George H. Vine, jr., Salt Lake city.
M. B. Sowles, Salt Lake city.
W. G. Van Horne, Salt Lake city.
Alex Myles, Salt Lake city.
John Steitz, Salt Lake city.
Edward Brook, North Salt Lake.
H. Leicherini, Salt Lake city.
W. B. Webber, Salt Lake city.
S. A. Chase, Salt Lake city.
Arthur Farnsworth, Salt Lake city.
F. M. Lyman, jr., Mill Creek, Utah.
George S. Beckman, Salt Lake city.
Joseph Hepworth, Salt Lake city.
W. B. Hooper, Salt Lake city.
L. Skeen, jr., Plain City, Utah.
Edwin Wright, Salt Lake city.
James Moffatt, Salt Lake city.
A. W. Caine, Salt Lake city.
C. A. Neville, Salt Lake city.
H. J. Shimming, Salt Lake city.
Ole Ellingson, Lehi City, Utah.
Mrs. M. E. Randall, Salt Lake city.
Granvill Gillett, Salt Lake city.
Maurice Levy, Salt Lake city.
R. M. Biele, Salt Lake city.
Thomas McKelvie, Salt Lake city.
George S. Spencer, Salt Lake city.
J. Button, Salt Lake city.
W. S. Muir, Randolph.
Stephen W. Alley, Salt Lake city.
M. J. Kennedy, Salt Lake city.
Moylan C. Fox, Salt Lake city.
A. H. Worthen, Salt Lake city.
H. Mitchell, Salt Lake city.
E. O. Olsen, Salt Lake city.
A. B. Ewing, Salt Lake city.
Henry T. McEwan, Salt Lake city.
W. T. Gunter, Salt Lake city.
C. A. Lund, Salt Lake city.
Richard Griffiths, Salt Lake city.
James H. Randon, Kaysville, Utah.
Peter McCardell, Springville, Utah.
Albert Graupe, Salt Lake city.
James R. Smurthwaite, Box Elder, Utah

M. W. Butler, Logan city, Utah.
J. B. Taylor, Salt Lake city.
J. S. Acker, Salt Lake city.
F. A. Hammond, Bluff, Utah.
Dr. Julius Hannberg, Provo city, Utah.
B. Y. Randall, Salt Lake city.
Rebecca Daynes, Salt Lake city.
W. J. Lewis, Salt Lake city.
Edwin H. Brewerton, Salt Lake city.
John S. Lewis, Salt Lake city.
Milton Ridges, Salt Lake city.
W. W. Salmon, Salt Lake city.
M. E. Van Schoonhovan, Salt Lake city.
C. H. Wilson, Salt Lake city.
E. A. Tripp, Salt Lake city.
J. A. Grennan, Salt Lake city.
H. B. Nielsen, Salt Lake city.
John T. World, Salt Lake city.
R. Simpson, Salt Lake city.
Sydney Dawes, Salt Lake city.
A. W. Gallacher, Salt Lake city.
O. E. Cary, Salt Lake city.
Nicholas Groesbeck, Springville, Utah.
Carl Wilberg, Castle Dale, Utah.
J. F. Gibbs, Deseret, Utah.
Matthew White, Salt Lake city.
Phineas Young, Salt Lake city.
Ed. L. Elder, Salt Lake city.
Mrs. Bullock, Salt Lake city.
A. W. Stevenson, Salt Lake city.
F. Holman, Salt Lake city.
Amy J. Smith, Salt Lake city.
L. Loda, Salt Lake city.
S. S. Riter, Logan city, Utah.
Jomes Blamires, Kaysville, Utah.
H. H. A. Harris, Salem, Idaho.
W. G. Lane, Shoshone, Idaho.
J. E. Daniels, Provo city, Utah.
St. George Temple, St. George, Utah.
F. W. Fuller, city.
James A. Fuller, city.
H. H. Mears, city.
W. T. Fletcher, city.
George K. Reese, jr., city.
Fred Miller, Camas, Ida.

Manti Sentinel
March 12, 1892

Claytie Snow of Manti and Mamie Moffitt of Orangeville, Emery county, left for that place on Thursday morning.

Mabel Tuttle of Orangeville has been visiting friends and relatives in Manti for the past week.

A PLEASURE TRIP.

What Was Seen on a Recent Trip to Ferron.

FERRON, March 22, 1892.

DEAR SENTINEL: Like THE "SENTI-NEL'S" Pets, I am anxious for you to print my letter, and hope it may prove interesting to your readers. We left Sanpete on the morning of the 20th and arrived at Thistle at 9:30 o'clock where we waited for the east-bound train until 12:30. It kept us on the lookout to see all the scenery through Spanish Fork canyon. The lofty peaks of the Rockies were covered with snow, while the grass and ferns were peeping out in places from the foot hills from a white like covering, which had fallen the pre-vious night. The train almost crept around the winding, sharp curves, giving us a good opportunity to see those grand magnificent works of God. We cannot doubt he is a lover of the beautiful. When no eye but his own could see them, he has carved these peculiar forms. Every cliff, every tree and shrub, vine, leaf and flower is a thing of beauty so nicely are they con-trasted in their weird wildness. I would advise the young people of San-pete if they want to take a pleasure trip, to ride over the Rio Grande West-ern. Its accommodations are excellent and the officials are gentlemanly and courteous, and I am sure they would enjoy nothing more than a pleasure trip to Castle Gate. I could not begin to describe the scenery at that point, and do it justice. It is indeed a "Scenic

Route." Great perpindicular, moss covered cliffs rise up thousands of feet each side of the track and here nestles the tiny village of Castle Gate. Brown and white painted tenement houses, seemingly all alike, the great yawning mouths of the coal mines, and the electric lighting building from which the mines are lighted, make a pretty contrast with the cliffs. We arrived at Price at 3:45 and found it to be a town of about 500 inhabitants and it seems to be prosperous. We were kindly received at the Mathis house, where we met Mr. Peradice, editor of the Eastern Utah Telegraph. In company with Manager Moore of that paper, the editor showed us their town, and did all they could to make our waiting as pleasant as possible. Mr. Moore, told us, very confidentially of course, he thought seriously of soon visiting the Manti temple accompanied by Miss Annie Gull of Spanish Fork. We also had the pleasure of meeting Tooreoloose, Bob Ridley, Toots Carter and Ned, five Indian policemen and the head farmer of the Uintah Indian reservation. Deputy Marshal Eager of Salt Lake had subpœned them as witnesses in a case to be tried at Provo. The Indians were nicely dressed and looked clean. They gave an account of a recent "bear dance" which they had just completed, having danced a week. They ended the performance with a grand feast which the govern-

ment had provided. They also told us the squaws always have the choice of partners regardless of leap year. We thanked them for their information, but they would not let us off until we had sang—and we gave them, "How Can I Leave Thee?

At 8 o'clock Monday morning we took the stage for Ferron. Of course the wind blew, but the driver informed us it was "only a breeze." Later we found it was true. After "traveling a week," we arrived about 11 o'clock at a small settlement called Cleveland. It is hardly as large as Cleveland, Ohio, but it has room to grow and its prospects are flattering, for we saw a man and a duck pond. We reached Huntington at 12 and waited at the post office for the Ferron stage. In a few minutes up dashed the "lightning express" from the latter place consisting of a four-wheeled "barouche" drawn by an old gray mare whose name, the driver said was "Puddin'" and a big horse named "Deceiver." When we remarked on the looks of the mare the proud driver replied: "That ther' brute? Oh, she's none o' yer slouches, I can tell yer. If Morris had only known ther worth o' that brute he'd never'd troubled erbout inventin' the telegraph

After the hardest ride of our lives we finally arrived at our destination about sundown, tired, cold and Oh, so hungry! It is a town of about sixty families, nearly all young people, and their health is generally good. Spring is advancing rapidly. The apricot trees are beginning to bloom. Mr. A. C. Olsen of Mount Pleasant has been here a number of days. Justice Lowry officiated a short time ago at the wedding of Miss Mima Stevens to Mr. August Nelson The relief society celebration was a complete success. James Jeffs of Castle

Dale met with a severe accident the other day while driving. His horse became frightened, ran away and he was thrown out. He was badly hurt about the face and head. The doctor has fears of blood poisoning. The Home Dramatic club are having their stage enlarged. New scenery is being painted by G. Jack of Manti. They will put on the drama, "The Forest Keeper." Several Ferron people went to Orangeville last week to witness a dramatic performance. The performance, so their critics say, was altogether too "spirited."   C. L.

THE YOUNG STATUE

Public Interest in it Continues Un bated.

THE SITE IT WILL OCCUPY

The General Committee's Work—Ten Thousand Dollars Subscribed—A Sketch of the Site.

Public interest in the Pioneer monument and statue of Brigham Young continues as live and eager as when the plan was first mooted. According to Mr. H. M. Wells, secretary of the general committee, nearly $10,000 have been subscribed towards the $50,000 needed and the association is taking steps to inaugurate a grand territorial subscription to collect the entire sum.

Those having the affair in hand have formed an active and representative combination called the Brigham Young Memorial association. It is made up as follows:

JAMES SHARP, president.
WILLARD YOUNG, vice-president.
HEBER M. WELLS, secretary.
ELIAS A. SMITH, treasurer.

ADVISORY COMMITTEE.

PRESIDENT WILFORD WOODRUFF.
PRESIDENT JOS. F. SMITH.
PRESIDENT GEO. Q. CANNON.

GENERAL COMMITTEE.

James Sharp,	Willard Young,
Spencer Clawson,	Nettie Young Snell,
Susie Young Gates,	Heber Young
Leonard G. Hardy,	Charles S. Burton,
Nelson A. Empey,	Elias A. Smith,
Thomas G. Webber,	David H. Cannon,
William W. Riter,	George M. Cannon,
Franklin S. Richards,	Andrew Kimball,
Francis Armstrong,	Heber M. Wells,
Brigham F. Grant,	John Clark,
T. W. Jennings,	Frank Y. Taylor,
LeGrand Young,	Orson F. Whitney,
James H. Moyle,	John W. Young.

As the public is aware the first steps of the association were to engage the talented young sculptor C. E. Dallin. Next they sent out thousands of the following circulars to all corners of the territory:

To the People:

A proposition which has met with general favor, has been made to erect a bronze statue of heroic size, upon a suitable pedestal, in Salt Lake city, in memory of Brigham Young. The suggestion to erect such a memorial has been received with favor by all classes, and strongly advocated without a dissenting voice by the press of our community.

So confident have the originators of the idea been that it would meet with popular approval, that a central committee has been appointed, consisting of some twenty-six persons, for the purpose of bringing this matter to the attention of the entire people. It is with this object in view that this circular is issued.

It is not necessary to dwell upon the character of Brigham Young. His fame has reached every corner of the land. Whether we think of him as a religious leader, or a statesman, or a pioneer, or a city builder—in whatsoever capacity he is regarded, he is the same grand personality.

Time serves but to increase the tribute paid by the world to his genius, and the grateful love tendered his memory by the people he so faithfully led. The value of a monument is not to be measured by its pecuniary cost, but by the motives prompting its builders. Were this not true, our grandest memorials would not depend so much upon the services to mankind of those whose lives they are intended to commemorate, as upon the wealth of the dead or that of his surviving friends. With this idea in view, and feeling that Brigham Young in life belonged, not to his family and intimate friends alone, but to the people of Utah and to the entire west, it has been decided to make the subscription a popular one. To every man, woman and child throughout our mountain home, it is designed to extend an invitation to contribute something toward the erection of this monument to him whose genius has left its impress in every part of our beloved Utah. No amount, however small, is to be refused; for, as above stated, the purpose is to have the statue erected by all who love and revere the memory of the illustrious dead.

The time seems auspicious for the purpose of such a work. For while no arbitrary arrangement has been made and no unchangeable design adopted, we have now in our minds Mr. C. E. Dallin, a young man born in this territory, who has attained an enviable reputation as a sculptor. He has had the benefit of the instruction of the leading sculptors of Paris, and his works have had the stamp of their approval, as well as that of the leading artistic people of our own land. His services can be secured for the completion of this great work, and, no doubt, he will, if employed, give us a monument worthy of his reputation and of its great subject.

The association will appoint sub-committees in each county, and they will doubtless, as necessity may require, appoint other sub-committees, so that every person in the community may be reached.

BRIGHAM YOUNG MEMORIAL ASSOCIATION.
JAMES SHARP, President.
HEBER M. WELLS, Secretary.
SALT LAKE CITY, Utah, December 18, 1891.

THE DESIGN.

The committee on statue, of which Captain Willard Young is chairman and J. H. Moyle secretary, has submitted the following report to the association, which has been approved:

Your special committee on statue beg leave to report that they have adopted, as the general plan of the Brigham Young memorial statue, the design submitted by Mr. C. E. Dallin, a rough sketch of which is given herewith. The general idea, taken from the Gambetta monument, recently erected in Paris, France, is to make not simply a statue of President Young, but rather a monument to the pioneers, with President Young as the central, or crowning figure.

The base and shaft of the monument twenty-five feet high, the base to be of granite, the shaft, or column, twenty feet high, is to be of white oolitic sandstone, with pioneer group cut in bas-relief on the face; the statue of President Young, ten feet high, is to be of bronze, as are also the sitting figures, eight feet high, at the base of the shaft. On the face there is to be a bronze tablet, giving briefly such data concerning President Young as may be decided upon. On the back there is to be a similar bronze tablet, giving the names of the pioneers and the date of their entrance into the valley.

Mr. C. E. Dallin has offered to furnish and put in place all the bronze work and to do the stone cutting on the bas-relief pioneer group, for the sum of $25,000. We believe this to be a reasonable figure, and we therefore recommend that Mr. Dallin's offer be accepted, with the understanding, however, that the models of the figures and the details of the whole design shall be first approved by this committee.

The execution of the whole work should be under the general superintendency of Mr. Dallin; but it will be necessary for the committee to employ an architect to get out the drawings for the stone work, and then to contract for the execution of the stone work as designed. Your committee now respectfully ask for authority to do this.

The cost of the whole monument, including all items of expense, except the site, will, your committee estimate, be under $50,000.

WILLARD YOUNG, Chairman.

J. H. MOYLE, Secretary.

These details will be those governing the erection of the monument and statue, except that on the back of the shaft a beehive and eagle will be cut in bas relief.

THE SITE

was a subject on which there was a wide diversity of opinion, but it was most satisfactorily settled by the adoption of the following report:

SALT LAKE CITY, Utah, Feb. 12, 1892.
To the Chairman and General Committee on the Memorial Statue to the late President Brigham Young:

GENTLEMEN—Your committee on location has carefully considered the suitability of several sites for the proposed statue, among them, one immediately opposite, east of the temple, upon East Temple street; another in the vicinity of the Eagle gate, and still another on President Young's private cemetery, and lastly the southeast corner of the Temple block. After carefully considering the whole of these sites it is the unanimous opinion of your committee that the last mentioned, viz., the southeast corner of the Temple block, is a site in every way suited to the requirements of the monument. We therefore recommend that this last mentioned site be selected, provided, of course, the consent of the presidency of the church can be obtained. It will not be necessary in this report to elaborate upon the advantages of the site recommended; neither will it be necessary to detail the disadvantages of the other sites. These points can be discussed orally when the whole of the committee meets and this report has been presented. Respectfully.

THOMAS G. WEBBER,
ORSON F. WHITNEY,
ANDREW KIMBALL,
HEBER YOUNG,
THOMAS W. JENNINGS,
L. G. HARDY,
Committee on Location.

It is understood that the reply of the church authorities has been favorable, and that the statue will stand on the south east corner of the Temple block, within the shadow of the great temple and tabernacle which Brigham Young founded. Surely no other site in the city could be more appropriate. The plan is in the early future to take down the wall which has surrounded the block for so many years, and to replace it with a handsome iron fence on a low stone wall, so that the grounds will all be visible to the public.

The sketch accompanying this article shows the monument and statue as it will be when finally placed in position—at least according to the idea entertained by Captain Willard Young. His estimate is that the statue will be placed at a point about thirty or thirty-five feet within the present wall, but that it will be left outside the enclosure. It will, however, be protected by a stone coping. It will face the Templeton hotel, and will be visible from four different approaches, North and South Main and East and West South Temple, and it will probably more than ever be called Brigham street.

Mr. Dallin's model in clay, from which the sketch is taken, is about forty inches high. He will go to work at once, and expects to take about two years to finally complete the work.

The committee will at once push the work of inaugurating a vast popular subscription. The chairman, F. S. Richards, has appointed the following persons in the various counties, and E. A. Smith, cashier of the Deseret Savings bank, is treasurer, to whom all sums are to be sent:

THE COMMITTEES.

Bannock, Idaho—Joseph Haight, Oakley; Charles Carlson, Franklin Brim, Albion; Mrs. S. A. Barnes, Kai-tuck P. O.

Bear Lake, Idaho— R. S. Spence, Paris; George Osmond, Bloomington; E. Burgoyn, Montpelier; Miss Julia Budge, Paris.

Beaver—P. T. Farnsworth, Frisco; William Fotheringham, R. Maeser, Mrs. Sadie Maeser, Beaver.

Box Elder—R. H. Jones, A. H. Snow, John C. Rich, Mrs. Minnie J. Snow, Brigham.

Cache—L. R. Martineau, J. H. Paul, W. M. Maughan, Logan; Mrs. Jane E. Molen, Hyrum.

Cassia, Idaho—John L. Smith, Oakley; William T. Harper, Albion; Moroni Pickett, Marion; Mrs. Louisa Pickett, Oakley.

Davis—John R. Barnes, Kaysville; John W. Thornbey, T. B. Clark, Mrs. Aurelia Rogers, Farmington.

Emery—L. M. Olsen, Price; Oscar Wood, Huntington; William Crawford, Mrs. Josie E. Childs, Orangeville.

Juab—W. C. A. Bryan, Alma Hague, William Adams, Mrs. Mary Pitchforth, Nephi.

Kanab—Franklin B. Woolley, Joel E. Johnson, James L. Bunting, Mrs. Harriet D. Bunting, Kanab.

Malad, Idaho—William H. Gibbs.

Maricopa, Ariz.—C. R. Hakes, Lehi; Francis Johnson; George Passey; Mrs. Francella P. Robison, Mesa.

Millard—Thomas C. Callister, Jas. Melville, William Black, Mrs. Birdie Robinson, Fillmore.

Morgan—Samuel Francis, J. R. Porter, Ed Hunter, Mrs. Ester C. E. Francis, Morgan.

Oneida, Idaho—M. W. Pratt, Fairview; M. F. Cowly, Samuel Parkinson, Mrs. Elizabeth Fox, Franklin.

Panguitch—Samuel Crosby, M. M. Steele, Sarah Crosby, Panguitch; Rufus A. Allen, Junction.

Parowan — William Mitchell, Robert Heyborne, Cedar City; Morgan Richards, Parowan; Mrs. Mary Smith, Wimmer.

San Juan—F. A. Hammond, Bluff; Luther C. Burnham, Burnham; George Hall, Mrs. Mossella H. Hall, Mancos, Col.

San Luis, Col—Joseph Thomas, A. R. Smith, S. C. Berthelsen, Sanford; Mrs. Georgie Snow, Manassa.

Sanpete—L. T. Tuttle, Manti; Dr. Sam Allen, Mount Pleasant; Peter Peterson, Ephraim; Mrs. Ellen B. Matheon, Manti.

Sevier — Andrew Hepler, Glenwood; George T. Bean, Jonas Estlund, Mrs. Celia Bean, Richfield.

Snow Flake, A. T.—Joseph W. Smith, Lewis Hunt, Bebe Gardner, Mrs. Mary H. Larson.

Salt Lake—William M. Stewart, James L. McMurrin, Joseph H. Felt, Mrs. William Jennings.

St. George—Anthony W. Ivins, Thomas Judd, Jos. C. Bentley, Mrs. Jane Bleak, St. George.

St. Johns, A. T.—Willard Farr, John T. Lescour, Joseph Udell, Mrs. E. L. S. Udell, Springerville.

Jt. Joseph, A. T.—W. D. Johnson, Thatcher; John Taylor, Pima; Joseph Layton, Mrs. Wilmeth, East.

Summit—W. W. Cluff, Alma Smith, Miss May Cluff, Coalville, George W. Young, Wanship.

Tooele—Harry Haynes, Murray; James Wrathall, Gustan Anderson, Mrs. Maria A. Wooley, Grantsville.

Uintah—R. S. Collitt, Lycurgus Johnson, George Freestone, Vernal; Mrs. A. Bartlett, Ashley.

Utah—George S. Taylor, Reed Smoot, Mrs. Tennie S. Taylor, Provo; James Chipman, American Fork.

Wasatch—John Duke, Heber Giles, David Murdock, Mrs. Ruth Hatch, Heber City.

Weber—C. C. Richards, Ben E. Rich, David Eccles, Mrs. Minnie D. Richards, Ogden.

Salt Lake Tribune
April 3, 1892

PUBLIC MONEYS FOR UTAH.

Forty-Eight Thousand Dollars Sent on for the Agricultural College.

ANOTHER SCHOOL SECTION ASKED FOR.

This Time Ferron Wants It—Vacant Land Grants and Irrigation—Praise for Utah Methods—Pensioners in Utah—Irrigation Survey for Utah Lake—Depository for Documents.

CORRESPONDENCE TRIBUNE.]

WASHINGTON, March 29, 1892.

Secretary Noble has informed Congress that he caused to be paid to the authorities of Utah the sum of $48,600, in three installments of $15,000, $16,000 and $17,000, respectively, under the act of August 30, 1890, "to apply part of the proceeds of the public lands to the support of agricultural colleges."

ANOTHER SCHOOL SECTION WANTED.

Senator Carey has prepared a report urging the passage of the bill to enter one of the Utah school sections of land for the inhabitants of Ferron, Emery county, for townsite purposes. The Senator says the section is already occupied in part by the town, this being the only land adjoining to the town that is suitable for townsite purposes. Houses have been built, he says, irrigation ditches constructed, gardens improved, streets laid out on the land in question, under the belief that Congress would authorize the conveyance of the property to the town authorities.

THE VACANT LANDS

THE VACANT LANDS.

As a good deal of objection has been urged against the bill giving the vacant public lands to the various Territories and States in which they are situated, Representative Lanham, who has charge of the measure, felt it incumbent upon himself to give some attention to the matter, by way of explanation. He cities Utah as a conspicuous example of what may be expected of the Territories in the effort to reclaim the arid lands, and as it is of general, as well as local, application, his words are worth quoting. He says:

"The objection which may be urged against the cession to the Territories before they are admitted as States, the doubt that the people would act wisely in the discharge of the trust, that the legislation on the subject might be reckless, and thus defeat the object to be attained, is largely met by pointing to the success which has attended the irrigation and reclamation of arid lands in the Territory of Utah. Irrigation in the United States by white men began in Utah in 1847 and has proved a most gratifying success under wise and conservative legislation, based largely upon actual experience. The waters have been so distributed and utilized by the settlers as to produce the very best results. Considering the scarcity of water and the vast area irrigated, there have been comparatively few conflicts over water rights.

"The showing in the recent United States census of agricultural development gives a fair conception of what has been accomplished in that Territory. Crops were raised by irrigation in the census year ending June 30, 1890, on 263,473 acres, or 411.68 square miles, a trifle over five-tenths of one per cent of the entire area of the Territory. The aggregate number of farms was 10,757, and of these 9724, or about nine-tenths, depended on irrigation, the remaining tenth being either stock ranches or farms in the northern end of the Territory, where the climate is less arid, or situated so high on the mountain sides that crops can be raised by what is known as "dry farming."

"The irrigated farms of Utah are small, averaging from twenty to thirty acres each. It has not been the policy of the people of Utah to encourage the acquisition of large bodies of land, and the monopoly of water has been impossible. The laws were made to encourage and protect settlers. The small holder had an equal opportunity for his proportionate share of water with the large holder. 'The greatest good to the greatest number' is the prevailing idea and has always been strictly enforced. Water rights are considered sacred, and no theft is regarded more despicable than the theft of water in the irrigating season; no misdemeanor is more quickly or severely punished.

"A people who in the past, under the most adverse circumstances, have done so much to reclaim the arid lands, who have turned what has been considered arid deserts into fruitful fields, may be trusted to manage the arid lands within their borders; besides the power will still remain in Congress to disapprove any legislation which the Territories may enact. These considerations would seem to remove any serious apprehensions in regard to making cessions to the Territories."

PENSIONS IN UTAH.

According to a statement of the Pension Office, there are 544 pensioners of the late war living in Utah. Arizona has only 289 and Wyoming 364.

IRRIGATION SURVEY.

The irrigation survey people, in a communication to Congress, say: "In Utah a careful survey has been made of Utah lake. This survey was for the purpose of determining the area which would be covered by damming or holding back the flood water. After a careful study it was found that, on account of the excessive evaporation from such an enormous surface, the lake was too large to act in an economical manner as a storage reservoir. On the other hand, while it may not be avisable to hold back the water to a point above that of the average height, yet there is sufficient evidence to show that natural forces at times may raise the water level and increase the area to abnormal proportions by backing water over the great fringing marshes on the east

and south. This land being, therefore, the natural flood ground of the lake, should be reserved up to the high water line. Accordingly the segregation was made to include not only the bed but the lowlands up to mean high water."

DEPOSITORY FOR "PUB. DOCS."

Although there are institutions in every State and all the Territories designated as "depositories of public documents," to which all the publications issued under the authority of Congress are sent, there is not one in Utah. The Latter-Day Saints' College, Salt Lake City, receives the publications of the Geological Survey, but these books are but a small percentage of the public documents published each year.

THE HERALD had a pleasant call yesterday from D. C. Robbins. J. L. Lemon and J. C. Duncan, of Emery county. Mr. Lemon left on the counter some excellent samples of last year's growth of apples, raised in Ferron, which show that he is a master in that sort of culture. Mr. Lemon expects to be represented in the fair next fall.

A jury was impaneled in the case of T. Hambrick vs. Orange Seeley. This is a replevin suit brought on appeal from a justice of the peace in Emery county, where the case was decided against Mr. Seeley. Mr. Hambrick lives in Castle Dale and loaned a race mare, "Red Kit," to a man by the name of Brown for the purpose of running against another animal. Brown left the mare as security with Mr. Seeley for some stock he put up as a forfeit, worth about $200, and Mr. Hambrick replevied the mare. The defense claims that Mr. Hambrick sold the mare to Brown.

Mr. Hambrick was the first witness. He testified that in February 1891 he had loaned the mare to Brown to run a matched race for $700. Brown had told him that he had left the mare with Mr. Seeley to be taken care of till the race came off. Mr. Seeley had turned out the stock which he had let Brown have to put up as a forfeit, as the race did no come off, and Mr. Seeley had held the mare till Brown paid him for the stock and refused to give her up. Then Mr. Hambrick brought a replevin suit against Mr. Seeley.

The plaintiff rested.

Orange Seeley testified that Brown had worked for him, and in January, 1891, he left the mare with him as security for stock which he wanted to put up as a forfeit on a horse race. Brown took one of the animals with him, and the rest were turned over to pay the forfiet. Brown had left and has not been heard of since. Brown had claimed that he had bought the mare from Hambrick and paid him $300, down on her and was to pay the balance when he returned.

J. H. Bruno testified that Hambrick had told Hill early in February, before the mare was put in possession of Mr. Seeley, that he had sold the mare; witness thought he had said he sold her to Brown, but was not sure of this.

J. H. Kilpack testified to meeting Brown with "Red Kit" early in February. Brown said he had bought the mare and had a bill of sale. Mr. Hambrick had corroborated this at a later conversation.

R. T. Hill testified that he had offered to run against "Red Kit" and Hambrick had said that he had sold the mare to Brown. He had afterward made up a race with Brown; at the time the forfeit was put up Seeley had said he held the mare in security for the stock that was put up as a forfeit.

Mr. Seeley was called by the plaintiff and said he had not asked to see the bill of sale from Hambrick to Brown.

Mr. Hambrick was re-called and testified that Brown had not paid him anything for the mare and had received no bill of sale for her.

Mr. Jones, of Castle Dale, testified that Brown had told him that he had borrowed the mare to run a race.

Wm. Hinkin was called by the plaintiff. He testified that Brown said he had bought the mare at the time Jones testified to speaking to him.

This closed the evidence and counsel argued the case before the jury.

Judge Judd is counsel for plaintiff, and Geo. Sutherland for defendant.

At the close of the arguments, and Judge Blackburn's instructions to the jury court adjourned till 2 o'clock.

Manti Sentinel
April 16, 1892

In the obituary notice of Mrs. Cecelia Sharp Crawford, which appeared in last week's issue, the following names as children of the deceased were unintentionally omitted: W. W. Crawford of Orangeville, Nathaniel Crawford of Manti, and Maggie Peacock of Orangeville.

Manti Sentinel
April 23, 1892

Mrs. Retta Callaway, nee Merriam, who has been living at Orangeville for the past winter, returned to Manti last Sunday where she expects to remain for the summer. To see her assisting in the singing Wednesday night reminded the members of the choir of olden times.

THE SHEEP CASE.

The Evidence for the Defense.

SEELEY AND MOLAN

Testify in Regard to the Language of Nephi Allred.

Court resumed session at 2 o'clock.

The case of C. J. Fitzpatric vs. Alfred Johnson was dismissed, on account stated to be due. Defendant to pay costs to the February term, 1892.

Nephi Allred who had testified for plaintiff in the forenoon, in the Olson vs. Loveless sheep case, was cross-examined in regard to herding sheep for Andrew Olson and Peter Justeson. He related how many sheep had been delivered out of the herd before the attachment. There were some of the sheep weak and scabby, when Mr. Seeley attached them. He did not remember telling Mr. Seeley that he had told Ole that the sheep ought to be dipped, when Mr. Seeley attached the sheep. If he said anything it was that he had asked Ole to help him dip them. Andrew hired him to take care of the sheep.

Mr. Brown—Do you live in Spring city?

Mr. Allred—I do when I am there.

Re-direct—I was in Ferron after supplies, when I spoke to Ole about dipping the sheep; I had had no experience in dipping sheep. He never furnished me any supplies while I herded the sheep. All the instructions I received in regard to taking care of the sheep, I received from Andrew Olson when I was hired. The sheep taken by Loveless were worth from $3 to $3.25 a head. I told Seeley the sheep were Andrew Olson's. I told Seeley whom he first came up that I had been looking for him, thinking he was a sheep inspector, and the sheep were scabby.

Cross-examined—Andrew Olsen had told me to turn out some sheep to Mr. Lowry, if he came after them; he told me this before I went to work.

Dan Jensen was the next witness—On the second of March 1890 he started to herd for Andrew Olsen; he herded till the 20th of August. He and Allred herded the sheep together. Twelve or thirteen hundred head come into the herd about the last of July. They were branded with an O. There were about 350 weathers taken out of the O herd after they were turned in to the general herd. John Lowry got 200 head after that.

Andrew Olsen identified checks sent to Ole Oleson for wool off Ole's sheep in 1890. The checks were admitted in evidence. He also testified that Ole's family was sick and that was the reason he was not in court, now.

He was cross-examined in regard to Ole's absence, and stated that he had sent a subpoena to his brother by mail. He had received a reply from Ole, and he was sent after the letter. This closed the evidence for the plaintiff.

Justice W. Seeley was the first witness for the defence. He testified to serving the papers in the suit of Mike Molan vs. Ole Olsen in March 1891. He was then a deputy sheriff in Emery County.

He asked Allred where Ole Olson's sheep were; He told him, and said, "I am glad you came, I told Ole last fall that the sheep were scabby and they ought to be dipped." When Mr. Seeley told Mr. Allred he had not come to see about scab, but to serve an execution on the sheep. Mr Allred said they were Andrew's sheep, he finally said they were sometimes known as Ole's sheep, and Mr. Seeley then attached 1931 head of sheep and turned them over to Ole Madson to take care of. They were very poor, then, in flesh, and very scabby; a fair market value of sheep was $1 50, in the condition they were in. He afterwards saw Ole Olson in Ferron and served a summons on him

The defense endeavored to get some testimony from Mr. Seeley in regard to the admissions made by Ole Olson to him, on the ownership of the sheep. The plaintiffs objected and the objection was sustained.

Court adjourned till Tuesday forenoon at 10 o'clock.

Court opened at 10 o'clock.

Mike Molar, the principal defendant in the Olson et al. vs. Loveless et al. sheep case, testified to delivering his herd of sheep, amounting to 2,015 head to Ole Olson. A number of conversations with Ole tending to show that he (Ole) claimed to own the sheep, after the time Andrew claimed they were sold to him, were asked to be introduced in evidence; objected to and objection sustained.

Mr. Molan corroborated the testimony of Mr. Seeley in regard to the conversation had with Nephi Allred, at the time the sheep were attached; and also in regard to the condition of the sheep.

A number of other witnesses testified to the condition of the sheep, at the time of the attachment; the poor condition of the wool taken from the sheep, etc.

Court adjourned till 2 o'clock.

Brigham City Bugler
May 7, 1892

ON ACCOUNT OF LACK of patronage from local business men, the Manti *Sentinel* is thinking seriously of pulling up its stakes and flopping over the hills to drop down in sequestered Gunnison or unknown Castle Dale, where those one-horse towns, of a few business houses each, guarantee double the patronage Manti now offers, says that paper. That condition of things gives Manti "dead away," yet when THE BUGLER asserts that Manti is not as prosperous a town as Brigham, here is what the rather improvident editor of the *Sentinel* says:

We trust Brigham is as nice as that out of the way boneyard can expect to be. It would, taken altogether, if properly placed in one mound, make quite a respectable Sanpete mile post. The editor of

Salt Lake Times
June 13, 1892

A proposition to change the county seat
of Emery county from Castle Dale to Price
is being agitated.

Salt Lake Times
June 20, 1892

It is claimed that a majority of the delegates favor the removal of the county seat of
Emery from Castle Dale to Price.

Salt Lake Herald
June 23, 1892

WESTERN MEASURES

Two Important Ones Pass the Senate.

One Allows the Authorities of Ferran, Utah,
to Enter a Section of School Land—
Utah Bill Goes to the President.

HERALD BUREAU,
Cor. 15th and G Sts., N. W.,
WASHINGTON, D. C., June 22.

Senator Carey of Wyoming, succeeded in
carrying through the Senate today two
measures of interest to the people of the
west. One was the bill authorizing the
authorities of Ferron, Utah, to enter a
section of school land, and the other was a
bill authorizing the settlement of the Fort
Fetterman hay reservation under the
homestead law. Senator Carey called
them both upon his own motion and they
were passed without debate and without
opposition.

The Utah bill has already passed the
House and now goes to the President for
his signature.

Salt Lake Times
July 11, 1892

The petition asking that the county sea
of Emery county be removed from Castle
Dale to Price is being extensively signed.
We would not be surprised to see more sig-
natures attached to that petition than there
were votes polled last year.—Price *Telegraph*.

Ephraim Enterprise
July 20, 1892

FROM THE SHEARERS.

Lowry's Cove. Emery Co., Utah.

Editor ENTERPRISE: We, the shearers, arrived here last Wednesday and found the corral but half built, so had to spend Thursday in building shade, fixing up camp, etc. Friday and Saturday we sheared about 3,000 sheep; and to-day we are observing the Sabbath in our rude way.

We are camped in a small grove of pines on a bluff overlooking as pretty a mountain cove as one might ever expect to see. The cove is at head of one of the forks of Ferron creek, about fifteen miles southeast of Manti. It is bordered on the west and south and partly on the north by the topmost ridge of the Wasatch range and on the north and east by lower ridges, dotted with pretty little groves of white pine, black balsam and ash. Hundreds of springs, several small lakes beautiful meadows, terrace-like benches covered with almost every variety of mountain vegetation, clumps of trees, and snow-banks here and there, and the whole encircled with a huge collar, as it were of crystalline white, making a picture so beautiful that we will not attempt to describe it, yet such a place is the cove.

The boys are all in the best of spirits and peace reigns in camp. We have plenty of music, and concerts are not out of date, up this way. Besides the thirty shearers, there are many more persons in camp, sheep-owners, camp-bosses, herders, one woman and two children. All are well. More anon.

WILDERNESS.

Salt Lake Times
July 25, 1892

The petition praying that the question of moving the county seat from Castle Dale to Price be submitted to the qualified electors of Emery county at the next general election was granted. Every voter in Price should consider himself a committee of one to use all honorable means to secure the county seat at Price.—*Telegraph.*

UTAH COMMISSION.

The Registration Offices Not All Filled Yet—Today's Appointments.

David Butler was appointed deputy registrar for Spring Lake precinct in Utah county, vice J. C. Warfield, declined.

GARFIELD COUNTY—Panguitch precinc', Wm. O. Orton; Escalante precinct, R. M. ᴸᵁ'on; Hillsdale precinct, H. J. Clove; Coyot precinct, A. V. Carpenter; Cannonville precinct, W. G. Henderson, jr; Homerville precinct, W. R. Riggs, jr.

EMERY COUNTY—Blake precinct, J. F. Farrer; Wellington precinct, H. F. Hanson; Price precinct, Soren Olsen; Huntington preci ict, Olonzo Brinkerhoff; Castle Dale precinct, Casper Anderson; Orangeville precinct, Frank Carroll; Ferron precinct, J. H. Cook; Muddy precinct, Rasmus Johnson; Lawrence precinct, Elias Thomas; Cleveland precinct, Hans Morsing; Castle Gate precinct, H. J. Schultz; Scofield precinct, S. J. Harkness; Minnie Maud precinct, T. E. Grames; Winter Quarters precinct, S. J. Harkness; Spring Glen precinct, C. H. Cook; Woodside precinct, C. S. Lively.

MORGAN COUNTY—Peterson precinct, M tin Goarder; Milton precinct, James Gohansen; Canyon precinct, James Peterson; Morgan precinct, T. D. G. Webb; Croyden precinct, Thomas Walker.

Ogden Standard
July 29, 1892

Utah Commission Appointments.

The Utah commission has appointed the following additional deputy registrars:

Box Elder county—Box Elder precinct, James Shetfield; Bear River precinct, George S. Church; Collinston precinct, L. W. Standing; Call's Fork precinct, Israel Hunsaker; Deweyville precinct, John Genner; Grouse Creek precinct, B. H. Cooke; Junction precinct, John Lund; Malad precinct, Ed E. Spencer; Mantua precinct, Hyrum Jensen; Portage precinct, Charles T. Gibbs; Promontory precinct, T. G. Brown; Park Valley precinct, W. H. Meachem; Plymouth precinct, E. Stoddard; Curlew precinct, W. D. Ocheltree; Terrace precinct, John E. Henderson; Three-mile Creek precinct, W. Housley; Willard precinct, Peter Lowe.

Davis county—South Weber precinct, Joseph Earl; South Hooper precinct, Adam Smith; Layton precinct, J. H. Allen; Kaysville precinct, T. F. Rouche; Farmington precinct, Dr. D. Wilcox; Centerville precinct, W. J. Cheeney; West Bountiful precinct, Andrew Grant; South Bountiful precinct, Luther S. Burnham; Steel precinct, T. S. Terry; Syracuse precinct, John Cole.

Summit county—Echo precinct, E. C. Morse: Coalville precinct, William Allison; Grass Creek precinct, Gormer Thomas; Hoytsville precinct, George Daniels; Oakley precinct, W. H. Stevens; Park City precinct, Henry Shields; Parley's Park precinct, Gideon Snyder; Peva precinct, F. W. Merchant; Upton precinct, W. H. Smith; Wanship precinct, George Moore; Henefer precinct, George Roberts; Kamas precinct, E. Sorenson; Lockport precinct, W. Reynolds; Woodland precinct, Thomas P. Potts.

Wasatch county—Midway precinct, Willard Birenmshaw; Wallsbury precinct, D. O. Wray; Woodland precinct, Henry Coe; Elkhorn precinct, James McClain; Heber precinct, Fred Hayes.

Emery County.—Blake precinct, J. F. Farrer; Wellington precinct, H. F. Hanson; Price precinct, Soren Olsen; Huntington precinct, Alonzo Brinkerhoff; Castle Dale precinct, Casper Anderson; Orangeville precinct, Frank Carroll; Ferron precinct, J. H. Cook; Muddy precinct, Rasmus Johnson; Lawrence precinct, Elias Thomas; Cleveland precinct, Hans Morsing; Castle Gate precinct, H. J. Schultz; Scofield precinct, S. J. Harkness; Minnie Maud precinct, T. E. Grames; Winter Quarters precinct, S. J. Harkness; Spring Glen precinct, C. H. Cook; Woolside precinct, C. S. Lively.

Morgan County.—Peterson precinct, Martin Goarder; Milton precinct, James Johansen; Canyon precinct, James Peterson; Morgan precinct, T. D. G. Webb; Croyden precinct, Thomas Walker.

The Weber county registrars will be appointed to-day.

Grangeville *Free Press*: Mr. Jacob Schwalbach, of Pataha, arrived here last Thursday to look over the field with the view of establishing a flour mill in our town. After making known his mission the matter was taken hold of by prominent citizens and that evening a public meeting was called at Grange Hall at which it was resolved that the citizens of Grangeville donate to Mr. Schwalbach five acres of land, and furthermore haul all his freight from Lewiston to Grangeville free. This offer was very gratifying to Mr. Schwalbach and he gladly accepted it, on the distinct understanding that the mill he proposed to erect would be a roller process mill, with a capacity to grind fifty barrels of flour per day. On Friday the ground was surveyed and the site for the building selected. The necessary grading and rock hauling has already been done, and during the coming week the timber for the frames will be hauled. The mill will be run by steam power.

EMERY.

The quarterly conference of the Emery Stake of Zion convened at Castle Dale on Sunday and Monday, August 7th and 8th. Present, the Stake Presidency, C. G. Larsen, Orange Seeley and William Howard, and most of the Bishops and High Council of the Stake. The principal speakers were President C. G. Larsen, Seely Howard, Brother Black, a returned missionary of Huntington, U. Curtis, Superintendent of the Sunday Schools of the Stake, W. P. Aldred, J. D. Chase, Elder Olephant, Wm. Taylor, President of the High Priests' Quorum, Elder Charles Pulsipher, Bishop L. P. Averson and Father Samuel Jewke, all of whom spoke words of encouragement to the large assembly.

We had a good time and all the people felt to acknowledge that the Lord has been with us in this part of His vineyard.

We have prospects of a bountiful harvest this year. W. TAYLOR,
Clerk pro tem.

PRICE POINTERS.

[ENQUIRER Correspondence.]

The pedagogues of this school district were in session here on Wednesday and Thursday for the purpose of passing their annual examination. Supts. L. M. Olsen and W. W. Crawford conducted the examination·

Mr, J. M. Easton, president of the Emery County Mercantile Co., is spending a few days here surveying the situation of affairs and will start for Ferron, to visit their branch store tomorrow,

Ah, thou wedding bells! We hear them in the distance. September 1st, is to be honored by "the event" of the season. viz: The marriage of Mr, Henry Saddler, Jr., and Miss Nellie Allen, the light hearted congenial Nellie.

The query among the boarders at Hotel Lynch, is, "who will bake our biscuits when Nellie is gone?" We wish them every imaginable success. with a long and happy life.

PRICE, Aug· 19th, 1892

Accident at Orangeville·

Wm. Moffitt met with a painful and serious accident at Orangeville, Emery Co· last week. He was working on a scaffold several feet above the ground, He walked to one end of the scaffold, when the board on which he was standing tipped up and threw him head first into a bucket of slacked lime. His head was covered with lime and his nose, ears and eyes completely filled. He was rescued from his dangerous position and taken to a doctor. An examination disclosed the fact that the sight of one eye was entirely destroyed. The doctor has hopes of saving the sight of the other eye. At last accounts the unfortunate man was doing as well as could be expected.

The residents of Price and vicinity are agitating the question of removing the county seat of Emery county from Castle Dale to the former city

THE JURORS SUBPOENED

For the September Term of the First
District Court.

Deputy Marshal Bachman returned last night from the southern counties of the district. He has subpœnaed the following jurors for the September term of court:

GRAND JURORS.

Geo. W. Mickel, Provo.
E. J. Ward, "
Thomas Beesely, "
Heber Allred, Lehi.
Andrew Adamson, American Fork.
L. J. Deal, Springville.
J. Frank Bringhurst, Springville.
J. J. Banks, Spanish Fork.
Wm. Jex " "
George Carter, Fountain Green.
Parley R. Allred, Sr., " "
Henry Green, Ephraim.
E. T. Barry, Manti.
J. W. Lowe, Mount Pleasant.
James Rigby, Jr., Fairview.
Nephi Reese, Wales.
Wm. Lisenbee, Annabella.
Samuel Sprague, Richfield.
Mads Christensen, "
Frank Carroll, Orangeville.
Arthur Van Buren, "
Thomas C. Miles, Huntington.
Wm. Memmoth, Jr., Scipio.
George Crane, Kanosh.

PETIT JURORS.

R. A. Hill, Jr., Provo Bench.
Chas. E. Crandall, Provo Bench.
Robert Dugdale, Provo.
Albert Glazier, Provo.
J. S. Fiddler, Provo.
Wm. P. Bennett, Provo.
Chas. J. Taylor, Provo.
John F. Westfall, Pleasant Grove.
J. B. Seleck, Provo.
George Dorton, Lehi.
Newell Brown, Lehi.
Leo. T. Sholly, American Fork.
James H. Clark, American Fork.
Albert G. Thomas, Fairfield.
George McKinzey, Springville.
Morgan Warner, Spanish Fork.
John O. Thomas, Spanish Fork.
Henry Fairbanks, Payson.
O. H. Pulver, Payson.
James Leetham, Lake Shore.
John F. Williams, Lake Shore.
Levi Openshaw, Santaquin.
J. M. Halladay, Santaquin.
Luke Hickman, Silver City.
H. H. Sorvles, Silver City.
Joseph Hoff, Lemington,
Frank Holbrook, Fillmore.
G. W. Cropper, Deseret.
La Fiber Ouddeback, Vermillion,
Asa R. Harvley, Central,
Wm. H. McKenna, Redmond.
James P. Christensen, Ephraim.
August Anderson, Ephraim.
Edward Reed, Manti.
John A. Larsen, Mt. Pleasant.
John Ford, Wallsburgh.

(No. 1472.)
NOTICE FOR PUBLICATION.

Land Office at Salt Lake City Utah,
August 9th 1892.
Notice is hereby given that the following named settler has filed notice of his intention to make final commutation proof in support of his claim, and that said proof will be made before the Probate Judge of Emery county, Utah, at Castle Dale, on October 3rd, 1892, viz:
Sylvester H. Cox, H. E. No. 7197
for the N½ of S E¼, S W¼ of S E¼ and S E¼ of S W¼ Sec. 31 Twp., 18 S, R. 8 E. S. L. M. Utah.
He names the following witnesses to prove his continuous residence upon, and cultivation of, said land, viz:
Frank Carroll, N.T. Guymon, William Tatton and J. H. Taylor, all of Orangeville. Emery county, Utah.
T. C. Bailey,
Atty.   FRANK D. HOBBS,
          v 1 no 5.   Register.

Desert Weekly
September 17, 1892

DEATHS.

RASSMUSSEN.—At Castle Dale, September 4th, of cholera infantum, Caroline C., daughter of Annie C. and Andrew Rasmussen, born October 3rd, 1891.

Bikuben, please copy.

Manti Messenger
September 17, 1892

(No. 1473.)

NOTICE FOR PUBLICATION.

Land Office at Salt Lake City Utah,
August 9th 1892.

Notice is hereby given that the following named settler has filed notice of his intention to make final commutation proof in support of his claim, and that said proof will be made before the Probate Judge of Emery county, Utah at Castle Dale, on October 3rd, 1892, viz:

Sylvester H. Cox, H. E. No. 7197 for the N¼ of S E¼, S W ¼ of S E ¼ and S E ¼ of S W ¼ Sec. 31 Twp. 18 S, R. 8 E. S. L. M. Utah.

He names the following witnesses to prove his continuous residence upon, and cultivation of, said land, viz:

Frank Carroll, N.T . Guymon, William Tatton and J. H. Taylor, all of Orangeville, Emery county, Utah.

T. C. Bailey,   FRANK D. HOBBS,
   Atty.   v 1 no 5.   Register.

Salt Lake Herald
September 20, 1892

THE COURT OPENS.

A Big Grist of Business Yesterday.

The Grand Jury—The Judge's Charge—New Citizens—The Castilla Scheme—Personal and General Notes.

Yesterday was the day set for the opening of the First district court and the beginning of the regular civil and criminal business of the September term.

Judge J. W. Blackburn was on the bench and Benjamin Bachman, jr., at the clerk's desk; John Pike, court reporter; Don C. Huntington, crier; James Sutherland and Ray Bachman, bailiffs.

At the opening of court at 10 o'clock there was a goodly representation of attorneys present, together with Assistant United States District Attorney John M. Zane, Ogden Hiles, King & Houtz, M. M. Kellogg, A. G. Sutherland, S. R. Thurman, J. W. N. Whitecotton, A. Saxey.

The February term of court was formally closed and the September term opened, after which the grand jurors were called up to be examined.

GRAND JURY.

The following are the grand jurors who were examined and passed:

A. Vanouren, Orangeville; Mads Christensen, Richfield; W. W. Lisonbee, Annabella, Sevier county; Nephi Reese, Wales, Sanpete county; George Crane, Kanosh; William Memmott, Scipio; William Jex, Spanish Fork; L. E. Deal, Springville; George Carter. Fountain Green; Henry Greene, Ephraim; George W. Mickel, Provo; Peter Allred, Lehi; Andrew Adamson, American Fork; E. J. Ward, Provo; Thomas Beesley, Provo.

EXCUSED.

The following were excused: T. C. Miles, J. W. Lowe, E. P. Allred, E. T. Parry, Frank Bringhurst, James Rigby.

George W. Mickel was sworn in as foreman of the grand jury.

CHARGE TO THE GRAND JURY.

In the charge to the jury the judge instructed that they should not be influenced through malice or ill-will. He called attention to the violations of the laws of the United States in relation to postoffices, public lands, unlawful cohabitation, adultery, fornication, etc.; crimes against the territory, such as murder, assault with intent to commit murder, assault with intent to do bodily harm, gambling, etc. The liquor laws were brought to the attention of the jury, selling liquor without a license, selling to minors, selling liquor on the Sabbath day.

In framing indictments the judge stated that it would require twelve to agree, and if there is evidence sufficient in their minds to convict it is their duty to find an indictment.

Salt Lake Times
September 29, 1892

OFF FOR EMERY COUNTY.

John Hanson will start for Emery county in the morning in the interests of the Republican party. He will start the ball rolling at Price on Friday night, and at Castle Dale Saturday night. He will also speak at Ferron, Emery, Huntington and Scofield.

On the Stump.

Dr. O. J. Irwin, Colonel Nim Ferguson and William Wellock spoke at East Bountiful last night.

Frank J. Cannon spoke at Vermillion at 10 o'clock yesterday morning; at Glenwood at 2 o'clock during the afternoon, and at Richfield last night at 7:30.

John Hanson will start for Emery county this morning in the interests of the Republican party. He will start the ball rolling at Price tonight, and at Castle Dale Saturday night. He will speak at Ferron, Emery, Huntington and Scofield.

At Bingham City, on Saturday night, Judge Judd will tell the people what he knows about wire nails, and last night at Spanish Fork Judge Henderson and C. O. Richards spoke upon the issues of Democracy.

The Big Attraction at the Fair Yesterday,

A BIG LIST OF AWARDS MADE.

FRUITS.

J. C. Lemon, Ferron, apples, $10.

J. C. Lemon, Ferron, apples, $2.
J. C. Lemon, Ferron, pears, diploma.

IN EMERY COUNTY.

Democrats Are All Alive and Active.

The Charges Fabricated by the So-Called Independants Indignantly Denied— Some Ringing Resolutions.

The Emery county Democratic convention was held at Huntington on Saturday, Oct. 15, at 2 p.m. It was an interesting occasion and a large number of citizens in addition to the delegates, gathered from all parts of the county and attended. More than usual importance was attached to the convention, because of the organization of an Independent party to which a number of Democrats had to some extent attached themselves, and which had formulated a ticket containing the names of both Democrats and Republicans as candidates for county offices.

A temporary organization was effected by placing in the chair C. E. Larsen of Castle Dale, and appointing D. M. Tyler of Huntington as secretary.

Committees on credentials and permanent organization and order of business, and on resolutions were appointed and a recess of forty-five minutes was taken.

On re-assembling, the presence of Hon. C. W. Penrose was announced and he was called on to address the meeting. In a brief but forcible speech he presented the leading issues in the present political campaign, national and local. He also showed the folly of Democrats who are in the majority in the county, fusing with the Republicans for any purpose, and argued that the changes said to be needed in the county management could be effected by the Democrats themselves, and that if they wanted the county seat removed—as that was one of the features of the fusion movement— they could vote for it just as well on a straight Democratic ticket as on any Independent or other ticket. He exhorted them to union, to place a ticket in the field representing all parts of the county, and to vote unanimously for Joseph L. Rawlins as delegate to Congress. The speech was punctuated with applause and much enthusiasm was aroused among the large audience assembled.

The committee on credentials then reported the names of twenty delegates entitled to seats in the convention, five distant precincts being not represented. The committee on permanent organization &c, reported the names of J. W. Nixon for permanent chairman; Andrew Hood secretary; William Taylor chaplain and Mr. Ovialt sergeant-at-arms; also the order of business to be: Roll call, prayer by the chaplain, report of committee on resolutions, nomination of county officers, appointment of county central committee, miscellaneous business, adjournment.

The report was unanimously adopted in its entirety. The roll was called and twenty delegates responded. Prayer was offered by the chaplain. The committee on resolutions presented the following, which were received with applause and unanimously adopted by the convention

RESOLUTIONS.

Resolved, That we heartily endorse and accept the platform adopted by the National Democratic convention held at Chicago, June 21, 1892, and also the platform adopted by the Territorial Democratic convention held at Provo October 5, 1892.

That we will do all that lies in our power to elect Joseph L. Rawlings as delegate to congress from Utah territory.

That we favor the impartial expenditure of public funds, so that every section of the country shall receive its due proportion of the taxes, for public improvements.

That we repudiate the charges fabricated by the socalled Independent party against the present officers of this county, and deny with indignation that they have "prostituted their official trusts to selfish interests or the perpetuation of their political power, also that they are either incompetent as officials contemptible as men." We regard these accusations as insulting to the gentlemen so assailed and utterly false and without foundation in fact.

That we pledge ourselves to support at the polls for county officers only the nominees of the Democratic party of every county.

A number of gentlemen were placed in nomination for the various county offices, and their claims and qualifications set forth by their respective champions. The result was that L. P. Overson, of Cleveland, a present incumbent, was nominated on the first ballot for selectman. L. C. Jorgenson, of Emery, and R. C. Burch, of Lawrence, were nominated as selectmen after several ballots, and their nomination made unanimous.

Carl Wilburg, of Castle Dale, was renominated by acclamation for county clerk and recorder.

A. Tuttle, of Orangeville, received the nomination for sheriff after a sharp contest.

J. W. Nixon, of Huntington, was placed on the ticket for prosecuting attorney; E. W. Fox, of Orangeville, for assessor; William McCarlain, of Cleveland, for collector; L. M. Olsen, of Price, for superintendent of schools; R. C. Miller, of Castle Dale, for treasurer; William Taylor, of Ferron, for coroner, and George Fox, of Orangeville, for surveyor. These nominations were all finally made unanimous. No one named on the fusion ticket received a nomination.

A county committee was organized with J. K. Reid as chairman and John Peterson as clerk.

As an appointment had been made for a public meeting, that C. W. Penrose, of Salt Lake city, might be heard on the issues of the day and a host of people had assembled, at 8 p. m. the convention adjourned.

Manti Reporter
October 27, 1892

No. 1569,

NOTICE FOR PUBLICATION.

Land Office at Salt Lake City Oct. 15, 1892.
Notice is hereby given that the following named settler has filed notice of his intention to make final proof in support of his claim, and that said proof will be made before the county clerk of Emery county at Castle Dale, Utah, on December 2nd, 1892, viz: Frank Carroll, H. E. No. 8368, for the S W ¼ of N W ¼ section 29, township 18, S, range 8 east.

He names the following witnesses no prove his continuous risidence upon and cultivation of said land, viz:

A. C. Van Buren, Robert Logan, James B. Crawford and George Snow, all of Orangeville, Utah.

FRANK D. HOBBS,
Register.

18—21

Manti Reporter
November 3, 1892

No. 1569,

NOTICE FOR PUBLICATION.

Land Office at Salt Lake City Oct. 15, 1892.

Notice is hereby given that the following named settler has filed notice of his intention to make final proof in support of his claim, and that said proof will be made before the county clerk of Emery county at Castle Dale, Utah, on December 2nd, 1892, viz: Frank Carroll, H. E. No. 8888, for the S W ¼ of N W ¼ section 29, township 18, S, range 8 east.

He names the following witnesses no prove his continuous residence upon and cultivation of said land, viz:

A. C. Van Buren, Robert Logan, James B. Crawford and George Snow, all of Orangeville. Utah.

FRANK D. HOBBS,
Register.

15—21

Deseret Weekly
November 5, 1892

DEATHS.

OLSON.—At Ferron, Emery county, October 16th, 1892, Matilda J. Olson, beloved wife of Bishop Frederick Olson. She was born February 2nd, 1840, in Denmark; baptized when a young girl, she emigrated to Utah in the first large company that left Denmark under Elder Fostgreen with her parents and went to Sanpete, where she was married when quite young. She raised a large family, leaving six daughters and three sons. She was a faithful wife and a loving mother, and greatly respected by all who knew her; and died as she had lived, true and faithful to the covenants that she had made.

The funeral took place on the 18th, and the people showed their love for her by assembling in large numbers at the meeting house, where the services were conducted. Her remains were followed to the graveyard by a large company. The husband and family have the sympathy of the whole ward in their bereavement.
—[Com.

Precincts Not Heard From.

Beaver — Adamsville, Greenville, Minersville.

Box Elder—Curlew, George Creek, Junction, Kelton, Park Valley, Promontory.

Davis—South Weber.

Emery—Castle Dale, Cleveland, Huntington, Lawrence, Muddy, Morlan, Orangeville, Spring Glen, Winter Quarteas, Woodside.

Garfield—Cannonville, Coyote, Escalante, Henrieville, Hillsdale, Orson, Panguitch.

Grand—Blake (G. R.), Cisco, Noal, Richardson, Thompson, West Water.

Iron—Summit.

Juab—Fish Springs, Mammoth.

Kane—Georgetown, Pahreah.

Millard—Burbank, Scipio, Smithfield.

Morgan—Croydon, Morgan.

Piute—Bullion, Circleville, Deer Trail, Junction, Kingston, Koosharem, Wilmont.

Salt Lake—Butler.

San Juan—Bluff, Monticello, McElmo.

Sevier—Burrville, Gooseberry.

Sanpete—Milburn, Petty.

Summit—Upton.

Tooele—Deep Creek, Granite, Lake Point.

Utah—Cedar Fort, Clinton, Fairfield.

Wasatch—Daniels.

Washington—Bloomington, Gunlock, Hamblin, New Harmony, Pinto.

Wayne—Dale, Pleasant Creek.

A ROLL OF HONOR.

List of Missionaries Who Have Died Away from Home.

1887.

May 26. JEREMIAH H. KIMBALL, of Salt Lake City, accidentally killed by falling from a train while traveling through Missouri, on a mission to Europe.

June 29. JASPER PETERSON, of Castle Dale, Emery county, in Odense, Denmark.

July 20. BRIGHAM WILLARD YOUNG, of Salt Lake City, o. fe r, at Nuhaka, New Zealand. Body br u t home.

Aug. 19. JOHN BULLOCK, in England; on a visit to relatives.

Salt Lake Tribune
November 19, 1892

In the vote on the question of the removal of the county seat of Emery county from Castle Dale to Price, the removal scheme was defeated, the vote standing 319 in favor and 332 against.

Provo Daily Enquirer
November 23, 1892

A MARRIAGE license was this morning issued to Edward B Jones, of Castle Gate, Emery county, and Josie P. Curtis, of Orangeville, Emery county.

Manti Reporter
December 30, 1892

NO 1636

DESERT LAND, FINAL PROOF

NOTICE FOR PUBLICATION

U.S. Land Office at Salt Lake City
December 20th, 1892.

Notice is hereby given that Fredrick A Killpack of Ferron Emery Co. Utah, has filed notice of intention to make proof on his desert-land claim No. 2366, for the S½ NE¼ Section 10 Township 20 S. Range 7 East before the county clerk of Emery Co. at Castle Dale Utah, on Saturday the 4th. day of February 1893.

He names the following witnesses to prove the complete irrigation and reclamation of said land Edwin Olsen, H W Curtis, William Henrie, Wyatt Bryan, all of Ferron Emery Co. Utah.   Frank D Hobbs
25—31   Register

Manti Reporter
January 28, 1893

FOR SALE CHEAP.—A farm in Emery county, located close to Ferron, containing 160 acres of land, all fenced with first class fence in two equal divisions, 80 acres farm land and meadows; 80 acres of pastures. A large brick house, well furnished. coal house, milk house, ice house combined; seperate from house, and large granery. stock yards etc, good orchard and shade trees. Has a primary water right for nearly all the land. For further particulars address
M. W. Molen,
Mapleton, Utah.

Salt Lake Herald
March 8, 1893

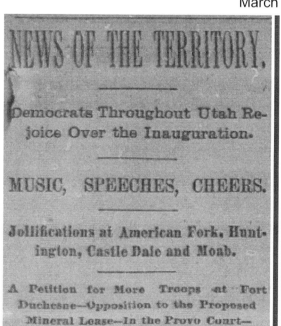

NEWS OF THE TERRITORY,

Democrats Throughout Utah Rejoice Over the Inauguration.

MUSIC, SPEECHES, CHEERS.

Jollifications at American Fork, Huntington, Castle Dale and Moab.

A Petition for More Troops at Fort Duchesne—Opposition to the Proposed Mineral Lease—In the Provo Court—The Watson Steggell Escapade.

AMERICAN FORK, March 7.—For the last fortnight diphtheria has been making its terrible ravages, quite a number of children having succumbed to the disease.

Last week we were called to bury one of our oldest residents, Josiah Nichols. Mr. Nichols was born in England, and emigrated to Utah in an early day, and settled in American Fork, were he has resided ever since. The deceased was seventy-nine years old, and leaves a family of twelve sons and two daughters to mourn his loss.

A shot gun club has been organized in American Fork, with J. D. Cooper, M. D., as president and Will Miller as secretary. They have a membership of twenty and meet each Wednesday for practice.

The rifle club of this place is also doing their best to raise the price of lead.

DEMOCRATS REJOICE.

Last Saturday night the Democrats here celebrated the inauguration of Cleveland by the ringing of bells, firing of anvils and lighting of bonfires, while the brass band paraded the streets, and last night a picnic ball was given in honor of the occasion. The opera house was crowded to its full capacity, several leading Democrats from surrounding settlements being present. Just before intermission the floor manager called the assembly to order, stating there was a little matter of business must be attended too. Thereupon Mr. Clark stepped forward and, making a speech eugolistic to the services rendered the party by their chairman, Mr. Lapish, presented him in behalf of the Democrats, with a handsome gold headed cane as a token of their appreciation.

Mr. Lapish was taken completely off his guard, but rallied and thanked the donors for their magnificent present, saying that he did not deserve it, as there were others that had done more for the party than he had and what he had done, had not been done for reward but from a desire to see Democracy triumph. Mayor Evans of Lehi and the Honorable George Cunningham being called for, responded with short, but interesting speeches suitable to the occasion. A repast was then served, after which dancing was continued to a late hour.

A PAINFUL ACCIDENT.

Last Saturday evening Mr. Fred Henroid met with a very painful accident. While engaged in a scuffle with Will Chipman he slipped and fell in such a manner that one of his legs was broken half way between his foot and knee.

The large brick school house has been finished and handsomely furnished, and will be occupied by the schools this week.

CASTLE DALE FESTIVITIES.

Democratic Dancing, Speeches, Music and Cheers.

CASTLE DALE, March 6.—The 4th of March (inauguration day) was celebrated in the Democratic style by the Democrats of Castle Dale, to the chagrin of our Republican friends. The stars and stripes were hoisted at sunrise. The day was passed in quietness, until about 5 o'clock p. m., when the Castle Dale brass band gathered at Social hall, under the leadership of C. P. Andersen, who in short notice had the band playing their sweet music to the gathering crowd who met wearing their Democratic badges, "Democracy to the Front, 1893."

At 6 o'clock, Manager C. E. Larsen (ex-selectman of the county) called the assembly to order, and in a neat little speech told all present that they had met to pay honor to president, Grover Cleveland, and vice-president, Stevenson, who are now the chosen ones to take the reins of government, which all true Democrats rejoice in, and in closing proposed three cheers for the president and vice-president, which were given with a good will by the assembly.

The ball was then pronounced open. Dancing commenced, and a true Democratic spirit made itself manifest, for everyone felt to make one another happy.

At about 9 o'clock supper was served at the residence of Mrs. Andersen, where all found large tables loaded down with such a variety of food which would make even you, our city cousins, stare. The credit is due to Mrs. Andersen and Mrs. Rasmussen, with their aids, who worked like beavers to make everything pleasant and tasteful.

During the dance Mrs. C. P. Andersen, the nightingale of Castle Dale, gave us some of her sweetest vocal music. Recitations were also rendered, which were very appropriate.

A speech was given by Mr. John Peterson in favor of Democracy.

At 12 o'clock the manager called for attention, saying it was time to close our exercises, but before closing, he thought proper to give three cheers for Grover Cleveland as president of the United States, which were given with a will. Then three cheers were given for Stevenson, the vice-president, and Joseph L. Rawlins, our delegate, who came in without a recommend. was given three rousing cheers.

The band then rendered a fine air, which closed one of the most enjoyable times experienced in Castle Dale.

The honors are mostly due to C. E. Larson, Carl Wilberg, Samuel Jackson. William Lake, Rhode McDonough, A. E. Smith, Peter Anderson and R. C. Miller, who spared neither time or means to make the whole a success.

Deseret Evening News
May 8, 1893

Captured at Ferron.

Sheriff Mathis arrested a man at Ferron, says the Price *Telegraph*, by the name Robinson. The arrest was made upon advices from Sheriff Girardet, Delta county, Colorado, and the charge was grand larceny. It appears that the man had been working on a farm belonging to a widow. The lady had occasion to visit Denver and left him in charge of the farm, but prior to her departure for the city she also made arrangement with a local merchant to supply the man with what he wanted from the store. A short time after the lady had gone, Robinson went to the merchant referred to and got about $40 worth of supplies, hitched up a good team of horses, tied another good one behind the wagon and started for Arizona, but for some reason he stopped at Ferron, with the result stated. Sheriff Mathis reached Price with the prisoner on Saturday night and Sheriff Girardet left for Colorado with him on Sunday.

Summons.

Territory of Utah, }ss.
County of Emery, }

In the Justice's Court, of Ferron precinct.

A. G. Conover, plaintiff,

vs.

John Doe, defendant.

Demand $0.50

To John Doe, Greeting.

You are hereby summoned to be and appear before me the undersigned at my office in Ferron Precinct, Emery County, Utah Territory, to answer a complaint filed against you herein by said plaintiff within five days (exclusive of the day of service) if this summons is served on you within Ferron Precinct, within ten days if served on you outside of said Ferron Precinct, but within the county of Emery and within twenty days if served elsewhere.

Said action is brought to recover from you the sum of fifty cents damages alleged to be owing and due from you to Sam Singleton, for damages done by the following described animals, to-wit:

One black horse, 7 or 8 years old, with white spot in forehead, also on nose, and left hind foot white; branded H C on left thigh,

One brown horse, two white hind feet and spot in forehead, 6 or 7 years old, branded [brand] on left thigh, and shoes on front feet.

And you are hereby notified that if you fail to so appear and answer as above required the plaintiff will take judgment against you for fifty cents, damages, cost of keeping said animals and costs of suit.

To the Marshal or any Constable of said County, greeting; Make legal service and due return hereon.

Given under my hand this 15th day of May. A. D, 1893.

F. A. KILLPACK,
Justice of the Peace.

Deputy Registrars.

The following deputy registrars have been appointed by the Utah commission. They are all Democrats, except when otherwise noted:

WASATCH COUNTY.

Wallsburg—Isaac O. Wall.
Midway—David L. VanWagener.
Woodland— James D. VanTassel.

There are three more precincts to be filled in Wasatch county and the appointments in these will be made by the respective registrars.

BEAVER COUNTY.

Adamsville—Joseph H. Joseph.
Beaver—Joseph L. Knss.
Greenville—John H. Barton.
Minersville—Louis Leesing.
Star District—W. W. Gingles.
Champion—R. S. Lipscomb.
Sulphurdale—Tobias Ammon.

EMERY COUNTY.

Mubby—S. M. Williams.
Ferron—(To be filled by the resident county registrar.)
Molen—J. H. Cook.
Orangeville—Frank Carroll (Independent.)
Huntington—V. D. Crain.
Cleveland—L. P. Overson.
Castle Dale—R. C. Miller.
Lawrence—Philander Burch.
Price—Soren Olson.
Wellington—H. F. Hanson (Republican.)
Woodside—C. O. Moore (R.)
Blake—J. T. Farrer (R.)
Minnie Maud—F. E. Grames (R.)
Spring Glen—C. H. Cook.
Castle Gate—H. J. Schultz (R.)
Scofield—S. J. Harkness (R.)
Winter Quarters—J. M. Beatie.

THE body of William Durden, who committed suicide near Scott Elliott's ranch on Wednesday night by shooting himself with a double-barreled shotgun, was brought to Provo last night, prepared for burial by A. E. Ford, and interred without further delay. Durden was impelled to commit suicide on account of great suffering from a broken leg. He leaves a wife and several sons and daughters at Castle Dale.

IN the land office yesterday Samuel L. Aiken of Castle Dale, Emery county, filed a homestead application covering lot 1, the east half of the northwest quarter and the northeast quarter of the southwest quarter of section 7, township 19 south, range 9 east.

Salt Lake Herald
September 15, 1893

Andrew Neils Olsen of Castle Dale, Emery county, filed final proof on his pre-emption application for the northeast quarter of the southeast quarter of section 2, township 19 south, range 8 east.

Provo Daily Enquirer
September 20, 1893

Republican County Convention.

Pursuant to instructions by the central committee a convention of the Republican party of Emery county, is hereby called to meet at Castle Dale, in said county, on Wednesday, the 27th day of September, 1893, at 2 o'clock p. m.

Said convention is called for the purpose of placing in nomination the following candidates to be voted for at the coming election. Assessor, to fill vacancy. Superintendent of public schools. Coroner, to fill vacancy. To choose delegates to the Council and Representative convention, for the election of a county central committee for the ensuing year, and for the transaction of such other business as may be brought before the convention.

Said convention will consist of 37 delegates, apportioned as follows: Blake 1; Castle Gate 3; Cleveland 1; Castle Dale 5; Emery 2; Ferron 3; Helper 2; Huntington 4; Lawrence 1; Lower Crossing 1; Minnie Maud 1; Molen 1; Orangeville 3; Price 4; Wellington 2, Winter Quarters 2.

It is recommended that the several precincts hold their caucuses for the election of delegates, on Saturday evening, September 23, 1893, at 8 o'clock p. m.

By order of the Republican County Central committee,

W. J. TINWELL, Chairman.
A. E. GIBSON, Secretary.

A Girl's Fight With Indians.

A dispach from Ferron City, Utah, to the Phiiidelphia Times says: An interesting relic of a tragedy more thrilling than fiction could devise was recently discovered near here through the fall of an old elm tree about seven or eight miles from town. This tree was struck by lightning some years ago and was blown down during a thunder-storm a week or two ago, and it was while chopping it up for firewood that Moashey Thorne, on whose ground it stood, found the remains of what had beyond doubt once been a human head. The long hair on the top of the skull was still plainly to be seen as such, and was origionally of a yellow color. It was wrapped about an Indian arrow head, which was still sticking in the wood and which held the skull in place. From the length of the hair it is judged that the victim was a woman, and the older settlers recall in this connection a tragedy of the plains when the first pioneers were reaching out in the direction of California. The Dodwell family, consising of thirteen members, old and young, with twenty or more of their neighbors, started from near Clinton, Missouri, seeking new homes. While passing throught this part of the country, they were

ATTACKED BY THE INDIANS

but warned of their approach the men succeede in fighting then off and they withdrew. But it happened that Mary Dodwell, a girl of seventeen, was riding behind the rest of the train and was surrounded by the hostiles and cut off from her friends. She succeeded in running through the circle, and, putting her horse to a gallop tried to regain the emigrants who could only look on helplessly, knowing that if they left their waggons it would only expose them to the attack of the Indians But the redskins got between her and the train, and she turned her horse and rode off in an other direction with the yelling savages in full chase behind her. For miles the girl was able to keep bo pursuers at a safe disance, but her horse began to fail, and, seeing this, she dismounted and hid herself behind a pile of rocks and waited for death. She was armed with a pistol, and as the redskins came on she killed the formost of them, and kept the others at bay all that day and the next night, killing a second and a third as they attempted to surprise her by creeping upon her in the darkness. Early the next morning she made out the band within a few yards of her and,

and tried to make her understand by signs that if she would surrender to them she should not be harmed, but she was afraid to trust this promise* and crouched back among the rocks. This parley finished, the Indians greeted her with a shower of arrows, one of which pierced her right hand. But in spite of the pain this wound gave her she fired her pistol at them, crippling the chief. The Indians, always afraid of facing certain death and not knowing how much ammunition she might have, and being satisfied, besides, that it was only a question of time before she would be starved out or could be surprised when assleep, made no attempt to surround her and carry the position by storm. At last the girl, feeling fatigue overcoming her and with only one charge left for her weapon, took the desperate resolution of puting the ball through her own head and proceeded* to place the pistol to her ear.

But her desire to escape falling alive into the Indians' hands was frustrated by some defect in the priming of her weapon, and the powder only blackened her cheek. She then made signs to her captors that she was ready to accept their terms, and calmly walked out from her barricate at their invitation. But the treacherous creatures now bound her hand and foot, and proposed to

but were prevented by the chief whom she had crippled, and who, admiring her courage, which had defied them for nearly two days and a night, asked to make her his wife. His followers showed so much dissatisfaction at this proposition that he abandoned it and only insisted that she should not die by fire. She was then bound to a small tree and the Indians amused themselves by shooting arrows at her to see how near they could come to hitting her without actually doing it. After an hour of this sport, a young brave, through awkwardness, or pity for the captive, sent a shaft into one eye, penetrationg the brain and killing her instantly. Her body was left to decay where it was. The story of her brave fight and death was told years after to her parents by one of the party, who, however, disclaimed any share in the murder, but not satisfied with this statement, Mary Dodwell's father killed the rascal. It is believed by the persons who remember this story that the skull is that of the girl, whom they declare had yellow hair of unusual length and beauty. If this be the history of the skull, it must have been that the trunk of the tree afterwards encircled the object pinned to its bark by the arrow-head, for the skull was found buried nearly three inches in the body of the elm.—Family Herald

TERRITORIAL POLITICS.

The Republicans at Their Convention Nominate Winners.

The Summit county Republicans have nominated A. B. Emery for representative from the Tenth district, and D. S. L. McCorkle for county superintendent of schools. Both candidates are residents of Park City. The central committee is composed of W. I. Snyder and O. H. Gitsch of Park City; Mark Hopkins, Coalville; Neils Pierson, Peoa; Chris Larsen, Kamas; Mr. Winters, Hoytsville; George Olsen, Echo; Leonard Frazier, Oakley; Lonzo Frisby, Upton; Wm. Archbald, Parley's Park; Wm. Reynolds, Rockport; Thos. Potts, Woodland.

Emery county Republicans have made the following nominations:

For superintendent of public instructions, J. S. Scott of Huntington.

For assessor, Henry M. Reid of Orangeville.

For coroner, Dr. H. B. Asadoorian of Castle Gate.

The following were chosen as delegates to the legislative convention to be held at Mount Pleasant, October 5th: H. G. Mathis, S. I. Paradise, J. W. Seeley, W. J. Tidwell, William Hinkin, M. Cox, H. Fraudsend and O. H. Cook. The delegates were instructed to vote for Hon. Orange Seeley of Emery county for councilor.

At the Republican county convention held at Spanish Fork on Saturday, Charles D. Evans, the veteran educator of Springville, was nominated by acclamation for the position of county superintendent of schools. D. P. Clark of Provo was nominated to fill the unexpired term of sheriff. John O. Graham was elected chairman of the county central committee.

The Tooele county Republicans held a convention on Saturday, September 30th, at Stockton. The school house was filled with delegates. P. P. Christiansen was nominated for superintendent of schools and ten delegates were elected to attend the legislative district convention, which embraces the counties of Tooele, Juab, Morgan and Davis. The following resolutions were presented by Judge Herman and unanimously adopted:

Resolved, That the Republicans of Tooele county heartily indorse the course of Senators Stewart, Teller and Dubois in the United States Senate and that we will do all in our power to enlist the aid of the Republican party to have silver remonetized and to continue the tariff on silver, lead ores and wool and the bounty on beet sugar.

Resolved, That as Republicans we believe it our duty to aid the development of our mining interests, especially in this county, thereby creating a home market for the farmer and rancher; we also believe it our imperative duty to aid all home manufacturing industries by patronizing them and by securing favorable legislation to encourage them by electing a Republican legislature at the next November election.

Resolved, That we ascribe and charge the present crisis and depression in business to the threatened legislation by the Democratic party; that it is a fact recorded in the history of our country that whenever the Democratic party, with its free trade heresies, obtained control of the legislative and executive department of our government, business was invariably depressed and banks assigned. The workingman, mechanic and miner were thrown out of employment, the United States treasury invariably handled a deficit instead of a surplus, and no one prospered excepting the usurer and bloated money lenders of Wall street and Lombard street, London.

Respectfully submitted.

C. A. HERMAN, Chairman.
T. H. CLARK,
LOUIS STRASSBURY,
Committee on Resolutions.

Provo Daily Enquirer
October 7, 1893

On Friday the dead lock existed until noon, when Mr. Brandley, proxy for Milliard county, withdrawing that county's vote, gave the choice of the convention to O. Seely, of Castle Dale, by a vote of 17 to 10. Mr. Brandley, however, could not promise the support of Millard to Mr. Seely.

Salt Lake Herald
October 20, 1893

LAND OFFICE ITEMS.

Decision in Madsen vs. Central Pacific Company—Filings.

The register and receiver of the land office yesterday rendered a decision in the case of Andrew Madsen vs. The Central Pacific Railway company, involving the southwest quarter of section 29, township 11 north, range 2 west. This case arose upon an application of Madsen to enter the land, which is within the selection made by the Central Pacific, on the grounds that the selection was allowed on false and fraudulent testimony, and that a pre-emption claim had already been attached when the selection was made. Several very nice points of evidence arose in the hearing, but they were all settled. The decision is wholly in favor of Madsen, whose pre-emption application will be allowed.

Gabriel M. Utley, of Black Rock, Millard county, filed a homestead application for the west half of the northeast quarter and east half of the northwest quarter of section 7, township 25 south, range 10 west.

Philip L. Orth, of Huntsville, Weber county, filed a homestead application for the southeast quarter of the northeast quarter, the east half of the southeast quarter and southwest quarter of the southeast quarter of section 22, township 6 north, range 2 east.

Harmon W. Curtis, of Ferron, Emery county, filed a homestead application for the southeast quarter of the southeast quarter of section 22, and the east half of the southwest quarter and southwest quarter of the northwest quarter of section 23, township 20 south, range 7 east.

William Pectal, of Caineville, Wayne county, filed a homestead application for the north half of the southeast quarter and southwest quarter of the southeast quarter of section 10, township 29 south, range 8 east.

Salt Lake Herald
October 25, 1893

Frank Carrol is a respected citizen of Orangeville who is quartered at the Morgan .

LAND OFFICE ITEMS.

Contemplated Change of Quarters—Four Homestead Filings Yesterday.

On account of the inconvenience and poor heating of the present quarters, the register and receiver of the land office contemplate a removal of the office in the near future, and are now looking for a better location.

Rose Feller of Lake Point, Tooele county, filed an additional homestead application for lot three and the southeast quarter of the northwest quarter of section 1, township 2 south, range 4 west.

James M. Hunley of Orangeville, Emery county, filed a homestead application for the south half of the southwest quarter of section 10 and the northeast quarter of the northwest quarter and northwest quarter of the northeast quarter of section 15, township 18 south, range 7 east.

John L. Ellertson of Mona, Juab county, led a homestead application for the east half of the southwest quarter and west half of the southeast quarter of section 9, township 11 south, range 1 east.

Daniel O. Larsen of Castle Dale, Emery county, filed a homestead application for lots 1 and 2 and the east half of the northwest quarter of section 30, township 18 south, range 9 east.

Ninth Council District.

The candidates were Orange Seely of Castle Dale, Emery county, Republican, and Joshua Greenwood of Millard, Democrat. Following is their vote so far as received:

	Seely.	Green- wood.
Previously reported	1002	774
Winter Quarters	17	29
Blake	14	5
Huntington	34	75
Lawrence	3	17
Castle Dale	60	29
Orangeville	25	51
Total	1170	976

The remaining thirty precincts in Sevier, Millard, Emery and Grand counties gave Rawlins a net majority of 36, and Allen 9 votes. Seely is elected.

CONFERENCES OF THE CHURCH.

EMERY STAKE.

The quarterly conference of the Emery Stake of Zion convened at Castle Dale, November 4 and 5, 1893. Present on the stand: C. G. Larsen and William Howard of the Stake presidency, Elder Francis M. Lyman of the Council of the Apostles, the Bishops and most of the leading Priesthood of the Stake.

After the usual opening exercises President C. G. Larsen reported the condition of the Stake; he said the people as a whole were trying to lead consistent lives, but some were careless about attending their meetings and performing other duties incumbent on the Saints of God. He exhorted such to repent. The organizations of the Stake were nearly complete. The health of the people is good; the crops are abundant, but there is no market for grain, hence very little money is in circulation. Good schools are in operation in all the wards, but the Church schools are not so well attended as could be wished.

The following Bishops reported their wards, corroborating the statements of President Larsen: Peter Johnson, Huntington; Henning Olsen, Castle Dale; Frederick Olsen, Ferron; Wm. Lamph, Castle Gate; George Frandsen, Price; E. D. Fulmer, Spring Glen, and H. P. Rasmussen Molen.

Elder Lyman then addressed the conference on punctuality and order in meetings. He said much confusion could be avoided by a proper arrangement of the seats before meeting. He explained the necessity of keeping ward records and of each person keeping a diary.

In the afternoon, after the administration of the Sacrament by the Priesthood of Castle Gate, Elder Lyman occupied the time in giving general counsel to the Saints. He thought it better to speak of the virtues of the people than of their vices. As a people we do not sin because we love wickedness but are always sorry when we make a false step. Church discipline was explained by the speaker. Persons doing wrong in a strange ward should be dealt with in the ward where the acts were committed and then reported to their own ward.

Nov. 5th.—The Bishops continued their reports as follows: A. E. McMullin, Wellington; L. P. Overson, Cleveland, Jasper Robertson, Orangeville; Calvin Moore, Lawrence; and Emery ward was reported by Counselor Hans C. Wakeman. All were in a fairly prosperous condition.

Elder Lyman advised the Bishops and counselors to lead out in attending meetings by taking at least two members of their families to Sunday and fast meetings. He continued on "Church discipline."

Elders Orange, Seely and Wm. Howard spoke briefly in the afternoon meeting after which the General and Stake authorities were sustained.

Elder Lyman then defined the duties of missionaries, High Counselors, and the Stake Presidency. He explained that politics did not form part of our religion. Gave excellent advice to the young on marriage and chastity.

Elder Larsen made closing remarks, admonishing the Saints to follow the excellent council given during the conference.

The weather was fine, the meetings were crowded, and an enjoyable spirit prevailed. The Castle Dale choir furnished sweet music for all the meetings.

Elder Lyman held meetings at Orangeville on the evening of the 6th and at Huntington on the 7th in which excellent advice was given, especially to the young.

A. E. WALL, Clerk.

Manti Messenger
November 24, 1893

D M Crawford of Orangeville, is one of the many subscribers placed upon our books this week The MESSENGER will find him during the next fifty-two weeks and give him the news

H M Fugate of Ferron, writes 'I like the MESSENGER very well It is good, plain print The portions devoted to news, farming and irrigation are immense I think you a little radical on politics, still I would like to see you hit Alma Greenwood a lick, as I understand he is trying to knock out my friend Orange Seely, after he has been selected as the choice of the people"

1953

Desert Land, Final Proof ---Notice for
Publication.

United States Land Office,
Salt Lake City Utah, Nov 2 1893.

Notice is hereby given that Josephine Williams of Ferron Emery
county, Utah Territory, has filed
notice of intention to make proof
on her desert land claim No 2093,
for the unsurveyed southeast one-
half of northeast one quarter section 7, township 20 s, range 7, e,
before the Probate Judge of Emery
county, at Castle Dale, on Monday,
the fifteenth day of January, 1891

She names the following witnesses
to prove 's complete irrigation and
reclamation of said land- John J
Rhoads George Hertz, Wyatt Bryan
and J W Williams, all of Ferron,
Utah.

9   Biron Groo, Register.

Grangeville Free Press: On Tuesday
morning a hunting party consisting of
Fred Riggins, Fred Bowman, Charles
and William Chamberlain started home
and endeavored to cross Clearwater at
the crossing of the trail in the Big
Cove. William Chamberlain was ahead,
the packhorse ahead of him. When in
the center of the stream Chamberlain's
horse struck a rock and turned over,
getting away. Chamberlain fortunately
got hold of a rock and held himself
there until Fred Riggins pulled the
saddle from his horse, striped off most
of his clothes, and after four different
efforts got his horse swimming across
the river above Chamberlain and let a
rope down to him. When they landed
on this side Chamberlain was completely exhausted, and almost chilled
to death. The boys had crossed the
river at the same place a few days before, but the heavy rains had raised
the river four feet and shut the boys
up so they were unable to get their
horses more than a short distance
either way.

Salt Lake Herald
December 24, 1893

Another large canal is being built at Ferron. The canal will get its water from Ferron river, and will cover a large body of fertile land north of Ferron. A large force of men are now at work and it is expected that water will be on the land in time to raise a crop next year.—Price Telegraph.

Salt Lake Tribune
December 26, 1893

LETTING OF MAIL CONTRACTS.

Routes and Service in Utah—The Rates Awarded to Bidders.

The Postmaster-General has awarded contracts for carrying the mail in Utah from July 1, 1894, until June 30, 1898, as follows:

Ferron to Molen, C. R. Felt, $59.
Ferron to Emery, D. K. Udell, $274.

Manti Messenger
December 29, 1893

Frank Tuttle returned the first of the week from Ferron, where he is feeding sheep for the spring market. He called at the MESSENGER office and ordered the paper sent to Orson Lowry and Gustave Miller at Ferron and Sam Williams at Emery. We appreciate such favors and hope Frank will remember us every time he goes to Emery county.

Manti Messenger
January 5, 1894

1953
Desert Land, Final Proof —Notice for
Publication

United States Land Office,
Salt Lake City, Utah, Nov. 21, 1893.

Notice is hereby given that Josephine Williams of Ferron Emery county, Utah Territory, has filed notice of intention to make proof on her desert land claim No 2993, for the unsurveyed southeast one-half of northeast one quarter section 7, township 20 s, range 7, e, before the Probate Judge of Emery county, at Castle Dale, on Monday, the fifteenth day of January, 1894

She names the following witnesses to prove the complete irrigation and reclamation of said land   John J Rhoads George Hertz, Wyatt Bryan and J. W. Williams, all of Ferron, Utah.

9   Byron Groo, Register.

Salt Lake Tribune
January 24, 1894

Land Office Filings.

William S. Seely of Castle Dale, Emery county, filed an application in the Land Office yesterday for a homestead entry of 160 acres in section 20, township 18 south of range 9 east.

William J. Holly of Springville filed final proof in the Land Office yesterday for a desert entry of forty acres in section 1, township 8 south of range east.

Salt Lake Herald
January 30, 1894

There have been some litigious and dissatisfied spirits at Price who have been wire working for some time to have the county seat of Emery removed from Castle Dale to their small burg. Failing in that, this new movement has been started to capture the prize. We think that if the people want division they should have it. If they want the county seat at Price they should be accommodated. But they should have a chance to express their wishes before the matter is decided.

Salt Lake Tribune
January 31, 1894

FIRST DISTRICT COURT.

Grand and Petit Jurors—Criminal Settings—Motions and Orders.

Judge Smith opened the First District Court in Provo yesterday.

GRAND JURORS.

The following grand jurors for the February term were drawn, to appear February 19th: J. L. Allred, Hinkley; Thomas Murdock, Heber; Charles Allred, Chester, J. C. Hawley, Oasis; John Williams, Mayfield; William J. Lewis, Vineyard; John Grier, Provo; John Duncan, Ferron; William Wing, Lehi; John Nicholson, Eureka; Meshach Pitt, Nephi; Joseph S. Tibbetts, Lake Shore; Andrew Van Buren, Orangeville; William Gardner, Glenwood; Samuel Cowley, Provo; John Johnson, Lake View; A. Ballinger, Price; John Davis, Annabella Springs; Charles Glines, Vernal; Simon P. Beck, Spring City.

PETIT JURORS

The following names were drawn as petit jurors, to be in attendance February 20th: George H. Bruno, Castle Dale; John O. Johnson, Santaquin; S. W. Warsely, Provo; Anthony Paxton, Jr., Kanosh; Henry Curtis, Mapleton; Joseph McDonald, Daniels Creek; Sims Walker, Oak Creek, J. J. Houston, Tucker; E. S. Reed, Fayette; James Washburn, Huntington; C. H. Sperry, Nephi; Joseph R. Murdock, Heber; Lorenzo Peterson, Fairview; Peter Thompson, Ephraim; William Metcalf, Gunnison; Lorenzo Webb, Nephi; A. O. Smoot, Jr., Provo; Nephi Robertson, Spanish Fork; William H. Boyle, Santaquin; John Smith, Santaquin, William Bethers, Daniels Creek; Richard Westwood, Moab; James Campbell, Heber; Chris Nelson, Santaquin, John P. Johnson, Spanish Fork; John Rogers, Deseret; Swen O. Nielsen, Fairview; A. N. Rasmussen, Levan; E. W. Penny, Kanosh,

EMERY COUNTY.

Interesting Facts and Occurrences at Orangeville.

To the Editor of The Herald:

Recognizing your paper as a very satisfactory representation of the territory of Utah, I desire to express through its columns a few facts that the district of country from which I write is entitled to have recognized and recorded, and of which many of the people of the territory are not aware.

This particular district is Orangeville, Emery county, forming a part of the section of country known as Castle Valley. Some few years ago, before our resources and advantages were known in part, a person writing from this locality doubtless would have preferred to leave out the name "Castle Valley," it having some humble significance and being alluded to at times with a degree of sarcasm; but that time has passed never to return again. We have grown out of such reproach and above its stigma.

Since the year of 1878, from which the history of our town begins—a short period of fifteen years, we have improved from the humble execvation of mother earth to happy, comfortable and beautiful homes. From a population of tens we number hundreds. From a school held in a log cabin with about ten pupils, we pass into one of modern construction having between 200 and 300 pupils between the ages of 6 and 18 years.

Instead of going to distant quarters to purchase our merchandise, or paying two or three prices for the same, we have three prosperous mercantile companies in our town, also a drug store and millinery shop, carrying any and all supplies necessary for use, at prices as low as in the metropolis.

Our land now under cultivation is measured by sections and miles, and this is not more than one-fourth of the good tillable soil laying dormant all around us.

Scarcity of water is to us unknown. the supplus will cover as much again land as is now irrigated.

Is this not an opportunity to many seeking homes and desiring to get something around them that they can "call their own?" Why should you ask, what kind of land is this of which you speak? Certainly it would be absurd to say it is all the very best land in the country; but those who are sufficiently acquainted with it to be competent judges will bear me out in the assertion—that most of it is and will be when worked up the very best land in the territory.

The immense crops of vegetables of all descriptions, fruits, hay and cereals every year harvested from the land that is under cultivation, show at once its fertility and serve as the best possible proof of the producing quality of the soil.

Let me now invite your attention from our wide stretching farms to our almost unlimited resources of coal. Going a distance of a few hours' drive from our town, we may look upon ledge after ledge of this decayed vegetation standing out in bold relief. Follow on up through the main canyon through which our creek (called Cottonwood Creek) flows on either side you find the coal still inexhaustible. Turn off up one of the canyons coming into the main canyon from either the right or the left, and you still find a continuation of these unlimited coal fields. One of these ledges about six miles from town, now being worked, is twenty-five feet through and its width is from the mouth of the canyon to its head.

You doubtless will feel to remark, fuel, then, must be out of the question with you. Indeed, compared with most of localities where coal must be bought at $6 or $7 a ton, it is a great advantage. And besides this supply of coal, wood, too, is very plentiful, so that in about six hours one man with a team can go and get a good load of either pine or cedar.

These things, readers, are not fakes, are not hearsays, fancies or illusions. They are facts true and candid, which when investigated, need no confirmation.

We are not booming, but we are growing with a good solid footing under every step. We want settlers, we own, but we do not want them to speculate on or "take in." We want them to build up the country and develop its resources; we want them to foster enterprise and education and division of labor, which is bound to be beneficial and which a large community, if interested in the right direction, has the power to do.

So much for this time. You will hear from us again. We have some more facts to tell you yet and a few propositions to make. Respectfully.

A RESIDENT OF ORANGEVILLE.

Salt Lake Herald
February 11, 1894

SUSPENSION OF ENTRIES.

Instructions Received at the Land Office Yesterday.

The following order was received at the local land office yesterday from the commissioner of the general land office:

"Owing to the existence of certain irregularities in the range line between ranges 12 and 13 west, in townships 14 and 15 north, it has been found necessary to issue to Deputy Surveyor Andrew P. Hanson special instructions to govern the surveys under his contract No. 194, and for the resurvey of said range lines.

Pending the resurvey of said range line, and the investigation of irregularities existing in the sub-divisional survey of townships 14 and 15 north, range 12 west, you (the local receiver) will suspend, until otherwise ordered, all entries and disposal of lands in sections 6, 7, 18, 19, 30 and 31 in township 14 north, range 12 west, and sections 30, 31 in township 15 north, range 12 west, Salt Lake meridian."

HOMESTEAD ENTRIES.

Applications for homestead entries were filed in the land office yesterday as follows:

No. 10,802, by William Gee, jr., of Gunnison, 160 acres in section 34, township 18, south range 1 west.

10,801, by Edward W. Fox, jr., of Orangeville, Emery county, 159 acres in section 21, township 18, south range 8 east.

LAND CONTEST.

Contest testimony was filed yesterday in the case of L. P. Palmer vs. Robert E. Ross, involving homestead No. 10,448. The case was decided in favor of the contestant, and an appeal is taken.

DESERT ENTRY.

Desert land entry No. 3,890 was made by Samuel J. Paradice, of Price, containing 40 acres in section 17, township 14 south, range 10 east.

TO BURY THE HATCHET.

Delegations From Price and Helper Raise the Flag of Truce.

At an informal caucus of the forces who have been urging and oposing the division of Emery county, in the Cullen hotel last night, all asperities were set aside and a calm review of the question entered into upon its merits. There were representatives from Castle Dale, from Huntington, from Price, Helper and various other precincts in that thriving empire when its material interests were taken up for discussion. In support of the movement looking to the ultimate division of the county which the divisionist contends is unweildy, two columns of figures were introduced, one showing the assessed valuation and revenues of Emery county after the legislative knife had been run through it, the other showing the valuation and revenues of Carbon county. The total assessed valuation of the former was shown to be $1,081,220.50, with a revenue for county purposes amounting to $3,843.60, while valuation of the latter is fixed at $959,594.50, with revenues for county purposes aggregating $4,678.78.

One item in expenditures shows a striking contrast between the moral structure of the two wings that are now spreading apart the cost incurred by the Emery division, as it has been designed, amounting to but $54.25, while that in the block, which it is proposed, shall constitute Carbon county, amounts to $763.30.

Discussing the political result in the event of division, the stalwarts who agreed that all acrimonies should be temporarily set aside, launched a column of figures which, is was said, had been taken from the last official returns. From these returns it was demonstrated that in the ten precincts incorporated in Emery county under division there had been cast at the last election 288 Democratic votes and 191 Republican votes. In the seven precincts which it is proposed to incorporate in Carbon county, the result at the same election was 89 votes for the Democratic ticket and 169 for the Republican.

At the same meeting the delegation from Helper and Price who have been as wide apart upon th question of a county seat as is the space that divides the two ambitious towns, agreed to bury the hatchet and to permit that issue to be decided by popular sentiment. The discussion, while purely informal, was very exhaustive and the figures produced show the county to be one of the most prosperous, wide-awake and progressive in the territory.

A. O. U. W.

Temple lodge met Monday night and elected Martin Rollins and W. C. Ferron to receive the junior workman and workman degrees, and conferred the same on them. Richard Sexton was elected to receive the workman degree. Brother C. G. Smith handed in his resignation as receiver, which was accepted. An election being held, Brother Dickinson was elected to fill the position for the balance of the term. The offer of Salt Lake Valley lodge No. 12 to accept $165.50 in settlement in full of their claim against Temple lodge, was accepted and $100 was raised at once and the balance will be raised within thirty days. When this is done it will leave Temple lodge out of debt. The lodges in Utah are working hard to make Utah a separate jurisdiction within the present year, which will undoubtedly be done, as it only lacks 700 more to make the required number to make the change, which when done will cut the number of assessments down over one-half, which will make it the cheapest beneficiary order in the Territory. Temple lodge will meet next Monday night in the hall on West Temple street instead of on Main street.

TO DIVIDE EMERY.

OPPONENTS OF THE MOVEMENT WERE NOT REPRESENTED.

They Claim That the Caucus at The Cullen was a One-Sided Affair, and Protest.

Those who represent the sentiment opposed to movement to divide Emery county assert that their side was not represented at all at that caucus at the Cullen on Monday night. The statement that the delegations from Price and Helper had agreed to bury the hatchet as to the county seat question is not challenged but it is claimed that there were no representatives from Castle Dale and Huntington, the meeting being made up wholly of those who favored a division, and naturally they had no difficulty in agreeing among themselves. It is also claimed that the financial statement which those favoring division have had published is not correct, and misleading on the vital points at issue.

The up shot of the whole matter is that this alleged meeting does not change the status of the matter at all. Those who opposed the division originally stand in the same position today and when they have anything to put forth with reference to the matter, they say they can and will speak for themselves.

Raising Goats in Emery County.

We are glad to know that we have a large herd of goats in our county now located in the Cedar mountains says the Eastern Utah *Telegraph*. Goats are very hardy animals and are more profitable than sheep. The length of their wool is about twelve inches long and brings a very large price in the market. A goat will sheer four grades of wool; the highest grade will probably bring 75 cents and the lowest 35, making an average of 55 cents. In an ordinary climate they can be shorn twice a year, with an average of about five pounds of wool to the clip. Besides the fine wool they produce they are also very valuable for the fine butter and milk they produce. Mr. Bromly, the owner of the herd is now located in our town (Castle Dale) for a time.

Land Office Filings.

Charles H. Edminster, of Castle Dale, Emery county, yesterday filed in the land office his final homestead entry No. 8,309 for forty acres in section 9, township 19 south, range 8 east.

Peter Hansen, of Emery county, also filed final homestead entry for 160 acres in section 11, township 22 south, range 6 east.

Salt Lake Herald
March 11, 1894

Land Office Filings.

Brigham Sandberg of Richfield, Sanpete county, yesterday filed in the land office, homestead entry No. 10,846 for 160 acres in section 14, township 24 south, range 2 west.

William H. Worthen of Ferron, Emery county, filed desert entry No. 3,940 for 80 acres in section 4, township 20 south, range 7 east.

James E. Kay, of Mona, Juab county, filed desert entry No. 3,298, for 120 acres in section 20, township 11 south, range 1 east.

Joseph J. Shields of Riter, Salt Lake county, filed a contest against the desert entry filed by William J. Brimley on January 13, 1890, for land in section 30, township 1 south, range 2 west. He claims that Brimley has never complied with the provisions of the desert land act.

Salt Lake Herald
March 13, 1894

John W. Lake, of Castle Dale, Emery county, made final proof of desert entry No. 3,214, for 120 acres in section 26, township 18 south, range 8 east.

Salt Lake Tribune
March 17, 1894

ENTRIES.

Charles H. Oliphant of Orangeville, Emery county, filed an application in the Land Office yesterday for a homestead entry of forty acres in section 29, township 18 south of range 8 east.

Mathew Evans of Lawrence, Emery county, filed final proof for his homestead entry of 120 acres in sections 17, 8 and 7, township 18 south of range 9 east.

Salt Lake Tribune
March 22, 1894

Elijah J. Winber of Castle Dale, Emery county, filed an application for a homestead entry of 160 acres in section 33, township 18 south, range 9 east.

Brigham Moffitt is reported very
sick at his home in Orangeville

A grizzly bear weighing 700 pounds was
killed by James Martin and Soren Hanson
in the mountains about four miles southwest of Ferron, last Monday. The bear
was shot nine times before it was killed.

HON. ORANGE SEELY.

An Enthusiastic Demonstra-
tion in His Favor.

The many citizens of Castle Gate,
with their noted brass band, came down
to Price, to accord Hon. Orange Seeley
a hearty welcome. The Castle Dale
band, accompanied by a mounted escort and a number of citizens of that
place went to Huntington bridge to
meet him and extend to him a royal
reception. On his arrival at Castle
Dale a grand reception awaited him
there, at the social hall. There was a
general turnout of citizens from many
parts of Emery county, and cordial
congratulations were extended to their
honored representative in the last Legislative assembly. Dancing was freely
indulged in, and pithy and appropriate
addresses were delivered, notably by
the distinguished guest, Hon. Orange
Seeley and the new probate judge, Mr.
H. Savage. It was midnight before
the assemblage dispersed.

Emery county's esteemed Councilor
had the credit of being the largest and
heaviest man in the Legislature. The
sergeant-at-arms, it will be remembered, was under the necessity of purchasing a chair of suitable dimensions
for the hefty member, and the Governor urged Judge Seely to carry this
mammoth chair back home with him,
which was done.   D.
CASTLE DALE, March 24. 1894.

Salt Lake Tribune
April 3, 1894

Coal Entry Appeal.

An appeal was filed in the Land Office yesterday in the case of S. S. Markham vs. W. W. Paine. The case involves a coal entry of 160 acres near Castle Dale. At the hearing in the Land Office the case was decided in favor of Markham, but on appeal to the Commissioner of the Land Office Paine's entry was pronounced to be the prior one. The case now goes to the Secretary of the Interior on appeal.

Salt Lake Tribune
April 6, 1894

Joseph H. Behunin of Ferron filed an application for a homestead entry of 160 acres in section 29, township 21 south of range 7 east.

Joseph A. Thomson of Ferron, Emery county, filed an application for a homestead entry of 160 acres in section 11, township 20 south of range 7 east.

Deseret Weekly
April 7, 1894

BUSY SANPETE.

The new county road from Ephraim to Castle Dale, Emery county, is to be pushed to a finish as soon as workmen can get into the canyon. The live citizens of this county are anxious to see it completed, for it will greatly benefit both counties, and will make of Ephraim more than ever a junction city.

DISTRICT COURT.

Grand and Petit Jurors For the Nephi Term

DRAWN FROM THE BOX.

A Civil Suit Wherein a Brother is Suing a Brother Appealed From the Justice's Court of Spanish Fork is on Trial—Other Business of Court.

After Saturday's issue of THE DISPATCH went to press the following business was transacted in the First District court.

People's Exchange vs. Geo. Erickson, dismissed at cost of plaintiff.

J. W. N. Whitecotton vs. D. S. Dana, suit for attorney's fee alleged to be due and owing, was taken up, jury empaneled, some evidence offered and continuance until Monday morning taken.

Demurrer overruled in the Redden vs. Searle et al case and defendant given until May 1st to answer.

The following jurors were drawn for service at Nephi:

Grand Jurors:—Marinus Jensen, T. T. Davis, Provo; Joseph Judd, Manti; Owen Sanderson, Fairview; George W. Cropper, Deseret; Leslie Bunnell, Lake View; W. W. Jenkins, Nephi; Wm. Probert, Holden; Frank Carroll, Orangeville; George Hansen, Eureka, A. A. Cahoon, Mt. Pleasant; P. C. Christensen, Moroni; John Barnard, Salina; Reese J. Lewellyn, Fountain Green; John Ellertson, Mons; Jas. B. Gaddie, Lehi; James Barlow, Richfield; W. H. Carson jr., Fairfield; John E. Moulton, Heber; Martin, Huntington.

AT THE LAND OFFICE.

Some Homestead and Desert Filings and Two Contests.

In the land office yesterday Samuel Ware, jr., of Orangeville, Emery county, filed a homestead application for the west half of the northeast quarter and east half of the northwest quarter of section 13, township 19 south, range 7 east.

Salt Lake Herald
April 27, 1894

THE FERRON TOWNSITE.

Final Papers Issued Yesterday at the Land Office.

The final papers on the application of Orange Seely, formerly probate judge of Emery county, for the townsite of Ferron, in that county, were issued yesterday, the filings having been completed, and a patent will now issue.

Peter L. Anderson, of Bear Lake City, Box Elder county, filed a homestead application for the southwest quarter of section 32, township 12 north, range 3 west.

John McDonald, of Molen, Emery county, filed a homestead application for the northwest quarter of section 12, township 20 south, range 7 east.

Frank Rowe, of Goshen, Utah county, filed a homestead application for lots 1 and 2, the southwest quarter of the northeast quarter and the northwest quarter of the southeast quarter of section 1, township 10 south, range 1 west.

Salt Lake Tribune
May 1, 1894

Land Office Filings.

Christian Tobbs of Castle Dale, Emery county, filed an application in the Land Office yesterday for a homestead entry of 160 acres in section 27, township 18 south, range 8 east.

James E. Sheen of Smithfield, Cache county, filed an application for a homestead entry of 160 acres in section 11, township 13 north, range 1 west.

William H. Kesler of Milford filed an application for a desert entry of 160 acres in section 5, township 26 south, range 10 west.

Salt Lake Tribune
May 6, 1894

Mrs. Elizabeth Yoxall, aged 74, was found dead in bed at Ferron on the 24th of April, as reported by the Price Telegraph. She was living alone and poor.

Salt Lake Tribune
May 20, 1894

A Utah Orchardist on Spraying.

J. C. Lemon, a notably successful farmer and fruit grower of Ferron, Utah, writes the Irrigation Age of his method of spraying trees as follows:

"I irrigate my trees as soon as possible so as to keep back the early blossoming; then when the trees do start, they do so with more vitality and vigor. I prefer early irrigation so as to get as much early growth in the first part of the season, then the trees are in good condition for fall, provided they are not started in September to make a second growth in a season. This is the cause of some trees dying at the tops. Water trees late in the fall and early in the spring. I use the F. E. Meyers spray pump. I use or prefer Paris green for spraying apples, although London purple is good. I spray the first time as soon as the trees are in full bloom, and again in about ten days, but if it should rain inside of a day or two after I have sprayed, I spray again. I made my spray a little stronger than this formula, one pound of Paris green to about 150 gallons of water. I have never had any worms on my trees or in my apples, but I thought an ounce of prevention better than a pound of cure. I always manure and cultivate thoroughly and delve between the trees and place all the bones and refuse of like character at the roots of my trees, and the result is good, vigorous, healthy trees that bear an abundance of apples, that I will place in competition with any in the United States for quality, color and flavor. I have never had pear or plum leaf blight, but should anything of the kind occur I will fight it with a formula I have for that purpose."

Salt Lake Herald
May 29, 1894

Hon. John T. Caine and O. W. Moyle have just returned from Emery county where they have been organizing Democratic societies. Meetings were held and clubs formed at Huntington, Cleveland, Lawrence, Castle Dale, Orangeville and Ferron.

Salt Lake Herald
June 3, 1894

Land Office Items.

In the land office yesterday the following original homestead filings were made:

William E. Davies, of Portage, Box Elder county, on the southeast quarter of the northwest quarter and southwest quarter and southwest quarter of the northeast quarter of section 9, township 14 north, range 3 west.

Samuel H. Preston, of Orangeville, Emery county, on the south half of the southeast quarter of section 17, the northeast quarter of the northeast quarter of section 20, and the northwest quarter of the northwest quarter of section 21, township 19 south, range 8 east.

James B. Jardine, of Clarkston, Cache county, on the northwest quarter of the northeast quarter of section 28, township 14 north, range 2 west.

John E. Eyre, of Parowan, Iron county, on the east half of the southeast quarter of section 13, township 33 south, range 9 west, and lots 3 and 4 of section 18, township 33 south, range 8 west.

Final homestead—Hennery Onni, of Corinne, on the southwest quarter of section 24, township 10 north, range 3 west.

Emil Pauly, of Summit county, on the southwest quarter of section 20, township 3 north, range 10 west.

Desert entry—Lauritz H. Smith, of Draper, on the southwest quarter of the southwest quarter of section 27, township 3 south, range 1 east.

Provo Dispatch
June 5, 1894

NOTICE TO CREDITORS—ESTATE OF
Joseph Haycock, deceased. Notice is hereby given by the undersigned administrator of
the estate of Joseph Haycock, Jr., deceased,
to the creditors of, and all persons having
claims against the said deceased, to exhibit
them with the necessary vouchers within
four months after the first publication of this
notice at the Probate court at Castle Dale,
Emery County, the same being the place to
transact the business of the estate.
                          JOSEPH HAYCOCK,
   Administrator of the estate of Joseph Haycock, Jr., deceased.
   Dated this 2nd day of June, 1894.

Provo Dispatch
June 9, 1894

   Decree of divorce granted on June
2nd, in which case D. D. Houtz was appointed referee to take testimony,
Joseph Bonnacio of Castle Dale vs.
Johanna Bonnacio, was entered.

Salt Lake Herald
June 19, 1894

Land Office.
   The following applications were filed
in the local land office yesterday:
   Matt Anderson, of Sterling, Sanpete
county, desert entry of the southeast
quarter of the northeast quarter of section 7, township 19 south, range ½ east.
   Francis Morley, of Moroni, Sanpete
county, homestead entry of the southwest quarter of the northwest quarter
of section 33, township 14 south, range
3 east.
   John S. Grange, of Orangeville, Emery
county, final proof of desert entry of the
southeast quarter of the northwest quarter of section 31, township 18 north,
range 8 east.

Manti Messenger
June 22, 1894

   John Patton petitioned for authority to bring water from Ferron
canyon, and open up the old ditch
made some years ago   Referred to
committee on irrigation

Manti Messenger
June 29, 1894

Mr and Mrs Forrester of Castle Dale, are sojourners in the city this week   They are domiciled at the Bench House

Salt Lake Tribune
July 22, 1894

Flouring Mill at Orangeville.

Price Telegraph: The people of Orangeville should feel proud of the fact that in a short time they will have a flouring mill right at their doors. The machinery for the mill has been ordered and is expected to arrive soon. The building is almost completed. They expect to have the mill running in a short time.

Manti Messenger
August 10, 1894

A NEW LAKE.

One can be Made in the Mountains and more Water Obtained

Several parties have been in the MESSENGER office the past few days discussing a scheme for increasing the water supply of city creek The plan is to have the owners of primary water rights in the field to dig a channel though the mountain into Crawford's fork of Ferron creek and tap the lake which always has more or less water in it The estimated cost will not exceed $10 000 and enough water could be impounded to double the capacity of city creek at this season of the year   It is understood that the city owns a right in that water up to July 1st every year   This right could be held and the water trained into the lake, which might be made almost 100 feet deep

The city engineer and other parties interested should make surveys and estimates and report at a citizens meeting   There is no question about the actual need of more water in this valley   The creek might be filled to three times its present capacity and still there would be no surplus water, Every person owning hay land knows the small crop that was cut this season on account of lack of water   This can be remedied by next year with but very little expense to any one The amount necessary to cut the tunnel and construct a dam on the south side of the lake might be chiefly paid in labor and stock issued in proportion to the value of the work Now is the time for action

BOARD OF PHARMACY.

Work Done at the Meeting Held Here Yesterday.

The Utah Board of Pharmacy met at the office of C. H. McCoy yesterday, the members present being J. L. Boyden, G. H. Fennemore, J. B. Farlow, W. A. Wade and C. H. McCoy.

The time for registration, under section 2 of the pharmacy law, expired with the meeting of the board, so that in future the registration will be confined to those who are either graduates of recognized colleges of pharmacy, or those who pass a satisfactory examination before the board. The following persons were registered yesterday: B. B. Schroeder, Logan; Wynn Eddy, Brigham City, James Reger, Salt Lake city; William Crawford, Orangeville.

The secretary was instructed to prosecute all pharmacists who are delinquent with their registration and to have a thorough investigation made of the grocery men who are engaged in selling drugs, and to prosecute those not complying with the law.

The secretary was instructed to prosecute all pharmacists who are delinquent with their registration and to have a thorough investigation made of the grocery men who are engaged in selling drugs, and to prosecute those not complying with the law.

Secretary McCoy reports that much good is resulting from the operation of the law in the way of protecting people from impure drugs and unsafe druggists. He will be very glad to have all cases of carelessness reported to him as well as cases where unregistered or unqualified men are selling drugs, particularly poisons.

It is dangerous for any person to handle drugs who is unable to determine as to their genuineness and the danger attending their use. Pharmacy is a profession in itself.

Wynne Eddy was successful in buying out all the drug stocks carried by grocery stores in Brigham city, and pharmacists in other towns have done the same.

Struck By Lightning.

Castle Dale, Aug. 8.—During a thunderstorm this evening William Lake, a farmer living in this place, started to go up to the ditch to turn off the water, and had only been out a few minutes when struck down by lightning. He was heard moaning by a neighbor and assistance was procured and the injured man taken home. His clothing was very badly torn and burnt by the bolt. At this writing he is rapidly recovering from the shock and no apprehension of danger is entertained.—Price Telegraph.

Andrew Nelson, of Ferron visited the Temple city of Sanpete during the week. He called at the MESSENGER office and left two big silver dollars to guarantee the delivery of this paper to his home in Emery county for the next twelve months

Castle Dale Republicans.

EDITOR THE STANDARD:—Hon Joseph Standford and Judge Watson of Heber, addressed a large and enthusiastic audience of Republicans he e last night. A large number joined the already flourishing club of Castle Dale. The speakers handled the political issues of the day in a manner that will prove very dangerous to the party of promises who had hoped for a majority in this county this fall. The warm reception accorded the apostles of Republicanism manifests the change of public sentiment. Judge Watson is an able exponent of a protective tariff on lead and wool, and has a convincing way of expressing his convictions. He resides within sight of the smokestacks of the great Park City mines, and knows the effects of tariff tinkering, even done by experts like Wilson.

Mr. Stanford is a pleasing speaker. His remarks are clear and to the point. He was at his best last night and made some telling points in favor of protection and against free trade or revenue tariff.

The inconsistency of the late attempt at tariff legislation was pointed out much to the disgust of a lone Democrat who occupied a front seat. The announcement that Judge Patton, of Ogden, had withdrawn from the Democratic party, proved a bomb in the local camp of Democracy.

Emery county will be counted in the Republican column in the future.

ROYER.

Castle Dale, Aug. 26th.

Salt Lake Tribune
September 3, 1894

SPEECHES AT FERRON.

Judge Watson of Heber and Hon. Joseph Standford of Ogden.

Ferron, Aug. 29.—Our quiet little town was the scene of a most enthusiastic Republican meeting held in the Town Hall last evening.

The speakers were the Hon. Joseph Standford of Ogden and Judge Watson of Heber, who are canvassing Emery county in the Republican cause.

Judge Watson was the first speaker. He dwelt upon the present situation of the people under a free trade Administration. He spoke of the promises made to the miners if they would vote the Democratic ticket, and in what manner these had been kept. He pointed out the condition of the laboring masses in free trade England. His speech was practical and to the point and won most hearty applause.

Mr. Standford followed with an eloquent address, setting forth the Republican principles in an able manner. He spoke of the way in which the People's party of Utah had merged themselves into the Democratic party without having studied its principles. He cited statistics from history, showing the progress in the wealth of the country during the years of Republican administration. Mr. Standford was frequently interrupted by hearty applause. When, at the conclusion of his speech, three rousing cheers were given for Republicanism, the Democrats of Ferron felt that their death knell had been tolled. At the close a large number were enrolled in the Republican list.

After the close of the meeting a Republican Club was organized, with the following officers: J. C. Lemon, president; James Henry, vice-president; George M. Leonard, secretary and treasurer.

Deseret Weekly
September 8, 1894

THE EUPOREAN MISSION.

[*Millennial Star, Aug. 20.*]

RELEASE AND APPOINTMENTS.—Elder Samuel Gerrard has been appointed to labor as traveling Elder in the Liverpool conference.

Elder Enos Bennion has been released from his labors in the Cheltenham conference and has been appointed to labor in the London conference.

ARRIVALS. — Elders Bengt M. Ravsten, of Clarkston, Cache county, Utah, and Niels A. Morck, of Salt Lake City, arrived in Liverpool, August 1st, per Anchor steamer Anchoria, via Glasgow, on their way to the missionary field in Scandinavia.

Elder Samuel Gerrard arrived in Liverpool, August 8th, per Anchor steamer Circassia, via Glasgow. He was accompanied by Elder Frederick Ottosen, of Castle Dale, Emery county, Utah, who is on a visit to his native country, Denmark.

Salt Lake Tribune
September 14, 1894

Land Office Filings.

Land Office entries yesterday were as follows:

Ephraim L. Allred of Ferron, Emery county, No. 4044, north half of southeast quarter of section 30, of township 19 south, range east.

James H. Campbell, Minersville, Beaver county, No. 11,151, north half of the southeast quarter of section 8, in township 30 south, range 9 west.

Salt Lake Tribune
September 19, 1894

Land Office Filings.

The Land Office filings were as follows yesterday:

George W. Fillmer of Orangeville, Emery county, homestead entry No. 11,162, west half northwest quarter and southeast quarter of northwest quarter and northwest quarter of southwest quarter of section 20, township 19 south, range 8 east.

Arthur Meads of Salt Lake City, desert entry No. 4046, lots 1 and 2 and south half of northeast quarter of section 3, township 15 south, range 1 west.

Provo Dispatch
September 27, 1894

Today the case of the People vs. A. Nielsen of Mt. Pleasant, charged with a misdemeanor in driving, on January 8, 1894, away from the cattle range near Castle Dale two head of cattle not his property.

Salt Lake Herald
September 28, 1894

A jury was empaneled in the case of The People vs. Andrew Nielsen. Assistant United States Attorney Thurman prosecuted and Jacob Johnson defended. The defendant is charged with driving stock from the range near Castle Dale, Emery county, on the 8th of January, 1894, contrary to law. The defendant was found guilty of the charge by Justice Anderson, of Castle Dale court, and appealed to the district court. The testimony went to show that defendant drove some cattle not belonging to him from the range in Castle Dale to a winter range 30 or 40 miles away.

The defense opened by putting the defendant on the stand. The defendant stated that he thought the cows in question belonged to some of the parties who he was driving for, and did not intentionally drive them off.

The jury brought in a verdict of acquittal.

Salt Lake Tribune
September 30, 1894

THE SAN PETE MAN HUNT.

Sheriff Burns's Murderers Are Closely Pursued.

MICKEL IS BADLY WOUNDED.

The Desperadoes Left Word at Orangeville for the Posse to Come Shooting, as They Would Not Be Taken Alive—The Pursuers but a Few Hours Behind—Apathy of the Citizens.

Mount Pleasant, Utah, Sept. 29.—Special to Tribune.—It is reported that Pete Mickel and another man, answering the description of Moroni Koffard, were seen early this morning, passing west, between Fairview and this city. It is thought by some that these may be the murderers of Sheriff Burns, and by others that it is a blind to draw attention away from the present line of pursuit. Especially is this latter view taken as a party returning from the posse say that Marshal Braby and men are in close pursuit, having received valuable information and assistance at Orangeville. Dr. Moore took a bullet from Jim Mickel's side, the same having passed through the arm. The murderers started south, leaving word with Dr. Moore not to say anything about having seen them, threatening his life.

Marshal Lee has gone to Birch Creek to investigate the report of the passing of the fugitives north of this city to the West mountains. The description of the horses and men corresponds exactly. Lee has sent for men and posses are being organized here and at Fairview to scour the hills. The report that they were seen is positively confirmed.

MUST COME SHOOTING.

One of the party searching for the murderers of Sheriff Burns has sent in private information that the fugitives were traced down into Castle valley, where Jim Mickel had a pistol ball removed from his side, it having passed through his hand. They left word in Orangeville of their deed and that "for any one following them to come shooting as they would not be taken alive." The boys were allowed to leave Orangeville unmolested and the searchers were much disgusted with the seeming apathy of the people there to assist in the capture. It is believed the desperadoes are heading south, but if travelling together slow progress will be made, as Mickel's wound is a serious one. Ab Koffard, while pretending to aid the posse, is believed to be endeavoring to mislead them. He persists in a different story from that told by the other eye-witness to the tragedy. The correspondent says that if the men at Larsen's sawmill had done as they should the murderers would not have escaped.

A party arriving to-day from the search says it is believed by Marshal Braby and his followers that they are only a few hours behind the fugitives and have strong hopes of soon overtaking them.

Much excitement was created in this city this afternoon by the information that a party of two on horseback had crossed the valley at Birch creek and gone into the west hills. The local officer went up and the report being substantiated and a description of the horses and men given corresponding exactly with that of the fugitives, sent in for an armed posse, which was soon raised and, assisted by a posse from Fairview, went into the hills. Word is received to-night that they have been traced as far as Indianola. This new discovery, if not misleading, confuses matters, as the posse in the south are positive they are not far from the fleeing murderers. All points north and west have been notified to keep a sharp lookout, and if the fugitives have slipped the southern posses, they will still find themselves surrounded.

Word has been received from Spring City that Mrs. Mickel's mind has temporarily given away and she is constantly raving.

IN CLOSE PURSUIT.

Manti, Utah, Sept. 29.—Special to Tribune.—Milton Colloway arrived here this evening from Orangeville. He reports that Mickel and Moroni Koffard, the slayers of Sheriff James Burns, had stopped two hours in Orangeville. Mickel had been shot through the right hand and in the side. Dr. Moore extracted the ball and gave Mickel a big dose of morphine.

The fugitives boldly asserted that they had killed Burns and dared any man to arrest them. They left Orangeville at 10 o'clock at night. The Manti posse reached the town at daylight next morning.

The murderers left word for their pursuers to come shooting, as they would be in hiding in the San Rafael bluffs. They went to the cabins at Paradise, packed up provisions and started down the south bank of the San Rafael river. The posse are in close pursuit. No others have yet been seen in that section.

Evening Dispatch
October 2, 1894

WORD comes that Marshal Fowler's posse are close upon Koffard and Mickel, the murderers of Sheriff Burns, near Orangeville, in Emery county. Mickel's wound is causing him great suffering and the doctor who extracted the bullet says that unless he has the very best of care he cannot possibly live longer than six or eight days. Mickel's brother has taken medicine to him once or twice and he is being tracked.

Evening Dispatch
October 3, 1894

BURNS' SLAYERS.

Chief Fowler's Posse Have Them Surrounded.

KOFFARD IS WOUNDED.

Shot by the Officers in a Battle Had With the Murderers at Long Range—W. O. Norrell Gives the Particulars in an Interesting Letter to S. R. Thurman.

The murderers of Sheriff Burns are as good as captured. Their lair is surrounded; they are both wounded; their horses are taken from them, and no friends can reach them from the outside. It depends wholly upon the amount of grub they have with them as to how long they are out of the grasp of the officers. They have shown fight; in fact have shot at the officers, and the officers do not propose to throw themselves in range of the murderers' guns. The scheme is to starve them out.

This news was brought to Provo last evening by Deputy U. S. Marshal Bean of Richfield who had a conversation with the city marshal of Manti who had just returned from the seat of war. The following letter will be found very interesting:

CASTLE DALE, EMERY COUNTY,
September 30, 1894.

Hon. S. R. Thurman,
  Assistant U. S. Attorney,
    Provo, Utah.

DEAR SIR:—As we surmised, the murderers of Sheriff Burns came this way. When we reached Orangeville on the evening of the 27th we learned that they had stopped there at about 9 o'clock the night before and that Dr. Moore had extracted a bullet from Mickel.

We could get no trail from there but started that night into the rough, broken country south of the San Rafael river. We searched in vain for their trail until yesterday afternoon when we struck it in the stupendous box canyon, known as McCarty canyon, about thirty miles south from this place.

At about sunset we found their horses and have them in our possession.

We could not locate their camp last evening, but very early this morning we caught sight of them, but they refused to surrender, We opened fire which they returned as they ran to a more advantageous position.

Their retreat seemed in-accessible to us except by approaching it exposed for a long distance to their fire, and we had the misfortune to get two of our rifles out of fix.

We were out of provisions and so I rode here this afternoon to get grub and two guns, leaving Fowler and two others at the seat of war. I leave again tonight prepared for a seige, the sheriff and others returning with me.

We believe that Koffard was wounded this morning, but as the firing was at long range we could not be positive. We think tomorrow or next day at least will tell the result.

Our future work must be done on foot, as a mountain sheep couldn't climb where the men are hiding.

Yours truly,
  W. O. NORRELL.

Salt Lake Herald
October 4, 1894

Fair Notes.

The art department is finer than at any previous fair.

The largest apples on exhibition are those in the display of fruit made by J. C. Lemon, of Ferron. They have been compared to cannon balls in size, but not in lack of mellowness.

Enterprise is the motto of Hewlett Bros. Their exhibit of bottled beverages is an attractive feature. The firm's efforts are not confined to this line, however, as the display of their baking powders, spices, etc., show.

The bicycle raffle, conducted by the associated charities at the fair, is progressing to the satisfaction of the committee in charge. At an early hour yesterday afternoon 124 chances had been sold.

The following ladies are requested to meet at the Exposition building at 9 a. m. today for the purpose of awarding prizes for the articles in the woman's department: Committee on Arts—Mesdames Arthur Brown, F. S. Richards, Frank Knox and Wendell Benson. Committee on Industrial Department—Mesdames C. W. Bennett, O. J. Salisbury, W. S. McCornick and Bertha Bamberger.

SOME residents of Castle Dale reached Provo today and they say that to a person who knows the country where Burns' murderers are in hiding it is absolutely impossible to surround him so that he cannot get out unseen. They also say that Kofford and Mickel know the country thoroughly well.

Twelve Thousand Delighted People Visited the Great Fair Yesterday.

J. C. Lemon, Ferron, Utah, best variety apples, second prize, $4.
J. C. Lemon. Ferron, Utah, best peck apples, first prize. $2.
Nelson Ferron, pears, second prize, $2.

OFFICERS RETURN

Kofford and Mickel Succeed in Escaping.

WILL YET BE CAPTURED.

That Is The Expectation of Deputy Marshal Fowler--Deputy Marshal Norrell's Account of The Long and Arduous Search.

Deputy Marshals Fowler and Norrell returned last evening on the R. G. W. train after being away since the evening of Sep'ember 26th, hunting for the murderers of Sheriff Burns.

Marshal Fowler was seen this morning; he was very reticent in speaking of the trip, but expressed the opinion that the outlaws would yet be captured.

Marshal Norrell gave the following account of the hunt: The officers arrived at Castle Dale on the afternoon of the 27th, and accompanied by Sheriff Thos. Lloyd of Carbon county and Rodney and Sidney Swasey went south in the direction the fugitives were supposed to have gone on the evening before, after Mickel's wound had been dressed by Dr. Moore of Castle Dale.

The officers were greatly aided in getting on the trail of the murderers by watching three of Kofford's brothers, who live in a little town on the San Rafael, called Paradise. They did a great deal of night riding and doubtless carried food and medicine to the murderers. On Saturday evening. September 29th, the officers found the horses, some food, medicine and clothing, belonging to Kofford and Mickel in a cave; but the assassins had seen the officers approach and had made their escape. On Sunday morning. September 30th, the murderers were seen in the rocks above, and shots were exchanged, without any serious effects. so far as known, on either side. Mickel and Kofford retreated farther into the rocks; their place of refuge was in a country where it was impossible to follow them except by making a considerable circuit to reach the place where they had climbed the cliffs.

The officers had been for twenty-four hours without food, and it was de-determined to send Mr. Norrell to Castle Dale for supplies, and the other officers remained and took a position where they believed they could prevent the outlaws from making their escape. On Monday morning an aggressive campaign was begun and the cliffs were scaled by the pursuing party. About half a mile from the place where Mickel and Kofford were seen the day before the officers found a place where a boot heel had scratched a smooth rock and where a tobacco chewer had expectorated. This is the last trace that has been had of the slayers of Burns. The remainder of the week was spent in searching the almost impenetrable mountain fastnesses, but without any result, and last Sunday the posse returned to Castle Dale, and yesterday evening they took the train for home.

Mr. Norrell says that the efforts of Sidney and Rodney Swasey, in aiding the officers, cannot be too highly commended. The boys are well acquainted with the country and no better scouts could have been obtained.

Information reaches us from Sanpete that George Kofford, a brother of Moan Kofford, came into town Sunday evening and visited his own home and the home of Mickel. No information could be obtained in regard to the object of the visit The sheep claimed by Mickel and Kofford are said to be scattered, and the relatives of Mickel and Kofford who were left in charge have left the camp presumably to go to the aid of the fugitives.

Salt Lake Tribune
October 20, 1894

Postmaster at Orangeville.

TRIBUNE BUREAU,
517 Fourteenth St., N. W.,
Washington, D. C., Oct. 19, 1894.
E. W. Fox, Jr., was to-day appointed postmaster at Orangeville, Emery county, Utah, vice Frank Carroll, resigned.

Salt Lake Herald
October 21, 1894

DEMOCRATIC MEETINGS.

The Democratic Territorial committee announces the following speakers at meetings on the evenings designated:

HON. J. L. RAWLINS

Will speak as follows:

EMERY AND CARBON COUNTIES.

Hon. A. G. Norrell, W. G. Sharp and others will speak as follows:

Monday, Oct. 22—Schofield, or Winter Quarters.

Tuesday, Oct. 23—Castle Gate.

Wednesday, Oct. 24—Helper and Spring Glen.

Thursday—Oct. 25, afternoon—Wellington.

Thursday, Oct. 25—Evening—Price.

Friday, Oct. 26—Afternoon—Cleveland.

Friday, Oct. 26—Evening—Huntington.

Saturday, Oct. 27—Morning—Lawrence.

Saturday, Oct. 27—Afternoon—Orangeville.

Saturday, Oct. 27—Evening—Castle Dale.

Deseret Weekly News
October 28, 1894

The citizens of Orangeville, says the Eastern Utah *Telegraph*, are congratulating the selves upon the successful operation of their new flouring mill. The mill is capable of turning out seventy-five barrels per day and has plenty of grain in sight to keep the machinery going until another crop is grown.

Salt Lake Tribune
October 30, 1894

MAY GIVE THEMSELVES UP.

Efforts to Induce Kofford and Mickle to Surrender.

Mt. Pleasant, Utah, Oct. 29.—Special to Tribune.—Simon T. Beck, who was over from Spring City to-day, says a gentleman who was over from Orangeville a few days ago reported that he had seen and conversed with Kofford and Mickle, the slayers of Sheriff Burns, in the mountains last week. Jacob Johnson says it is reported the boys were seen in Ferron canyon by other boys. It is beginning to be believed around here that an inducement will successfully be made to have the fugitives give themselves up. The brothers of the boys seem to think they stand a good chance of getting clear and claim they are endeavoring to get them to surrender. Mrs. Mickle is anxious to have her son give himself up, owing to the fact that the witnesses to the affair conflict somewhat in their reports. It is generally remarked that Kofford and Mickle may get off with a heavy prison term sentence.

EMERY STAKE CONFERENCE.

The quarterly conference of the Emery Stake of Zion was held at Huntington, Nov. 4th and 5th, 1894. Present on the stand was the Stake Presidency, Bishops and many of the leading members of the Priesthood. The weather was fine and all the meetings crowded to overflowing.

After the usual opening exercises Elder Larson bade the Saints welcome and expressed his great pleasure in meeting under such favorable circumstances. He regretted that none of the general Church authorities were present, but said we had been much favored with their presence in the past. The Divine Spirit can and will operate through our local speakers so that we shall have a spiritual feast. He had visited a number of the wards since last conference, and found the Saints generally attending to their religious duties; could find fault with many for not attending their meetings, but would rather praise than scold. He urged the Saints to observe the Word of Wisdom and carry out the advice of the First Presidency in relation to round-dancing; he also made many encouraging remarks concerning the numerous blessings we now enjoy.

Elder John R. Young, of New Mexico, gave a brief description of the Saints of his ward; said he was born in the Church and had noted with pleasure the steady growth of the Saints, extending as they do from Canada to Mexico. He related instances of the efficacy of prayer and of the sick being healed through faith.

Elder J. W. Nixon showed how inconsistent were the ministers of the world in teaching that "faith" alone would insure salvation. He knew this to be their teaching as he had met and conversed with several of them on a recent trip to Minnesota.

2 p. m.—The sacrament was administered by the Priesthood of Huntington, after which Bishops' reports of the Huntington, Cleveland, Wellington, Spring Glen and Castle Dale wards were made.

A. E. Wall then spoke on the law of tithing and the benefits of prayer.

He was followed by Charles Oliphant, who explained how many weak Saints lose faith through watching the faults of others. This is a wrong view to take; he exhorted parents to train their children in the truths of the Gospel.

A Priesthood meeting convened in the evening at which much valuable instruction was given pertaining to the duties of its members.

Nov. 5, 10 a. m.—The wards of Lawrence, Orangeville, Ferron, Molen and Emery were reported by their respective Bishops. The reports showed ward organizations complete with few exceptions, health of the people good and bountiful harvests.

Elder Samuel Alger, a recently returned missionary, gave an interesting discourse on the first principles of the Gospel.

The High Priests' quorum was represented by Elder William Taylor. The Eighty-first quorum of Seventies by Elder William A. Guymon, and the Ninety-first by Elder Peter R. Peterson; Elder George Gull represented the Second quorum of Elders. The brethren exhorted their co-laborers to prepare for usefulness in the ministry.

2 p.m.—Elders O. Seely, Alma G. Jewkes and William Howard spoke encouragingly on a number of interesting subjects.

The general and Stake authorities were then unanimously sustained, after which Joseph E. Johnson, president of the Y. M. M. I. A. of the Stake, invited all to assist in the great work of improvement.

Elder Larson made closing remarks; admonished the people to be temperate in their habits, avoid going in debt and take care of their crops.

The Huntington choir, conducted by J. E. Johnson, furnished the music for all meetings and was much appreciated by all.

Signs of thrift in Emery county are seen on every hand, such as new dwelling houses, new farms, and two new roller flouring mills.

A. E. WALL, Clerk.

Salt Lake Tribune
December 14, 1894

AGAIN IN HOT PURSUIT.

KOFFORD AND MICKLE SUR-
PRISED BY A POSSE.

The Slayers of Sheriff Burns Made Their Escape, but It Is Still Believed They Will Be Captured.

Mt. Pleasant, Utah, Dec. 13.—Special to Tribune.—From a letter received by the Pyramid to-day from Castle Dale, the first definite information concerning the posse of officers after the slayers of Sheriff Burns has been obtained. From the source mentioned it is learned that on last Sunday as one set of officers approached a crowd of friends of the boys at Paradise, two men, supposed to be the fugitives, broke and fled for cover and eluded the pursuers. Sheriff Carter, the two Swazey boys, and other officials are supposed to be by this time with Sheriff Fowler's men in the Sinbad breaks, where the boys are supposed to be hiding.

It is believed at Castle Dale that the slayers are hiding near there, and that they will be captured, but not alive. It is reported that Mickle is anxious to surrender, but is influenced not to do so at present by Kofford. The amount of public sympathy expressed for the boys in Emery is surprising, and it is quite evident they are among friends over there. The weather is bitter cold, the mountains full of snow and something definite one way or another is expected soon.

Ogden Standard
December 27, 1894

Thomas Fugate, of Ferron, Emery county, homestead entry of the southwest quarter of section 3, township 21 south, range 7 east.

Salt Lake Tribune
January 2, 1895

At the Cullen: H. L. Forde of Payson, Mr. and Mrs. N. C. De Lano of Bellevue, Ida., Frank B. Carroll of Orangeville, A. Forsher of Salina, John Brooks of Stockton.

Deseret Evening News
January 23, 1895

ORANGEVILLE PROSPERITY.

Plenty of Room for More Settlers and Good Land Cheap.

Capital Wanted for the Erection of a Woolen Factory, to be Commenced in the Spring.

Editor Deseret News:

I thought perhaps a few words from this secluded little hamlet would not be amiss as we hardly ever hear anything from our little town.

The health of the people as a general thing is good with the exception of a cold among the children, which of course sometimes proves fatal when it terminates in croup, as has been the case the past two weeks. Bro. and Sister Robert Logan lost their little one on the 5th inst., and Bro. and Sister Wm. Bunting's little one died on the 10th.

We have three district schools in good running order, which are well attended and are really full to overflowing. We are very much in need of a new school house, as our primary department is held in our social hall or meeting house, which are the same.

Our roller mill, which has done such noble work for us, is now frozen up for a short time, perhaps till the 15th of February. We hardly know how to appreciate the good flour we have had since the first of October last. We most assuredly have a good mill. Its capacity is sixty barrels, and it has ground as high as seventy-five. The machinery is from the Great Western Manufacturing company, and we are proud of the structure.

Some of the people are now agitating a woolen factory, and I expect we will make a start in that direction next summer in the way of getting timber for the building and perhaps putting in the foundation. We have plenty of good timber here for that purpose, in fact material of all kinds, but would invite capitalists to help us out with a little money for the machinery. We have an excellent site here for a factory, can get a water fall of sixty feet and can place it almost in our town, on the head waters of an irrigating canal where water I think will never fail.

We would also invite settlers to come and settle with us, as we have plenty of room. There is lots of land yet to enter, and much good land for sale at low prices. There are also chances to work on new canals and obtain water rights, etc.

Perhaps I had better close. There is lots I would like to say, but will write more at some future time about our country.   A. ANDERSON.

ORANGEVILLE, Emery county, Utah, Jan. 21, 1895]

Ogden Standard
January 31, 1895

PATENTS RECEIVED.

The following homestead patents have been received at the Land office:

William Wyatt Bryan of Ferron, 160 acres.

DEATH OF SISTER LARSEN.

HUNTINGTON, Utah, Jan. 26, 1895.

A gloom has been cast over the Latter-day Saints of this Stake by the sudden death of Sister Maria Karren Sorreen Larsen, beloved wife of President C. G. Larsen of the Emery Stake of Zion. On the evening of the 21st inst. about 10 o'clock, after most of the family had gone to bed, Sister Larsen, unbeknown to any of the family, went to visit a sick grandchild that lived a short distance away, and in returning it is supposed she was stricken with heart disease, for one of her sons who happened to go out to the street found her lying dead on the sidewalk. In the morning in looking at the place where she was found, it was seen that after she was stricken with pain, she stepped from the path into the snow to the fence, about two steps, and then followed the fence about two or three rods, with short steps, until she fell.

Sister Larsen was born in Arnager, on the Island of Bornholm, Denmark, in 1838, and was 56 years, 2 months, and 21 days old at the time of her death. She leaves a sorrowing husband, to whom she was married in the spring of 1857. She emigrated to Utah the same year. She cheerfully accepted and obeyed all the laws of the Gospel revealed through the Prophet Joseph Smith, and faithfully assisted her husband in all the duties devolving upon him as a leader among the people for a great many years. She went with her husband and family through the Manti Temple late in 1894, and received all her blessings. She also leaves six sons and four daughters, most of whom are married, and twelve grandchildren; all attended her funeral, which was held at 1 p.m. on Wednesday, January 23, 1895, in the Castle Dale ward house, which was crowded to overflowing with sorrowing relatives and friends. After appropriate singing and prayer the following brethren, in the order named, spoke words of consolation, and sympathized deeply with those that mourn: Bishop F. Olsen, of Ferron, Bishop Jonsson, of Huntington, Bishop Robertson, of Orangeville, Elder Alexander Jamison, of Castle Dale, Elder William Howard and Orange Seely, of the Stake presidency, and Bishop H. Olson, of Castle Dale. All had known Sister Larsen for years, some of them for over thirty years, and all testified of her great worth as a kind and affectionate wife and mother, and a true Latter-day Saint. A large number of relatives and friends followed her remains, which were laid away in the cemetery just north of Castle Dale.

The last time Sister Larsen met with the family apparently in good health and feeling well was in the family circle in evening prayer about half an hour before she was found dead. It can be truthfully said of Sister Larsen that she remained true and faithful to the end.   W. H.

ORANGEVILLE PROSPERITY.

I thought perhaps a few words from this secluded little hamlet would not be amiss as we hardly ever hear anything from our little town.

The health of the people as a general thing, is good with the exception of a cold among the children, which of course sometimes proves fatal when it terminates in croup, as has been the case the past two weeks. Bro. and Sister Robert Logan lost their little one on the 8th inst, and Bro. and Sister Wm. Bunting's little one died on the 16th.

We have three district schools in good running order, which are well attended and are really full to overflowing. We are very much in need of a new school house, as our primary department is held in our social hall or meeting house, which are the same.

Our Sabbath school is also in a flourishing condition under the management of our worthy superintendent J. C. Snow, and his aids. The Orangeville Dramatic troupe played on the 11th inst. for the benefit of our Sabbath school, and netted them a nice sum, which will be a great benefit to our school, as it was very much in need of some means to carry on the school.

Our roller mill, which has done such noble work for us, is now frozen up for a short time, perhaps till the 15th of February. We hardly know how to appreciate the good flour we have had since the first of October last. We most assuredly have a good mill. Its capacity is sixty barrels, and it has ground as high as seventy-five. The machinery is from the Great Western Manufacturing company, and we are proud of the structure.

Some of the people are now agitating a woolen factory, and I expect we will make a start in that direction next summer in the way of getting timber for the building and perhaps putting in the fondation. We have plenty of good timber here for that purpose, in fact material of all kinds, but would invite capitalists to help us out with a little money for the machinery. We have an excellent site here for a factory, can get a water fall of sixty feet and can place it almost in our town, on the head waters of an irrigating canal where water I think will never fail.

We would also invite settlers to come and settle with us, as we have plenty of room. There is lots of land yet to enter, and much good land for sale at low prices. There are also chances to work on new canals and obtain water rights, etc.

Perhaps I had better close. There is lots I would like to say, but will write more at some future time about our country.   A. ANDERSON.

ORANGEVILLE, Emery county, Utah, Jan. 21, 1895.

THE DEAD.

Peaceful be their Rest.

Deseret Weekly
February 16, 1895

EMERY STAKE CONFERENCE.

One of the most spirited and instructive conferences ever held in the Emery Stake convened in Castle Dale February 3rd and 4th. Elder F. M. Lyman, of the Apostles, the Stake presidency and all the Bishops of the Stake were in attendance. Five crowded meetings were held, owing partly perhaps to the good sleighing and clear, exhilarating weather.

After the usual opening exercises at 10 a.m., President Larsen bade the Saints welcome; expressed his great pleasure in meeting the people under such favorable conditions; gave a good report of the various wards—he and his brethren had visited every ward in the Stake since the last conference. Four Bishops then corroborated the President's statements and said a marked improvement had followed these visits. Complaint was made that some families were living in the wards, that had not brought recommends from their former homes.

Elder Lyman then spoke on the subject of tithing and records. He read from III Nephi the instructions of our Savior to the Nephites on these subjects; said we were a record making people and Stake and ward records should be neatly and carefully kept. As one of the Bishops reported that some in his ward had an idea that debts should be paid before tithing, Brother Lyman pronounced such belief false doctrine. Our first debt should be to Him who gives the increase.

Counselors Seeley and Howard made encouraging remarks in the afternoon, followed by Elder Lyman, who continued on his former subjects, and urged that family genealogies be written.

A Priesthood meeting was held after the afternoon services. Strictly keeping the Word of Wisdom was enjoined upon all who were in leading positions. A catechism of each member in the High Council, Bishops, Bishop's Counselors and Seventies showed a determination on their part to reform. Bishop Frederick Olson, of Ferron, and Counselor Alexander Jameson, of Castle Dale, were sustained to be ordained Patriarchs.

The second day was occupied largely by giving Bishops' reports, sustaining authorities, etc. Alexander Jameson reported religious class work.

President Larsen made timely suggestions to those who had heard the precious truths of the conference.

The parable of the ten virgins was read, with other selections, by Elder Lyman, who then prayed that all would try to secure "oil in their lamps."

Excellent music was rendered by the Castle Dale and Orangeville choirs.
A. E. WALL, Stake Clerk.

Salt Lake Tribune
March 8, 1895

The Governor to-day appointed the following Regents of the State University: W. W. Watkins, A. J. Green, Moscow; C. W. Chaff, Lewiston; C. L. Heitman, Rathdrum; W. E. Borah, Boise; S. H. Coffin, Caldwell; J. F. Ailshie, Grangeville, William Budge, John Donaldson, Paris.

Deseret Weekly
March 16, 1895

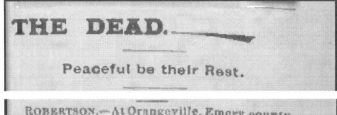

THE DEAD.

Peaceful be their Rest.

ROBERTSON.—At Orangeville, Emery county, Utah Territory, March 3, 1895, of inflammation of the bowels, Arthur Gilbert Robertson, son of Jasper Robertson and Rhoda Ellen Gaymon; aged 13 years and 7 months.

Salt Lake Herald
March 18, 1895

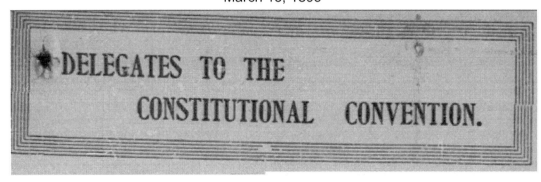

DELEGATES TO THE
CONSTITUTIONAL CONVENTION.

JASPER ROBERTSON,

Of Orangeville, Emery county, was born at Walkerville, Green county, Ill., May 8, 1847. His father, grandfather, uncle and brother, all rendered valuable service as enlisted men at various times in the history of our nation. His father died when he was about 5 years old. His ... ter and family, consisting of five ... emigrated to Utah in 1852, and located at Lehi City, Utah county. After a short stay of one year at that place, removed to Fountain Green, Sanpete county. Crossed the plains in the spring, and also the fall of 1866, in the interest of the people of Utah. Was married to Rhoda Ellen Guymon, April 17, 1871. Served two terms as justice of the peace of Fountain Green. Was in the Black Hawk war in Sanpete county, and was severely wound-

JASPER ROBERTSON.

ed with a ball from an Indian's rifle. In 1880 he removed to Emery county. Served six years as probate judge of said county. Served as a delegate from Emery county at the last constitutional convention held at Salt Lake city, in 1887. Was appointed bishop of Orangeville ward, August 12, 1882, and is acting in that capacity at the present time. Is now engaged in agricultural pursuits.

Salt Lake Herald
March 21, 1895

Final homestead entry of Elisha A. ones, of Castle Dale, Emery county, lots 3 and 4 of section 6, township 9 south, range 9 east, and lot 1 of section 1, township 19 south, range 8 east, containing 120.92 acres.

Deseret Weekly
March 23, 1895

THE DEAD.

Peaceful be their Rest.

ROBERTSON.—At Orangeville, Emery county, Utah, March 3rd, 1895, of inflammation of the bowels, Arthur Gilbert, son of Jasper and Rhoda E. Robertson; born August 27th, 1881; aged 13 years, 6 months and 4 days.

Salt Lake Herald
March 26, 1895

UTAH COMMISSION.

Judges of Election For the Emery County Bond Election.

For the first time in twenty-five days the Utah commission met in the executive building yesterday afternoon and immediately went into executive session to consider the Emery county bond question. Although disclaiming authority to do so, yet wishing to lend that county whatever authority they did have they acceded to their request, and appointed the following persons as judges of election in the various precincts of that county:

Cleveland precinct—Henry H. Oviatt, W. E. Cawley and Anton Crammer.

Huntington precinct—E. M. Johnson, Joseph Johnson and Christoffer Willcox.

Lawrence precinct—O. N. Tuft, B. D. Bunnell and E. W. Moore.

Blake precinct—Joseph Gammage, George Stanton and Thomas Farrer.

Woodside precinct—William Turner, James Colman and J. E. Randall.

Castle Dale precinct—A. E. Smith, James Jeffs and C. E. Larsen.

Orangeville precinct—E. M. Moore, Frank Carroll and A. C. Van Buren.

Ferren precinct—Frank Hitchcook, N. W. Curtis and Moses Burdict.

Molen precinct—N. C. Larsen, Joseph Caldwell and Seth Wareham.

Emery precinct—Heber C. Petty, Peter Hansen, jr., and Nephi Williams.

Evening Dispatch
March 27, 1895

SUES FOR DIVORCE.

Melinda Burns of Ferron, Emery county, has filed suit for divorce, alleging desertion and failure to provide.

Daily Enquirer
March 28, 1895

Melvina Burns wants a divorce from Miles S. Burns. They were married at Ferron, Emery county, two years ago. Plaintiff now resides there, and she says that he, wilfully and without cause, disregarding the solemnity of his marriage vows, desserted her and has been apart from her, without any sufficient cause or reason, for one year, failing to provide for her the necessaries of life. She has a little child, only 14 months old, named Miles L. Burns Jr., which she wants the custody of. She asks for no alimony.

Salt Lake Tribune
April 3, 1895

DEATH OF CAPTAIN TODMAN.

Lake Tahoe Pioneer and Father of Mrs. Goodwin.

The Virginia City Enterprise contains the following announcement of the death of Captain Todman, father of Mrs. Judge Goodwin of this city and well known by many Salt Lakers:

News was received last evening of the death in Orangeville, Cal., of Captain Todman. Although Captain Todman was never a Nevadan, he was well known to all well-to-do Nevadans who visited Lake Tahoe. He was often in Virginia in years gone by and was well known here.

Captain Todman has been for many years identified with the steamboat business at Lake Tahoe. He owned the first boat navigated upon the waters of that famous resort. He was the father of Mrs. Judge Goodwin of Salt Lake. At the time of his death he owned considerable property about the lake, and also some fruit ranches in California.

Years ago, when everything was booming in Nevada and California, there was always a big rush of pleasure-seekers to the lake, and Captain Todman made a great deal of money, which he invested advantageously in California.

He was known to all the tourists of the coast, and the portly old Captain's picture spinning mariner's yarns often graced the pages of the city papers.

He will be missed from the lake by the thousands who depended on him to steer them safely across the lake in rough weather.

Salt Lake Tribune
April 5, 1895

Land Office Filings.

Desert entry No. 4169, by Alice M. Page of Orangeville, Emery county, on lot 4, section 4, township 19 south, range 9 east, containing 39 81-100 acres. Timber culture entry No. 172, proof

Deseret Weekly
April 13, 1895

We are pleased to state that Brother Richard T. Evans is recovering from the severe attack of brain fever from which he has been suffering. His parents are up from Castle Dale and are assisting his wife to nurse him back to health.

Evening Dispatch
April 23, 1895

THOMAS H. JONES, of Ferron, Emery county, was yesterday admitted to citizenship by Judge King in the First District court.

Salt Lake Herald
May 2, 1895

LAND OFFICE.

The local land office yesterday received entries as follows:

Homestead entry of Isaac R. Behunin, of Ferron, Utah, to the southeast quarter of the northwest quarter and the southwest quarter of the northeast quarter and the northwest quarter of the southeast quarter and the northeast quarter of the southwest quarter of section 29, township 21 south, range 7 east, containing 160 acres.

Salt Lake Tribune
May 12, 1895

Spray in the Blossom.

Editor Tribune:—Fruit and Tree Inspector Fred W. Price claims, in your issue of April 26th, that it is injurious and against the law to spray fruit trees while they are in bloom. Now, Professor E. S. Richman of the Agricultural College at Logan claims it is the best to spray while the trees are in bloom. I have followed Richman's advice, and, as a result, my fruit has been awarded a diploma two years in succession at the D. M. & A. fairs, held in your city, and also a medal at the World's Fair. Will you kindly tell a subscriber to the Semi-Weekly Tribune who is right, E. S. Richman or F. W. Price? I think I have proved Professor Richman's theory the right one. Respectfully yours,

JOHN C. LEMON.

Ferron, Utah, May 6, 1895.

‌ENTION ROSTER.

List ‌cers, Members and Standing Committees.

Th‌ing is a complete list of the office‌ members and standing committ‌ the convention, and of the ‌ost‌addresses of the members and office

OFFICERS.

Jo‌enry Smith, President, Salt Lak‌

Pa‌ P. Christensen, Secretary, Gra‌le, Tooele county.

C‌ app. Assistant Secretary, Ogden‌r county.

Jo‌ A. Smith, Enrolling and Engro‌ Clerk, Providence, Cache county.

‌ B‌wson, Sergeant-at-Arms, Ephra‌an Pete county.

‌ss S. Watson, messenger, Heber‌ satch county.

‌ Johnson, watchman, Salt Lake Cit‌

‌ Scott, janitor, Salt Lake City.

‌ H. Thorn, page, Salt Lake Ci‌

‌ Camp, page, Salt Lake City.

‌B. T. McMasters, committee cl‌ Salt Lake City.

‌ Henrietta Clark, committee cl‌ Salt Lake City.

N‌ES AND ADDRESSES OF MEMBERS.

‌ Adams, Ogden, Weber county.

‌ Allen, Kingston, Piute county.

‌ Anderson, Frisco, Beaver coun‌

‌ R. Barnes, Kaysville, Davis ‌ty.

‌ R. Bowdle, Salt Lake City.

‌ Boyer, Springville, Utah county.

‌odore Brandley, Richfield, Sevier ‌ty.

‌ G. Button, Salt Lake City.

‌illiam Buys, Heber, Wasatch coun‌

‌ster Call, Bountiful, Davis county.

‌orge M. Cannon, Salt Lake City.

‌ F. Chidester, Panguitch, Garfield ‌nty.

‌arley Christiansen, Mayfield, San ‌ ‌e county.

‌ H. Clark, Jr., Grantsville, Tooele ‌unty.

‌. L. Coray, Mona, Juab county.

E. E. Corfman, Provo, Utah county.

Charles Crane, Kanosh, Millard coun‌y.

William Creer, Spanish Fork, Utah ‌unty.

George Cunningham, American Fork, Utah county.

A. J. Cushing, Sandy, Salt Lake coun‌y.

William Driver, Ogden, Weber coun‌y.

D. C Eichnor, Salt Lake City.

Alma Eldridge, Coalville, Summit county.

George R. Emery, Salt Lake City.

Andreas Engberg, Salem, Utah.

David Evans, Ogden, Weber county.

A. J. Evans, Lehi, Utah county.

Lorin Farr, Ogden, Weber county.

Samuel Francis, Morgan, Morgan county.

W. H. Gibbs, West Portage, Box Elder county.

C. C. Goodwin, Salt Lake City.

J. F. Green, Draper, Salt Lake coun‌ty.

F. A. Hammond, Bluff City, San Juan county.

Charles H. Hart, Logan, Cache coun‌ty.

Harry Haynes, Murray, Salt Lake county.

J. D. Holladay, Santaquin, Utah county.

R. W. Heyborne, Cedar City, Iron county.

S. H. Hill, Salt Lake City.

William Howard, Huntington, Emery county.

Henry Hughes, Mendon, Cache coun‌ty.

J. A Hyde, Nephi, Juab county.

A. W. Ivins, St. George, Washington county.

W. F. James, Salt Lake City.

Lycurgus Johnson, Vernal, Uintah county.

J. F. Jolley, Moroni, San Pete county.
F. J. Kiesel, Ogden, Weber county.
David Keith, Park City, Summit county.
Thomas Kearns, Park City, Summit county.
William J. Kerr, Logan, Cache county.
Andrew Kimball, Salt Lake City.
J. N. Kimball, Ogden, Weber county.
Richard G. Lambert, Salt Lake City.
Lauritz Larsen, Spring City, San Pete county.
C. P. Larsen, Manti, San Pete county.
Hyrum Lemmon, Payson, Utah county.
T. B. Lewis, Ogden, Weber county.
William Lowe, Willard, Box Elder county.
Peter Lowe, Willard, Box Elder county.
J. P. Low, Smithfield, Cache county.
A. C. Lund, Ephraim, San Pete county.
Karl G. Maeser, Provo, Utah county.
Richard Mackintosh, Salt Lake City.
Thomas Maloney, Ogden, Weber county.
William H. Maughan, Wellsville, Cache county.
Robert McFarland, West Weber, Weber county.
G. P. Miller, Monroe, Sevier county.
Elias Morris, Salt Lake City.
Jacob Moritz, Salt Lake City.
John R. Murdock, Beaver, Beaver county.
Joseph R. Murdock, Charleston, Wasatch county.
James D. Murdock, Park City, Summit county.
Aquilla Nebeker, Laketown, Rich county.
J. D. Page, Mount Pleasant, San Pete county.
Edward Partridge, Provo, Utah county.
J. D. Peters, Brigham City, Box Elder county.
Mons Peterson, Moab, Grand county.
J. C. Peterson, Fairview, San Pete county.
Frank Pierce, Salt Lake City.

Frank Pierce, Salt Lake City.
William B. Preston, Salt Lake City.
A. H. Raleigh, Salt Lake City.
F. S. Richards, Salt Lake City.
Joel Ricks, Salina, Sevier county.
B. H. Roberts, Bountiful, Davis county.
Jasper Robertson, Orangeville, Emery county.
Joseph E. Robinson, Kanab, Kane county.
Willis E. Robison, Loa, Piute county. (Mr. Robison represents Wayne county).
George Ryan, Eureka, Juab county.
W. G. Sharp, Castle Gate, Emery county.
H. T. Shurtliff, Miller, Salt Lake county.
E. H. Snow, St. George, Washington county.
John Henry Smith, Salt Lake City.
H. H. Spencer, Ogden, Weber county.
G. B. Squires, Sugar, Salt Lake county.
D. B. Stover, Stockton, Tooele county.
C. N. Strevell, Ogden, Weber county.
C. W. Symons, Salt Lake City.
Moses Thatcher, Logan, Cache county.
Daniel Thompson, Scipio, Millard county.
I. C. Thoresen, Hyrum, Cache county.
Joseph E. Thorne, Pleasant Grove, Utah county.
S. R. Thurman, Provo, Utah county.
W. G. Van Horne, Salt Lake City.
C. S. Varian, Salt Lake City.
Noble Warrum, Jr., Logan, Cache county.
Heber M. Wells, Salt Lake City.
Orson F. Whitney, Salt Lake City.
J. J. Williams, West Jordan, Salt Lake county.

COMMITTEES.

Committee 1, Rules and Methods of Procedure—John Henry Smith, chairman; C. S. Varian, W. H. Gibbs, Charles H. Hart, David Evans.

Committee 2, Federal Relations—J. D. Page, chairman; L. L. Coray, James D. Murdock, Mons Peterson, Henry Hughes, John S. Boyer, William Buys.

Committee 3, Preamble and Declaration of Rights—Heber M. Wells, chairman; Joel Ricks, C. P. Larsen, R. W. Heyborne, Daniel Thompson, William Driver, O. F. Whitney, I. C. Thoreson, William Creer, T. B. Lewis, Andrew Kimball.

Committee 4, Legislative—W. G. Van Horne, chairman; Richard G. Lambert, Frank Pierce, George B. Squires, J. N.

Kimball, David Keith, Lauritz Larsen, Theodore Brandley, Lorin Farr, F. S. Richards, B. H. Roberts, William J. Kerr, Charles H. Hart, Ed Partridge. E. H. Snow.

Committee 5, Judiciary—C. C. Goodwin, chairman; W. G. Van Horne, Frank Pierce, Alma Eldridge, G. P. Miller, J. A. Hyde, Elias Morris, C. W. Symons, Noble Warrum, Jr., Aquilla Nebeker, Thomas Maloney, David Evans, S. R. Thurman, Joseph R. Murdock, S. H. Hill.

Committee 6, Executive—C. S. Varian, chairman; W. G. Van Horne, George R. Emery, Richard Mackintosh, Thomas Kearns, A. C. Lund, Daniel Thompson, J. L. Jolly, W. G. Sharp, Samuel Francis, J. R. Barnes, J. D. Holladay, A. W. Ivins, J. D. Peters, W. B. Preston.

Committee 7, Elections and Right of Suffrage—J. F. Chidester, chairman; A. S. Anderson, Joseph E. Robinson, Richard Mackintosh, Parley Christiansen, Robert McFarland, Peter Lowe, James D. Murdock, Chester Call, Andreas Engberg, Fred J. Kiesel, A. H. Raleigh, William Howard, F. A. Hammond, S. R. Thurman.

Committee 8, Apportionment and Boundaries—Alma Eldridge, chairman; Joseph R. Murdock, Charles Crane, William H. Maughan, John R. Barnes, Jasper Robertson, John F. Chidester, Mons Peterson, R. W. Heybourne, J. A. Hyde, Joseph E. Robinson, Samuel Francis, R. A. Allen, Aquilla Nebeker, F. A. Hammond, C. P. Larsen, Harry Haynes, Joel Ricks, T. H. Clark, Lycurgus Johnson, George Cunningham, John R. Murdock, E. H. Snow, Willis E. Robison, L. B. Adams, W. H. Gibbs.

Committee 9, Education and School Lands—Frank Pierce, chairman; Heber M. Wells, A. C. Lund, C. N. Strevell, John R. Bowdle, Elias Morris, Karl G. Maeser, T. B. Lewis, A. J. Evans, E. H. Snow, William J. Kerr.

Committee 10, Public Buildings and State Institutions—Elias Morris, chairman; H. T. Shurtliff, Daniel Thompson, A. J. Cushing, George Ryan, James C. Petersen, J. F. Thorne, J. P. Lowe, H. H. Spencer, E. E. Corfman, William Creer.

Committee 11, Water Rights, Irrigation and Agriculture—John R. Murdock, chairman; L. B. Adams, Theodore Brandley, Lauritz Larsen, J. J. Williams, H. T. Shurtliff, James F. Green, L. L. Coray, William F. Maughan, Henry Hughes, Lycurgus Johnson, Hyrum Lemmon, Lorin Farr, William Lowe, Willis E. Robison.

Committee 12, Municipal Corporations—D. C. Eichnor, chairman; A. J. Cushing, J. N. Kimball, J. D. Page, John R. Bowdle, A. H. Raleigh, Lorin Farr, George Cunningham, Noble Warrum, Jr.

Committee 13, Corporations Other than Municipal—W. F. James, chairman; G. M. Cannon, William Driver, D. B. Stover, David Keith, G. P. Miller, J. L. Jolly, R. A. Allen, Charles H. Hart, Aquilla Nebeker, Thomas Maloney, Fred J. Kiesel, S. R. Thurman, E. H. Snow, William Buys.

Committee 14, Public Lands—L. B. Adams, chairman; A. S. Anderson, S. H. Hill, H. G. Button, B. H. Roberts, J. P. Lowe, William Creer.

Committee 15, Revenue, Taxation and Public Debt—G. M. Cannon, chairman; George B. Squires, Harry Haynes, Jacob Moritz, C. N. Strevell, Robert McFarland, James D. Murdock, Peter Lowe, William J. Kerr, Chester Call, A. W. Ivins, David Evans, Abel J. Evans, Moses Thatcher, Hyrum Lemmon.

Committee 16, Salaries of Public Officers—Richard Mackintosh, chairman; George R. Emery, T. H. Clark, Thomas Kearns, H. H. Spencer, W. B. Preston, John S. Boyer, Ingwald C. Thoresen.

Committee 18, Labor and Arbitration—C. N. Strevell, chairman; D. C. Eichnor, Jacob Moritz, Lauritz Larsen, Ed Partridge, Andreas Engberg, J. D. Peters.

Committee 19, Printing—Richard G. Lambert, chairman; John R. Bowdle, Charles H. Hart.

Committee 20, Militia—George Ryan, chairman; C. W. Symons, D. B. Stover, Jasper Robertson, Ed Partridge.

Committee 21, Manufactures and Commerce—J. A. Hyde, chairman; Jacob Moritz, Parley Christiansen, William Driver, Fred J. Kiesel, Andrew Kimball, Joseph E. Thorne.

Committee 22, Ordinances—R. W. Heybourne, chairman; J. F. Chidester, D. C. Eichnor, H. G. Button, F. S. Richards, Moses Thatcher, William Buys.

Committee 23, Schedule and Future Amendments and Miscellaneous—Joel Ricks, chairman; James F. Green, Joseph E. Robinson, J. J. Williams, G. P. Miller, B. H. Roberts, Samuel Francis, Karl G. Maeser, John D. Holladay.

Committee 24, Accounts and Expenses—A. C. Lund, chairman; A. J. Cushing, John R. Barnes.

Committee 25, Engrossment and Enrollment—Mons Peterson, chairman; Heber M. Wells, Theodore Brandley, William Lowe, William J. Kerr.

Committee 26, Compilation and Arrangement—Charles Crane, chairman; C. C. Goodwin, Richard G. Lambert, O. F. Whitney, I. C. Thoreson.

Address to the People—John Henry Smith, C. C. Goodwin, O. F. Whitney, Charles Crane, W. J. Kerr, Heber M. Wells, Samuel R. Thurman, Theodore Brandley.

Salt Lake Herald
June 5, 1895

GOLD STRIKE REPORTED

New Discoveries Said to Be Near Lower Crossing.

SOME REMARKABLE FINDS.

ORE WHICH IS CLASSED AS TWO THOUSAND DOLLAR ROCK.

Statement as to What the New Mexican Mining Law Means—Adjustment of the Stewart Loss Has Been Delayed a Few Days—Lead Mill Preparing to Operate on Custom Ores—Austin Plant Completed Its Run—General Mining News.

According to a communication received by The Herald from E. P. Sweet, dated at Woodside, Emery county, Dr. Hasbrouck, of this city, now representing Dr. Shores in Emery county, and A. E. Smith, of Castle Dale, have struck it rich in mining. Mr. Sweet writes that the gentlemen named have just returned from a prospecting trip in the vicinity of Lower Crossing on the Rio Grande Western and during their absence they located a large number of very promising prospects. Two of these claims are said to show gold in great quantities and if the report is true, the gentlemen have made as rich a find as has been recorder this year.

In his letter Mr. Sweet states that Doctor Hasbrouck informed him that on one of the properties located by himself and Mr. Smith, they uncovered a true fissure vein twenty feet wide, twelve feet of which contains ore very rich in cinnabar and carrying $2,000 on gold to the ton. On another claim the vein is not quite so wide and the ore averages but $200 ton in gold. gold. It is said that these properties are located about twelve miles from Lower Crossing on the Rio Grande Western, in the old Somerville mining district, near the mines or H. Hutchinson, one of which is reported to carry ore which assays $1900 in gold to the ton.

Doctor Hasbrouck expects to do some extensive development work on the properties at once and will make shipment of some of the ore in the very near future. According to the report which came in last night these discoveries have stirred the people up to a great pitch and well they may, if true, for such ore is not encountered in every prospect opened. It may be as well to take the stories which are flying about with a grain of salt until they have been demonstrated.

Daily Enquirer
June 8, 1895

Utah Postmaster Removed.

WASHINGTON. D. C., June 7.—Special to Tribune.—Martha Curtis has been removed as postmaster at Ferron, Emery county, Utah, and Mrs. M. J. Taylor appointed.

Salt Lake Tribune
June 15, 1895

Dr. William P. Winters has gone over to Orangeville, Emery county, to take up the practice left by the late Dr. E. M. Moore.   GAD.
Mt. Pleasant, June 13, 1895.

Salt Lake Herald
June 28, 1895

LAND OFFICE.

The following filings were made in the local land office yesterday:

Christen Christensen, of Chester, desert entry of 80 acres in township 16 south, rnage 3 east, Sanpete county.

Joseph Burkeholder, of Moab, desert entry of 160 acres, unsurveyed, in township 26 south, range 23 east, Grand county.

Francis D. Clift, of Salt Lake City, final proof of desert entry of 160 acres in township 1 north, range 2 west, Salt Lake county.

The heirs of Neriah Lewis, of Richmond, final proof of timber culture entry of 40.29 acres in township 13 north, range 1 east, Cache county.

Rodney Swazey, of Orangeville, homestead entry of 80 acres in township 17 south, range 7 east, Emery county.

Doctor G. W. Shores:
Dear Sir.—Another two weeks finds me feeling much better. My heart beats more regularly now, my hands and feet are warm and I am not bloated as I was. I feel more natural than I have for over a year. Respectfully,
MRS. B. HUNTINGTON,
Orangeville, Utah.

Daniel Thomander has accepted a position as teacher in the district schools of Ferron Emery county He intends to make his home in that county before long

Emery County Convention.

A county convention of the Republican party of Emery county will be held at Castle Dale on Tuesday, Aug. 20th. 1895, at 10 o'clock a. m., for the purpose of electing seven delegates to the Republican State convention held at Salt Lake city Aug. 28, 1895; also for the election of a county chairman. Delegates to be elected and apportoined as follows:

Ferron. 8
Huntington 6
Emery......... 5
Orangeville..... 4
Castle Dale...........................4
Molen...............................2
Cleveland............................ 3

                    Total   32

O, SEELY, Territorial committemen.
H. S. LOVELESS, Jr,, County Sec'y.

Daily Enquirer
August 10, 1895

Emery County Census.

Precincts	Population
Huntington	987
Cleveland	507
Castle Dale	533
Lawrence	190
Orangeville	672
Ferron	549
Molen	206
Emery	481
Blake	123
Woodside	132
Total	4,390

Males, 2308.

Females, 2082.

366 more males than females.

Deseret Weekly
August 17, 1895

ORANGEVILLE NEWS.

ORANGEVILLE, Aug. 7, 1895.

I promised in my last letter to the NEWS that I would say something about this country in the near future. Will now say to those seeking homes that this is the place to come, as there is land here for sale on reasonable terms. And right now would be a good time to see the land, as you can now see what it produces. You will

see the crops on it, which are fine.
There will be an abundant harvest
this year. Times are livening up a
little here to what they have been,
although money is yet scarce.

The lumber and shingle men are
busy at their trade, and the products
are beginning to come into town now
from the mountains. Good lumber can
be had twenty-five miles distant for
from $6 to $10 per thousand, and shingles at $1.50 per thousand.

Fencing is as yet quite plentiful,
from fifteen to twenty miles distant.

The New State Roller mill here has
done a wonderful business since it
started last October. Flour at this
season of the year has always been from
$2.50 to $3.50 till this season. It is now
only $1.50, and that first class roller mill
flour, instead of burr mill flour, and
plenty of it on hand; and it is taking
good in the market everywhere.

We are very much in need of some
very good tradesmen here of different
kinds, more especially a good shoemaker, or cobbler, and brick makers.

We are going to have another paper
published at Price—a Republican paper
I believe; its name will be the Castle
Valley *News*. I think we will be able
to have one published at Orangeville
in the near future.

I would not advise any one to sell
out their property till they come and
see our country, as we would like to
have them satisfied when they come.

          A. ANDERSON.

Conference at Ferron was well attended on Sunday and Monday. Besides the Stake authorities, Apostle John Henry Smith was present, and delivered remarks adopted to the condition and circumstances of the Saints It was one of the most enjoyable conferences held in this Stake.

Price, Aug. 17.

Emery county, by Wm. K. Reid attorney-at law, has filed suit for $324 80 and costs against P. C. Borresen, sheriff of Emery county, C. P. Anderson, justice of the peace of Castle Dale precinct, F. A. Killpack and C. E. Kofford. The county claims to have been damaged by the defendants appropriating scrapers, plows, spikes, etc., under the pretense of collecting a judgment obtained against the plaintiff in favor of Killpack out of the justice's court. Kofford was Killpack's attorney.

MUSIC AND MUSICIANS.

The next notable musical event will be the concert to be given at the First Congregational church on Tuesday evening by W. C. Carl, the famous New York organist, whose recitals on the coast have been so uniformly successful. He will be aided by well known musicians, and the full programme will be as follows:

Concert Piece (Ms. new).........
.....................B. Luard Selby
Written expressly for Mr. Carl.
(a) Pastoral, new.George McMaster
(b) Gavotte, dans le style an-
cien ....Charles Neustedt
Arranged by Mr. Carl.
Fugue in D major......J. S. Bach.
Mr. W. C. Carl.
Piano Solo—Rhapsodie No. 2.....Liszt
Mill Lillie Oliver (pupil of Mr. Rad-
cliffe.)
Cavatina—"In questo Semplice"..
.... Donizetti
Mrs. Agnes Keane McNally.
(a) Caprice in B flat...Alex. Guilmant
(b) Marche aux Flambeaux......
W. C. Carl.
Recitation .... Selected
Mrs. McNally.
(a) Bridal Song (Wedding Sym-
phony) .... Goldmark
(b) Toccata, G major.....T. H. Dubois
W. C. Carl.

* * *

Following is the programme for the open air concert to be given by Held's band at Liberty park at 4:30 p. m. today:
March—Beau Ideal.............. Sousa
Overture—Night Wanderer..V. Moskau
Gems of Germany, "German
Songs" .... Kuhner

Gavotte—"The Lover's Dream"
........................J. O. Casey
Waltzes—Il Nino................Jaubau
Grand medley, Ye Olden Times
.... Beyer
Dance—Characteristic .... Perkins
March—Randolph .... Hall

* * *

Following is the programme for the

open air concert to be given by the Sixteenth Infantry band at Fort Douglas at 5 p. m. today:

"Star Spangled Banner."
Overture, "Allessandro Stradella". ....Flotow
Medley, "Bric-a-Brac"..........Missud
Waltz, "Edinburgh" ....Bonnisseau
Selection fr Don Juan..........Mozart
Danza, "A Pearl of Madrid".......
....Bachmann
"Nearer My God to Thee" (Paraphrase) ....Reeves
"Hail Columbia."

* * *

The entries for the great Eisteddfod to be held at the tabernacle next month are closed and the list is as follows:

No. 1—Grand chorus of 125 mixed voices, four have entered: viz, Denver chorus, Henry Housely leader; Salt Lake chorus, C. J. Thomas leader; Ogden chorus, Squire Coop leader; Salt Lake Amateurs, H. S. Ensign leader.

No. 2—Military band contest, two entries—Denhalters, F. Christensen leader; First Regiment, John Held leader.

No. 3—Male chorus, five entries—Ogden male chorus, Squire Coop leader; Orpheus club, A. H. Peabody leader; Malad Choral club; Harmony chorus, H. S. Ensign leader; Salt Lake chorus, C. J. Thomas leader.

No. 4—Ladies' chorus, three entries—Ogden Female chorus; "Cecelias," Salt Lake; "Belle Cantos."

No. 5—Miscellaneous chorus, eight entries—Lehi ward choir, J. L. Gibb, leader; Malad ward choir; Spanish Fork choir, W. T. James leader; Cripple Creek choir (Col.), A. Jones leader; Second ward choir, Ogden, W. Hinchcliff leader; Twentieth ward choir (Salt Lake), Joseph J. Daynes leader; Sixteenth ward choir (Salt Lake), G. W. Tompson leader; Twenty-first ward choir (Salt Lake), Thomas McIntyre, leader. (The two last named choirs have not finally determined to compete,

but are at work on the pieces and may yet be in the fight.)

No.6—One entry, Ogden male quartette. (It is regrettable that there is no representation from Salt Lake in this contest.)

No. 7—Ladies' quartettte, six entries, viz: four from Salt Lake, one from Cripple Creek, and one from Denver, Colo,

No. 8—Soprano and tenor duet, three entries, divided equally between Ogden, Salt Lake and Cripple Creek.

No. 9—Tenor solo, seven entries—Three of Ogden, three of Salt Lake, one of Cripple Creek, Colo.

No. 10—Soprano solo, eleven entries—Five of Salt Lake, one from Logan, two from Ogden, one from Rock Springs, Wyo., one from Cripple Creek, one one from Denver.

No. 11—Baritone solo, seven entries—Two from Salt Lake, one from Gilman, Colo., one from Ogden, two from Denver, one from Cripple Creek.

No. 12—Contralto solo, ten entries—Five from Salt Lake, two from Denver, one from Provo, two from Cripple Creek.

No. 13—Harp solo, two entries—David Jeremy, Salt Lake, W. L. Jones, Scofield.

No. 14—Piano solo, eight entries—Four from Salt Lake, one from Ogden, two from Provo, one from Smithfield, Cache county.

No. 15—Male chorus composition, twelve entries—Three from Salt Lake, one from Preston, Idaho, one from Philadelphia, Pa., one from Wilkesbarre, Pa., one from Portland, Ore., one from Ohio, four with no address.

No. 16—Best poem, ten entries—two from New York, one from Springville, Utah, one from Morgan, Utah, one from Tooele, five from Salt Lake.

No. 17—National Welsh song, fifteen entries—One from Union Daly, Pa., one from Morgan, Utah, one from Iowa, one from Castle Dale, Utah, one from Provo, two from Edwardsville, Pa., one from Wales, Iowa, one from Nanticoke, Pa., two from Salt Lake City, one from Pennsylvania.

No. 18—Best Pioneer libretto, nine entries—One from Morgan, Utah; one from Castle Dale; one from Tooele; one from Provo; two from St. George, Utah; three from Salt Lake City.

No. 19—Best historical sketch, four entries—One from Sandy Creek, N. Y.; one from Chicago; one from Ohio; one from Kansas.

No. 20—Best prose, one entry—Lloyd Jones, Denver.

No. 21—Best recitation, The Bells, nine entries—One from Draper, Salt Lake county; one from West Jordan, Salt Lake county; two from Denver; one from Portland, Or., one from Bingham City; three from Salt Lake.

A number of entries have come in since the first, but had to be barred out on account of rule No. 10, which forbids anyone contesting whose names are not in the hands of the secretary by Sept. 1.

When there are more than five for any contest, a preliminary examination will be held before the adjudicators on the morning of Oct. 3 at the Assembly hall. The tickets for this mammoth event will be on sale at all the principal stores next week. The season tickets, which will admit to the two days' festival, will be $1 each. Single admission 50 cents.

The committee has offered a premium of $25 and $10 for the ward or church choir selling the most tickets. Treasurer Elias Morris would like the leaders of these organizations to call at his office, 21 West South Temple street, and get tickets.

The adjudicators will be Haydn Evans, T. J. Davies and Dr. J. J. Mason, all of the east.

Professor William Apmadoc, of Chicago, will conduct the great festival. Ex-Governor A. L. Thomas will be president of the first day's exercises and Governor C. W. West will preside on the second day. Excursions from all points will begin on Tuesday, Oct. 1.

The following filings were made in the local land office under date of Sept. 9. Ephraim Green, of Vernal, homestead entry of 160 acres in township 4 south, range 21 east, in Uintah county. Karrick M. Swanson, of Ferron, desert entry of 40 ocres in township 20 south, range 1 east. in Emery county.

The case of Abner Kofford vs. Lawence Lund, Andrew Olsen and Jack Llewellyn. The plaintiff Kofford is brother of Mone Kofford of Kofford & Mickie fame. Mone bought a horse in August 1894 from one Justensen at Spring City, Justensen purchased the animal from one Hansen who owned him several years during which time he was dispossessed of him for about two years by a man borrowing the animal and failing t return him. Abner and Mone Kofford were partners and while Abner was at Orangeville the horse was taken from him to Castle Dale. Lund and Olsen, it is alleged, were in in a combination which succeeded in getting the animal in possession of Llewellyn.

RALLY AT FERRON.

The citizens of Ferron turned out en masse last evening to hear the speakers. The brass band was in attendance, discoursing sweet strains of music.

Mr. Scott, superintendent of schools for Emery county, was the first speaker. Mr. Scott being for education spoke of the people being educated in politics and fully understanding the principles of the party to which they belong. He quoted the platform of the Republican party, explained free trade and protective tariff and gave statistics under each. Mr. Scott's remarks were well received and frequently applauded.

Hon. Joseph Stanford was next. His address was the best political speech ever delivered in Ferron. Mr. Stanford is a most eloquent and magnetic speaker, and a thorough expounder of Republican principles. His earnest and masterful style, combined with sound logic, carries conviction. His remarks on the home industries of Utah were especially well received.

A few days previous the people of Ferron had the honor of listening to

a Democratic orator. The burden of his talk was accusations against the Republican party, the first and foremost of these being the creating of millionaires at the expense of the masses. Mr. Stanford took up all these charges, and proved to his audience that such criminations were wholly without foundation. He also took up the silver question as advocated by our Democratic friends, giving his opponents a few posers which they could not easily have gotten around.

Mr. Stanford's remarks were interrupted by frequent and hearty applause. Conversions are steadily being made to our party here in Ferron, and we anticipate a grand Republican victory in November, 1895. Yours obediently,

_____,
Secretary Republican club.
Ferron, Utah, Sept. 15, 1895.

Land Office Filings.

William G. Cheshire of Ferron, Emery county, homestead entry No. 11,839, on north half of northeast quarter of section 29, township 19 south, range 8 east.

Salt Lake Tribune
September 26, 1895

Republican Rally at Ferron.

On Thursday evening, September 19th, the chairman, Mr. J. C. Lemon, called to order the largest audience that ever assembled at the Ferron Social hall, to listen to the remarks of the Hon. Jacob Johnson of Spring City. Mr. Johnson began his remarks by showing up the fallacy of the public bond system, which has so terribly crippled the Nation during the Administration of Cleveland. He spoke of the number of bills introduced in our last Legislature, namely: the iron foundry bill the bill for a tannery, all of which were vetoed by our Democratic Governor, thus dealing death-blows to our home industries. Mr. Johnson showed some samples of leather tanned by the canaigre root, which were pronounced by our worthy shoemaker (Mr. Theide) to be of a superior quality. The speaker claimed that such industries should have *friendly legislation.* If we are to maintain a prosperous State we must do so by industry and protection.

Mr. Johnson claimed that the Republican doctrine has for its object the upbuilding of the home, the village, the city, the State, and the whole country. The speaker pleaded most earnestly for a more mature consideration of the two political questions, claiming that by reading the history of each one and comparing them, was the only possible way of voting understandingly.

By a special request Mr. Johnson corrected and most successfully eradicated the idea in the minds of the public, that the Republican Legislature had tried to cripple the public school system. The speaker was warmly applauded at the conclusion of his remarks.

The meeting was adjourned by a selection from the brass band, after which three cheers and a tiger were given for the Republican cause of Emery county, led by our honorable friend, Orange Seeley of Castledale.

After the rally a free dance was given, and a general social time was had by all who participated. The people of Ferron are enthusiastic in the cause, and wish for more of such rousing times as was had on Thursday evening last. Most respectfully,

MARIE LORENTZEN,
Secretary Republican Club.

PETIT JURORS.

The following additional jurors were drawn: L. S. Glazier of Provo, Samuel Probert of Holden, William Baum of Heber, W. S. Peacock of Orangeville, T. G. Wimmer of Payson, Samuel Corvaby of Spanish Fork, J. H. Ellsworth of Santaquin and B. A. Stringham of Scipio.

Political Notes.

R. G. Miller, candidate for State Senator in the Twelfth district, writes Chairman Cannon from Castle Dale that good meetings are the rule, and the prospect of the party's success excellent.

BANNER WEEK IN EMERY.

John James and John Nicholson Visit Every Precinct.

Correspondence Tribune.]

Huntington, Emery County, Oct. 31, 1895.—This has been a banner week for Republicanism in Emery county. On Monday last John Nicholson and John James of Salt Lake arrived here and visited every precinct in the county, meeting with enthusiasm and success everywhere. They have been accompanied by local Republican State candidates.

Mr. Nicholson has given special attention to the new "Declaration of Independence," and so effectually annihilated that peculiar document, depicting its inconsistencies and inaccuracies that many of the Democrats have failed to swallow it on the day set apart for its ratification.

The bond question, the Wilson-Gorman-Brice bill, the Utah Sugar factory and the hostility of the Democracy towards it, besides other questions affecting the people's welfare, were dwelt upon by Mr. Nicholson with telling effect. His arguments have all been clear, logical, forcible and acknowledged even by a number of the Democrats to be unanswerable.

Mr. James has not only contributed to the interest and success of the rallies by his pointed and perspicuous speeches, but also by his excellent singing, which captivated the audiences everywhere. His addresses have related, as a rule, to the tariff issue, upon which he has adduced strong evidence in support of the Republican principle of protection as opposed to the disaster-breeding policy of free trade and tariff for revenue only. He also delivered telling and logical addresses on the subject of silver.

The vigorous work of these two gentlemen has made converts to Republicanism in the towns of this county, which heretofore has been stronly Democratic. There is no room for doubt that if the large majority heretofore given to the Democracy is not completely annihilated, it will at least be reduced to a comparatively insignificant figure.

Following are the towns already visited by them: Price, Cleveland, Castle Dale, Emery, Ferron, Molen and Orangeville. Monday night a rally will be held at Huntington, which will be addressed by Messrs. Nicholson, James, Johnson, Miller and others.

REPUBLICAN.

ORANGE SEELY'S OPEN LETTER.

He Replies Vigorously to Candidate Rhodes's Plea.

Editor Tribune: Enclosed please find a card from Judge Rhodes, which you will publish, also this letter, in your daily. I have been personally present at every meeting held by Mr. Kofford in this campaign, and can say that the statements made in the said card are not true. That Mr. Kofford has not assailed the character of Mr. Rhodes, nor has the man White traveled with us. He was present at a meeting in Castle Dale when Mr. Kofford spoke, and he (White) made a few remarks in favor of Mr. Rhodes.

Mr. Kofford attacked Mr. Rhodes on the grounds that he (Rhodes) was not identified with the people; that he paid no taxes in the district; that he had traveled from State to State, from county to county, hunting for office; that it was a very small minority of the Democracy of Sanpete county that solicited Mr. R. to come to Sanpete to be eligible for office, they being actuated by selfish motives and wishing to knife Hon. W. K. Reid and Hon. Ferd Erickson, who were both residents of this district, and who held certificates equal with Mr. R.

Mr. Kofford urged his reasons why Mr. R. should not be elected with his usual vim and vigor, but did not say anything derogatory to the character of Mr. Rhodes, and did not call him a carpet-bagger or any opprobrious names.

I have never heard that Mr. Rhodes was starving while in this county, and that he had not had a decent meal while here. But there is one thing sure, that Mr. R. will go belly-up in this district at the coming election. Yours truly, ORANGE SEELY.
Castle Dale, Emery Co., Oct. 31st.

[The "card" is a circular from Rhodes, wherein he denies having said that he didn't have a decent meal while in Emery county; that if defeated he had no use for the country and would leave it; and that he was a carpet-bagger.]

Salt Lake Herald
November 10, 1895

Simon Webb of Ferron, Emery county, desert entry No. 4,329, on northeast quarter of northeast quarter of section 25, township 19 south, range 7 east.

HOWARD ELECTED.

Emery County Will Send a Democratic Representative.

It is now quite evident that errors have been made in the unofficial returns received from a number of precincts. These mistakes, while slight, cut an important figure in districts where the vote is very close. There is little room for doubt but that Nebeker of Rich county has been elected senator, and in the Sixteenth representative district William Howard, Democrat, is undoubtedly elected over J. E. Johnson. This contest has excited much interest, and at first it was thought that Johnson was elected. The complete returns from Emery county, given below, indicte, however, that the Democratic candidate was successful:

	Howard.	Johnson.
Huntington	98	45
Castle Dale	49	56
Ferron	41	58
Cleveland	42	19
Orangeville	59	43
Molin	14	21
Emery	37	49
Laurence	16	14
Blake	8	18
Woodside	7	..
Totals	371	323
Howard's majority	48	..

Stake Superintendent U. E. Curtis gave the report of the Stake announcing that it is more progressive this year than it has ever been before. He explained the courses of study that had been pursued by the union of Castle Dale and Orangeville during the past winter in relation to carrying out the instructions given at Provo. He further announced that he had instructed the various wards to do likewise. He concluded by presenting the methods used in Orangeville Sunday school.

A sad fatality occurred at Castle Dale, Tuesday, in which one person lost her life and another was so badly injured that his recovery is doubtful. Mrs. Wellington Seeley was driving from Castle Dale to Orangville with a friend and on rounding a corner turned too quickly throwing the occupants out of the wagon. Mrs. Seeley received several bruises and was also hurt internally from the effects of which she died in a short time. Her companion was none the less fortunate, receiving a broken arm in two places, and also driving his thumb into his hand. besides receiving many other bruises, and at this writing his recovery is doubtful. Mrs. Seeley was a middle aged lady and was well known in this vicinity and especially in Wellington, the town being named after her husband.—Price News.

ANNA ELIZA REYNOLDS SEELY.

CASTLE DALE, Nov. 23, 1895.—Anna Eliza Reynolds Seely, wife of Justus Wellington Seely, of this place, met her death last Tuesday, November 19, from injuries received from being thrown from a buck board while on her way to Orangeville along with Elder William Cash, of this place, who also received some very bad bruises, a broken foot and a dislocated thumb.

Sister Seely was born in Pleasant Grove, Utah county, in 1853, and afterwards moved with her parents to Mount Pleasant, Sanpete county. During her childhood and youth she was very mild and gentle in her ways, and kind to everybody. She was married to her husband, Brother Seely, on the 26th of February, 1872, in the Endowment House, Salt Lake City. She afterwards resided in Mount Pleasant and Thistle valley, where she made many friends among the Indians of that place.

On October 18, 1879, she, with her husband, three children and Sister Mary Wilcox of Mt. Pleasant started for Castle valley, her future home. There being very little or no wagon road through the mountains they were nine days in reaching this place. One cause for being so long on the way was that they were detained one-half day by the birth of a little daughter; but the next day continued their journey, reaching their home, a rude log cabin without floor or windows except blankets for windows and the earth for floor, on the 27th of the same month.

Through the blessings of the Lord she soon recovered. Since that time she has ever been a devoted wife and mother, administering to the comforts of life in her family and to many friends.

She was the first Stake secretary in the Relief Society in the Emery Stake. In 1892 she was chosen by Sister Millicent Jameson as first counselor in the Y. L. M. I. A. of Castle Dale, which position she filled with honor until 1893, when she was called by the Bishop to preside over the Primary association, in which calling she was very diligent and faithful and won the love and respect of the little folks.

Owing to her many domestic duties in caring for her family, she was honorably released from that position, but during the few months past has been filling an office in the Woman Suffrage association, manifesting great interest in the same.

Sister Seely has been an example on the Word of Wisdom and hygienic living, for some years past. She leaves a good record as a faithful attendant at Sunday school and meetings and will ever be remembered by those who knew her, for a meek, gentle and forgiving spirit.

She leaves a husband and ten children, only one of which is married, and has gone to meet her little boy who passed away some years since. The people of Castle Dale sympathize with the bereaved family and friends.

There were present at her funeral Friday last three of her brothers and sisters from Mt. Pleasant and her sister, Dr. Ellis Shipp, of Salt Lake City; also her brother and his wife from Springville, besides many of Brother Seely's relatives.

The funeral was one of the largest ever held in this place. Elder C. G. Larsen, president of Emery Stake, and Elder Alexander Jameson made very appropriate remarks, after which her body was taken to its last resting place, where Brother Alex. Jameson offered up the dedicatory prayer.—[Com.

Salt Lake Herald
December 12, 1895

LAND OFFICE FILINGS.

Entries were yesterday made as follows in the local land office:

Charles E. Nelson, of Ferron, homestead entry of 160 acres in section 28, township 21 south, range 7 east, Emery county.

John C. Lemon, of Ferron, homestead entry of 158.62 acres in township 20 south, range 6 east, Emery county.

Salt Lake Tribune
December 12, 1895

A widows' pension was today granted to Jane Wifkin of Orangeville, Utah.
W. E. A.

Hans Olsen, the oldest person in Mt. Pleasant, and one of the early settlers, died Wednesday evening at the age of 94 years. Always honorable and honest in his dealings with his fellowmen, he had an enviable reputation, and his friends were numbered among all who knew him. Among his children living are the wife of Orange Seely of Castle Dale and the wife of the late N. B. Nielson of this place. He has numerous children and great-grandchildren. The funeral takes place today.

Desert land entry No. 4,366, of James A. Watt of Ferron, Utah, for east one-half of southwest quarter, southeast quarter of section 10, township 21 south of range 7 east, containing 160 acres.

Homestead No. 12,100, by W. M. Miles of Orangeville, for north half of of northeast quarter, southeast quarter of northeast quarter, and northeast quarter of northwest quarter of section 7, township 19 south, range 8 east.

Eastern Utah Advocate: Wellington Seely of Castle Dale passed through Price today on his way to Springville. Mr. Seely reports many new cases of measles in that town......A number of prominent irrigationists met on Monday night to consider a plan for materially advancing the interests of Castle Dale in particular and Castle valley in general.....The new meeting house though full of scaffolding will soon be in readiness for religious gatherings. The Huntington people before long, will have the satisfaction of having the largest and most comfortable meeting house in all eastern Utah......A defective flue on Wednesday nearly lost to Cleveland its large and expensive school house. From the overheated pipe fire caught to the partition during the morning session of the school and before discovered the flames had attained a dangerous headway. Fortunately enough water had been turned down the ditches a day or so before and by strenuous efforts of W. E. Cowley and others after half an hour's hard work put out the fire and saved the building. A few more minutes start or tardy aid would have made homeless the school children of Cleveland.

Salt Lake Tribune
February 17, 1896

Representative Howard.

William Howard was born in Belfast, Ireland, January 13, 1847. He came to Utah with his parents in the summer of 1852, attended the schools such as there were in Utah in the fifties and early sixties, but most of the education he has was got by study at home.

He was appointed Second Lieutenant in the Nauvoo Legion in 1865, and took charge of a small company of men in the Black Hawk Indian war in Sanpete in 1866, when he was only 19 years of age.

He was married to Miss Mary Peal on December 21, 1868. He moved to and settled in Bear River valley in the spring of 1870, and built the second house in Randolph, the county seat of Rich county. While living there he held the positions of County and Probate Clerk, Assessor and Collector, County Recorder, County Prosecuting Attorney, and Notary Public; he also held the position of postmaster from 1872 to 1880, when he moved from that county to settle in Emery county. He superintended the building of the first meeting-house in Emery county in the fall of 1880. In the fall of 1888, at a county convention, he was elected chairman of the People's party of Emery county and held the position until the people divided on party lines.

He has held the position for the last ten years of statistical correspondent of the United States Agricultural department. By virtue of that position he was appointed and received a commission as a member of the World's Congress auxiliary. He was elected November 6, 1894, a member of the Constitutional convention; he attended that convention and never missed one meeting during the sixty-eight days of its session, and missed roll-call but once. He signed the Constitution of Utah at forty-seven minutes past 12 o'clock on the 5th day of May, 1895.

He was nominated Representative of the first State Legislature at a convention held at Orangeville September 21, 1895, and was elected as a Democrat by 48 majority on the 5th day of November following, in a total vote of 694.

He was a member and chairman of the delegation to the Democratic State convention held in Ogden September 5, 1895.

Provo Pickings.

PROVO, Feb. 18.—A social gathering of about fifty friends of Abraham E. Haliday was held at the Haliday residence last evening. The occasion being the fortieth anniversary of Mr. Haliday's birth.

Three small boys named Brown, Allen and Burless, aged about 12 years, ran away from their homes in the Third ward yesterday. They started for Orangeville and tried to get more of their playmates to join them. Up to this writing they have not been found.

Sidney Swazey, of Orangeville, was tried before Judge Johnson at Castle Dale Thursday on a charge of grand larceny. Swazey was accused of stealing two steers, the property of N. S. Nielson, of Mount Pleasant. Swazey claimed to have got the steers from Al. Peterson who acts as foreman for Nielson. The jury brought in a verdict of not guilty. Ferd Erickson and O. H. Hoffman prosecuted and Sam A. King of this city defended.

Sidney Swazey, of Orangeville, was tried before Judge Johnson at Castle Dale Thursday on a charge of grand larceny. Swazey was accused of stealing two steers, the property of N. S. Nielson, of Mount Pleasant. Swazey claimed to have got the steers from Al. Peterson who acts as foreman for Nielson. The jury brought in a verdict of not guilty. Ferd Erickson and O. H. Hoffman prosecuted and Sam A. King of this city defended.

Judge Jacob Johnson of Sanpete, passed through Provo today on his way home from Castle Dale, where he has been holding a term of the Seventh district court.

Attorney Sam A. King returned to Provo today, from Castle Dale, where he went to try a larceny case.

Attorney A. B. Edler of Salt Lake, is in Provo today and has been in consultation with his client Hayes the greater part of the day.

The work on Ferron's roller mill is well under way, the millsite is said to be among the best in the state, and the machinery is the best that can be had.

Porter Price, who has been here at Ferron some eleven months, left last Wednesday for Draper, Salt Lake county.

Mr. Watterson, of Farmington, was in Ferron the other day. He is to furnish machinery for the new mill.—Castle Valley News.

Ephraim Enterprise
February 26, 1896

The Castle Dale Court.

Provo, Feb. 21.—S. A. King returned yesterday from Castle Dale, where he has been defending Sidney Swasey, son of Rodney Swasey of this city. Young Swasey was accused of grand larceny, by stealing two steers, the property of N. S. Nielson of Mt. Pleasant, but he proved that he bought the steers in question from Al Peterson foreman for Nielson, and was acquitted. Ferdinand Erickson of Mt Pleasant and O. L. Hoffman of Price prosecuted. S A. King was assisted in the defense by Charles Koffard, a brother of the notorious Mone Koffard, one of the slayers of Sheriff Burns Charles was recently admitted to practice at the bar at the term of the court held at Manti.

The only other matters of business that came before his honor, Judge Johnson at the term of court held at Castle Dale was the hearing of the pleas of guilty of three other men of grand larceny, by stealing a mule, horse, bridles, saddles, etc. Two were given one year each in the penitentiary and the other, being young, was sent to the reform school.—Tribune.

Manti Messenger
February 28, 1896

Two men from Castle Valley were arrested here and taken to Moab a few days ago, charged with stealing a branded calf near Moab and hauling the same in a wagon to their home near Castle Dale.

Ephraim Enterprise
April 8, 1896

Notice of Publication

(2857.)

LAND OFFICE AT SALT LAKE CITY UTAH.
MARCH 26, 1896.

Notice is hereby given that the following named settler has filed notice of his intention to make final proof in support of his claim, and that said proof will be made before the County Clerk of Emery county, Utah, at Castle Dale, Utah, on May 16, 1896, viz: Niels B. Adler, H. E. No 9042, for the S. ½ N. W. ¼ Sec. 3, S. E. ¼ N. E. ¼ N. E. ¼ S. E. ¼ Sec. 4, Twp. 20 South, Range 8 East.

He names the following witnesses to prove his continuous residence upon and cultivation of said land, viz:

Orange Seely, Wellington J. Seely, George H. Bruno, Albert Cloward, all of Castle Dale, Utah.

BYRON GROO,
Register.

First Publication April 1.

Provo Daily Enquirer
April 16, 1896

DR. Allen returned today from Castle Dale, where he removed a 40 lbs. tumor from the abdomen of the wife of President C. G. Lareen. She has been a sufferer for five years and this operation was resorted to as a last chance. It was very successfully done, but she is a precarious condition. Dr. Allen leaves this afternoon for Manti.

Notice for Publication.

No. 2886.

LAND OFFICE AT SALT LAKE CITY, UTAH.

APRIL 25, 1896

Notice is hereby given that the following named settler has filed notice of his intention to make final proof in support of his claim, and that said proof will be made before the County Clerk of Emery county, Utah, at Castle Dale, Utah, on June 6, 1896, viz: James S. Fullmer, H. E. No 9259, for the S. W. ¼ S. E. ¼ and S. E. ¼ S. W. ¼ Sec. 19, Twp. 18 South, Range 8 East.

He names the following witnesses to prove his continuous residence upon and cultivation of, said land, viz

Samuel R. Jeukes, O. W. Sitterud, Thomas Fullmer, George Fullmer of Orangeville, Utah.

BYRON GROO,
Register.

First Publication April 29.

In the European Mission.

ARRIVALS.—The following named Utah Elders arrived in Liverpool per American Line steamer Boigenland on April 17, 1896: For the British mission—Edwin F. Parry and George Hilton of Salt Lake City; H. C. Jacobs, Jr. of Ogden; Henry Blackburn of Orderville; Joseph G. Schofield of Spring City. For the Scandinavian mission—Anton P. N Peterson of Scipio; Thos. Halversen of Spanish Fork; P. P. Siggard of Brignam City. For the Swiss and German mission—John Zwahlen of Ferron. The Elders for Scandinavia continued their journey toward Copenhagen on the afternoon of the 17th, and Elder Zwahlen proceeded towards Berne on the 18th. All were feeling well.

Also on the same company's steamer Waesland, on April 22, 1896, there arrived: For the British mission—William Campbell and John W. Robertson of Salt Lake City; John H. Hammond of Mancos, Colorado; Joseph S. Broadbent and Joseph F. Russon of Lehi; Abel M. Roper of Oak City; Peter Allan of Bluff City. For the Scandinavian mission—Christian Johnson of Thurber; George A. Sanders of South Cottonwood; Charles A. Thompson of Oasis; Henry Wing of Provo. For the Swiss and German mission—Arthur W. Hart of Logan; Isaac R. Barton of Salt Lake City. With this company came James Ovens of Fairview, Wyoming, Mrs. Agnes E. Barton and Miss Barbara B. Barton of Salt Lake City, who are over on a visit.

EMERY COUNTY.

Official Salaries are Fixed—They are Kept Low.

The county commissioners of Emery county, pursuant to law, met May 4th at Castle Dale for the purpose of fix g the salaries of county officers.

A resolution was finally passed fixing the salaries of county officers as follows: County commissioners, $150, sheriff, $450; county clerk, $800; recorder, $400. These amounts to include all assistance and deputy work, and are for the year.

Superintendent of schools, $400 per annum; surveyor, $100; janitor, $120 for 1896.

The coroner's salary was not set, as that officer had failed to qualify.

Andrew Neilson of Ferron and A. E. Gibson of Cleveland were appointed bee inspectors for the districts of Ferron and Molin and Cleveland and Desert Lake respectively.

C. H. Oliphant of Orangeville was appointed tree inspector for Emery county.

John S. Curtis, Justice of the Peace or Orangeville, resigned, and Ole Sorensen was appointed to fill the vacancy.

Bills were allowed to Skelton & Co' of Provo for stationery and ordered paid.

The contract with A. E. Smith for abstracting the county reords developed considerable discussion, but as Mr. Smith had done all the contract required the books were accepted and the amount, $500, was allowed.

Superintendent of Schools J. H. Scott and George Miller were appointed a committee to assist Mr. Smith to audit the abstract books, and they were found correct according to the records.

The county school examination will be held in Castle Dale on the 12th and 13th of June.

Provo Daily Enquirer
May 13, 1896

Court at Price.

Judge Johnson is holding a term of court at Price. The following jurors were empaneled: W. H. Sturges, Scofield; M. H. Beardsley, Helper, Samuel Harrison. Winter Quarters, E. D. Fullmer, Spring Glen; E. C. Lee, Minnie Maud; Levi Simmons, Price; George Drury, Spring Glen; Eugene Miller, Castle Gate; Fred Grames, Minnie Maud; C W. Allred, Price; S. J. Padfield, Jr., Winter Quarters; J. J. Bearnson, Winter Quarters; John Holey, Castle Gate, Henry Fiack, Price The vanire was ordered,

A number of naturalizations were effected, most of the applicants being residents of the coal-mining camp of Castle Dale as follows: Henry Wade and Richard White, natives of England, Christmas Davis, Thomas W. Lewis and James Evans of Wales, and Louis Allanti, Christopher Sainaghi, Pieter Gerz, Calso Daniel, Carlo Ruggeri and J. Palva of Italy

The motion to re-tax costs and set aside verdict in the case of Wilson vs. Milner was set for 10 a. m. May 12th.

The second libel case against editor S. H Brownlee was called up for trial, but owing to the uncertainty of the whereabouts of the defendant, who a short time since made his exit through a 6x11 inch hole in the county jail, the hearing was postponed indefinitely,

Salt Lake Herald
May 21, 1896

IT GOES MARCHING ON.

EVER INCREASING INTEREST IN THE GRAND CARNIVAL.

Committee on County Queens Named —Miss Clarissa Thatcher in the Lead for State Queen—Great Increase in the Voting Yesterday.

The remarkable interest shown in the last few days by all classes of citizens in the midsummer carnival has resulted in a redoubling of the efforts of those in charge of its affairs to make it a success. The fact that the carnival means much for Salt Lake city and Utah has at last dawned upon prosaic citizens who have for years been content to allow matters to shape themselves and they are now beginning to realize that the city whose citizens put their shoulders to the wheels of progress is the city that succeeds in the race for wealth and importance. For an expenditure of not more than $10,000 Salt Lake city will receive from the midsummer carnival advertising the value of which cannot be computed in dollars and cents, her merchants will reap a harvest of shekels from the thousands of strangers who will visit the city and every citizen, no matter what his vocation, will be benefitted. The midsummer carnival means the beginning of a new era of prosperity for Utah and that the fact is fully realized by our people is demonstrated by the very gratifying success that the committee on finance is meeting with.

COUNTY QUEEN CONTESTS.

Yesterday the following gentlemen were named as chairmen of the respective county committees to care for the voting contests for county queens:

C. H. Woolfenden, Beaver, Utah, Beaver county.

John Rich, Brigham City, Box Elder county.

Noble Warrum, Logan, Cache county.

A. Ballenger, Price, Carbon county.

J. R. Barnes, Kaysville, Davis county.

Frank Carroll, Castle Dale, Emery county.

Jesse W. Crosby, Panguitch, Garfield county.

O. W. Warner, Moab, Grand county.

Postmaster Page, Parowan, Iron county.

Fred Nelson, Eureka, Juab county.

H. E. Bowman, Kanab, Kane county.

Alvin Robinson, Fillmore, Millard county.

J. Williams, Morgan, Morgan county.

J. W. Fulmer, Circleville, Piute county.

— McKimmon, Randolph, Rich county.

— — ——, Bluff, San Juan county.

A. L. Williams, Mount Pleasant, Sanpete county.

John Meteer, Richfield, Sevier county.

F. McPherson, Park City, Summit county.

Harry Haynes, Murray, Salt Lake county.

P. A. Droubay, Tooele, Tooele county.

— — ——, Vernal, Uintah county.

Mayor L. Holbrook, Provo, Utah county.

A. Hatch, Heber, Wasatch county.

Ashby Snow, St. George, Washington county.

— McClellan, Loa, Wayne county.

William Glassman, Ogden, Weber county.

INSTRUCTIONS SENT.

To each of the chairmen has been sent a letter reading as follows:

Salt Lake City, May 20, 1896.

Dear Sir—The executive committee of the Mid-Summer Carnival has appointed you chairman of the committee for your county, to select your county queen, who shall be the guest and maid of honor of the state queen. You are instructed to call a meeting of the citizens of your county, using your best judgment as to the means of advertising the meeting and the place of holding it. We recommend the selection of two others besides yourself, who shall constitute this committee.

If there are one or more newspapers published in your county we will make arrangements with the publisher of each paper to print coupons which will be received by your committee up to the 15th of June at 10 a. m., at which time the ballots will be counted by your committee and the result reported, as soon as possible, to us.

It is very important that you immediately send us the photograph of the lady chosen as queen of your county, that her picture may appear in the daily papers and programmes that are being prepared.

Should there be no paper published in your county, your committee will have authority to adopt any plan they see fit for electing your queen, but we suggest that your citizens be allowed to vote on the matter in some way. We will send today instructions to the different papers and we would like for you to urge upon the newspapers of your county to publish the copy and form of the coupon we send.

Should the paper, or papers, in your county fail to make such publication, then your committee may take such other steps as they see fit. We have also written to the mayor or other public officer of the different cities and towns of the state, urging them to assist us in making this the grandest celebration Utah has ever known, and we have asked them to attend the public meeting that you will call to select the above mentioned committee, and to take other steps to get the people of your county to join us in this celebration. Thousands of visitors will be in Salt Lake from all parts of the west, and we suggest to you that it would be an excellent opportunity to have some kind of float or other display to advertise your county and give the world some idea of your great resources.

The entire state militia will be called out to take part in this celebration, and the best speakers of the state will assist in Utah state's first celebration of Independence Day.

The railroads will make the lowest rates ever given, and the fireworks, the immense Chinese dragon and the unique and beautiful floats, will all combine to make the grandest carnival and celebration that the inter-mountain country has ever attempted, and one which no citizen of your county could afford to miss.

If your queen-elect cannot furnish her photograph, or cannot attend, your committee will declare the lady receiving the next highest number of votes elected queen.

Hoping that we may have your hearty support, we are respectfully yours,

H. F. M'GARVIE,
Director General.

E. G. ROGNON,
President Executive Committee.

STATE QUEEN CONTEST.

The vote for queen more than doubled yesterday, the pool last night resulting as follows:

Miss Clarissa Thatcher	176
Miss Dollie Walker	113
Mrs. A. J. Atkins (Provo)	79
Miss Lottie Nickum	68
Miss Fannie Sharkey	58

Keep your favorite above this line if you wish her to succeed.

Miss M. A. Torgenson	55
Miss Estella Engleman	47
Miss Laura Beebee	42
Miss Minnie Kiesel	24
Miss Luna Thatcher	19
Mrs. H. M. Wells	11
Miss Sadie Thomas	30
Mrs. Emiline Wells	7
Mrs. E. P. Mulhall	10
Miss Lizzie Livingston	23
Mrs. R. C. Easton	2
Mrs. Nancy Lamoroux	7
Miss Rose Nye	5

Miss Dell Miller	2
Miss Carol Young	15
Mrs. Dr. Stiehl	2
Mrs. R. A. Keyes	1
Mrs. F. J. Jennings	1
Miss Emma Dowden	8
Mrs. Harry Jennings	7
Miss Jean Groo	7
Miss Lee Dunford	16
Miss Lenora Trent	4
Mrs. Don H. Porter	1
Mrs. Murge Jennings	1
Miss Fusia Oglesby	2
Miss Ida Chandler	4
Mrs. F. S. Murphy	3
Mrs. L. M. Rich	11
Mrs. D. B. Hempstead	6
Mrs. L. Y. Brockbank	6
Mrs. Grace Scofield	10
Miss Alice Saunders	2
Miss Maud Pratt	4
Miss Marian McDonald	12
Miss Grace Wallace	2
Miss Ethel Lynn	6

CARNIVAL NOTES.

Los Angeles spent $30,000 on her last fiesta and took in $300,000. Salt Lake's enterprise should be rewarded in a like ratio.

Manager Snow, of the Consolidated Implement company has tendered to the carnival managers the use of seventeen new wagons for the floats.

Director-General McGarvie of the midsummer carnival gained his experience as a promoter at the World's fair and San Francisco midwinter exposition.

San Francisco is preparing for a celebration on the lines adopted for the midwinter carnival. Zion will yet be able to give pointers of enterprise to her sister cities.

Thirty thousand strangers visited San Jose, Cal., during the recent floral festival held there. Salt Lake's floral festival will not eclipse it, but it will be well worth seeing.

The name of Mrs. M. Shaughnessy was withdrawn yesterday from the state queen contest. Shortly after the withdrawal 100 votes for her were received at headquarters.

After today the names of all the contestants for state queen who have not received ten votes or more will be dropped from the published list until their votes have reached that number.

The committee on publicity and promotion has offered a prize of $25 for the best editorial on the midsummer carnival. Salt Lake editors are barred from entering the contest, as a committee on award will be selected from among them.

The press bureau has offered a prize of $50 or transportation to and from this city and all expenses during the carnival to the "adsmith" who constructs and publishes the best advertisement relative to the carnival. Salt Lake printers are barred from contesting.

Salt Lake Tribune
May 21, 1896

SEVENTH DISTRICT COURT.

Jury Drawn—Motions and Orders— County Attorney May Practice.

Correspondence Tribune.]

Castle Dale, May 18.—Judge Jacob Johnson opened the April term of the Seventh District court here this morning, when the following business was transacted

William S. Hinkin was sworn in as bailiff for the term.

PETERSON DIVORCE CASE.

In the divorce case brought by James M. Peterson against Karren M. Peterson, both residents of Castle Dale, the court after hearing the evidence took the matter under advisement. Plaintiff claimed that his spouse, without sufficient cause, deserted him, and refused absolutely to adorn his domicile, but Karen M. being placed upon the stand affirmed that far from there being no cause, plaintiff on the very day of the final separation and alleged desertion struck and kicked her, and otherwise ill-treated her in a manner unbecoming a loving husband. The parties are evidently ill-matched, and both desire to have the matrimonial bonds severed, but the conflict in the evidence as to the ill-treatment was such as to render it questionable whether plaintiff could properly charge desertion, and his honor said he would think over the situation and render a decision in the morning.

JURORS SELECTED.

The following jurors were selected to act during the April term: John W. Lake, Castle Dale; S. H. Cox, Orangeville; James C. Woodward, Orangeville; E. A. Jones, Castle Dale; Joseph H. Taylor, Orangeville; John Walker, Huntington; Robert Johnson, Orangeville; Heber Frandsen, Castle Dale; George Fox, Orangeville; A. A. Sherman, Huntington; James B. Crawford, Orangeville; Joseph Dennisen, Castle Dale; Alma Y. Jewkes, Orangeville; George W. Johnson, Jr., Huntington; Warren S. Peacock, Orangeville; Hy M. Reid, Orangeville; W. L. Stelson, Orangeville; Jacob Sorensen and J. Peterson, Castle Dale, and Thomas C. Wakefield, Huntington.

NATURALIZATIONS.

Joseph Dumayne, a native of Great Britain, Peter Larsen of Denmark, George Hery of Germany, and Carl Christian of Denmark, were all admitted as citizens of the United States upon passing an examination as to their qualifications.

CLOSING AN ESTATE.

In the matter of the estate of E. M. Moore, deceased, an order of final distribution was entered on motion of Charles E. Kofford, attorney for the administratrix, Mrs. Mabel Moore.

MOTION TO STRIKE OUT.

The motion to strike out certain portions of the affirmative answer in the case of Emery county vs. P. C. Borreson, C. P. Anderson, F. A. Killpack and C. E. Kofferd, was argued by Attorney Will K. Reid of Manti on behalf of the plaintiff and Attorney Whitecotton of Provo for the defendant. The motion was taken under advisement.

COUNTY ATTORNEY MAY PRACTICE.

John K. Reid, Emery's duly elected County Attorney, made, through Attorney W. K. Reid, a somewhat novel motion. It appears that the County Attorney here has never been admitted to practice in any of the courts of record, but asked, notwithstanding that fact, that he be allowed to represent in the Seventh District court any cases in which Emery county might be interested. His honor held that inasmuch as Mr. John K. Reid was duly elected and qualified as County Attorney, and in view of the laws now in force, which contemplate the prosecution of criminal cases by the County Attorney, the motion would be allowed.

CRIMINAL CASE DISMISSED.

In the case of the State of Utah vs. George Moffit, charged with grand larceny, on motion of the prosecution the information was dismissed. The same action was also taken in reference to the case of the State vs. George Moffit, on a charge of forgery.

Salt Lake Tribune
May 21, 1896

AN IRRIGATION DECISION

Question Affecting Priority of Rights Involved.

ROCKY MOUTH CREEK CASE.

Party May Take Out Water Above One who has Made a Prior Appropriation if there is a Surplus—Third Precinct Council Contest Argued in the Supreme Court—District Court Opened at Castle Dale—County Attorney Admitted to Practice by Virtue of His Election.

The decree of the court founded upon the decision of Judge Young in the case of the Draper Irrigating company against John H. Smith was filed in the clerk's office yesterday. By it John H. Smith is adjudged the owner of a primary right to the waters of Rocky Mouth creek from September 1st to May 1st each year, and to the amount saved by him by dam, ditch and flume between May 1st and September 1st, each year, not to exceed thirty inches. The chief point of public interest involved in the suit of which this is a determination, was whether a man can go above another who has a prior right on a stream, but who wastes the water, and by saving take out such water as the party below would allow to go to waste. Judge Young holds that this can be done.

Provo Daily Enquirer
May 22, 1896

Court at Castle Dale.

Judge Johnson finished the business of the adjourned April term in the Seventh district, Tuesday afternoon.

James M. Peterson was granted a divorce from Karen M. Peterson, it was ordered that the defendant be awarded custody of the minor children, and that the plaintiff pay to the defendant for the support of the children the sum of $10 per month, plaintiff to pay the costs.

Emery county vs. P. D. Barrison et al. This case was submitted to the court upon the pleadings and judgment rendered in favor of the defendant.

Jurors were selected for the July term of court.

Court then adjourned for the term.

Ephraim Enterprise
May 27, 1896

Notice for Publication.

No. 2883.

LAND OFFICE AT SALT LAKE CITY, UTAH,
APRIL 23, 1896.

Notice is hereby given that the following named settler has filed notice of his intention to make final proof in support of his claim, and that said proof will be made before, the County Clerk of Emery county, Utah, at Castle Dale. Utah, on June 13, 1896, viz: Noah T. Guyman Jr. H. E. No. 9649, for the Lot 1, Sec. 5, Twp. 19 South, Range 8 East

He names the following witnesses to prove his continuous residence upon and cultivation of, said land, viz:

David Griffiths, Andrew Anderson, Andrew C. Van Buren, George Sitterud

of Orangeville, Utah.

BYRON GROO,
Register

First Publication April 29.

Salt Lake Herald
June 5, 1896

Huntington Echoes.

HUNTINGTON, Utah, June 3, 1896.—Our Sunday school had a very enjoyable celebration on June 1 (President Young's birthday), the most notable feature of which was the braiding of the pole by twelve boys about 10 years old and twelve girls about the same age. The bands were out in full blast. The programme consisted of songs, toasts, recitations, etc. The oration, by J. E. Johnson, was well applauded at intervals, showing that it was appreciated.

Our river is higher than for years and irrigation is the order of the day.

It is reported that a boy named Kafford was drowned in Cottonwood creek a few days ago while crossing the mountains.

The newest excitement was caused at the last session of the district court at Castle Dale, where Judge Jacob Johnson rendered his decision in favor of P. C. Borreson and against the county who had sued Sheriff Borreson for selling county property on an execution issued out of the justice's court of Castledale. If space would permit an outline of this case, it would be interesting to at least some of your many readers; but let it pass, for the present at least. It appears that some of Borreson's friends are petitioning the county court to submit to Johnson's decision and not take the intended appeal, but as the great statesman Clay said: "I would rather be right than be president of the United States;" so feel the people of Emery county, as is being shown by the monster remonstrances against the above petitions now being circulated and signed in every settlement in the county, asking the court to carry the case through all the upper courts if need be.

The Democrats held their convention at Castledale on the 29th of May and appointed ten delegates to attend the state convention to be held in Salt Lake on June 6, 1896, and those delegates were instructed for silver, and Moses Thatcher et al. to represent them at Chicago.

Our town board meets often enough to accept of a resignation now and then and to pass on the reports of the several committees and officers of the town. A report was accepted at the last session from the road supervisor in which twenty-six men had been worked and the supervisor's charges were $22 for working them. The people think the town was worked harder than the men.

Crops look fine and bid fair to yield a good harvest this fall. There will be some fruit raising here, the wind and frost to the contrary notwithstanding.

Our town claims to have one of the best ward choirs in the state. Prof. Hardee intends to try for the championship at the coming Eisteddfodd contest at Schofield on July 28, 1896, so the Diggers will have a chance to measure tongues with the Hay Seeds again.

Made a Safe Journey.

The following named elders arrived in Liverpool, May 14, 1896, per American Line steamer Pennland: For the British Mission—William Stoneman, T. H. Cartwright, James H. Davis, Francis D. Hughes, Robert Cameron, Wm. T. Noall, Alfred A Garrick, Wm. F. Tuckett, J. C. Poulton, O. E. Rose, Salt Lake City; Raguel Barber, Centerville; Nathan Hawkes, West Weber; Thomas England, Plain City. For the Scandinavian Mission — Christian Poulsen, Orangeville. With the company are Elders Jesse Smith and George Comer of Lehi, who came on genealogical business; also Mrs. R. Daynes and Master Dean Daynes, who are here on a visit.

Also on May 20, 1896, by the same company's steamer Belgenland: For the British Mission—Frederick Langton, Raymond McCune, Ellas M. Jones, Salt Lake City; Alma Montgomery, David E. Randall, North Ogden, Alexander Faddies, Coalville, John P. Burt, Brigham City; Edmund Price, West Jordan; Don. B. Colton, Vernal; Barnard J. Stewart, Draper. For the Scandinavian Mission—August E. Rose, Richville; Peter Christensen; Emery. For the Swiss and German Mission—Wm. F. Olsen, Coalville. With the company were Mrs. S. A. Evans and Miss Minnie P. Musser, who are here on a visit.—Star.

E. J. Palmer of Cedar city is chairman of the Iron county committee and not Frank Carroll, of Castle Dale, as has been announced by the committee.

LEGAL QUESTIONS ASKED.

Eligibility of Legislators to Office—The Fish and Game Law.

The Attorney-General's office has rendered two opinions on subjects of general interest. One is in reply to a letter from J. Wesley Warf of Castle Dale, Utah, who asked if a member of the last Legislature, who resigned at the close of the session, is eligible to appointment or election as prosecuting attorney. The Attorney-General holds that such a man is eligible under certain conditions. In his letter he says:

"You know, of course, that the members were elected to serve until the second Monday of January, 1897, but if you resigned you would be eligible to appointment or election during 1896 unless the emoluments or salary of the office was increased during the term for which you were elected."

The other opinion is on the fish and game law, in answer to an inquiry from the State Fish and Game Warden. The law says it shall be unlawful for "any person" to have in his possession at one time fifteen pounds of trout. The term "any person" is ruled to be applied to fishermen only and not to dealers.

Castle Valley News: Mr. Jukes of Orangeville died last week of old age. ......Bishop Lamph's house in Cleveland was burned this week......John Huntington of Orangeville died of pneumonia a few days ago......John Downard had a narrow escape from a vicious cow which he was driving through Soldiers' canyon Wednesday. The horse he was riding was gored to death but he was not hurt.

SCOVILLE.—At Orangeville, Emery county, Utah, on May 31st, 1896, Amasa Scoville, son of Roswell and Sally Gregory Scoville. Born February 18th, 1815, at Vienna, Trumbull county, Ohio. He died as he had lived, an honest man and a true and faithful Latter-day Saint. Ypsilanti, Mich., papers please copy.

EMERY COUNTY FLOODS.

THE WORST KNOWN IN THAT SECTION.

Dams, Canals and Bridges Washed Away—Fields of Grain Converted into Mud Floats.

Correspondence Tribune.)

Huntington, Utah, July 17.—The greatest flood in the history of Emery county occurred here yesterday afternoon. A cloudburst in the mountains northwest of town on what is known as the Gentry mountains, was the cause, and soon the Huntington river was filled to overflowing. The mud, water and driftwood swept everything before them.

All the dams in the Huntington river, which were used for turning the water into the various canals, are carried away by its tremendous force.

The bridge just north of town, which cost the county $800, is almost gone. It was only through the efforts of the citizens that it was saved. The damage to the bridge alone is $150.

All of the land along the river is flooded; in many instances people have lost their entire crops. Where a few moments before stood nice fields of grain, nothing can now be seen but a field of mud and driftwood.

Every canal in the vicinity is washed out.

The Cleveland canal is broken in several places, and it will take weeks before water can reach Cleveland. The inhabitants are entirely without water.

The Huntington canal is also washed out in several places, and the town is without water even for culinary purposes. The damage in the neighborhood will augment several thousand dollars.

Word comes that Castle Dale experienced a like flood a few days ago, and that the damage there is even greater than at Huntington.

It is reported that the farm of Orange Seeley and many others are entirely covered with mud and debris, even the hay which was cut and piled cannot be seen.

CASTLE GATE CHIPS.

CASTLE GATE, July 20, 1896.—One of the most interesting as well as amusing trials took place here on Friday night, the case being one of scandal, between Eugene Santschie, plaintiff, and Louis Allant and wife, defendants. Damages to the amount of $290 being claimed. S. R. King, of Provo, and Willey L. Brown, of Salt Lake city, were the lawyers employed on the case, a jury of four good men and true were called in to give their decision on the result of the evidence adduced, and it was racy enough, sure. The parties were foreigners and the witnesses were natives of all Europe, two interpreters had to be sworn to make the evidence intelligible to the jury. It was near midnight when the jury was empaneled, and then the legal fight commenced, in which the judge came in for a good share. After the atmosphere was cleared from the sulphuric taste caused by the evidence, the case was put into the hands of the jury, at about 2:30 a. m., who brought in a verdict of guilty as charged in the indictment, with damages to the amount of $125, not including costs. The case will be appealed, as it ought to be.

Professor John P. Meakin, of Salt Lake city, tonight organizes his club on dramatic culture and elocution. It is to be hoped that many will avail themselves of this opportunity of education.

Alex Jameson, of Castle Dale, accompanied by his estimable wife, were in Castle Gate yesterday on ecclesiastical business. He is one of the patriarchs of this stake.

On account of the muddy state of the river, caused by the freshets of last week, the mine laid idle Friday, the boilers being choked up, and in consequence they could not run the electric motors.

Quite a number of local politicians went to the metropolis to take in the ratification, and they have returned filled up with nothing but Bryan, Sewall and silver.

Yours respectfully,
W. T. LAMPH.

SCOFIELD EISTEDDFOD.

A grand Eisteddfod was held at Scofield, Carbon county, July 28th and 29th, 1896, under the auspices of the Carbon County Musical association. There was a fair attendance of well dressed and respectable people, and the proceedings gave general satisfaction.

The Eisteddfod was opened by singing the chorus Star Spangled Banner, by the audience, led by Prof. H. E. Giles.

Address by Governor Heber M. Wells, who spoke in favor of the Eisteddfod, and said he considered it an honor to be called to preside over its meetings. His patriotic speech was well received by the audience.

Tenor solo, Ye Breezes that Blow, sung by W. T. Evans, to whom was awarded the $5.

Mr. Ferguson of Provo was called for a comic song and responded to the satisfaction of the audience.

The prize of $5 was awarded to Hugh Hunter, Scofield, for playing "Pibroch of Donald Dhu," on the highland military bagpipes.

Contest recitation for adults, "Asleep at the Switch," three contestants; the prize of $3 was awarded to Libby Walton, Scofield.

Soprano and alto duett, "Love was playing hide and seek" (Gwent), was rendered by the Swinger Brothers; no contest. The boys have done well under the circumstances. They are the favorites of the whole camp.

Organ and solo selection by Prof. Giles.

There was no contest on the ladies' chorus, "Spring Morning;" the prize of $15 was awarded to the Scofield Chorus Club, which sang very well.

The afternoon session was closed by singing "The Land of my Fathers," by Wm. T. Evans, the audience joining in the chorus.

The Tuesday night session was opened by singing "America" by the audience, led by Prof. Giles.

Address by Hon. J. R. Sharp, who took the chair, as Governor Wells had to go home. He paid a tribute to the Welsh and the Scotch for their patriotism and love of music and literature. His address was a master-piece, and ought to be printed.

There were two contestants for the bass solo, The Mighty Deep; the prize of $5, was awarded to John Wood, Scofield.

Mr. Hunter played Mrs. McClow Highland Fling on the bag pipes, Mr. Ferguson dancing in the Highland costume.

Prof. John P. Meakin of Salt Lake city, another Celt, recited The Drummer. It was very comical, and was encored.

The Winter Quarters, male voice club, sang Invocation to Harmony (Stephens) the baton was awarded to William T. Evans, the conductor, but the prize of $50.00 was withheld until the next Eisteddfod.

Singing the comical song, The Man that broke the bank of Monte Carlo, by Peter Elliott, Salt Lake city.

Singing, Clamoring Over the Hillside, by Swinger brothers; very good and was encored.

The Winter Quarters, male voice club, sang Invocation to Harmony (Stephens) the baton was awarded to William T. Evans, the conductor, but the prize of $50.00 was withheld until the next Eisteddfod.

Singing the comical song, The Man that broke the bank of Monte Carlo, by Peter Elliott, Salt Lake city.

Singing, Clamoring Over the Hillside, by Swinger brothers; very good and was encored.

Singing, the Pilgrim's Chorus, by the Scofield choir, under the leadership of John Hood; no contest.

Adjudication by John J. Davies of the eighty lines o' English poetry, subject, Utah; prize, $3; of the compositions that of James Dunn of Tooele, the best; the poem was read by Prof. Meakin, who recommended it to be printed, for the use of literary meetings, concerts, etc.

Adjudication by John J. Davies of the eighty lines of Welsh poetry; subject, Music; prize, $3, which was awarded to Isaac Evans, Castle Dale.

Contest selection, Best song of singer's choice; four competing; Peter Elliott and Richard T. Evans equally worthy.

Contest recitation for children, Little Joe; three competing; the prize awarded Annette Ferguson, Castle Gate.

Contest selection, Welsh song, two competing, Wm. T. Evans took the prize.

Thomas Giles of Provo took the prize of $3 for playing the organ solo, Washington Post March.

The last session was opened by singing in Welsh, The Lamb of My Fathers, by Wm. T. Evans, the audience joining in the chorus.

Contest in singing the soprano solo My Western Home (Stephens), Jennie Morgan, Winter Quarters, and Alice Browning, Salt Lake, competing; both sang well, the prize awarded to Miss Browning.

Tenor and bass duet, Flow Gentle Deva; prize $5, awarded to Evans Brothers.

Baritone solo contest, Noble Boy of Truth, four contestants; the $5 prize awarded to John S. Evans, Castle Dale.

Comic recitations by Professors Meakin and Giles—encored.

Contest selection of comic song—two competing; the prize of $2 awarded to Prof. Meakin.

Singing the second piece in the grand choral contest, "Daybreak," (Broome,) by the Scofield choir; the second prize of $50 was awarded the choir, and the gold medal to the conductor John Hood.

A vote of thanks was given to Gov. Wells and Hon. J. R. Sharp for their good services as president and conductor, and also to the adjudicators Smythe and Davies for their just adjudications during the Eisteddfod.

Mr. John Hood, chairman of the committee, and Levi Jones, secretary, worked like beavers; Ed. Morgan, Hugh Hunter, Thomas Brown, John W. Lloyd, Hector Evans, John L. Price, Wm. Edwards, Frank Mereweather, H. H. Earl and others have done commendable work, and labored under unfavorable circumstances to make the musical festival a success. The committee will make their financial sheet balance even.

They intend to hold it annually and set the one for next year earlier in the season.

The Rio Grande Western round house was well seated and decorated for the occasion. The weather turned out to be very favorable and the people enjoyed one of the most interesting and enjoyable Eisteddfods ever held in Utah.   BRUTUS.

Manti Messenger
August 14, 1896

Young Charlie Elder is making a record in this section which is not an enviable one. He is constantly up to some deviltry, and his last escapade is likely to cost him his freedom or send him to the Reform School. Charlie is only about 12 years old. Sunday he took a horse from the pasture belonging to F. W. Cox, and rode off over the mountains toward Manti. Some men on the range recognized the horse and brought the youth back. He is now in custody and will probably be brought before Judge Johnson at the coming term of the District Court.—Ferron item in Castle Valley News

Attorney-General Bishop yesterday prepared an important opinion, interpreting certain sections of the county government act relative to liability and indebtedness. The opinion, which was rendered per request of Prosecuting Attorney Reed of Emery county, is as follows:

Hon. J. K. Reed, County Prosecuting Attorney, Orangeville, Utah:

Dear Sir—I have considered your communication of August 10, 1896, in reference to the construction of chapter 121 of the laws of 1896, being "an act to establish a uniform system of county government," your particular inquiry being as to whether or not a claim allowed or a warrant issued on a claim allowed by the county commissioners is a liability and indebtedness of the county within the meaning of the said act.

Section 5 of said act, found on page 517 of the laws of 1896, provides "no county shall incur any indebtedness or liability in any manner, or for any purpose, exceeding in any one year the taxes for the current year, without the assent of a two-third majority of such qualified electors thereof as shall have paid a property tax therein in the year preceding such election, voting at an election to be held for that purpose, nor unless before or at the time of incurring such indebtedness provision shall be made for the collection of an annual tax sufficient to pay the interest on such indebtedness as it falls due, and also to constitute a sinking fund for the payment of the principal thereof, within twenty years from the time of contracting the same. An indebtedness or liability incurred contrary to this provision shall be void." Section 6 of the same act provides that "all contracts, authorizations, allowances, payments and liabilities to pay, made or attempted to be made in violation of this act, shall be absolutely void, and shall never be the foundation or basis of a claim against the treasurer of such county, and all officers of the said county are charged with notice of the condition of the treasury of the said county and the extent of the claims against the same."

LIMIT OF INDEBTEDNESS.

In answering your inquiry intelligently, it may be proper to observe that the first question which arises under this law is, what is the limit of indebtedness or liability to be incurred in any one year. Under the first clause above set out I am of the opinion that the legislature intended to limit the indebtedness or liability to be incurred in any one year to the amount of the taxes actually received for that year, without taking into consideration any outstanding indebtedness which may have been incurred during any year or years preceding. The language is plain and free from any ambiguity and is entitled to that interpretation and meaning which the words used ordinarily and in common acceptation denote. "No county shall incur any indebtedness, etc., exceeding in any one year the taxes for the current year." The same idea may be expressed by transposing the sentence so as to make it read, the taxes collected in any one year shall be equal to the indebtedness or liabilities incurred during that year. To illustrate, suppose the revenue of a county for the year 1896 was $50,000 for county purposes; that on January 1 there was an outstanding or floating indebtedness of the of the county for $10,000, and that during the year, say November 1, the county commissioners had incurred an indebtedness since the fourth day of January, 1896, to the extent of $40,000, would this amount, together with the outstanding liability of $10,000 at the beginning of the year, constitute the legal limit of liabilites of the county during the year 1896? I think not. The language of the above clause evidently means that the liabilities in any one year shall not exceed the taxes for that year; it may be said that the last clause of section 6 above set out, wherein the county officers are charged with notice of the condition of the treasury of the said county, and the extent of the claims against the same has a bearing upon the said clause in section 5, that would tend to give to that section a different meaning than the one which we have adopted as expressive of the legislative intent; these two clauses, however, I think may be construed together in perfect harmony, and if there is an apparent conflict the same may be reconciled without difficulty.

I think that in the use of the words "condition of the treasury," the legislature meant that the county officers must be presumed to know what revenue had been collected during the year, and that in the use of the words, "extent of the claims against the same," it meant that they must know, at any time during the year, the extent of the liabilities which had been incurred during that year.

THE ACT AS A WHOLE.

Reading the whole bill together, I think it clearly appears to have been the intention of the legislature, beginning with January 4, 1896, to thereafter limit the indebtedness to be incurred in any one year to the actual revenues of the county derived during that year. This view of the law is strengthened by the provisions of subdivision 14 of section 21 of the same act which provides, in substance, that the county commissioners of any county having an outstanding indebtedness on January 4, 1896, evidenced by bonds or warrants thereof, may, under certain conditions if they deem it for the public interest, fund and refund the same and issue bonds of the county therefor, etc. Reading this section in connection with sections previously set out, I am of opinion that it was the intention of the legislature to circumscribe and limit the power of any county to create liabilities in excess of their revenue. If the county was on a cash basis and had no outstanding indebtedness on January 4, 1896, then it would be impossible in any one year thereafter to have an outstanding indebtedness or liability and no funds with which to meet the same. If the county on that date had an outstanding or floating indebtedness, the provisions relating to the issuance of bonds as above suggested was intended as a relief on that account.

REGARDING WARRANTS.

Now as to whether a warrant issued or claim allowed is a liability or indebtedness, permit me to say that "liability" is defined to be "a responsibility; the state of one who is bound in law and justice to do something which may be enforced by action." [Bouvier's law dictionary.] Under this definition can it be said that an allowed "claim" or "warrant" issued upon the treasurer by the county auditor as provided by law, will constitute a liability or indebtedness against the county? I am of opinion that either or both is a liability of the county, unless they come within the inhibition of the law, and that they remain a liability or indebtedness until discharged by payment thereof. Any indebtedness or liability incurred in any one year in excess of the revenue for county purposes in the same year shall be void, and all contracts, authorizations, allowances, payments and liabilities to pay are absolutely void and are forever prohibited from being the foundation or basis of a claim against the county. I have the honor to be your obedient servant,

A. C. BISHOP,
Attorney General.

Deseret Weekly
August 22, 1896

EMERY STAKE CONFERENCE.

The quarterly conference of the Emery Stake was held in Orangeville Sunday and Monday, Aug. 9th and 10th, 1896. Present on the stand was Elder F. M. Lyman, of the Apostles, President C. G. Larsen and counselors, Bishops and leading brethren of the Stake.

After the opening exercises at 10 a. m., Elder Larsen reported the condition of the Stake, saying that so far as he knew, by visiting with the Saints and from reports, the Stake was in a healthy condition both temporally and spiritually. He was pleased to see so many attending conference under such favorable circumstances. The Stake presidency were united and working harmoniously with the Bishops. He gave timely advice on the Word of Wisdom and charity.

Patriarchs Alexander Jameson and Frederick Olsen expressed pleasure in laboring as Patriarchs; had given quite a number of blessings and noticed that greater blessings are usually given to the young than to the old.

Elder F. M. Lyman occupied the remainder of the meeting impressing on the people the necessity of planting public groves and shade trees. He said seven years ago a small public grove was planted in Grantsville; today it furnishes shade for meetings, conferences, etc. Ditches and canals should be bordered with trees.

At 2 p. m. the Sacrament was administered by the Priesthood of Orangeville ward, after which Elder Lyman spoke at length on the marked changes that had taken place since 1891, in the attitude of the world towards the Latter-day Saints, especially since the Salt Lake Temple was finished in 1893; these changes seem to indicate that the "winding-up scene," spoken of by Joseph Smith had been fulfilled.

Second day's service, Aug. 10.—Elders Orange Seely and Wm. Howard spoke briefly on the duties and privileges of Latter-day Saints. They exhorted all to works of righteousness. Bishops Alonzo Brinkerhoff, H. A. Nelson, H. P. Rasmussen, Jasper Robertson, Henning Olsen, Peter Johnson, C, W. Moore, L. P. Oveson, A. E. McMullin, Geo. Frandsen and Edwin Fullmer reported their respective wards. The reports showed that in most of the wards meetings were well attended, health good and organizations complete. Yet there is some indifference manifest by many in Church matters. Elder Wm. Taylor, president of the High Priests' quorum, said he and his counselors visited the entire Stake twice a year and found all grades of High Priests in the quorum; some scarcely ever attended meetings while others were very zealous.

Elder Lyman then pictured very vividly the many disadvantages of families removing from place to place. We should cultivate a spirit of contentment and make the best of each blessing placed within our reach. Emery county compares favorably with the most of the counties in the State. Referring to the new Jerusalem, he said it would be built in Jackson county, Missouri, and the great Temple will be erected on the spot dedicated for that purpose by the Prophet Joseph Smith. The law of consecration is the only plan by which the financial difficulties now extant could be adjusted.

2 p. m.—Elder J. W. Nixon read the declaration on Church discipline, which was presented by President Larsen and unanimously accepted. The general and Stake authorities were presented and sustained. Elder Larsen expressed his gratitude in seeing the Saints so united in voting to sustain the Priesthood. Elder Lyman then gave instructions on the proper way to administer the Sacrament; said every ward should have a low bench or stool on which the Elder officiating could kneel; all should indorse the prayer by saying Amen. In the blessing of infants, Elders should not seal them up to eternal life. Sisters do not hold the Priesthood because they have not been ordained. The speaker advised every one to keep out of debt and practice domestic economy.

The meetings were crowded and the good spirit prevailed. Much praise is justly due the ward and Primary choirs of Orangeville, under the guidance of Alma G. Jewkes, for the sweet singing furnished during the entire conference.

A. E. WALL, Clerk.

Legal Publications.

No. 3007.

TIMBER CULTURE, FINAL PROOF.—
NOTICE FOR PUBLICATION.

United States Land Office,
Salt Lake City, Utah,
August 22, 1896.

Notice is hereby given that Hans Christian Jensen has filed notice of intention to make final proof before the County Clerk of Emery county, Utah, at his office in Castle Dale, Utah, on Saturday, the 17th day of October, 1896, on Timber Culture Application No. 1057, for the East half of Southwest quarter of Section No. 35, in Township No. 21 s, Range No. 6 e. He names as witnesses Niels Christensen, Jedidia Knight, Carl A. Andersen, Lourly Nielsen, all of Emery, Utah.

47—52   BYRON GROO, Register.

(No. 3000.)

Deseret Land, Final Proof.—Notice for Publication.

UNITED STATES LAND OFFICE, SALT LAKE CITY, UTAH, AUG. 17, 1896.

Notice is hereby given that Ole Sorenson, jr., of Orangeville, Emery County, Utah, has filed notice of intention to make proof on his desert-land claim No. 3386, for the S. W. $\frac{1}{4}$, N. E. $\frac{1}{4}$, N. W. $\frac{1}{4}$, S. E. $\frac{1}{4}$, and S. $\frac{1}{2}$, N. W. $\frac{1}{4}$, Sec. 17 Tp. 19 S. R. 8 E. before the County Clerk of Emery County, Utah, at Castle Dale, Utah, on Saturday, the 17th day of October, 1896.

He names the following witnesses to prove the complete irrigation and reclamation of said land:

Jos. H. JEWKES.
Jos. G. BURNETT,
ALMA G. JEWKES,
WARREN S., PEACOCK.

of Orangeville, Utah.

BYRON GROO, Register.

Salt Lake Herald
September 3, 1896

Notes From Huntington.

HUNTINGTON, Utah, Sept. 2.—The recent rains here have been very detrimental to the farmer, as much hay and grain have been destroyed by the floods.

The town board has just appropriated $60 to repair the county roads leading into and out of Huntington.

At the late term of the district court held at Castle Dale, Judge Jacob Johnson charged the grand jury to be zealous in the investigation of the illicit liquor traffic which is being carried on in Emery county, and urged that indictments should be found against all such offenders. If the justice expected very many such indictments to be found by that particular grand jury he did not know some of the men here as well as the people of Emery do.

There is quite an excitement here over the recent gold discovery in Huntington canyon by S. R. Hill, Alex. Johnson, Hite Loveless, jr., John W. Scott and others. The quartz as also the washings, seem to be very flattering.

The Democrats of Emery county are up to the front and as usual expect to score a victory.

Salt Lake Herald
September 10, 1896

COURT.

The following business was disposed of in the Fourth district court last evening and today:

Ferron Co-op vs. E. Selman; transferred to Emery county.

EMERY COUNTY REPUBLICANS.

Solid for Silver—Delegates Chosen—County Officers Nominated.

Correspondence Tribune.]

Huntington, Utah, Sept. 15.—The Republican county convention was held on September 14th at Castle Dale. Orange Seeley and George M. Miller were elected temporary chairman and secretary respectively, and afterwards made permanent.

Committee on credentials as follows: C. C. Bookman, Alma Jewkes, Orson Robbins.

Committee on permanent organization and order of business: J. H. Scott, J. D. Killpack and Samuel Singelton.

Committee on resolutions—George M. Miller, J. W. Seeley, Jr., J. H. Killpack.

REORGANIZATION.

The committee on resolutions reported as follows, and report was unanimously adopted.

We, the Republicans of Emery county, in convention assembled, hereby adopt the following declaration of principles:

First—We deplore the action of the National Republican convention held at St. Louis which declared against the free coinage of silver, thereby taking from the people the last hope of the Republican party ever recognizing silver through independent action, and, believing as we do, that the United States cannot prosper under our present financial system, we advocate the immediate restoration of the free and unlimited coinage of both gold and silver at the present legal ratio of 16 to 1, leaving to the individual judgment of each Republican his own idea as to the best methods to be pursued in order to bring about the desired result.

Second—We renew our allegiance to the great principles of protection and reciprocity enunciated and put in practice by the Republican party, under whose wise and patriotic influences the United States has grown to be the greatest and most prosperous nation on earth. We believe in the grand triune of principles—protection, reciprocity and the free coinage of both gold and silver.

Third—With the exception of the free coinage plank in the Democratic platform we condemn it as a menace to prosperity and dangerous to our free institutions.

Fourth—We denounce the present Democratic county administration as incompetent, and ask the voters of Emery county to repudiate by their ballots such a worthless expenditure of public means.

Fifth—We invite all voters of Emery county, irrespective of party ties, to unite with us in electing the best men for the positions, to the end that an honest and economical administration may be obtained.

OFFICERS AND DELEGATES.

George M. Miller and J. H. Killpack, both of Huntington, were elected chairman and secretary respectively of the Republican county central committee.

The following delegates were elected to attend the Mt. Pleasant convention: Mr. and Mrs. Orange Seeley, A. G. Jewkes, J. D. Killpack, Samuel Singelton, J. C. Woodward, George M. Miller and A. D. Dickson.

Four alternates-at-large were also elected as follows: J. W. Seeley, Jr., Mrs. A. C. Sorensen, Mrs. Amelia Jewkes and Andrew Nellson.

Frank Corroll and Orange Seeley were elected to attend the Ogden convention and are empowered to cast the entire vote of Emery county.

COUNTY OFFICERS.

The following candidates for country offices were nominated:

Sheriff—H. S. Loveless, Sr., of Huntington.

Prosecuting Attorney—A. D. Dickson of Huntington.

Treasurer and Collector—Mary A. Sorensen of Orangeville.

Clerk and Recorder—F. A. Killpack of Ferron.

Assessor—H. M. Reid of Orangeville.

County Commissioners—A. Brinkerhoff of Emery, Samuel Singelton of Ferron, Orson Robbins of Huntington.

Salt Lake Tribune
September 22, 1896

EMERY COUNTY DEMOCRATS.

They Name a Complete Ticket—Alleged Senatorial Instructions.

Correspondence Tribune.]

Price, Utah, Sept. 21.—The Democratic convention for Emery county was held at Castle Dale September 11th, and the following county ticket nominated:

Commissioners—O. A. Wood, Huntington; H. P. Rasmussen, Molen; Nephi Williams, Emery.

Sheriff—E. Tuttle of Orangeville.

Clerk and Recorder—Ole Citron of Orangeville.

Treasurer and Collector—R. C. Miller of Castle Dale.

Assessor—M. C. Bryan of Ferron.

Prosecuting Attorney—William Howard of Huntington.

Surveyor—George Fox of Orangeville.

The convention was held and business dispensed with quickly, without any fighting. The nominees on the ticket were all chosen as delegates to the convention at Provo.

ALLEGED INSTRUCTIONS.

The Eastern Utah Advocate is authority for the statement that the Democratic county convention instructed their delegates, who were elected to attend the Senatorial convention, to support L. M. Olson of Price for the State Senate. If that convention did so instruct their delegates, it was not done during their session, and hence must have been decided upon at the private caucus held in the Advocate office. It was not, however, even ratified at the meeting, for at the convention the delegates were not instructed. L. M. Olson was once a Representative to the Legislature from Emery county, before Emery and Carbon became "two," and the record made by Mr. Olson then would fill a very large book with blank pages. That he is not the man for this office will not be disputed by the people whose interests are *affected* by the work of the Legislature.

Deseret Weekly
September 26, 1896

EMERY COUNTY NOTES..

HUNTINGTON, Utah, Sept. 16, 1896.

Our town has recently been struck with a marriage mania, four couples having launched themselves upon the turbulent sea of matrimony, daring the breakers upon which so many of their predecessors have stranded.

The wedding supper of Mr. T. O. Wakefield of Huntington and Miss Nettie Johnson of Orangeville, and Mr. J. A. Washburn and Miss Luella Wakefield of Huntington was held at T. G. Wakefield's, father of two of the contracting parties, on Monday last, when about 75 couples did ample justice to the good things of life.

Mr. Joseph A. Young, son of the W. G. Young of Salt Lake City, and Miss Laurette Brinkerhoff of Huntington were united on the 14th inst., Bishop Brinkerhoff of Emery, performing the ceremony.

Yesterday, the 15th, Mr. J. Roy Young, son of J. R. Young of New Mexico and Miss Elizabeth Wilcox of Huntington, were made one by Bishop Peter Johnson.

The two first couples were married in the Manti Temple, from where they returned a few days ago. They are all very popular young people, and start out in life with the hearty good wishes of their many friends.

Our harvest which has been somewhat prolonged on account of rains, is about gathered. Crops are very good generally, though the second cutting of hay is slightly damaged with rust.

Politics are brightening up with Bryan and Sewall in the lead. The health of the people is good.

We regret that Elder J. F. Wakefield Jr., who has been laboring in the South Mississippi conference, is very sick with chills and fever. It is to be hoped that he will not have to return home, as so many of our Elders have been obliged to do.

DEE BEE UU.

INTEREST ON WARRANTS

Those Issued by the County Prior to June 5 Last

NOT INTEREST BEARING

EXCEPT WHEN ISSUED IN PAYMENT OF WORK ON ROADS.

Opinion Delivered Yesterday By Attorney-General Bishop—All County Warrants Issued Subsequent to June 5, 1896, if Not Paid When Presented, Will Bear Interest From Date of Presentation Until Payment.

Attorney-General Bishop yesterday, in response to an inquiry from J. K. Reed, county attorney of Emery county, rendered an opinion which will be interesting to holders of county warrants for the reason that it deals with the question of the payment of interest on such warrants, or rather the non-payment of it. The opinion is as follows:

Office of Attorney General,
Salt Lake City, Sept. 30, 1896.

J. K. Reed, Esq., County Attorney of Emery County, Orangeville, Utah:

Dear Sir—I have before me your favor of some days ago which has been unavoidably delayed on account of press of business in this office.

You ask to be advised upon the following: "Controversies have arisen in this county between the board of commissioners and parties holding county warrants issued before January 4, 1896; the latter claiming that they should draw 8 per cent interest, as provided therein; the former holding that the 8 per cent interest was cut down to 5 per cent interest by the county government bill. My opinion has been asked and I have advised the cutting down of the interest from 8 per cent to 5 per cent, except in cases of certain warrants which, by order of the court, show on their face that they draw 8 per cent. This was done about nine months ago at a session of the board, when a resolution was passed, stating that all warrants issued after that date should have inserted on their face the legal interest they drew, and a great many were already in circulation without this provision inserted on their face."

Replying thereto, permit me to say that I know of no statute authorizing county courts to issue interest bearing warrants prior to 1896, excepting that of chapter 81 of the laws of 1894, which provides, in substance, that the several counties are authorized and empowered to issue warrants to the amount of one-fourth of one mill on each dollar of value of taxable property situate in the county, said warrants to bear interest at the rate of 8 per cent per annum from date of issue, until called in for payment; also provides that said warrants shall not be issued for any other purpose than in payment for labor performed upon the public roads within the county so issuing them. These warrants were made redeemable within two years from the date of issue at the option of the county. This law also provides for a special tax, not to exceed three-eighths of one mill on each dollar of taxable property within the county, with which to redeem said warrants.

If the warrants of which you speak were issued under and by virtue of this law and in accordance with the conditions therein named, they would, as a legal proposition, bear interest at the rate of 8 per cent, and would not be affected by any law enacted subsequent to their issue, or in other words, to state the rule more broadly, all county warrants issued under and by virtue of the provisions of chapter 81 of the laws of Utah of 1894, prior to June 5, 1896, the date of the taking effect of chapter 131 of the laws of Utah of 1896, known as the county government bill, would draw interest as provided therein.

Section 59 of the county government bill, provides that if upon presentation of any county warrant, the same is not paid for want of funds, it shall be registered and from that date, until funds are on hand to pay the same, they shall bear 5 per cent interest per annum. This law took effect June 5, 1896, and became the law upon this subject from that time hence.

The provisions of this law, however, are not retroactive, and can have no effect in law, upon warrants issued prior thereto, notwithstanding it operates to repeal the provisions of the law of 1894, supra.

It does not clearly appear from your inquiry whether all of the warrants of which you speak were issued under the provisions of chapter 81 of the laws of 1894, or whether a portion thereof were issued for purposes other than those mentioned in said chapter, to-wit: "For labor performed upon the public roads within the county issuing them."

The rule is well settled that in the absence of a statute authorizing the county court to issue interest bearing warrants, there can be no liability for interest as against the county. Counties are not liable to implied common law liability. Their liabilities, whether grounded in tort or in contract, are mere creatures of statute, and they possess no power and can incur no liability or obligation, except such as are specially provided for by statute. They are, in this particular, the same as the state government of which they are merely a part. The state is not liable except by its own consent, and so the county is exempt from liability, unless the state has given its consent by legislative enactment.

Answering your questions, I am of opinion, therefore, that the county courts, prior to June 5, 1896, had no power to issue any interest bearing warrants, except such as are provided for in chapter 81 of the laws of 1894, supra, and if any warrants have been issued for any other purpose than those mentioned in said chapter, providing for any rate of interest, the interest clause therein would create no liability against the county.

Further, that all warrants which may have been issued pursuant to said chapter 81, providing for 8 per cent. interest, are a liability against the county, and that the law of 1896 does not operate to avoid or abrogate the same, neither could it have the effect of reducing the rate of interest of said warrants.

I am further of opinion that all warrants issued by the board of county commissioners subsequent to June 5, 1896, if not paid when presented, will bear interest from date of presentation until funds are in the treasury to pay the same, and this by operation of law.

I have the honor to be, very respectfully yours,   A. C. BISHOP.
Attorney General.

THE DEAD.

Peaceful be their Rest.

OLIPHANT—At Orangeville, Emery county, Utah, August 25, of bronchitis, Ida, infant daughter of Charles H. and Lucinda A. Oliphant, aged three months and sixteen days.

OPINIONS BY BISHOP.

TWO GIVEN OUT BY THE ATTORNEY GENERAL.

Taxes on Lands Upon Which Final Proof Has Been Made, But No Patent Issued—County Indebtedness—Interest on County Warrants.

Attorney-General Bishop yesterday issued two opinions. One was to County Attorney Houston of Panguitch, replying to a question as to whether lands upon which final proof has been made, but no patent issued, is taxable for the year 1895, and if so, can the taxes be collected, and how. To this Mr. Bishop replies that the supreme court of the United States, in several cases, has held that such lands are taxable, and the taxes may be collected in the same manner as upon other property; if the owner refuses to pay the same, the property may be sold and whatever interest the party has in the property will pass to the purchaser.

ASSESSOR'S SALARY.

The county attorney's second inquiry is: "The county commissioners of this county have appropriated the full amount of the assessor's salary, as provided by law, for the collector and assessor, and the statement for the warrants drawn for the payment as provided by law has been sent the state auditor, with the result that no warrant has been drawn by the auditor for the part payment of the same. Our commissioners thought that the work in this county could not be done for less than the full amount provided for both offices without doing a very great injustice to the assessor and collector. The assessor says that he cannot think of performing the work for the salary as prescribed by law, and it will be impossible to get anyone to take the office, and as a result the taxes will remain uncollected. The commissioners took the view of the matter that the circumstances justified their action. Will you kindly send us information as to the best way to pursue to get us out of this dilemma?"

Replying thereto, the attorney-general says "that it does not come within the province of this office to give advice, except upon questions of law. You are doubtless already aware that under the law the board had no power to fix the salary of the assessor in any greater amount than that prescribed as the maximum salary of the assessor in the classified schedule contained in section 4 of chapter 124 of the laws of 1896.

"I have already advised the state auditor that under section 9 of chapter 124 the state is liable only for one-half of the salary of the assessor, as determined by section 4 of said act, and any statement containing an amount in excess of this amount would of course be rejected by him on the ground that the state is not liable therefor."

COUNTY INDEBTEDNESS.

The other opinion was rendered to County Attorney Reed of Orangeville and is concerning county indebtedness. This opinion may be of some importance in many counties, and the full text is given, as follows:

"I have before me your favor of October 8, in which you submit the following questions and ask to be advised thereon: First: Does sections 1 and 2 of chapter 65 of the laws of 1896 extend the limit of indebtedness of the county beyond that provided for in section 5 of chapter 131 of the laws of 1896 without a vote of the taxpayers of the county? Answering this question, permit me to say that it does not.

"Second: Has there been a decision of the supreme court of the territory of Utah rendered some three years ago, holding that county warrants being negotiable paper, should carry legal interest?

"In answer to this question I would say that I know of no such decision, and am satisfied that none was ever rendered by the supreme court."

Salt Lake Tribune
October 24, 1896

TRIBUNE BUREAU.

Post Building, Pennsylvania Ave.
Washington, D. C., Oct. 23, 1896.

Treasury department officials are in quest of claimants and owners of 516 World's fair medals and diplomas, which have been returned from the Postoffice department as unclaimed. The following residents of Utah and neighboring States are included in this number:

Utah: J. C. Terrace, Ferron; James Jenson, Cache Junction.

Nevada: H. C. Willmings, Lemville valley, Elko county; Conn Trudo, Saline valley.

Wyoming: W. W. Becks, Fossil.

Salt Lake Herald
October 24, 1896

Meeting at Cleveland.

CLEVELAND, Emery County, Utah, Oct. 20.—The first meeting opening the campaign was held here this evening. Joseph F. Dorms was chosen chairman and Agnes McFarlane secretary. William Hinkings of Castle Dale was the speaker of the evening.

Salt Lake Tribune
October 28, 1896

COLLETT AND CURTIS.

They Have Finished a Good Tour of Emery County.

Correspondence Tribune.]

Huntington, Utah, Oct. 26.—Hon. R. S. Collett of Vernal and Hon. H. E. Curtis of Orangeville, Republican candidates for the State Senate and House of Representatives, respectively, spoke here last Saturday evening to a crowded house in the interest of their candidacy. This was the last in a series of meetings which have been held throughout the county. The gentlemen are both ardent free silver advocates, but did not in their eagerness for free silver forget the important principles of protection, reciprocity and the judicious use of bounties.

The gentlemen explained their positions thoroughly and made good impressions. Certain victory, even in a Democratic county, awaits them on November 3rd.

Mr. Collett is a strong contrast to his opponent, M. E. Johnson, both physically and intellectually. The Democrats have begun their campaign by the employment of William Hinken of Castle Dale, the Democratic janitor of Emery county, who is making a campaign of education in favor of the Democratic nominees, and incidentally lauding his own skill and ability, and considering the stumper's position, the taxpayers ought to pay particular attention to his remarks.

Hon. J. E. Booth of Provo will be here Tuesday and stump the county.

Salt Lake Herald
November 1, 1896

Meetings in Emery County.

HUNTINGTON, Emery County, Utah, Oct. 30.—We have just had four rousing Democratic meetings in this county, one each at Huntington, Orangeville, Castle Dale and Ferron. The people turned out and filled the large halls to hear that gifted orator, John Howells of Salt Lake, and some of the local candidates. From present appearances Democracy will increase its vote.

MARRIAGE license has been issued to Andrew L. Van Leuven aged 21 of Mapleton, and Ida E. Jackson age 19 of Castle Dale, Emery county.

A RUSH OF TAXPAYERS

Yesterday Was the Last Day of Grace.

TAXATION OF MORTGAGES

SUBJECT SEEMS TO BE RAISING CONSIDERABLE TROUBLE.

An Opinion by Attorney-General Bishop Covering the Whole Ground—The Collection of Special School Taxes.

County Collector Spencer was a very busy man yesterday, it being the last day upon which people could pay their taxes without having a penalty attached to it. As a result the people poured into the office from the time of its opening in the morning until after the closing hour last evening. The receipts for the day were by far the largest during the year.

The subject of mortgage tax has been widely discussed and the collector has had a big job on hand explaining the point. It appears that the taxation of mortgages is not only causing trouble in this county, but that there are others. Attorney-General Bishop yesterday rendered an opinion which covers the essential points relative to the collection of taxes on this class of property. The opinion was gotten out in response to a letter of inquiry from County Attorney J. K. Reed of Emery county and reads as follows:

J. K. Reed, Esq., County Attorney of Emery County, Castle Dale, Utah:

Dear Sir—Your favor of the 1st inst. is before me in relation to the assessment of mortgages and the collection of the taxes thereon.

Your question, "How will the collector compel payment on any mortgage on which assessment has been made and what can be levied upon?" may be answered, "The same as any class of personal property."

Every tax has the effect of a judgment against the person, and every lien created by this act has the force and effect of an execution duly levied against all personal property of the delinquent; the judgment is not satisfied or the lien removed until the taxes are paid or the property sold for the payment thereof." (Section 92 of the "revenue act.")

Every tax upon personal property is a lien upon the real property of the owner thereof, from and after 12 o'clock m. of the first Monday in March of each year." (Section 93 of the same act.)

Every tax upon personal property is a lien upon the real property of the owner thereof, from and after 12 o'clock m. of the first Monday in March of each year." (Section 93 of the same act.)

"The treasurer may collect the taxes delinquent on personal property, except when the real estate is liable therfor, by seizure and sale of any personal property owned by the delinquent." (Section 125 of the same act.)

"On payment of the price bid for any personal property sold the delivery thereof with a bill of sale vests the title thereto in the purchaser." (Section 129 of the same act.)

That a mortgage is property and subject to taxation, there can be no question, when so assessed.

It will be observed from these provisions of the law that the tax thereon has the force and effect of an execution duly levied against all of the personal property of the delinquent.

I think the law would authorize the treasurer to take into his possession the mortgage so taxed, and under the provisions of sections 126 and 127, sell the same at public auction, provided the owner of the mortgage was not the owner of the real estate, in which case the tax would be a lien against the real estate and he could proceed to sell the real estate in satisfaction of the taxes on the mortgage.

As to your second question, "Have the county commissioners, under the law, the right to charge school districts with the collection of special school taxes?" permit me to say that I know of no provision in the present law which will authorize such a charge.

I have the honor to be very respectfully yours, A. C. BISHOP, Attorney-General.

Salt Lake Tribune
November 19, 1896

A DREADFUL GUN ACCIDENT.

A Little Boy of Emery County the Victim of It.

Correspondence Tribune.]

Castle Dale, Nov. 17.—A very shocking accident occurred here the other evening. Little Soren Peterson, an eight-year-old son of Marinus Peterson, was playing with a twelve-year-old son of Seymour Olson at the former's home, and the boys commenced fooling with a Winchester rifle, which it appears, an elder brother had been using during the day in shooting rabbits. The 45-70 cartridge shells had been loaded with buckshot and a shell was left in the rifle. Young Olson, pointing the gun at Soren, exclaimed, "I'll shoot you!" and the charge exploded. Had the whole charge hit him squarely it would have blown his head off, but luckily it glanced, and, starting at the corner of the mouth, tore the entire cheek into shreds. Dr. W. P. Winter was hastily summoned from Orangeville and dressed the little fellow's awful wounds. He is said to be progressing favorably, but his face will be terribly disfigured.

A Malpractice Case Dismissed—Marsh's Will Contested.

Correspondence Tribune.;

Castle Dale, Nov. 18.—Monday morning the Seventh District court in and for Emery county opened at 10 o'clock. Judge William McCarty was on the bench.

The first case was the State of Utah vs. Joseph Biddlecom; fornication. It was shown by Prosecuting Attorney J. K. Reid that the indictment was defective, and the defendant should have been charged with adultery, as the offense was committed with a married woman. Upon his motion the case was dismissed and the bondsmen exonerated. This was done in order to give the prosecutor a chance to take the case into the Justice's court and properly bring it before the District court.

Goldsmith & Co. vs. A. A. Mulholland; suit on account, dismissed on motion of the County Attorney, in accordance with stipulations.

Nephi Rhoades vs. Katy Rhoades; divorce, dismissed at plaintiff's costs, on motion of A. D. Dickson, who stated that the parties had now agreed to agree again.

J. K. Reid, administrator for the estate of J. A. Hammill, deceased, showed that he had made final settlement and was discharged.

Adjourned till Tuesday morning at 10 o'clock.

A MALPRACTICE CASE.

Tuesday morning the case of Jesse Brinkerhoff vs. Dr. W. P. Winters, in which the plaintiff sued for $10,000 damages for malpractice was called, and it stated in the complaint that the cause of action was, that on the 21st of December, 1895 at Huntington, Emery county, the plaintiff had the bone of his right thigh broken, and called the defendant in the capacity of surgeon. The leg was set, but through the carelessness of defendant, the leg healed, and was shown to be three inches shorter than before the injury occurred; it is crooked and has a large lump upon it, which plaintiff alleges is due to the defendant not properly adjusting the ends of the broken bone, and permitting them to overlap, hence plaintiff is rendered a cripple for life.

Defendant in his answer denied all the allegations, and claimed the fault, and consequent results of the injury, were for the reasons that plaintiff did not follow instructions and took off bandages and splints placed upon plaintiff's limb by defendant.

Testimony was taken at great length, plaintiff saying that his thigh-bone was broken late in December of last year, while at work in the coal mine in Huntington canyon, and he was brought to Huntington and Dr. Winters set his leg, but first was asked by defendant if he "knew his business," the doctor saying he did. The process of setting the bone was then described, and the splints, and the board reaching up to his side, and the flat-iron hanging over the foot of the bed by a string attached to the foot, and how the string broke, and the anxiety about the leg being shorter than the other one, etc., and the doctor saying it was all right.

The doctor claimed that his treatment was all right; he used Buck's extension method, and thought when the limb and the body had become adjusted to the new conditions the leg would not be short, but all would be right. He also complained that too many had a hand in the case, and that he didn't know of the weight falling off, claiming it was left off too soon. He also said the patient came out sooner than he wanted him to.

After arguments the court summed up the testimony and briefly stated the points of the case, and dismissed the case on the grounds of "no cause of action."

Wednesday—The only matter coming before the court this morning was the signing of records, etc., and court was adjourned subject to call and order of the Judge.

NOTES.

Judge McCarty has approved the bonds of a number of the Carbon county officers-elect while at Price, but has consented to attend to the remaining ones on his return from Castle Dale.

Emery county officers-elect have flocked into court during its short session here, and had their bonds approved. Judge McCarty placed the bonds of the County Commissioners at $2000 each.

The court-room was well filled during the Winters-Brinkerhoff case, in which the people of this county all seem very much interested.

W. K. Reid, J. W. Whitecotton, Sam A. King, A. D. Dickson, J. W. Warf and William Howard were the attorneys present.

No jury had been asked for in the Brinkerhoff vs. Winters case by either side, consequently the trial was taken up without one.

William K. Reid has been appointed deputy Prosecuting Attorney for Emery county by the County Commissioners.

In the testimony of J. B. Meeks for the defense in the Winters case, Attorney Reid asked witness what was said by the patient during the conversation which took place just before the doctor set the leg. Meeks replied, "He said, 'Give me another drink of whisky and have Brother H— administer to me, and I'm ready for the doctor.'" Attorney Reid said, "So he got the spirit first and then the administration?" and everybody laughed except the court.

Tuesday morning when court opened a remittitur from the Supreme court of the State of Utah in the case of Emery county vs. P. C. Burrison et al, was filed in this court by Attorney W. K. Reid. The decision of the lower court having been reversed by the Supreme court, the case was remanded back for a new trial.

Judge McCarty ordered that the bondsmen of the County Commissioners may justify before a notary public in the town or precinct where they reside.

THE MARSH CASE.

An application was made to the court for the probating of the estate of W. Van Marsh, deceased, and the Judge gave instructions to procure depositions to prove said Marsh was dead.

The estate of William Van Marsh being probated brings to mind the following. Marsh was a German, and was well educated. At times he became despondent, and once tried to shoot himself, but made a failure of it. The young man became enamored of a young lady living near Castle Dale, named Mary Jane Biddlecom. The couple were engaged, and Marsh went early this fall to Diamond mountains, where he was herding sheep for Hacking Bros., and on October 15th last he committed suicide. Before shuffling off this mortal coil, however, he made a will in his own handwriting, and signed the same, mailing it to his intended wife. He left to her all his personal effects and some property here, which will be valued at about $500. The young lady is trying to get possession of the estate, but parties here claim the estate to be indebted to them, and a settlement is asked.

THE OFFICERS-ELECT.

Correspondence Tribune.]

Castle Dale, Nov. 17.—The Commissioners for Emery county, after completing the canvass of the late election returns, have declared the following named gentlemen to be the county officers-elect:

Commissioners—H. P. Rasmussen of Molen, Nephi Williams of Huntington.

Attorney—William Howard of Huntington.

Clerk and Recorder—O. J. Sitterud of Orangeville.

Assessor—M. C. Bryan or Ferron.

Treasurer—R. C. Miller of Castle Dale.

Surveyor—George Fox of Orangeville.

L. P. Overson of Cleveland received the neat majority of 255, for Representative to the State Legislature, and it will be seen by the table herewith given that the entire Democratic ticket was elected, with majorities ranging from 255 to 759. O. J. Sitterud, the present Clerk and Recorder, receiving the last named majority on re-election. As there was only one man placed on the ticket for Surveyor, he received almost the entire vote.

The total vote cast in the county is shown to have been 1251.

JUSTICES AND CONSTABLES.

Below is the list of Justices and Constables elected in the precincts of Emery county:

Green River—For Justice, J. T. Farrer; Constable, Frank Cook.

Ferron—For Justice, William H. Worthin; Constable, George W. Perry.

Desert Lake—For Justice, William J. Powell, Jr.; Constable, L. J. Marsing.

Cleveland—For Justice, M. L. Snow; Constable, William McFarlane.

Lawrence—For Justice and Constable every man in the town received one vote each, supposed to have been cast by their respective wives.

Huntington—For Justice, E. H. Cox; Constable, R. A. Howard.

Castle Dale—For Justice, C. P. Anderson; Constable, Heber Frandsen.

Emery—For Justice, P. V. Bunderson; Constable, H. C. Christensen.

At Orangeville, Molen and Woodside there were no precinct officers placed on the ticket.

After the above canvass was completed, the regular session of court was held and appropriations made aggregating $144.95. Emery county has an indebtedness of something like $8000, and is now trying to bond for $8000, under the new State law. An extension of time for receiving bids for the bonds has been made from November 9 to December 7, 1896.

DOG COLLARS.

In the clerk's minutes an order of the Commissioners appears which might cause some curiosity with those not fully initiated in the laws of Emery county, and, of course, it caught my eye and, on inquiry, gathered some information regarding it. The order reads thus: "Clerk was ordered to distribute dog collars to the different Constables, with instructions for them to enforce the law."

It appears that last summer some time the Commissioners concluded there were too many dogs in the county, and they decided to take advantage of the State laws which empower them to enact ordinances against or for the festive canine. So the gentlemen studied and pondered, and eventually drafted an ordinance which empowers the County Clerk to purchase a carload, or such a number of dog collars as he may deem necessary to supply the canine population of the county. The Clerk, maybe, is to take the census of the dog-owners who think their dogs are worth buying a collar for, and then he is ordered as above to go to each precinct, hunt up the Constable, furnish him collars according to the dog census of his precinct, and instruct the Constable to enforce a most peculiar dog-tax law. The Constable is then required to visit all the farms in his precinct, which are probably from one to five miles apart, sell the collar to the poor farmer, who has from one to five dogs, at $1.50 each; and it is his duty to kill all dogs that are too poor to wear one of these county collars.

Another funny provision is that the Constable is to have 50 cents for his trouble in case he sells a collar. These collars cost the county 50 cents, the Constable gets 50 cents and the dog-owner does 50 cents worth of cussing. There is no provision made for exempting a dog that has lost or had its collar stolen, and a prominent resident of Castle Dale suggests that each man owning a dog buy a collar and nail it up on the front door of his dwelling, where it would have the only remunerative or beneficial result expected. When a man has a lightning rod towering above his house it serves as a warning to rod agents, and the idea about these collars might be a sign to the Constables.

A Malpractice Case Dismissed— Marsh's Will Contested.

Correspondence Tribune.]

Castle Dale, Nov. 18.—Monday morning the Seventh District court in and for Emery county opened at 10 o'clock. Judge William McCarty was on the bench.

The first case was the State of Utah vs. Joseph Biddlecom; fornication. It was shown by Prosecuting Attorney J. K. Reid that the indictment was defective, and the defendant should have been charged with adultery, as the offense was committed with a married woman. Upon his motion the case was dismissed and the bondsmen exonerated. This was done in order to give the prosecutor a chance to take the case into the Justice's court and properly bring it before the District court.

Goldsmith & Co. vs. A. A. Mulholland; suit on account, dismissed on motion of the County Attorney, in accordance with stipulations.

Nephi Rhoades vs. Katy Rhoades; divorce, dismissed at plaintiff's costs, on motion of A. D. Dickson, who stated that the parties had now agreed to agree again.

J. K. Reid, administrator for the estate of J. A. Hammill, deceased, showed that he had made final settlement and was discharged.

Adjourned till Tuesday morning at 10 o'clock.

A MALPRACTICE CASE.

Tuesday morning the case of Jesse Brinkerhoff vs. Dr. W. P. Winters, in which the plaintiff sued for $10,000 damages for malpractice was called, and it stated in the complaint that the cause of action was, that on the 31st of December, 1895 at Huntington, Emery county, the plaintiff had the bone of his right thigh broken, and called the defendant in the capacity of surgeon. The leg was set, but through the carelessness of defendant, the leg healed, and was shown to be three inches shorter than before the injury occurred; it is crooked and has a large lump upon it, which plaintiff alleges is due to the defendant not properly adjusting the ends of the broken bone, and permitting them to overlap, hence plaintiff is rendered a cripple for life.

Defendant in his answer denied all the allegations, and claimed the fault, and consequent results of the injury, were for the reasons that plaintiff did not follow instructions and took off bandages and splints placed upon plaintiff's limb by defendant.

Testimony was taken at great length, plaintiff saying that his thigh-bone was broken late in December of last year, while at work in the coal mine in Huntington canyon, and he was brought to Huntington and Dr. Winters set his leg, but first was asked by defendant if he "knew his business," the doctor saying he did. The process of setting the bone was then described, and the splints, and the board reaching up to his side, and the flat-iron hanging over the foot of the bed by a string attached to the foot, and how the string broke, and the anxiety about the leg being shorter than the other one, etc., and the doctor saying it was all right.

The doctor claimed that his treatment was all right; he used Buck's extension method, and thought when the limb and the body had become adjusted to the new conditions the leg would not be short, but all would be right. He also complained that too many had a hand in the case, and that he didn't know of the weight falling off, claiming it was left off too soon. He also said the patient came out sooner than he wanted him to.

After arguments the court summed up the testimony and briefly stated the points of the case, and dismissed the case on the grounds of "no cause of action."

Wednesday—The only matter coming before the court this morning was the signing of records, etc., and court was adjourned subject to call and order of the Judge.

NOTES.

Judge McCarty has approved the bonds of a number of the Carbon county officers-elect while at Price, but has consented to attend to the remaining ones on his return from Castle Dale.

Emery county officers-elect have flocked into court during its short session here, and had their bonds approved. Judge McCarty placed the bonds of the County Commissioners at $2000 each.

The court-room was well filled during the Winters-Brinkerhoff case, in which the people of this county all seem very much interested.

W. K. Reid, J. W. Whitecotton, Sam A. King, A. D. Dickson, J. W. Warf and William Howard were the attorneys present.

No jury had been asked for in the Brinkerhoff vs. Winters case by either side, consequently the trial was taken up without one.

William K. Reid has been appointed deputy Prosecuting Attorney for Emery county by the County Commissioners.

In the testimony of J. B. Meeks for the defense in the Winters case, Attorney Reid asked witness what was said by the patient during the conversation which took place just before the doctor set the leg. Meeks replied, "He said, 'Give me another drink of whisky and have Brother H— administer to me, and I'm ready for the doctor.'" Attorney Reid said, "So he got the spirit first and then the administration?" and everybody laughed except the court.

Tuesday morning when court opened a remittitur from the Supreme court of the State of Utah in the case of Emery county vs. P. C. Burrison et al., was filed in this court by Attorney W. K. Reid. The decision of the lower court having been reversed by the Supreme court, the case was remanded back for a new trial.

Judge McCarty ordered that the bondsmen of the County Commissioners may justify before a notary public in the town or precinct where they reside.

THE MARSH CASE.

An application was made to the court for the probating of the estate of W. Van Marsh, deceased, and the Judge gave instructions to procure depositions to prove said Marsh was dead.

The estate of William Van Marsh being probated brings to mind the following. Marsh was a German, and was well educated. At times he became despondent, and once tried to shoot himself, but made a failure of it. The young man became enamored of a young lady living near Castle Dale, named Mary Jane Biddlecom. The couple were engaged, and Marsh went early this fall to Diamond mountains, where he was herding sheep for Hacking Bros., and on October 15th last he committed suicide. Before shuffling off this mortal coil, however, he made a will in his own handwriting, and signed the same, mailing it to his intended wife. He left to her all his personal effects and some property here, which will be valued at about $500. The young lady is trying to get possession of the estate, but parties here claim the estate to be indebted to them, and a settlement is asked.

THE OFFICERS-ELECT.

Correspondence Tribune.]

Castle Dale, Nov. 17.—The Commissioners for Emery county, after completing the canvass of the late election returns, have declared the following named gentlemen to be the county officers-elect.

Commissioners—H. P. Rasmussen of Molen, Nephi Williams of Huntington.

Attorney—William Howard of Huntington.

Clerk and Recorder—O. J. Sitterud of Orangeville.

Assessor—M. C. Bryan or Ferron.

Treasurer—R. C. Miller of Castle Dale.

Surveyor—George Fox of Orangeville.

L. P. Overson of Cleveland received the neat majority of 255, for Representative to the State Legislature, and it will be seen by the table herewith given that the entire Democratic ticket was elected, with majorities ranging from 255 to 759. O. J. Sitterud, the present Clerk and Recorder, receiving the last named majority on re-election. As there was only one man placed on the ticket for Surveyor, he received almost the entire vote.

The total vote cast in the county is shown to have been 1251.

JUSTICES AND CONSTABLES.

Below is the list of Justices and Constables elected in the precincts of Emery county:

Green River—For Justice, J. T. Farrer; Constable, Frank Cook.

Ferron—For Justice, William H. Worthin; Constable, George W. Perry.

Desert Lake—For Justice, William J. Powell, Jr.; Constable, L. J. Marsing.

Cleveland—For Justice, M. L. Snow; Constable, William McFarlane.

Lawrence—For Justice and Constable every man in the town received one vote each, supposed to have been cast by their respective wives.

Huntington—For Justice, E. H. Cox; Constable, R. A. Howard.

Castle Dale—For Justice, C. P. Anderson; Constable, Heber Frandsen.

Emery—For Justice, P. V. Bunderson; Constable, H. C. Christensen.

At Orangeville, Molen and Woodside there were no precinct officers placed on the ticket.

After the above canvass was completed, the regular session of court was held and appropriations made aggregating $144.95. Emery county has an indebtedness of something like $8000,

and is now trying to bond for $8000, under the new State law. An extension of time for receiving bids for the bonds has been made from November 9 to December 7, 1896.

DOG COLLARS.

In the clerk's minutes an order of the Commissioners appears which might cause some curiosity with those not fully initiated in the laws of Emery county, and, of course, it caught my eye and, on inquiry, gathered some information regarding it. The order reads thus: "Clerk was ordered to distribute dog collars to the different Constables, with instructions for them to enforce the law."

It appears that last summer some time the Commissioners concluded there were too many dogs in the county, and they decided to take advantage of the State laws which empower them to enact ordinances against or for the festive canine. So the gentlemen studied and pondered, and eventually drafted an ordinance which empowers the County Clerk to purchase a carload, or such a number of dog collars as he may deem necessary to supply the canine population of the county.

The Clerk, maybe, is to take the census of the dog-owners who think their dogs are worth buying a collar for, and then he is ordered as above to go to each precinct, hunt up the Constable, furnish him collars according to the dog census of his precinct, and instruct the Constable to enforce a most peculiar dog-tax law. The Constable is then required to visit all the farms in his precinct, which are probably from one to five miles apart, sell the collar to the poor farmer, who has from one to five dogs, at $1.50 each; and it is his duty to kill all dogs that are too poor to wear one of these county collars.

Another funny provision is that the Constable is to have 50 cents for his trouble in case he sells a collar. These collars cost the county 50 cents, the Constable gets 50 cents and the dog-owner does 50 cents worth of cussing. There is no provision made for exempting a dog that has lost or had its collar stolen, and a prominent resident of Castle Dale suggests that each man owning a dog buy a collar and nail it up on the front door of his dwelling, where it would have the only remunerative or beneficial result expected. When a man has a lightning rod towering above his house it serves as a warning to rod agents, and the idea about these collars might be a sign to the Constables.

Manti Messenger
November 20, 1896

Legal Publications.

No 3068.

TIMBER CULTURE, FINAL PROOF.—
NOTICE FOR PUBLICATION

United States Land Office,
Salt Lake City, Utah, October 26, 1896
Notice is hereby given that JOSEPH
EVANS, of Emery, Emery county, Utah,
has filed notice of intention to make final
proof before the County Clerk of Emery
county, Utah, at his office in Castle Dale,
Utah, on Saturday, the 19th day of December, 1896 on timber culture application No 1127, for the south half of southeast quarter, and south half of southwest
quarter of Section No. 3, in Township
No 22 south, Range No. 6 east

He names as witnesses George Collier,
John Keel, Samuel M. Williams, Christian Larsen, all of Emery, Utah

BYRON GROO Register

First publication, Nov. 6, 1896   e10

Deseret Weekly
November 28, 1896

ATTORNEY GENERAL'S OPINIONS.

Attorney General Bishop transmitted
the following opinion today in relation
to collection of taxes on mortgages:

J. K. Reed, Esq., county attorney of
Emery county, Castle Dale, Utah:

Dear Sir.—Your favor of the 1st inst.
is before me in relation to the assessment of mortgages and the collection
of the taxes thereon.

Your question, "How will the collector compel payment on any mortgage
on which assessment has been made
and what can be levied upon?" may
be answered, the same as any class of
personal property.

"Every tax has the effect of a judgment against the person, and every
lien created by this act has the force
and effect of an execution duly levied
against all personal property of the
delinquent; the judgment is not satisfied or the lien removed until the taxes
are paid or the property sold for the
payment thereof." Section 92 of the
"Revenue Act."

"Every tax upon personal property

is a lien upon the real property of the
owner thereof, from and after 12
o'clock m. of the first Monday in
March of each year." Sec. 93 of the
same act.

"The treasurer may collect the taxes
delinquent on personal property, except
when the real estate is liable therefor,
by seizure and sale of any personal
property owned by the delinquent."
Sec. 125 of the same act.

"On payment of the price bid for any
personal property sold, the delivery
thereof with a bill of sale vests the
title thereto in the purchaser." Section
129 of the same act.

That a mortgage is property and subject to taxation there can be no question, when so addressed.

It will be observed from these provisions of the law, that the tax thereon
has the force and effect of an execution duly levied against all of the
personal property of the delinquent.

I think the law would authorize the treasurer to take into his possession the mortgage so taxed, and under the provisions of sections 126 and 128 sell the same at public auction, provided the owner of the mortgage was not the owner of real estate, in which case the tax would be a lien against the real estate and he could proceed to sell the real estate in satisfaction of the taxes on the mortgage.

As to your second question, "Has the county commissioners, under the law, the right to charge school districts with the collection of special school taxes?" permit me to say that I know of no provision in the present law which will authorize such a charge.

I have the honor to be,

Very respectfully yours,

A. C. BISHOP,

Attorney General.

Manti Messenger
December 4, 1896

James Jeff of Castle Dale passed through here Friday with five wagon loads of extracted honey which he is to deliver in Grand Junction. His honey crop this year amounts to over fifteen hundred gallons

Emery County Budget.

The celebrated whisky selling case of the people of the State of Utah, vs Dr. W. P. Winters of Orangeville came up for hearing on Wednesday before Justice Hunter at Huntington, whither it had been carried from Orangeville on change of venue taken by the defendant

J. K. and W. K Reid prosecuted, and Chas. Kofford appeared for the defence. The case presented many amusing features and consumed the better portion of the day

The complaint alleged that on the 27th. day of last November the defendant without a license to do so, sold to one Collington a half pint of whiskey; contrary to statute etc

Some difficulty was experienced by the prosecution in establishing that the liquid in evidence was really whiskey, and in order to do so Albert Nagely, Joe Meeks, H. S Loveless, Dr. Winters and the officers of the court made experiments upon the bottle which Attorney Kofford furnished to aid the experts in making comparison. Nagely and Meeks experted the stuff and pronounced it something besides whiskey, but the other gentlemen who each took copious libations said they beleived that the bottle coutained whiskey.

Dr Winters, testifying in his own behalf, said that he had sold to Collington a half-pint of medicine which he admitted contained five sixths whiskey, but which he said was covered by a prescription made by him for the man who applied to him for treatment for a hard cold: the doctor stated that whiskey was a favorite prescription of his for colds and snake bites, and that he, as a practicing physician, surgeon and druggist, could not do business without such liquor being used

Collington testified that he did not apply for a prescription, but that he called for whiskey and got it, and that he believed it was straight winskey, without any other ingredients and not medicine at all, probably effecacious for colds and rheumatism, but better to get drunk on

During the trial the Doctor testified to having prescribed beer and whiskey for his patients at various times, and on one occasion he prescribed 72 bottles of beer for a patient.

The court after hearing all of the evidence in the case, and the arguments of counsel, fined the defendant $100 and costs. Dr. Winters appealed the case to the District Court.—Castle Valley News.

Legal Publications.

No 302

NOTICE FOR PUBLICATION.

Land Office at Salt Lake City, Utah,
November 27, 1896.

Notice is hereby given that the following-named settler has filed notice of his intention to make final proof in support of his claim, and that said proof will be made before the County Clerk of Emery county, Utah, at Castle Dale, Utah, on January 18, 1897, viz

Franklin Hitchcock homestead entry No 5085 for the NW ¼ SW ¼ Section 27, SE ¼ NE ¼, E ½ SE Section 28 Township 20 south, Range 7 east. He names the following witnesses to prove his continuous residence upon and cultivation of said land, viz Moses I Burdick John Barton, Harmon H. Curtis, William Hitchcock, all of Ferron, Utah

BYRON GROO, Register,
First publication December 11, 1896.   e15

Salt Lake Tribune
January 18, 1897

The Price Trading company, through whose enterprise a telephone line was constructed to Huntington from Price in October last, has now completed the extension of the line from Huntington via Castle Dale to Orangeville, and the long-distance telephones have been placed in position. These 'phones are purchased outright, so that the line with all its equipments is owned entirely by the local company. It is of great benefit to Castle valley, and will be extended in the spring to Ferron, some fifteen miles further south. Telephone connection can now be had between Orangeville, Emery county, and Vernal Uintah county, a distance of over 150 miles.

Numerous shipments of cattle have been made from this country in the past few weeks and stockmen continue their trips through here in quest of "feeders" and calves, which are marketable at good prices.

Correspondence Tribune.]

Huntington, Utah, Jan. 22.—Many of the cattle raisers throughout the county report losses, and it is generally believed that a tough gang of cattle thieves are operating on the Cedar mountains. However this may be, Sheriff Tuttle is on the lookout and some of the festive thieves are likely to get nipped. One large cattle-owner in the extreme south end of the county states that on "rounding-up" lately he was loser over a thousand head, including the natural increase.

The enterprising citizens of Ferron are building a roller-mill, and it is now nearly completed. They expect to have the machinery all in place ready to commence operating early in May. This mill finished, Emery county can boast of three roller-mills and one "Burr" mill, while Carbon county as yet has none.

Several Orangeville young men were out for what they call a good time some time ago, and in their hilarious diversion they tied cans and bells to horses' tails and feet. There would propably be no necessity of mentioning this foolish incident were it not for the fact that one of the party, who was not in the intoxicated condition that some of the others showed, was very seriously injured. A large cow bell had been strapped to one of the front feet of a horse and a young fellow rode the animal down the street at a full gallop, and when nearing the crowd of boys the bell slipped loose and went whirling with terrific force toward George Tatten, who was struck on the cheek-bone and above the left eye, fracturing the skull in an L shape. The unfortunate victim was led home in a semi-conscious condition and was in a precarious state for five or six days, but is again able to be out, though it will be a long time before he will fully recover or want to participate in such barbarous pastimes.—Eastern Utah Advocate.

Salt Lake Tribune
January 29, 1897

GOSSIP FROM SCOFIELD.

Bridges Put In—Objections to the Manifesto—More Snow Needed.

Correspondence Tribune.]

Scofield, Jan. 27.—Nearly every day it has snowed this week, but there has yet to be a very heavy fall in Pleasant Valley, or water will be scarce in Castle Valley next summer. This is the mildest winter ever known here.

The bridges over Price river, which were all washed out during the floods last fall, have finally been replaced under contracts recently let out by the County Commissioners. In most instances the bridges are but temporary affairs for this season's use.

Emery Stake Latter-Day Saints' conference, which stake comprises Carbon and Emery counties, will be held at Price Sunday, February 7th and 8th.

Judge Johnson's court for the Seventh district is to open at Price, Monday, February 8th. The cases to come up have not been set for any special date. After court is adjourned at Price, the Judge will proceed to Castle Dale, where he will commence hearing cases on the 16th.

George L. Black, general superintendent of the U. P. coal department, and J. M. Moore, general Western agent of that company, were in Scofield this week. The gentlemen were entertained by Superintendent J. R. Sharp.

Last Sunday afternoon the now celebrated "manifesto" was for the first time read at the meeting-house in Scofield, and everything did not go quite as smoothly as might have been expected. A vote being taken, it was found to be divided, and in some quarters the sentiment seemed strongly in favor of rebelling against it, and it is rumored that one or two parties made strong protests, but the excitement soon waned, and all goes smoothly once more.

Tom Brown, the popular young clerk at the company offices in Winter Quarters, is somewhat of a genius in mechanical construction. He has recently completed a small electric dynamo or generator, every piece of which he has made himself from material purchased for the purpose except the iron casting. The little dynamo is in splendid running order, and furnishes power for ten 16-candle-power incandescent lights. Tom claims the proud distinction of being the first one to construct an electric generator in eastern or southern Utah, and probably in the State.

The thermometer ranges below zero in Pleasant Valley during the night, and but little above during the day.

Richard Howells is the proud father of a ten-pound baby girl, which arrived at his domicile yesterday.

Burns's birthday was most appropriately celebrated by the Scotch residents of Scofield. A concert, ball and luncheon was the programme of the evening, and there was an immense throng gathered in the schoolhouse, and enjoyed the entertainment. Hugh Hunter enlivened the occasion by rendering several selections on the bagpipes, and the lads and lassies danced the "reel" and "Highland fling" till the "wee sma' hours."

For three months past work at the Winter Quarters and U. P. mines has been fairly good, with but few lay offs, and in consequence the miners rejoice.

There is a strong sentiment in this camp for Thatcher, and he is generally the most popular one mentioned for Senator. However, there are a number of ardent Henderson supporters here. Great interest is shown in The Tribune's reports of the ballots taken, but people begin to wonder if our legislators intend to continue drawing their salary and do nothing through the entire time alloted them to transact their business.

Manti Messenger
January 30, 1897

Word comes from Ferron, that the diphtheria is making ravages among the people there

HE IS CONGRATULATED

Rawlins Receives Messages From All Parts of the State.

SENATOR DUBOIS EXPRESSES SATISFACTION.

The Senator-Elect Has Not Yet Appointed His Private Secretary— Editorial Comment of the Denver Times.

Senator-elect Rawlins continues to receive scores of congratulations, both by mail and wire, and his time is largely occupied in receiving those who call to extend their felicitations and good wishes. The first suggestion of the many western interests he will be called on to look after and promote at Washington came from mining men, who are heavy users of cyanide of potassium. They allege that an attempt is now being made before the ways and means committee of the house to increase the already high duty on cyanide of potassium from 25 per cent to 40 per cent, which, if carried into effect, will prove very disastrous to the mining interests of the west.

Mr. Rawlins, although he has not yet taken his seat in the senate, has wrapped about him the mantle of senatorial etiquette, and declines to make public his attitude on the Cuban question, tariff legislation and other important questions that will soon come before the senate. It is believed that his sympathies are with the Cuban insurgents, but for obvious reasons he does not care to discuss the subject. He stated yesterday that he had not yet appointed his secretary and was not certain that he would do so at this time.

That the election of Mr. Rawlins has apparently given great satisfaction to many leading Democrats as well as Republicans in all section of the state is shown by the congratulatory letters he is receiving. Among those that reached him yesterday were the following:

J. Z. Stewart, city attorney at Logan, writes: "You will please accept my congratulations, and I am pleased to say that of the very many Democrats I have met since the good news came, nine-tenths of them are rejoicing over your triumph. The majority of the Democrats of Cache county support you, and I know whereof I speak."

The following came from J. M. Blair, postmaster at Logan: "I have been waiting anxiously for the news of your success to the senatorship, and I now take the pleasure of offering you my congratulations. I am sure our cause will be taken care of in your able hands, especially our state and the silver cause."

Joshua Greenwood writes from Fillmore, Millard county: "Notwithstanding our men in the legislature favored Thatcher for United States senator, the news of your election last evening to that important station was received in this section with much joy and satisfaction. Many expressions can be heard on every hand that the right thing has been done. Your honorable record and standing have been vindicated by the party, which, in my opinion, has not given more than was justly due. You can be assured that, with few exceptions, Millard congratulates you. The nation and the state, and especially the Utah Democracy, congratulates."

This came from Richard Bridge, Heber City: "No people in Utah rejoice over your election more than the people of Wasatch county. You are deserving of the success you have just attained, and we feel that our fair young state will be ably represented in the United States senate."

William Creer, a "sagebrush Democrat," writes from Spanish Fork: "I take pleasure in congratulating you upon the choice made by the legislature for senator. Looking back to the time when the Democratic party was first organized in Utah, and contemplating the changes that have taken place politically since then, we have reason to feel happy."

A. J. Weber, of Ogden, known during campaign times as "the Weber cyclone," expresses himself as follows: "While, owing to peculiar conditions, you were not my first choice for senator, still I can earnestly and sincerely congratulate you upon your victory. You sounded the keynote in your address yesterday and I know you will always remain true to the sentiments then expressed."

William Howard writes from Castle Dale: "I am pleased to think that I cast my mite to help elect as United States senator a man whose record in congress in the past could not be met by his enemies, and whose record in the future we hope they will not reach. Please receive my most hearty congratulations on your election. Our county commissioners also send you greeting."

James A. Allred, from Spring City, Sanpete county, sends the following: "I am satisfied, from my long acquaintance with you, and from your past service to the people, that your labors will be for their best interests."

James L. Loar writes from Ogden: "I have always been persuaded that your election to the United States senate would bring about the highest possible good to our party and have known that such selection would be rewarded by such services to our entire state that could not fail to look after the rights and interests of our citizens to the highest degree."

Fire Chief James Devine, in a congratulatory letter, says: "Utah, without regard to politics, should congratulate you and herself. I, as a Republican, expect to be proud of our Senator Rawlins."

Among others who sent congratulations by mail were H. O. Young, Parley Park; J. B. Carver, Plain City; J. S. Hyde, Eureka; S. W. Riter, Logan; I. M. Pitts and Elijah Sells, Salt Lake.

FROM SENATOR DUBOIS.

United States Senator Dubois wires Senator-elect Rawlins from Washington as follows: "I know your work, integrity and ability. They were fully demonstrated to me by your service as delegate to congress. I congratulate you and the people of Utah on your election to the senate."

Ex-Governor McConnell, of Idaho, and Charles Crane sent the following message from Boise: "We congratulate the Democratic party on the election of the ablest exponent of the party in Utah."

The following editorial, published by the Denver Times, is from the pen of Arthur I. Street, formerly of this city: "In electing Joseph L. Rawlins as its representative in the United States senate, Utah has chosen one of the best and most useful men that could have been named. The defeat of Mr. Thatcher is unfortunate because of the church issue it involves, but Mr. Rawlins has been in congress on behalf of Utah and has demonstrated his unusual capabilities as a worker for the interests of those who honor him. He is an apostate from Mormonism and was bitterly opposed by the Mormon leaders during the campaigns of 1894 and 1895. If he has gained the support of the church in his candidacy for the senatorship it has been solely because the church was unwilling to see Mr. Thatcher elected.

"During his two years as a delegate from the territory of Utah Mr. Rawlins accomplished the unprecedented work of having seven bills in behalf of his constituency passed through both houses of congress and signed by the president. The records show no parallel to this either on the part of a delegate from a territory or on the part of a regular voting representative. If greater evidence were needed of Mr. Rawlins' ability it would be sufficient to point to his work at the Chicago convention, where, as a member of the committee on resolutions, he succeeded in having the plank of the Democratic platform relative to tariff adopted. That plank, it will be remembered, expressed the new principle that no tariff act should be so framed as to discriminate between the different sections of the country. It was upon this principle that Mr. Rawlins as a Democrat opposed the Cleveland policy of removing the tariff from wool.

"Mr. Rawlins is a most sound and determined advocate of the free coinage of silver, and in the senate he will do much to replace the loss of Senator Dubois. He is not the dashing, brilliant fellow that Dubois was, but he has the nerve and grit that belongs to Senator Teller and the tactical skill that will make his efforts felt at the capital. He is one of the few men in public life who never quits until he has gained his end. Many men now in congress know his power, and there is probably not a gold man among them that would not rather have seen any other candidate than Mr. Rawlins chosen by the people of Utah.

"Colorado's sister state is to be congratulated upon the naming of Senator Rawlins, who is one of Utah's greatest and strongest native sons.

"Hanna, who thought he had well rid himself of a sharp enemy when he defeated Dubois in Idaho, may find that he has an equally doughty and elastic combatant in Rawlins of Utah. The Hanna blanket, like the gold standard blanket, can cover only a small section of the United States at one time, after all."

Eastern Utah Advocate
February 11, 1897

ORANGEVILLE.

The party given by the relief society last week was a very pleasant affair. Five quilts were raffled, neting the society a very snug som of money.

The home talent played Enoch Arden on Friday and Saturday, the proceeds going to the widows of Orangeville. Good houses greeted them each evening and results were quite a satisfactory.

At the meeting of the board of the Relief-society the o'd board was reelected with three additional new members.

Considerable sickness prevails among both old and young, most of which is chiefly from colds. There is nothing serious, however.

A good delegation from our ward attended the quarterly conference at Price on Sunday and Monday.

We regret to note the departure in the near future of O. Sorensen and wife. Mr. Sorensen will be miller at the new roller mill at Ferron.

The majority of the people are well pleased with the result in the joint session of the legislature. In our opinion Rawlins is the man.

Salt Lake Herald
February 16, 1897

FERRON

Snow still continues to fall.

The farmers are jubilant over the prospects of a plentiful harvest the coming autumn and together with the promised McKinley prosperity good times are expected.

Diphtheria is still raging, Mrs. Barley's 7-year-old son fell a victim to its ravages.

Mrs. Cheshire is going almost day and night visiting the sick. Under her skillful treatment few cases prove fatal.

The rabbit inhabitants of our vicinity declare C. C. Bookman to be a distructive agent in their vicinity. When his presence is discovered the bunnies seek their burrows.

In the contest offered the residents of Ferron by Foster and Cooley for the greatest number of words, exclusive of proper nouns to be formed out of the letters of the word 'California," four open cans of assorted California fruits were awarded in four prizes of 24, 12, 6 and 6 cans each, to the following persons in order. A. E. Edwards, Miss Bertie Behunin, Mrs. T. Pearl Edwards and Mrs. Amanda Cox, with 138, 146, 120 and 114 words respectively.

Boys having good sleighs and bells are at a premium with the young ladies Sleigh riding is the chief source of amusement all public gatherings being prohibited.

NEWS FROM NEARBY

Lugio Pallio Gets Two Years For Assault.

COURT AT CASTLEDALE

REPUBLICAN SCRAMBLE FOR OFFICE ON THE INCREASE.

K. P. Annual Ball at Park City—Ontario Pay-day—Dedication of the New Meetinghouse at Payson—Work in the Canyon Abandoned on Account of the Depth of the Snow—Two More Earthquake Shocks at Brigham City—Carl Loveland's Funeral Services.

Price, Utah, Feb. 13.—Lugio Pallio, an Italian coal miner from Castle Gate, who has been confined in the county jail here since Feb. 1 for shooting one Italian and seriously cutting another at a beer party at that place, was tried before Judge Jacob Johnson in the Seventh judicial district court at Price, Friday and Saturday of last week, Feb. 12 and 13. Pallio was tried for each case separately and was found guilty by the jury of both offenses.

In the first case the jury's verdict was "guilty of assault with intent to kill," recommending mercy. In the second case "guilty of assault with intent to kill."

He employed Attorney John E. Booth of Provo to defend him, and County Attorney J. Wesley Warf was assisted in the prosecution by Attorney J. W. Whitecotton of Provo. The court sentenced him to one year for each offense. Sheriff Devant will leave here Tuesday next with the prisoner.

The damage case of Clarence Marsh vs. the Rio Grande Western railway was thrown out.

Judge Johnson will hold a short session of the Seventh district court at Castle Dale, beginning Monday morning, Feb. 15.

There is a great scramble being made here by the two elements of the Republican party for the postoffice, two new candidates having come up. E. W. McIntire and Arthur J. Lee are the other new aspirants. Fourth-class postoffices should be put in the civil service and save all this annoyance to executives in Washington.

When Major William McKinley takes his seat on March 4 he will immediately be confronted with these four petitions of the four worthy Republicans of Price desiring some of the pie. When the fourth-class postoffices are put under the civil service it will not be necessary for the president to distribute the pie to every little town in the United States.

The people of Price are somewhat worked up over the prospects of the Uncompahgre Indian reservation being thrown open in the near future, and hope and pray that Senator Frank J. Cannon's amendment to the Indian appropriation bill will be approved by President Grover Cleveland before he starts on his trip around the world. If this reservation is thrown open it will be a great benefit to Utah, giving the men in the thickly settled portions of the state who own a house and lot and live from hand to mouth on their daily wages a chance to sell their house and lot and come to eastern Utah and get a farm of their own and live an independent life. Price will be greatly benefited, as it is the only natural gateway to the Uncompahgre reservation.

Eastern Utah Advocate
February 18, 1897

FERRON

For some time past the health officers would not permit public gatherings, but as the diptheria is now on the decline it is hoped that it will soon be safe for us to enjoy ourselves as of yore. In anticipation of that happy time some of our people are already making preparations to celebrate with amateur theatricals, a fancy dress ball, etc It has leaked out that the directors and stock holders of the Roller Mill company intend to celebrate the completion of the mill on a grand scale If their plans for the mill are carried out successfuly there will be plenty of reason for every citizen of Ferron to rejoice and jollify. It will be something to be proud of 'a thing of beauty and a joy forever."

The many friends of Miss Lizzie Behunin are glad to welcome her home again after a long stay in Provo attending the B. Y. academy.

Two of our young people, Lawrence Glines and Miss May Thornton have surprised their friens by quietly joining hearts, hands and fortunes. We extend hearty congratulations and best wishes to the happy and popular couple.

We expect to soon be in telephonic communication with the outside world Our popular townsman, Wyatt Bryan, has the contract for the poles to extend the line from Orangeville to Ferron, and a party of our town people are now on the mountains busily hauling down the poles

F. A. Killpack has returned from a visit to Salt Lake whither he went on business for the Roller Mill company.

...ree of our most popular boys, John Bohleen, Alf Swensen and Will Taylor are just now feeling very well satisfied with toemselves and the worl l in general They now have nobby sleighing outfits It is said all g rls like a young m in t hus quipped and more especially if he can drive with one hand. These boys can do even better than that, they have strong teeth, and can drive without using either hand It is only necessary to say, without g)ing into details, that .hey are having a good time, and making the most of the exc ll nt sleig ing, but they are generous enough to let their rigs to l ss fortunate boys—sometimes.

The gratitude of our community is due our cheif health officer Wm. H Worthen for the prompt, energetic and tireless manner in which he has attend d to the comfort and welfare of those who were quarantined on account of the diptheria

Emery County Court.

There was very few cases before the district court, which met at Castledale on February 15, and they were disposed of in short order

The the state of Utah vs. Kate Rhoades for adultry was dismissed.

The state of Utah vs W. P. Winters, on appeal from the justice's court of Huntington, when he was convicted of selling liquor without a license, and fined $100 and costs amounting in all to $151.80, was called for trial, but Mr. Winters had enough law for a little while, so he made haste to pay up and came nearly getting into trouble again It appears he gave the sheriff a check for $150.00, the balance in silver. The sheriff then gave a receipt in full and then handed the check back for Winter's endorsement. Winters endorsed it and handed back a piece of paper that the sheriff supposed was the check He put it in his pocketbook with out looking at it. This happend at Orange ville. The Sheriff then went to Castledale, and when he went to pay the check to the treasurer it was missing Of course, he was in trouble, and telephoned to Frank Carrol the maker of the check, to stop payment. Mr. Carrol telegraphed to Salt Lake to have the payment stopped at the Deseret National bank. Winters also came to Castledale and was questioned pretty strongly about the check, but denied any knowledge of it. Finally the county attorney met him on the stairs of the court house, and again questioned him, when he put his hand into his overcoat pocket and produced the check. Now the opinion of those acquainted with the circumstances is that Winters did not hand the check to the sheriff when he endorsed it A very few tricks of that kind would land somebody behind the bars

The case of P. C. Barreasen vs. C. P. Anderson et el. was before the court several times, and was finally settled without trial.

In the foreclosure suit of Hannah W. Gadsden vs Thos F. Earl, et al, judgement was given for plaintiff and the sheriff ordered to sell the property

There was considerable probate matter settled.

The most important case, although it took but few minutes to settle it, was that of Huntington town vs. William Cole, petit larceny. Cole was convicted under a town ordinance and fined $55. He, by his attorneys Geo. M. Miller and C. E. Kofford appealed the case to district court. When the case was called the defense employed W. K. Reid to assist them. Mr. Reid raised the point of jurisdiction of the town to make such an ordinance.

After argument and quoting authorities on both sides the judge ruled against the town. The judgment was that the town had no right or authority to make an ordinance on anything except that which was specifically mentioned in the law giving towns the right to incorporate.

for the same offence, and quite a number insist it shall be done. The question of jurisdiction was not raised in the lower court, and as soon as the appeal was taken and a copy of the ordinance was obtained. The prosecution anticipated that if that point was raised the case would go against the town, but they did not expect it to be so sweeping D W. Palmer, the fellow that was arrested at the same time as Cole, plead guilty, was fined $50 and costs. He did not pay a cent nor was he sent to jail. What he did do he done voluntarily. He now threatens the town with a suit for damages. He will get, what he can get. Cole says he has had enough

Spectator.

The defendant was discharged. The result is that the town of Huntington's ordinance book has got several ordinances in it that is no good, under this judgement. What has been done does not bar another prosecution under the statute

Salt Lake Tribune
February 18, 1897

JUDGE JOHNSON IN EMERY.

Prospects of a Short Term—Cases on Hearing—The Jurors.

Correspondence Tribune.]

Castle Dale, Feb. 15—The January term of the Seventh District court for Emery county was opened here this morning, Judge Jacob Johnson presiding.

There is very little business to be transacted at this term, and in all probability but one case, that of the town of Huntington vs. William Cole, will be tried.

State vs. Katy Rhodes; on motion of prosecuting attorney, dismissed.

State vs. William P. Winters; appealed from the Justice's court; dismissed, defendant having paid the fine and costs imposed.

Judgment for $502.63 principal, $40 attorney's fees, together with interest and costs, was rendered in favor of the plaintiff in the case of John W. Latt vs. Thomas Rowley.

Judgment was also rendered in favor of Hannah W. Gadsen in her suit against Thomas Earl et al. for $600 principal, $22.27 interest, $75 attorney's fees and costs.

Estate of Samuel Babbett, deceased; final account of administrator approved and administrator discharged.

P. C. Burreson vs. C. P. Anderson et al.; set for February 16th.

Town of Huntington vs. William Cole; set for February 16, 1897.

The following jurors were selected to serve at this term of court: Harmon W. Curtis, Ferron; William A. Staker, Lawrence; F. C. Burch, Castle Dale; Chris Johnson, Huntington; A. E. Smith, Castle Dale; Jonathan H. Killpack, Huntington; Andrew Mortensen, Lawrence; Jesse D. Jenkes, Lawrence; William Hitchcock, Ferron; James W. Kilman, Orangeville; L. B. Reynolds, Lawrence; George Ipson, Huntington; H. A. Nelson, Ferron; Parker A. Childs, Orangeville; Seth Wareham, Nolen.

Salt Lake Tribune
February 18, 1897

The following jurors were selected to serve at this term of court: Harmon W. Curtis, Ferron; William A. Staker, Lawrence; F. C. Burch, Castle Dale; Chris Johnson, Huntington; A. E. Smith, Castle Dale; Jonathan H. Killpack, Huntington; Andrew Mortensen, Lawrence; Jesse D. Jenkes, Lawrence; William Hitchcock, Ferron; James W. Kilman, Orangeville; L. B. Reynolds, Lawrence; George Ipson, Huntington; H. A. Nelson, Ferron; Parker A. Childs, Orangeville; Seth Wareham, Nolen.

Eastern Utah Advocate
February 25, 1897

FERRON

Snow from twenty to twenty four inches deep on the level make sheep and cattle owners feel very blue. Big losses are anticipated.

Sickness here has inspired the school trustees to give our school building a thorough cleaning from floor to cel'ing a thing it has not had for a number of years. It is believed when school starts again the teachers will exert increased energy and tact when influenced by the spirit of c'eanliness, and all parents of chil'ren in this district interested in the cause of education and advancement should see that our schools are well attended as soon as they are again in session.

The machinery for the Ferron roller mill is expected to be on the site this week; when it will be rushed to completion in order to get the early spring grinding With the energy and enterprise of our thriving community many improvements are expected in the near future.

The Ferron brass band gave the residents a lively serena le on Sunday.

Such strains have power to quiet
The restless pulse of care,
And come like the benediction
That follows after prayer

We heartily thank them for their effort to dispel the gloom and disponden cy that has for so long overshadowed our vicinity.

Ex bishop Wm G Petty, of Emery was the guest of his son, Geo. A. Petty, of Ferron, Monday and Tuesday. He reports the people of Emery in a healthy and prosperous condition.

HUNTINGTON.

At the last term of the county court the commissioners decided to issue bonds to pay the outstanding indebtedness of the county existing prior to January 4, 1896. The first issue having been found deficient, as previously stated in these columns. Now comes an opinion of the attorney general regarding the issue of county bonds. The opinion says in part.

"I am of the opinion that sub-division 11 of section 21 of the county government bill gave to the board of county commissioners the option of funding or refunding any outstanding indebtedness

on January 4, 1896, and at that time they could have issued bonds for the full amount of said indebtedness. However, if they choose not to do so, and to pay off a portion thereof they could not afterwards issue bonds for the entire amount."

If that opinion be the law, and we suppose it will be until reversed by some higher court, the work done by the commissioners at their last meeting. In which it was decided to issue bonds, will have to be revised. They authorized an issue of $8,000 while the first issue authorized was for $8,300 The next, and we hope the last, will be for about $6,000 as from $1,200 to $1,500 has been paid on this outstanding indebtedness.

Few people like this bonding business, while a great many would not bond at all but something must be done. The writer would rather the people would vote a tax of about four mills to pay this debt outright than to pay interest for the next twenty years when at the end of this period the principle will b due and must needs be paid.

Judge Cheeny's judgment given against the Salt Lake county commissioners last Wednesday, if it be law, legalizes all the bills allowed by the commissioners of Emery county at their last meeting and also about $1,000 more that is awaiting action, about $1,500 in bills being left by the old court It appears that the Judge is indeavoring to favor some one for he ends his judgment in a way that makes it no judgment at all He says

'It is my opinion that at least a part, if not all, of the warrants held by plaintiff are not invalid and that the plaintiff have the relief prayed for"

We think it will take another ruling to tell what that sentence means It is an admission on the part of the Judge that at least a part of the warrants are illegal, if so, what part? That is the question he was called upon to decide.

"Our friend," Geo M. Miller, when not trying to make trouble for the people of Huntington, is industriously circulating a petition asking for the removal of M E. Johnson as postmaster at Huntington and that he be appointed in his stead He is using arguments to induce people to sign his petition that are not true. There are very few people here that will sign for him but he does not stop at that, he goes outside. We can not understand why people outside of Huntington should sign a petition against the Huntington postmaster. Mr. Miller says his main objection to Mr Johnson is that he is a democrat. The practice of neglecting school duties in order to injure certain parties is getting tiresome to the people.

Hon M. E. Johnson came down from Salt Lake on Saturday evening. He came to see a stranger a little girl that arrived at his home last week. The family think just as much of her as though they had known her for years. Mother and babe are doing nicely.

There is much sickness in our town caused by la grippe. Hardly a family is exempt. A few cases of severe illness among the little ones

Nobody married lately. There are some that would like to be married There are several of our young men that ought to get a rustle on themselves and get something to start a home with

The Castledale dramatic company played the "La ly of Lyons" to a fair house here on Saturday evening The play was well rendered.

The Huntington town board met on Saturday afternoon and passed a new ordinance relating to officers, by cutting off a number of them. This step was taken in order to conform the town ordinance to the decision of Judge Johnson in the case of Wm. Cole appealed from the Huntington Justice's court

Some time ago the president of the town board appointed a committee on ordinances. One of the committee, according to the others, have made himself so offensive in his acts and words that the balance of the committee refuse to act with him and have resigned. The talker wont resign. To get out of the muddle the town dads have appointed the town's attorney to revise the ordinances.

The school fittingly celebrated Washington's birthday

Hay and grain will be scarce here this coming spring The farmers sold both hay and grain too close and the result will be that grain will have to be shipped in for seeding purposes. The tithing hay has heretofore come in handy for the farmers for their stock during the spring work and as this has been sold to stockmen this supply has been cut off

The Relief Society had a good program prepared for the celebration of their anniversary and on account of la grippe it has been postponed for two weeks.

After considerable hard work on the part of two of our leading citizens a martial band was organized last fall. The boys have made good progress. On last Friday night a dance was given, to raise funds with which to purchase a bass drum, and on account of the great number of dances recently, and a play the following night it was not a financi-al success. Do not get discouraged, boys. Try it again after a while.

The people of Huntington had better begin to lay by their nickels. The town board will soon promulgate an ordinance taxing dogs. If a dollar a head is paid on all Huntington dogs we need not fear the big damage suit.

"The greatest words of thought or pen, are these sad words, it might have been." If we had known that the snow should have been so deep and stayed on so long, what lots of fun we might have had, in that nice sleigh we did not make, because we did not know.

The Huntington water works have been in bad shape this winter. The freezing of the canal that supplies the town, caused by the intermittent supply of water has been the source of much annoyance. We have had little if any running water for two months. Thus, water for culinary purposes and for stock must be hauled two miles. Something should be done to make the water supply regular in order to avoid frozen ditches.

A Visitor

Deseret Weekly
February 27, 1897

EMERY STAKE CONFERENCE.

HUNTINGTON, Emery County, Utah, February 10th, 1897.—The quarterly conference of the Emery Stake was held in Price, February 7th and 8th, 1897 Besides a large congregation of the Saints, most of the bishops and the stake presidency, Elder F. M. Lyman, Anthon H. Lund, of the council of Apostles, and Jonathan G. Kimball of the council of Seventies, were in attendance.

The Sunday school section of the conference convened at 10 a. m. After the usual opening exercises, Superintendant Eldredge reported the Price school as being fully organized, and in a prosperous condition.

Elder F. M. Lyman explained that the object of holding Sunday schools during ward and stake conferences was that the children might see and hear the visiting brethren, and not be driven into the streets during the usual time for holding Sunday schools. He explained that the president of the Stake should preside at such meetings, but the superintendent of schools should conduct the services. He thought these exercises should consist of concert recitation and singing, the Lord's prayer, the Ten Commandments and Articles of Faith would be appropriate selections to recite.

Elder Anthon H. Lund, Jonathan G. Kimball and C. G. Larsen, each gave timely instructions on Sunday school work.

At the close of meeting Brother Lyman called the Sunday school teachers together, and as a member of the Sunday School Union board gave a list of instructions prepared by the board.

At 2 p. m.—The last meeting session of the conference convened.

Elder Anthon H. Lund was the first speaker. He referred to the Vision of Lehi in which he saw the "tree of life" "iron rod" etc.; said the Bible, Book of Mormon, Doctrine and Covenants, and the teachings of the Prophets were the "iron rod" or word of God to which all should hold fast.

Elder Jonathan G. Kimball said he felt to warn the Saints against worldly pride. How very strange it is, that while the Lord is showering the greatest blessings upon His children they are most apt to turn against Him. God is obliged to chastize his Saints in order to keep them in the line of their duties. Those who cannot discern right from wrong, through the assistance of the Holy Ghost, without continually running after the authorities for help, are on slippery ground.

At evening meeting 7 p. m.—President C. G. Larsen reported the condition of the Stake; said union exists in the Stake presidency; felt that the bishops, high counselors and other Stake officers were good men. Interest in meeting is on the increase. The change of fast day is working well in the various wards. Said he was well satisfied with the principles of the Gospel.

Elder F. M. Lyman was the next speaker. He complimented the people of Price for the erection of a large town hall, setting out shade trees, and making other improvements. Advised them to continue the good work. He reminded the Saints that this Gospel will never be taken from the earth, nor given to another people; yet many may apostatize. Cited a number of cases in which those in high positions had fallen through their boasting, and feeling that they had very great abilities. Humility is the only safe platform upon which to stand. This is not our church; it is the Lord's, and will remain so forever.

At 10 a. m., Monday the 8th, inst. Brothern J. G. Kimball spoke at length on the necessity of sustaining and honoring the Priesthood of God. All should become thoroughly conversant with the principles of the Gospel. Since the days of Kirtland the Saints have never had greater trials than the troubles of today. Many are questioning and finding fault with those whom the Lord has

chosen to lead this people. This is a most dangerous condition. He exhorted the Seventies and Elders to be prepared to teach the Gospel to their families, neighbors, and the whole world. Let us repent and shun hypocricy.

Brother Anthon H. Lund occupied the remainder of the meeting in urging all to cultivate a spirit of meekness and humility. Jesus says that the meek shall inherit the earth.

On Monday at 2 p. m.—Elder O. J. Anderson presented the general and and stake authorities who were unanimously sustained.

Stake counselors Orange Seely and William Howard both made appropriate remarks on the duties of Latter-day Saints.

Brother Lyman then gave some very interesting and fatherly counsel to the Saints.

Conference adjourned for three month's to meet in Huntington.

The songs of Zion were rendered by the choirs of Price and Spring Glen, under the able leadership of Samuel Cox.   A. E. WALL, Clerk.

The schools were closed one day last week that the teachers might visit other schools. Orangeville received the visit and they returned to their duties with renewed vigor.

ORANGEVILLE.

The play presented by the district school on February 24 was very creditably rendered and very largely attended.

The conjoint session of the Y. M. and Y. L. M I, association Sunday evening brought out the largest congregation of the season. All felt well repaid for attending The singing which was a pleasing feature, was conducted by A. O Jewkes and was very enjoyable The lectures were of an instructive character while the humorous recitations were loudly applauded The "morning star," edited by Miss Emma Higg was very excellent. It was a pleasant and profitable evening

Mrs Potter is very ill.

The weather is moderating and mud will be our great annoyance,

The health of the people is getting better, the la grippe loosing its grip

Our worthy bishop's wife, Mrs. Robertson, has been confined to her bed for some time with a severe attack of pneumonia. She has sufficiently recovered to be up again.

"The Drunkards Morning," will be presented by our home troop on Friday evening The proceeds go to the Sunday school.

NOTICE FOR PUBLICATION.

No. 3185

Land office at Salt Lake City, Utah, Feb. 15, 1897

Notice is hereby given that the following named settler has filed notice of his intention to make final proof in support of his claim, and that said proof will be made before the Register and Receiver at Salt Lake City, Utah on April 3, 1897. viz: Joseph Thayne, H E. No 9522, for the N W 1 4 Sec. 23, Tp. 18, S., R. 8 East,

He names the following witnesses to prove his continuous residence upon and cultivation of, said land, viz: Charles Jensen, Orangeville Utah, Henry Thayne, Salt Lake, City, Utah, Oscar Mann, Provo, Utah, Morwil Thayne, Murray, Utah,

Byron Groo, Register.

f18m25.

CASTLEDALE.

The farmers are elated over the prospects of a good harvest.

The district schools will continue four weeks and possibly longer.

At least ten brick residences will go up within the coming year.

The schools were closed one day last week that the teachers might visit other schools. Orangeville received the visit and they returned to their duties with renewed vigor.

The home dramatic company presented "The Lady of Lyons" two nights to appreciative audiences. The play was an entire success. Encouragement is due them for the very faithful work Such entertainments should be more frequent.

The foundation stone for Dr. Winters new drug store is being placed on the ground His plans are well matured and when the building is completed it will be a credit to the owner and to the town.

Petty thieving has been too frequent of late. Beware, ye perpetrators, hard will be your lot if this is continued much longer.

Sand! Sand seems to be a favorite receipt in making up weights, filling deficiencies, enlarging bulk and lowering character. Oh, how blind, how bold and how false they are

A company has been organized to build a dancing pavillion. They are men with push and vim and will surely make it w n. The floor will be completed May 1. The broad canopy of heaven will be its roof until fall when brick walls will be built and the roof placed thereon They expect to have everything modern, good floor and refreshments will be served

The Emery County Teachers association met at Castledale, February 27, about one-half the teachers being present. The association is doing good work The most modern methods and devices are given and the teachers are striving to keep in touch with the times. Following is the program for the next institute to be held at Castledale, the last Saturday in March

1—Psychology, "The Representative Powers," by Seth Allen, Emery.

2—History, "How to teach," Geo E Weggland, Molen

3—Drawing, D. T. Thomander, Castledale.

4—Recitation, Miss Killian, Orangeville.

5—Song, Jesse Jewkes, Orangeville.

6—Song, A. Jameson & Co, Castledale,

More of the people and trustees should turn out to these meetings and see what the teachers are doing.

Program for Y. M. and Y. L. conj'nt to be held March, 7, 1897, Sunday evening

1—Lecture, "The Representative Powers," A. Jameson.

2—Song, Miss Sarah Larsen

3—Church History, Miss Syble Feely

4—Song, Hyrum Larsen.

5—Recitation, Miss Rosa Anderson.

6—Essay, John Y. Jensen.

7—The Mutal Advance, John Burke.

8—Critic. D. T. Thomander.

The young ladies hat trimming social was a unique affair and credit is due them for the way it was conducted

The house being beautifu'ly decorated made an entirely new appearance. The tables groaned beneath the spread of things both dainty and delicious. A good program of songs, recitations and toasts were in order arranged. The main feature of the evening was the trimming of hats. Each lady brought an untrimmed hat with ribbons etc. While the gentlemen were at work at this avocation now thrust upon them, many were the laughs that arose from different parts of the house. The hats when finished were worn by the trimmers, who marched around the house until the judges decided the winners of the prize to be Carl Olsen to have the first prize, a beautiful silk hankerchief and Hyrum Larsen the booby prize, a shoe brush. Well, ladies, success is the right word, and may such times often come to brighten and lighten our weary ways.

Omano.

HUNTINGTON.

The wife of Bishop Peter Johnson died on February 27, and was burried the following Sunday. She was a woman beloved and respected by all who knew her. She had been suffering for a long time with dropsy which finally took her away. Her brother and sister came over from Sanpete to attend the funeral. Three children died here last week. The Eighteen-months old child of brother and sister Ira Brinkerhoff, the eighteen-months old child of brother and sister J. H. Killpack and the little child of Ed. Mangum. There has hardly been a family but has had sickness. La grippe is the general complaint. Nearly all are getting better now.

Our schools have done well this winter and our only regret is that they can not run longer. A few days more and they will have to quit for lack of funds to pay teachers.

The seminary taught by A. E. Wall has done splendidly. He has had between fifty and sixty scholars. We think the people have done well to support this school so liberally. Everybody nearly is complaining of hard times. The next thing in order now will be to rustle and pay up what little may be owing the teacher.

We are pleased to see the Advocate come out a first class weekly, all home print We wish it success. The Advocate is a good stayer but it would help it some if the editor would get a good wife and settle down He can see what respect the legislature of a certain state hold bachelors, when they attempt to put a ten dollar tax on them.

The snow is going very fast We will soon have mud to spare.

Manti Messenger
March 6, 1897

No 3197
NOTICE FOR PUBLICATION

Land Office at Salt Lake City Utah,
February 5 1897

Notice is hereby given that the following named settler has filed notice of his intention to make final proof in support of his claim, and that said proof will be made before O J Sitterud, County Clerk of Emery Co Utah, at Castle Dale, Utah, on April 17, 1897 viz William Henrie, homestead entry No 9539, for the N SE and E SW Section 10, Township 20 South, Range 7 East.

He names the following witnesses to prove his continuous residence upon and cultivation of, said land, viz John C Duncan, F A Killpack, William Killpack and William Stringham, all of Ferron Utah
a-10   BYRON GROO, Register.

TWO UTAH MURDERERS

How Moen Kofford and Pete Mickle Were Caught.

IDENTIFIED BY PHOTOS

THE CAPTURE IS A MOST IMPORTANT ONE.

History of the Most Brutal Crime Ever Committed in Sanpete County—Reward of $1,500 For Their Arrest—Both Men Under Indictment For Murder.

Moen Kofford and James Peterson, alias Pete Mickle, the slayers of Sheriff James Burns, have been fully identified by the police authorities of Wilmington, Del., through the agency of photographs and other descriptions forwarded by Sheriff Judd of Sanpete county.

The capture is an exceedingly important one, as it revives the indignation of the population of Sanpete

PETE MICKLE.

county against the men who took the life of one of the most popular public officials in that section of the state.

STEALING SHEEP.

The murder was committed on Sept. 26, 1894, in Reeder range, ten miles southeast of Spring city. At the time of the killing Kofford and Peterson were under indictment for stealing sheep, having been accused of exercising a wholesale penchant for appropriating other sheepmen's property for more than four years preceding the tragedy. During that interval it was said that Kofford, Peterson, Young and a number of others had stolen at one time more than 700 sheep. They were tried twice for such offenses, but escaped conviction each time.

HISTORY OF THE CRIME.

What led up to the murder was a complaint filed in the United States district court early in September, wherein among others Kofford and Peterson were charged with stealing 300 or 400 sheep and cutting off the branded ears, which were hidden near the spot where the animals were taken. A great pile of ears were afterward exhumed from the cache. These severed organs were used as evidence against the sheep bandits, being exhibited by the owner of the stolen ani-

MOEN KOFFORD.

mals to United States authorities. Upon that showing a writ of replevin was issued and placed for service in the hands of Sheriff Burns, who proceeded to the sheep ranch of Kofford and Peterson on the Reeder range.

Service was made and denied by both men, who were then placed under arrest and started back to Spring City in custody. While en route the party stopped at a ranch for dinner. Sheriff Burns was sickened by swallowing a dead fly that had become mixed in his food. He left the cabin for a short time. While his attention was distracted the prisoners mounted their horses and got away. Burns was so piqued over the result of his labors that he returned to the Kofford ranch, enraged and bent upon "turning loose" on the fugitives. Arriving there he found Kofford and Peterson at work in a corral and started to be abusive. Hot words ensued and hostile demonstrations succeeded. It ended in Kofford discharging a revolver and Peterson a Winchester rifle into the body of Burns. He was riddled with bullets and shots were taken at three other men who witnessed the deed.

PURSUIT OF THE MURDERERS.

The murderers then fled southeast, while a posse was organized at Spring City to pursue them. At first it was surmised that the slayers were directing their flying footsteps toward Colorado.

When about 30 miles south of Castle Dale, in the McCarthy canyon, the posse came up with Kofford and his companion. They were surprised and lost their horses, but got away into the surrounding rocky country before the rifles of the officers could be trained upon them. So inaccessible became the haunts of the bandits that the posse had to forsake their own animals and follow the trail afoot among places where a mountain sheep might barely find a resting place. Word came back from the pursuers that the murderers were surrounded and their capture assured. A gauntlet of Winchesters was laid for the hunted men. Even with these prophecies of success, those who knew the temper of the man-killers also predicted that they would never be taken alive, and the last forecast was the true one.

OPENED FIRE.

The assassins kept in a secluded spot and were fully posted on the officers' movements by three brothers of Kofford, who dwelt in San Rafael valley. On Sept. 30 the two men were seen on the mountains above the posse, which opened fire. It was returned by Kofford and Peterson. No person of either party was hurt and the bandits retreated further into the rocky country. From time to time traces of them were had, but finally, through the assistance of friends, both got safely over the state line into Colorado, and from thence to Oklahoma, where they were again spotted, but eluded detection.

REWARDS OFFERED.

For their capture, dead or alive, the county of Sanpete offered $500, the territory $700, and societies of which Burns was a member contributed about $500 additional, making a total of about $1,500 blood money. This reward will revert to the Delaware officials.

WILL GO HARD WITH THEM.

It is likely to go hard with Kofford and Peterson when arraigned for trial, as the circumstances of the killing are so clear that it cannot possibly admit of successful defense. The prisoners are very young men. Kofford being not more than 25 years of age and Peterson not so old. There is an indictment for murder now hanging over their heads. As the rewards for their capture have never been revoked, nearly every officer in the United States has been constantly on the alert for them. Sheriff Judd will bring the prisoners back alone and promises to run no chances on the trip. He ought to arrive here in about one week, having left on Sunday for Wilmington.

Deseret Evening News
March 10, 1897

FROM THE ATTORNEY GENERAL

Defining the Powers of County Commissioners.

William Howard, county attorney of Huntington, Emery county, Utah, in a letter to the attorney general asks:

"Has the board of county commissioners the right to require the county assessor to assess and collect the dog tax? Second: If not, what will be the proper way to assess and collect the dog tax? Third: Has the board the right to appoint an officer not mentioned in the law defining his duties?"

Mr. Bishop says:

"The tax upon dogs may be collected, First, by the exercise of the police power possessed by the county, by the adoption of proper ordinances in relation thereto. Second, by assessing them as other property is assessed according to their value, in which case they would be collected as other similar taxes."

Eastern Utah Advocate
March 11, 1897

FERRON.

That a few warm days appeared last week is evidenced by the mud in our streets, which renders the progress of the pedestrian irksome.

The ball and supper on Monday evening gotten up in lieu of the "character ball" announced by the young ladies and postponed to give all a chance to participate in its revelry, was a decided success especially the supper in which all was heavier and while the merry joke and laugh went around viands disappeared as if by magic.

Celia Mildred Cheshire, daughter of Mr. and Mrs Wm G. Cheshire, died on Thursday March 4, aged eight months and five days. We extend our sympathies to the bereaved parents.

Salt Lake and Ogden papers please copy.

Jens Larsen, Arthur Parsons and Joe Braith valte all of Manti arrived here Thursday evening and left on Tuesday enroute to their sheep herds near the Colorado river. They report about six inches of snow and the people in general enjoying good health. No snow at Salina and spring work commenced

Wyatt Bryan one of our enterprising merchants has again restocked his store and seems to be doing a good business

The horse race at Molen drew most of our populace thither on Thursday leaving our streets almost destitute of loafers

EMERY COUNTY'S DOGS.

LOTS OF TROUBLE IN COLLECTING THE TAXES.

Something of a Muddle Which Calls
Forth an Opinion From Attorney-
General Bishop.

Emery county is having a great deal
of trouble with its dog population. The
problem in reality is how to collect
the imposed tax on the curs. Last
year the board of county commissioners of that county passed an ordinance
creating the constable of each precinct
a dog tax assessor and collector, with
instructions, if they found the dog
without a collar and the owner refused

or neglected to pay $1 in tax, the constable was to kill the dog. The theory of this plan was good enough, but the results were very unsatisfactory. The new board of commissioners subsequently passed another resolution requiring the county assessor to list the number of dogs owned by each taxpayer on the assessment roll at the same time the assessment was being made for other purposes, and requiring the assessor to collect $1 for each canine so listed.

This seems to have created quite a muddle, the assessor contending it was not a part of his duties to collect dog tax. Yesterday Attorney-General Bishop received a letter from County Attorney Howard of Huntington, who seeks enlightenment upon the following point:

First, has the board the right to require the assessor to assess and collect dog tax? Second, if not, what will be the proper way to assess and collect said tax? Third, has the board the right to appoint an officer not mentioned in the law defining his duties?

In his reply the attorney-general points to section 28 of the county government bill as giving the commissioners power to levy dog tax, and then he continues:

"The effect of the resolution adopted by the county commissioners in 1886, would be to seem to constitute the constable of each precinct a collector of the tax in question. It presupposes the existence of another resolution or ordinance permitting any one to own a dog upon the payment of a tax, and that upon the payment of such tax, the dog should be provided with a collar. If such resolution or ordinance had been duly passed by the county commissioners it would be an exercise of the police power vested in the county commissioners by said section 28, for the purpose of regulating the ownership of dogs with a view of preventing injuries to cattle or sheep as well as for the purpose of taxation. Such resolutions would not come within the taxing power of the county, but would come within the police power thereof. It would not be an imposition of a tax upon property on the theory of taxation of property according to its value, but, being for the purpose of regulation or in the exercise of the police power, it need not conform to the principle of uniformity which must be observed in the former case. The owner of every dog in the county, if the same had a value as property, would be liable, and it would be the duty of the assessor to assess the dog at its actual value, and the assessment and collection of the tax thereon would come within the duties of the assessor and collector of the county, whose duties are imposed by law; but when the tax or license is imposed under the police power, it is valid whether imposed for the purpose of regulation or revenue, or both. And although the property had been taxed under the general laws on the ad-valorem principle, such fact would not prevent the county from enforcing the resolutions which are referred to, for the purpose of licensing and regulating the privilege. The duty of enforcing the provisions of the resolutions thus passed by our board in pursuance of the police power which is vested in it, would properly fall upon the peace officers of the county to be designated by the board.

"You are, therefore, advised that the tax upon dogs may be collected, first: By the exercise of the police power possessed by the county, by the adoption of proper ordinances in relation thereto. Second, by assessing them as other property is assessed according to their value, in which case they would be collected as other similar taxes."

Salt Lake Tribune
March 13, 1897

HOUSE LACKS COURAGE

Sloan Says the Senate Has Intimidated It.

HE THREATENS TO RESIGN.

Outburst Caused by the Senate's Action on the Jubilee Appropriation Bill—Too Many Members Interested in Road Bills to be Brave—Mining Bill Passed Over the Governor's Veto—Bill Providing a Hospital for Miners Passed—Action on Appropriations.

Representative Sloan has threatened to secede from the House. He says it is not because he doesn't like the members personally, but because they lack courage collectively. The threat was made last evening, when in a brief communication the Senate announced that it had passed the semi-centennial resolution with amendments. Representative Sloan, in common with other members of the House, had supposed that the enrollment clerks were busy preparing the measure for signature. He had heard the communication read the evening before, stating that the resolution had been passed by the Senate without amendment, and had heard also the order for its enrollment. The proper method of procedure was debated for a time with much warmth. During this discussion Mr. Sloan announced his intention of withdrawing from the House if again it bent a suppliant knee to the Senate. He charged House members with lack of proper spirit, and said the only fear of losing local appropriations impelled them to advocate obedience to an overweening Senate. This charge he made more definite afterward when he related how one member asked him to yield so that the Senate would not kill the road appropriation he desired. The member expressed belief in the justice of Mr. Sloan's position, but had been intimidated by Senators who threatened to destroy the petty sum he sought for the improvement of a highway in his county.

FEELING INTENSIFIED.

The incident had the effect of further intensifying the feeling between the two houses, but similar incidents have occurred before, and, it is expected that, as in the past, the House will again yield after the customary platitudes, dubbed wisdom by their authors, have been spoken by the members who welcome an opportunity of bending their necks in order to display what they regard as a Christian spirit.

After idling away the morning session and an hour of the afternoon, the House finally succeeded in taking up the appropriations bill at 3 o'clock in the afternoon. The measure aggregates in excess of $1,100,000 in appropriations. Only a small portion of the bill has yet been considered.

CITY ELECTION PRECINCTS.

The House was still in complaisant mood and Senator Hamer's bill, providing for the division of cities and towns for the purpose of municipal elections was passed without a dissenting vote, as soon as the morning session began yesterday.

Then Senator Rideout's bill, permitting Boards of Commissioners to levy an annual tax for the purchase of textbooks and school supplies, was rejected, 10 to 18.

Oveson's bill, appropriating $1000 for a road between Castle Dale, Emery county, and Ephraim, Sanpete county, was passed after a short debate.

The fish and game bill was next taken up and, after being amended so as to permit seining in the Green, Grand and Colorado rivers, the bill was passed, as agreed upon the night before.

Duffin's bill, appropriating $1500 for a Washington county road, was rejected.

Then the public lands bill was taken up. On recommendation of the conference committee the House receded from its position as to the salary of commissioners.

PASSED OVER THE VETO.

Nebeker's mining bill, which had been vetoed, was called up by Callis. The veto message was read, after which debate on the merits of the bill occurred. Then the vote was taken, resulting in 23 affirmative votes for passage over the veto. Its accuracy was questioned and again the roll was called, resulting this time in the passage of the bill over the veto, Romney changing his vote in the nick of time to give the necessary thirty votes. The vote was:

Ayes—Bennion, Callis, Cook of Rich, Cook of Box Elder, Dresser, Duffin, Gibson, Greenwood, Hardy, Kimball of Cache, LaBarthe, Lund, Mangan, Martin, Maxfield, McKay, O'Brien, Oveson, Parry, Price, Ray, Romney, Shepard, Stewart, Sorensen of Sanpete, Sorensen of Grand, Taylor, Thomson, Thoresen, Wilson—30.

Nays—Anderson, Creer, Dotson, Forshee, Hansen, Hopkin, Kenner, Kimball of Carbon, Lemmon, Robinson, Roylance, Wheeler—13.

BRIGHAM YOUNG STATUE.

The Senate resolution, providing for a commission to arrange for the placing of a statue of Brigham Young in the National Capitol, was passed to third reading.

Robinson's bill, appropriating $750 for a road between points in Kane and Garfield counties, was passed, after which a fruitless effort was made to suspend the rules in order to reconsider the adverse vote on Duffin's bill.

Greenwood's bill, appropriating $1000 for the Clear Creek canyon road, was passed next.

Then the Sorensen resolution, appropriating extra amounts for various officials, came up. There was little objection to the $40 for Janitor Stewart, but there was decided opposition to paying Stenographer Hattie Thatcher $50, because of her being the employee of the committee clerks. The resolution was killed with the adoption of an adverse committee report.

Greenwood's memorial, asking Congress to set apart Red or Fish lake, in Sevier county, as a National park, was passed at the beginning of the afternoon session.

HOSPITAL FOR MINERS.

Sloan called up the Park City hospital bill, which, owing to the lateness of its introduction, had been tabled. The bill was then taken from the table.

Sloan, Callis and O'Brien spoke for the bill, the latter suggesting as an amendment that the hospital be located at Coalville. The amendment was withdrawn. Then the vote was had, resulting in the passage of the bill, 24 to 15.

APPROPRIATIONS.

It was after 3 o'clock when the general appropriation bill was taken up.

Representative Taylor of the committee reporting the appropriations bill made an explanation in general terms of the bill, and replied briefly to attacks made upon the committee.

The first item on the list, the Governor's salary, is fixed by the Constitution, and couldn't be changed, but the next appropriation, that for the Governor's private secretary, was the subject of an animated controversy. A motion to reduce the appropriation of $3000 to $2000 failed, after which the amount was fixed at $2500.

Then, with the knife ever in active operation, the work went on.

TANNER FIGHT RENEWED.

Shepard made an attempt to legislate the Supreme court reporter out of office by cutting off his salary.

Sloan and Kenner seconded the effort, while Roylance defended the appropriation, as did Sorensen of Grand, who believed there was no assurance that Mr. Tanner would be retained at the head of the Agricultural college after this academic year. He said that his belief arose from the unsatisfactory work being done by Mr. Tanner in that position.

The motion to strike out the entire salary failed; then Sloan moved to make the amount $500, or $250 a year.

The matter was undecided when it was decided to "walk around," which, in the language of plebeian non-parliamentarians, meant a recess for dinner.

DENOUNCED THE SENATE.

The evening session opened with an incident that occasioned a continuation of the recriminations that have been so often directed against the Senate. It occurred when a Senate communication was read stating that the Senate had reconsidered its action on the House joint resolution appropriating $20,000 for the semi-centennial celebration. Twenty-four hours before a communication announced that the Senate had passed the resolution without amendment. The House at that time had ordered the enrollment of the bill.

During the discussion that followed it developed that the Senate secretary had gotten the resolution from the House clerk by a ruse, after its reference to the Committee on Enrollment.

Sloan moved that the clerk notify the Senate that the matter was entirely out of its hands, having been regularly passed by both houses and in process of enrollment.

Other members were opposed to this form of action, preferring rather that the House should yield. Hansen, Duffin, Kimball of Cache and Price spoke in this vein, after which Sloan asserted that the only reason why further yielding to the Senate was advocated was in order to insure the passage of appropriations. He said that he had grown weary of membership in a body, supposed and intended by the Constitution to be co-ordinate with the Senate, but in reality always ready to yield and truckle at the dictation of the upper house. Then he concluded with a vehement declaration of independence and the assurance that if the House again submitted, he would withdraw from further participation in its deliberations.

The matter was referred to the steering committee and the appropriations bill again taken up.

ACTION ON APPROPRIATIONS.

The attempt to reduce the Supreme court reporter's salary to $250 failed, after which Shepard moved to make the amount $500 for the two years, and no part to be paid until at least one decision had been reported. This amendment carried.

Cook of Rich moved to cut the appropriation for the maintenance of the University of Utah from $31,000 to $60,750, and make the appropriation cover only 1897 and 1898, and not cover the academic years ending June 30, 1899.

This idea became gradually very popular, as it meant a reduction of one-quarter of the entire appropriation. No final action on the item was taken when the members absquatulated.

At this time, with appropriations recommended at $243,101, reductions of $5000 had been made, as follows:

Deductions—	From	To	Deduction
Governor's secretary	$3000	$2400	$ 600
Secretary of State, clerical assistance	6000	5000	1000
Secretary of State, contingent	3500	2400	1100
State Treasurer, clerical	800	600	200
Attorney-General, contingent	1500	1200	300
Fish and Game Warden, expenses	500	400	100
Bank Examiner, salary	2100	1200	900
Supreme Court Reporter	1000	500	500

Sarcasm for the Senate.

Representative Sloan tried to introduce this bill yesterday:

Be it enacted by the Legislature of the State of Utah:

Section 1. The House of Representatives of the Legislature is hereby abolished.

Sec. 2. The membership of the Senate is hereby reduced to three members, being the distinguished gentlemen who have controlled all legislation to date.

Sec. 3. The three members of the Senate referred to in section 2 of this act are hereby constituted life members thereof, with plenary powers and the right to appoint their successors.

Sec. 4. All State officers are hereby abolished, the whole affairs of the State to be controlled by the three distinguished, industrious and self-sufficient members already referred to in section 2.

Sec. 5. All powers not herein expressly reserved to the State are conferred upon the aforesaid three members of the Senate.

Sec. 6. This act is already in effect.

[TRIBUNE SPECIAL.]

Price, Utah, March 27.—News is just received here from Emery county of the shooting of Sheriff Tuttle of Orangeville by Joe Walker. It occurred in a box canyon down on the San Rafael river some time yesterday morning, and happened in this wise: J. M. Whitmore recently lost his three saddle-horses from his barn in Price, and Walker was suspected of the theft. Men have been on the trail for some days, and a few days ago J. M. Whitmore, M. C. Wilson, J. M. Thomas and C. L. Maxwell went south and, with Sheriff Tuttle, took up Walker's trail east on to the San Rafael. For two days the bandit was cornered in a narrow box canyon where it is next to impossible to get out when both ends are guarded, and yesterday morning the posse entered the canyon and finally came upon the fugitive. The men were separated, and Tuttle being near to Walker, dismounted because of the difficulty in getting over the rocks, and was trying to get in a position of safety where he might get his man. Walker shot him, however, before he had time to act. The ball penetrated the right thigh near the hip, and the bone was also fractured Walker had discarded his horse and was making his way on foot up the rugged mountain side. Thomas is reported to have followed on Walker's trail while Wilson, another of the party, rode to Cleveland and telephoned to Orangeville for Dr. Winters to meet the men bringing in the wounded Sheriff. Two other posses were organized in Huntington and Castle Gate and are scouring the country in the wake of the escaping man.

THE LATEST WORD

from Orangeville by telephone is that Tuttle had arrived and is resting quietly. The full extent of his injury is not yet reported. Whitmore and Wilson are expected to return to Price tonight, when more particulars can be had.

There is an organized gang of cattle and horse-thieves down in that country, and the citizens vow that it must be broken up.

CONFERENCE RATES.

Via the Oregon Short Line Railroad to Salt Lake and Return.

IDAHO.		From.	Rate.
From.	Rate.	Ogden	1.50
Huntington	$23.20	Hooper	1.20
Weiser	22.15	Syracuse Junct.	1.10
Payette	21.45	Layton	.75
Caldwell	19.70	Kaysville	.60
Boise	20.25	Farmington	.50
Nampa	19.25	Centerville	.35
M'tain Home	16.50	Woods Cross	.25
Shoshone	12.40	Terminus	1.50
Ketchum	15.90	Tooele	1.20
Hailey	15.25	Erda	1.10
Minidoka	8.50	Halfway House	.95
WYOMING.		Lake Point	.80
Opal	9.50	Garfield	.75
Diamondville	9.50	Saltair Junction	.60
Fossil	9.00	Chambers	.50
Cokeville	8.75	Frisco	6.70
IDAHO.		Milford	6.00
Montpelier	7.75	Smith's Ranch	6.00
Soda Springs	7.60	Black Rock	5.75
Bancroft	7.00	Clear Lake	5.25
Preston	4.25	Oasis	4.50
Franklin	4.25	Lemmington	3.90
UTAH.		Juab	3.25
Richmond	4.25	Nephi	3.00
Smithfield	4.10	Mona	2.50
Logan	3.80	Santaquin	2.35
Mendon	3.55	Payson	2.35
IDAHO.		Benjamin	2.25
Beaver Canyon	12.00	Spanish Fork	2.25
Dubois	11.00	Springville	2.10
Market Lake	9.00	Provo	1.90
Idaho Falls	8.50	Lake View	1.70
Blackfoot	7.40	Pleasant Grove	1.50
Pocatello	7.00	American Fork	1.35
McCammon	5.75	Lehi	1.25
Downey	5.00	Lehi Junction	1.20
Oxford	4.25	Eureka	3.25
STATE LINE.		Ironton	3.25
Cannon	4.00	Silver City	3.25
UTAH.		Mammoth	3.25
Cache Junction	3.25	Doremus	2.60
Collinston	2.75	Rush Valley	2.50
Dewey	2.50	Fairfield	2.25
Honeyville	2.25	Cedar Fort	1.95
Brigham	2.00	Draper	.70
Willard	1.75	Sandy	.50
Hot Springs	1.50	Junction	.25
Harrisville	1.50	Murray	.25

WALKER NOT YET CAPTURED.

Price, March 28.—M. C. Wilson, J. M. Whitmore, J. M. Thomas and C. L Maxwell arrived here today from the scene of the shooting of Sheriff Tuttle of Emery county. They were accompanied by an old mining man and prospector who was at Walker's camp when these men found it. From Mr. Wilson your representative gleans the following particulars regarding the affair. For several day the above named gentlemen with Sheriff Tuttle were on the trail of Walker. The suspected criminal, and eventually traced him to a very narrow box canyon some fifty or sixty miles from Cleveland down on the San Rafael river, in what is known as Mexican bend. This country is as wild, rugged and precipitous as any in the world and has favored the escape of many noted criminals. Thomas and Wilson were stationed outside of the canyon while Sheriff Tuttle, Whitmore and Maxwell, entered in search of Walker, who, leaving his horse and saddle, was making his way among the crags and cliffs. No trace of Whitmore's stolen animals had been found and no words passed between the posse and Walker. When the three men were within 150 feet of their man who was hid behind rocks and could not even be seen, he

COMMENCED FIRING.

His first shot struck the barrel of Maxwell's rifle and cracked it several inches. Firing then became general and several shots were exchanged, to no effect. Maxwell is known by Walker to be a bad man with a gun, and as he and the Sheriff were in range, it is supposed he missed Maxwell and hit the Sheriff. Walker is a good shot but must have been nervous or would have picked off all his men.

When Tuttle was shot the other men took refuge and awaited for nightfall it being too dangerous to do more in their position. The shooting occured at 4 o'clock Thursday afternoon and Sheriff Tuttle had to lie there in the bottom of the canyon until Friday morning before being removed.

In the meantime Wilson and Thomas, who had heard the shooting and saw from the cliffs that Tuttle was wounded, prepared their rig to enter the canyon. At daybreak Wilson rode to Cleveland the nearest telephone point, to notify friends and Dr Winters at Orangville to meet the party bringing Tuttle in, and Thomas alone drove up the canyon to the three imprisoned men. Nothing more was seen of Walker, and it is supposed he the flesh and breaking the bone. The wound is severe one and would have proved dangesous had it been summer time, on account of delay in securing medical aid, but the Sheriff is progressing as favorable as can be expected under the circumstances, and it is hoped will soon recover. He is at his home in Orangeville under the immediate care of his family and Dr. Winters.

Walker's action in commencing the fight appears to show his guilt in the crime of horse-stealing, and he will probably be a scarce article in this community hereafter. No further trace of the crimminal could be found, so the other posses from Huntington and Castle Dale were called back and disbanded.

Walker's horse, saddle and camp outfit were left on the ground and the boys report crows and hawks feasting on fresh beef which he must have killed a couple of days previous. They say one fugitive can stand off a thousand men when fortified in these wonderful fastnesses of the wilderness.—Tribune.

ESCAPED IN THE NIGHT.

The party then started with Sheriff Tuttle, who suffered intensely from his wound, until Dr. Winters met them Saturday morning. An examination disclosed the fact that the rifle ball had entered the back of the right thigh about eight inches below the hip and gone clean through, badly lacerating

Salt Lake Tribune
March 31, 1897

—The Wounded Johnson Boys.

Correspondence Tribune.]

Price, Utah, March 29.—Word received here today from Orangeville indicates the condition of Sheriff Tuttle as very serious indeed, and the doctor thinks this is the most critical time for the wounded man, but he was looking for a change which must soon come, and expressed a hope that it might be for the better. Sheriff Tuttle having been so exposed over night after being shot, caused him to contract a severe cold, and that with the time elapsing before any surgical assistance could be secured, caused the injured thigh to swell and become much inflamed. Since the Sheriff reached home he has of course received every possible attention, but as before stated, his condition is very critical.

Ebenezer Tuttle is well known throughout the State, especially by numerous peace officers, as this is the second time he has served as Sheriff of Emery county. When he acted in this capacity before, Carbon and Emery counties were one, and he was always found ready and willing to face any danger or brave anything for duty's sake. He has won the confidence and respect of our citizens, and is a most popular man with all classes, who will now earnestly pray for his speedy recovery.

The rifle Walker has belongs to J. M. Thomas, one of the pursuing party, and he simply took it away with him one morning recently when he had been stopping at that gentleman's ranch over night.

THE WOUNDED BOYS.

The two Johnson boys, the victims of the terrible gun accident here yesterday, were forced to wait and suffer for want of medical attention until today noon, when Dr. Allen of Provo, who had been telegraphed for, arrived. The doctor first paid his attention to Laurence, the eldest boy, and trimmed and dressed the lacerated fingers. His injuries are more serious than they at first appeared. Dr. Allen then placed young Oscar under chloroform and enlarged the wound in the neck made by the foreign substance. An incision was then made under the sternocleido-mastroid muscle, and the piece of cartridge shell traced to the back of the windpipe. The substance making the wound in the neck had not cut the jugular vein, as at first supposed, but had severed one of the large veins in the front of the neck and laid bare the carotid artery. It was a very narrow escape from certain bleeding to death, and Dr. Allen expresses the opinion that he has but a very slim chance of recovering as it is. Mr. and Mrs. Johnson will accompany Dr. Allen to Provo Tuesday morning, taking Oscar with them so that his case may have proper attention and be under the immediate care of the physician. The many friends of the family will wish that this terrible misfortune may not result fatally.

George W. Eldredge of Price had a cancer of the skin removed from the lower lid of the left eye today. Dr. Allen of Provo skillfully performed the operation.

UTAH ·NEWS.

Bandit Shoots a Sheriff.

Orangeville, Utah, March 27.—Sheriff Tuttle of Emery county was shot by Joe Walker, a horse thief, yesterday morning. Walker was suspected of stealing three horses from J. M. Whitmore of Price, and the sheriff with a posse was on his trail. The shooting occurred in a box canyon down on the San Rafael river. For two days the bandit was cornered in a narrow box canyon where it is next to impossible to get out when both ends are guarded, and yesterday morning the posse entered the canyon and finally came upon the fugitive. The men were separated and Tuttle being near to Walker, dismounted because of the difficulty in getting over the rocks, and was trying to get in a position of safety where he might get his man. Walker shot him, however, before he had time to act. The ball penetrated the right thigh near the hip, and the bone was also fractured. Walker discarded his horse and was making his way on foot up the rugged mountain.

Castle Dale Chips.

Something unusual for the news of Castle Dale to appear in the columns of the MESSENGER; however a little from us may be of interest.

Spring has come and the farmers feel confident of a good year

Sports among the young folks are in full force

J W Seely left today for Nephi to attend a board meeting of Wool Growers Association From there he will go to Salt Lake City to be present during conference

Castle Dale will have a good representation at the semi annual conference at Salt Lake

The work has commenced for putting up the wall of our new State Academy building

A crowd of boys left for Wyoming Saturday to find work at shearing sheep

Mr James Allred of Ephraim was in town Saturday

Bro O J Anderson's face is seen among us now Having been away most of the time for six years He is now at home making a general stir

The Home Dramatic Company has cast the realistic drama, 'Imogene or the Witches Secret ' Will present it in about two weeks The play is strongly cast and no doubt will be well rendered The same company played the " Lady of Lyons ' very creditably

The Orangeville Dramatic Company presented the ' Drunkard's Warning' to a medium house. Some parts were well taken The leading lady was excellent

The teachers institute, to have been held March 27, was postponed on account of Supt Scott and teachers from the north being held fast in the mud and forced to retreat Many of the teachers were present and some disappointment was felt An appointment was made for April 17, at Castle Dale

The Board of Examiners for teachers of Emery County have seen fit to have an early examination, the last Friday and Saturday in April By so doing accommodating many teachers who must go off to work during the summer months

Sheriff Tuttle after his encounter with the bandits on the Mexican Bend on the San Rafael is getting along as well as can be expected The wound received is a painful one, the thigh being pierced by the ball and the bone broken Being unattended to for thirty-six hours and no treatment for more than forty-eight, we may imagine he does not rest too easily

SCRIBO

Eastern Utah Advocate
April 8, 1897

Sern Anderson and Miss Sabina Oliphant were recently married in the Manti Temple. They have reached Orangeville and are now keeping house. We extend congratulations to the young couple.

FERRON.

On Friday evening the 2nd instant the Ferron Dramatic club gave a pleasant entertainment in the social hall. The attendance was not large owing to short notice given.

Sunday last witnessed the passing from this mortal sphere of Mrs. Clara A., wife of Geo. A. Petty, after a short illness of less than 24 hours. Mrs Petty was born at Manti Nov. 30th 1861, and with her husband moved to Ferron about 9 years ago. She was much beloved by all who knew her. The funeral obsequies were held on Monday, and a large procession followed the remains to their last resting place. A husband and five children are left to mourn her loss. The people of Ferron extend their heartfelt sympathies to the bereaved family.

County school superintendent, J. H Scott, stopped here Monday night on his way to visit the Emery school. He also expected to visit the Ferron schools, but was disappointed in finding them not yet in session.

The Ferron Roller mill will commence running the last of this week. Come with your grists. The mill is recommended to make as good flour as any mill in the west. This enterprise is a credit to the stockholders, who, with only about half the capital stock subscribed for have managed to push the work to completion, and will now commence reaping a reward for their expenditure.

The farmers are all busy either sowing or preparing to sow seed. The fact that, "He that reaps must sow" is well demonstrated and understood by our farmers. An abundant harvest is expected. The ground is in excellent condition for cultivation.

Many Advocate subscribers have missed the paper in the past two weeks, and were not at all sorry they did not get it when they discovered that jail bird Brownlee was temporarily in charge again. That Brownlee and Braffet combination in Price, must be peculiar, as the latter was a year ago an enemy of the former. Is it now a case of "Birds of a feather" Mr. Editor?

Eastern Utah Advocate
April 15, 1897

...mer was in Price this week. He reports things in Ferron to be on the gad vire.

...Boswell will go to Ferron next week to adjust and place in position the telephone instrument at Ferron.

Workmen will start to string the wire next week for the extension of the telephone line from Orangeville to Ferron in Emery county.

ORANGEVILLE.

With few exceptions the health of our people is good.

Olive, the pretty 11 year old daughter of Joseph and Mrs. Grange, died of pneumonia Tuesday morning after a sickness of only five days. The parents thus bereaved have the sympathy of the community.

The grand stand, stables, fences etc. at our association race track on the bench east between here and Castledale, are nearing completion An extra force of carpenters have been employed in order to get the track in readiness by the 16th of this month. That day promises to be the greatest sporting day yet had in Castle valley. The program includes two horse races, one foot race and two prize fights.

There are eleven new residences now in course of erection here.

Arrangements are being made for a new brick meeting house to be built this summer.

It will only be a short time before work will be commenced on our new school-house.

It is an open secret that Orangeville is to Castle valley, what Oakland is to the people of San Francisco, the city of homes.

Dolph Axelson the rustling mason of Cleveland, is building a two story drug store and residence for Dr. Winters at Castle dale.

Rumor has it that our enterprising townsman, Mr A. Nagely, has proffered to donate his town lot for depot grounds, to a proposed company to be organized as the Castle Valley railway company

Desert Evening News
April 20, 1897

Ferron—Past week very favorable to all farm work and growth of vegetion; farmers are seeding very fast; lucern is beginning to show quite green.

Eastern Utah Advocate
April 22, 1897

EMERY COUNTY COURT.

Reward Offered for Walker—An Ordinance Licensing Stock.

The board of county commissioners meet Monday and transacted the following business.

A petition was filed by Olsen and Brandon asking for license to sell liquor in Castledale was granted upon a new bond being filed.

The commissioners recommended to the governor, John Snow of Orangeville, and Orson Robbins of Huntington, for appointment as special agents to disburse the money appropriated for roads in Emery county. The first to disburse the $1000 to be expended in Straight canyon west of Orangeville, and the latter to disburse the $750 to be expended in Huntington canyon.

Andrew Christensen was appointed road supervisor for Castledale precinct.

A. E. King resigned the position of road supervisor of Ferron precinct and A. G. Conover was appointed in his stead. Scott M. Miller was appointed justice of the peace for Woodside precinct.

Henry Thompson was appointed a member of the board of health of Ferron.

A reward of $250 was offered for the arrest and conviction of Joe Walker for shooting at and wounding Sheriff Tuttle.

A reward of $15 was offered for evidence that will convict any one of selling liquor in Emery county without a license.

An ordinance was passed requiring all persons, firms or corporations that make stock-raising a business in Emery county that own over 15 head of horses or horned stock, or over 50 head of sheep to take out a license. The license to commence on the 1st day of July 1897. The charges will be on horses 50c. per head, horned stock 25c. per head, sheep 2c. per head There may be some fault found with this ordinance but other counties in the state are doing the same and the commissioners think that Emery county might as well start in now as any other time.

The following bills were allowed

Dr. Booth, Salary for 8 days in March,	$4.00
To roads in Castledale precinct,	$5.00
To roads in Molen precinct,	2.00
W H. Worther, attending quarentine,	30.00
M. C. Bryan	1.25
Wm. Howard, Cash advanced on criminal case,	15.00
Wm Howard expense account	34.00
Sam Larsen for posts	.80
R. Blake	1.00
W. Hinkin, putting up the posts	3.00
N Williams expenses	7.00
H P. Rasmussen,	5.00
O A. Wood	5.00
Total	$157.03

Court adjourned sine die.

Dr P C Christensen of Orangeville came to Price Tuesday. He is going through the county on professional business.

FERRON.

We had quite an interesting trial here last Friday in a case against Alec John son who resides in Huntington. Alec is frequently in trouble and this time he took a change of venue from Huntington to Ferron. The charge was drunkenness and disturbing the peace, and because the defendant was found guilty, some of his relatives and friends are feeling very sore about it. They give the witnesses for the prosecution the credit of all being liars, and the names they attach to the prosecuting attorney it would not be polite to mention. It seems that when some people go away from home a while and are called to some important position, that they get overly important themselves, but they have to get over it. The kickers in this case should not talk too loud, for there is a little law left yet as it did not use it all up in convicting this defendant. Young Johnson was fined $10 and costs, amounting in all to $94 05, and it is hoped this will prove a lesson to him and any other young men who think they have a perfect right to do as they please and insist upon breaking the law. It cannot be done with impunity and be stopped.

...ew grist mill is all ready for operations but has not yet started. The gentleman who superintended its construction is here inspecting the work and getting everything in shape to start up.

There is not quite so much sickness here now as there has been, but there is still some.

The Molen horse carried off the honors at the races in Orangeville last Friday and we are informed that Ferron and Molen men carried off considerable money as well.

Salt Lake Tribune
April 22, 1897

Rich Ore from La Sal.

[Correspondence Tribune.]

Orangeville, April 20.—Mr. A. E. Gibson, who resides at Cleveland, is showing samples of ore obtained in the La Sal mountains, north and east of Moab. The rock is from claims in which Mr. Gibson is interested, and recent developments are certainly most encouraging, for these samples show the richness of the proposition. Mr. Gibson claims that the last assay secured gave a return of 35 per cent copper and nearly $500 in gold.

ROAD COMMISSIONERS NAMED.

Disburse State Appropriation—Reward for Walker—Stock License.

Correspondence Tribune.]

Castle Dale, Utah, April 20.—The Emery County Commissioners met Monday, and among other things attended to I find the following items of general interest:

The board will recommend to the Governor that John Snow of Orangeville and Orson Robbins of Huntington be appointed special agents to disburse the money appropriated by the late Legislature for the construction of roads in Emery county. Mr. Snow is to disburse the $1000 to be expended in Straight canyon, west of Orangeville, and Mr. Robbins to disburse the $750 to be expended in Huntington canyon.

A reward of $250 was offered for the arrest and conviction of Joe Walker for shooting at and wounding Sheriff Tuttle.

An ordinance was passed requiring "all persons, firms or corporations that have stock in or make stock-raising a business in Emery county, that may own over fifty head of sheep or fifteen head of horses or horned stock, to take out a license." All licenses are to be dated from the 1st day of July, 1897. The charges will be, on horses, 50 cents per head, horned stock, 25 cents per head, and sheep, 2 cents per head.

This ordinance will affect a great number of cattle and sheep men in other counties who use the ranges in this county, and the Commissioners expect there will be fault found with their action, but they claim some counties have already a similar law in force, and they might as well start in now as any other time.

CO-OPERATION

is evidently believed in by the people of this county. The Deseret lake dam, which was washed out last fall, leaving the residents of that place without any means of irrigating their crops this season, has been repaired and built up even stronger than it was before the floods took it out. This good work has been accomplished by the united efforts of the people of Ferron, Castle Dale, Huntington and Wellington who have donated sufficient labor to make the necessary repairs.

NOTE AND PERSONAL.

Mrs. Mabel Moore of Orangeville, daughter of Sheriff Tuttle, went to Salt Lake Tuesday.

Thomas Wright and family of Cedar City have located on a farm near Huntington recently.

A handsome new grist mill has just been completed at Ferron, and is almost ready to commence operations.

The ground is in excellent condition and our farmers are all very busy putting in crops. Probably this will be a great year for grain in this county.

Poles are being erected for the telephone line extension between Orangeville and Ferron. The line will soon be completed in every detail, and when opened for use will make the distance covered over fifty miles from Price.

The district schools at Ferron have been closed nearly all winter, on account of sickness and disease being prevalent among the children. Diphtheria and other contagions have carried off nearly thirty children this winter in that one small town, and the children are now afflicted with croup.

A good-sized colony from Wayne county is moving into Castle valley, and some thirty families have already located on the flat north of Orangeville. They are taking up farms and making a ditch from Cottonwood river to cover their land. More such home-seekers are wanted in the valley, for there are thousands of acres of splendid land to be had if people are willing to work and secure water for it.

A BOLD ROBBERY

Committed at Castle Gate, Utah.

TWO MEN SECURED $7,800.

They Robbed the Pay Master—Over a Hundred Men Witnessed the Deed.

PRICE, Utah, April 21.—One of the most daring and successful hold-ups on record occurred today at about 12:30 o'clock at Castle Gate. This is, or should have been pay day for the coal miners there and $9,800 came down on No 2 Rio Grande Western which reached here at 12:26 p. m. When the train reached Castle Gate the money was delivered by the express agent to E. L. Carpenter, paymaster of the P. V. Coal company, who was with T. W. Lewis, an employee of the company. They crossed over the tracks and went onto the platform in front of the Wasatch store. The passenger train pulled out for Helper, and about 100 men or more were congregated around the store and in the road near the post-

office, which is close at hand. Two rough individuals who had been loitering around town and in the saloon all day yesterday were also there with their horses. Just as Mr. Carpenter was nearing the outside stairs at the east side of the building leading up to the P. V. Coal company's office over the store, one of these individuals dismounted and placing a six-shooter in Carpenter's face said: "Drop them sacks," and "hold up your hands." At the same time the second robber was whirling a six-shooter in his hand and firing shots promiscuously to create consternation. Carpenter and his deputy complied with the highwayman's request, when the bold outlaw immediately secured the money and handing it to his pal, started off down the canyon. The horse belonging to the man who did the work got loose during the excitement and he had to run 300 yards down the road to catch it, but in the meantime the other hold-up was riding at breakneck speed away with the boodle. Mr. Lewis managed to escape into the store with one sack of silver containing $1,000 and the other sack of silver was either dropped or thrown away by the departing robber and was picked up a short distance from the store, but the satchel containing greenbacks and gold amounting in all to $7,800 was successfully made away with.

No one in all that crowd of men had a gun, and everybody was rattled and did not hardly realize what had happened until too late.

Three shots, however, were fired at the retreating highwaymen from upstairs windows of the office to no effect. Down the canyon they rode for fully half a mile through the thickly settled part of the town before getting away from the houses. Just north of the Half Way house the fugitives cut all telegraph wires, apparently to keep the news from reaching Sheriff Donant at Price, and in this, for a time at least, they were successful.

the foothills and came down past Garden creek, keeping two or three miles away and back from the railroad and farms in Price canyon, making a straight cut across the country, striking the main Price and Huntington road in Emery county at about 2:30 p.m., in Washboard flat, for just about that time the telephone wire running south to Price through Emery county was also cut. This was done too late for their purpose, however, as word had already reached here and messages were sent to Cleveland, Huntington and Castle Dale to at once organize posses and be in readiness to intercept the robbers. By this time, 7 p. m., they are well out of reach and in the vicinity of their rendezvous in San Rafael county, if not overtaken or intercepted by some of the numerous posses sent out. In about 30 minutes after the robbery at Castle Gate an engine was secured and Mr. E. L. Carpenter and Mr. Robert Dickson of Price, an eye witness to the robbery, and others boarded it and began a chase down the canyon, but they got no sight of the men and came on to Price.

On they sped and with no one in pursuit until they reached Spring creek canyon, half a mile north of Helper. Crossing the mouth of this canyon they evidently took the trail leading across

Sheriff Donan hastily gathered a posse of four men who, armed with Winchester rifles and well mounted, started off south toward Cleveland at 2 p. m., so they were but a few miles behind the escaping desperadoes, but will probably not overtake them, as the outlaws were riding two good mustangs.

Mr. Carpenter immediately offered a reward of $2,000 for their capture, or $1,000 for the return of the money. At 3 p. m. another posse left Price for Emery county, and they returned at 6 o'clock, upon hearing of the robbers being so far ahead of them.

At 4:30 p. m. the telephone wire was repaired. It had been cut nine miles south of Price. The first message received over the wire was to the effect that two men having white and bay horses and answering to the description of the robbers had been seen off east of Cleveland. At 6:30 p. m. the mail arrived from Emery county and the carrier stated that he met the two bandits just this side of Cleveland and about 15 miles from Price, and that these two men kept several rods away from him and the road, but he noticed them particularly. One man was smooth shaved and wore a blue coat and black hat, and the other a broad and light hat, so these were most assuredly the thieves.—Herald.

Salt Lake Herald
April 24, 1897

COMMISSIONERS NAMED

For the Semi-Centennial Pioneer Jubilee Celebration.

THE SELECTIONS ANNOUNCED BY THE GOVERNOR.

They Will Supervise the Expenditure of the Amounts Appropriated to the Various Counties Outside of Salt Lake.

HE governor has appointed jubilee commissioners for the several counties in the state, whose duty it will be to spend the money appropriated by the last legislature toward the coming celebration. The parties named are: Beaver, John R. Murdock, of Beaver; Box Elder, Rudger Clawson, of Brigham City; Cache, Lyman R. Martineau, Logan; Carbon, W. G. Sharp, Castle Gate; Davis, John W. Hess, of Farmington; Emery, C. G. Larsen, Castle Dale; Grand, M. W. Warner, Moab; Garfield, Thomas Sevy, Panguitch; Iron, Francis Webster, Cedar; Juab, C. H. Blanchard, Silver City; Kane, Thomas Chamberlain, Orderville; Millard, Ira N. Hinckley, Fillmore; Morgan, Richard Fry, Morgan; Piute, Charles Morrill, Junction; Rich, Archibald McKimmon, sr., Randolph; Sanpete, William D. Livingston, Manti; San Juan, F. A. Hammond, Bluff; Sevier, Theodore Brandley, Richfield; Summit, A. D. Moffatt, Park City; Tooele, Hugh S. Gowans, Tooele City; Uintah, R. S. Collett, Vernal; Utah, Lafayette Holbrook, Provo; Washington, David H. Cannon, St. George; Wasatch, Abram Hatch, Heber; Wayne, W. E. Robison, Loa; Weber, G. H. Islaub, Ogden.

These commissioners will supervise the expenditure of the amount which was appropriated toward the celebration and divided up among the counties outside of Salt Lake, the sums for each county ranging from $150 to $350, according to population.

We note with pleasure that last week the Emery county commiss'oners recommended John Snow of Orangeville and Orson Robbins of Huntington as special agents to disburse the appropriations made by the late legislature for building roads through Straight canyon and Huntington canyon. As soon as the governor acts upon the recommendations the work can be proceeded with and the roads built without delay.

FERRON

Diphtheria is again in our midst, and two cases are reported.

The District schools are once more in session, but there is a very small attendance.

Farm hands and teamsters are in great demand at present. Every farmer seems to be behind with his spring work.

Sunday was the first day we have had water in the town ditch for over two weeks, it having been turned out for cleaning the ditch. The people found it a big chore to haul water from the river for culinary purposes.

The Ferron Roller Mill company celebrated the completion of their new grist mill, by giving a ball and supper for the stock holders and a few of their most intimate friends. Fruits and liquid refreshments were freely dealt out. The participants dispelled all care and enjoyed a "jolly good time" It was kept up until the early hours of morning.

Talk regarding Mrs. M. E. Cheshire's ability to treat diphtheria, and to practice midwifery, has induced that lady to get testimonials from some of her patients. The lady has been successful in a large majority of the cases which she has treated. Among those who testify of Mrs. Cheshire's ability are Mr. and Mrs Albert Edwards, Mrs A. M. Stevens, David Reed and Arthur Cox.

ORANGEVILLE.

Bishop J. Robertson has two very sick children. The little ones are down with whooping cough, and a great many other children in town are afflicted with the same disease

C. G. Van Buren and Wm Taylor are both "under the weather," through an attack of the mumps.

"Poverty Flat" will hereafter be known as "Silver Dell." It is evident that the McKinley wave of coming prosperity, has struck the residents of the flat.

Bert Childs and his charming bride have settled down and started to keep house.

The wedding reception of Wm. Curtis and Miss Mercy Miles took place Friday last. A grand ball was given in the evening. The bride was very prettily attired. Our best wishes and congratulations go with them.

We begin to mourn the loss of the bridge over Cottonwood river The stream has risen so much lately, as to make it extremely difficult to cross with safety Teams will have to go to Orangeville via. Castledale bridge in the near future.

We had quite a heavy rain storm last Sunday.

Joint session of the M. I. A. was held Sunday evening, and the house was well filled. The program was an excellent one and the numbers were well rendered.

J. W. Seeley of Orangeville passed through Price to-day, en route to Mount Pleasant to attend the funeral of J. K. M'Clanahan, who was shot Tuesday night at Salina M'Clanahan was attempting to enter Mrs. Nelson's house, when 'er son Arther procured a Winchester rifle and shot him as he was running away

HUNTINGTON.

The teachers examination was held at Castledale last Friday and Saturday. Those who took the examination will receive their grade certificates as soon as the examining board can prepare their report.

The fields and orchards have once more put on their spring raiment, and everything is verdant again even to the eagle eye of the coming fall politician.

Huntington river is very high, but there is no immediate danger to farms on the creek

Quarterly conference will be held here next Saturday and Sunday There will doubtless be a large turnout from the surrounding towns.

The district court will not be held at Castledale until Monday, 24th instant.

The matter of securing a daily mail through Emery county as suggested in the Advocate last week, is a good idea, and is something the people need badly. Our citizens should take the hint and see what can be done.

Charl-s Clawson was given a preliminary hearing before Justice Cox last week on the charge of adultery preferred against him by Miss Sarah Lewis of Cleveland. A brief account of his arrest and of the claims in the case, was published by the Advocate last week. At the hearing three witnesses outside of the prosecuting witness, were examined and the evidence adduced against the defendant was of a very damaging character. It was shown that Miss Lewis, the plaintiff is 21 years of age, and has resided with the Clawson family for the past fifteen months. She claims that at diverse times up to and during October last, the defendant has been guilty of criminal intimacy with her at times when his wife was absent from home temporarily, and when she had accompanied him into the field etc.

The other witnesses testified to having noted Clawsons actions toward the girl, and had seen his undue intimacy shown in a lirivious manner on several occasions. No witnesses were put on the stand for the defense, and Clawson was bound over in $800 bonds to await the action of the district court, where the case will probably be taken on information

C. E. Kofford has been retained as attorney for the defendant, and the defense will, it is hinted, make the blame for the girls condition, appear to lie elsewhere, which at this time seems a hard matter to do. Miss Lewis will soon become a mother, and she stoutly clings to the assertion that Clawson is the author of her ruin. It is maintained by the prosecution that the defendant tried to bribe a witness, to testify at the hearing that the girl had blamed another person, but the bribe did not work

There is considerable talk over this most shameful scandal, and people are fully awake to the moral effect of so pernicious a crime. They hope the wretch who is guilty of this moral depravity, will be given the full extent of the law, and rid the community of one who has placed a blot upon the good people of Emery county.

At last accounts Clawson had not succeeded in procuring bondsmen. The trial of this case promises to be a racy affair.

Salt Lake Tribune
May 7, 1897

NOTE AND PERSONAL.
Wm. Curtis and Miss Mercy Miles were married at Orangeville last Friday.
B. F. Luke, superintendent of the Orangeville Co-op, is in Salt Lake this week.

Castle Dale Chips.

Quarterly Conference will be held May 8th and 9th at Huntington

Rain, rain, the beautiful rain! Most of the crops are in, and much good in consequence

District Court will convene about May 24th.

It is rumored that $1,000 has been appropriated to make or repair the road through straight Canyon This done we will be joined to the Sanpete County road via Ephraim

Emery County Mercantile Company has purchased Carl Wilberg's building for a store It is soon to be stocked with goods A Jameson is to take charge. Jacob Sorenson will put in shelves and counter

Teacher's examination was held April 30th and May 1 Eleven applicants for certificates were there.

Miss Lina Larsen of Ephraim gave her friends a visit here, and also took the teachers examination

Lars and Charley Christensen of Chester came to Castle Dale a few days ago Lars brought his household goods and will make this place his future home. We are glad to hear it Success to you. Charley left for Chester Tuesday

The fellows of whom so much has been said have made well their escape It was well planned They having been at work during the winter and spring, and made an entirely new trial through the rocks and ledges This was unknown to any but themselves. After they passed Cleveland their escape was sure, for posses in pursuit seeking familiar trails were easily eluded.

                                    Scribe

ORANGEVILLE.

A light frost Sunday morning did little damage to other than tender lucern.

Quarterly conference at Huntington was well attended by our people. The good people of Huntington made everybody feel welcome.

Spring is here at last and the verdant fields and lawns are a pleasing sight.

County commissioners meet again on Saturday May 22.

Sheriff Tuttle is now getting out a little on crutches.

Several people from Wayne county arrived last week. It is probable that more will follow and that they will locate on the bench north of town.

Whooping cough is still with us and many are the sufferers

The wedding dance of Mr. and Mrs. Swen Anderson took place Friday evening The beautiful bride looked pretty in her elegant dress of white casimere trimmed with pale line silk. We wish them all manner of happiness and worldly success.

NOTICE TO CREDITORS

Estate of McCarl Johanson, deceased Notice is hereby given by the undersigned, administrator of the estate of McCarl Johanson, deceased, to all creditors of, and all persons having claims against the said deceased, to exhibit them with the necessary vouchers within four months after the first publication of this notice, to the said administrator at his residence in Huntington precinct, Emery county Utah the same being the place for the transaction of the business of said estate

PETER JOHANSON,
Administrator of the estate of McCarl Johanson, deceased.

Dated at Huntington, April 11, 1897

Geo. M Miller, Attorney for the estate of McCarl Johanson, deceased.

fp apr, 15 lp may 6,

NOTICE FOR PUBLICATION.

No 2268

Land Office at Salt Lake City, Utah, April 11, 1897,

Notice is hereby given that the following named settler has filed notice of his intention to make final proof in support of his claim, and that said proof will be made before Wm Howard U S Circuit Court Commissioner for Emery County at Huntington, Utah, on May 27 1897 viz William White on H E. No. 8*42, for the N¼ SW 1-4 of Section 8 Tp 17 S R 9 E

He names the following witnesses to prove his continuous residence upon and cultivation of, said land, viz Charles H Brown George Westwood, George Watson, J F. Quinn, all of Huntington Utah

BYRON GROO, Register

Frank D Hobbs, Attorney

a22m27

EMERY COUNTY'S VETERANS.

Black Hawk Warriors There Number About a Hundred.

Correspondence Tribune.]

Huntington, Utah, May 12.—Monday evening the Black Hawk war veterans of Huntington met with a few of their comrades from surrounding towns and effected a temporary organization. M. E. Johnson was made temporary chairman, and William Howard, temporary secretary. Several of the veterans related reminiscences of their experiences during those years of fighting with the Indians, and altogether they spent a very pleasant evening.

A week from Saturday, at 4 p. m., another meeting is called to form a permanent organization in the county, and as there are estimated to be nearly a hundred of the Black Hawk veterans in the settlements of Emery county, it bids fair to become a strong organization in these parts. A summer encampment has been suggested, in which it is desired that all the veterans and their families will take part. They are organizing to assist in furthering the ends sought to be attained by their comrades in other parts of the State.

EMERY STAKE CONFERENCE.

SAINTS URGED TO BREAK UP ROBBERS' ROOST.

Elder Fjelstead Pleads that by Ancient Usage the Prophets Gave Laws, and Should Have Voice Now.

Correspondence Tribune.]

Huntington, Utah, May 12.—Apostle Anton H. Lund and Elder C. D. Fjelstead of the presidency of the seventies were present at the stake conference this week, and both did considerable preaching to the people. Much good counsel and advice was given for the temporal as well as the spiritual guidance of the people.

APOSTLE LUND warned the church members against the spirit of indifference which is so manifest and cautioned them to be on one side or the other in all matters of importance. He read from Ephesians iv., 1-14, on the ancient organization of the Church of Christ, and argued that the present organization of the Church of Jesus Christ of Latter-day Saint was in exact accordance with the ancient order of things generally. Mankind should listen to the promptings of the spirit, and they will invariably be led aright. The authorities of the Mormon church are men who seek the Lord, and are ever striving for the good of Israel. There must be a universal faith, a union of all in the faith, and then the purposes of God can be accomplished. The speaker strongly advocated public improvements being made, and desired every one of the saints to interest themselves in public works, so that their towns and the country will be built up and beautified.

ELDER FJELSTEAD

spoke upon the evils of strong drink, and hoped men would be industrious and not lose their self-respect. They should not even enter a saloon, nor indulge in profanity. He then lectured the saints for showing a lack of faith in the authorities of the church, and said: "The authorities have a hard time to stand vindicated before the people, who claim they have no political rights, or no right to take part in politics. Moses and Abraham gave laws for the temporal guidance of the people. Other ancient prophets and apostles took part and assisted in making the laws of the land, and so did even Christ. Have the prophets now, not the same privilege as their predecessors?" The speaker cited numerous instances in support of his theory that the apostles as citizens of the Republic, have a perfect right to take active part in politics, though he did not say they should or could do so as church dictators.

WERE MOST SEVERE.

Both of these speakers were most severe on the existing evils of the day; the filthy scandals and the unchastity of some of the people; the wickedness which now exists in various parts of Utah, and finally the dens of thieves and outlaws infesting the San Rafael. The saints were urged to use every effort in their power to break up this lawless gang, and to unite together on all propositions for the bettering of their condition morally or otherwise.

CONFERENCE NOTES.

The various bishops' reports showed the stake generally to be in a thriving and prosperous condition.

The Huntington choir, consisting of over fifty voices, are well trained, and their music is excellent. It is now proposed to take this choir with a few other picked voices, from the county, and enter the contests at Salt Lake City in July during the Jubilee. They propose to give a series of concerts to get sufficient means for the purpose.

Stake President C. G. Larsen asked that efforts be made to swell the Brigham Young monument fund, so as he could soon remit the full quota from this stake.

Conference adjourned to meet at Cleveland Saturday and Sunday, August 7th and 8th.

Salt Lake Tribune
May 19, 1897

LARGE NUMBER COMING

Host of Delegates will Attend Western Congress.

GREAT INTEREST MANIFESTED

Letters from Various Sections of the Trans-Mississippi Country Indicate that the Coming Meeting will be the Greatest of the Series—Missouri's Strong Delegation—Large Party Coming from Louisiana—South Desires Closer Relations with the West—Delegates Chosen.

Recent developments indicate that the ninth annual session of the Trans-Mississippi Commercial congress, which convenes in this city on July 14th, will be a record breaker in point of attendance and interest. An immense correspondence is coming into the office of Secretary W. H. Culmer, and the yellow slips containing the names of appointed delegates are piling up at a rapid rate. A large amount of labor is required in caring for this mail matter. Circulars and printed information are being constantly sent out and as fast as the names of appointees are received a letter is sent to each one requesting him to fill out a blank declaring his intention to attend the congress. The O. R. & N., the Rio Grande Western and the Oregon Short Line have already announced a rate of one fare for the round trip, to the congress, with the limit extended to allow the delegates to attend the Jubilee.

Encouragement comes from St. Louis in a letter from Chairman H. R. Whitmore, who writes in part: "Each day the outlook seems more promising, judging from the correspondence which I am receiving, than it ever has before, so far in advance of the time of meeting and indications now point to the largest and most interesting meeting we have yet had. I have written to each of the Governors urging the appointment of delegates who will attend. Gov. Stephens of this State (Missouri) has already appointed our delegation, which I regard as an especially strong one being headed by ex-Gov. Stone, who with several others are warm friends of Mr. Bryan and will doubtless take an active interest in our meeting."

GREAT INTEREST SHOWN.

Other letters are of similar interest. An old newspaper man of Pleasant Hill, Mo., who is coming to the congress writes: "I think it is high time that the West was taking a position in National affairs that will enable it to exert the influence to which it is entitled. We must look after our own interests in a broad sense and by conference, discussion and organization ascertain the best mode of protecting our interests and determining what we can and will do."

D. C. Scarborough, an attorney of Natchitoches, La., has been appointed as a delegate, and in accepting, says: "My impression is that if you can secure a very low rate for round-trip tickets with some stop-off privileges the representation from the Southern States will be simply immense. I recognize a very deep seated disposition among the people of the South to see the West, and know something of that country and build up a close trade relation between the two sections by which they will become buyers and sellers direct to each other, without passing through the hands of Eastern dealers who are unnecessary parties to the transactions."

J. H. Bradley of Omaha writes: "We

L. H. Bradley of Omaha writes: "We intend to send as large a delegation from Nebraska, as possible."

Gov. R. B. Smith of Montana, sends the information that Hon. John M. Quinn, editor of the Butte Miner, has consented to prepare an address upon some one of the topics suggested by the executive committee.

L. P. Eastin, editor of the Ventura, Cal., Independent, who will come as a delegate says: "I passed through or near Salt Lake in 1847 en route to California and would be pleased to see how it looks fifty years later."

Texas is coming forward with appointees. A list of the names received since those last published in The Tribune is here given:

ADDITIONAL DELEGATES CHOSEN

Manti, Utah, Hon. Joseph Judd.

Price, Utah, Hon. R. G. Miller.

Farmington, Philander Hatch.

Texarkana, Tex., Frank D. Hiller, Ed Benjamin, W. D. Tilson and H. F. Briley.

Beaumont, Tex., W. A. Ward, J. D. Polk, W. S. Davidson, C. H. Figley, N. R. Strong and G. C. Osgood.

Longview, Tex., R. B. Levy, Jr., Walter Cunyns, A. J. More, A. T. Castleberry, E. A. Reese, J. P. Kuykendall.

Stephenville, Tex., N. C. Baldwin.

Alvin, Tex., A. J. Birchfield.

Wood county, Tex., B. F. Read.

Richmond, Tex., Hon. Oscar D. Kirkland, Hon. Jas. M. Moore, D. R. Pearson, J. H. P. Davis, C. A. Beasley, J. R. Farmer, S. J. Winston, Dr. A. A. Bailey, J. T. Dyer, George Dunlap.

Thompson, Tex., J. W. Slavin.

Boothe, Tex., F. J. Boothe.

Fulshear, Tex., S. J. Avis.

Harlem, Tex., W. H. Bertrand.

Foster, Tex., J. C. Hunker.

Victoria, Tex., J. M. Brownson, G. A. Levi, J. J. Wilder, E. L. Dunlap and J. A. McFadden.

Nursery, Tex., W. H. Kyle.

Farmington, Utah, J. W. Ross.

Carterville, Mo., W. A. Dougherty, Jacob Litteral, C. H. Lillibridge, B. D. Mowry, J. B. McDearmond and W. B. Kane, president Carterville Commercial club.

Pleasant Hill, Mo., R. B. Bishop and F. W. Little.

Omaha, Neb., Alvin Saunders, ex-Governor and United States Senator; C. W. Lyman, G. M. Hitchcock, Arthur Smith, J. E. Markel, E. Dickenson, Dudley Smith, Charles Metz, H. T. Clark and Daniel Farrell.

Mount Ayr, Ia., H. R. Wilson, M. L. Bevis, F. E. Sheldon and Clyde Dunning.

Eureka Springs, Ark., Harvey Beauchamp.

Stuttgart, Ark., N. S. Savage, W. D. Motherot, G. W. Hand, G. C. Lewis, Philip Rench and John Underwood.

Logan, Ia., Col. C. F. Luce.

Lamoni, Ia., Rev. J. W. Wight and Mayor W. W. Scott.

Newton, Ia., Senator J. R. Girrell.

Fargo, N. D., R. S. Lewis, H. Harrington, J. J. Jordan, James Kennedy, G. Q. Erskine, John D. Benton, Martin Hector and John E. Haggart.

Natchitoches, La., D. C. Scarborough, Hon. G. W. Kile, C. V. Porter, Dr. J. S. Stephens, Jr., Julius Aaron and A. E. Simon.

Houma, La., John J. Kleiner, Alp. Dupont, A. F. Davidson, Arthur J. Daspit, Julien Blum and D. A. Chanvin.

Butte City, Mont., James H. Lynch.

Brigham City, Utah, Rudger Clawson.

Pleasant Grove, Utah, James O. Bullock.

Port Angeles, Wash., M. J. Carrigan and James Stewart.

Tombstone, Ariz., M. D. Scribner.

Lisbon, N. D., Hon. M. L. Earle, Hon. P. H. Rourke and Hon. H. S. Grover.

St. John, N. D., Joseph Fanning, William Gedbreth and Frank Peltier.

Rolla, N. D., A. Cooper, W. J. Haskins and Thomas Hesketh.

Nephi, Utah, William Paxman.

Parowan, Utah, George M. Decker.

Denton, Tex., Dr. J. P. Blount.

Belton, Tex., George C. Robinson and L. M. Smith.

Denton, Tex., J. T. Bottorff.

Livingston, Tex., C. B. Dunnam and L. Mawry.

Colita, Tex., F. W. Bentnell.
Carrigan, Tex., T. H. Williams.
Hortense, Tex., J. A. Handley.
Leggett, Tex., J. C. Leggett.
Hillsboro, ex., Ex-Mayor C. J. Scor-
rells, Hon. T. S. Smith and H. G. Gib-
son.
San Diego, Tex., W. W. Meek, E. N.
Gray, N. C. Collins and C. L. Coyner.
Hebbronville, Tex., William Hebbron.
Benavides, Tex., Archie Parr.
Mineola, Tex., J. G. Bromberg.
Wahoo, Neb., J. B. Cook and Olaf
Birgren.
Wansa, Neb., Robert Lynn.
Nebraska City, Neb., John C. Wat-
son, M. L. Hayward, E. S. Brown and
C. W. Seymour.

Monticello, Ark., C. T. Harris and
wife, John J. Whitaker and wife, J. J.
McCloy and wife and Walter Lambert
and wife.
Wilmer, Ark., Barney Kidd and wife.
Brady, Tex., F. M. Newman.
Wichita Falls, Tex., Frank Brown
and A. F. Fossett.
Huntington, Utah, William Howard.
Cleveland, Utah, L. P. Overson.
Castle Dale, Orange Seely.
Orangeville, Jasper Robertson.
Ferron, Utah, Samuel Singleton.
Emery, Utah, Alonzo Brinkerhoff.
Camden, Ark., Milton A. Elliott.
Harrison, Ark., John Murphy.
Waldron, Ark., Dr. G. Cox, D. A. Ed-
wards, Daniel Hon, G. S. Evans, W. L.
Beavers and T. G. Bates.

Territorial Enquirer
May 20, 1897

Jottings.

Emery county is to have a telephone
line. Poles for the telephone connection with Orangeville and Price have
all been placed in position, and the
stringing of wire is being hastened
with all possible dispatch. The workmen expect to have the line all completed by Friday.

Eastern Utah Advocate
May 20, 1897

ORANGEVILLE

Lucerne will soon be in blossom here.

Fruit trees are laden with blossoms
and there will doubtless be a large crop
of all kinds of fruit this year.

Mrs. Mabel Moore has returned home
from a visit with relatives in Salt Lake
City.

Last Wednesday the 14 instant, Robert
Davis and Miss Mary Miles were married. A reception was given in the
afternoon, a grand ball was given in the
evening

Bishop Robinson's children, have recovered from their recent illness, and are able to be out again.

By the aid of crutches Sheriff Tuttle is again getting around, but he goes about very slowly, and will yet be some time before he is entirely recovered and gains his former strength. We are pleased to see the sheriff out again.

Albert Nagley and family are this week moving to Salt Lake City where they will hereafter reside. Albert is a hustler and has made many friends in Emery county, who will wish him success in his new location.

FERRON.

Several prominent business men from Price have made visits to Ferron the past few days.

Assessor M C. Bryan now spends much of his time in Castledale.

A Livingston and Orange Seely of Castledale were here last week procuring grain.

Several Springtown boys were in town the other evening.

The big north canal which carries the water supply to Silver Dell, broke last week and did much damage to the crops out that way. It also caused the town creek to break.

Wyatt Bryan has increased his stock of goods, and is putting in an entire new line.

A. D. Dickson has taken up his abode in Castledale for the summer.

Frank Carroll paid Price a visit last Sunday.

Dr Winters has put a soda water fountain in his drug store.

People are all busy on their farms at present.

The county road between Orangeville and Castledale has been changed a little near here, to make it run around the section line.

Cottonwood river is still pretty high but is forded as usual.

All the fields around Ferron look well, and show fine prospects for large crops.

George Petty Jr. who has been in Salt Lake City for a short time, returned to his home in Emery last Friday.

George Petty's saw-mill in Ferron canyon will be put in operation next week

Ferron river is on the rampage, and has been high for some time.

A number o'men have gone to the saw-mill to work. They left here on Tuesday.

Wyatt Bryan returned home this week from a business trip to Price and Salt Lake City.

A shipment of oranges, bananas, cherries ect, was brought to Bryans store this week, and there was more in the lot than has ever before been sent to Ferron.

The infant baby of A. G. Conover, died of whooping cough last Sunday and was interred Monday.

Hurrah' for the telephone! The poles are all set between here and Orangeville, the wire is being strung and the telephone instrument will be placed in position Friday. The line will then be in operation through from here to Price and the advent of the line will be celebrated in royal style. A dance will be given Friday night and everybody is invited to join the Ferronites, and have a good time with them. We are proud to be at last connected with the living world

Two new cases of diptheria were reported late last week one of which was of the malignant kind.

The oil field discoveries are again attracting attention 85 miles south east of Ferron. John Fugate has gone out with a party to look up the locating of the lands, and see what can be done in the way of development. Should the gentlemen report favorably, there is a probability of work being done soon and machinery being placed on the ground. There is plenty of crude petroleum on the surface of the springs, and the gentlemen who are interesting themselves in the matter, have hopes of obtaining, at a depth of about 200 or 300 feet, a good article for lighting purposes. Should their operations prove successful, this will form another industry for Utah, and will be a great benefit to Emery county and eastern Utah. There is said to be great quantities of paraffin wax in the whole locality.

There will be a gala-day here on Tuesday next the 25th It will be held in Lemon's grove, and will be a sort of May day celebration because nothing was done on the first of the month. A May pole will be erected and the children will have a grand picnic.

The new roller mill recently completed here, is turning out fifty barrels a day, and is doing excellant work It is one of the best equipped mills in the country, and is a great credit to the community.

Many hives of bees have been entirely exterminated this spring by some unknown disease, and other hives have been thinned out so that the honey crop will be small this year. Bee-keepers cannot discover the cause of the trouble and are at a loss to know what to do. The loss in some cases has been almost entire and in others the partial loss will greatly decrease their honey yield.

The fruit crop here this season will be simply immense, and orchards are looking healthier and better than ever before. There has been no late frost to injure the buds, and trees are all covered with blossoms

Our Ferron correspondent this week reiterates what we have seen forcibly remarked in one or two of our exchanges that the recent action of the Emery county commissioners in levying a tax on cattle, horses and sheep, exceeding a certain very limited number, is meeting with a great deal of criticism and now pretty thoroughly established opposition. Emery county is, no doubt, very much in need of funds, but we are hardly of the opinion that a discriminating tax levy is the proper method of trying to raise revenue. Again, we fear it will be extremely difficult to enforce the act in the face of serious objections that will certainly be made. Furthermore, we are sanguine that it will not stand a test in any court.—Manti Messenger.

Salt Lake Tribune
May 22, 1897

Annie E. Calloway of Escalante was awarded a divorce from her husband, Levy H. Calloway, on the grounds of failure to provide. She was also awarded the custody of the minor children, three of a family of six being under 14 years of age. The defendant lives in Orangeville, and has not lived with or supported his family for ten years.

Deseret Weekly
May 22, 1897

Ferron—Peach trees in bloom; farmers are busy putting in grain; seeding of small grain is about one-half completed.

Manti Messenger
May 22, 1897

Telephone Connection at Ferron

Other Items of Interest

Yesterday (21st inst) witnessed the placing of Ferron in telephonic communication with other parts of the country and was fittingly celebrated by a free ball given by Wyatt Bryan in Bryan's hall, all enjoying a good time on the light fantastic Next give us a rail road and Emery county will come to the front as one of the best in Utah.

The two-year old child of A. G Connover's that has been sick for several weeks died and was burried Monday last.

The May day celebration to be given on Tuesday the 25th inst promises to be an enjoyable affair. Good times are always had under the supervision of the young ladies

A couple of the Ferron teachers made a trip last we ... wn into Sin Bad in the ... of h ... rs Roost on a prospecting to ... r. The ... were highly jubilant ... cting t wa and remarked " It prosp ... a ... s not promising, we will lo ... cate th Castle Gate robbers and claim the offered reward by bringing them to justice '' They are not so jubilant now and think an army of soldiers would not be ably to oust the out laws and when accosted on th streets are loath to say much about prospecting.

A. L. L.

Ferron, May 13th, 18 ...

Eastern Utah Advocate
May 27, 1897

The Ferron band has been engaged to play at Emery on the first of June We will then have a celebration and expect a large turn out A good time is gauranteed to all who attend.

Davis County Clipper
May 28, 1897

Williams Osborn and David Jackson, both of Orangeville, pleaded guilty before Justice Jensen at Richfield, to catching trout in streams feeding Fish lake. The sentence of Osborn, an invalid, was suspended; Jackson was fined $10, and in default will serve ten days in jail. One hundred fish landed by clubs and spears were confiscated

Manti Messenger
May 29, 1897

Williams Osborn and David Jackson both of Orangeville, pleaded guilty before Justice Jensen at Richfield, to catching trout in streams feeding Fish lake The sentence of Osborn, an invalid, was suspended, Jackson was fined $10, and in default will serve ten days in jail One hundred fish landed by clubs and spears were confiscated

FERRON NEWS.

Eli Fredrickson met with an almost fatal accident Sunday morning while chasing cattle into the canyon his horse accidently fell with him He was rendered unconcious for some time and was picked up by his companions limp and as they thought lifeless, bleeding from the ears, nose and mouth. Signs of life appeared and he was taken to the home of his aged parents where he has lain in a lethargic condition for a couple of days, but is now said to be gaining life and conciousness

A new born girl adorns the home of E. K. Funk Jr. All are getting along nicely.

The May-day celebration here was an enjoyable affair The large crowd met in the morning at the Social Hall and thence proceeded to J.C. Lemmon's, recitations, songs, etc. were rendered. After luncheon, swinging and other games were participated in until late afternoon when adjournment was taken to the hall where in the evening the crowning of the queen, weaving of May pole, dancing, reciting and singing occupied the time until a late hour

A. E E.

Ferron, May 25th, 1897.

While J D Kilpack, of Ferron, was in town the first of the week, his attention was drawn to a letter of rather a startling nature in the Deseret News communicated by his son J. D Jr who is at present on a mission in the Carolinas It appears that one evening at the close of a meeting, he and companion were taken into custody by a sheriff and charged with murdering a man who had just been found with his throat cut Fortunately, a party was on the scene who was able to identify the murderers, if found, and when the two Elders were brought in, he at once saw the error, and they were exhonorated

Eastern Utah Advocate
June 3, 1897

FERRON.

The conviction of Lars Thompson has caused a ripple excitment here, the people being about equally divided as to guilt or innocence.

Wyatt Bryan has just placed an elegant mantle in his resldence

Dr. Winters of Orangeville spent a few hours in our town early this week

Ed Cooley, H. Curtis and Frank Bur dick visited the county seat recently

The Ferron creek is still high but is gradually falling. Most of the snow in the mountain is gone.

The building for the new saloon will soon be completed.

George Petty was down from his saw mill and reports little snow on the mountains.

Ephraim Allred left for Spring'own on Monday.

S th Allen, the Emery school teacher, left for a visit to Sanpete county early in the week.

Last Thursday was a field day for Molen it being the close of the last year's school term. An interesting program was had during the day and followed in the evening by an elegant supper and dance. Castledale boys furnished the music.

Chris. Jergensen and James Henrie came in from the sheep herd and spent a few days in our midst.

Booth Larsen, of Manti was in from Ferron mountain where he is herding sheep.

John C Lemon has begun the erection of an elegant brick residence which will cost near $4,500. When completed it will be one of the best residences in the valley.

A crowd of brave (?) Ferronites with all manner of arms, got together on Sunday evening with the avowed purpose of routing a poor helpless old tramp When near to the aforesaid tramp their courage left them and they one and all concluded that the safest place was at home in bed and which conclusion was immediately acted upon.

Miss Dasie Aldredge, so we understand, will clerk for the Emery County Mercantile store at Castledale.

All crops look well and give promise of an abundant yield this season

Round Up
June 4, 1897

At Castle Dale, in Emery county, Charles C. Clauson got a year for adultery and Lars Thompson was given three years for stealing a calf. Don't steal.

Castle Dale Chips.

Gar lens are suffering for want of water, the town ditch having been broken about ten days ago by a severe rain storm

Ditch work seems to be the occupation for most of the men in town now a days All the ditches and canals have been broken more or less

Masons D Axelson, of Cleveland, at Dr Winters drug store, and Lars Christenson of this place at Jos Christenson's harness shop are laying up the brick at a rapid rate

Decoration Day was fittingly observed May 31st under the auspices of the Sunday School Credit is due the superintendency for the way the house was prepared

Brigham Young's birth day was celebrated by the Primary Association A meeting and program was rendered in the forenoon and a dance indulged in in the afternoon They like such times they say

D F Thomander, our school teacher, is busy fixing up his lot By the way he goes at it you would expect he is to have an aristocratic home

A bevy of ladies with their chaps gave Ferron a visit June 1st and tripped the light fantastic with them A good time was had no doubt.

Emery County Mercantil Co are filling the shelves of their building here, and will soon be in running order

Alfalfa will soon be ready to cut

A good job has been done in making a flood canal on the west side of the meeting house square More of them should be made to carry off the waters that accumulate in the hollows leading from the bench Be careful that they do not lead so as to do damage to anyone They must go to the creek where all debris can be deposited

SCRIBO

Castle Dale, June 1st, 1897

FERRON.

Much has been said of late regarding the friendliness of the people of the south end of Emery county to the Robbers Roost gang. It is going abroad that we are in sympathy with them. The report is erroneous and does our people a very great injustice. In fact when any of our people go abroad we are looked upon as nearly as bad as the robbers. It is a well known fact that the people look upon them as their worst enemies. There can be no doubt in the minds of the law abiding people but that they are a menace to life and property. It is true that they pass through our settlement occasionally and that it is said that the two who held up the P. V. Coal company at Castlegate were camped near Ferron for some time last winter yet this is no evidence that our people are in sympathy with them.

James Henry and George Robinson narrowly escaped being drowned in Ferron creek a few evenings ago. The stream was bank full and very swift and the boys were in the water before they realized the unsafe condition of the stream.

Max Ottenheimer, the Seigel Clothing company's drummer, was in Ferron this week.

A number of Ferronites left for Sanpete and Sevier early in the week for a visit with friends and relatives.

It is said to the credit of the Ferron ladies that they have threatened to cover with a coat of tar and feathers any one who attempts to start a saloon here. Stay with it ladies you are in the right.

J. L. Brasher and Attorney Howard were Ferron visitors late last week.

J. L. Allred, our village blacksmith, is kept exceedingly busy these days. As many as seven teams were seen standing at his shop waiting for work. Our other black smith, George Petty, is running a saw mill.

Wyatt Bryan, our very enterprising merchant, has secured the government contract for transporting government freight from Price to the post and it is said that he will open up a store in Price.

A dance in Bryans Hall on Friday evening will be quite a swell affair.

John Barton, Horace Duncan, Wm. Henry and Wm. Killpack returned from Moab late last week.

The high water was the cause of a few days stoppage of the Ferron Roller Mill.

The canyon roads were badly washed by the recent floods and a great deal of work will be necessary to put them in as good condition as they were in last fall.

A crowd of Ferronites will leave here this week to work on the reservoir.

Alpha Ballinger, of Price, spent a few days in Ferron this week

Eastern Utah Advocate
June 17, 1897

A Worthy Institution.

For eight or ten years the Emery County Mercantile company have pursued safe and energetic business methods and today the firm is one of the strongest in eastern Utah.

Like the majority of eastern Utah business institutions the firm in its infancy did not have any too much of the filthy lucre but a long, hard pull on safe business lines gradually but surely placed the institution on a sound financial footing

Recognizing the future wealth of Castle valley the management have recently acquired property in Castledale where they will, when extensive improvements are completed, open up a big line of general merchandise in the elegant building formerly owned by Carl Wilberg. The branch store at Ferron is being enlarged and the stock now on hand will be greatly increased It is the intention of the management to have as well stocked stores at Castledale and Ferron as the main store at Price.

It is safe to say that the enterprising ranchers of Castledale and Ferron will appreciate well stocked stores by giving them hearty support.

The great success of this institution is mainly due to a strict and rigid observance of the only safe business policy—fair dealing and honest goods, which is without doubt the key note to the success of this deservedly popular institution. The motto "Honest goods at honest prices" has become a household word with the many patrons of the store throughout the valley.

J. M. Easton, of Salt Lake, and the manager, L. M. Olsen, are the principle stock holders. Both gentlemen are well known throughout the valley. The manager has seen the business grow from its infancy and to his strict integrity and honest dealing with his fellowmen is due the unprecedented growth of the institution.

Salt Lake Herald
June 21, 1897

Huntington, Utah, June 17.—People are wondering when the money appropriated by the legislature for building roads and bridges in Huntington canyon is to be expended. Now would be a good time to begin the work, so that the farmers could earn a few dollars for taxes as soon as the first hay crop is up.

The Huntington choir is practicing for a series of concerts to be given in Price, Castle Gate and Scofield about the last of this month. We predict a good time to all who have the pleasure of hearing them.

Our county commissioners showed the white feather at their last session by repealing the ordinance passed at a former sitting licensing sheep and stock. The stockmen are jubilant and claim an absolute knockout.

Mr. D. C. Woodward, our principal, is still in the schoolroom with a full house of the primary students.

Huntington is building up. Several new houses are in course of erection. The swamps that have for some years past been springing up in our streets are fast fading away and our town is drier than for years.

Haying is in full blast. The hay crop is good and the prospects for grain crop fine.

Deseret Evening News
June 22, 1897

IN ROBBERS' ROOST.

Judge Johnson Tells What He Knows About It.

ORGANIZED GANG OF OUTLAWS.

People Living In Southern Utah are Terrorized—The Carpenter Robbery Planned.

That there is an organized gang of bandits in the secluded mountain retreats of Utah seems almost incredible to those familiar with the history of this peaceful State; but that such is the case is known to be only too true, regrettable as it is. The depredations of these robbers of late, have been such as to terrorize the people residing in the southern portion of the State, and every effort thus far made by the officers of the law to capture the gang has been non-effective.

MOORE AND THOMPSON.

Judge Jacob Johnson of the fifth district, who has been holding court here for the past two weeks in Judge Hiles' division of the Third judicial district, in a conversation with a NEWS representative a few days ago related some interesting incidents that go to show what proportions the existing conditions are liable to assume if some steps are not taken to break up the lawless gang.

"It is about four or five weeks ago," said the judge, "that I was holding court at Castle Dale in Emery county. Two men named Jack Moore and Lars Thompson were on the calendar to be tried on the charge of cattle stealing. They were to have been tried before Judge Higgins at Beaver, but came to my district on a change of venue. The men had a bad reputation and were known to be connected with the "robbers' roost" gang.

"On the day of the trial I received word from several citizens warning me that if the men were convicted an effort would be made to rescue them.

THREE YEARS FOR THOMPSON.

"When the case was called Moore failed to respond and his bond was declared forfeited. Thompson stood trial and after a hearing, lasting three days, the jury found him guilty of grand larceny, when I sentenced him to three years in the State prison. I told Sheriff Tuttle to take Thompson to Price as soon as possible. Thompson was taken the same day on the regular train to Price. It was a fortunate thing he did, for early the next morning sixteen armed men came into Castle Dale with the full intention of rescuing Thompson at the peril of losing their own lives. They were very much chagrined when they learned Thompson had been spirited away, and threatened dire vengeance on those that had been responsible for it.

Ex-United States Marshall E. A. Ireland, hearing that there was likely to be trouble, came in with a number of men prepared to render the officers of the law any assistance within his power. During the past few months Ireland has had 1,000 head of cattle stolen from him, and he for one, declares this kind of work will have to stop. "It is supposed," continued the judge, "that the gang is made up of about 20 or 30 men, but we have it from men who are familiar with the whole thing, and they say there are between 225 and 250 of them.

"Robbers' roost is on a line between Wayne and Emery counties and their route extends from Canada, on the north, to Mexico on the south. Stations are established at various points through this scope of country.

METHOD OF DOING THINGS.

"You no doubt wonder what in the world they needed with barbed wire. A hole is drilled into the cliffs on either side of the canyons and the wires are stretched across and serves as a corral for the horses and cattle. The robbers never all camp together. They are always four or five miles apart. They signal and hold communication with each other, with smoke or by fires built on prominent points. When any written communication passes between them it is done by means of cyphers, so that few outside of their own members can understand.

TOTAL NUMBER OF THE GANG.

"One station in Wayne county is known as Brown's park. Here they have about 17 or 20 men. Their organization and method of doing business is reduced to a science. They travel in threes and fours and no two men are together longer than ten days or two weeks at a stretch. Men are transferred from one station to another in the same way. From a well known resident of Spring City, whose name I am forbidden to give it is known that one ton and a half of giant powder has been shipped to them this spring. This powder is used for prospecting, blasting out trails and also for the purpose of making escapes when there is an outlet unknown to the officers. It is also known that large quantities of groceries have been shipped to the robbers from Green river and Price, as well as a blacksmith shop outfit, between 6,000 and 8,000 pounds of grain and 4,000 pounds of barbed wire fencing. These goods are boxed and taken to the robbers through the canyons.

"Two letters were recently picked up by a cowboy and were transcribed by the citizen referred to. They have everything they need and their main operations are guided by men living in Denver and Salt Lake. From these sources they received information regarding Cashier Carpenter of the Pleasant Valley Coal company. The first arrangements made was to hold up and rob the United States paymaster while on his way to Fort Duchesne to pay off the Indians. This was known for a month or so before. Orange Seeley, of Ferron, Emery county, was informed of the contemplated robbery and he sent word to Major Randlett, who provided the paymaster with an escort and thus frustrated the robbers' plans. It was then they waited for Mr. Carpenter, with the result that they got away with several thousand dollars.

PEOPLE ARE TERRORIZED.

"The people living in Wayne and Uintah," the judge continued, "are terrorized and nearly scared out of their lives. The acts of the robbers are getting more and more desperate right along and in my opinion it is only a question of time, before there is bloodshed, for the people have put up long enough with their depredations.

"Within the past few months it is estimated that they have stolen upwards of 4,000 head of cattle and shipped them East.

"No officer can pursue them with any degree of safety. It will take a number of brave men to rout the fellows out, and it would not surprise me if it took a troop of Uncle Sam's men to finally exterminate them."

DESIGNS ON MANTI.

It was quietly but definitely noted in official circles as much as two months ago that an organized effort was being made by the robber roost gang to raid some bank in central or Southern Utah. The one at Manti was considered a particularly shining mark, while the one at Richfield was also considered valuable. Why the raids were not made is probably accounted for by the stir and official activity that followed the Carpenter hold-up. Those who are in a position to know think that the gang is simply waiting for the excitement to subside, and then, when all is quiet, ride into town in regular Jesse James style and execute their plans, which, if carefully undertaken, would not be a difficult task. This being the fact, banking and business men in outlying communities can well afford to be on their guard.

Eastern Utah Advocate
June 24, 1897

The road from Orangeville to Castledale which formerly passed through the premises of James Killian has been changed and now runs around the foot of Castledale bench.

FERRON.

Miss Janie Tuttle, daughter of Sheriff Tuttle of Orangeville, spent a few very pleasant days with the Misses Conover and returned to her home Sunday with her father.

The genial superintendent of the Orangeville Co-op, B F. Luke, visited Price yesterday and returned home to-day.

Salt Lake Herald
June 27, 1897

SOME LIVING PIONEERS.

Mary Eliza Westover, who now resides at Huntington, Emery county, is a surviving pioneer. She is the daughter of Charles and Julia A. Shumway, and was born in the town of Sturbridge, Worcester county, Mass., on Oct. 27, 1835. When 2 years of age, she removed with his family to Illinois, and in the fall of 1842, went to Nauvoo. Her family was the first of the Saints to cross the Mississippi. They spent the following winter at Winter Quarters, where her mother and only sister were buried. The next spring, her father and brother started west, and Mrs. Westover followed later, arriving in the

valley in October, 1847. She went with the first company to Manti, Sanpete county, and four years later moved to Payson, where she lived during the Walker Indian war and then moved to Big Cottonwood. this county. In September, 1856,(she married Charles Westover and in the fall of 1862 they were called to go to St. George with the original settlers of that place. She then moved to Pine Valley and later to Pinto, where a flood destroyed their property.

Eastern Utah Advocate
July 1, 1897

Mrs. C W Fox and her family re turned from a visit with her parents in Sanpete county and took Monday's stage for her Orangeville home

Salt Lake Herald
July 3, 1897

A Few Facts From Ferron.

Ferron, Emery County, Utah, June 29.—We are today enjoying the opening of Ferron's first saloon. The gang from "Robbers' Roost" can now get plenty of beer here, and the sale of whisky on the sly will probably be stopped.

Ferron will celebrate the Fourth of July in a good, patriotic style.

The Emery County Mercantile company of Price are fitting up a first-class store here, and with a new manager it will be a boon to the place.

Salt Lake Herald
July 4, 1897

Marriage licenses were yesterday issued to John A. Reid, of Orangeville, and Edna Hall, of this city, and F. A. Muzzy and Clara Minor, of this city.

Eastern Utah Advocate
July 8, 1897

ORANGEVILLE.

A very enjoyable time was had here on the Fifth. At daybreak a salute was fired and at sun up Old Glory was unfurled to the gentle breeze and the band awakened the sluggards with patriotic music. The parade formed at A. Anderson's corner at 9 a. m. and made an excellent showing. Miss Emma Riggs, as Goddess, with her maids of honor, Misses Stella Scoville and Fannie Snow all elegantly and appropriately dressed occupied the leading float which was followed by a float in which the beautiful Mrs. Mabel Moore did honor to Utah and who was attended by six lovely little maids. The parade disbanded at the hall where an interesting program was rendered. The decoration of the floats and hall was neat and tasty. The committee on decoration deserve much praise. The pleasurable event closed with a grand ball in the evening.

John Thompson is again quite low.

Mark Perry, Chester Ashcroft and Burr Whiting, of Mapleton, Utah county, arrived in Orangeville on Saturday evening. Mr. Ashcroft spending the Fourth here while Messrs Perry and Whiting celebrated with Castledale people. The gentlemen are looking at the country with a view to locating.

J. A. Woodward, the big sheepman, came to celebrate the Fourth with friends who gladly welcomed his return.

Wm. Miles and Fred Stilson have returned from P. V. Junction where they have been getting out timber.

James Justice is home from Desert Lake.

The freighters came in in time to celebrate with home folks.

The pool room is exciting unfavorable comment by a number of people. It is thought that other games than pool are played and some of the boys who frequent the place act strangely and with great difficulty walk.

FERRON.

The celebration here was a joyous occasion and passed off without any unpleasant incidents. A good program was rendered in which all participating did their parts well. The childrens dance in the afternoon and adults at night were pleasant features.

John Taylor and Joe Wrigley took two loads of oats to Price for the Emery County Mercantile company and returned Wednesday morning with goods for the branch store here.

The pleasant faces of Wyatt Bryan and Ed Cooley are greatly missed since their departure for Price.

D. T. Fox, formerly of Orangeville and who has has recently been employed in the Emery County Mercantile company store at Price, came in last Thursday and took charge of the above company's branch store here.

D. H. Wilkins took a short lay off and Ephraim Allred drove the mail a trip.

The saloon has finally been opened to the public. Tom Brandon is the proprietor.

A great deal of wheat on Silver Dell is headed out and will shortly be ready for the harvester. A big yield of lucern is harvested. All other grain and fruit promises well.

PIONEER JUBILEE RATES.

Via the Oregon Short Line.

To Salt Lake City and return from following points:

From	Rate	From	Rate
Wood's Cross..	25	Pocatello	$5 00
Centerville	35	Ross Fork	5 50
Farmington	50	Blackfoot	5 75
Kaysville	40	Idaho Falls....	6 50
Layton	65	Market Lake..	7 00
Syracuse Jun't.	75	Dubois	8 75
Hooper	85	Beaver Canon	10 00
Ogden	1 00	Monida	10 25
Harrisville	1 00	Lima	10 75
Hot Springs...	1 25	Red Rock......	11 75
Willard	1 50	Dillon	12 75
Brigham	1 75	Melrose	13 50
Honeyville	1 50	Divide	14 25
Dewey	2 00	Silver Bow	15 00
Collinston	2 10	Butte	15 00
Cache Junct'n.	2 50	Anaconda	15 00
Mendon	2 60	Americ'n Falls.	6 00
Logan	2 75	Minidoka	7 00
Smithfield	3 00	Kinama	8 00
Richmond	3 25	Shoshone	9 00
Franklin	3 50	Bellevue	10 50
Preston	3 50	Hailey	10 75
Cannon	3 00	Ketchum	11 50
Dayton	2 00	Bliss	10 00
Oxford	3 50	Glenn's Ferry.	11 00
Downey	3 75	Moun'n Home.	12 00
Thatcher	3 75	Orchard	13 00
McCammon	4 00	Nampa	14 00
Bancroft	5 50	Meridian	14 50
Soda Springs ..	6 00	Boise City.....	15 00
Montpelier	6 75	Caldwell	15 00
Cokeville	7 75	Ontario	15 75
Fossil	7 75	Payette	15 75
Diamondville .	7 75	Weiser	16 25
Opal	7 75	Huntington	17 00
Murray	25	Clear Lake....	3 75
Bing'm Junc'n.	50	Neola	3 75
Sandy	50	Black Rock	4 00
Draper	60	Smith's Ranch.	4 00
Amer'n Fork..	1 00	Milford	4 00
Lehi Junction.	1 00	Frisco	4 50
Lehi	1 00	Cedar Fort.....	1 40
Pleas't Grove..	1 00	Fairfield	1 50
Lake View.....	1 25	Five Mile Pass	1 50
Provo	1 25	Rush Valley ...	1 00
Springville	1 25	Del Monte......	1 75
Spanish Fork .	1 40	Doremus	1 75
Benjamin	1 50	Ironton	2 00
Payson	1 50	Eureka	2 00
Santaquin	1 60	Mammoth	2 00
Starr	1 75	Silver City.....	2 00
Mona	2 00	Jordan	25
Burriston	2 25	Saltair Junct'n	40
Nephi	2 50	Garfield	50
Juab	2 75	Lake Point.....	55
Leamington ...	3 00	Halfw'y House	65
Oasis	3 50	Tooele	80
		Terminus	1 00

Selling Dates—From nearer points, July 20 to 24; from farther points, July 19 to 22. Limit of all tickets, July 26.

For full particulars call on nearest O. S. L. agent.

D. E. BURLEY, G. P. & T. A.

Salt Lake Herald
July 10, 1897

THE BALL GAME.

Reorganized Jubilees and Ogden's Crack Nine Play Today.

The first meet of the Jubilees and the Ogdens will occur this afternoon on Beck's grounds at 4 o'clock. The Ogdens have beaten every team that they have met except the Parks, and as the same thing can be said of the Jubilees, so they ought to be very evenly matched. Neither one is a favorite in the betting.

The two nines will line up as follows:

Jubilees.	Position.	Ogdens.
Wilson	First base	Shoupe
Ostler	Third base	Brewster
Mathews	Left field	Crandall
Scare	Right field	Belcher
Kidder	Center field	Raymon
Knickerbocker	Catcher	Greenwell
McFarlane	Pitcher	Emmett
Miller	Shortstop	Ferron
Barnes	Second base	Ferguson

Taylor, the new pitcher expected, has not arrived, but McFarlane will ably fill his place.

Salt Lake Herald
July 11, 1897

DOWN IN EMERY.

Gold Bug Proclivities of the County Commissioners.

Huntington, Utah, July 8.—The county board of equalization met at the courthouse in Castledale on June 28 and was besieged by the widows and indigents of the county, asking for abatements.

A very noticeable feature of our present county court is their especial love for Republican office seekers. Appearances indicate that Emery county patronage is for the goldbugs only. The court is at present making a tour of the eastern part of the county.

Our big church bell has at last been placed in position on the Huntington tabernacle.

Our good citizens have finally concluded that his excellency, the governor, is too long winded for them and have raised a party of volunteers and gone up Huntington canyon to repair the road so that the traveling public may go between Emery and Sanpete counties again as of yore. The road has been impassable since the floods of last summer, and the last legislature appropriated money, through the efforts of our senator and representative, for the repair of these roads, to be expended by an agent to be appointed by the governor. The agent has not been appointed, the importunings of our citizens for one notwithstanding.

The denizens of Robbers' Roost are seemingly satisfied for the present and are waiting for an opening.

The Glorious Fourth of July was spent in a way long to be remembered by the people of Huntington. The 45 young ladies dressed in white with blue and red sashes were an especial feature. The 13 original states were a little more prominent than the others, and the bright silver star of Utah in the center making a beautiful picture to look at. The whole day's proceedings were a success, winding up with a trip of the light fantastic toe at night.

The first crop of hay is all up and irrigating for the next is now in order.

The company of five who recently formed in town to purchase a thresher outfit has gone where the woodwine twineth.

Logan Journal
July 15, 1897

A serious accident occurred on the afternoon of the 5th. George Moffit, who was intoxicated, was riding a wild horse when it became unmanageable and dashed through a crowd of pleasure seeking men, women and children. The little grandson of Bishop Robertson was ridden down and received very painful injuries. Luckily the boy escaped with only a contusion of the head and arm and it is thought will soon recover. Sheriff Tuttle succeeded in placing Moffit under arrest and restoring order.—Orangeville Cor. Eastern Utah Advocate.

FROM OVER THE STATE

Military Escort For Fort Duchesne Freighters.

HORSES SPIRITED AWAY

NIGHT ATTACK UPON THE NEW CONTRACTOR'S OUTFIT.

Fishermen Seining Trout In the Strawberry—Fires at Hooper—Fairview Creamery In Operation—The Pioneer Coal Mine at Wales—Park City School Finances.

Price, Utah, July 13.—On the 1st of last May the sealed bids for the transportation of government freight between Price and Fort Duchesne were opened by the quartermaster of the department of the Colorado, Colonel E. B. Atwood, at his office, Denver, Colo., and it was found that Wyatt Bryan, of Ferron, Utah, had secured the contract, as he had made the lowest bid, which was 67 cents per hundred weight. The bids put in by other parties for this contract were 69 cents, 70 cents, 71 cents, 72 cents and 75 cents. As soon as it was known that Mr. Bryan was the lowest bidder there was a great deal of kicking done amongst his competitors and the freighters as well as his competitors wanted the contract themselves and the freighters did not like to see the contract secured at such a low figure, fearing that it meant lower wages for them. It was rumored that beginning July 1 when Mr. Bryan would take charge, the freighters would strike. Nothing more was thought of this until yesterday. Mr. Bryan sent out his first load of freight Sunday under the new contract. It was Captain Beck's, the new Indian agent's household goods and Elisha Jones' team, of Huntington. Late Monday Mr. Bryan received word that after camping Sunday night the freighter's teams were turned loose and driven off while he was asleep by unknown parties. The entire day was spent in searching for the team and up to the present time no track of them had been seen. Mr. Bryan started at once for the disabled outfit and will transfer the goods to Joe Anderson's wagons, who will take them through at once, and I will venture to say that it will be very dangerous business for anyone to attempt to run his horses off or otherwise disable his outfit. If such practice is repeated no doubt the government will take a hand in the game and it is very likely to get someone into serious trouble. Mr. Bryan telegraphed to the quartermaster at Fort Duchesne and a guard will be sent from the post today to meet Mr. Bryan's wagons and no one doubts for a moment but what the soldiers will see that the wagons and horses are let strictly alone. Mr. Bryan has established himself here by putting up a good substantial store building and stocking it well with goods.

At the school board election today only one ticket was in the field. Bishop E. S. Horsley was elected for the long term and Mrs. Barbara McIntyre for the short term.

Dan C. Robbins of Salt Lake City, was here today in the interest of the Castle Valley Land and Irrigation company and will return to Salt Lake City tonight and bring out some capitalists from that city who are contemplating investing in Price property.

Salt Lake Herald
July 17, 1897

A FEW PLUMS.

Appointments of Supervisors to Spend Public Appropriations.

Several appointments have been announced by Governor Wells.

Orson Robbins of Huntington will supervise the expenditure of an appropriation of the legislature of $750 in the building of a bridge and improvement of a road in Huntington canyon, in Emery county.

John E. Snow was appointed to supervise the expenditure of state funds to the amount of $1,000, in the building of a road and bridge in Straight canyon, between Castle Dale, Emery county, and Ephraim, Sanpete county.

SENSATION AT HUNTINGTON.

Mysterious Gang of Armed Men Ride Through the Town.

Huntington, Utah, July 14.—Quite a ripple of excitement was created last Saturday by the appearance on our streets of half a dozen tough looking men, all well armed and mounted, accompanied by what appeared to be a very manish looking woman, who was also well armed (and legged, as she rode astride). The gang was driving before them about eight or ten heavily packed animals, and heading towards Sanpete.

The ice cream party given by Mr. and Mrs. W. H. Leonard in honor of a few friends, was a most enjoyable affair.

Mrs. J. W. Nixon gave the entertainment of the season at the family residence on First West street, last night, where about 50 invited guests were royally feasted ice cream, etc. The evening was spent in songs, toasts, recitations and social chat, until 12 o'clock, when the good night was said.

At our school meeting, Mr. J. P. Johnson was elected school trustee for the three years' term.

The people of this burg are still pushing work on the Huntington canyon road, and a very good showing is being made.

Quite a number of our citizens will attend the Jubilee at Salt Lake, and go early enough to attend the Y. M. M. I. conference. Among the latter will be Stake Superintendent J. E. Johnson and D. C. Woodward.

The county commissioners have utterly ignored section 5 of the fish and game law, which requires them to appoint a county fish and game warden at their first sitting. It is reported that the commissioners (after reducing a certain claim of one of the supervisors) were glad to compromise with him by asking the governor to appoint him special agent to disburse the appropriation for the Huntington canyon roads and bridges. It is whispered by the birds that the same road supervisor has said that he could not work more than five or six men at a time, which would insure him a nice long job.

NOTICE.

Of intention to make application for a permit to cut timber upon the public lands under Act of March 3, 1891.—To all whom it may concern:

Notice is hereby given that immediately after the publication hereof for three consecutive weeks as required by law, the undersigned will make application to the Honorable Secretary of the Interior, at Washington, D. C. for a permit to cut and remove 300,000 feet of red pine, white pine and black balsam timber from a rough, mountainous tract of country upon unsurveyed, nonmineral public lands of the United States, in Sanpete county, Utah and if surveyed would be located about sections 6 or 7, Township 18 South Range 5 East, and more particularly described as follows: Beginning at the head of what is known as Bear creek fork of Ferron canyon, just South of H. P. Hansen's shingle mill thence, East one fourth mile, thence South one half mile, thence West one half mile, thence North one half mile, thence East one fourth of mile to place of beginning, located about 12 miles Southeast of Ephraim, Sanpete County

Utah·   JOHN THOMPSON
                BEAUREGAARD KENNER.
Postoffice address, Sterling, Saupete
County, Utah.
First publication July 14th 1897.

Eastern Utah Advocate
July 22, 1897

ORANGEVILLE.

Mr. and Mrs Jasper Robertson, Mrs F. W Fai', Mrs George Fulmer, J. L. and Charles Curtis left Orangeville on Sunday for Mt. Pleasant where they will take the train for Salt Lake to attend the Jubilee

Gardner Jewkes and his sister, Miss Emma, Miss Killian, Miss Sorensen and Miss Johnson left for Fountain Green Saturday to visit relatives and friends until after the 24th.

Brigham Higgs has removed his family to Provo where they will reside permanently Mr. Higg's eldest daughter is taking a B.Y. course and her zeal and earnestness will place her to the front in Provo as it has in Orangeville where she was president of the Y L M I. association.

Mr and Mrs Bert Childs have gone into the mountains to spend the summer at the shingle mill.

Mr. Cork and family from Tintic will make Orangeville their future residence Mr. Cork purchased a building spot from Reese Griffith and will erect a comfortable brick cottage.

Sheriff Tuttle and wife and Miss Al sadie Anderson are visiting in Saupete county

A number of the Orangevideites will spend the 24th in the canyon and a program is prepared for the proper observance of this great event.

Although the two hold over trustees were men the male population insisted on the election of another man. The ladies looked at the matter different and had two candidates in the field, Mrs. Jack and Mrs. S. A. Fulmer. The race was a pretty one, Mrs. Fulmer had only five plurality. One hundred and five votes were cast against only thirty at the election one year ago.

At the reorganization of the Y L M I association Miss Caroline Sitterod was chosen president and will select her assistance at a later meeting.

Wm. Orson, O. Miles and Mr. and Mrs. Wm Curtis are expected to return in a short time from Idaho where they were called by the death of their father,

— Sheriff Tuttle, of Orangeville, has been in town all of this week. He still uses his crutches, but his wounded leg is fast becoming sound —Manti Messenger.

Salt Lake Herald
July 26, 1897

THE FRATERNAL SOCIETIES

Utah No. 1 met Thursday night and several members from a distance were present, who spoke of the advantages of being an Odd Fellow when away from home. Mr. Fred W. Hail of Orangeville was present.

Daily Enquirer
July 27, 1897

Price Advocate —Brigham Higgs has removed his family to Provo where they will reside permanently. Mr. Higg's eldest daughter is taking a B. Y. course and her zeal and earnestness will place her to the front in Provo as it has in Orangeville where she was president of the Y. L. M. I. association.

ORANGEVILLE.

Genial Doctor Winters is a pet of fickle fortune. There are those who assert that if Doc fell in a lake he wouldent get wet. His latest luck was the finding of a half dozen game chickens and a child's rocker while returning through Cottonwood canyon from a visit to a patient.

R. C. Christensen, the dentist and watchmaker, is putting the finishing touches to his handsome new building. The base boarding and doors are finished in a very close imitation of oak, skillfully executed, and is altogether a work of art to which Orangevilleites can point with pride.

In the case of the People vs Geo. Moffit tried at Castledale Monday last the jury returned a verdict of acquittal after an hour's deliberation. Defendant was accused of maliciously running over a child at Orangeville on the 4th of July. Moffit claimed that the horse was unmanageable and the preponderance of evidence adduced at the trial supported his asseveration. There was much local interest in the case.

The telephone line, which has been out of "whack" for a few days, is now in working order between Price and Ferron.

Orangeville was the scene of some exciting running races on Tuesday. The main event was between a Greenriver raised horse owned by Paul Judd and Noah Guinon's black mare. The home animal won by two lengths in a quarter of a mile dash.

Bob Logan's black easily defeated the sorrel owned by Henry Larimey of Escalante. There was several minor events. Sam Snow rode the winning mount in the first race and Larimey in the second. Doc. Winters offered to jockey the horse he was betting against and was indignant that this offer wasn't even considered.

In all probability diptheria has again broken out in Ferron. Dr Winters was called there Tuesday p m. to attend the very sick four-year old child of Andrew Neilson. On his return he stated that all the symptoms indicated that dread disease, although the sickness was not far enough advanced to make an absolutely certain diagnosis.

It rained at intervals all Monday evening and Tuesday, doing immeasureable benefit to the growing crops.

FERRON.

With characteristic energy H. M. Fugate has pushed well nigh to completion an enterprise that will add greatly to this handsome town and withal be a source of profit to its inaugurator. Fronting Mr. Fugate's residence is a natural lake bed covering an area of some three or four acres. A short time ago he conceived an idea of beautifying the surroundings, flooding the land and making a lake for the adornment of his own property and the comfort of his neighbors. But the original conception has been much enlarged upon. In corresponding with A. M. Musser, late fish commissioner, as to the best fish with which to stock the lake, Mr. Fugate obtained some data as to the great profit there is in propagating the finny brain nourisher for the market. Hence, although his original plans will be carried out, he will also include a commercial side to the venture and raise fish for the residents of the valley. Within a short time the lake will be stocked with a variety of spawners and Emery county will soon be as well supplied with black bass, salmon, trout, sunfish etc, as the residents of the metropolis. Strange as it may seem it is the universal testimony that fish thus propagated are much more toothsome and palatable than when taken in their natural haunts. Mr. Fugate s lake is admirably adapted for the purpose there being a large spring at its head which will amply replenish all evaporations and keep the water constantly renewed and refreshed. He also intends to make the lake a pleasure resort for young and other folks. Boats will be placed on the lake and a pavillion erected from which music will be discoursed on suitable occasions. In the spring poplars will be planted around its banks and other improvements made. It will be a valuable acquisition to Ferron, materially and esthetically.

Sheriff Tuttle was in town Saturday to make a formal demand on C. P. Jensen one of the bondsmen of Jack Moore. Moore, it will be recalled, was to have been tried for cattle stealing at the last term of court but when his case was called it was found he had levanted, Mr. Jensen and Cattleman Burr of Wayne county were his sureties in the sum of $750.

Doll Fausett and Sergeant Bessell, of Price, were in town on Sunday. They were repairing the telephone line.

D. H Wilkins returned from the Jubilee last Saturday evening and reports a good time.

The Advocate grows in popularity with the Ferronites with each issue. They would be lost without it.

Ed Cooley and other Ferron boys left on Monday for the mountains where they will assist in getting out timber and work at the different mills.

A number of Ferron people left for Richfield this week on a visit.

The conjoint rendered an interesting program on Sunday evening.

The telephone line between Price and this point was in bad condition last week but has now been repaired.

Mrs. Wm. Behunin is quite ill. Dr Winters, of Orangeville, is the attending physician.

John Snow, of Orangeville, visited friends and relatives in Ferron on Saturday.

Miss Lillie Allred returned home from Springtown on Sunday where she has been for the past two months visiting relatives.

Eastern Utah Advocate
August 12, 1897

We note that the good people of Castledale and Orangeville are about to incorporate an irrigation company to control the waters of Cottonwood creek. This is a wise and commendable movement. And, one of the first acts of the company should be the estopping of the persons from Sanpete county who are using valley waters.

John L. Brasher, of Huntington, was appointed fish and game warden for Emery county with compensation at $50 per annum.

Eastern Utah Advocate
August 19, 1897

ORANGEVILLE.

There was an unique reunion at Beaver dam on the top of the Wasatch range midway between Manti and Orangeville recently. Our hustling little town is largely peopled by native sons of the Sanpete metropolis and the meeting which lasted two or three days was solely for social communion, exchange of reminiscence and general pleasantry. There were sixty five persons present from Manti and fifty five from Orangeville, among the latter being J K Reid and family, H M Reid and family, E M. Cox and family, S H Cox and family, H G. Falsom and family, A. C. Van Buren and family, A A. Van Buren and family, and many others.

There is some talk among the citizens of changing the name of our town. There is no particular choice for another name, and for this reason we suppose there is little interest. It might be just as well to let the matter rest.

The telephone company should take cognizance of the condition of the telephone wires between Castledale and Orangeville. Two poles are down in the bed of Cottonwood creek and the wire has been sagging lower for several days until at present it nearly touches the ground.

Court at Price.

The following cases have been disposed of by Judge Johnson at Price this week:

J. G. Allred, who was recenty arrested for burglarizing the store of William Trapp at Green River, securing $40, pleaded guilty and was sentenced to four years in the penitentiary.

In the case of the State of Utah vs. County Attorney William Howard, objections were filed to the complaints. Mr. Reid came into court and stated that the complaint was unfounded, that there was nothing to warrant the filing of any charges against Attorney Howard, that he was not in any manner chargeable with neglect of his official duty and asked that the proceedings be dismissed. The court thereupon dismissed the proceedings, and at the request of Attorney S. A. King of Provo. who was representing Mr. Howard, the costs, $39.60, were taxed against the complainant, Samuel Singleton of Ferron.

The demurrer of the state of Utah vs. J. G. Burr and Peter Jensen, which arose out of the notorious case of alleged cattle stealing, and for which Henry Thomann is now confined in the penitentiary. Burr and Jensen being bondsmen in the case, the demurrer as to Jensen was overruled and 30 days allowed to file amended plea.

Mary Anderson vs. C.C. Anderson, for divorce. Plaintiff filed complaint against her husband, alleging cruelty and failure to provide. Defendant filed a cross bill alleging cruelty. Judgment was given to plaintiff, giving her the custoy of the 7-year old boy, and a house and two lots in Huntington.

Sheriff Cottrell of Wayne county, is in Price today upon some mission. Rumor has it that he has come to confer with the new sheriff of Carbon county concerning the course of procedure, which may be carried out at an early day towards effecting the arrest of several alleged members of the so called "Robbers Roost" gang of desperadoes.

Big Yield of Sugar Beets.

Castle Dale Correspondence Price Advocate: As an instance of the prolificness of Emery county soil and its peculiar adaptability to the cultivation of sugar beets, it may be noted that in two rows but 11 rods in length, Mr. John Peterson raised five bushels of the saccharine bearing vegetable. If more had been planted and the same ratio had held out, it would mean a yield of 300 bushels to the acre. When Castle valley gets a railroad it will rival the famous southern California belt as the home of sugar beet factories.

HUNTINGTON.

County Commissioner Wool has a project to furnish our town with good water by piping it from a fine flowing spring some seven miles distant. A mass meeting will be called shortly in this connection The proposition meets with favor among those whom your correspondent has interviewed. Among the methods to raise the funds for this work that if popular sucription of money and labor see ns to meet with the greates' favor

H N. Fowler has the sympathy of the community in the death of his little child on Friday last

CASTLEDALE.

The busy hum and familiar whistle of the steam thresher can be heard.

The mason work on the aca'emy building has been discontinued for a time to allow the carpenters to put in the joist and stair casts. By the way, every town in Emery county should be more interested in putting up this building Of course, Castledale was decided upon by the Church Board of Education to erect this edifice. No jealousies ought to exist but all give earnest aid,

A few more days and Dr. Winters building will be at its height in mason work.

Moab's correspondent inquires for us We have perhaps been in a somnambulistic state, but a somniloquist we are not.

Bishop Peter Johnson who has been absent in Sanpete county some days, has returned

Apiarys in this vicinity are busy extracting Senator Johnson has put up 800 pounds of honey within a week In one day last week J. A. West extracted 41-5 gallon cans.

There are some 8 0 tons of hay in the tithing yard.

A number of Castledaleites passed pleasant hours at a wedding dance in Orangville Tuesday evening

Soren Hansen leaves for Provo this week where he will attend B. Y. Academy.

G. A. Wegg-land left for his field of labor at Molen Sunday.

The ditch referred to in last week's notes from this place near Borreson's shop is not on the county road and therefore is not required to be bridged, but it should however be done,

Complaints are still coming from the saw-mill men No permits thus far have been granted them and they are at a loss to know the reason of this delay. The people are in need of lumber for building and improving our new country. If the mill cannot run we cannot build and consequently we will retrograde.

In the case of the people vs Elw Olsen, charged with grand larceny, defendant on preliminary examination was held to answer in the sum of $750 at the ensuing term of the district court. Great interest was manifested the court room being crowded by persons from various portions of the county. Decisive arguments of much length, legal

They are great traders in Emery coun'y It is said there is a horse swopped for every baby born, which, considering the—well, its pretty tall trading

I forget whether it was Milt. Tuttle at Orangeville, George Brandon or Abe Hammon of Huntington, whom I heard talking up the merits of a remarkable gun on some trading dicker. At any rate here is about how this wonderful weapon was described "Now," he said, "this gun if aimed right will shoot up the street and around the block, with practice you can shoot around any house and it has great force. Once when I was out deer hunting I shot a buck in the rear at 500 yards and he turned so quickly the ball came back and took my hat off. It is a great gun." I didn't hear the other qualifications of this miraculous gun

The seller caught my look of pained incredulity and toned his voice to what is known in polite society as an inaudible whisper.

The long-expected suit in which the people of Huntington and vicinity are very much interested was filed last Saturday in the district court. The plaintiff is the Huntington Roller Mills and Manufacturing company, a corporation, and the defendants are the Huntington Canal and Agricultural associa ion, a corporation, Joseph E. Johnson, John P. Pearson and H. T. Statworthy. The complaint alleges, in short, that the plaintiff is the owner of a flour mill situ ated on defendant's canal, the wa ers of which are used by plaintiff for the purpose of obtaining motive power to run its mill, that plaintiff had acquired a right of way through defendants canal, and has used the same for a period of three years prior to the 6th day of August, 1897; that during the months of July, August and September of each year it becomes necessary, in order to produce sufficient motive power to run said mill, to turn into defendants' canal other water, that on the 6th of August, 1897, defendants unlawfully interfered with and stopped the flow of said water, and in consequence the mill has not been able to run. The complaint further asks that a temporary injunction against the defendants be granted, restraining them from interfering with the flow of said water, and that the injunction be made permanent, that the rights of the respective parties be determined by decree of the court and that plaintiff recover $2,500 damages. The injunction was granted and service made on defendants on Monday by Sheriff Tuttle.

The road up Huntington canyon is now completed, and Orson Robbins, who has had charge of the work, informed your correspondent that he had repaired the road for a distance of about 40 miles, in many instances having made entirely new dugways and at one place a new bridge across the Huntington river has been made. Mr. Robbins repaired the road as far as the old Huntington coal mines, and as the road from those mines to Fairview is kept up by the coal miners, Mr. Robbins says the road is now in first class condition through to Fairview. This is a good thing for Emery county, as the road up Huntington is practically its only outlet with a load.

The various canal and irrigation companies of Castledale and Orangeville are considering the feasibility of consolidating into one general company. The move is undoubtedly a good one and will tend to lessen the expense as well as avoid unnecessary and useless litigation, which might result from the numerous independent companies operating alone.

The total valuation of real and personal property in Emery county this year is $1,183,590, an increase over last year of $25,691

County Treasurer R. C. Miller and wife paid our town a visit last Sunday.

Cattle and wheat buyers are numerous

in Huntington. Colonel Yeager is here buying cattle.

County warrants have been redeemed to the amount of $7,000 from recent bond sales.

Mrs. O. J. Harmon, who has been quite sick for some time, is now around again

Born, last week, to Mr. and Mrs. John Quinn, a baby girl. Mother and child doing nicely.

Our district schools commence next Monday, with the exception of the north school, which is being repaired.

The fruit crop in Huntington is good.

E. L. Geary is building a seven room brick residence.

HUNTINGTON PROSPEROUS.

Property Sells at Good Prices— Abundant Crops.

Huntington, Utah, Sept. 3.—The kickers and malcontents are now starting up their annual cry of disincorporation and are trying to induce the county commissioners into assuming the debts of the town. The people would then vote to disincorporate. Such illusion! There are plenty of citizens in Huntington to snow under such a proposition at the polls.

William Marshall is putting up a very fine residence, which will add to the beauty of the west side of town.

There is a controversy between the Huntington Roller Mill company and the Huntington Canal company in regard to the right of the mill company to use the canal without pay. The mill is stopped for the present. The people are getting somewhat short of flour.

The hum of the thresher is to be heard and the farmers are smiling at the prospect of good prices for their abundant crop.

County Attorney Howard is putting some additions to his residence and the saw of the carpenter and builder is heard in many parts of our town, showing that Huntington is improving and attracting the attention of homeseekers, who are numerous among us at present. Property here is changing hands and in many instances at very high prices. A small ranch in close vicinity to town sold the other day for $1,100.

The second crop of hay is all up and the third has a good start. With a continuation of the present beautiful weather for a couple of weeks the third crop will be assured.

Salt Lake Tribune
September 15, 1897

CATTLE COMPANY STRIFE.

Controversy Over the Possession of Books and Papers.

The Ireland Land and Cattle company has filed an action against the Denver & Rio Grande Railroad company and E. A. Ireland, to recover the possession of certain books and papers in a box consigned to Edith Ireland in this city from Ferron, Utah, on September 10th, which it is claimed Ireland is unlawfully retaining. In the event that the articles cannot be recovered the plaintiffs pray for judgment in the sum of $1000, their alleged value, with damages in the sum of $500.

Provo Daily Enquirer
September 16, 1897

PRICE Advocate: On Tuesday of last week Attorney Howard of Emery county was called to Ferron to prosecute Horace Duncan, charged with fornication. There was sufficient evidence to warrant the justice in binding Duncan to the district court. It is thought that the case will be withdrawn, as Duncan signifies a willingness to marry the girl.

Salt Lake Tribune
September 16, 1897

SECURED THE BOOKS.

Suit of the Ireland Land and Cattle Company Dismissed.

The litigation between the Ireland Land and Cattle company on one side and the Denver & Rio Grande Express company and E. A. Ireland on the other has ceased, temporarily at least.

The trouble arose over a box containing certain books and papers, consigned to Edith Ireland in this city from Ferron, Utah.

The land and cattle company appears to have desired the box, and E. A. Ireland and the Denver & Rio Grande Express company said nay. The company then filed an action in the Third District court to recover possession of the box. This was on Tuesday. Yesterday the suit was dismissed, and inquiry developed the fact that the cattle company had indemnified the express company against loss by filing a bond, and in this way secured possession of the coveted box.

What may follow is merely a matter of conjecture in view of the fact that the persons interested declined to discuss the differences that are presumed to exist between Mr. Ireland and the company.

Eastern Utah Advocate
September 16, 1897

The largest flood of the season and also the greatest one within the recollection of the oldest settler occurred here Sunday evening. The bridge held out against the mighty force of the current. The water had fallen nearly two feet when it began cutting around the north abutment of the bridge, which sunk about four feet, but fortunately was not carried away. A large force of men turned out Monday and Tuesday and the bridge now can withstand another siege. Considerable damage has been done along the river. The brick yard was flooded and a consequent heavy loss resulted. Meadows were covered with debris and ditches filled with mud.

Brother Seth Allen, formerly of Emery, has moved his household goods to Castledale. We welcome you and your wife, Brother Allen, and hope you will not be sorry for your move.

School commences Monday, September 20, with Seth Allen and D. T. Thomander, as teachers. Parents should send their children at the beginning, as much better results will follow. Let no little task keep them from learning all they can. Rather sacrifice a little, but give them as much schooling as possible.

Carl Willberg and Carl Olsen have bought Peter Anderson's sawmill. They have a good force of men and expect to run the mill to its utmost capacity for two months at least.

Work has at last commenced on the Straight canyon road. We hope to see a good road through there, as it will be of great value to Castledale and Orangeville. Much timber country will be thrown open, and a way to travel to Sanpete by a shorter route brought about.

—Very few attended Sunday school conference on account of the stormy weather.

The photo man Spults has been taking shots around town the past week. He left us Monday.

Melons at Biddlecom's and Luud's are all right, and a good flavor and withal a good supply

FERRON.

The unusual quantity of rain that has fallen within the last few days make the farmers seriously uneasy about their grain, a good deal of which is cut but still in the field and some of it not shocked.

Misses Eva Brandon of Castledale and Lee Reid, Rosa Cox and Willie Grange of Orangeville were some of Ferron's charming visitors this week. Wyatt Bryan, a sojourner in Price, was also here for a few days.

H. M. Fugate and family returned last week from a pleasant trip to Manti

Ezra Frank, E. A. Wild, J. O. Lemon and Chris Peterson are some of our citizens who are erecting handsome and substantial dwellings, some of which are nearly completed. A number of others are making additions and improvements to their dwellings Wren & Co. have nearly finished an elegant store building. The Co-op, it is learned, will soon make extensive additions to its store buildings. Several large barns are being built, and altogether our mechanics are in clover. Let the good work go merrily on

The next thing in order is the much-needed improvement of our streets and foot bridges over the ditches. Economy, convenience and sightliness strongly demand this

An entertainment was given by the young ladies on Monday night. A varied program was followed by a pleasant dance, which was a most pronounced and enjoyable success. Failure is never recorded of anything undertaken by our ladies.

HUNTINGTON.

Attorney George M Miller purchased the residence of W. R Guymon. This means that Mr. Miller is permanently located at Huntington.

W. R. Guymon and B F. Black are making preparations to go to Mexico.

O P. Black and family of Fruitland, New Mexico, are here visiting friends and relatives.

At a joint meeting held recently by the Huntington and Cleveland Canal companies, it was decided that active steps should be taken to prevent the Ginpitchers from appropriating the head waters of Huntington river and that unless the practice is stopped at once the matter will be taken into the courts.

The family reunion of W. M Black of Donblan, Mexico, was celebrated at the residence of George Gale last week. The family is perhaps the largest in the state, excepting only that of the late Brigham Young. There were present at the reunion 102 children, grandchildren and great grandchildren. These are the descendants of about one-third of his family. Mr Black has been here since the Jubilee, having come from Mexico to attend the pioneer festivities.

Our flour mill is again in operation, the injunction having accomplished the desired result. Our people can now obtain flour at home instead of spending two or three days going to Orangeville, and oftentimes being compelled to wait several days for their grist on account of the rush at Orangeville which necessarily followed

The directors of the Huntington Canal and Agricultural association met Satur

The damage to Emery county crops by the recent floods will amount to several thousand dollars. The state road up Huntington canyon is washed out, the dugways just completed are impassable and the new bridge, which cost the state about $300, is entirely swept away, nothing remaining but one abutment. Nearly every dam in Huntington river used by the irrigation companies is gone and the only bridge on the entire river is the one at Huntington, and it is damaged. Hundreds of bushels of grain along the river were swept away and several hay stacks went down in the terrible flood.

Peter Johanson, Jacob Maxwell and Peter Hauson are the heaviest losers in the canyon, while W A. Guymon and son report about eight acres swept away along the river below town

The loss at Lawrence is reported to be even greater than at Huntington.

The Huntington and Cleveland canals are badly damaged.

The flume across Cedar creek owned and used by Desert Lake is gone, and it was reported that the water was running out of the reservoir Sunday evening, and it is feared that the dam is gone.

Considerable damage has also been done the grain in the field by causing it to sprout. Heavy damage to property from the south is also reported.

day for the purpose of taking some steps toward making a defense to the suit filed against them by the Huntington Roller Mills and Manufacturing company. The directors repudiated the action of the individuals who interfered with and stopped the flow of the water in the Huntington canal, and instructed the secretary, J. H. Scott, to procure the assistance of an attorney to make this defense.

An educational meeting of the district school teachers was held last Wednesday evening, at which a number of good suggestions were given upon the duties of parents to their children and to the schools It is to be hoped that our schools will be well and regularly attended by every child in the district within school age.

J B Brockbank, who has been at Eureka for the last ten months, has returned home.

Mrs. Peter Hanson is very sick

Dr. Winters was in our town last Wednesday on professional business John Murning was his patient.

Mrs. Wm. Floyd has returned from Orangeville

Rue Killpack of Manti is here visiting his brother, J. H Killpack.

Robert Gordon sold his sheep herd last week to G. G. Frandsen of Price for $1400. Robert says he s tired of the range.

EMERY COUNTY FLOODS.

Much Damage to Crops and Roads— Other Notes.

Huntington, Utah, Sept. 13.—The most damaging flood in the history of Huntington came down last night about 1 o'clock, carrying with it trees, brush, haystacks, bridges, etc. The new bridge just built in the canyon is gone, and as reports come in many acres of grain already in the shock have been swept away. The roads through the county are almost impassable, owing to the way the washes have heretofore been fixed. The big bridge across the Huntington river is still in place, but damaged.

The controversy between the Huntington Roller Mills company and the Huntington Canal & Agricultural association has assumed serious proportions. The mill company has placed an injunction on the canal company restraining its officers from meddling with the disputed water until the sitting of the district court in November. The canal company is making arrangements for a finish fight when the ball opens. Several mill owners have been seen talking up a compromise, which the canal company does not seem at present to favor, claiming that it has tried to compromise several times. Reid & Cherry of Manti are the attorneys for the mill company and Hon. W. H. King and his brother, S. A. King of Provo, are defending the canal company.

The mail from the north today is over five hours late, owing to the floods.

We have one case of scarlet fever in town, but it is under proper quarantine regulations.

The non-partisan fever has not yet put in an appearance here, and if it should the writer is of opinion it would be promptly quarantined as other fevers are.

Your correspondent, together with a few friends, had the pleasure of an invitation to a big melon cut last Sunday at the home of Thomas Rowly. Mr. Rowly has as beautiful a lot of melons as can be found anywhere, some of which weigh 25 and 30 pounds each.

Professor Hardy, the choir leader, is somewhat discouraged owing to the fact that many people throughout the county have failed to pay him for his services teaching music classes in the different settlements last fall.

There will be more grain raised in Huntington this year than any previous season.

An Orangeville B Y Student

Ehlor Advocate.

Provo has just awakened from a summer's nap which she always takes during vacation and is now alive and as active as ever It is a very pretty little city, situated near Utah lake, with the great Wasatch range on the north and east. which is at this time of the year crowned with autumn tints, making the scene very picturesque.

The B Y, academy opened August 30 with 300 pupils, which was very encouraging, as the greater part of them were new students. Many more are expected during the present week and the old students are flocking in

Prospects are that this will be one of the most successful years the academy has ever known There is nothing to prevent this institution from becoming the leading educational institution in the west. A new $15,000 building for the college department will be erected on the east of the present building and will be ready for use by the 1st of January

We are pleased to say that few students have presented themselves for examination, the greater number entering school on certificates from the various district schools

Students desiring to attend school may find good board at from $2 50 to $3 00 per week, or they may greatly reduce their expenses by renting a room and keeping house

Young people, if you desire to gain an education and learn to be useful, the academy is the place for you. Do not remain at home because you are short of means and have had little school advantages. Provision is made for such students and you will find the B Y A a very pleasant place.

A course for this class of students will open the 1st of October, continuing twenty weeks Friends, consider this matter and write at once for a circular. Commence saving your cents and before you are aware you will be ready for a year's course in school, which will be sure to lead to something higher.

On the evening of September 9 a reception was given to the students by the faculty. The assembly room was crowded with pleasant faces. After a few hours of greeting friends and a short program, the crowd repaired to the lawn where all indulged in a watermelon festival The occasion was a perfect success.
EMMA HIGGS.

Provo, September 10

Little Loss to Grain.

The reports in last week's Advocate of great loss to grain in Emery county by the recent floods, by later and careful investigation have, we are glad to say, been found to be without foundation. The loss to grain is slight in both Carbon and Emery counties. Hay was damaged to some extent. The greatest loss was to canals. A careful estimate of damage to canals at Orangeville and Castledale will probably reach $900, while at Huntington it is thought that the damage will run up to $1,000. Ferron and Emery sustained little loss to canals. Cleveland was also a heavy loser from washouts on the upper end of its canal. The reservoir dam at Desert Lake held out against the flood, the spill ways doing their work of carrying off the surplus water satisfactorily. The damage to canals in Price valley is quite heavy and will reach several hundred dollars.

Fatality at Ferron.

On Monday last the 5 year-old son of Edson Huntsman of Ferron was run over by a hay rack and instantly killed. The accident occurred about two miles this side of Ferron. The boy was riding with Mr. Crawford and fell through the rack, the hind wheels passing over his temples, with the sad results stated. The accident was particularly deplorable in that his father was riding directly behind Mr. Crawford and was a witness to his child's painful death.

Grand Valley Times
September 24, 1897

Wm. H. Allred, our fellow townsman, who has been over to Castle Dale on business, writing us from there under date of Sept 13th, received to late to publish last week, says that there has been heavy rains in that section; that the flood in Castle Dale creek was a glorious sight, being about four hundred yards across the water, if the flood had lasted two hours longer the long bridge would have gone out. Mr. Allred informs us that the hand of Providence saved the bridge but does not state whose hand started the flood. As it was the bridge sank about 5 feet at the center.

He reports heavy crops in that section but in danger of being injured by the heavy rains.

The people of Castle Dale seem to be very energetic, he writes, building nice brick houses and improving their places generally.

Huntington, Utah, Sept. 25.—It is very amusing to some and annoying to others to see the way some of the office holders of Emery county, whose duty it is to look after the expenditure of public money are doing. Instead of calling out men enough to do the road work in a few days as few as possible are employed and plenty of idle men who are asking for work to earn something with which to pay their taxes, which are now due, are refused work.

The county commissioners met on the 20th and 21st at the county seat and had quite a turbulent time adjusting a batch of old and new claims against the county. A new fund was created for the ostensible purpose of paying off some of these old accounts.

Hon. Isaac C. McFarland of the state land board is here and in company with the county land appraisers are busily engaged setting a price on the land in the vicinity of Huntington. It is expected that they will do considerable work throughout the county before adjourning.

E. A. Howard is again on our streets. Mr. Howard has been with the Co-op. Wagon & Machine company of Salt Lake for the last two or three years. He is now a member of the board of county land appraisers, who, together with Hon. J. E. Johnson, also a member of the board, will do the right thing by the farmers of Emery county, as well as the state of Utah.

L. D. Crandall, who is in the employ of W. M. Roylance of Springville, is here buying grain. M. E. Johnson is also buying grain and paying the highest price in cash for car lots. The farmers are having a picnic as fast as their grain is ready for market.

Postofficer Inspector Fitzgerald was in the city on Wednesday last.

There are two cases of scarlet fever in town, but not considered dangerous. They are both under strict quarantine.

There is five district schools in full blast at present, all full. Mr. Call of Willard, Box Elder county, has been employed by the trustees.

The church seminary board is making arrangements to start that school in the near future.

The Huntington roller mills procured an injunction against the Huntington Canal & Agricultural association just in time to have the fun of keeping the canal in repair during these heavy storms and floods. The stockholders of the canal are enjoined from having anything to do with the canal and the mill company look as though they had taken too large a bite.

A few of our citizens have concluded to remove to Old Mexico, where they have a host of relatives and friends.

HUNTINGTON.

Hans Jacobson, while coming down Huntington canyon Saturday with a load of lumber, ran off a dugway which had been partly washed out by the recent flood, and came nearly being killed. The wagon tipped over and fell into the river, a distance of about 20 feet, and Mr. Jacobson, who was unable to get off the wagon, was thrown down the embankment, with lumber upon him. He, however, happened to fall between two large rocks, and was thus saved from being crushed. As it was, Mr. Jacobson's left knee was dislocated and the bone badly fractured, his left arm being also bruised. Mr Jacobson was brought to town Saturday evening and his injuries attended to by Dr. Booth. His wagon was also damaged. This accident is a verification, in part, of the damage of the recent flood to our state road, which is in worse condition now than it ever was, all the reports to the contrary notwithstanding

Wm Floyd made a business trip to Salt Lake last Wednesday.

Land appraisers J. E Johnson and E A. Howard, together with Commissioner McFarland, are here at work at praising school land.

Robert Hill and John Wilson have purchased a new thrasher and are doing some good work.

The north school house will be completed this week, and school will begin next Monday, with George M. Miller as teacher.

CASTLEDALE.

Charles Swasey has been seen about home and town the last few days.

Hyrum and Rastus Larsen left home for a sojourn in Price and the gilsonite mines.

Mr. and Mrs. Bonnie of Mount Pleasant spent a few days with us.

Mrs. A. E. Miner of Fairview has been visiting old friends here and attended the Day family reunion at Lawrence.

Miss McMullin of Wellington has been about town the past week.

The district school is under full sway, with an attendance of 60 in primary department and 25 in the advanced.

The choir is busy rehearsing songs for the November conference. Brother Jameson is doing his best to get them in proper trim.

Several new dwellings are going up and others are soon to follow. James H Wilcox's is of solid brick, James Peterson's and the Evans' being frame Seth Allen is repairing and adding to his new home.

Hector Evans spent a fortnight among us and returned to his home in Scofield Monday.

Elder Bonnie of Mount Pleasant, a newly returned missionary, gave an excellent discourse at the meeting Sunday.

Joe Lund and family are giving Sanpete a visit.

Preparations are being made for a self-supporting flume over Grime's wash The Mammoth Canal company find it a great expense to put in a new flume after every flood. They will now try a plan which they think will be a success.

Mr. and Mrs Larsen feel jubilant over the arrival of a new girl at their home All doing well.

Daily Enquirer
October 14, 1897

AMONG yesterday's postoffice appointments were the following: Utah—Avon, Cache county, George Davis vice Wm. Johnson resigned; Hyrum, Cache county, Soren Hanson vice Corydon Beavens resigned; Meadow, Millard county, Charles D. Smith vice May Greenhalge resigned; Molen, Emery county, Edward Caldwell vice Mrs. C. A. Young resigned; Orangeville, Emery county, William F. Fall vice E. W. Fox, jr., resigned; Rawlins, Cache county, William H. Hill vice Robert Baxter, jr., resigned; Tooele county, Mrs. Rosa M. Marks vice A. McD. Frazer removed.

OFFICIAL DIRECTORY.

CARBON COUNTY

Comm'rs. { A. Liddell, Chm. Wellington
{ A. Hood Scofield
{ Edgar Thayn, Wellington.
Treasurer—Albert Bryner, Price.
Clerk and Recorder—W. H. Donaldson, Price
Assessor—W. J. Tidwell, Price
Supt. of Schools—H. G. Webb, Scofield.
Pros. Attorney—J. W. Warf, Price.
Sheriff—Gus. Donant, Castlegate
Coroner—R. B. Asadoorian, Castlegate.

EMERY COUNTY.

Commissioners { G. A. Wood, Huntington
{ H. P. Rasmussen, Molen.
{ Nephi Williams, Emery.
Treasurer—R. C. Miller, Castledale.
Clerk & Recorder—Ole Bitterud Castledale.
Assessor—M. C. Bryan, Ferron.
Supt of Schools—J. H. Scott, Huntington.
Pros. Attorney—Wm. Howard, Huntington.
Sheriff—Azariah Tuttle, Orangeville.

Eastern Utah Advocate
October 14, 1897

HUNTINGTON.

A number of our worthy townsmen attended the conference at Salt Lake last week.

The scarlet fever flags have now all been taken down, and our town is entirely free from any sickness of a contagious nature.

The mail did not arrive until dark Saturday evening on account of the bad roads and swollen creeks, and then it came on horseback.

Our county road is again in a deplorable condition, especially the road between Huntington and Castledale.

Hans Jacobson, who was recently injured by having a load of lumber fall on him, is getting much better.

James Bradley will soon move to town for the winter.

J. H. Scott, our genial county superintendent of schools, got a rusty nail run into his foot last week, and as a result Mr Scott is confined to his home.

B D Black, W. R. Guymon and Ezra Brown left Huntington on Wednesday for Old Mexico, where they intend to remain permanently.

John J. Thorderson has filed an action of trespass against Arthur Marshall.

FERRON,

There is a number of cases of diphtheria in our town. Sam Singleton, H. A. Cullum and James Nelson have each lost a child, and a greater number of the children in the families of Ole Osen, Peter R Peterson and Andrew Nelson are ill with the disease.

The canyon roads are badly washed from the recent floods

It is said that considerable wheat and other grain is sprouted

A greater number of the herds of sheep that have ranged on the mountains west of Ferron have gone to lower altitudes for the winter feed.

Chess Bryan has opened up a saloon in Wyatt Bryan's old store building

George A. Petty is in Salt Lake this week.

Ed Cooley returned from the saw mill last Saturday, where he spent the summer.

Will Cooley visited friends in Ferron a few days and on Wednesday departed for Davisville, Cal.

ORANGEVILLE

Born, to Mrs N. S Curtis, a fine baby boy. This is their first son of a family of six children, and Mr. Curtis is very proud of the newcomer.

Milton Tuttle and Miss Flora Fail were joined in wedlock Monday evening, October ? The bride was charmingly attired in white silk. A greater portion of the town was present and a good time was had. Mr and Mrs Tuttle are of the best families of our town and are deservedly popular. Milton Tuttle is one of the prominent and successful young business men of the county, and surely the future partakes of the roseate hue for him and his lovely bride. The Advocate wishes the worthy pair all manner of happiness and prosperity.

Dame rumor says there will be another wedding in the very near future Watch the postoffice for invitations.

After a long absence A. E. Stilson has returned home.

Orson Miles has moved his family to his new residence near the old mill site.

William Barker has returned from Escalante, where he has been for some time.

The first frost of the season bit the most tender vegetation.

The pool hall is a very popular place of resort for our men and boys

There has been an unusually heavy rain fall the last week

An amusing incident occurred at Orangeville a short time ago A Castledale man on his way to the canyon learning there was bacon to be had at Orangeville wished to get some but had left his purse a* home. He stepped into a store, and inquired of the merchant if he had beacon or ham. Merchant. "Yes, sir." C. D. man ' Let me have twenty five pounds" Merchant. 'Yes, sir," The required amount being weighed the merchant said, "Here it is." C. D. man "Please charge it" Merchant. "Why, I don't know you." "Well, charge it." Merchant. "We don't do that kind of business, and I don t know you." C. D. man· 'Shall I get references* Will Sheriff T——do?" Merchant: "I guess so, but who are you anyway?" C. D. man "My name is ——." Merchant "Oh! oh! go on, go on" C. D. man "Well, a name is worth something I find." And he went his way.

We understand that two weddings are to come off this week. Particulars in our next.

There are lots of grain and hay in the field yet, and some of it has been considerably damaged by the heavy rains of the last three weeks.

Fine weather now, but roads awful muddy.

Additional Huntington Correspondence.

Mr. J. H. Leonard and Miss Alice Rowley, Mr. Joe Gordon and Miss Hannah Augusta Johnson have taken out marriage licenses and have been inviting their friends to the wedding next Friday. The writer is on the list and will eat but very little during the three or four days next preceding the eventful day

The Huntington Dramatic association held a meeting Saturday evening and reorganized, with D. C. Woodward, president, J. E. Johnson, manager; Wm. Hunter, assistant manager; P. E. Johnson, treasurer; M. E. Johnson, secretary. They expect to put on some plays soon

A town caucus for everybody was held Monday evening, when the almost unanimous sentiment was to disincorporate, but the time had gone by to do that, according to law. So, after considerable heated talk, the following ticket was nominated for the ensuing two years George W. Johnson, president; William Hunter, Albert Collard, A. P. Johnson and J. B. Meeks, trustees. The town is almost hopelessly in debt, and the people see no reasonable way to get out of it, as the revenue from the taxes is not more than half enough to pay the current expenses, and besides that the roads around Huntington are a disgrace to the county. Nearly all the poll tax is used inside the town, and the county is not able to put the work on the roads that is necessary to keep them in repair.

Taxes and the exchange of school books are the cause of much worry and the scratching of many heads. People don't know where all this money is to come from. Senator Johnson made a great fight against this scheme of exchanging books every few years at an expense of nearly half a million dollars to the state, in the legislature last winter. Salt Lake City furnishes the whole catalogue of books per capita for less than $1, and why the outside counties should pay several times that much is yet to be explained.

We have no sickness in town to speak of. The storms seem to have settled, the mud is drying up and things are settling down to their wonted quietness.

We understand that Christopher Wilcock, who is now on a mission to Great Britain, will soon return on account of the delicate health of his wife.

HUNTINGTON.

The Huntington Dramatic association held a meeting Saturday evening and reorganized, with D. O. Woodward, president, J. E. Johnson, manager; Wm. Hunter, assistant manager; P. E. Johnson, treasurer; M. E. Johnson, secretary. They expect to put on some plays soon

A town caucus for everybody was held Monday evening, when the almost unanimous sentiment was to disincorporate, but the time had gone by to do that, according to law. So, after considerable heated talk, the following ticket was nominated for the ensuing two years George W. Johnson, president; William Hunter, Albert Collard, A. P. Johnson and J. B. Meeks, trustees. The town is almost hopelessly in debt, and the people see no reasonable way to get out of it, as the revenue from the taxes is not more than half enough to pay the current expenses, and besides that the roads around Huntington are a disgrace to the county. Nearly all the poll tax is used inside the town, and the county is not able to put the work on the roads that is necessary to keep them in repair.

We understand that two weddings are to come off this week. Particulars in our next.

There are lots of grain and hay in the field yet, and some of it has been considerably damaged by the heavy rains of the last three weeks.

Fine weather now, but roads awful muddy.

Additional Huntington Correspondence.

Mr. J. H. Leonard and Miss Alice Rowley, Mr. Joe Gordon and Miss Hannah Augusta Johnson have taken out marriage licenses and have been inviting their friends to the wedding next Friday. The writer is on the list and will eat but very little during the three or four days next preceding the eventful day

Taxes and the exchange of school books are the cause of much worry and the scratching of many heads. People don't know where all this money is to come from. Senator Johnson made a great fight against this scheme of exchanging books every few years at an expense of nearly half a million dollars to the state, in the legislature last winter. Salt Lake City furnishes the whole catalogue of books per capita for less than $1, and why the outside counties should pay several times that much is yet to be explained.

We have no sickness in town to speak of. The storms seem to have settled, the mud is drying up and things are settling down to their wonted quietness.

We understand that Christopher Wilcock, who is now on a mission to Great Britain, will soon return on account of the delicate health of his wife.

Salt Lake Herald
October 21, 1897

TICKET AT HUNTINGTON.

Democrats and Silver Republicans Nominated—News Notes.

Huntington, Utah, Oct. 19.—Last night a primary of the people of the town was held for the purpose of nominating a president and board of trustees. The meeting was called ostensibly for that end by the Democratic party, but when the meeting convened it was noticed that about as many Republicans as Democrats were present, and as our town officers had heretofore been nominated by a joint meeting of all political parties, it was decided to proceed and nominate from the house.

The following nominations were made:

President—George W. Johnson, jr.

Trustees—William Hunter, Albert Collard, A. P. Johnson and J. R. Meeks. Three are Democrats and the others Silver Republicans.

Before the nominations were made a proposition was made to disincorporate the town, on the grounds that the revenues were not sufficient to support the organization, but it was voted down by a large majority.

The primary conference for the Emery stake, held at Huntington last Saturday, though not largely attended, was a grand success. The storm and mud were very unpleasant, but those who attended had a treat, as the programme and exercises generally were very instructive.

Mr. J. H. Leonard and Miss Alice Rowly and Mr. Joe Gordon and Miss Hannah Augusta Johnson, four of Huntington's popular young people, have gone to the county seat today to secure marriage licenses. We understand that there are several couples here who will do likewise in time for winter comfort.

The Robbers' Roosters are apparently defunct, save it be in the memories of the officials at Castle Gate and vicinity.

Provo Daily Enquirer
October 27, 1897

Utah Postmasters.

Washington, Oct. 26.—Five of the sixty-two fourth class postmasters appointed today were for Utah to fill vacancies caused by resignation and removal. The appointments were as follows: Annabella, Sevier county, E. B. Keyes, vice B. Gardner, resigned; Ferron, Emery county, H. W. Curtis, vice M. J. Taylor, removed; Huntington, Emery county, G. M Miller, vice M. E. Johnson, resigned; Manti, Sanpete county, J. P. Madsen, vice William J. Stacey, removed; Stockton, Tooele county, Mary A Frank, vice Dora L. Frank, resigned.

Salt Lake Herald
October 27, 1897

UTAH POSTMASTERS BEHEADED

MORE PLACES PROVIDED FOR HUNGRY M'KINLEYITES.

Manti, Stockton, Huntington and Annabella Receive Attention—Patents and Land Selections.

Special to The Herald.)

Washington, Oct. 26.—Fourth class postmasters for Utah were appointed today as follows:

Annabella, Sevier county, E. B. Keyes, vice G. B. Gardner, removed.

Huntington, Emery county, G. M. Miller, vice M. E. Johnson, removed.

Manti, Sanpete county, J. F. Madsen, vice William J. Stacey, removed.

Stockton, Tooele county, Mary R. Frank, vice Dora L. Frank, resigned.

Eastern Utah Advocate
October 28, 1897

Cox & Carroll of Orangeville shipped ten cars of cattle from this place early in the week.

HUNTINGTON.

We had two fine dances last week —one on Thursday night, celebrating the marriage of J. H. Leonard and Miss Alice Rowley, and one on Friday, celebrating the marriage of Joseph Gordon and Miss Hannah A. Johnson Both these dances were well attended, but it is nothing unusual to have free dances well patronized in Huntington.

On Monday evening the town board met and passed a few bills, also instructed the clerk to prepare for the election, and appointed D. O. Woodward, H S Loveless and E. H. Cox, judges of election.

There seems to be a kick from some of Huntington's smarties about the work done by the mass convention or caucus held on the 18th inst. There has never been a party caucus held in Huntington to nominate town officers. As section 1 of chapter 7 municipal elections provides that the term of office of all the present elective officers shall expire at 12 o'clock meridian on the first Monday in January, 1898, and as neither party called primaries or conventions something had to be done, as the time had nearly, if not quite, expired. The vice-president of the democratic club of Huntington gave public notice for everybody to come. They came, both democrats and republicans, and there was as good a turn out as there generally is at such gatherings. It now appears that some of the leading republicans threaten to contest the nominations made, because the republicans did not call the meeting In the nominations made there are known to be two republicans, one democrat and the politics of the other two is not known We hope they will kick so that the public may learn what kind of men they are.

On Tuesday morning we had a very heavy snow storm for about half an hour, then it partly cleared up, a cold wind blowing the balance of the day. The first heavy frost of the season was on the 18th of October.

Our coal miners are thinking of getting a rustle on them, as the cold weather makes the people think of their winter's supply of coal and wood Howard's coal mine in Cedar reek seems to be the favorite, as they have the shortest and best road and the best coal.

CASTLEDALE.

Joseph Christenson, the harness maker, has been putting up a shop on Main street. It will soon be ready for occupancy, and then you may look for a big display of goods.

Young Vern Kofford coming down the canyon last week met with a strange accident. The road having been washed out brush had been filled in to make a crossing. The horse the boy was riding stepped through the brush and, becoming frightened, made a lunge and fell into the creek a channel, with Kofford underneath the horse. He dug a hole and was in the act of crawling out when the horse began to struggle and fell upon him again, pinning him to the ground. He laid in this position nearly three hours, when O. J. Anderson, coming down the canyon, saw the boy in his critical position and hitched his team to the horse and soon liberated the young fellow, who was more scared than hurt.

The young ladies have a fair prepared for this week. When the ladies undertake anything we are sure of a good time. An excellent program has been prepared and includes a sumptuous feast to appease our appetite and a dance Wednesday evening which will be no an all affair

William Savage, 10 years of age, and eldest son of Mr. and Mrs. H Savage, met with a serious accident Sunday afternoon. He and his smaller brother Gilbert were out hunting rabbits. It appears from their story that Will was leaning on his gun with the muzzle in his arm pit. His little brother, who had the ramrod in his hand, struck the hammer, accidentally discharging the gun. The charge entered Will's shoulder, tearing a great hole and coming out near the neck. An artery was cut, causing the loss of much blood. Dr. Winters attended the injured lad, who it is thought will not recover

HUNTINGTON ACCIDENTS.

A Boy and a Baby Receive Serious Injuries.

Huntington, Utah, Oct. 29.—Yesterday Edwin, the 11-year-old son of Jerome Bradley, while riding at a fast rate through one of the streets, was thrown from his horse so violently that his arm was dislocated at the elbow and the bone fractured, causing an ugly wound. Dr. Winter, of Orangeville, set the limb and the little fellow is resting comfortably today.

Another accident occurred yesterday to the infant child of Mr. and Mrs. Sam Myers, late of Salt Lake, at the sheep camp of Rowberry & Myers in the mountains west of here. Mr. Myers had ridden up to the camp on horseback and dismounted and put the child into the saddle and was leading the horse and also holding to the child. In some way the horse became frightened and began kicking and running around trying to get away. Mr. Myers held to the animal and the child became entangled in the saddle trimmings and was dragged and thrown around in a frightful manner. When it was finally rescued from the perilous situation it was discovered that one leg was broken below the knee and the child otherwise bruised and maimed. The parents started at once for home, arriving late in the night.

Salt Lake Herald
November 3, 1897

EMERY CONFERENCE.

None of the Twelve Attended—Post-office Appointments.

Huntington, Utah, Nov. 1.—The quarterly conference of the Emery stake convened at Castle Dale on the 30th and 31st of October and, though the attendance was not heavy, a very good instructive time was had. It was truly a home conference, as none of the apostles were present; but Emery stake can furnish as good speakers as can be found in any stake in Zion, and some of them occupied the time to good advantage during the different sessions. The sustaining of the officers passed off smoothly, owing to the fact that it was understood that the unpleasantness that has existed in Castle Dale for some time must await adjustment until some of the apostles could be present.

There are over 200 pupils enrolled in our district schools, which are presided over by Principal D. C. Woodward and a corps of assistant teachers.

The weather is so warm and pleasant nowadays that the fields are full of farmers preparing for spring crops, and next year will not find as much grain in the fields when the rains and floods of September and October come as was destroyed this season. The farmers are waking up.

Salt Lake Herald
November 6, 1897

HUNTINGTON ELECTION.

No Opposition to the Democratic Ticket—Case of Diphtheria.

Huntington, Utah, Nov. 3.—The election of town officers yesterday passed off very quietly. Nothing of note transpired to cause any kind of excitement, there being no opposition to the straight Democratic ticket. The following were elected:

President.—George W. Johnson.

Trustees.—William Hunter, Albert Collard, A. P. Johnson, J. B. Meeks.

Mrs. Wilcox is gradually growing worse, and Mr. Wilcox, who is on a mission in Great Britain, has been telegraphed for, and his friends are anxiously waiting for his arrival home.

George Ipson has just been awarded a patent on a non-refillable bottle. Mr. Ipson's application for patent was contested in the patent office, but the outcome was in his favor.

There is one case of diphtheria in town now.

Eastern Utah Advocate
November 11, 1897

Ferron's Progressive Ranchman.

J. W. Williams, one of Ferron's progressive farmers, was in Price early in the week. Mr. Williams is one of the old settlers of that thriving settlement and a close observer of the climatic conditions which tend to the growth of the cereals in which the farmer is most interested. He states that the excessive rains of the past two months, while doing some damage to the summer's yield of hay and grain, will in the end be of benefit, as the people will hereafter be prepared at the breaking up of winter to begin farm work as soon as the frost gets out of the ground. The work of repairing and putting the various canals in shape for irrigation the coming season will be attended to this fall, and a number of farmers are fall plowing. Mr. Williams states that he will in the future put in fall wheat. While it will ripen and be harvested before the late season rains, he is of the opinion that it will produce better. He says that the diphtheria has disappeared, and from the rigid quarantine regulations of the Ferron authorities, thinks there will be no further trouble, as the new physician who is thoroughly qualified, has charge of the sanitary regulations. The doctor's opinion of the frequent appearance of the disease and in so malignant form is that it is due mainly to improper sanitation.

Logan Journal
November 11, 1897

Beauregaard Kenner, of this city, while hunting in Big Bear Creek, Ferron Canyon, run across a grizzly bear; being out hunting, of course, was prepared to meet his victim. Beauregaard leveled his gun on it and we all know the result. Mr. Kenner brought the hide to the town and received $5 bounty from the county. The weight of the hide is about 125 pounds, showing that the animal must have been a monster. Beauregaard takes great delight in such sports and usually meets with success whenever he takes a trip into the mountains. There can be no mistake about his ability using a gun, and we believe he is a sure shot every time he takes aim. No one takes more pride in having a good gun than he. Those wishing to see the hide can do so by calling at his residence.—Manti Messenger.

Deseret Evening News
November 15, 1897

Joseph William Jackson, aged 22, of Castle Dale, and Ida May Van Leuven, of Mapleton, aged 18, have received a marriage license.

Salt Lake Herald
November 18, 1897

HUNTINGTON SPRINTERS.

Orangeville Not In It With Jones and Howard.

Huntington, Nov. 16.—The foot race between James Jones of Huntington and A. M. Stillson of Orangeville was run at Castle Dale yesterday and was easily won by Jones, who carried off $25 of Orangeville cash.

The foot race between Lu Howard of Huntington and Rob Woodward of Orangeville, also pulled off at Castle Dale, was won by the former, who brought the cash home with him.

Eastern Utah Advocate
November 18, 1897

A NORWAY LETTER.

Chris Poulsen Sends Word of

MISSIONARY WORK

And the Beauties of the Land of the Midnight Sun. Strange Customs.

THRONDHJEM, Norway, Oct. J, '97.
Editor Advocate:

Perhaps a few lines from this "land of the midnight sun" will be of interest to you and your many readers, and also answer queries in regard to my whereabouts, to the many friends in eastern Utah as well as elsewhere.

I left my home in Orangeville in April, 1896, and after a very pleasant trip both by land and sea (not including seasickness), reached my native country, Denmark, on May 18, just the time of year to see all nature in her beauty. The fields of flowers make me think this to be the "Flowery Kingdom," and after an absence of twenty-three years the scene was very inviting. Strange though it may seem to those who do not understand the Latter-day Saints, our homes in the valleys of the mountains seem even more beautiful and attractive than those here. After a short visit to my relatives near Aalbarg, I was sent here to Norway, and when my eyes first beheld the mountains and forest covered hillsides as we passed up the fjord (bay) toward Christiania I could hardly realize the beauty, the scene is so grand—one constant landscape—and so it continued wherever I went during the summer months, when the daylight lasts twenty-four hours, and in the longest days here in Throndhjem the sun is only out of sight about four hours, but these days soon pass away, and then we have the equally long winter, when darkness almost reigns supreme, and the sun appears in the horizon only a few hours, and instead thereof in this city of 33,000 inhabitants gas lamps and American coal oil are used.

There are many customs here so strange to us Americans, such as teaming with a two-wheeled wagon, one horse and a teamster, men with hand wagons hauling goods, women laboring out in the fields, hanging hay up on a sort of fence to dry, cutting grain with a sickle and hanging it on posts to dry, digging a large field of potatoes with the spade after having cut and dried the vines for winter feed. These with others have now become old and seem like that is the way they ought to do in Norway in order to give employment to their people.

During the summer months we spend most of the time traveling and laboring in the country, spreading the seeds of the gospel by distributing tracts and books, and it has been the writer's experience to find many people here who have never seen or conversed with a Mormon, although it is now nearly 40 years since Elder Dorius from Ephraim first preached the gospel in this city and a branch has been in existence here for many years. But as a rule the people are very kind and hospitable and one can go wherever he feels disposed. Of course they prefer not to have any "new doctrines preached, but let us have the old like our parents and ancestors, even if it is a little wrong," they say. During the past summer I have visited nearly every part of this large branch and also attended conference on September 1r in Christiania, traveling the whole distance, nearly 64 miles (about 378 English), on foot. I had therefore a good chance to learn the customs of the people and to lay before them the important message we are sent out to deliver, and having many experiences of a pleasant nature as well as otherwise, and on the whole found the people kind and hospitable.

Our conference was attended by 29 Utah elders, including Presidents Rolon S. Wells and McMurrin from Liverpool and President C. N. Lund, from Copenhagen, and the remarks and testimonies of the brothers—from the young man of 18 who just arrived to the old brother of 64 who is now serving his second mission here—were listened to by attentive congregations. Much valuable instruction was given, so that all who attended for the purpose of learning had a good opportunity. Each of the elders returned to his field, feeling well repaid for the time and money spent, and with renewed courage in pressing on the good work.

We have a nice little branch here of about 64 members, and each one of them has a great desire of emigrating to Zion. Among them are all kinds of tradesmen and laborers, and I sometimes think it would be a fine little colony for Castle valley. One thing is sure and that is, if we had more of these Norwegians or

others to set us more Americanized examples of economy and learn us how to stop the leaks on our farms, we would be better off.

I have enjoyed the best of health and feel thankful for having this privilege of being a representative of people "the world speaks evil of," and trust the feeble efforts of mine in spreading the truth will in the future bring forth fruit

Many thanks for The Advocate sent me free, and I may you succeed in the good work of showing forth the advantages and resources of our valleys

With kind regards to the many friends in the homes visited by The Advocate, I remain, very truly yours,

CHRISTIAN POULSEN.

Manti Messenger
November 20, 1897

The Castle Dale teachers and a number of pupils gave Orangeville schools a visit a day last week. They returned to work with renewed energy

Orangeville foot racers saw the backs of Huntington runners in the races here Nov. 15

Later Families and Young Hopeful

The residents of Poverty Flat near Ferron were one day last week regaled with rather an unique chase—that of pater families in hot pursuit of his young hopeful. The first knowledge of the affair was when said young hopeful passed our reporter on the road between the above named place and Castledale bound at a break neck speed for the latter place and who vouchsafed this only information, "Pops after me." In a very few minutes "pop" passed him a comet and the chase was on in good earnest. The boy being light and well mounted had a little of the advantage of the sire. It was a pretty close race, and for the first few miles it seemed that the runaway son would be overhauled and captured. The fear of punishment in the event of capture spurred the young hopeful almost to desperation and which was by intuition transferred to the mount which apparently realized that the situation was critical, and the way it threw dust at the pursuer was a caution. Up and down hill, over desert, pursued and pursuer flew, with the kid every minute putting a greater distance between himself and pater. When Castledale was reached the young hopeful disappeared so effectually that after a long hunt pater was compelled to return home empty handed.

Mr. and Mrs. Lars Thompson and L. P. Thompson of Ferron passed through Price en route to Salt Lake, where they will visit several days

CASTLEDALE COURT,

The Calendar Quickly Cleared.

A BIG WATER SUIT.

When Case is Heard Decision is Taken Under Advisement..

The seventh judicial district court for Emery county convened at Castledale November 15, Judge Johnson presiding.

The first case coming up for trial was that of the state of Utah vs. Ed Olson, charged with grand larceny. Continued to the next term.

State of Utah vs. Lars Thompson. The lower court was sustained and Mr. Thompson was resentenced to three years in the penitentiary.

The case of George H. Wade vs E. W. Jones was set for trial at the January term. This is one of the old bond suits against Mr. Jones when he was collector of Emery county.

The case of Thomas Rowley vs. A. Tuttle et al, was withdrawn by plaintiff without prejudice.

Judgment of $750 was taken for the state in the case of the state of Utah vs. J. B. Buhr and P. Jensen. This is the bond forfeited by Jack Moore at the May term of court.

Horace Duncan pleaded guilty to the charge of fornication and was sentenced to five months imprisonment in the county jail.

In the matter of the estate of James Von Musch, deceased, an order was granted relinquishing homestead entry to the United States.

By stipulation the court adjourned to Huntington to hear the case of the Huntington Roller Mill company vs Huntington Canal and Agricultural company. The case occupied the time of the court during Tuesday and Wednesday, many witnesses being examined by both sides. At the conclusion of the arguments Judge Johnson took the case under advisement.

The plaintiff sued the irrigation company for $2,500 damages for shutting off the supply of water used by it for power purposes, and asked a decree of the court giving the mill company a right of way perpetually through the defendant's canal for sufficient water to run the mill. Plaintiff claimed that it had erected the mill under an agreement with the canal company, by the terms of which the latter agreed to furnish all the water needed for power purposes, free of cost. As the water flowing through the canal was insufficient for the mill, the latter increased the flow by taking more water out of the river, thus, it is claimed, overtaxing the capacity of the canal. The plaintiff claimed that it was the duty of the canal company to enlarge the canal for this increased flow, and the canal company contended that this should be done by the plaintiff, and thereupon shut off the water. The defendant denied that the mill was damaged and denied that the mill had the right to any water, except that which flowed through the canal to the town.

Salt Lake Herald
November 25, 1897

B. F. SAUNDERS' SHEEP.

Twelve Thousand Ewes to Winter In Eastern Utah.

Richfield Advocate: J. H. Lock spent a few days in Richfield last week. He, with nine other men, 19 horses and Scotch coolies galore, is in charge of the B. F. Saunders sheep herd, now near Ferron, about 125 miles east of here. Mr. Saunders is in Salt Lake City for the winter, leaving his flock of 12,000 ewes in Mr. Lock's hands. They are divided into four herds of 3,000 each. All winter long they will travel slowly east. Blake, Utah, will be headquarters until the river freezes, and then the sheep will be driven across the ice and on towards Colorado. Mr. Lock says the feed so far is very good, and that a thick spread of snow already on the divide insures plenty of water for his herds, which are doing well.

A COUNTY DOG TAX.

A Dollar Each on the Emery County Canines.

Huntington, Nov. 23.—At a meeting of the county commissioners yesterday at Castle Dale it was decided to collect the tax on dogs throughout the county, and a man was appointed to make a canvass of the county and collect $1 on each dog. The assessor failed to list the dogs in the spring, as was also the case with the special bee tax, which was charged up to the assessor.

BAD MAIL SERVICE.

The people of this place are greatly inconvenienced through the recent action of the postoffice department introducing a through or brass lock system, from Price to Castle Dale. About half the time our mail is put into that pouch, instead of the way pouch for Huntington, and hence goes by us, either to Castle Dale or Price. The Huntington postmaster has antagonized the proposition from the start, but to no avail.

The church seminary opened last Monday with an attendance of 25 pupils under the principalship of Mr. David Prior of Spanish Fork. The roll is daily augmented by new pupils from neighboring towns.

A SALOON OPENING.

It is currently reported that Wyatt Bryan will open a saloon here next Monday morning. If he does, it is to be hoped that a stop will be put to the wholesale liquor traffic that has been going on here lately. Drunkenness and hoodlumism have been too much indulged in here for an incorporated town. It is to be hoped that the rebuke administered by Judge Johnson in the recent trial will have a good effect.

E. L. Geary's new brick residence is fast nearing completion, and is a credit to its owner.

Salt Lake Herald
December 1, 1897

UTAH POSTMASTERS.

Deputy President Glen Miller Makes Three Appointments.

(Special to The Herald.)

Washington, Nov. 30.—Postmasters appointed today:

Utah.—Circleville, Piute county, William Johnson, vice Mrs. S. C. Gellies, removed.

Hamblin, Washington county, John Day, vice E. Hanfield, resigned.

Thurber, Wayne county, James Grant, vice M. W. Mansfield, resigned.

Wyoming.—Fort Fred Steele, Carbon county, A. R. Couzins, vice Anna M. Hess, resigned.

Harmon W. Curtis was today commissioned postmaster at Ferron, Utah.

Idaho postoffices discontinued: Indianola, Lemhi county, mail to Shoup; Pinedale, Boise county, mail to Alpha.

Patents issued today: Utah.—Orson P. Tretwell, Cedar City, animal cleaning device; William J. McDonald, Salt Lake, measure.

Wyoming.—John F. Webber, Sheridan, pant holder.

An original pension is granted William H. Guile, Gibbonville, Ida.

Eastern Utah Advocate
December 2, 1897

Thompson Takes an Appeal.

Lars Thompson of Ferron, who last week was resentenced to three years in the penitentiary for grand larceny, has taken an appeal to the United States supreme court. Thompson was first tried in November, 1885, by a jury of twelve men and convicted. Later a new trial was granted, and before the second hearing Utah had been admitted to statehood, and Thompson was tried by eight men and again convicted. He was then sentenced to three years in the penitentiary, and took an appeal to the state supreme court upon the ground that he was entitled to a trial by a jury of twelve men in view of the fact that the offense complained of was committed before the eight jury law and gone in effect. The state supreme court held an opposite view, however, and the supreme court of the United States will now pass upon the matter.

Salt Lake Herald
December 3, 1897

THIS WOMAN LIVED 108 YEARS

DEATH OF MRS. HAMILTON AT CASTLE DALE.

Was Married Five Times and Outlived All of Her Husbands and All But Three of Her 15 Children.

(Special to The Herald.)

Castle Dale, Utah, Dec. 2.—Mrs. Nancy Hamilton of this place died last Sunday at the remarkable age of 108 years. Mrs. Hamilton was born in North Carolina in the year 1790, residing in South Carolina and Tennessee until 1850, when she became a convert to Mormonism and removed to Utah, and up to her death remained faithful to her church vows. In 1883 she, with her husband, moved to Arizona, and when 100 years old again became a resident of Utah, residing at Mapleton and later at Castle Dale. In this long span she was married five times, and survived all of her husbands and raised 15 children, and outlived all with the exception of three. Her first marriage was at the age of 14, and the last at the ripe age of 93.

Emery County Teachers.

Castle Dale, Dec. 1.—The Emery County Teachers' association convened at Castle Dale Nov. 27. New officers were elected for the ensuing year, and matters pertaining to pedagogy were discussed. An interesting programme has been outlined for their next meeting, which occurs Dec. 18. The teachers find these discussions very interesting and instructive.

Eastern Utah Advocate
December 16, 1897

Last week a bunch of about thirty cattle, bearing the Ireland Cattle company's brands which had been recently obliterated, was seen in the foothills southwest of Orangeville and on the following night the cattle were driven across the canyon into the foothills north of Orangeville. Parties who saw the cattle being moved were unable to recognize the drivers, as it was after dark. Subsequently the Ireland company's herders found the cattle in the foothills north of Orangeville, where they had been left, and drove them back to their range in the vicinity of Emery. This brings to mind a similar occurrence in which about forty head of the Ireland cattle were early in November driven from their range and also bore obliterated marks and brands. When this information reached Emery a posse was quickly organized and pursuit given. A short distance from Emery a sheep herder was seen who stated that two of the Swaseys were driving the cattle toward the San Rafael reefs. The posse continued their chase and shortly came up to where the cattle were quietly feeding, but no drivers were to be seen. They continued their search and some miles from the herd found two of the Swaseys, whom they arrested and took to Emery for trial. When the sheep herder was put on the stand to testify he stated that he could not swear that the Swaseys were the drivers. The Swaseys were thereupon acquitted and released.

The Orangeville orchestra has arranged for the use of Dr. Winters' hall the coming season. They expect to have some excellent dances, good music and good management, with ample accommodations for a big crowd.

Salt Lake Herald
December 16, 1897

IN EMERY STAKE.

Interesting Conference of Mutual Improvement Association.

Huntington, Utah, Dec. 13.—Last night wound up the semi-annual conference of the Y. M. and Y. L. M. I. A. of the Emery stake. There were present on the stand, besides the superintendency of the stake and the different associations, President of the Stake C. G. Larsen and council, together with General Secretary Thomas Hall of Salt Lake City, and many bishops and other leading brethren of the stake.

The first meeting on Saturday was an officers' meeting, and was well attended. The instructions given were mainly as to the duties of the different officers of the associations. The afternoon was mainly occupied by Mr. Allen of Castle Dale, who delivered a very instructive lecture on the subject of "Home Sanitation." The evening was taken up with a musical entertainment, which was pronounced by all to be a success.

Sunday morning the Sunday school commenced at 9 o'clock and the usual exercises were rendered. The visitors took great interest in visiting the different departments under the guidance of Superintendent O. J. Harmon.

The meetings on Sunday were occupied by Elder Thomas Hall mainly. Brother David Prior of Spanish Fork and Superintendent J. E. Johnson occupied a short time. The instructions given were of a nature that would cause young people to be more obedient to parents and to leave off the vices and failings of youth.

This very instructive and entertaining conference wound up last night at about 9 o'clock, at which meeting Brother Hall exorted parents and guardians to look more closely after the interest and welfare of the youth of Zion, especially as to their morals and habits. A good time was had by all, and the verdict was that no better conference was ever held in this stake.

TROUBLE OVER SHEEP.

A Peaceable Transaction Magnified Into a Sensation.

Price, Utah, Dec. 14.—The sensational report alleging C. E. Kofford, the well known Castledale attorney, and other Emery county men threatened Mike Holloran with death if he resisted, and then drove off his herd of 2,000 sheep, is without foundation.

For some time there has been trouble between Holloran and Charles McArthur, whom Mr. Holloran had employed to look after his sheep, and early in September, at Pleasant Valley Junction, they came together in a fistic encounter, which resulted in the loss of some cuticle and much gore, and both were laid up for repairs in a Provo hospital. The scrap apparently settled the existing difficulty and shortly afterwards Holloran gave McArthur $2,500, with which to buy sheep, and when the sheep were purchased and had become the property of Holloran he then transferred them to McArthur by a bill of sale. Desiring to possess himself of property which the law would award him, McArthur's agent Attorney C. E. Kofford, and other Huntington men, proceeded to the Nine Mile country and there made a demand for the sheep, which Holloran refused, and thinking that force would be used to dispossess him he called on Pete Francis for help. Mr. Francis stated to McArthur's representative that if Holloran desired to deliver him the sheep they could have them, but could not take them by force. Mr. Kofford then returned to Price and was followed by Mr. Holloran, and an attempt will be made tomorrow to amicably settle the dispute.

As near as can be learned, no force was attempted. No arrests were made because there was no evidence that the law had been infringed.

ONE DOLLAR PER TON.

That Is the Price of Coal In Emery County.

Huntington, Utah, Dec. 18.—The best coal is being sold at some of the mines for $1 per ton. There are many of the comforts of life that Emery county people don't get, but they do have comfortable, happy and warm firesides. The Y. M. M. I. makes glad the hearts of the poor and widows each winter by piling up huge lots of wood and coal by their doors.

Many new settlers have come in this winter to locate, and they tell of more coming in the spring.

The streets are covered with ice and water to such a disgraceful extent that some are nearly impassable, besides the damage being done to property, and there are murmurings of law suits. The watermaster claims that the roller mill company is responsible, and the mill company denies it.

The new postmaster will take charge of the postoffice on the first of the new year; so says rumor. Many are the expressions of regret received by the outgoing postmaster, who has been the only postmaster that Huntington has known, he having held the office since 1879. Three-fourths of the patrons of the office remonstrated against the change, but Mr. Johnson is a true silver advocate, and that tells the story.

Last night the church seminary gave the semi-monthly ball. The students were out en masse. The bishops and counsel and the leading men of the ward are taking part to make these dances successful.

The town is full of picture men and tree agents, who seem to be well pleased with the results of their labors.

George M. Miller has lately been appointed a notary public for Emery county.

EMERY COUNTY EARTHQUAKE.

A Correspondent Thinks It Was a Meteoric Explosion.

To the Editor of The Herald:

I have read in your valuable paper an account of a supposed earthquake that recently occurred in this section. I have just had a conversation with a man who claims to have been near the center of the disturbance when it occurred. He is a resident of Castle Dale, but has a ranch 15 or 20 miles down Huntington creek, in the direction of the San Rafael. At the time of the disturbance he was taking a load of hay from his ranch, when there were three heavy reports, one after the other, followed by heavy rumbling. His horses were frightened so badly that they ran quite a distance, and nearly upset the wagon. He declares the reports were in the air above him, and never struck the earth. The heavens were immediately filled with a great volume of smoke, which whirled in a circle just above the earth. The three reports were very sharp and loud, and the rumbling that followed resembled the noise made by a snow slide. No doubt it was heard by everyone through Castle valley, and all supposed it to be an earthquake. I think it was the explosion of a meteor. Some people declare they have found oil springs not far from where the explosion occurred, and think perhaps one of these blew up.

JOSEPH THAYNE.

Orangeville, Emery County, Utah, December 22.

THE HOLLADAYS IN LUCK

HAVE LOCATED 1,000 ACRES OF VALUABLE GROUND.

Gives More Gas to the Ton Than the Best Colorado Product—Formation of a Company For the Operation of the Property — The Week at Mercur — Increased Activity Throughout This Great Gold Camp —Tintic Mining News — The Miner's Weekly Review of the News of the Camp—A Prosperous Season—Bright Future In Store For the "Old Reliable"—Mining Notes and Personals.

Castle Dale, Dec. 24.—The coal deposit which was recently discovered in the vicinity of Sunnyside, Emery county, now proves to be of vastly more importance than was at first supposed. Messrs. G. J. Holladay of Salt Lake, together with his father and brother and a number of other gentlemen, have located about 1,000 acres of land, embracing an entire mountain, and are now engaged in taking out coal for shipment to the Salt Lake gas works. This coal contains 420 feet more gas to the ton than the best Colorado product, and is the best for coking purposes that has yet been discovered.

For the development of the mine a company has been formed, with a capital stock of $200,000, and work on a large scale will commence on Jan. 1. The P. V. Coal company, which, a short time ago, was negotiating for the purchase of this property, and failed to secure it, now has a number of men prospecting in the vicinity of Sunnyside, but up to the present time they have discovered nothing.

A MYSTERIOUS VISITOR.

Mr. Cunningham Makes Trips Into the Robbers' Roost Country.

Castle Dale, Utah, Dec. 24.—Mr. Robert Cunningham made one of his periodical visits to Castle Dale this week, and again set the people to wondering who and what he is. He tarried here a few days, and Tuesday morning mounted his horse and rode into the Robbers' Roost country, since which date nothing has been heard from him. Some say he is a detective, others that he is a cattleman, and still others that he is a representative of the Ireland company. Mr. Cunningham rides a good horse, and talks a good deal upon every matter except his mission in Emery county, on which subject he is as dumb as an oyster.

Albert Larsen, formerly of Spring-town but now of Eureka, is spending the holidays in Ferron.

Republicanism flourishes in Ferron since our new postmaster took possession of the postoffice.

The Ferron saloon, we understand, is to be moved into the building recently used by Pettey & Brandon.

* The young ladies of Ferron will give a dance at the social hall New Year's eve.

NEW INDIAN AGENT.

Captain Cornish Was Surprised By His Appointment.

Castle Dale, Dec. 28.—Captain G. A. Cornish, who was on Friday appointed agent at the Uintah and Ouray agencies, to succeed Captain Beck, arrived at Price this morning and departed at once for his post. Being interviewed by a Herald representative, the captain said he was greatly surprised when he received a dispatch ordering him to the reservations, and had no idea what the reasons were for the removal of Captain Beck. He was as much at sea regarding the reasons for his own appointment. He is unacquainted with the present conditions on the reservations, and could say nothing regarding his policy as commandant.

The captain is a fine, soldierly-appearing man, tall and commanding, and is about 50 years of age. There is something about him that impresses one at first sight with a feeling of confidence in his ability to carry out anything he undertakes. There is nothing overbearing in his conduct, but, on the contrary, he is courteous and considerate in his treatment of others. Whatever are the reasons for the appointment of Captain Cornish, there can be no doubt that his selection is an eminently wise one.

CHRISTMAS AT HUNTINGTON.

Festival and Entertainment Given By the Sunday Schools.

Huntington, Dec. 25.—Last night a Christmas festival was held in the large brick tabernacle by the combined Sunday schools and Primary associations of this place. The building was very brilliantly lighted and decorated for the occasion. A magnificent Christmas tree adorned the center of the stage, around which were gathered the choirs and tiny performers. The programme consisted of songs, operettas, choruses, recitations, etc., by the children, all of which was very appropriate and entertaining, and the most unique of which was three little tots dressed as wax dolls, who went through a series of little songs and movements that brought out repeated applause from the large audience. The names of these little performers were as follows: Myrtle Nixon, Maggie Johnson, Myrtle Wakefield. The entertainment wound up with a candy treat by old Santa Claus, J. A. West, who dealt out a package of candy to each child in the room under 14 years of age, as they marched by his candy stand under the tree, to the sounds of beautiful music, played by Mr. L. A. Johnson on the organ.

The whole performance was a success, and reflects credit on those who took the lead in the matter.